Flotsam and Jetsam

Flotsam
and
Jetsam

Robb White

BREAKAWAY BOOKS
HALCOTTSVILLE, NEW YORK
2009

Flotsam and Jetsam: The Collected Adventures, Opinions, and Wisdom from a Life Spent Messing About in Boats

ISBN: 978-1-891369-83-4
Library of Congress Control Number: 2009924617

Published by Breakaway Books
P.O. Box 24
Halcottsville, NY 12438
www.breakawaybooks.com

FIRST EDITION

Contents

ACKNOWLEDGMENTS AND DEDICATION

As always the author (and the editor) owe thanks to "family and friends, either living or dead" who participated in the events that became these stories, then gleefully listened as they were told, retold, refined, and embellished.

Next we need to thank all the editors who generously shared their enthusiasm "for this stuff and even published some of it." Versions of these stories have appeared in *Maine Boats & Harbors, Smithsonian, Natural History, Ash Breeze, WoodenBoat, Classic Boat,* and many, many of them in *Messing About in Boats.*

Thanks to our publisher, Garth Battista, for consistently encouraging the compiling of "all this stuff" and for giving much needed advice along the way.

This book is dedicated to "messers everywhere" who have learned (like we of the Reynolds crew) that "the important thing ain't comfort, it's joy."

—Jane White, April 2009

Foreword

Bailey White

When I was a little girl about three years old I wanted a horse more than anything in the world. "You can't have a horse," my mother said. "You're too little. It would be dangerous. You have to wait."

But my big brother, twelve years old at the time, did not think I should have to wait. A neighbor, Huegel, had taught him to weld, and he went out behind the shed and welded me up a horse. The body was made out of an oil drum, with angle-iron legs and a rebar neck. The head was a coffee can with two nuts for eyes. The nostrils he made with a church key. The horse's face had a wise and knowing look, and could be adjusted according to my mood, by twisting the coffee can on the rebar—now defiant and challenging, now sweet and sympathetic. It was the best horse I've ever owned.

And the horse was just the beginning. My brother was always the one to go to—when I needed to know how to cook a haunch of venison, or had a broken heart, or wanted a swan for a pet, he would understand and know what to do about it.

My brother had an early interest in firearms and sharp-edged tools, and a power of concentration that could be alarming. The peculiar combination of intelligence, ability, energy, and unswervable interest in dangerous things made him a troublesome child, and when he was fifteen years old our parents sent him away to school, thinking that strangers might be able to straighten him out.

I was six years old by then, just starting school myself, and I needed him. I got a pot of glue and went out behind the shed and started gluing duck feathers to an old piece of roofing tin with the idea that if I could just get enough feathers on there I would be able to fly up to Alexandria, Virginia, and bring my brother back. There were not enough feathers, though, and it was a whole year before they gave up on strangers and let my brother come home.

We both hated school, but having my brother back home to drive me the fifteen miles back and forth every day made it bearable. One day we pretended to go to school, but when we got to the first stop sign we turned around and came home. On that day my brother had only one thing on his mind—chinquapins and how best to eat them. Chinquapins are tiny, scarce, and difficult to extract from their prickly burrs, but my brother was already enough of a scientist to know that he had to have a goodly number to conduct any kind of valid experiment, and we spent the whole day in the woods gathering chinquapins. That evening we cooked them a dozen different ways. The best was stewed in cane syrup.

No matter what my brother had on his mind, it was worth your while to throw yourself in with it. Though you might be scarred for life, you would never be disappointed or bored. On summer nights me and all my cousins used to follow him up and down the road catching spiders. We would find them by the glow of their eyes in the beam of a flashlight. My brother had the most cunning round tackle box, with many pie-shaped compartments and a rotating lid. He would put a big spider in each compartment, and when the tackle box was full we would go up on the porch, tump the spiders out in pairs, and watch them fight. The disintegrating plastic of the old tackle box smelled like vomit, and the combination of that smell and the sight of huge spiders locking themselves in high-kneed combat, then grappling for a better hold with all their long legs in the glare of the porch light, has left me with a lifelong fear of spiders, but I would not have missed one of those nights for the world.

When I turned thirteen my brother took me aside and said, "It's time you learned about the workings of the internal combustion engine." We spent a whole day under the hood of Miss Essie Baker's Model A Ford, and he made me a little handwritten book held together with safety pins, full of diagrams and drawings of pistons and gaskets. I did not take to it, but I still keep the book in the glove compartment of my car.

Whenever I needed help, whether I knew it or not, my brother was there. He taught me which kind of people deserve respect, and the many little ways you can recognize them; what matters and what doesn't, and how to tell the difference; when to cut loose and when to keep your own counsel; the importance of maintaining your dignity in public. And I wasn't the only one: My cousin Bruzz imprinted on my brother when he was a two-year-old baby just like Konrad Lorenz's goslings, and would have followed him step for step through the gates of Hell, and he did follow him into some mighty dangerous places.

When another cousin got married, one of those big blow-out weddings with all the out-of-town bridesmaids and the big white dress, and the gifts on display, and the catered rehearsal dinner, my brother showed up with his gift for the bride: two perfectly matched baby mouse skeletons curled up in the fetal position on a wad of cotton in a little white box. "These are your earrings," he said. The marriage didn't last five years, but she still has the earrings.

The year before my brother died, one of the cousins from the spider-fighting summers brought her little baby from Tennessee to meet him. My brother took the little fellow out into the backyard and showed him how to catch a jack out of its hole by twiddling a straw, caught him a jar full of doo-dlebugs by gently brushing sand down the sloping sides of their cone-shaped nests until the doodlebugs were revealed waving their menacing jaws, gave him a ride on a gopher tortoise, and told him how indigo snakes take refuge from the heat down in gopher burrows. The next year when they visited my brother was gone, but the little boy, too young to understand such things, ran around and around the house looking behind the shed and under the steps. He asked, "Where is that man who knows all about holes?"

My brother was an enigma in many ways. Nobody could be more exces-sive than he. He could take on the study of any little thing and go deeper and deeper into it with a joyful exuberance, way beyond the bounds of reason. The subjects of his interest could range from the evolution of panty hose to the sex lives of armadillos. He understood and encouraged that sort of excess in others, if he considered the subject worthy of it. He always indulged my interest in the life habits of pack rats, and my desire to grow peonies way outside of their climate zone. Other kinds of excess were abhorrent to him, though, and one was the mass shooting of ducks over bait on a lake near where we live. Every dawn from Thanksgiving through Christmas the gunshots sound like the distant roar of cannons. In the last years of his life he took to dumping corn into our little wet-weather pond, luring the ducks to safety. He forbade us to walk near the pond during duck season for fear we would scare the ducks away and they would fly back to Lake Iamonia to be slaughtered.

He was not materialistic. For the last twenty years of his life he wore the same clothes every day: a pair of baggy brown canvas short pants that his wife made him, with suspenders attached to two huge buttons in the front that made him look like Mickey Mouse, and an Army-surplus olive-drab T-shirt. He drove a ratty old cheap car and lived in the back room of his boat shop.

Yet nobody understood better the absolute love a person could have for a knife or a typewriter or a fine old heart-pine house, and the terrible plague of temptation to own such things. His granddaughter, learning to talk, used to say, "Cain't want that," and that phrase has come to be an admonition in our family when we long for things we cannot or should not have.

My brother was an energetic and prolific writer, and his wife, as a kindness to his many readers, has dug deep in the files and boxes to bring together all these stories. I am jealous: within these pages, you, his readers, can now have him back. But we, his family, have to get along without him. Sometimes I look down the hill at the ducks cavorting in safety on the wet-weather pond where my brother taught them to take refuge from the hunters at Lake Iamonia, and I think—*If only I could get enough duck feathers* . . . Then I say to myself, "Naaa . . . Cain't want that."

Wonders of the Last Century

in which the twig is bent

I have lived long enough now to have seen us improve our situation in this world until it is almost intolerable. I remember my childhood as very happy (of course, due to blind luck, my whole life has been like a happy childhood) and we didn't even have electricity. My grandfather and idol did not even approve of automobiles. He said that they were not only treacherous but undignified . . . that a man should not be seen sitting down by strangers unless his head was as high as it was when he was standing up . . . like on a horse or the seat of a wagon. He had a lot of opinions sort of like that and he was a powerful influence on not only little old me, but everybody who knew him. To this day, even though he has been dead for over fifty years, somebody will say "Mr. Jim might be watching you" when one of us gets too self-indulgent with foolishness.

He really did not like machinery of any kind and though he put up with a lot of farming junk out of necessity, he absolutely despised any machine used for pleasure or sport, especially gear-driven fishing reels and automatic shotguns. He didn't even like pump guns. When he had a dove shoot or a duck shoot or took somebody quail hunting with his champion pointers a guest who brought such a thing was never invited back. It was almost as bad as walking around with the breech closed on a real gun. It wasn't that he was snobbish with his old English double guns . . . plenty of people who could only afford a slack-jointed single-barreled Iver Johnson were his dear companions. He just didn't like the idea of a gun that could put the shell in the barrel all by itself.

Electricity was certainly lurking around for a long time before it came into more or less controlled use and I am sure that it is at the top of everybody's list for wonders of the century unless, of course, they have never had the experience of not having any . . . then they don't know how wonderful it is. There are those who don't want to fool with it and don't care how wonderful it is. We didn't have any electricity when I was a little boy. I remember when it came . . . no big deal to me at first but of course, I didn't have any heavy workload to be lightened by its wonderful power. My grandfather did not like it (which is the reason we were so late getting any). He said he thought it was dangerous and sure enough, something went wrong with the wires that they pulled through the walls of the old big house and some of the electricity got loose and set it on fire. I remember standing out in the yard with everybody else as we watched it burn. My sister and I were almost too amazed to continue licking the cake icing out of the bowl that we happened to save when we ran from the fire. My grandfather said, "I told you so. Boy that's a hot fire. Give me a little lick out of that bowl."

Then there is the airplane. My grandfather said, "I have measured the distance from my ass to the ground and it is thirty-two inches and that is far enough. I can't imagine what Will Rogers is thinking messing around with those aeroplanes. I used to think he had good sense." Now people clutch their money in one hand, pull their little wheeled suitcase in the other, and flock to the points of departure like sheep to be fleeced, separated from their families, and herded into situations that are completely beyond their control. They are just as proud of their frequent-flier miles as my grandfather was his big old gray horse.

There is the outboard boat motor. Before the invention of that wonder, people had to paddle, pole, or row a boat unless they were smart enough to learn to sail. My grandfather said, "I would rather swim than pull that little stinking rope. Who in the world would have ever thought that somebody would want to have that much noise right there in the boat with them. I don't care if the damn thing baits the hook for you and scales the fish and jumps in the cold water to retrieve the ducks. You hate it when it is running and you cuss it when it ain't. To hell with those things." That just about covers my sentiments, too.

You know, a bicycle is a pretty good thing. My grandfather loved them. He said. "There is no more attractive sight than the way the hips of a fine woman act on the seat of a bicycle but the machine itself is dangerous. I don't think they are much good except for pavement. They look like they will throw you in a sand bed." They have these "dirt bikes" now and I had to borrow one from one of my grandchildren. They will still throw you in a sand bed but, of course, most everything is paved now.

Air-conditioning has certainly caught on down here in South Georgia. If my grandfather had been alive when it came along, I don't know what he would have thought, so I'll just tell you what I think. I think it is what gives us all these allergies and colds all the time but that ain't the real trouble. Air conditioners isolate us from the real world to the point that most people don't know when it starts raining or when it gets cool or some cat has scared all the birds out of the yard or anything. They just sit in there, breathing the same air over and over, watching the TV.

Now, that's a powerful wonder. My grandfather would have had something to say about that one for sure . . . something like "No news is good news." They have to have an hour's worth of news even if only ten minutes' worth of something happened. The TV is a very powerful influence in the lives of most people. My daughter-in-law says that every person in my granddaughter's class is named after some character on the TV, even the teacher. Television emulation has got all these women wiggling their heads so emphatically when they talk that they look like a line of coots swimming across the pond as they sit, in their cars in traffic, talking on their telephones.

The telephone is certainly worthy of note. My grandfather thought that they were a nuisance. "Just as soon as you get concentrated, the damn telephone rings and the thing it wants you to do is never as important as the thing you were doing before it rang." Though I only use the damn things for outgoing information, I still am affected by them when I am busy trying to drive my car. A long time ago, I decided to be suspicious of people who were wiggling in their cars. To me it is a sign that the driver is occupied with something other than driving the car. Before car phones, he might have been wiggling because he knocked the coal out of his cigar down in his crotch or he might have been a nut case with the uncontrollable twitches or an irresponsible teenager who was so wrapped up in the music that he couldn't concentrate properly on anything else. Now there are so many wigglers that you have to be scared all the time. You better be afraid of them because the reason they are wiggling is because they are occupied with the telephone and not only are they apt to do something like run over you from not paying attention, the person talking to them on the phone is liable to enrage them and you might wind up run over by proxy.

So, was there no good invention of the last century? I think there was and I know my grandfather would agree with me . . . the ubiquitous white plastic bucket is a wonderful thing.

The Best Boat Lamp in the Whole World

in which I explain how we got along without electricity

Dang, I am getting old. I tried to explain how old to my grandchildren to whom big numbers are just as much nonsense as they are to me. I told them that I had been driving cars so long that, if I went back from when I started as far as I have come forward to now, there wouldn't be any cars to drive. At that, they looked as if I had told them a bunch of big numbers so I told them that we didn't have any electricity when I was a little boy. That fact had enough significance to prompt a bunch of questions like, "Well, how did you see to read *The Roly Poly Pudding* and weren't you scared after your momma read it to you after it got too dark to see the horrible rats?" I explained that not having electricity didn't mean that we didn't have lights in the house, just that people had to know a thing or two about a thing or two to manage them and I (boy, ain't opportunity a wonderful thing?) got my old Aladdin Mantle Lamp down off the pie safe, switched off the main switch, and threw us all the way back in time to the good old days of my childhood . . . showed those children the best non-electric light ever in this world. They were amazed, too.

You know it's a puzzle to me how, in these consumer-style boat-goody stores, you can buy these little, useless, trinket-like kerosene lanterns that hang in cute gimbals like it was necessary for such a thing to be level to emit its pitiful little glow but you can't buy the best non-electric light ever invented (no gimbals required). There was an Aladdin, nonpressurized mantle lamp in every room of our house when I was a boy. Before that, the old house had gas lights and the old acetylene generator was still down in the basement and the retrofit piping was still in the walls. I don't remember those lights, but the old folks said that they were a pain in the neck and smutty and stank and that they were delighted when the Aladdin lamp was invented (Victor Samuel Johnson, Chicago, 1909). My mother and father used them when they ran away to Marina Cay in the British Virgin Islands to escape the Depression. Not too long ago, if you walked down the road in the Bahamas or one of the lesser of the Antilles at night, you would see the bright glow of some family's heirloom Aladdin shining prominently out the window, the beautiful colors of its decorative glass shade (lots of old Aladdin shades are valuable collector's items now) shining like something of Christmas.

Aladdin lamps were one of those wonderful inventions, like naphtha boat engines, that came along at the exact wrong time. External-combustion naphtha engines were developed just before two-cycle gasoline engines and it didn't take long for those cheap-junk polluters to displace that elegant, clean, easy-to-handle, and silent improvement over steam. Electricity did the same thing to the wonderful Aladdin lamp . . . except in places too remote for it to get to like the Bahamas and our old home place way down in the woods of South Georgia. I remember our first electricity too. It came from a thirty-two-volt Kohler plant that stayed out in a little brick addition to another little brick house with the plates of its batteries in big glass jars. I remember with glee what my grandfather said about it after my progressive uncles and father had gone off to fight the war and left us with it, "Those gas lights were a pain in the neck but this thing is a pain in the ass." "Amen to that about any electrical appliance and its support apparatus on a boat," I say. We stayed with the Aladdins until the boys came marching home again and I still haven't given them up. To hell with voluntary dependence on things beyond my control.

An Aladdin lamp is such a good thing that that's what my wife and I give all the newlyweds in our family for a wedding present. I know the ones who weren't raised around me are puzzled at the significance of the peculiar gift but, after the initial frolic and marveling at all the special olive grabbers and extra electric frying pans wears off, they start to wonder about what's in the box that we sent. When they open it, there is a damn kerosene lantern. Most of them have seen something kind of like that before and I am sure they would rather have a propane lamp or even one of those pump-up messes than a wretched, weak, stinking hurricane lamp. It certainly looks just like a plain old ordinary kerosene lantern, just like from out of *The Grapes of Wrath* or *Key Largo* or something. I always give the cheapest kind . . . one with the plain glass bowl and the no-nonsense chimney (you can spend some big money with The Aladdin Mantle Lamp Company to go beyond the basics). Once it is out of the box there is only one peculiar-looking thing . . . a little box with prominent writing on it in several languages. In there is the wonderful camisa . . . the main trick that makes the Aladdin lamp "the best non-electric lamp in the world." Stuck to the little camisa box, there is also, with lamps from me, a piece of paper that says in big letters, DO NOT OPEN

THIS BOX UNTIL YOU READ THE INSTRUCTIONS.

Handling the camisa is tricky. In addition to the regular, pretty good, Aladdin instructions, there is a set of my own in the box. It takes a little learning to get the most out of any good thing and I have been an Aladdin lamp dealer since . . . well . . . big numbers, and I got tired of people bothering me all the time because they couldn't master a camisa so, out of self-defense, I wrote my own instructions. I have heard from some of our newlyweds about how it went. One dear couple had the use of a cabin in the mountains of North Carolina for their honeymoon but, when they got there . . . all tired and over-stressed from the trip and festivities of the day . . . they were shocked to find that there was no electricity and it was dark and they were in a strange place and the car flashlight had been left switched on by a batch of frolicking flower girls and they were in a hell of a fix. The bride happened to remember that her old nut-case uncle had insisted that they take his gift with them to this place, "just in case," and she and her new husband squatted in the headlights of the car and read the instructions and put the thing together, poured in the oil (I give paraffin oil but an Aladdin lamp will burn kerosene, diesel fuel, mineral spirits, turpentine, olive oil, peanut oil . . . damn near any oil . . . but never, never gasoline and that's perfectly fine with me) and, with great care, flashed off the precious camisa and walked into their first home carrying about fifty watts worth of reliable, virtually maintenance-free, silent, nonstank, all-night light. They said that it was a good thing that it was an all-night light, too, because every time they shut it down too low (the output is adjustable), enormous pack rats came out of the woodwork and ran, loudly, all over the cabin including the bed. With all that they had a good honeymoon, caught some little brook trout and fried them in an electric frying pan . . . on the fire. Of course they had sense enough to take the little plastic feet off and unplug the cord out of it.

I don't want to discourage you about how tricky it is to handle the camisa and all. There are plenty of ten-year-old children in places like Nicaragua and the Philippines who do it every night. Space doesn't permit me to give you the complete instructions for how to run an Aladdin Mantle Lamp so I'll just hit it a light lick. As you can guess, it has a mantle (camisa) like those aggravating, pump-up kind. You don't have to pump it though, so all that jerking around does not destroy the mantle. Indeed, a sensible operator can get many, many hours out of a single camisa (means "little girl's shirt" in Spanish and I like the word). The wick is formed into a circle in the burner (Aladdin makes the burners in kerosene refrigerators too) and when it is lit and the whole "gallery" with the camisa and chimney is put on, the circle of fire winds up inside the mantle and it begins to glow white hot. The marvelously intense incandescence completes the oxidation of the fuel most perfectly and there is no smoke and, with good fuel, no stench at all and, boy, oh, boy, what a light. You have to spend a hell of a lot of money to set up enough electricity on a boat to beat the reliable Aladdin, nonpressurized Mantle Lamp.

Note:

Though I am still a vestigial Aladdin dealer, I only do it to keep up old traditions (and camisas) and I only sell them in my shop. I don't ship lamps and parts anymore. They are readily available from outfits that supply folks who remain unconvinced of the delights of high-tech living like the Amish. Aladdin Mantle Lamp Company has split off from its parent, Aladdin Industries, the makers of coolers and water jugs. Hell, what am I saying? Aladdin Lamp was the daddy of all that . . . just got too behind the times to keep up with the offspring . . . sort of like me. Anyway, now they are a little outfit up in Tennessee who ship the wonderful lamps over all three worlds. Back when they were still part of the powerful cooler conglomerate, they had a deal with True Value hardware stores that, in order to get to sell the popular coolers, they had to offer the slow-selling lamps too. The ridiculous Y2K foolishness alerted a bunch of hardware stores to that fact (and over-stressed the poor little lamp company about like the rigors of a wedding) so, if you jump up and down and talk a bunch of noise, you might get the local hardware store to order a lamp for you. Tell them you want a Genie II and at least one spare camisa.

The Boat in the Coach House

in which I sink as far as possible

I remember my first boat. I had been in other boats ever since I was a little baby, but the boat in the coach house was the first one to belong to me and, you know, that makes a lot of difference. I think I was about four or five years old when I became a boat owner for the first time.

There were two segments of my family, the wild and the civilized. My family was the former. While my father and uncles were off attending to World War Two, my grandfather, my mother, me, a bunch of aunts, and all sorts of folks who worked the old place were all that was left of the wild segment of our family. My grandfather was an unusual man. Though he was capable of doing anything useful and was loved and respected by everybody who knew him, he was incompetent in the management of money (sort of like me, I guess). I believe that he suffered from excess enthusiasm. If he had been in a primitive situation—something like an old savage sitting around his fire, roasting little morsels of meat on a stick for his grandchildren—he would have been fine, but he just didn't fit in the modern world (never learned to drive a car for one thing).

The other segment of our family was connected to my grandfather's sister who, along with her husband, was a rich Yankee. Our place (twelve thousand acres then) was what they call a "hunting plantation." Which, I believe are maintained by rich Yankees as a winter refuge from the rigors of piling up money and as a tax dodge. There were, and are, a bunch of them around here. This is longleaf pine country, and those kinds of woods were thought to be "salubrious" back when people were scared to death of things like tuberculosis, so the industrial tycoons of the late nineteenth century started coming here for their health right after the Civil War. There were hotels in Thomasville, Georgia, that catered to them and, when my grandfather's grandfather first started coming down here for extended vacations in the winter they stayed in a fancy hotel (The Piney Woods), then they built a house in town . . . then, in 1886, they bought the old Blackshear place down on the Florida line and started vacating in the real piney woods.

My grandfather had been a rich Yankee, too, but he loved roaming through the woods and messing around in the water down here so much that he never went back to Philadelphia to tend to his business, and it dwindled to nothing even before the crash of '29. He worked for his sister as overseer of the plantation. His four children ran the woods like coons all the time. There was a tutor who lived on the place and was supposed to teach them the three R's, but they were so bright and eager to get out that all formal education was accomplished before breakfast. These children quickly reverted to "wild type" like the escaped fruit flies in a genetics lab. The deformities of civilization evaporated from them like the ether used to knock out the special flies that lived with their birth defects in jars in the lab. One story is that if they found a shutbox (eastern box turtle, *Terrapene carolina*) while they were wandering the woods, they immediately raked up a pile of pine straw, set it on fire, and put the turtle in there to roast. If he (or she, a he has red eyes) crawled out, they raked him back in with a stick. He was done when the steam began to come out from under his tail and they busted him open and ate him on the spot. My mother, who was the Red Cross lady in Thomasville for many years, was such a nice person that nobody ever suspected the depths of her savagery. She was never sick a day in her life and attributed that to the early challenges to her immune system.

Anyhow, these wild, savage children were extremely cruel to the tame little Yankee cousins when they came down. I mean, goddamighty knows, some of those stories will curdle the blood. I'll quickly whip out two so you can see what I mean, but I'll try to spare you all I can. One time, they hung a little innocent boy by his belt onto the horns of a deer skull nailed to the wall of the coach house. It wasn't child abuse . . . at first. He was willing, but an airplane flew over about then (1918) and they had to run see and forgot the little fella until they noticed his empty place at suppertime. Another time, they told the whole crew of innocents that when you chewed sugarcane, you were supposed to swallow the pummins. I better explain that or it might not be as impressive to people who have never chewed cane. There are three components: First there is the peeling, which is exactly like bamboo—stuff nobody but a panda can chew. Next there is the juice, which is astonishingly delicious. Unfortunately the juice is soaked up in the pummins, which is just about like a piece of hemp rope. Southerners used to caulk boats with cane pummins. My mother and aunt and uncles had those little gullible Yankees all in a row swallowing like matching cormorants, each with a pinfish trying to go down backward. Jesus. My sisters and I did it to one of our Yankee cousins, too, and it was pitiful. I hope St. Peter is on his break when my time comes so I can slip by the substitute.

The little wild children didn't have anything much. They made bows and arrows with the single worn-out pocketknife that they shared, and they had a box of matches, a few fishhooks, and a spool of "Aunt Lydia" sewing thread. Later, when they were old enough (about seven), they had a gun. Oh, they ate well, because this was actually a working plantation with big fields of peanuts and a garden from which everybody on the place (maybe thirty people, all told) had all they needed. There was livestock of all kinds: My grandfather raised pigeons for the squabs. You know a squab is a peculiar phenomenon. When they get ready to kill and eat, they are much bigger than a grown pigeon . . . sort of like how a caterpillar is bigger than the butterfly into which it metamorphoses. They don't actually look all that appetizing with their pin feathers sticking straight out and all that dook stuck on their bottoms because their legs are too flaccid for them to waddle out of it. But I tell you this, a squab roasted with a strip of bacon is a treat. There are a lot of foodstuffs kind of like that, you know, those that don't look too good as raw material, but with proper preparation turn out fine. A hot dog is a good example of that. But the point is that the little wild children were well fed but poor.

Well, the little Yankees had all sorts of toys and junk. Everything a child could have was provided for them, not only down here, but back in Philadelphia. Momma said that they had a real steam train, big enough to ride on. Years later she showed me the little rusty tracks running all out through the flower beds over at the big house. They also had a tiny boat.

Everybody in the family was grown up when I, the first of the new generation, came along. My sisters and I and a bunch of children of the folks who worked the place ran just as wild as before. What did you think . . . that someone like my mother would, all of a sudden, fly into a frenzy of supervision? I was the oldest, by far, and for a long time I was by myself. I was out there in the coach house one time when I found a ladder nailed to the harness wall and, after I had climbed into the loft, I found the most charming little boat.

I'll get right back to it in a second but, first, I better explain the Coach House. Back in the horse-and-buggy days, a buggy was an expensive thing and a "coach" was something reserved for people like my ancestors—people who were apt to top it the knob every chance they got. One story is that when they came (I guess my grandfather was a little boy at this time) down for the winter on the "Carpetbagger Express," they would spend the first night in their house in town while their servants got the coach ready. It was big enough to haul them all, all the men in their Prince Alberts and beavers and all the ladies in their plume-bird hats. There was a little perch up front for the driver, and a little perch back aft for the man who blew the horn to warn the peasants to get out of the way. If that ain't topping it the knob, I don't know what is. I actually knew one old man who remembered those days. He said, "You heard that horn, you better get your ass out the road or them goddamn Masons would run over you in that big-assed thing." Anyway the coach house is where the coach stayed so that the mohair and plush and leather wouldn't get rained on. When I was a little boy, it was full of agricultural implements, rusty tools, old harnesses, and some old, dusty buggies and wagons. No telling what happened to the coach and the horn.

So I found that little boat up in the loft with some old fishing poles (we had our own bamboo grove, which is right down in back of my son's house right now—most excellent stuff) and old, dusty lumber. I remember it exactly. During the time of the coach and on up into the thirties, there was a man named Dan Kidney in Ohio who built double-ended duckboats. They were decked over and had an oval cockpit. When I was a boy, there was one in every pond on the place. As with the fancy canoes my Yankee relatives brought down, the duckboats didn't last long down here, and by the time the war was over and I was old enough to make much use of them, they were rotted out. The one in the coach house was a miniature that the Yankees had built specially to suit the needs of their children. Initially there was a whole fleet of them but all but one had succumbed to the fecundity of the South. Nobody knew how this one got up in the loft of the coach house, but there it was. It didn't take me long to get it down so I could get to messing. I wasn't even old enough to go to school but I was old enough to need a boat of my own.

I dragged it to the closest creek and slid it in. The old cedar planking had shrunk and gapped so bad that I couldn't keep it bailed out. When I got in, the bottom spouted like the whales in *McElligot's Pool*. It didn't make any difference in the long run though because the creek was too little to float the boat anyway. I fought and dragged it all the way to the delta where the creek spread out at the head of the pond. There the button bushes, briers, stagger bushes, and grass were too thick for me to get any farther, and I had to abandon the whole project right there. I guess an archaeologist, armed with sophisticated infrared devices, could find a hint of extra richness in the shape of a tiny boat in the humus of that place. I might fight my way back through the impenetrable thicket myself one of these days with my metal detector and see if I can find one single clenched tack for my artifact cabinet.

Epilogue

When I got out of the Navy in 1963 and set up in the boatbuilding business, all the old Kidney boats on all the Yankee places down here had rotted out. I hate to talk bad about legendary things, but they weren't very well made. When the Yankees found that there was a boatbuilder in town (me—right downtown in an old storefront), one of them asked me if I thought I knew what a Dan Kidney boat looked like and, if so, could I build one? "Will a yellow butterfly light on a dog turd?" was my reply. I surveyed a few wretched scraps at the ponds on our place and found little pieces of galvanized tin, rusty steel nails, little pieces of rotten northern white cedar, and even a little crust of painted canvas. From that, and my childhood memories, I was able to build an ersatz Kidney boat. Abercrombie & Fitch had stopped selling the real thing by then so I had no competition. The duckboat business was one of the things that lured me into deceiving myself that I could make a living as a boatbuilder. I built a lot of them—saturated the market. The only problem was that I didn't have good business sense like old Dan. Mine were made of old-growth, red-heart cypress fastened with copper and bronze, and they never rotted out. The old boats had two galvanized tin pipes down through the foredecks (they were symmetrically double-ended) and all the way through the bottom so you could stick a pole down into the bottom of the pond to stabilize the boat in the blind. Though the Yankees didn't do much bream fishing, I found that the pipes (mine were copper) were the best way to hold the boat over a bed so rambunctious grandchildren won't turn the boat over when the old redbellies get to biting like they do sometimes. Does that mean that I have one of those boats? Can a fat baby fart?

Midway School

in which the tone for my academic career was set

The first school I went to was old Midway about halfway between nothing and not-much down here in South Georgia. Midway was so far from anything and was so little that they only had one school bus and the logistics of trying to get to a dirt road where it might pass were so complicated that most of us might as well have stayed home, which some of us did, most of the time. I, for instance, often had to ride a horse named Sparkplug through the woods to the bus driver's house and hope to get there before he left. Old Sparkplug stayed in the man's pasture with some po-looking cows and hoped I would hurry back soon so he could go home to the clover and rye. Going to school was a big deal and a major social event. Most of the children walked to school barefoot. There was only one boy who wore shoes to school (none of the girls wore shoes) and he was a sanctified little snob who was always parroting what his big-league mother told all her high-society friends in town about how high-class they were and how she was going to send this little aristocrat to school in town as soon as the county got a school bus running so he could get away from all the little one-mule farm children who were so low-class that they didn't even wear shoes to school. Most of us little one-mule children didn't worry about what this little squirt said. We could all outrun him and our pocketknives were sharper and we won his marbles every day (he did not deign to mumble the peg) but there was one little girl in his grade (third) who did not like people looking down their noses at her one bit. She feisted up at him pretty regularly on the playground. I don't remember all the things she said about his highfalutin momma and her prissy ways but I do remember how she finally got his goat. "The Bible says if your feet stink it means that you don't love Jesus," she declared. "Where does it say that?" Little Lord Fauntleroy snapped. "It certainly isn't in Deuteronomy." "Might be in Acts," she replied. We knew she had hit him where he lived because somebody caught him smelling his shoe out behind the privy. You know, none of our little spraddle-toed feet stank and I bet Jesus's didn't either.

Though the old school has been erased from the land so completely that I can't even be sure exactly where it was, I remember it perfectly. It was a small, but tall, wood building with big, high windows and wide, brick steps. There were several outbuildings like the lunchroom, a little duplex "facility" for the girls and boys, and the toolshed. We had agriculture class at Midway. We children (both boys and girls) raised corn, cotton, and peanuts in about a seven-acre field behind the school. Though we didn't have a mule, we did have a whole setup of old, donated, wo-out junk. We borrowed a mule from one of the neighboring alumni to break the land, lay out the rows, and pull the planter and the lime and guano spreaders. After the crop was in the ground, we kept the weeds hoed out and side-dressed guano and lime by hand until the time came to lay the crop by . . . then we borrowed the mule to pull the sweep and Joe-harrow. Some of us hardly ever participated in any of the academics inside the schoolhouse and I am afraid that that group included me and Ted. In those days, schoolteachers and administrators (I don't remember any administration at Midway at all) had sense enough to know that there were some people who were just plain not cut out for academic careers. They just let us work in the field and didn't make us feel guilty.

They couldn't have made Ted feel guilty if they had caught him with his head down in the hole on the boy's side of the duplex facility trying to see what had darked the hole over on the girl's side. Ted was a character, I tell you. When the corn got high enough to hide in, he would sneak down the rows to where you were busily engaged chopping weeds . . . which, that is an engaging thing . . . and he would slip up behind you and grab you from the back like a bear and pick your feet clean off the ground. There wasn't anything you could do but something that would tickle Ted. It wasn't just me Ted did that to either. You could hear him hooting all over the field.

To this day, sometimes the hair will stand up on the back of my neck and I'll just know that Ted is coming up behind me . . . particularly in the tall rows of the grocery store. I was in there just the other day puzzling, in my ignorant way, over how many grams of carbohydrate were in one size serving of this versus how many were in another size serving of that when I felt Ted slipping up behind me. I spun around to find a very tall, dignified-looking stranger who was trying to look over my head and do the same thing I was trying to do. "Oops," I said "I thought you might have been Ted coming up behind me." The tall man laughed and said, "You know Ted?" I told him about our association at Midway and he told me how, though he had gone to school in Calvary because of the pigmentation situation, he and Ted had been raised in the same place down by the river and had both played hooky from school and gone fishing together all the time. He told me, "Back in '52, I was in Korea trudging down the road when somebody came up from behind me and grabbed me . . . felt like a bear had me. If I coulda got loose, I would have shot him. Finally he said, 'Hey boy, I bet you don't know who this is got you.' I was so wary after that that I think Ted might have been a factor in my surviving that conflict."

Shoes

I hate not to be in the middle of the mainstream about so many things but there is no denying the facts. I think the invention of shoes is right up there with the invention of cosmetic body piercing for a ridiculous frivolity. I am not just talking about high-heeled shoes and white cowboy boots and all, I mean plain old regular walking-around shoes like everybody wears all the time. It is easy to tell that shoes are an unnatural thing. I mean, your little toe and the one next to it are not supposed to be deformed into little alewife-bellied, tadpole-looking things by being walked on by each other while they are squeezed together in sweaty confinement in the toes of any durn shoes. Your big toe is not supposed to be confined into useless deformity, either. It is supposed to be spraddled wide and ready to grab hold of a bush or something to keep you from slipping down in case you come to a slick place. All right, now I heard the arguments about how you might step in something nasty in your bare feet. Well, I am not going to argue all the possible excuses but, you know, I think it is easier to get a little dog dook off the bottom of your foot than it is to try to scratch it out of all those little all-terrain turd trackers they put on the bottoms of shoes . . . like the terrain all these people walk on wasn't concrete. Besides, when you are barefoot, you can tell when you stepped in something and not have to wait until you get in the car with the windows rolled up to find out that you have made a hell of a mess of the carpet.

"But shoes protect our feet from danger." Shoot. If you didn't wear shoes you wouldn't need all that protection, because pretty soon you wouldn't be a tenderfoot anymore. When my sisters and I were little children, our feet were so tough we could walk all the way to the store down one of those exposed aggregate-style asphalt roads. Neither the rocks or the heat ever bothered us at all. We could wade around on oyster bars, too, and nobody had any athlete's foot or fungus toenails or anything. Of course our feet were always black dirty but we knew that and had to wash them off before we were allowed in the house, but where do you think all that dirt would be if we'd had on shoes? On the shoes and right into the house along with the sand that was inside the shoes. People who won't go barefoot are as bad as people who hug the thermostat all their lives and snatch on a coat every time the temperature gets down below seventy-two degrees like they were poikilotherms. You know if you don't use a capability, you lose it, and there are zillions of people who are as helpless as lizards without a thermostat when it gets down around forty. It is pitiful how these moms and schoolteachers bundle the little children up if they have to go outside in anything less than hot weather when little children will run around until their lips get blue without any ill effects at all. People don't catch colds from the cold and they don't catch diseases from going barefoot, either. Charles Darwin observed that the natives of Tierra del Fuego didn't wear any shoes . . . or clothes, either, and never got sick until they caught some of them and took them to England and then they died. Us hothouse flowers just need to toughen up a little bit.

How to Play Mumbley Peg (I Knew You'd Want to Know)

Playing mumbley peg is just about a lost art like spinning tops and shooting marbles, all of which were practiced in every rural school in this part of the country a long time ago. Every boy in school had a pocketknife. Usually it was a worn-out old passed-down thing with the blades so short and springs so slack that it was mostly useless for anything but mumbley peg. How that game worked was that two boys (girls did not mumble the peg . . . equal opportunity hadn't been invented yet) squatted down with their spectators around a piece of hard-packed dirt well polished by being stomped by bare feet for many years. The two competitors took turns flipping their pocketknives in a complex and rigidly ritualized series of movements with the main goal being that the knife wound up sticking up in the ground after each move in the progression. The first move was just to flick the knife, blade-first, and stick it in the hard dirt. The next was to hold it in the palm of the hand and flip it so that it made one revolution and wound up sticking up in the dirt. The third was to do that same thing off the back of the hand and the progression got more complicated and difficult and included flipping the knife with one finger on the butt end and the nose on the sharp end (the dullest blade was used for this). If a child missed sticking his knife up (the rule was that two fingers must be able to pass between the end of the handle and the ground) he had to start all over with the series. The winner was the one who finished all the moves first and the loser had to mumble the peg, which was a small wooden peg that had previously been carved (with the sharp blade) and agreed on by the two players. The peg was driven into the ground by the handle of the knife of the winner. The number of driving licks was determined by the number of moves the loser was behind in the competition. Four or five licks would usually bury the frazzled top of the peg about an inch below the surface of the dirt. The poor loser, then, had to root around it with his nose until he could get to it to pull it with his teeth. It paid to have a strong nose and buck teeth with at least two opposing frontal incisors if you planned to lose a game of mumbley peg by more than about two licks.

The Pocketknives of the Children
of Rural South Georgia in Olden Days

Some children had knives that had been pretty good when they were new. One boy had a three-bladed Case except all the blades were broken off but the littlest one and it had gotten so rusty that his fingernail wasn't stiff enough to open it so he had to do it with a dime and he was so poor that he couldn't keep a dime on him . . . had to borrow one or he couldn't play mumbley peg. The most common knives among the children (a lot of girls had pocketknives) were cheap-made Barlow-pattern two-bladed knives and the best of those was the IXL. It had genuine bone handles but most of them had handles made of stamped tin, which had originally had a celluloid wrapping to make them look like genuine bone but had been replaced by the patina of the pocket by the time the knife trickled down to Junior. One boy had a one-bladed Queen City (Titusville, Pennsylvania, home of the first oil well named "The Queen"—I knew you would want to know that) Big Chief and it didn't pay to lose a game by even one lick with him. A Big Chief had a solid aluminum handle at least half an inch thick and it was checkered like the stock of a gun so it hit the peg mighty hard and didn't ever slip off. It was so heavy that it hardly ever bounced out of the ground, either. We were all very glad that it got lost when it wore its heavy way out of that boy's pocket. Me, I had a cheap-made "Fish Knife" (that's all it said on the little shield on the side). It was big and had two long blades. One of them was for cutting and the other was notched for scaling and had a notch in the end for removing a swallowed hook. It also had a bottle opener notch in the scaling blade and was very useful. I was very proud of it, too, and kept the cutting blade razor-sharp. I used the scaling blade for mumbley peg work. It wasn't an ideal rig. The notched tip of the scaling blade didn't stick up in the ground worth a flip and the peculiarly serpentine curved handle didn't drive a peg worth a flip, either. Of course that was a moot point since I never won a game . . . but I did have a strong nose and buck teeth and, for a short time, two opposing incisors.

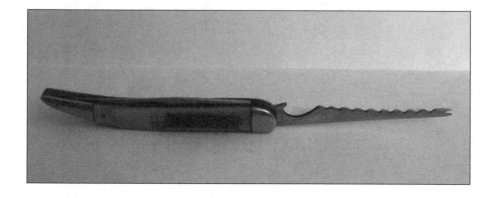

Color-Blind

in which I admit to a genetic defect

I am color-blind . . . been like this all my life. I hardly notice it anymore and, if I can manage to keep my mouth shut, I never notice it at all. When I was a little booger in school, my teacher sent home a note about it. Lucky for me, she was a keen observer. Too bad she was not the type to mince words. I still have that note in my rat nest. She said, "Though your son appears to be a bright little boy, he has been unable to learn his colors. Given that and some of his other behavior, I would suspect that he is idiotic. Time will tell."

Folks with deformities or disabilities are usually overlooked by adults. Some are even ignored as if they were furniture, shrubbery, or thin air. Fortunately, this is not so with the color-blind. A lot of people are infatuated with the interrogation of men like me (this is not an inaccurate sexist statement, color-blindness is a sex-linked[1] genetic dysfunction and since men have no natural defense against sex-linked birth defects, about 8 percent of the men in this country are color-blind while there are hardly any color-blind women at all), and it isn't uncommon for us, when we have been indiscreet enough to reveal our infirmity, to have a person that we have never seen before in our lives thrust a portion of their clothing at us with a strongly hooked thumb and demand, "What color is this?"

It happened in the post office just this morning. I was talking to another old man about fish. I was describing the peculiar behavior of a species of little bream I have been watching called "stumpknockers." "Ain't they the ones with the little reddish chartreuse line around their gills?" asked he. "I don't know," says me, " I tell them by how they look like they already have the pepper sprinkled on them, ready to fry. I can't tell what color their opercular border is, you know I am color-blind." With that, this little woman stranger stopped in her tracks, wheeled about-face just as smartly as any properly trained little soldier, and, as if someone had yelped, "Present . . . Arms!" with a hook of her thumb, thrust the logo from her T-shirt a remarkable distance from her chest straight up under my nose. "What color is this?" she demanded. I probably could have backed up enough to focus my slow-working old eyes if I had thought I had a chance at a correct answer, but long years of slickly skirting the issue have trained me well. "I don't know but, my goodness! You certainly do have a large and deep navel for someone, otherwise, so sparely built."

I really didn't say that, even though the thought did occur. My home training and natural shyness prevented me. I wouldn't ask a one-legged person to show me how high he could jump or somebody in a wheelchair how fast she could go (about twenty-five mph or so it looks like to me) either but it is somehow acceptable to question color-blind men in order to determine the extent of their disability. I guess folks think it is not a serious business but it is. Color-blind people are prohibited by law from being doctors, nurses, airplane pilots, submariners, able-bodied seamen, combat officers in the military, and a bunch of other stuff. Diagnosis of color-blindness is determined by an abstract little test using a book with a bunch of little colored dots on its pages called the "Ishehara Test." Unlike other handicaps, with color-blindness a person's ability to perform a job is not tested, just his ability to see a 7 instead of a 9 among the little dots on the page of the cursed Ishehara Test. My futile efforts to qualify for some license or other were always viewed as a curiosity by my examiners. "Hey, y'all, come look at this here!" was the usual reaction to failure. "Now, tell them what number you see right there." Now that I have given up on the submarines, airplanes, captain's licenses, and all that other able-bodied stuff, people's openness about their curiosity has become my curiosity.

I was a middle school teacher for a long time. At first, I used all my skill to hide my color-blindness from my students to keep the distraction from taking away from class time. I didn't mention the color of stuff if I wasn't absolutely sure about it. Though I drew elaborate color chalk graphs and illustrations of volcanoes, circulatory systems, ant colonies, weather systems, food webs, DNA molecules, and stuff like that on the chalkboard, I did it early in the morning and was in cahoots with the social studies teacher next door who helped me select and slickly mark my big chalks. At that time, I thought I was smart enough to wiggle out of questions like "Mr. White, what was it you said that pinkish magenta stuff right under that yellowish mauve thing right there by the purple blob was?" "Can anyone help Angelica with that question?" was one of my responses. "Angelica, could you come to the board and outline the structure you are talking about with this turquoise chalk so that everyone can see it better?" was another. How about, "What do you think it is?" None of my schemes worked.

I'm not sure if this is common knowledge or not, but I soon found out that it is impossible to fool eighth graders for long. Finally I just let them in on the secret right on the first day. "Hello, I am your science teacher. My name is Robb White. I am color-blind. Any questions?" "What you mean by that?" was one immediate response. I told the kid (a spontaneous inquisitor . . . the best kind), "The normal structures of the eye that detect color, especially red and green, are missing from mine." (That, right there, is a puzzle to me since the color green, they tell me, is composed of yellow and blue which I can see a little of, but green looks gray to me.) "What color am I?" was always the best question. "The right color" was always what I said. Then there would be a flood of "What color is this?" spoken extra-loud as if color-blindness somehow carried along a hearing problem like a little genetic suitcase. Then all sorts of objects would be thrust right under my nose as if I were myopic as well as color-blind and hard of hearing. Sometimes questions would be spoken with a phony Spanish accent to see if that would help.

After it was all over, after all the kids in my classes (that's a lot since science and social studies classes were always filled to the max) had acquainted themselves and their friends from other grades with the intricate details of my color blindness, "Mr. White, this is my little brother Alphonso, tell him about how you got to be color-blind. Tell him how 'the trait'[2] works too," we settled down to do what we had to do. The little Florida school where I was teaching was a small school district, one where local tax money went to pave the roads to white people's places, favor the little businesses the county had, and support an impressive infrastructure of county government. Oh, they would buy a computer every now and then with some federal money and set it up in some prominent place at the public school and call the TV station, but mostly, it was a tough assignment going to school in that county either as a student or a teacher. The affluent white children went to the "Christian" school. Most of the kids in public schools were black. Many of our students hadn't had much experience with situations that gave the opportunity for learning compassion for the problems of other people. Even so, they became my allies. "Jesus, Mr. White, that ain't the right color for that. I hate to hurt your feelings, but I just can't stand it." All through the year things would occur to them. "Mr. White, how can you tell when a white woman gets shy and blushes if you are color-blind?" somebody would ask. "Skin gets kind of shiny looking, and besides, they look like they are wandering off in their mind," I might venture. "How about a black woman, Mr. White?" "Same thing." "Mr. White, when a white person gets sun-burned, can you tell that?" "Sure, if you poke them with your finger the skin gets extra-white for a while afterward, otherwise they look sort of mis-erable and tired." "Can you tell ashy?" "Yep." "What about freckle-faced?" "Sure." "Mr. White, Can I ask you something? I always wondered about them freckles. They go down the neck . . . How far down they go on them kind of people?" "All the way." "Mr. White, you ain't no real schoolteacher."

Once my wife, a schoolteacher too, had to go off on one of those useless out-of-town workshops that teachers are always being subjected to so that the administration can claim that they are doing something to "make edu-cation the very best that it can possibly be" by introducing a bunch of new acronyms and eating a bunch of doughnuts. I, a sort of helpless person in some ways, was left at home alone to fend for myself and I quickly ran out of socks. Luckily the Dollar Store was right on my way to work. Too bad I had to go in there with my naked feet in my schoolteaching oxfords. Lucky for me it was cold enough so that I could wear my overcoat coat to hide how I had snatched my pants down to cover my sockless condition with the britches legs. Another lucky thing was that they were having a regular sock rummage sale on a table right by the door. Too bad they had already been picked over and weren't matched up anymore. Luckily I have a good eye for size. Too bad I left the bag on top of the car while I was covertly pulling my pants back up. Good thing I saw the bag fly off and strew its contents all over the highway. The trouble was, I had not adequately fastened my britches before I hopped out and I was hobbled before I could get back to the socks and a passing truck blew them all to hell and gone. At least I found two of them . . . Unfortunately, the two didn't match. Luckily, even with all that, I wasn't late for school. Too bad I didn't get to consult with my conspirator in the social studies room next door . . . Good thing the year was well enough along for everyone to be comfortable with imperfect situations. As the chil-dren (eighth graders ain't children but what can I say?) of my first class filed in, all of them gave my socks the once-over . . . "Mr. White, ain't you got no momma?"

One of the side effects of color-blindness is the inability to appreciate makeup. The subtleties of all the hues that are used are lost to us and all that remains are the differences in darkness and lightness. For a long time, I thought that the recent escalation in the use of lots of makeup was the sign

36

of an explosion of spouse abuse, those terrible bruises on the cheeks, those black eyes, busted lips . . . I worried that it would happen to one of mine. Finally it did and I jumped in with both feet like a fool. I was embarrassed when I found out that all those abrasions and bruises were just decorations. Good thing I hadn't gotten around to applying some decorations of my own on the head of the husband of that dear frumped-up little child quite yet.

My sister's son is, predictably, also color-blind. When he was first starting school, his teacher sent a note home saying that she thought he needed to be tested to see if he needed to be labeled "EMH" or "TMH" or one of them because he seemed unable to learn his colors. I started to jump in and raise a bunch of hell but I finally decided just to show the boy that the names of the colors were written on the paper cover of the crayon. No need to start the interrogation ritual before the kid was firmly on his feet. I looked forward to having some color-blind company, but now that he is a grown man, I find that all we ever do is argue about what color something is. One lady, upon overhearing a discussion between us during a parade, said, "You know y'all ain't making a bit of sense with all that."

During the seventies, the optometrists invented this little colored contact lens that, they said, when worn in one eye, would rectify the condition. My father, whose love of gimmicks and doodads ruled his life, insisted that I come to California to be fitted. I said that I didn't see how half a pair of rose-colored glasses could possibly cost so much. "I'll spring for the doctor. You buy the plane ticket." I took the bus. The damn thing was terrible. I never did find out if it straightened out my color perception because it made me list to the right so bad that I couldn't pay attention. Besides, even after I had learned to walk in something besides a tight circle, every person I met would stop dead in their tracks, grab me firmly, and offer to help me get that bug out of my eye so I wouldn't keep staggering out into the traffic. I bought a plane ticket back home.

My grandfather was also color-blind. Because of his determination, he refused to use automobiles even after they had proved to be almost practical. His dignity also made him try to keep people from knowing that he couldn't see colors. He was a formidable man. Both of his daughters were getting pretty old before they got married because he intimidated the beaux so. He wasn't mean, and both my father and my uncle liked him fine once they got up the nerve to stand up and speak. If anyone had known he was color-blind, they would not have dared to grab any portion of their garment, thrust it at him, and demand that he tell them what color it was. Long after he died, I was talking to one of his old employees about snakes. The fact came out that I had to use other ways to tell which was which besides color ("red next to yellow, kill a fellow" . . . child, please). "You know, Mr. Jim was like that," said the man, looking both ways to see if the ghost was passing by on his horse. "We never let on that we knew. When he would get to going on about this pink this and this pink that, everybody just agreed with him. They don't do that for you do they?"

Lots of times, I have wished I could see all the colors of the rainbow. Some folks have kindly asked me if I hadn't wondered what I had missed. I guess I have, but I am a happy man. Durn fool with it, some say. The other day, my granddaughter asked me to pass her a green marker (why ain't the name of the color written on them?). I said, "You show me which is green and if you aren't right, I'll get to snorfle on your neck." I don't know if she was trying to fool me or not, but it worked.

1. *Sex-linked* is a genetic term for any inherited characteristic that is carried on the pair of chromosomes that determine what sex a person will be. Women have two active sex chromosomes ("X") while men only have one and this other little anemic thing ("Y") for the other half of the pair. Normally, any bad word in the genetic language that appears on one chromosome is hushed by the corresponding good word on the other chromosome of the pair. In women these arguments result in mostly normal people, while in men, the big chromosome gets its way no matter what it says because little puny "Y" just stammers around and can't say anything worth mentioning. (How's that for anthropomorphic?)

2. *The trait* is a colloquialism for sickle cell trait, the presence of one recessive gene on one chromosome that, when present on both chromosomes of the pair, causes sickle cell anemia, a deformity of the erythrocytes in the blood of some people with ancestors who lived around Africa. Fortunately, "the trait" is not sex-linked and there are always two voices in the argument so sickle cell anemia is rarer than color-blindness but sickle cell anemia is a hard disease and not an entertainment for anybody. Interest in my genetic defect made it easy for me to explain about "the trait." Easy tests are available to identify folks who carry the bad word. If those folks keep away from unions with other folks who also carry "the trait" their children won't have to suffer the misery of sickle cell anemia. Too bad human nature is like it is and selectivity is not as easy as the test. Too bad sickle cell anemia and all the other birth defects aren't as easy to be happy with as mine.

Pine Oil

in which a family remedy evolves from cow dip

I am the one who fell heir to the old big pine oil jug. It is more a responsibility than a privilege but it is about the least of those that came along after Momma died. The pine oil is in a five-gallon glass jimmy-john that sits in the pantry closet in its crate in a squatty, slowly shrinking gray bed of ancient excelsior. The best I can figure, it has been sitting in the same place since around the time of World War Two. There is a little paper tag that Momma tied to the neck of the bottle about 1965 or so that says, DO NOT PUT ON BALLS.

I can remember when there were two jimmy-johns of pine oil but I busted one when I was a little boy trying to climb up to the peach jar shelf. It turned over and the full glass bottle inside the crate broke and five gallons of pine oil flowed out through the closet door and twenty feet down the pantry hall all the way through the kitchen. My family, as soon as they found out that I wasn't cut to pieces, stood around and discussed the progress of the pine oil as it soaked through the floor and seeped under the threshold of the kitchen door and then dripped onto mossy old brick steps. It was a marvelous thing then, and continues to be even now. Evidence of that day persists, not only on the floor where there is a sheen on the pine boards more beautiful than any other place in the house but on the steps where no moss has grown since that day. Even under the house, in the sand, the thickly random pattern of doodlebug holes is startlingly interrupted by long straight lines with no doodlebug holes where the pine oil dripped through the old gapped open hand-planed tongues and grooves of the ancient flooring above.

I was supposed to take the remaining half-full jug to my house when I inherited it, but I have somehow procrastinated so long that my neat sister who wound up with the responsibility of the house has quit nagging. We all have our little jugs of pine oil that we siphoned out to take with us when we moved out after we grew up a long time ago, and since the cow dipping days are long gone, it doesn't take much to do the job. I probably use more than any of the rest of them and my forty-year-old gin bottle is still better than half full. I keep it in a safe place where my grandchildren can't accidentally bust it like I did back in the forties. That old stuff is as extinct as the mastodons. I couldn't do without it. None of us could.

Pine oil is the essential oil of turpentine from the old vanishing longleaf pine trees. It used to be common stuff. People used it as a universal disinfectant (a by-product of the pulpwood industry is substituted these days in these common pine-named bathroom products but that half-assed dilution ain't in it with the full-strength real stuff). Pine oil will kill anything from insects to microbes and do it without poisoning the poor infested creature you put it on. The reason we had so much of it in the old days was that we used to dip hundreds of cows in it. We would herd them up from out of the piney woods and drive them along the fence to a chute where they had to jump into this deep concrete pit full of pine oil dip. A bunch of us would crowd around this place to make sure that none of the cows turned around and tried to go back. We would drive them off into the dip (an emulsion of pine oil in water) and push their heads under with a broom. After they came out the ramp at the other side, they were free to go on back to the woods and their business. They were free of external parasites too . . . all the ticks on them would die and dry up . . . not only that, but new ticks wouldn't get on them until it got cold enough to be too late. For the first few days, horseflies and yellow flies wouldn't even bite them. The flies that were with them when they got dipped were sure glad to see us that were working the trough though. We used to have to catch up a little dip for ourselves. My grandfather would wipe dip off the neck of the first cow as she scrambled up the output side and put it on himself and any little children that were hanging around. All it takes is a little whiff of pine oil to take me back to those old dusty days in the late summertime.

It was always hot. The locusts (that's the seventeen-year cicada) would be hollering their last desperate tune up in the trees and the cows would be bellowing and bamming the boards of the chute. People would have to holler at them and shoo them to make them do right. It was a loud, dusty business. Those poor cows would have been driven from way on back in the place and, except for a few hardheads, they would smell the water and trot right straight into the chute to the dip trough. We let them drink a little bit of the dip before we pushed them on into the water with the pole. We thought it might kill what ailed them inside just like it did on their hides. I don't think it hurt them any. They still drank the dip when we switched to DDT right after World War Two . . . didn't kill them. Didn't kill the yellow flies or horseflies either so we had to bring ourselves a little pine oil in a bottle because that new dip wasn't any help at all.

Ticks are all over the woods around here. The big ones aren't so bad . . . you can feel them walking on you (we all learned that talent early) and pick them off before they bite you. I used to teach school and in the early spring before the time sprang forward, there was a short chance, when it got to be daylight enough, to fish for just a little minute or two in the mornings on the way to school. I would pull off my britches and my shoes and wade out with my pole and catch me a little mess. I would clean them in the sink in my lab during my planning period and hide them in the refrigerator in the teacher's lounge. After Mrs. Huggins found out about that and started getting my few redbellies and stumpknockers, I had to bring my son's little old college refrigerator to my classroom.

So, with my years of practice, I was able to feel a tick walking up to find a tender place or a confining spot where he could brace himself to bore in while I was boring those kid's eyeballs out trying to show them why it is cold in the winter and hot in the summer (knowledge that somehow escapes an astonishing number of people). I found out that if I pinned the tick to my hide with my finger to keep him where I could find him when I got a chance, he would bite me right then, so I developed this subterfuge of acting like I had heard a commotion in the hall that I needed to check on. One time a big starry-head tick bit me in that tender spot where my ass hangs down over the top of my leg right in the middle of demonstrating how oblique light isn't as hot as direct light. "Excuse me just a minute," and I darted out the door, jammed it with my heel, looked both ways, snatched my britches down, and got that damn tick off me. I was so quick that nobody caught me in the hall and no copulations or conceptions occurred in my classroom while I was gone . . . that I know of. That worked for grown ticks, but sometimes, right in the middle of the experiment that shows how day length varies with axis tilt, I would discover that I had the seed ticks (right in the middle of manipulating the slide projector and the globe) and then there was nothing for it but to barricade myself in my chemical closet with my little bottle of pine oil and let the procreation proceed.

"Mr. White! What you been doing in there all this time . . . Got-Dog Man, what is all them fumes? You smell like you got some kind of chemical dependency." I am a truthful man, at least about things that matter, and the lesson would just have to take the seed-tick shift. The country children would understand perfectly. "My daddy uses diesel fuel." (I tried it myself once in an emergency . . . about half effective.) "Mr. White, you was in there prancing around naked as a jaybird wasn't you? Nothing personal now, but I'm glad you locked the door."

Seed ticks are a serious thing. You know, ticks are supposed to be in the same class with spiders. The adults have eight legs but when they first hatch out they are tiny little things with only six legs like insects. The female tick stays on the host animal, usually a deer, rabbit, cotton rat (vole), or squirrel around here. She keeps a little shiny male underneath her until she gets inseminated and full of blood . . . then she's a big, shiny, round, tight, incompetent thing, just full of eggs . . . a "squirt tick" like you find on a dog's neck or around the anus of a deer. After she gets ripe, she drops off on the ground and little ticks hatch out right there inside her as if she was only an egg-case like spiders have. Finally she busts open and the little six-legged larval ticks come crawling out by the thousands and climb up on the first weed they get to. They stay there like a little brown smudge on the grass with their two hind legs stretched out like little hooks. If you come by, they will all . . . seems like . . . grab you and swarm all over you and eat you into an itchy-bump mess. They are so small that they are almost invisible and they walk so lightly that it is real hard to feel them. Soon the psychosomatic walking from anticipation is far stronger than the real thing. We have some red-headed Yankee cousins who have repeatedly gotten themselves in pitiful shape with the seed ticks. We used to think that it was because they were so ignorant that they got in such a fix but we finally discovered that the real reason was that they couldn't feel the seed ticks walking because they didn't have any little hairs on their skin for the ticks to bump into as they crawled up, and all those freckles that they had instead apparently served no sensory function. After all the seed ticks bit, the freckles and bite bumps sort of merged on those children and they turned a uniform bad-looking color. If it hadn't been for pine oil, they probably would have swole up and died.

The cure, after detection, is simple. All you have to do is immediately strip naked, dip a little rag (I'm a dirty-sock man myself . . . ain't got time to be prissy at a time like that) in some pine oil, and wipe every, even vaguely, suspect area. Leave them clothes in the pile right where they fell . . . don't even feel around for your pocketknife or your money or anything. If something is too embarrassing to leave in plain sight like that, you can rake it off in the bushes with a long stick, but you better not touch anything, especially not your shoes. After that, you have to stand around naked and wait until the pine oil has had time to kill the seed ticks. While you are waiting, it is best to peer closely to make sure there aren't any little places you left out. After a little while, you can rinse yourself off and put on some other clothes . . . if you have any . . . and go on about your business. One of my uncles is supposed to have driven a bulldozer, buck naked, for four miles so he would have a little concealment coming up through the yard . . . ran over the *Ophiopogon* border trying to get close to the door so he could slip in. One wit observed, "Hell man, we knew you was naked . . . you didn't have to destroy the flower bed . . . you must think somebody wants to look at yo old bony ass."

The seriousness of getting in the seed ticks is how the warning tag came to be on the old original jimmy-john. It used to fall to my momma to anoint the little children who came home with seed ticks. She would catch them before they had a chance to come in the house and examine them carefully with her eagle eye. If they were infested, she would pull off their clothes right there on the steps . . . didn't make any difference whose children they were . . . sex, social standing, race, attitude don't make a bit of difference at a time like that. Since they were so ignorant as to have seed ticks and not know it, she would assume that they were covered and she would get the *big* rag. Mucous membranes were immune to the ticks and hence to treatment, but anything that had normal skin on it got wiped down real good . . . head, ears, between the toes, external genitals . . . everywhere. After experimentation she finally began to exempt the lips, the eyelids, and the pigmented part of the anus to take care of themselves but she didn't leave anything else alone. After each one of the children (this always seemed to happen to groups of exploring children . . . including strangers unaccustomed to this sort of treatment) was dealt with, they were told to run (half blind from the pine oil fumes) all the way around the house . . . three times . . . which exercise proved to take long enough for the pine oil to work on the seed ticks. After they came back, she would rinse them off with the hose and put a big everready T-shirt on their naked selves and release them in the custody of their, sometimes dumbfounded, parents. When she first applied this effective ritual on behalf of my own two boys and their cousins, they wailed, "MaOdie, you ain't going to put that pine oil on my testicles are you?" "Yeah, that's just exactly what seed ticks like . . . they think the little wrinkles of the scrotum are perfectly delicious. Come here boy . . . it won't hurt you. Pine oil is wonderful stuff . . . absolutely harmless." Momma was one of those people that folks always minded, so they submitted. Her credibility began to suffer though and they told me that that pine oil burned the hell out of them there. One said, "Man that stuff burned so bad that, when the others stopped running around the house, I just had to keep on going." I finally had to confront her about it and she agreed to abide by the results of an experiment, of course she wasn't properly equipped to be the guinea pig, so I had to stand for the job myself. . . burned the pluperfect hell out of me. My credibility ain't all that hot but I finally managed to convince her to put that tag on the jug. I advise you to do the same. Of course, the last longleaf pine was turpentined about 1949. I don't know where you are going to get your jug to put the tag on. Just some more lost lore of the piney woods . . . which place, if you ain't got any pine oil, you better stay away from.

Slow and Barefoot

in which an errant gene slows me down . . . hooray

My mother was the slowest kind of person. When she was a young girl, she had broken her leg in a bad way when she ran over a wagon and killed the mule with a motorcycle (did not hurt the man driving the wagon. She hollered from the wreckage "You all right" and he replied "Just let me get out from under this mule and I'll see.") and I am sure that that old injury slowed her down some but her brothers and sister said she had always been slow. They said that when all of them walked to the pond to go swimming, they would already be through and ready to come back before she would ever show up and she would have to go swimming all by herself.

My two sisters both got divorced at about the same time and got into the habit of walking all over our old home place for exercise. Momma went too just for company and commiseration but it didn't work out. Those fast-walking women would lap her two or three times every afternoon. One of them told me that once when they passed her the first time, she was bending over in the middle of the little dirt road with her head down and they were worried that she had had some kind of heatstroke or something but she was just watching the doings in an ant bed. When they made the three- or four-mile circuit and came around the second time, she was still in the same place doing the same thing and she showed them the winged bodies of all the male ants of the colony scattered all around the little mound where their sisters had dragged them. "They killed them and now they are hauling off the bodies," said Momma. "Good idea," growled my oldest sister.

I was like my mother in one way anyhow, I was so fascinated by ants and things that I would have squatted in the road all day too but unfortunately, I did not inherit the slow gene. I was so twitchish when I was a little boy that when I found something interesting, I would stomp all the grass around it to death during my observations. When Momma went walking, she would always come back with stories about how she had watched a whole nest of newly hatched baby lizards dig themselves out of the ground or seen a snake swallow another snake or caught the mating of a pair of pileated wood-peckers (rough business . . . roosters and chickens are tame stuff). I would squirm with envy, and head right straight out to see what I could see too, but

45

all I would come home with would be scratches on my legs and tater-rows on my neck. My mother was not one to volunteer advice, not even to her children, but I finally slowed down enough to ask her why she saw so much and I saw so little. "You walk too fast" was all she had to say about it.

She was right. I guess, if those days had been these days, the school would have had me identified with some kind of named ailment and doped me down with some pills or something. My mother dealt with my wiggle-someness in another way . . . she just wouldn't let me in the house except when I was so hungry that I had to sit still to eat or so sleepy that I couldn't wiggle another wag. I am still like that. One of my customers told another man, "You know, that Robb White moves just like an electric spark." My good young doctor (an Eagle Scout and animal-watcher) tried to regulate my calorie intake to modify my blood chemistry a little bit and I lost so much weight in the first week that he was astonished. "You must have a metabolic rate about like an insectivore," he said. What I am trying to say is that my nature made it very hard for me to get close to the nature for which I yearned when I was a little boy . . . that is, until I started having to go barefoot.

There is another errant gene in the family that causes serious inflammation of the Achilles tendon in some of us when we wear shoes. It happens when we are about half grown and the only thing to do is to leave those shoes off for the rest of our lives. My father's brother, the college professor, had this gene. He used to wear these little Japanese toe-rigged, cloth-slipper-looking things . . . until he became tenured.

Having to go barefoot was the best thing that ever happened to me. It is impossible to walk too fast through the brier-woods without any shoes on. I started seeing box turtles copulating, baby birds hatching out, gopher tortoises laying eggs, grasshoppers, millipedes and all kinds of other arthropods mating, baby quail and turkeys hiding, all kinds of hawks standing on the ground eating doves, squirrels, and cotton rats . . . there were deer everywhere.

So, what happened to the slow gene? I have a very deliberate four-year-old grandson and I saw him squatting out in the yard looking at something just the other day. "What you see there, Will?" "Look at what these ants are doing, Pop-Pop. The little ones that don't have any wings are killing the big ones that do have wings and dragging them off."

Farts

in which the work of maestros is lost forever

It is a well-known but little-recognized fact that farts are funny. I think the reason recognition of that fact is not as universal as the fact itself is because of suppression by religious entities of all sorts. I mean if the whole doctrine of the followers of any deity is to promote single-mindedness, gravity, and solemnity, a fart in church is no laughing matter . . . unless there are children present. That's why they invented Sunday school . . . to get them the hell out of there just in time. After the children are gone and some bilious and self-sanctified old poot has to cut one, Episcopalians act like nothing happened, Baptists, Methodists, Presbyterians, and such just raise their eyes heavenward and some of the more retentive members may glare at the perpetrator, Catholics cross themselves and mumble a little litany against the thing. I guess the Garrison Keillor–style Lutherans say, "Could be worse." My mother-in-law (a dear person and keen observer of the foibles of humankind) was sitting in the waiting room of the town geriatric specialist when an old man who was also waiting surprised himself and all the other old people in there. As an apology, he said, "I knew old age would be bad but not *that* bad."

One of the first hints of a sense of humor in a baby is when he (or she . . . they are not *born* prissy) laughs at a fart so I guess such recognition is natural. I think suppression of such natural instincts is bad and so did my momma. She alienated herself completely from her new mother-in-law (an Episcopalian) who had the remarkable talent of being able to get up from the supper table and vent a single syllable . . . sort of like the bark of a small, adenoidal dog . . . with each step as she walked to the room where the brandy was. The mother-in-law was able to act as if the little dog belonged to someone else but my poor mother was not able to suppress just a hint of a guffaw at how closely the little thing was following behind . . . and gaining.

Because of her unconventional tolerance, her children and all our cousins on the old home place (which is still home for some) became quite talented. Like all talented people, we delighted in performing and wanted to expose our abilities to a wider range of people.

Which, at that, I must interrupt this essay to explain something. Animals (even dogs, some of which have a very well-developed sense of humor) do not think farts are funny. Perhaps it is because, due to the discrimination of whichever deity is in charge, they have been rendered mute. Humans don't think the farts of animals are particularly funny, either. Nobody laughs at the venting of mules, carriage horses, and oxen when they are pulling you along behind. Of course they are herbivores so it ain't so bad but dogs are carnivores and scavengers and, though there is a little bowl of impotent processed pellets right there in the corner, are apt to eat no telling what-all out in the yard. Even the most carefully coiffed little Precious is liable to lie there in the corner of the sofa and reek the room with the results of the further decomposition of something she found dead out in the yard. My grandmother had a tiny little bull terrier named Babs. Babs was bad to eat dead mice and even run over toad frogs in the driveway . . . loved rotten bird eggs that had fallen out of the numerous nests in the vast *Pittisporum* hedges around the old outfit. Because of this, she was unwelcome on the sofa in the living room when my powerful and imposing grandfather was in attendance. My grandmother loved to cuddle the little thing, though, so, when they were alone, old Babs would sit in her lap or lie in a little nest snuggled against her hip while she was doing her needlework and other Victorian accomplishments of the day. When my grandfather came into the room, Babs would get up and go behind the sofa. That was not good enough sometimes. If it became necessary to move Babs a little farther, he would get the bed warmer from off the wall where it hung by the fireplace and flail around under there with its long handle until Babs scurried out and went into another room. It finally evolved down to where every now and then while Grandmother and Grandfather were sitting on the sofa having their evening toddy, Babs would come out all by herself and hurry into the other room. . . walking on three legs as if she had been injured. In a minute, the reason for her exit would reveal itself. Once when I, at the ripe age of three, was snuggled in Babs' little vacated nest between my grandmother and my grandfather, I let out a silent, satisfying little fart. Just a few seconds later Babs emerged and hurried with her three-legged gait out of the room.

Soon we little farts of the house were very fortunate in our quest to distribute our talents more widely. My father was an early fan of technology and, though he could neither sing nor play music, acquired a reel-to-reel tape recorder. We set up a studio out on the side porch and every time it dawned on one of us while we were at play that the time had come, we would scurry in the characteristic clench-kneed strut of the Presbyterian matron up on the porch and try to render our offering into the microphone. Sometimes, much to the amusement of the enthusiastic crowd, especially with the littlest children, the thing would get loose prematurely or sometimes it would become reabsorbed (that's why sanctified people have such bad breath) and the poor child would stand there struck mute while the audience tried to suppress twitters as the reels slowly revolved. With a reel-to-reel machine, it is easy to manually wind back to the last offering and cut out such a semi-silent gap but sometimes the child would be able to, finally, squeeze out a little something and that part of the resulting tape (which was at least two hours long) would have especial value. All us children who had become bored listening to an endless series of single-syllable barks, sibilant whines, and sonorous bleats of operatic proportions would fall silent and wait with bated breath. Things that come hard are always more valuable than that which comes easy.

That simple, wordless tape was pretty good but our best performance was when we dubbed the Marty Robbins song "A White Sports Coat and a Pink Carnation" and skillfully replaced every noun in the song with another utterance that not only fit the melody but had exactly the right number of syllables . . . properly spaced. It was the work of consummate maestros, and took all of one summer's vacation to get exactly right. I, myself, did the best "carnation."

When my father ran off to California in 1956 to write for the movies and TV, he took his recorder and stole our tapes. We keep expecting them to turn up on *America's Funniest Home Videos*.

Epilogue

One of my sons inherited my father's technophilia. He has always been gutting out radios and stereos and all sorts of junk all his life . . . made good money when he was in high school enhancing the jam in automobiles of his peers. Now he is in his forties and still fools around with stuff like that. He has figured out how to distribute that wonderful sound in a new way. He knows how to, in a second, install a "vanity" ring to a cell phone. He worked on it for weeks to get the timbre exactly right for the circuitry and speaker of the average instrument. He planned to go to the

Republican convention and offer to, for free, instantly change anybody's phone so that it played the first few bars of "The Battle Hymn of the Republic" (he said) when somebody called that phone. It would have been bait-and-switch fraud but since no compensation was involved, would not have been a criminal act. Too bad he didn't qualify to get into the convention. Oh well.

Old Naturalists and Dugouts

in which I reveal some obsessions

I was a lucky little boy. You know how some children are born with obsessive compulsion as one of their properties sort of like redheadedness? Well, I wasn't redheaded but I sure was obsessed by two things . . . boats and the doings of animals. Animal obsession is fairly common among children. There are lots of little girls who would rather play with toy horses and dogs than damn Barbie dolls and there are scads of little boys who love bugs and frogs more than monster trucks. Even though the obsessive preferences of children seem to hedge in more or less stereotyped directions there are exceptions. My mother was a good example of that. Though she liked horses fine (would not have touched a Barbie doll with a ten-foot-stick) she used them mostly as vehicles to get where she wanted to go . . . the places where wild animals lived their natural lives beyond the influence of mankind. She was a naturalist . . . a universal naturalist. She liked birds, bees, herps, fish, mammals, and sea creatures both with and without vertebrae. She was also a cosmopolitan botanist. She was lucky, too.

There is something about the place where we were both raised (South Georgia, North Florida) that attracts ardent naturalists. You know, William Bartram walked right through there way before the Revolution and so did John Muir right after the Civil War and they found plenty of interesting things to write about.

The mentor of my mother was Herbert L. Stoddard. He called himself an ornithologist and was certainly one of the foremost of that breed but his interests in natural history were absolutely universal. He knew a lot about every natural thing and what he didn't know, he was trying to find out. There isn't time for me to even scratch the surface here so I'll just recommend his two best books. *The Bobwhite Quail* was his definitive work. It is a priceless collector's item and a classic example of the exhaustive field study of not only a little bird, but the immensely diverse and complex ecosystem upon which the little birds depend . . . the now almost extinct, old-growth, longleaf pine, fire-type woods. Stoddard was the man who caused the scales to fall from the eyes of all the other people who thought they understood the ecology of the southeastern coastal plain. Mr. Stoddard's childhood memory of growing up under difficult circumstances, down where Disney World is the main ecosystem now, is so eloquent and so human that nobody can read *Memoirs of a Naturalist* without being strongly affected.

Though Mr. Stoddard was a most wonderful man, he had a peculiar personality. For one thing, he didn't have any sense of humor at all except for the most basic puns . . . he just loved those. Not only that but he was a pedant of the first order. If it was possible to use some special word, he would do it. He eschewed the use of common language all he could. "We need to refrigerate these carcasses as quickly as we can to avoid postmortem penetration of the flesh," he explained once while we were skinning a batch of little warblers. Another time he was on the riverbank looking for bird nests when he came across a big rattlesnake in his way. He calmly punted the coiled snake out into the river where my father was trying to play like he was fishing with a fly rod. No matter which way my father scrambled, the high-floating, furious coiled snake changed his drift to come right at him." Don't worry, Robb," yelled Mr. Stoddard, "he's fully into pre-molt. His sensory pits are disabled and the integument over his eyes has become opaque and he can't see a thing." Yeah, right. My father never did find that fly rod.

First my mother and then I followed Mr. Stoddard around like little puppies. In his memoir book there is a picture of my teenage mother rigging a net up on a chimney top on one of the highest buildings in Thomasville, Georgia, to catch and tag chimney swifts for Mr. Stoddard.

There are no pictures of me following him around but there is some evidence. One of the things he did was to diligently pick up all the little dead or crippled migrating birds that had hit the guy wires of one of the first TV towers around. The tower was a thousand feet high and on top of the highest hill in Leon County, Florida (where Tallahassee is the county seat), and a lot of little birds hit the wires during their nocturnal migratory flights. Mr. Stoddard kept the grass cut real low under the tower to make finding his specimens easier. We always got there way before dawn and hurried with our flashlights to pick up the little birds before daylight brought the crows. Some mornings there would be hundreds in the grass and some of the poor little things weren't dead yet. Mr. Stoddard taught me how to kill them by sliding my forefinger (or thumb with larger birds) up under their breastbone and compressing the heart so it couldn't beat. If done right, the frantic little doomed creature would just seem to go to sleep in your hand. Though we killed hundreds of birds that way, we never forgot exactly what it was we were doing. Mr. Stoddard carefully skinned out every one and stuffed the skins and sent them to museums all over the world. He (and I) ate the little carcasses. Four and twenty blackbirds baked in a pie beats the dickens out of four and twenty warblers, I can tell you from firsthand experience.

Early one very foggy morning, we were picking up hundreds of white-eyed vireos when something very big hissed and lunged at Mr. Stoddard out of the bushes near the edge of the mowed part. Mr. Stoddard (though he had nerves of steel and was not afraid of anything) thought it best to levitate about three feet and, at the very top of his ascent, move horizontally about five feet away from whatever that big thing was before he allowed himself to come back to earth. It was a fully mature golden eagle that had hit the wire and broken his wing. The eagle was not the least bit intimidated by human beings and advanced upon us most aggressively hissing and snapping his beak. Even though I was very young, my sense of humor had developed beyond puns. "Are you going to mash his heart with your thumb, Mr. Stoddard?" I asked. "No," he replied. "I'll hold him at bay while you go back to the car and get the .22." In a big steel cabinet at the bird-skin collection of Tall Timbers Research Station down near Tallahassee (right across the road from the tower) there is a whole drawer devoted to just one stuffed bird skin. SHOT BY ROBB WHITE . . . WCTV TOWER . . . LEON COUNTY FLORIDA, 6:05 AM EST, MARCH, 21, 1955, the little tag reads. That is the only record of a golden eagle from this part of the country.

He, I was told, made skins of the last two ivory-billed woodpeckers collected in this country. When Mr. Stoddard was in the middle of his longleaf forest ecosystem studies in my mother's childhood, he met an old cracker turpentine hand, who said that he had seen a pair of ivory-billed woodpeckers. "Surely, you are mistaken, sir," stated Mr. Stoddard unequivocally. "What you saw was undoubtedly the common pileated woodpecker, which superficially resembles the extinct ivory-billed. There are no ivory-billed woodpeckers alive today." The next day, when Mr. Stoddard got home from his fieldwork, there on his doorstep was a pair of ivory-billed woodpeckers. Their skins are in the Field Museum in Chicago.

Mr. Stoddard was worth following around because he knew more about animal doings than anyone I've ever met . . . and . . . he had a dugout canoe. To me it was the most marvelous vessel I ever saw. It was eighteen feet long and twenty-seven inches wide and chopped out of half a cypress log by some

Indians around Cherokee, North Carolina, back around the turn of the century. According to the story, this one was the lesser of the two halves of the log. It was parallel-sided all the way to the ends (like a log) and both ends were shaped exactly like the bottom of a tablespoon. It didn't seem to have any hardness to the bilges at all. It was just about still a log on the outside. I know that description won't arouse any wild imaginings of great beauty but it was a beautiful boat to my notion.

It stayed sunk by rainwater in the big pond on Mr. Stoddard's place. The way you prepared it for fishing was to throw the water out over the ends with the paddle. The way it was shaped facilitated that maneuver. It was easy and didn't take long and the end of the paddle became worn to fit the bottom of the boat so well that you could get almost the last drop. Too bad you couldn't scrape the pond slime out. Fortunately the freeboard was so low that you could easily get back in after you slipped out. I know there are some experts among you gentle readers who will scoff at me when I tell you that this very narrow, almost cylindrical vessel was stable enough to stand up in and fish out of with a fly rod but it was. The bottom was about an inch thick and completely waterlogged (a cypress log will sink to the bottom and stay there for thirty thousand years). I guess that acted sort of like a ballast keel. I won't lie to you. It was ticklish fishing out of the boat. You sort of had to part your hair in the middle, but after you got on to it, you could do it . . . even in the wintertime. The best thing was that the old boat was so much like a log that fish didn't pay any attention to it at all. There was no need for a fly rod. A short handline was all you needed as long as you sat still and the nature of the old canoe helped you remember to do that. Because of its great weight and low freeboard, the old thing did not blow all over the pond and get away from the honey hole like these cursed aluminum and fiberglass (and . . . help me, Jesus, wood-canvas) canoes do. It sat there (well) just like a log while you pulled them in over the side. Mr. Stoddard did that all the time. He did not believe in store-bought foods.

When the old man died, his son inherited the old boat. He was in some ways a chip off the old block. He liked to wade the river with his fly rod and did not fish in ponds. He had no need for a dugout canoe so he took it out of the pond (a job of work) and stored it in the barn and it dried out. The son was also a serious saltwater fisherman and became most serious at the arrival of the first cold front of the fall. When the first frost came, he would always be at the coast down in the wonderful marshes of Apalachee bay catching redfish (red drum) as fast as he could pull them in. For this purpose, he had an aluminum skiffboat about twelve feet long with some kind of outboard motor on the transom. He was not interested in boats. He was interested in fishing. Because of that, when the first frost came about thirty years ago, he discovered that the acidic compost pile of leaves had combined with the bilgewater to eat about three feet of aluminum out of the bottom of his boat. He was desperate. He got the old dugout canoe out of the barn and tried to put it on the trailer but it was too long and didn't want to do right so he put it on top of the car . . . just bashed a longitudinal dent in the full length of the roof and tied her off and went fishing. Did good, too. He said that since the bottom hadn't soaked up any water he had to be real careful not to turn over.

The copy I built of Mr. Stoddard's dugout was an ill-fated attempt by a doggedly determined eleven-year-old boy to carve, chop, and gnaw an exact duplicate out of the wrong kind of log with none of the right tools and very little skill. The thing looked sort of like a boat on the outside but the inside looked like what Mark Twain said about a pencil sharpened by a woman . . . hold on now, it wasn't me that said it . . . "as if she had done it with her teeth." Fortunately the hollowing process removed all the durable heartwood and the termites, powder post beetles, and rot quickly eliminated all evidence of my shame.

Robb's mother in her teens.

Snoring

in which another genetic trait is handed down

I busted my durn nose. Normally I am a very careful person. Although I am "getting on up there," and have been working in the log woods and at the sawmill and in the boat shop all my life, I am (knock on wood) still all here. (I exempt little things that were not under my control . . . like circumcision.) Most people who do my kind of work have left a good many of their body parts in the sawdust when they went to the emergency room but not me. This winter, though, my system failed me and a little piece of oak limb about as big as a Co-Cola bottle fell out of a tree and busted me on the nose. I thought that it had killed me until I remembered that they say, when you are dead, you aren't supposed to feel pain anymore.

When I got to the emergency room the young experienced attendant said, "Yep, this is a job for a real nose man . . . You just hold this ice bag and chill out until he gets here. No sense in us fooling around with such as this. This here is a job for a real nose man." I held the ice bag until the nose man came. He knew just what to do. "Plenty of room to work in. How much reduction do you want?" says he. *"Reduction?"* I hollered as best I could. Anyway, to make a long story short, he fixed my nose back and improved it in at least one way. I am sure that my sense of smell is better. I can smell a baby's head three feet away now, whereas I used to have to get real close and snuffle all around in the baby's hair for a long time. With my new ability, I have been able to branch out into necks and ears.

It was a good little while before anybody noticed the most amazing by-product of this reconstruction. Actually, it was my wife and newest grand-daughter who made the discovery. I had just woken up from my nap and there, framed in the doorway, were my wife and the baby staring at me like I had done an amazing thing. "You don't snore anymore," my wife said. "We have been standing here looking at you for ten minutes waiting for you to snore and you didn't." Napping and snoring (along with noses of a capable size) are family traits that go way back. So is the tradition of bringing babies into the napping area to marvel at the snoring. One of my earliest memories is my mother carrying me in her arms to stand in the door of my grandfather's office where he napped on the sofa so that I would know where all that fuss was coming from and not be scared anymore. Although it was interesting to me, it was no novelty . . . My own precious momma could knock the dirt dobber nests out from under the rafters herself. Not only that but her own snoring would wake her up . . . only she wouldn't be completely awake. She would give out with an extra-loud snort, wake up, sit bolt upright in the bed, and irritatedly demand information from any bystanders. The trouble was that she wouldn't know who she was talking to . . . or listen to their replies. She never understood why my sisters and I were so traumatized by having our identities so vehemently denied and our tearful pleas so perfectly ignored when this happened while we were little. "Why," she said, "you ought to have known that I was just talking in my sleep."

My mother's grandmother was legendary. She was, from all accounts, a prissy little woman with a lovely garden and some little lady-like turn-of-the-century accomplishments and a pretty good reproductive ability. The legend came from her napping and snoring. She had this little club of like-minded women who used to come out into the country to her house about every-so-often for a little get-together. First they would have their little coffee in the living room, then they would take a little walk in the garden and read the "God Wot" poem on the marble slab and discuss its merits while they sat in the gazebo down by the fern grott, then they would go to the music room and play the piano and sing "I Dream of Jeanie" and such until lunchtime. My great-grandmother had a bunch of servants who fixed the lunch and brought it to these ladies in the dining room. She was the last one of the family to have any of the old money and the last one to be able to employ the people of the country as servants but I grew up with the children of the children of these people and that's how I heard this legend. After lunch, these ladies would retire to their own separate bedrooms in the big house for a little nap. My great-grandmother's room was upstairs at the absolute other end of the house from the kitchen but not so far away that the servants couldn't hear their cue when the time had passed for worrying about any last requests for hot-water bottles and steamed towels, then they would eat up the tiny sandwiches and the juvenile frenched green beans and the little sip of wine that was left over. The descendants of the feast removers told me that the cue was so loud that people who were out in the fields would stop work and comment, "They done started scrapping out now."

Her son, my grandfather, was the champion. He could take a nap anywhere. As soon as he got through with his lunch, he would wander off like a dog looking for a warm place to lie down. Sometimes he would go out in the yard and find a sunny spot on the grass or, according the season, some shade under a bush. He would lie down flat on his back and fall immediately to sleep. Pretty soon, the caterpillars would be shaken from the leaves they were eating. The vibrations would shake the ground for yards around, and earthworms would come up to get rid of the itch from the vibration of the dirt against their integuments. If it was dry, sand would sift down into the doodlebug holes and they would begin to throw it back out. We, children and babies, would stand in the dappled shade and marvel at all this.

Although he slept strong, he could wake up at the slightest intrusion (child spectators must not have counted, I guess). He didn't like for dogs to do any useless barking and he had a bunch of dogs. He ruled their lives with nothing but his will. When a dog made a mistake while pointing the birds, all it took from my grandfather was a glance and the dog knew. At night, when my grandfather was sleeping, sometimes a possum or provocative little fox would pass by the dog yard way the hell-and-gone down where they killed the hogs, and the dogs would, in abandonment of their good sense, tune up. Sometimes my grandfather would have to sit up in the bed on the porch where he slept and bellow "Hey you" once to remind them, but usually they would shut up the minute he stopped snoring.

For a while after my nose job, I felt bad about being silenced. After all, I was the only one left alive who had inherited the trait. No more little babies would stand in awe at the door to find out what was making all the racket. When I told them the stories about their great-great-great-grandmother, great-great-grandfather, and great-grandmother, they wouldn't possibly be able to imagine the magnitude of the situation . . . old legends would surely die. Then one afternoon, I was awakened from my silent nap by a new little noise in the bed beside me. I thought that it was my wife, who had inherited a certain weak snoring ability of her own. I lay in the waking-up daze and listened carefully. I was sure, after a while, that it was not my wife, but it sure did sound familiar . . . very accomplished. I decided to take a little peek. It was my baby granddaughter taking her after-lunch nap beside me, and I could tell that she had been eating onions. I lay back down and dropped easily off for a few little minutes more.

The Tin Canoe of World War Two

in which I begin a lifetime of building eyeball designed boats

I was born and raised in a place called the "Red Hills" region of Georgia. Contrary to the *Tobacco Road* sound of the name, it is so wonderful here that I have never stayed for very long anyplace else. This is the last outpost of the pitifully endangered virgin longleaf pine woods that used to cover the entire coastal plain of the southeastern United States from Virginia to Texas including all of Florida down to the Everglades. The place in the woods where I grew up down here on the Georgia–Florida line has a bunch of ponds scattered all around and we kept some kind of old boat or other in each one of them. Usually those boats were the everlasting, immobile, flat-bottomed, rough-sawn, five-quarter cypress style that stayed in the water and were full of water and skeeter wigglers all the time. Sometimes somebody would want to use one bad enough to dip the water out and pull the willow trees out of the cracks in the bottom but most of the time, they stayed right where they were and we fished off the bank. I was usually the one who went to all the trouble to make one of the old boats move because I wasn't patient enough to sit in the same place and watch my cork and wait for the fish to come to me. I could see them out there roiling the water beyond the range of my cane pole and I deluded myself that, if I could just get out there, I could catch them.

In addition to all these ponds but out back of the old place, there was a respectable river—one of those meandering kind with cutoff sloughs all through the woods. Those cutoffs were full of fish and ducks. I yearned for a little lightweight boat that I could carry, all by myself, from one little hole of water to another and even put in the main river when it was navigable. This was back in the days of the wood-canvas canoe, and some of our Yankee cousins brought them down and they were fun while they lasted, but they didn't last very long. The water that got between the canvas and the slats never got a chance to dry out in this humidity and they would grow a crop of mushrooms after about one season unless the boats were carefully dried out in the loft of the barn every time they got used. Such carefulness is not in the nature of my family, and we ruined some beautiful old canoes. When gas got rationed during World War Two, the cousins stopped bringing them down anyway, so I took the roof off my uncle's chicken house operation that he abandoned when he went off to fight and made me a tin canoe. You wouldn't think that the jackleg[1] efforts of a filthy, dirty, poorly supervised child would turn out to be worth a flip, but even now that I am a serious (well) professional boatbuilder with more than forty years in the business, I seldom build a boat that turns out all that much better than those tin canoes.

The first tin canoes were primitive. Now, they were satisfactory all right, but they needed improvement. I remember the launching of the very first one as if it happened yesterday. I think it was sixteen feet long and I know it was made of one sheet of what they call "five V crimp" roofing tin meant to span two feet on the roof of something like a chicken house. I bent the ends of the tin up and nailed it onto two rough cypress two-by-four stems sticking up almost vertical. Though it was caulked with regular, never-get-hard roofing tar, it leaked not only around the stems, but up through the holes where the nails used to be when the tin was still on the chicken house. The tar over the nail holes transferred itself to my skin when I was in the boat and earned me one of my early nicknames, "Spotty." The boat, though, was light and easy to drag by the stem through the bushes. The galvanize seemed to lubricate its bottom (a fact exploited by the airboat builders around here for years until the invention of high-tech) and it slid over the grass and pond weeds like they weren't even there. I couldn't wait to get in. It took a few tries.

I learned that I had to be careful. The narrow tin made the balance between beam and freeboard real tricky. If I made the boat too narrow, it was so tippy that I couldn't get settled before it turned over. If I made it too wide, it wouldn't have enough freeboard and would sink quickly to the bottom so that soon, the only thing that would be sticking up out of the water would be me and the two stems. There is a remarkable photograph of that in the family album. I'm the one in the middle with the hat.

When I finally managed to get it adjusted so that I could get in and push off, I knew I had something. The tin canoe moved through the water like a snake. Just paddling with my hands would make it sizzle across the pond. I had to be careful not to cut myself on the sharp edges of the tin, and to keep track of the bilgewater situation, but luckily the first pond was one of the shallow ones and I didn't lose my boat before I trained myself. I was obsessed. The abandoned chicken house had enough tin to make a big fleet of tin canoes and I instantly set out to improve the model. About the time all the men came home from World War Two and stopped all those women from spoiling me, I had evolved the tin canoe into a mighty fine boat.

You Can Build One for Yourself . . . Here's the Step by Step

The highly evolved five V crimp tin canoe is built like this. You need a sixteen-foot sheet of tin. Short tin might seem, at first, to be more workable, but we are messing around on the fringes of possible here and twelve or fourteen feet of tin won't keep you out of the water quite as long as sixteen feet will. After you get your tin home from wherever you got it (that stuff will slide out of a pickup and blow off a car too), the first thing to do is wash it with strong detergent to get the oil off, then fold it down the middle like a piece of paper. Don't crimp it along the center crimp too bad, just enough to get the tin to come together at the stems. Put some polyurethane adhesive sealant on the one-by-two stems and screw the tin to them with short stainless-steel flathead screws. See if you can drive the screws in so they bend the tin into a countersunk place so the heads will be sort of flush and won't catch weeds so bad. It helps to pre-do it with strong, hardened black steel screws that won't wring off before they get flush. I know it is a lot of trouble, but this is a high-performance boat . . . you got to do it right. Don't cut yourself. WD-40 will get that dook off you if you don't wait too long.

STOMPING THE BOAT INTO SHAPE

This is the tricky part. If you think you have enough screws in both ends, you can go ahead right away and not wait the long time for that polyurethane to set up. My patience hasn't completely developed yet, so I tell myself that it is best if the caulking is still sticky. That way, it will be able to follow the distortion of the tin as the hull is shaped.

Start stomping right in the middle. Bare feet, very gritty, are best but soft tennis shoes might work okay. Gradually stomp all the deadrise out of the tin in the center of the boat and work it forward and aft by walking and stomping. It is best to do this on soft ground sort of like a nice fluffy lawn. Do it in the backyard so you won't attract too much attention (this is a one-man project . . . you don't want no destructive supervision). Try to avoid places with big rocks, roots, or hickory nuts. Stomp accurately. Try not to let the edges that will become the gunwales get crimped too bad. Don't worry about all those little heel dents. You don't want the boat to look like it was made by machinery.

Soon you will notice that the bottom of the boat is assuming a hogged shape and that the two stem heels (or toes) are lower than the place you are stomping. Don't worry about it. I read an article in *Messing About in Boats* that said that hogging of the keel is beneficial to performance. A long time ago when I was brazing these tin canoes together, completely oblivious to the fact that the zinc vapors from the galvanize were deadly, I used to cut a dart fore and aft along the keel to eliminate this hog that I thought was so ugly. Now I know better. It keeps the ends of the boat in the water so the water-line length is as long as possible all the time. You might have to look for a little hill to move the stomping operation to so the lay of the land won't interfere with the hogging of the bottom. As you pull the sides up with your hands and stomp a beautiful roundness into the turn of the bilge, you will notice that the two stems are beginning to tumble home back toward you sort of like an 1890s battleship. I used to try to trim the ends of the tin to avoid this back when I was letting imaginary aesthetics override my better judgment. That tumblehome increases waterline length and looks good to me. At the final stages of stomping, it is hard to keep from crimping the "sheer strake." Just try to keep from fatiguing the metal by crimping the same place over and over. It takes experience. Don't let yourself get frustrated and frantic . . . Hell, man, tin is cheap.

FINISHING TOUCHES

Finally, you will have stomped and pulled a nice, lovely shape into the boat but it will be too limber and dangerous along the gunwales. A piece of quarter round screwed into the top V will cure that. No need for any 5200 (called "doo-get-around" in the trade) or even the ritual with the two kinds of flathead screws. Just use regular little sheet-metal screws into predrilled holes. After you get through with that, spring for some of that black plastic pipe that used to be so common. Put it out in the yard in the hot sun until it gets soft enough to cut with a sharp linoleum knife. Lubricate the blade by dipping it into a jar of diesel fuel and rip that pipe, full length, all down one side. When the plastic starts pulling on the knife, dip it again. Don't slip and cut yourself. While the pipe is still hot, slip it over the quarter round and tin of the gunwales. I don't know what your experience is, but to me that polyethylene pipe makes the best rub rail in the world, not just for tin canoes, but for any yacht tender. It is indestructible, cheap, and won't do any more damage to the paint (or gelcoat!) of a yacht than anything else. It is sort of eye-catching on a tin canoe. It is possible to fool folks into thinking you have something pretty cute if you paddle away real quick before they get a chance to examine it too closely.

ADJUSTMENT

This is a borderline vessel. The freeboard-beam ratio that I mentioned above might need to be re-stomped a little to suit the user. Fortunately, it can usually be done right there at pondside. There is one thing you ought to know, though. If your ass is much wider than ten inches (compressed) there ain't going to be a whole hell of a lot that you can do to bring the narrow range of the adjustment within the parameters of your big butt.

PERFORMANCE

You are going to be in for a surprise. I know that a lot of you think that I have been teasing all along with all this tin canoe foolishness, but I'm serious. I have been in a lot of small, fast-paddling boats, but there is nothing like a tin canoe. I don't know if it is the galvanized surface, the heel bumps on the bottom, the hog of the keel, or the shape that the sheet metal dictates, but it sure will fly. Even just paddling with your hands, the speed is astonishing. Weeds and lily pads don't seem to affect it at all. It just zips through the water. A double paddle helps keep it upright and makes it so that you can almost turn the thing a little, but you don't need it. The inability to turn the boat so it will go where you want it to is one drawback—along with the tippiness and the half inch of freeboard—but you know, ain't nothing perfect in this world.

When you hook a fish in one of those things, you have to work it a little differently. First, you have to be real careful not to get too excited or else you will either turn over or sink from not paying attention. The second thing is that, if there is any size to the fish at all, it is hard to tell who has whom. If the fish is anything but absolutely broadside to you, he (or she) will pull the boat off in a tack that is oblique to the line of the force and, in obeisance of the Newton Laws of Motion, the boat will continue like that until something stops it. You will probably pass right by the fish and go off in the wrong direction until the pull of the line finally stops the boat and reverses it. Then it will zip backward on the same line of travel, and either pass him again or cut him loose on the sharp tin stern (now stem) or hang the line on some weeds or a snag. If the fish is dead ahead when he gets hooked, he will just take you home with him. It is an adventure. The contest is much more even than when the fish is caught from a high-tech metal-flake monster bass boat. If you are trying to use a fly rod, I think the deal even favors the fish a little . . . if he could just figure out a way to take you home and eat you after he gets you in the water. Which . . . maybe an alligator . . .

ONE LAST THING

You don't want to litter the bottom of any body of water with carelessly sunk tin canoes. You need to tie a crab trap float to one of the stems with enough line so you can find it and swim the boat back to the bank to dump the water out. Doing that will test that ten-inch butt, too.

1. *Jackleg* is a name applied to people who drank so much moonshine that the lead and fusil oil from junkpile stills combined in their brains to disrupt the motor control of at least one leg. The result was an uncontrollable "jacking" of that leg when the poor fool tried to walk. When the jackleg began to affect both legs at the same time, the person fell down and was unable to go get any more moonshine so the affliction was, in a way, self-limiting. Cruel people began to use *jackleg* as an adjective to describe projects that look like the work you would expect from someone whose brain is in such shape. Often such observations are the result of the arrogance of jealous people who are too devoted to the imaginary dignity of ignorance and helplessness to have interesting projects of their own . . . Watch yourself.

River Trip from Hell

in which two veterans take a trip that makes a world war seem tame

When my father and uncles got home from World War Two, things, after the initial impact at least, were sort of tame, I guess. My father and mother, her youngest brother, and his new bride decided to go all the way down the Ochlocknee River[1] to the coast, a trip of over a hundred miles through some mighty wild country. They must have missed the hardship of the war. I know that river well, and such a trip ain't easy. The way they did it turned out to be real hard. They borrowed an aluminum boat (Reynolds,[2] one of the first of that tribe) from one of the new bride's uncles, and an outboard motor.[3] They loaded up with gas, whiskey, gin, cigarettes, groceries, and stuff and took off to have a pleasant trip. The place where they put in is a relatively pretty-good little stretch and they thought that they would just drift down like Huck and Tom except better . . . they would have whiskey, a motor, and women . . . important things to veterans of World War Two. The first night's camping wasn't even too bad. It was a cool, early-fall night and the skeeters were sort of slow. They had a little drink or two around the fire and laughed and talked and the men thought about how lucky they were that they weren't still wading through the mangroves in the Pacific or climbing the rocky ravines in Italy . . . with the trenchfoot . . . apt to get shot at any time. The women thought about how lucky they were that they weren't hanging around the house counting ration coupons and waiting for news. The next morning, things changed.

In the first place, the weather had warmed up and the mosquitoes too. The drizzle that woke them up turned into real rain. They decided to go back and try again another day but they couldn't crank the motor. After they had worked the plugs and dried off the old fabric covering of the spark plug wires, they finally managed to whip it into running on one cylinder but it didn't last long. The rain had come down from upriver where it had already increased the current so they couldn't make any way against it with the paddle and the banks were too steep and slippery to tow. They drifted and paddled down the river all day long in the rain. The mosquitoes ate them up. They had a bottle of 6-12 but it was as ineffective in Georgia as it had been on Guadalcanal. Things were pretty tough. The two vets started to get an old familiar feeling when the river began getting wide and shallow and so criss-crossed by logs that the boat couldn't go unless everybody got out and dragged. Then it got so shallow and rooty that they had to take the engine off and all the stuff out so that they could drag it. Finally they couldn't even tell where the main river was anymore. They stood there, perplexed, in the drizzle. I got this whole story from each of them through the years, and no mention was made of any arguing or blame being cast by anybody, which just goes to show you what kind of people we had both at home and afield during World War Two.

It rained for two days. There was nothing for it but to plug on. Momma told me that they carried that damn boat, turned up sideways, through the blackgum and cypress trees for one whole day, then went back for the motor and the stuff. All of them were ready to leave that whiskey and gin. My mother was all for leaving the outboard and the gas. My uncle's young wife was for leaving the whole she-bang and hiking up her skirt and striking off through the swamp until she hit a road. All of them were sick and tired of the whole expedition. Finally they found the real river and it stopped raining.

But it turned cold . . . real cold for down here . . . not only that, but my father developed this inflammation of the upper lip that didn't look good. He had been fooling with this little bump up next to his nose all that time. Despite warnings from the others, he had persisted until the damn thing had become infected. His lip began to swell up. After a long time of messing around with the motor, thinking that the dry weather would help it run, they finally gave up and started paddling, poling, and dragging again. Finally they came to a bridge (called the WPA bridge and many many miles from civilization even now). My uncle and his wife left Momma and my, by now pretty sick, father in the boat and struck out in opposite directions on the road to try to find a phone or something. One of them found a little house that was locked up and probably phone-less. They spent the night under the bridge in the boat hoping to hear a car coming. By morning, my father was delirious and his lip was swole up as big as a tomato. Somehow, somebody finally caught a ride and he was hauled off to the hospital where the doctor said that they weren't a moment too soon. The doctor also said that it wasn't a good idea to drink whiskey to try to cure a bloodstream infection . . . might make you sick and delirious. It was years after that before any of us made it all the way to the coast on the Ochlocknee River and we did it in a much more suitable boat.

1 The Ochlocknee River begins a little above Thomasville, Georgia. It is one of the smaller aboveground-drainage rivers in this part of the country (dwarfed by the Flint and Chattahoochee). Most of the rivers as small as it is are spring-fed and do not fluctuate in season so much. The smaller rivers around here have a way of disappearing into solution holes in the limestone underlying the soil and reemerging, sometimes miles away, in places called "rises" to continue their way to the coast. Some of them run into big swamps where the current disappears and it is hard to tell which way to go. These places are called "dead lakes." Ignorant navigation in those dead lakes is hard but the fishing is good. There are still a few old hands who spent their lives hook-and-line fishing commercially in those kinds of places.

2. The Reynolds was one of the first aluminum boats ever built. It was twelve feet long and shaped sort of like the tri-hull fiberglass boats of the sixties and seventies. The seats were made of plywood with some kind of primitive crystalline foam stuff for flotation under them. The stern seat was a wide U-shaped outfit that became very dear to me in my youth and is a characteristic of the skiffs I build now. The Reynolds came with a special trailer. There was a spring-loaded eye built into the center of the boat that engaged with an overhead hook that was an extension of the trailer tongue. The wheels were on the bottom legs of an upside-down U of pipe that straddled the boat and was welded to the overhead pipe. To retrieve the boat, you pushed the trailer down into the water by hand, engaged the hook with the eye, and pried down with the trailer tongue. That lifted the complete boat from the water . . . then all you had to do was figure out how to get the whole mess up the hill to the car. That old Reynolds and its steel trailer were heavy as hell . . . thick aluminum and big pipe. We used that boat until the middle fifties down at the coast. Most of that time was after the salt water had et up the trailer and we just dragged the Reynolds like they did back in the Ochlocknee river swamp. It was a pretty good boat . . . as aluminum boats go. It would beat hell out of you in a chop and finally metal-fatigued and electrolysed into junk but us children went many places and did many things in that old Reynolds. Sometimes I wake up in the middle of the night thinking that some of that old ancient foam dust has blown back into my eyes from under the front seat.

3. The engine was one of those old two-cylinder, opposed Johnsons. My recollection is that it weighed about 250 pounds. I bet that the adventurers of 1946 would bear me out on that. I don't remember the horsepower or anything, but the spark-plugs were covered by these little silly covers that must have been purely for decoration. They sure didn't shield the plugs from spray or rain at all. I believe that same outboard is described in John Steinbeck's book about the biology of the Sea of Cortez.

My experience now tells me that the river trip trouble was caused by water wicking through the fabric covering of the spark plug wires and into cracks in the old rubber insulation underneath, causing the spark to hop out short of the plugs way up under the flywheel somewhere, a problem that can only be fixed by pulling the flywheel off or storing the motor in a dry place for two years and ultimately by replacing the wires.

The Reynolds

in which I learn the true meaning of life . . .
when I am young enough to make some good use of the knowledge

We had a bunch of little boats when I was a boy, but the most important one was the Reynolds. I think I was about eight when I became captain of that worthy vessel. My family had always followed the laissez-faire method of child rearing and that old Reynolds made us all as free and wild as any civilized children could possibly be. My father was a writer so capable that he could make a living by just doing a little typing early in the morning before breakfast. Once he showed me, as an example, how easy it was. He wrote a story early in the morning and sent it off to a magazine in the first mail. The check, for fifteen hundred bucks—new-car money in 1952—came two days later. I have never been able to do that, but because of the freedom of his life and the freedom of use of the Reynolds, I do know a thing or two about a thing or two.

Most of the time in warm weather (most of the time), we lived in a house on the beach about halfway between Carrabelle and East Point in the panhandle of Florida. It was a big ramshackledy old log house that was built around 1910 by one of the pioneer Florida rich men as a gift for his beloved and peculiar daughter. She never went to that house, not even one time. When we bought it in 1947 the carpenter's scraps and sawdust were still on the floors of all the rooms. There wasn't an electrical wire in the place. It had a railroad-style windmill well pump. At first, the only electrical thing was my father's old battery-powered Halicrafters radio, and the only machines were his typewriter, the car in the yard, and the outboard on the Reynolds.

That Reynolds was one of the pioneer aluminum boats, built by Reynolds Aluminum Company. I believe it was built before World War Two because I am sure I remember it in 1946 when my father came back from the war and money couldn't buy any aluminum anything during the war. It was a pretty stylish old boat. The hull was shaped sort of like one of the tri-hull butt-pounders of the sixties and seventies. It actually had a center V and two side convolutions of the bottom. The bow was round, with a big, useless foredeck and a streamlined, futuristic-looking cast aluminum cleat. The transom had the good tumblehome of the time (you can say what you want to about tumblehome, but the fact of the matter is, the shape makes a convexity to the rails in the stern that strengthens a small planing skiff). It had a red streak of lightning, factory-painted down both sides, to make its intentions clear. The stern seat was big U-shaped plywood and there was only one center seat. Between the center thwart and the stern was a peculiar thing. A spring-loaded, cast-aluminum eye was welded into the bottom of the boat and stuck way up, most handily right in front of the man at the motor. Even now after some fifty years, my right hand still longs to grab that eye as I am standing at the tiller of any boat when it lurches wrong. Actually, I sort of miss the whole business.

That eye was part of a strange trailer arrangement. The Reynolds came with a humpbacked, welded steel pipe trailer that straddled the boat with its wheels. There was a tongue that stuck into the spring-loaded eye of the boat and, by prying down on the hitch of the trailer, one (or two, if the motor was on it) could lift the old Reynolds right out of the water and hook it up to the car and drive off with it. It sounds like a wonderful idea, but there were several things that went wrong in our situation. First, we had to unhook the trailer from the car to hook up to the eye, and then it was a struggle, with the heavy Reynolds hanging, to haul it uphill back to the trailer ball. Even when we got it hooked up, it didn't tow worth a damn with all that negative hitch weight. We always left the whole rig up in the sea oats and only used the fool trailer to launch the boat, and never hauled it over the road. Finally, the aluminum wheel hubs and the steel wheel bearings got together to finish off the whole trailer program, then we dragged the boat to the water. It was the children's boat and we did it eagerly.

The old Reynolds was twelve feet long and built out of aluminum so thick that it might as well have been lead. It took us all to get it to the water, but then, after we clamped the motor on, like *Where The Wild Things Are*, the wild rumpus began. We were a hard-charging little crew. I was the oldest so I was the boss. There were a variable number of my cousins, both boys and girls, some almost babies, and my two sisters and the girl (best friend of the oldest sister) who would wind up as my wife. Altogether, the whole bunch of children at the coast house averaged around seven or eight and usually all of them wanted to go. As I said, we were not supervised by our parents at all—didn't even have to come home for meals, but if we did, there it was, if we could find it. We were even exempt from evening muster and often stayed out all night rampaging up and down the wild shore in that old

Reynolds. When we ran out of gas, we just rowed and towed. Five little boogers on the towline are just about equivalent to five horsepower—better than that in the shallow water of the flats around here.

It would be easy to pass judgment on our parents and say that they were negligent. Of course, memory is selective, but I can't recall anytime when we were in any more danger than if we had been "properly" supervised. Children who know that they are on their own are pretty cautious, and there were so many of us that the chance of a little one drowning, unnoticed, was pretty slim. Besides, around here, shallow water is more of a problem than deep. As they say, "On the flats, a man would have to dig a hole if he wanted to drown himself." We were always so busy going where we needed to go that there was no fighting or meanness. All we wanted to do was to facilitate the progress. Those grown folks going on with their own doings weren't negligent, not at all. You know taking the whole summer off to go to the coast wasn't all that unusual in the Deep South back before megalomania and AC. Corn has made roasting ears before June so the farming is over until fall. Besides the sweat doesn't run into your eyes quite as bad down where the sea breeze blows. The grown people mostly stayed in the shade around the house but not us. We tried to wear out the water.

The whole Reynolds business took up several years and we all grew up while it happened. Little girls, the tops of their bathing suits hauled way down below their nipples (my skinny little wife-to-be too) by the hard charging, had to change their ways. The intensity of our progress through the shallow water from one important destination to the other was such that the little ones usually wound up naked. There was one very persistent little fella. We tried to leave him at home because he was so slow, waddling along behind, but just about the time we would be getting in the boat, here he would come down the path from the house hollering, "Wait the boat . . . Wait the boat." When towing time came, he refused to be a nonparticipant and just ride in the boat. We dragged him while he held on to the painter, little naked body trailing along behind, diaper long gone, short legs working. We did that so much with that little boy that he had calluses on his hands before he was two, and because he always trailed along the same way on the towline, he was darker on one side than the other, kind of like a flounder. At least his bottom eye didn't drift around to the dark side. He still lives around here. Says his whole life has gone downhill since those days.

There was another little boy who had a black wool bathing suit that never seemed to get wet. He could swim around in it all day long and when he got out, his bathing suit was just as dry as anything. We all marveled at it and got him to let us try it on to see what it felt like. As the years went by, the moths ate bigger and bigger holes in his bathing suit and, when he took it off, he had a pattern of their work tanned onto his hide. He was a pusher. I mean, when we towed the boat (which was most of the time) he pushed on the stern with one or two other little ones. Because of that, the moth hole patterns on his backside were darker than on the front. One time, he was pushing on the foot of the engine when it came unlatched and tilted down. He busted his lip something awful and didn't cry a single squawk even though he was only about five years old. He was a tough little booger, a neighbor kid, not of the family, so he had to go home to eat and sleep. I remember him trudging reluctantly off down the beach all by himself when the time came. He is an electrical contractor in Tallahassee now, still has that scar on his lip from where he bit that chunk of aluminum out of the foot of that motor. He does not have that bathing suit anymore, though. I think Jacques Cousteau wound up with it.

As I said, these expeditions sometimes kept us away from the house for a long time. Though we always took, at my mother's insistence, five whole gallons of ice water in an old galvanized cooler with a ceramic liner (a heavy thing), the food usually ran short. The deformities of our civilized tastes disappeared in the face of plain starvation. We squatted like varmints on oyster bars, silently at work with our screwdrivers. The kid with the bathing suit loved the little oyster crabs and ate them raw . . . just chewed them up whole, sand and all. We had to open oysters for the little naked ones, but they didn't mind a little grit. We ate, immediately, every scallop we found, mantle, viscera, eyes, and all (to me, even now that my experience has broadened, there is no better snack). The whole time we were moving, we caught crabs and towed them along loose in the bottom of the boat, along with all the seashells that the little ones thought they had to take home (there is a modern "shell midden" where we dragged that old Reynolds up in the yard of that old house). When we got to a good stopping place, we would dip up some seawater in a foot tub, build a fire around it, and boil all of those crabs. It was every man for himself when they got red. Sometimes, somebody nice like my wife-to-be would pick out some for the little naked ones, but usually they did it for themselves. The little ones ate so much shell that their excrement looked about like that of coons or otters. One little four-toothed boy developed a strong liking for the contents of the crop and stomach of the crabs—called it "goody." If I had known then what I know now, I probably would have stopped him. At least it didn't hurt him in the long run, and who was I to decide what it takes to make the time that is the pinnacle of a man's whole life?

Those old wonderful wild and naked days seemed to last forever. It was as if I spent half my life with that old Reynolds, but the facts are the facts: What got the old boat was electrolysis and metal fatigue. It had wooden rub rails and sheer clamps and three oak runners screwed into grooves to stiffen the bottom. After the rot and termites of the beach and gribbles of the sea had eaten those off, we patched the screw holes with some stuff called Celastic, which was a little piece of stiff cloth that, when wet with some special solvent, got very sticky and would stay on the aluminum pretty good. Though the bottom worked more in the chop and probably contributed to the fatal metal fatigue along the chines, the absence of the bottom runners was better for the boat than the replacement of them. One winter my father and uncle put new mahogany runners and rails on the old boat. It sure looked good like that. The brass screws and stove bolts just gleamed beneath the varnish. They kept on gleaming all summer as the old Reynolds sacrificed itself to keep them shining. By the summer of '55 most of the girls had pulled their bathing suits up, the babies were no longer naked, and the old Reynolds was leaking so bad that we couldn't keep up with it and we went on to other (actually better) boats. Some of us became responsible adults after that. Sometimes at a family gathering, two old executive types will exchange a certain look. One will say, "You remember that old Reynolds?" The other one will reply, "Did Elvis love his momma?"

The old coast house.

The Reynolds Crew Discovers St. George Island

and saves the day with a brave rescue

We were children of the flats. Around here, there are miles and miles of them. The shallow water covers sandy plains of grass that are almost continuous from Yucatan to the Keys. I read somewhere that the average decline of the bottom of the near-shore Gulf of Mexico is about a foot to the mile. The discovery of the wonderful diversity of the flats occupied us to the limit of our capacity. We tried our best to find out what lived in every hole (a never-ending quest—some of us are still at it after fifty years). When we found something interesting, we took it home for our folks to marvel at, and marvel they did. We dug enormous Gulf quahogs as big as softballs. The hard and soft clams of the north Gulf of Mexico get much bigger than they do in the Atlantic, even down south on the east coast of the peninsula. There has been some research on the quahogs, which has established that they are the same species and can be mix-bred. I knew a man who made that his life's work. Though Gulf hard clams get bigger sooner, they don't stay shut as well as Atlantic clams so they gape and drool while they are out of the water and aren't at their best unless they are eaten before they do too much of that. This man was trying to breed the drooling out of them. I guess he finally did but the whole project didn't pay off for him. Who wants to eat a quahog as big as a grapefruit besides my momma? A ghastly sight for the eyes of newcomers at our house.

We labored excitedly to dig huge little-known Gulf soft-shell clams and angel wing clams as big as Coca-Cola bottles that lived in holes so deep, the excavations we left in the flats became landmarks. We dug stinking, stinging nemertean worms and all kinds of polychaetes. We discovered the remarkable commensal association of the terrible toadfish and the pistol shrimp, an association that has interested me all my life. They live together in a good-sized tunnel cut through the roots of the turtle grass (*Diplanthera* usually). When the tide is out, it is possible to root around and dig them out. The toadfish acts like he doesn't care—he knows what he'll do for you if you mess with him—but the little shrimp hides so adroitly in the muddy water that he is hard to find. With that toadfish looking at you like that, it is hard to feel around adequately. My slapdash experiments have shown that though toadfish are not afraid of anything, they do not eat pistol shrimp (which is a good shrimp raw, kinda small for cooking). A regular pinead shrimp is a goner as soon as the toadfish sees him, even if he has to spit out some half-swallowed other morsel to make room. But you can starve a toad-fish down to where he is visibly hollow-bellied, and he won't make a pass at even a de-clawed pistol shrimp. I don't think I have it completely figured out, but I believe that, unlikely as it might seem, the pistol shrimp is the boss of the hole. It might be that the toadfish looks at a disarmed shrimp with cau-tion (can't tell—might have that pistol in his pocket). The relationship might be of mutual benefit. The hole undoubtedly allows toadfish to live higher on the flats where they would dry out at low tide if they didn't have the water in the shrimp hole, and the terrible toadfish might provide some protection for the shrimp, but I am not so sure that the shrimp can't take care of him-self. There is no question that it is the shrimp who makes the hole. They can do it without the help of any toadfish and, indeed, there are plenty of fish-less shrimp holes on the flats (and shrimp-hole-less toadfish farther out), which leads me to believe that the relationship between the two denizens is completely one-sided. The shrimp is just the host of the terrible toadfish. I'll tell you this for your own good. A big toadfish is a dangerous thing. Not only will they fin you with poisonous spines, they will bite the fool out of you. They are sort of diabolical with it. You don't have to stick your finger or toe in their mouth for them, they'll reach over there and grab you. It is hard to get loose, too. We soon learned not to let toadfish have free run of the bil-gewater of the Reynolds like the crabs. A crab sort of makes his intentions known and is hard to ignore, but a toadfish will lurk around and get you when you ain't paying attention.

We chased stingarees and hemmed flounders up in shallow pools. We marveled at the ferocity of the soft crab's husband and took her away from him anyway. We squatted in the short sea grass and fed the big burrowing anemones to see what they liked. Burrowing anemones live attached to the bottom of a hole that they excavate in the sandy bottom of the flats. When the tide is out, they retract and deflate their tentacles so that they are flush with the surface and don't look like much of anything. When they are cov-ered by water, they extend the tentacles and look like a sea anemone. Though they are tolerant of inspection, if you bother them too much, they will re-tract way down into their holes. They are eager feeders on most any kind of fresh meat, alive or dead, and can hold on to and ingest surprisingly large fish, crabs, and worms. Their favorite food is a shucked oyster. They get so excited when they detect the juice that you think they might turn loose and come hopping out of their hole.

We swam under the floating grass and found sea horses by listening to the snap they made when they ate some tiny creature. We made pools where we kept them with the sargasso fish, tiny puff fish, and other peculiar things that we caught. Sea horses mostly eat tiny crustaceans that crawl around on the stems of sea grass. They are slow and deliberate-acting little things and it is hard to imagine how they could possibly catch anything. They have a neat trick though. When they see an amphipod or tiny shrimp, they lean over in that direction and slowly stick their nose as close to the prey as they can without scaring him off. When they are close enough, they tense up their cheeks and with a little *pop* noise, open their tiny mouths and the crustacean vanishes from the grass . . . sucked in so fast it is hard to see exactly how it works.

The Yucatan Current, a major component of the Gulf Stream, makes a loop far to the north in the Gulf of Mexico. All sorts of strange plants and creatures wash up on the beach around here including sargasso weed with its unusual inhabitants. Looking carefully while swimming along in a patch of floating weeds is a fascinating thing for young children who are interested in strange creatures (and all children are before TV and puberty numb their skulls). There are few stranger-looking things than a sargasso fish except maybe for puff fish. There are two kinds of puff fish around here, the spiny kind and the smooth kind. Both of them are easy to catch and good to eat if they are big enough. You just skin them, cut off the head, and eat the backbone part. The soft bones are child-safe. Don't eat the liver, and never put one of the spiny kind in your bathing suit pocket.

We were delighted when we discovered a tiny, cunning octopus that held himself between two sunray Venus clam shells with his strong, little arms. The octopuses are just about the size of a scallop's adductor muscle and have very short arms. At night, they forage around in the grass, and catch little crabs and such, but during the day they close themselves up in a pair of often mismatched clamshells. They hold on to one side with four arms and grab the other shell with the other four and hold it closed just like a new adductor muscle. They have a pretty good grip, too, but if you do pry the two shells apart, they'll give a little squirt of ink and disappear so completely that six sharp-eyed children can't find them. Sometimes they'll stay in a gastropod shell and hold something like a sand dollar or a broken piece of shell over the hole sort of like an operculum. If you pull that loose, often they'll squirt and hide but sometimes they will retreat way back inside the volutes of the shell. If you root around down in there with your finger the minia-ture octopus will bite a cute little piece of meat out of you. Because of ex-perience such as that, there were four-year-old children in our crew who knew more of the animals of the flats than most of the graduate students at the FSU marine lab did when I was there in the late sixties.

Sometimes, but not often, we would see another boat. Usually it was a beach seiner, which was a fascinating thing to us children. This species of commercial fishing has been extinct in the Gulf since about 1954 or so. The fishermen cruised up and down the coast in shallow-draft inboard motor-boats about thirty-five or forty feet long. Even as late as this, some of those boats were old converted sailboats called luggers. (Down near the delta they carried the very fast and weatherly but reputedly dangerous French-style dip-ping-lug rig but up here, they were rigged as gaff schooners. They were well built out of good stuff and there are still a few around; one down in Apalachicola right now was built in 1877.) The net was carried in two big rowing skiffs that were towed along behind. When a school of mullet was sighted, the big boat was anchored well offshore and the skiffs were rowed ashore, one up the beach of the fish, the other down. They ran out the big heavy, tarred cotton seine over the stern. When the strike was complete, all the men (at least six, sometimes eight) grabbed the net and, running down the beach toward one another, drew the two ends together, completely en-circling the fish. Then, pulling as hard as they could, leaning way back, bare heels digging deep, they drew the net to the beach by both ends. As they pulled, they backed down the beach with the longshore current leaving the already pulled-in part of the net strung out in the shallow water behind them. Eventually they would have a good-sized bag full of frantic fish, which they would haul as close in as possible. Then they would empty as many of the fish out with a dip net and their hands as they could, throwing the catch into a big box in the stern of each skiff. Many of the fish would jump out, especially the wonderfully intelligent and agile mullet, the prize of the haul. Crabs and other "trash" were either thrown out or left alone until later. As they lightened the net, they pulled more of it in. Sometimes they would catch so many fish (mostly mullet, but a few speckled trout, redfish, floun-der, and sometimes Spanish mackerel) that the boxes would fill up; then they just threw the fish in the bottom of the boats. Though the men were skilled at what they were doing, sometimes they would get finned by a catfish or a stingaree. At that I must explain something to you. Only ignorant people call stingarees "stingrays," possums "opossums," and coons "raccoons."

These beach seiners were tough, I tell you. They just flung the fish off and kept on as if it hadn't happened. I have been finned by those things myself, and it is a hard injury to ignore. Sometimes there would be a shark in the net fixing to bite out. As soon as they saw him, one of the men would wade out into the boiling mass of cooped-up fish with the gaff. We children would stand and marvel at the fury as the man gaffed the shark, picked the head of the violently thrashing fish up as high as possible, and dragged him out of the net.

We were shy of these wonderful people but it was hard to keep the little ones aloof from such as that. One time, before we knew what had happened, the littlest one had clapped on to the net and was helping haul. The men tried their best not to step on him and we tried our best to dislodge him from the meshes without getting in the way, but he hung on until the end. As they left, I, as the oldest, waded out to apologize, but I was too late. As powerful strokes of the oars took the loaded net skiff out through the low surf, I heard the only words from those men. One said, "You know that little naked booger pulled pretty good to be so gap-toothed." The next time we saw that same boat, the men silently made room and motioned us up. We all clapped on . . . silently. It was easy to tell the difference in the progress of the project too. After that, there was a noticeable difference in the level of noise around our boat. We admired the silence of those men. To this day, I do not allow hollering on board my boats. My wife and I can, wordlessly, beat our thirty-foot sailboat out of most any narrow little place right into a dead wrong wind. Of course, I raised her from a child.

After the silent men had loaded up and gone, the beach would be littered with the rejects from the net. We, after a glance to make sure that we were finally alone, fell on these creatures, things too fast for us to catch on the flats. We examined the marvelous cutlass fishes with their terrible teeth. We found out the hard way about the shocking stargazer and the electric ray. We felt the sharp ventral ridge of the pogies (menhaden). We examined the Maurice Sendak faces of lizard fish (we called them "sharp-nosed boogers," a better name) and the delightful cowfish with only his fins and lips outside the fused scales that formed his triangular cross-sectioned shell. We took home the first one of those that we found and my momma called him a "trunkfish" and taught us to cook him by rolling him around in the fire, West Indian–fashion. As an example of simple cooking paying off, it is hard to beat a trunkfish rolled in a pine straw fire until the steam comes out around his tail.

We were not only biologists, ecologists, and gourmets, but archaeologists and paleontologists too. It didn't take us long to find the tailings from where the shell middens of the other wild people of this place were being cut out by the waves as the sea continued its rise across the flats from the far offshore of the Pleistocene. We found the broken pieces of pottery that had been discarded long ago with the shells of the same oysters, clams, and conchs that had become so familiar to us. We marveled at how many those people must have eaten to make such a pile of shells. We especially loved the thin pieces of pottery that had been decorated in antiquity by some little wild girl by digging in the soft clay with her little fingernail, repeatedly, in an intricate pattern. We could see in the long-ago print just exactly how the clay and her fingernail had been—how soft the clay and how long, how big, how thick her fingernail. We would look among us for someone who had a perfect match and vow to make us just such a pot one day.

In the bottoms of the dark creeks, we found the black bones of long-gone animals—the huge molars of mastodons and mammoths, the knuckles of manatees, the patterned shell bones of giant turtles, the jigsaw-puzzle pieces of the shells of armadillos. Half the things we brought home in the bottom of the old Reynolds were unidentifiable by the folks at the house, and even now one of us will come across a picture in a book somewhere and call a conference. We'll straggle in to have a look and exclaim, "Oh, that's what that was." We found a dugout canoe, partially embedded in the silt of the bottom of a pool in one of the little spring-fed creeks where we went many days in a futile attempt to hem in mullet. We tried to dig it out and raise it, but it was too big and slippery for us. Years later, one of us tried to interest an anthropologist at FSU in that canoe, but he never got around to making the trip way back in there. I did though, not long ago, and though the water was too high and dark to get a look, I could feel it with my feet. I think I'll let it stay there.

One day, while we were up in that same wonderful little creek catching crabs, we saw a yellow biplane with a good-sounding engine. Now I know it for an old Stearman, like so many that were sold off as surplus after the war and were flown to death dusting DDT onto tobacco fields. We watched it follow the same shore that was becoming so familiar to us by then; then it banked and flew out to sea and, as we watched, began to fly along the shore of a distant island that we had barely noticed in our preoccupation with the flats. Our attention was focused. We began to make plans.

We made a special arrangement with my mother to help us get ready to go to the island—extra gas, extra water, some groceries. Some of us thought about trying to get her to help us sidetrack the little naked ones but we knew it was no use—they had seen the airplane and heard the plans being made. Early the next morning, we set off. It was kind of strange to run the old outboard motor for so long. It seemed to me that we ran over the slick calm water for a mighty long time before the island started getting any closer but, after a while, we could see details of the beach—sea oats, dunes, clear little waves curling along the shore. When I shut off the engine and we slid up, it was certainly a different kind of place. We all hopped out onto the strange new land, St. George Island.

We became obsessed with that place. The flats were forgotten. We ran amok. Our parents had to make daily trips to town for gas after that. It is easy to think that they went on with their daily doings without giving us a thought, but I know the binoculars ("knobblers" in the family language from some long grown-up child's pronunciation) were well focused when the time came for the afternoon sea breeze to bring us back in.

St. George Island at that time was not only completely uninhabited, but almost unvisited. Someone had some cows over there and we were wary of them, but eagerly used their cow plops for fuel to cook our crabs because, on our end, there were no trees to make the pine straw and pinecones that we usually piled around our foot tub. We discovered many new things over there, but we were particularly excited by relics of the Army that were everywhere. During World War Two, St. George Island was used as a practice beachhead by trainees from Camp Gordon Johnston, which stretched along the coast from where Lanark is now, nearly to Ochlocknee Bay.

Now St. George Island is the most expensive real estate in Franklin County and overrun with all-terrain vehicles, Jet Skis, and party animals, but in the early fifties, when we were rampaging over there, about the only signs of humanity were rusty old bombs, nose-down in the sand among the cow plops. We found a tiny island covered with big bullets (fifty-caliber Browning machine gun, we would later learn). The vets told us that the pilots probably used that island as a target for strafing with aircraft. We loaded the old Reynolds up with those artifacts. (All that brass probably contributed to the eventual electrolytic destruction of the old boat. Just the slightest swipe of brass or copper on aluminum will take its toll.) One day, after we had rampaged up the bayside shore and picked up all the bullets we needed, we noticed that the sky was getting dark and dangerous looking. We were almost to the place where the trees and high dunes started so we decided to hurry on down there to take shelter. We had had a lot of experience with the swift, violent thunderstorms of the Gulf of Mexico and, by then, had established a quick little ritual.

Those storms are almost an everyday occurrence during the summertime and are caused by the difference in temperature of the land and the shallow water, both hot as hell. Usually, during the day, the land gets much hotter than the hot water and a sea breeze is drawn in by the updraft convection over the land. As this humid air from the sea rises, each molecule of water vapor gives up the heat energy that excited it into evaporating in the first place. Soon the heat released by all those little molecules as they condense causes a cumulus cloud that towers from the height of first condensation all the way to the stratosphere (the height above which water vapor cannot rise without condensing, because the air is so rare and cold) and sometimes from horizon to horizon. After dark, the land cools quickly and then it is the hot water that causes the convection upward. The result is a land breeze and thunderstorms that build over the water until the sun comes up in the morning. Either way, clouds that grow into the upper levels of the troposphere often get blown in unpredictable directions, so Gulf Coast seagoing people soon learn to keep a weather eye out. The summer storms of the Gulf come up quick and blow hard. In five minutes the shallow inshore Gulf can be transformed from a fiercely hot dead calm into such a sea that no boat can maintain planing speed and even seagoing tugs have to head up for a while. Often the lightning is continuously visible . . . a bad situation to be in, either at sea or on such a lightning-bait place as St. George Island.

When we saw a storm coming, we ran for the beach and quickly took the engine off and turned the boat upside down, stern to the wind with the foredeck propped up on the engine and water jug. The little ones would hide under the boat and us big ones would take shelter in the dunes as best we could unless there was lightning; then it was a tight little huddle with us all under the Faraday's cage of aluminum. Though the wind sometimes got up enough to hammer the boat pretty good it was never snatched loose from the strong hands of the little ones. After the storm had passed and we resumed our navigation, there would be a strange track left on the beach from where the children under the boat had swiveled the transom around to keep it to windward as the storm swept by. This time, when we arrived at the place where we planned to turn the boat over, we found another boat—the first we had seen on St. George Island. We quickly unloaded and turned the old Reynolds upside down. We noticed that there were some people too. We could see them waving at us from up the beach where they were ignorantly standing under some trees trying to bait up a little lightning. We could tell that the mosquitoes were eating them up. We didn't have time to exchange greetings before the blow brought the stinging sand and drove them back to the trees. When the rain came, though it stung us outside ones too, it was better than the dry sand. Immediately, those people's boat began to drag its anchor. If it hadn't been for quick work by my oldest sister and my wife-to-be in the strong southwest wind, it would have been gone down the bay. They squatted in the driving rain and held the little iron-lump-style navy anchor down in the hard sand until the blow was over. It was lucky for those people that there was no lightning, because my wife-to-be did not like it and does not to this day and would have quickly abandoned the project.

Those summer storms usually pass just as quickly as they come up and pretty soon, the mosquitoes were eating us all up again. We children put the Reynolds back in and began to load her up. I guess those people thought that we were getting ready to leave them because they came running. They turned out to be two couples of college students from FSU. Their boat was out of fix and they were stranded, had been all day long. The food was eaten, the drinks were drunk, and the shade was scarce and they were glad to see us. Since the Reynolds was too little to take all of us to the mainland, we agreed to tow them. Because of the direction of the wind, I decided to take them directly home to our house instead of where they wanted to go. At first, it was not too bad. Even though the sea was still up pretty good from the leftovers of the thunderstorm, it was in a fair direction and their big, heavy inboard boat, propeller dragging, came along noticeably on the towline.

The boat was a Correct Craft, plywood inboard runabout about eighteen feet long. We saw it all the time after the initial rescue. It turned out that one of the girls of that crew had a summer house about a mile down the beach east of us and attracted the male owner of the Correct Craft quite often. As is frequently the case with people who have boats like that, the boat had been left wallowing in the waves at the water's edge while the cavorting was going on. The tide went out and this fellow thought that the enormous horsepower of the flathead Ford V8 would shake the boat loose from the sand. What actually happened was that the sand shook that engine loose from its horsepower.

Before it got dark, the wind shifted more to the northwest and that slowed us down. We discovered that their boat was half full of water and we had to stop and give them something to bail with and tell them to center the rudder so our little engine could make a little better progress. After dark came, the usual backward wind sprang up from the land and it was slow going for real. Finally, we had to head directly for Porter Bar to make any headway toward the mainland at all. When the gas gave out, we were in our old stomping grounds, though still some few miles downwind of the house. Sleepy children piled out onto the flats and took up the towline in the dark as if they had been doing it all their lives. It was slow progress, too. Not only was that other boat heavy, we had to keep out where it was deep enough for the propeller and rudder and go slow so we could drag our feet for stingarees.

Except for lightning storms, stingarees ("stingrays" to the ignorant) are the most dangerous natural thing at the coast around here. There are more people waiting in the emergency rooms of Florida because of stingarees than from injuries inflicted by all other natural hazards combined. Only fools wade in water where they can't see the bottom without shuffling their feet for stingarees. If you slide your feet, you will touch the ray and scare him away before you can step on him. If you step on a stingray, he will instantly arch his tail and slide the lubricated spine, which is loosely attached at the base of his tail, into your ankle. The spines of stingrays and catfish are encapsulated by a slimy membrane of poisonous stuff (not usually infectious in stingarees, but very much so in catfish, especially freshwater catfish). Not only are those spines poisonous, but they are serrated—barbed in a most exquisite way. Only flesh knows flesh. A stingaree spine will stay with you like nothing else I ever saw. If they stay in you, you are in trouble. Some say that it is possible to grab the end with a pair of pliers and sort of unscrew the spine so that the barbs won't take so much meat as it is pulled out, but the idea never appealed to me all that much. I think they must be cut out and they hold on until the last barb. A lot of the folks down here have some bad-looking scars where the skin of a long, homemade incision didn't heal back straight—kind of like a cross-buttoned shirt. When I got hit while I was doing a bottom job on my sailboat on the flats of Dog Island, my momma, then in her dotage, said that the best thing to do was to soak your foot in the hottest water you can stand while you drink all the whiskey in the house and it worked so good that I was able to ignore the injury and go back and finish the job (turned out kind of sloppy). It was only after the thing had healed and I began to walk funny that I finally went to the doctor to find the spine embedded in the tendons of my ankle. My mother always carried a nine-inch stingaree spine in her pocketbook. She said that it was for self-defense, but I know that it was to impress little boys with.

More to the point, believe it or not, one of those FSU women declined to participate in the towing work, and we had to haul her, too, like Cleopatra on her barge. I am wary of women like that and try to stay clear of them. We delivered those people into the company of my father who introduced them to the martini. That little glass was a fixture of the coast house all through the fifties. It would be easy to think that our freedom was somehow connected, but it wasn't. Though the daily martini party started early and lasted late, there were quite a few adults, my mother included, who only rarely joined in. They fished and fooled around in the other boats and cooked and swept sand out of the house. When we came home for gas or something, there were usually people we had never seen before sitting around on the porch, laughing and poking at the olive in their martinis. Another day, on that porch, I saw a sunburned young woman (might have been Cleopatra) peel a slice of skin off herself that went much farther down inside her clothes than I would have expected. I wanted to hang around to see if it would have the nipple on it like the eye on the shed skin of a snake, but the children were already loading up and ready.

Robb took this picture (with permission) of a picture on the wall of the Spring Creek Restaurant.

Dog Island

in which I was too young to take advantage of the opportunity of a lifetime

Back in my boyhood summers of ignorant and reckless adventure there was an island about five miles offshore that we used to go to in the skiff. I always thought that it was the most wonderful place. It was never the same: The currents and storms washed the shoreline into different coves and bars all the time. Every trip down the beach of Dog Island was a voyage of discovery. Not only that, but we thought that it was where God lived.

One time we were walking on the seaside beach when we saw a man with floppy clothes disappear into the sand dunes. We thought maybe he was God but he was actually Ivan Munroe (like the name of the main street in the capital of Florida). He was one of the old pioneer aviators and lived in a little house on the other end of the island right beside his airstrip and flew off in his airplane every once and a while to see what was what. We thought that it was mighty appropriate that God had an airplane. Sometimes, when we were walking on the beach, he would fly low over us and waggle his wings. I have never had that much recognition from God since.

For some reason that I can't find out, about the time I was fourteen, Ivan Munroe decided to sell Dog Island. One of his first prospects was my father. Ivan Munroe landed his plane on the beach in front of our coast house on the mainland. It was the most marvelous airplane stunt I ever saw. The tide was high, and the beach was too narrow for him to land with both wheels on the sand and still have room for the inland wing to miss the trees, so he landed with one wheel on the hard sand above the waves and the other barely clearing the breakers. Just before the tail wheel settled and the seaside wheel sat down in the water, he kicked the rudder and pivoted the plane up on the soft sand facing the woods. The tail wheel stopped just inches from the range of the waves. I thought that I had me an airplane because there was no way that he could take off again but, by the time he and my father talked a while, the tide had gone out and there was plenty of room. Ivan Munroe and my father took off and went to look at Dog Island. The price (I'll never forget) was ten thousand dollars. My father thought it was way too high. "Hell," he said, "it won't even stay in the same place."

The Wakulla County Model Bow Skiff

in which I disclose a sin of omission

You know it is pitiful how much lore is lost without a second thought. One of the most lost of all lore is the history and design of the little skiffs of the coast of the Gulf of Mexico. Howard I. Chappelle named and published the lines of a boat for every inlet from Greenland to the Chesapeake but he sort of ran out of steam from there on down and around. I am just as bad. I think I am personally responsible for the loss of the lore of the Wakulla County model bow skiff.

Almost everybody had a model bow skiff down around Wakulla County in the Florida Big Bend back in the first half of the twentieth century and no telling how long before that. It was kind of like how everybody had an ax. I could never find out who built the first one or when but they were just about the standard skiff for commercial fishermen for a mighty long time. Wakulla County has, I believe, the most convoluted and hard-to-navigate shoreline in the United States. You don't have to take my word for it, just get on the Internet and fetch up with www.terraserver.com and call up an aerial photograph and see for yourself (a good name to enter is "St Marks, FL"). There might be some places down along the Everglades almost as bad, but you can spend a whole day messing around down around Panacea or St. Marks and not cover half a mile as the crow flies. Though the water is mostly very shallow and the bottom rocky and covered with oyster bars, there are deep holes sort of like limesinks all over the place and plenty of fish, crabs, and oysters and it is still possible for a hardworking person to make a scratch-by living with nothing but a little skiff.

The coast of Wakulla County is no place for a big-deal motorboat. Though it is the closest salt water to the monstrous Tallahassee (where national elections are decided) all the big-money Bayliners stay right in the middle of the channel and never have any idea of what the coastline is like. In ten minutes, a canoe can get so far from any sign of civilization that (except for jet airplane contrails and the ubiquitous trash from all the damn fools who, despite protestations of all kinds, don't know right from wrong) it is possible to convince yourself that you are the first person to ever see the place since the wild people were eradicated . . . but you aren't. People rowed, poled, sailed and paddled model bow skiffs around in those creeks and bayous for at least seventy-five years after the dugouts all got eaten up by the gribbles.

When I was a boy and a young man, I did it, too. My grandfather loved the place and every fall, when the crops were in, he rented a house at what they call "Wakulla Beach" (find that, if you can) and a skiff came with the house. We poled the little boat all through the creeks and caught crabs and fish and gigged flounders. Though I let the last model bow skiff I knew where was get eaten up before I got up the gumption to go down there and bog around in the mud to photograph it and take off the lines, I remember the boats pretty well. They were all just about as long as what you could build with sixteen-foot lumber. They were built hard-chined in the southern tradition. With that, I must digress. Most small southern boats are hard-chined. Bent frames don't last down here. There is an old erroneous saying that states that southern oak is not good for building boats. Southerners invented that saying and it got misquoted as it moved north. The saying is actually "*oak* is not good for building boats." Not even *Maine pasture-grown white oak*. Live oak is the only exception. Anyway, a model bow skiff was built of heavy, old-growth cypress. Like most southern chine-style boats, the sides were very thick and there was no chine log. The planking was just nailed onto the thick edge of the side of the boat. A lot of southern skiffs were deadrise-style both fore and aft, but a model bow skiff was flat-bottomed except for the bow, which had the steep deadrise of the bigger boats called "Florida skipjacks" like in the picture on page 248 in W. C. Fleetwood's book *Tidecraft*. Unlike the Florida skipjack, the bottoms of the little skiffs were cross-planked and the junction where the steep planking of the bow met the sides changed from having the sides beveled to having the ends of the planking cut at an angle to meet the square edge of the side. That kept the bevel of the side from becoming too acute and hard to caulk. You could see the little notch in the side of a model bow skiff about two-thirds of the way forward where that change occurred. I always thought it was the neatest little trick. The bow planking was put on extra-thick and then carved to form a hollow forefoot (model bow) and I thought that was another neat trick. Model bow skiffs were very low-sided and the thwarts were just nailed across the gunwales and, in the stern, there was a platform extending about six feet forward from the transom. You could sleep on that if you got caught short by the tide and had to spend the night in the marsh (not all that unpleasant in the wintertime if you had some good covers) but the other two functions of that stern deck were to strike a gill net from and to walk on to pole the boat . . . or throw a casting net. A model bow skiff was a deadly implement in a narrow creek full of mullet when poled backward by one person with another person (there have always been plenty of women in the fishing business around here) standing on the stern with a big cast net.

When outboard motors came along in the thirties, the old boats were modified to accommodate them by kneeing a board to the port side of the bow. The best motors for that purpose were the old style that turned 360 degrees. That way, the boats ran forward and didn't pound in the chop of the bay while heading to the creek and then the engine could just be swiveled around to head in the other direction to throw the net. Crab (both stone and blue) traps were worked by one person who ran the boat up to put the float on the starboard side where she caught it with the hook and trotted aft, hopping the thwart, to pull the trap onto the platform while he kicked the emptied and baited trap from the last haul off into the water. A good hand, didn't even cut his motor off while he did this. After the traps were swapped, an old heavy model bow skiff would run straight to the next trap while the man tended to his crabs and bait. Model bow skiffs were used to tong oysters, too. The low sides made it as easy as possible (which, ain't nothing easy about tonging oysters) and the boat was loaded from the bow back. Sometimes, the boat would be so loaded that it would swamp in the shallow water trying to get back to the hill and then the poor man would have to unload the boat, bail, and load it back up. I am going to tell you something. It takes a hell of a man (be he male or female) to tong a skiff full of oysters and pole it home. It takes all kinds of people to make the world go round, don't it? There are people who won't buy a car unless it has electric windows and I know a woman who has never been more than fifty feet from a thermostat in her life.

When I was a young man, I worked on a tugboat whose captain had hard-scrabbled, fatherless, through the Depression working a model bow skiff. He did it all, oysters, crabs, fish. Not only did he fish with a net, he commercially fished speckled trout (squeteague) and redfish (red drum) with a hook and line. In the summertime he and his mother and little sisters gathered wild rice up in the freshwater runs. He said that they would just pull the grass down in the boat and thresh out the rice with sticks and paddles into the bottom of the boat. It took a whole day to get about a load and then, while he poled the boat home, the women would sack up all that rice. He told me that they wouldn't miss a single grain . . . raked them out of the cracks with a knife. Then, the next day, they had to shuck it and that was the hardest job of all. Wild rice was too expensive for them to eat so they sold that for a little money to buy seed for the garden and shells for the gun.

Which, I hope the statute of limitations has run out on this sort of thing but those people down there killed a world of ducks in the wintertime and most of them were shot out of model bow skiffs. Almost all of Wakulla County is the "St. Marks Wildlife Refuge," which was set up back in the early part of the last century for a good reason. That country was duck and goose country for real. The people worked the skiff for ducks the same way they did for throwing the net . . . backward up the creek. "When we came around the bend where the bait was," Captain Junior told me, "we'd kill so many ducks that the feathers banked up on the edge of the marsh grass like snow." The feds had a hard time convincing those hardscrabble folks not to shoot those ducks that were worth a dime apiece at the same restaurants in Tallahassee that had bought the rice. Not only were the locals sort of naturally recalcitrant, but they were hard to catch back in all that shallow water. You know an enforcement officer who spent a lot of time doing his paperwork was hard-put to outpole a man who tonged a ton and a half of oysters six days a week.

So, I always hoped that I would find an old skiff in somebody's backyard. They would never rot out but they were so heavy that people never hauled them and the gribbles ate them from the bottom up. I watched it happen and never raised a sorry hand to save one. I am embarrassed. If you want to see what one looked like, there is a picture on the wall of the Spring Creek Restaurant down on this coast I have been talking about. I advise you to take your little skiff when you go to take a look. Spring Creek is about as close to as you can get to Primordea in a car. I advise you eat there. Order the fried mullet but don't order ducks and rice . . . unless you know somebody.

Further Reading: *Tidecraft,* William C. Fleetwood Jr., WGB Marine Press, P.O. 178, Tybee Island, GA 31328

Another Reynolds Rescue

in which I escape formal education but become educated nonetheless

One time we went in the Reynolds in company with another boat to St. George Island with the whole coast house crew, not just the children but the martini party from the porch, too. What had happened was that the constituents of the porch crew had gradually gotten younger and younger as the Reynolds crew got older and older. Some of us graduated to the porch as puberty infected us and that accounts for a little of the change, but the main thing was that my father's books were selling very well and some of the "young adults" they were aimed at were groupying around and they were so young that they got tired of sitting on the porch listening to the scintillating conversation. The books were adventurous and attracted adventurous fans and I guess they saw us children out there passing by in the old Reynolds and, kind of like a dog looking at a car he wants to chase and then back at the porch he is supposed to stay on, they just kind of drifted out the screen door.

I think I was fifteen the summer the Reynolds saved all those people. The reason I remember my age was because that was the year I skipped the ninth grade. I didn't skip it because I was so smart that the school put me up a grade—well, that ain't exactly accurate. I skipped it because I was so smart that I put *myself* up a grade. I hope the statute of limitations has run out on things like this because I have to admit something to you. I never was all that big on school (can you tell?) and I was a real hooky artist. Not only did I skip whole days at school, I was so slick that there were some classes I never attended when I was in attendance—things like English and PE, a lot of what they now call "social studies," and all of health. "Brush your teeth after every meal." That's horseshit. Other animals don't brush their teeth, and unless they have been inbred-for-cute too much, they don't have any trouble with them. I think that scum protects the teeth from decay. After my father ran away to California about 1957, he got him a new wife and she used to brush the teeth of her standard poodle with an electric toothbrush. Jesus, the poor dog shivered like she was freezing to death the whole time—the poor animal did the same thing when they took her to get bred. The offspring were supposed to be worth a thousand bucks a-piece. Too bad it didn't work and then her teeth fell out, too.

So, my education wound up sort of spotty. I never did find out the importance of why saliva changes sugars to starches and starches to sugars and I don't know the names of all the presidents of the United States or the capital cities of each and every one of the states, nor am I all that knowledgeable about the intricacies of old English royalty. I do know about the divorcée Wallace Simpson, though. I slept at the Indiantown Inn where she had worked as a waitress—might have slept in the same bed. Skipping school really didn't do me much damage in the long run . . . so far. I know a thing or two about a thing or two and did back when I was fifteen years old, too.

There was this girl that was hanging around the coast house then. She was, I guess, about twenty-two years old. She was one of the instigators of the "leave the porch" movement and I liked her fine. Back then, I was in the middle of my stingaree spine collection. I had a quart gin bottle (guess where it came from) almost full of stingaree spines. At first I was sticking the poor things with a regular, barbless flounder gig. I didn't want to kill the creature, I just wanted to pull his (or her . . . female stingrays get much bigger than males) spine off with my old rusty water-pump pliers and put it in my gin bottle. Too bad there wasn't any gin left in there, because it stank like the dickens when I unscrewed the cap. By the time of this rescue, I was trying to get the biggest of those marvelous spines I could, and St. George had (and still has) some of the biggest stingarees I have ever seen anywhere. A flounder gig won't hold a ray as big as the shadow of a Volkswagen, though, so I laboriously filed myself a little harpoon head out of an all-steel oyster knife and I stuck the flounder gig into a little hole I had drilled (burned up and broke about thirty-four of my father's drill bits) in it. When I stuck a stingaree, the head would go all the way through the wing and come off the gig, turn sideways and toggle to him (her) with fifty feet of three-eighth-inch manila line. She would have to come on in then. Boy, I had some big stingaree spines in my bottle by the time of this particular rescue.

Before I saved all those people, I had to save myself from this girl. The peculiarities of my education and social life had left me unprepared for the rigors of puberty. The few times I attended school, I was sort of a social outcast. I wasn't a wretch like these modern killer-jerks or anything. I wasn't even unhappy with my status. I just didn't fit in. My clothes were a good example. All the other boys my age wore tight blue jeans hauled down as low as possible to the pubic bone and they all had a waxed, flat-top hairdo, mowed off plumb bald in the middle of the top. Me, I wore my father's old passed-down khaki pants. They were too big so I hauled them up high and cinched them up tight (my hairdo was what could best be called "shaggy bristles"). Those pants and the Weldwood glue and model airplane cement (Ambroid) that I dribbled and wiped on my clothes sort of kept the girls off me. Which was a good thing, because, starting about the time of this incident, I have had a lot of trouble with them.

I had better tell you why I skipped the whole ninth grade (I'll tell you how later), and then I'll get back to how the old valiant Reynolds rescued all those people from St. George Island. I already knew all the science and algebra because of my mother and father who both knew how to cut right straight to the facts of the matter and I just couldn't see anything else they had up there at the school that would be of any use to me. Which, you know, I don't believe they have improved education all that much since then. I am going to step out on a limb here: School ain't worth a flip.

So what happened over there on St. George Island was that this twenty-two-year-old woman decided that she needed to reveal to me the true depth of my ignorance, which was not so deep as she imagined. During my year off from school, I had read the complete *Memoirs of Casanova,* all fifty pounds' worth, and that'll educate a person beyond what is normally expected.

"Have you ever kissed a girl?" was how it started.

"Yeah, I kissed my sisters on the cheek when they were sweet little babies" was my reply.

"No," she said, "I mean, have you ever kissed a girl, not related to you, on the lips."

"Nope, never wanted to do that, seems kind of nasty to me . . . you know, kind of like how chickens copulate."

"Well, you are mistaken," she stated assertively (she was in college studying to be a schoolteacher). "It's not nasty and the chickens don't think so either and I am going to show you."

Fortunately I was able to outrun her easily . . . didn't even have to drop my gin bottle or my harpoon.

All this carrying on sort of kept us from keeping a weather eye out. All of us children would have instantly noticed if we had been on our own, but we were too distracted by the complications of the new social situation. The first hint we socializing fools had was when the sun got cut off and the sand began to blow into the pimiento cheese sandwiches and the White Boat began to drag anchor.

I guess I'll have to tell you about that boat. I think it might have been the first fiberglass runabout ever made. My father loved a modern gadget more than anybody I ever knew and I believe he might have had an interest in the company. Anyway, it was a Winner fifteen-foot fiberglass boat, built, I believe, in 1953. It was as stark white as anything I have ever seen. You could hardly look at it in the bright sun. It was also extremely heavy . . . about half an inch thick. The Reynolds would run rings around it with a seven and a half and it had a thirty. It was a good sea boat though and very dry. The designer went to the max with the new medium and put a bow on there that couldn't be done with anything other than bent-to-broke strip planking. It had a hollow to the forefoot like the inside of a spoon and cheeks like Shirley Temple. Then it flared, uselessly, out to the foredeck (blue—thank goodness) like the bow of an aircraft carrier. It had a plastic windshield on it at first, but that useless thing soon disappeared along with the silly steering wheel and all those ridiculous cables and controls, including the starter switch. You know if you have to have all that in a fifteen-foot skiff, you are overloading your lifestyle with unreliability. As soon as my father ran off to California to write for the movies and TV (he wrote a lot of the Perry Masons), we cleaned up that old White Boat and I eventually put an old war-surplus storm boat motor on it and, for the first time, got that old, heavy tub up on a sure-enough plane.

I hate to keep interrupting this story, but the damn thing is already ruint and I need to explain the evolution of the ways to start an outboard motor so you'll understand some of the frustration to come. Old Ole Evinrude might have been the man who invented the cursed things and the first one was started by grabbing a little knob sticking out of the flywheel on top of the motor and giving it a spin. The damn thing has gone downhill ever since: Next, they put a little groove in the top of the flywheel to wrap a rope around (indeed, called "rope wrapper" in the family lexicon). You pulled the rope to spin the flywheel. The trouble with that is—after the engine is started and demanding attention to keep running—what the hell do you do with the rope, lose it, throw it down in the bilgewater? Next came the "recoil starter," which had a little spring-loaded spool that re-coiled the rope after you pulled. The trouble with that is the damn things hardly ever work right for very long. It is very common to see a lawn mower or a chain saw with the starter rope hanging out like the tongue of a hot dog. But, when in a fit of frustration you snatch the rope completely out of the weedeater, you just have to stop eating weeds but when the recoil starter messes up ten miles out on the flats—well, there you are. The next diabolical "improvement" was electric starting. I won't explain all that. I'll just tell you my opinion. I do not trust machinery of any kind. I never go out in a boat that cannot be propelled some other way. I'll be damned if I'll undignify myself by sitting helplessly out there in the hot sun dialing "911" on a cellular phone. I would rather row thirty miles, and indeed I have.

But on the day of the storm when I outran the schoolteacher, that white boat with both electric and recoil starters was dragging anchor rapidly out into the deep water of the pass. When my father and I finally caught the damn thing with the Reynolds, it was way out into the pass and the wind was blowing for real. He got off onto the White Boat and tried to start it with the key but the battery was dead from a short in the bilge pump, so he had to climb back in the stern to open the door in the shroud of the engine and reveal the pull rope. Then the remote-controlled choke rig way up there in the dashboard wouldn't let him choke the thing right and he pulled and pulled until he finally snatched the rope out of the recoil starter. By then it was way too rough to hang over the transom and do all that mechanicking so I took him in tow—finally. It was a sure-enough slow, crooked trip back to the little forlorn-looking crowd standing on the east-end point of the island in the driving rain.

And it kept on getting rougher all the time. If it had been these days, the little artificial German on the weather radio would have told us that this wasn't just another thunderstorm but a major meteorological event. If it had developed a little farther down by Yucatan, it would have made a hurricane and, as it was, it stormed for two days. When we finally got loaded up to head back, it was a borderline situation, and if St. George hadn't been so inhospitable a place to spend two days on, we would not have risked it. But we knew we were looking at a dismal prospect, so we decided to make a try. The wind was about straight out of the west—right down the bay—and we had to crab up into it to make any headway toward the mainland. It was far too rough to go directly because the shallow bay was making a breaker out of each of those waves, and if we let the bow fall off too much, we couldn't bail fast enough—even though we had plenty of eager people and containers (bailing a boat for five hours is a good way to wash pimiento cheese out of a bowl). Most of the people were huddling down in the White Boat. All you could see of them was the water they were throwing over the side. My mother and Bruzzwully and I were the only ones in the Reynolds. I was running the engine and dodging the towline made up to the trailer eye, which was trying to gnaw my ears off that day. My father and the rest of the crew finally got the White Boat trimmed to tow without yawing, but it was still slow going. We needed more line so we could get adjusted to the wavelength, but we didn't have it, and besides, by the time we got out there and under way, it was too rough to fool with any changes. It was a good thing that we had sense enough to get the gas cans out of the White Boat before we left because there certainly would be no handing over of anything from then on and the engine of the Reynolds burned a lot of gas that day.

That Reynolds engine was an Evinrude eighteen. Back in those days, Evinrude made two models out of the same engine. An eighteen was also a twenty-five, like a nine point nine is a fifteen now. They did that for years. As far as I could tell, there was not any difference in the two engines at all except for the bore of the carburetor—and the price. That's another example of what happens to people who spend too much time in school. They get so indoctrinated into accepting bullshit that they'll buy into a scam like that.

You know the memory of really hard times sort of misses getting properly embedded in the brain. I don't remember much of that trip. I remember that the rain was cold and the spray was warm and that is about all. I guess I sat back there and tried to head up into the biggest of the waves while Momma and Bruzzwully bailed and swapped gas tanks all day long. I just forgot about the White Boat trying to snatch us into a broach all the time. It was a long, miserable trip, though. You'll just have to take my word for it.

Years later I had another long miserable trip that I don't remember much about. My wife and I sailed straight across the Gulf from Dog Island to Pass-A-Grille down around Tampa Bay in our old raggedy Morgan thirty. I would have made another plan when it started breezing up that time, but my son and his new wife were waiting for us there on his sailboat and expecting us to show up. I didn't want to worry him when it started storming, so we beat right dead into it for what seemed like three or four days. I couldn't open the companionway but just a little crack and didn't dare quit the lookout for fear of getting run over in the poor visibility, so I stayed up there in the cockpit, wrapped up in the sail cover, and tried to duck the solid green water coming over the bow. I think that's the only time I ever looked *up* at a spotted porpoise. The only sail I could carry was just the reefed-to-nothing main and it wasn't doing anything. My little thirty-year-old, twelve-horse Volvo was all that was accomplishing anything at all. That and my wife down there with the Radio Direction Finder and the saltines with her feet jammed against one side of the dinette and her back against the other. All I remember of the trip was watching the crack in the companionway for her to pass me another saltine.

So the heroic rescuers and the shivering rescued finally waded ashore at the coast house. Most of them—those who could get a car to start—headed on back to high ground, but some of us had to stay to try to take care of the Reynolds and the White Boat, which had to ride at anchor through the rest of the storm. My father, gallantly, offered to let my twenty-two-year-old pursuer take his Porsche (356A Speedster just like James Dean killed himself with); when the Porsche wouldn't start, she was stuck with us remnants to wait the storm. Me and Bruzzwully and some other children played Monopoly with her when we weren't bailing the boats. Except for a little hiding of money, there was no hanky-panky. I think she might have learned her lesson.

I almost forgot that I was going to tell you *how* I skipped the ninth grade. I just never went on the first day. I had a special driver's license since I was fourteen and drove the car that hauled all the other children. When I finished dropping them off at their schools, I just kept on driving. It was a very educational year. When the time came to go to high school, I just went to the tenth grade. They didn't find out about it until I was ready to graduate out of the twelfth. They were very perplexed about what to put into my permanent record. Didn't bother me a bit. I enlisted in the Navy where I was perfectly safe from twenty-two-year-old girls.

A Few Recipes of the Reynolds Crew

in which I begin a lifetime as a gourmet

Back in the good old days (which are still around for some) my mother sort of looked after us to keep us from the extremities of bowel stress. We took various things with us from the house to help out with the hunting and gathering. Usually we had baked potatoes, apples, bananas and sometimes those old staples of skiffboat people all over: Vienna sausages and sardines. We finally quit taking saltine crackers because of all the mishaps, but we often had a hot watermelon rolling around in the bottom of the boat with the stomped-on baked potatoes and apples. We never brought anything back and we never got tired of the same old thing.

OYSTERS

Oysters are good. You can't eat lunch in a more natural way than squatting on an oyster bar until you get through. Now that they are apt to kill you or leave you with a disabled liver because of the nastiness of our civilization and the nature of their feeding, it is wise not to eat them raw but that is how they are best. Though they might appear to some to be sort of amorphous, they are regular pelecypods with the same symmetry . . . Not only do they have right and left, front and rear, they, like scallops, have top and bottom. Any child can quickly learn how they lie in the hand. A hungry, innocent child goes straight for the umbones and gnaws and wiggles with the screwdriver until the shells are separated at the hinge. I still do it that way. The oyster in the shell is (after scraping the adductor muscle free of the bottom shell) sucked up and, depending on the size, chewed or swallowed whole. After we had marauded our way west on St. George to where the trees began, we began to find some very big single oysters just lying around on the bottom. Some of them were as big as the bottom of a tennis shoe. Took quite a few chews, particularly for the little ones with only a few teeth right in front, to get them ready to swallow. My mother was the ace of the big-oyster-eating business. She just cut a few notches in them with her teeth to let out the flavor as they slid in and down.

CRABS

Keep the crabs alive until cooking time. A dead crab in the hot sun is a lot more dangerous than a live crab in the hot sun. They'll only stay alive in a bucket of water if you continually change it. If you are apt to forget, they keep better in a bucket with no water in it. Their gills can absorb oxygen from the air better than they can from stagnant water in a bucket full of other suffocating, urinating crabs. The best way to cut losses due to death is to let them have free run of the bilgewater in the bottom of a boat. Boil the crabs whole and alive in seawater. If the crabs have been in the same bucket for a while, rinse off the yellow urine before you put them in the boiling water. Don't get bit. A big blue crab will change your attitude about the apparent ease with which mankind exerts his dominion over all living things. Them, yellow flies, no-see-ums, and mosquitoes have not learned proper respect for us quite yet.

When the crabs are red, drag the foot tub to the deepest hole of water you can find and dump them out—skip to the side to avoid the hot water. As soon as you can stand to hold them, pull the carapace off by prying up on the tip of the inlaid abdomen with your fingernail (or use a crab claw if your fingernails have gotten so soft that they won't work). Eat the "goody" out of the cavity in the middle of the crab. There are different kinds of goody:

One is the contents of the crop and stomach which are encased in a little sac and extension sac right back of the teeth. It is usually pretty gritty with various kinds of stuff, but not usually sand. On seaside beaches, the grit is chewed-up shells of *Donax variabilis* (cochinas) and sand fleas (mole crabs, *Emerita* spp.), neither of which will hurt you. In marshes and creeks, the crabs (usually male) have been eating other crabs (usually fiddlers, *Uca* spp.) and oysters. Though it is possible that you might eat some carrion (maybe even a little bit of human being) my observations are that blue crabs mostly catch and eat live things. The contents of the crop and stomach of crawfish are a delicacy to the people (some elected officials) of Louisiana and crawfish are more indiscriminate than blue crabs. My own mother, rest her soul, always sucked that part up first. After I had learned the anatomy of crabs, I told her, "Momma, you know what that is you are eating?" "Yep," she said, "it's good." "That crab thought it was good when he ate it too," said me. "Delicious," said she around a mouthful. Before you turn prissy and pass judgment, consider the hot dog and the hamburger. If you think, for a minute, that huge meatpacking conglomerates throw away tons of those nutritious and valuable things (ears for a tame example) that, if wrapped in clear plastic and named by their real names, would send previously happy shoppers screaming from the store, you are wrong. Prissiness is a late-model invention in the evolution of mankind.

Another type of goody is the fat, which is a grayish white kind of stuff that (in a fat crab and they all ain't) is right on top in the cavity and even extends out into the corner spines of the carapace where it is easily dug out with the nonmovable pincher of a claw. In male crabs, the fat is all mixed up with the gonads, which look like convoluted strands of spaghetti. Both the fat and the gonads are quite good and very nutritious.

Another type of goody is all that yellow crumbly stuff in female crabs who have not made a "sponge" yet. Those crumbs are the eggs and are my favorite kind of goody. Female crabs keep the eggs inside their carapaces until they are mature. Then they are moved outside under the flap-like abdomen where the little larvae develop further. The eggs under the abdomen look like a sponge and have developed tough shells to protect the developing larvae. Make sure you don't throw the carapace of any nonsponge female crab away before you rake all that yellow goody out of the inside of the points of the spines. I think that the proof of what is good and what isn't is to try it on a child . . . one who hasn't been retarded by the Froot Loop and taught the word *yucky* yet. An ignorant baby will eat the yellow goody as fast as you can pick it out. While you are at it, eat those little muscles in the front of the carapace that move the eyes.

After you eat the goody, take off the dead man's fingers (gills, and like the sponge absolutely inedible) and bite the legs off well into the body of the crab. You can teach yourself how far into the body to bite by experimenting with the paddle-shaped swimming legs. They should come off with a good bit of the "lump" meat attached. Eat that and any that is sticking out of the proximal joint of the walking legs. Do not throw those legs away. Any child with two opposing teeth can munch out a good piece of meat from the big joint and in a pinch you can work it all the way to the toe. Clean out the big lump from the undivided swimmer fin hole. After that, it is sort of ticklish to get the meat from the walking leg holes in the body of the crab because there is a horizontal partition separating the pull-down muscle from the lift-up muscle. That is where small children get most of their shell from.

The claws are easy. Usually, if you bite the distal (outboard) side of each joint and then crack along with your teeth toward where the claw was attached to the crab, the meat will come out of each joint in one piece. Sometimes a crab has just shed and the claw is flimsy and damn near empty. We used to just chew the whole thing up and spit out what didn't go down easy.

The delicacy of this business is soft-shell crabs. Usually found being carried by their protective husbands. They find each other just before the time comes for the girl to molt into womanhood. The old boy holds her underneath him and carries her around until she molts. At that delicate time, he will eat your ass up if you mess with them. Though he can't help her shed her shell, he acts mighty anxious as he protects her. After she is all the way out, he mates with her while she is soft. Afterward, he carries her as before until she is hard enough to take care of herself. Somehow, all the girls in our crew have been thwarted in their efforts to find somebody to do them like that. Some of them, like my wife, have to protect the males that they wound up with—those who didn't get tired of it and run him off.

Soft crabs are best if rolled around in egg and buttermilk, battered with cracker crumbs, and fried, but we didn't have all that. We just boiled her along with her husband and the others while the anxious owner kept an eagle eye on the project. A fried soft crab is a special treat, but a boiled one ain't half bad. You just lift up the tips of the carapace enough to pull out the dead man's fingers and the teeth and eat her whole. One little girl in our crew used to specialize in soft crabs. While we were digging or fishing or messing around, she would continuously comb the grass for paired crabs. When she found some, she would put the male in the boat but she didn't trust the soft female out of her clutches. It was a rare thing to see her when she wasn't guarding at least one soft crab in her hand. If the crab was caught early in the morning, a long way before boiling time, it would just get littler and littler while the girl carried her as she ate, first the claws, then the legs, and finally just a little of this and that for a snack. Once in a rare chance she would catch a gigantic soft-shell male crab. At first, we used to tease her and act like we wanted to steal her treasure, but her reaction was so fierce that we soon stopped.

Altogether, crabs are good for people. They teach caution, patience, politeness, and nutrition.

BAKED POTATOES WITH SEAWATER AND OYSTERS

Cut a cold, walked-on, bilgewater-soaked baked potato in half and mess up the middle enough so that an oyster won't slide off. Try not to eat the potato until you have opened at least one oyster. Put him in and sprinkle seawater to taste. Eat a little hole where the oyster was and then open another oyster. Soon you'll have an empty potato skin. Fill it with oysters and eat it whole in one big mouthful . . . don't talk or get tickled while you are doing this.

BAKED POTATOES WITH MUSTARD (OR ANY OTHER KIND OF) SARDINES

Do the same way with the sardines as with the oysters above. Eat a little and pour a little. Try to eke it out so that the sardines and potato even out in the end. Only a fool wastes the juice out of a sardine can.

APPLES, SEAWATER, AND MUSTARD

You guessed it . . . what can I say?

UNDER WATERMELON

Slice and bust a large, hot watermelon into suitable-sized chunks and distribute according to the "Who shall have this?" ritual described in *Men Against the Sea,* (Nordoff & Hall; the second book in the *Mutiny on the Bounty* trilogy). Eat your part down to the green rind while you are completely underwater to escape mosquitoes, horseflies, yellow flies, and no-see-ums. Chew up and swallow the seeds too—they scour the guts and promote good health. You can stick your lips up every now and then to get a little breath of air.

CRABS AND APPLES

Eat the crabs first and then the apples. Eat a goodly portion of the shell of the crabs and the core, seeds, and stem of the apples.

CRABS AND BANANAS

Gobble the banana while you are waiting for the crab water to boil. You can scrape the goody off the inside of the peeling with your bottom teeth but don't eat the outside part. That won't do you a bit of good. Drink ice water to do you good and calm you down while you wait.

Personal Hygiene

in which one of the reasons that I am a hermit is revealed

Our family has always been sort of peculiar when it comes to personal hygiene. I won't belabor you back more than about three generations but my mother was a good example. "Poo," she said, "I remember back before they invented underarm deodorant. The first deodorant that came out was called 'Odor-O-No' and it came in a little jar. Then there was one of them called 'Arrid' which they claimed stopped you from sweating." I, with my recent knowledge of chemistry and the pedantry that comes with such, replied, "All it was was some kind of gurry with some artificial fragrance and powdered aluminum oxide. The aluminum oxide was supposed to stop up the sweat pores but it didn't work." "Better than Odor-O-No," she replied. One of my cousins discovered a product called "Five Day Deodorant Pads." Because he was always a little gullible, he tried them out when he first began to have a little puberty-driven pheromone signal but the poor boy thought that you were supposed to tape those pads up in the armpit for five days. "Came out sort of black," he observed. I guess what the name meant was that you could use the same pad to anoint the armpits for five days straight before the juice absorbed in it gave out. Whew.

There have been various views about how frequently one needs to bathe and change clothes. Some of us take it to extremes in both directions. I myself wore the same corduroy suit for a whole school year when my parents mistakenly sent me off to a boarding school in hopes that they could straighten me out. It didn't work but that suit had a pretty good ability to stand up straight all by itself and it was hard to tell if it was really corduroy or shiny rayon. My schoolteaching sister decided that washing clothes was a useless business in the wintertime so she proceeded to wear the same five sets of garments for one whole school year. Of course she bathed before she put on her dirty clothes but, by Thanksgiving, her first graders were beginning to notice a few things. "It must be Friday." one precocious chick observed. "Miz White has on the shirt that she dipped her elbow in the metchup with." "What?" you may ask, "is metchup?" Since I still retain a little of the pedant qualities of my chemistry days, I'll tell you. That's a mixture of ketchup and mustard for dipping french fries and hot dogs in. I always liked it swirled into patterns like a tie-dyed hippie shirt. Make sure you shake up the squeeze bottle of mustard good to keep from getting that first watery squirt.

One of my uncles believed that bathing reduced the body's resistance to disease and insect attacks. "If you didn't wash off all the natural oils and waxes," he proclaimed, "you would never catch the athlete's foot and no-see-ums wouldn't be able to bite you. You know, the way they work it is to dab a little drop of acid on you and eat the skin that gets dissolved. Natural oils and waxes prevent the penetration of the acid. Athlete's foot fungi are not adapted to dealing with that toe jam either. They like scrubbed meat and that's why athlete's foot always shows up in the spring when you start wading around in the water. Soaking your feet in antifreeze will cure it, though."

Believe it or not, I am the most frequent bather in my family. I do it because I get mighty dirty. I don't know what it is but, if my wife and I go walking down the little dusty roads, she'll come back just as clean as a whistle but my legs will be filthy all the way to the knees. Even after I rinse off, every pore will be easy to see. Which, rinse off is all I ever do. I like to do it out in the yard with the garden hose. I was so delighted when the pistol-style hose nozzle was invented. A common indoor, down-squirting showerhead just isn't in it with one of those things for rinsing various areas of the body. Careful manipulation of the trigger will put an appropriate shot of water exactly where it is needed and with the proper force . . . bidet . . . child please. Of course I don't have any hot water out there but I believe cold water is good for you any time of the year. I am hoping that surviving the shock will strengthen the heart muscle and make it appreciate just regular work. Besides, hot water removes the natural oils and waxes.

I certainly would never use soap. Soap is created when a chemical reduction occurs between an oil and a strong base like lye. Modern detergents, soaps, and shampoos are made by the reactions of something like calcium hydroxide and petroleum oil. To hell with putting something like that on your skin. You know, I believe the common acceptance of bathing with soap is about the purest example of the power of advertising upon the gullible that I know of. What the advertisers do is to pick out an area of vulnerability . . . personal attractiveness in this case . . . then they instill doubts and offer a solution. It is easy money. You know why most women have more wrinkles than men of an equivalent age? It is because they are more vulnerable to soap advertisement because they have been indoctrinated by megacorporations to believe that only young-looking women with skin like the rumps of babes are attractive so they scrub and scrub and then apply various ointments and emollients to replace all the natural oils and waxes they washed off. All that rubbing stretches the skin. They would be better off rinsing off out in the yard with cold water out of the hose. Men, on the other hand, have just the opposite indoctrination. They see all those young rock stars and athletes on the TV and notice that they aren't man enough to take care of business and have to hire older men called "managers." Youthful looks are a detriment to men so most of them don't do too much cosmetics and grow up to be Republicans.

I think there is some hope, though. I notice a modern trend in women's fashion where it looks like they have quit washing their hair. Stringy and dirty-looking hair is stylish these days. Of course they wash it with soap and then have to add some kind of stringy-style conditioner to get it back to looking like it was dirty. They could have just stood out there in the yard and squirted off with the hose and saved a bunch of money.

Getting Into and Out of Boats

in which a helping hand reveals all

My father was an enthusiastic photographer, both still and cinematic . . . no holds barred. When he died, his widow sent me a box of old movies. In there was a movie of scenes he had edited together of people getting into and out of boats. It was pretty good too . . . I could blackmail some of my aunts with some of the footage . . . made me wish I had had the old Bolex hanging around my neck all my life like he did. Inexperienced people who have become overly aware of their dignity do some comical things trying to get into or out of a boat.

One of the best examples on film is that scene where Katharine Hepburn is trying to get back into the *African Queen* after her little dip. She says, "Mr. Allnut . . . Mr. Allnut . . . MR. ALLNUT!!!!" I have an eighteen-month-old granddaughter who is experienced enough not to be too aware of her dignity. Our grandchildren love to play in the skiffs and little sailboats while they are anchored in that six inches of water outside our house. They stay out there almost all day long transporting sand and shells and creatures. They are all very adept at getting in and out, even the babies . . . until this latest one came along. She inherited the "little" gene that lurks in the background of my family. Though she is almost two years old, she only weighs seventeen pounds. It is not ill health or anything that makes these half-pints. My runt aunt (not even five feet tall) is over eighty and still hell on her little wheels. My runt great-grandmother, though crazier than a dingbat (another gene, but beyond the scope of this study), lived to be over a hundred. A side effect of the gene is a determination to be left alone in all endeavors. The other children out there scramble repeatedly over the side, often carrying sandy things in both hands, with no hesitation in the progress but this little baby can't even reach the rail. The others tried to help her but she squawked so loud that they gave up on that and left her to her struggling. I was watching with the knobblers one morning when I was fortunate enough to see the first success. She discovered the outboard motor tilted up on the transom. At first she grabbed it by the foot and tried, Katharine Hepburn–like, to dangle and stick her feet up, first one and then another in a futile attempt to catch the top of the transom and lever herself into the boat but she

110

couldn't do it. She stood back there for a long time. At first, I thought she was crying from frustration but she was actually thinking. Finally she took off her diaper, grabbed the foot of the engine, hooked her toes in the stern handle, flipped her other leg across the top of the transom, and was standing, triumphant, in the stern naked as a jaybird except for her hat before I could say Jack Robinson. From then on, she showed the others the best way to put sand in a boat.

Another baby incident happened at the Naples (Florida) City Dock. Late one summer, on our way back from Andros, my wife and I had gone up in there in the skiff to get some beloved ice and a can of beer to take back to the boat. It must have been on a weekend day because it was very crowded and I had to put my wife off and wait out in the river because there was no room. While I was waiting (where was my Bolex) I saw a nice-looking young couple trying to get off the dock into a small runabout with a baby about as old as the one in the first story (though considerably bigger and heavier). The man got in the boat first and reached up to take the baby from the woman who was still high up on the dock. As she leaned over and he leaned out, somehow they managed to do the old natural thing and get overbalanced and push the boat away from the dock. First the man's feet came out from under him and he fell, headfirst into the water, then the woman in a reflex, to keep her balance, stepped off the edge of the dock and plummeted straight down about six feet with the baby. It must have been twelve feet deep right there because the only thing visible on the surface of the water for a long, long time were the waves of the impact and the baby . . . bobbing calmly in her PFD. Before her parents managed to save themselves (I thought I heard a couple of loud thumps from somewhere under the boat) she had straightened out her hat. I know it is bad to make light of a potential tragedy like that but me, pop-eyed, in my skiff and about twenty retired Yankees running around on the dock were getting ready to get poised to do something.

In my father's movie, there seems to be a pervasive theme where all these women appear to be overly conscious of what the unusual stress on their bathing suits might let slip as they get into the boat. In most cases, the boat is anchored off the beach at our old house. Getting into or out of a boat in a situation like that, though less dangerous than dockside capers, is much more difficult. There is a good-sized segment of the population that, through inexperience, incompetence, out-of-shape problems, or some combination of those, just can't do it. The repetitive attempts of self-conscious ladies to try to get in the boat with their friends who are waiting to embark is sort of pitiful. For some reason, they all think that maybe the side of the boat is lower in another place, or maybe all the way to the stern or the bow (that anchor rope looks sort of handy), so they spend a lot of time sidling around sort of like a dog who is getting ready to lie down or a blue crab who is sizing up a worthy opponent. Young gallants in the boat are always reaching to help and sometimes, a willing hand is attempting a well-placed push from below. In most cases a strong pull from above causes some unacceptable movement of the cloth and the help is frantically, sometimes violently, refused. The helpful push from below is never met with much gratitude. I was involved with one of those situations for a long time once.

Back in the fifties a bunch of us decided to go to this little lake to do some waterskiing. There was only one of us who hadn't already learned to ski but the glamour and contemporary popularity of the thing (Esther Williams at Cypress Gardens) was so attractive to her that she insisted on trying over and over and over again to get going. Her failures were not only due to plain, natural incompetence but also to an innate stubbornness. She steadfastly refused to pay attention to our expert suggestions and kept on doing the same thing. She would get up to the planing position, pull back on the rope, and when the inevitable slack came fall over backward . . . time after time after time. All of the rest of us were about ready to drown the damn girl when finally she managed to stay up long enough to get out to the middle of the lake before she fell. Out there, it was too deep for a non-expert skier to get back up so she decided to get in the boat. From years of experience with others of her ilk, I knew that she couldn't do that either and tried to get her to hang on to the rope and let me tow her back to shore. She thought that sort of treatment was beneath her dignity so she spent half an hour going around and around the boat trying to find the easy place. It was past lunchtime so we all tried our best to help but she refused all attempts most adamantly. I found out why. This was back in the days when women were following the fad where they somehow manipulated their breasts into a conical shape. My skill as a keen observer of the bathing suits of my female relatives hanging on the line at the coast house had revealed that most of the bathing suits of the day had a funnel-shaped insert made of some material like heavy, fused monofilament nylon that accomplished this shaping . . . so did the evening gowns of that era. Often, there was a significant gap between the shapely outer shell of the garment and the actual flesh of the girl (my father said that you could drop a wet basketball down the front of some of those things) and such was the case here. Unbeknownst to this girl, her repeated attempts to lunge over the side of the boat had inverted these two heavily reinforced protuberances and revealed that there could not possibly be much inside. A fact that was proven shortly when the other boy got disgusted with the whole project and, throwing the girl's dignity to the winds, hauled her over the side by both arms.

I hope you remember that wonderful photograph on the back page of *Life* magazine back in the fifties . . . the one where the three nuns are involved with the flat-bottomed skiff. In the picture, one of the nuns is already out and has obviously just given a good hard jerk on the bow because the stern nun is just hitting the water after falling backward over the transom. The nun still sitting on the middle seat . . . the one with the wide eyes and the delighted grin . . . obviously has no business being involved with any solemn order.

My sister did the same thing to an octogenarian. She decided that this old man would appreciate a day trip out to Dog Island to see the sights. I don't know what she told him, but judging from the whiteness of his knuckles, he did not expect a rough, wet skiffboat ride across the bay. When we got there, it was high tide and I laid her alongside the beach to make it easy for this gentleman to get out. As usual, my sister grabbed the anchor and scrambled out like a squirrel. No point to any detail on this one. She snatched the boat right out from under this old dude. He couldn't have hit the water any better if he had been canonized. He is ninety-five now and still hasn't forgiven her.

So as not to appear sexist in this, I'll have to include the incident of this old high school buddy. He turned out to be one of these big wheeler-dealers who worked hard and made a bunch of money to buy things that he didn't have time to use. He was infatuated with the idea of scuba diving and, though he didn't have time to do it but about once a year, he had all the latest gear. When his annual day off came, he always chose me to be his "buddy" and go with him to watch him scuba dive. We would go out to the reef in his high-tech boat and I would swim around with my snorkel and look in little holes at all the faces and feelers while he adjusted his gear. Snorkeling is one of my favorite things to do and I quickly become so fascinated with all the discoveries I make that I am oblivious to everything else. It is a wonder that a shark hasn't swallowed me whole by now from not paying attention. Anyway, this time, I discovered that, by holding on to the rocks with my hands and paddling hard with my flippers, I could wash the sand out of little holes in the limestone bottom and reveal the worms and burrowing shrimp that were trying to dig back in. The current was so strong that the sand that I stirred up was quickly swept downstream and that left these creatures in plain view. When I finally became aware of my surroundings again (could have been hours) I discovered that old "high-tech" had also been washed downstream with the current but unlike the little animals, he was not in plain view. To make a long story short, after I had searched downstream for miles to find him, he couldn't get back in the boat with all that crap strapped on him and was so weak from exhaustion that he couldn't hold it up high enough for me to grab from over the high sides of his monster boat. I had to get in the water and undress him, then get back in the boat and haul his exhausted ass over the side. He was absolutely furious all this time and I know that it was frustrating to him that he didn't have the strength to take it out on me.

My own wife was deeply involved in an incident in which she earned a bottle of champagne. We had come to the island in our old surplus twenty-six-foot US Navy motor whaleboat late one winter afternoon. Though the onshore norther was blowing to beat the band, she adroitly caught the mooring and made us up while I gingerly got into the skiff we were towing. When she was passing the groceries and junk down to me, somehow, while we both had a grip on the same box, I let the skiff get too far away and she missed stays and *ploop* over the stern she went. Fortunately I was able to keep hold of the box of cans she was trying to hand me but in doing so, I lost hold of the whaleboat and, before I could get the oars shipped, I had been swept far off downwind in the skiff. Though it was rough, that water was cold and she scrambled over the slick, high, pitching stern of the whaleboat like it had handles and rungs. When we finally rowed in, there were our neighbors standing on the beach in front of our house with a little bottle of champagne. "We were watching that whole amazing incident through the binoculars," said Charlie, "and it was such good entertainment we thought we would bring you this bottle of champagne to help you celebrate. You know, Jane, you were back in that boat so quick I am surprised to see that you are wet. Why, I'm not so sure I could have done it any better myself," he said patronizingly. "Me neither," she snapped, looking him up and down before striding to the house with the bottle of champagne clutched by the neck.

Sailfish

in which someone learns a lesson . . . well, almost

My father loved boat kits. I guess he built ten or twenty or so during the time after World War Two before he took off for California. When he found one he liked, he built the same boat over and over again and gave the finished boats away when the accumulation got out of hand. One of his favorites was some kind of canvas-covered skiff . . . just frames and a few stringers covered with canvas. Another was a tiny V-bottomed plywood pram that I believe was called a "Seashell." He was welcome to give either one of those away. The canvas boats were almost useless because you had to be so careful where you went and you couldn't drag it. The damn little pram acted just like damn little prams all do—slow, wet, and crank—and it could not be propelled with a paddle.

When I was about eleven, one of my sisters (then nine years old) and I took a trip down the Ochlocknee River from the GA 93 bridge to the Hadley Ferry . . . kind of short as the crow flies, but a hell of a long way as the pram is dragged. As soon as our ride drove off and we got out of sight of the bridge, the river dwindled to a logjammed trickle and the little engine (Elto "Pal") spat its spark plug out in the only deep hole in the whole river and was no pal to us from then on. The river was so low that we had to drag that pram and that little engine all the rest of the way. The trip would have been just a long wade through some mighty interesting country if it hadn't been for our watercraft. As it was, we wore all the paint off the keel and chines until all my father's little Reed and Princes shined like new money. My sons polished up the bottom of my old Grumman Sport Boat doing that same thing many years later, but enough of all that, I was going to tell you about the Sailfish when I started.

The "Sailfish" was a plywood kit too. I never researched the design, but I believe that it was some sort of a predecessor to those ubiquitous fiberglass sailboards called "Sunfish" now . . . which, like an old .22 target rifle like the Boy Scouts use, is the standard to measure by when you think you have a hotshot rig. A lowly Sunfish sailed by a light, skillful kid in a good breeze will show just how much there is of that muchness you are so proud of.

So he built this Sailfish. I was about ten years old at the time and I got to sand the internal parts and paint the little plywood bulkheads and break off a few drill bits drilling the holes for the screws where he had stepped off some marks with dividers. He had this thing called a "Versamatic," which was a planetary screwdriving attachment for an electric drill (his was a D-handled Black & Decker . . . quarter-inch chuck . . . weak . . . made a funny smell when it was running . . . made a real funny smell when I burned it up trying to install a muffler cutout on my Momma's Ford station wagon forty-five years ago. I still have his old half-inch drill, which stands knee-high and won't drill a shaft log hole without extensive waiting periods between bouts with the spoon). This Versamatic was a pretty good thing. It had two collars that spun when the drill was switched on. If you grabbed the top collar, the screwdriver bit sticking out of the end turned at a much reduced speed to drive the screw, and if you grabbed the bottom collar it backed them back out. Though the drill always ran the same speed, you could vary the speed and torque of the bit by letting the collar slip in your hand a little bit. I think the man who invented it must have been an old Model T mechanic because that thing worked just like the planetary transmission in those old cars except that your hand took the place of the clutch bands. That old Versamatic was one of the things I wish my father had left when he took off for California about 1955. Oh well at least he left the "Yankee" screwdriver, which would run rings around that gadget.

So we finished the kit. I believe there were a jillion little three-quarter-inch #6 Reed and Prince monel screws in the deck and bottom of that boat. I have to digress again at the mention of that. Like my father, I sure do love monel. You know, the invention of "stainless" steel sure wasn't much improvement over that wonderful maritime metal. If metal was wood, monel would be live oak. I guess it is too expensive to make stuff out of anymore and I guess it is too expensive to make stainless steel like the kind that they made the 1930 Model A radiator shell out of too. Oh well . . . back to the Sailfish.

It looked just like a Sunfish except that it was made out of plywood. The mast step was the weak point in the boat. We children used to load ourselves out on the upwind side so many and so far and in such wind that the boat looked like it was heeling when actually the hull was level (and flying too). We used to have to pull it up on the beach and take the drain plug out about every fifteen minutes and take turns blowing our breaths into the hole to build up some pressure inside the hull so the water would come out faster. When we did that, water would well up inside the mast step like a little spring. My father accused us of abusing his boat and tried to patch the mast step all different kinds of wondrous ways. After he took off for California, my mother finally fixed the damned thing with about a hundred pounds of concrete (glad I didn't have to drag it down the Ochlocknee River) and a bunch of coat hangers. After that, the mast had to twist the deck and bottom from chine to chine instead of just a little place in the middle and it didn't leak quite as bad.

The Sailfish incident that has gone down in family legend doesn't have much to do with the boat though. Right soon after the Sailfish was finished (before we children molested the mast step) my father was drinking a few martinis on the porch of the coast house with a bunch of visitors while the husband of one of those people was down trying to teach himself to sail. It didn't do to pass by on the beach in front of that house if you were not in the mood to be scrutinized and criticized. My father was pointing out all the things that this man was doing wrong to all the other observers on the porch and not only explaining the proper way to do them, but implying that anybody who did not have the innate intuition to already know which way the wind was blowing and how a single piece of cloth would act when presented to that wind in the way this poor man was repeatedly doing it was a fool. Indeed, I have made similar observations myself, but such verbal punishment was superfluous because the boat could take care of all that on its own. I don't believe that I have ever been involved with a boat that would hit you in the head any harder with the boom than that Sailfish. There is something about the geometry of the lateen rig I guess. Of course, when you are sitting flat on the top of the slick deck with no real toehold and only about eighteen inches of clearance to hide in when the damn thing jibes, there ain't a hell of a lot that even the most agile among us could do but take the lick. This poor man took his share right there in front of the coast house audience. As the slapstick became progressively more funny and my father's comments more acerbic, everyone failed to notice that the poor young man's young wife was not taking part in the mirth. While they, in the throes of hilarity, were sloshing gin with a little vermouth and sometimes an occasional olive over the rim of their little glasses, she was sitting still, the surface of her martini remained high and level and her olive stationary—even after she had set it down and taken up a five-cell flashlight that she used to beat my father over the head until he was subdued. One witness to the incident said that she would have killed him if the lens hadn't busted and the reflector hadn't escaped and let the batteries out. I saw him when he got back from the hospital. The bandage was as big as a turban. I also fished the ruins of the flashlight out from under the settee . . . boy was it ever dinged up around the threads of the big end . . . some of the batteries were even dented.

Many years later, I used to ride the bus to California to visit my father at his house in Malibu (a trip just about equivalent to dragging a pram all the way down the Ochlocknee River except that there was no good place to go to the bathroom). One time, I was talking to one of his associates while he was outside barbecuing on the hibachi. The person told me that there had been a time in their association when things were said about life before California that seemed incredible even to a Californian. "Is that a fact?" said me. "Like all those little crescent-shaped bald spots all over his scalp . . . Robb said that they were old wounds from back in his sailing days." "That's a fact," said me.

The Model Airplane Malady

in which I report yet another genetic affliction

Scattered all through my big family are people who harbor a gene that, though usually suppressed enough to allow mostly normal function, will unexpectedly trigger the release of some powerful hormone and cause a single-minded frenzy of model airplane building. I am a carrier of this gene in its most virulent form and am afraid that I have passed it on. The reason I am afraid is because the model airplane gene is a very dangerous thing.

When one of my sons (the too-tall one, then skinny) was about twelve, he was struck by this thing in the middle of the night. Stupefied, he scrambled out of his bed and began carving a tiny propeller from a beautiful hickory ball-peen hammer handle that I had been saving as a treasure. After about three or four hours of chipping and scratching on the hardwood with a tiny knife, he was inspired with a better idea. He made an attachment for my big, powerful electric drill that rotated a small cylinder of very rough sandpaper while he, holding the drill in one hand and stabilizing it with his leg, manipulated the embryo propeller with his other hand against the rotating sandpaper. It worked so well that he became overconfident and let the sandpaper come in contact with his pajama leg. Instantly, the powerful drill twisted *up* the 80 percent polyester (same thing that the running rigging of an America's Cup racer is made of) britches leg while simultaneously twisting *down* the top part of the pants. Then the drill motor got loose from his hand and began to flail him on the thighs and, now naked, hips with the cord. Before it finally choked down and blew the fuse for the whole house, it had rolled up both its cord, thirty feet of heavy-duty extension cord, his britches, and parts of himself into an incredibly tight and complicated knot. We had to help him get loose. It was hard. The hardest part was trying not to laugh at the poor boy and make the flashlight wave around.

Editorial restrictions do not allow space for any stories about how I was humiliated by this malady, so I'll just skip to my father. He was a man who did not like to be exposed in undignified situations, so he tried to hide from the model airplane gene but like the rest of us, he couldn't help himself. When I was about twelve, I busted open my piggybank and bought one of the primitive model airplane engines (Ohlson & Rice) of that time. The wonders of miniaturization that we have these days had not been invented yet and this thing was big enough to run a chain saw (which had also not been invented yet). As soon as I got home with my prize, the powerful telepathy that is one of the main indications of this ailment struck my poor father while he was right in the middle of something important in his office and before I could finish reading the instruction manual for this monster, he was breathing down the back of my neck. I could feel the shivers running up and down his spine in the vibrations of his breath. We clamped the engine in the vise, mixed the complicated mixture of fuel, attached the eighteen-inch hard maple propeller, hooked up the big battery, squirted a little shot of fuel into the exhaust port, and my father gave the prop a flip. For the first time in the world, one of the damn things started . . . first flip.

It started off with a poot and a sputter that quickly changed into a bellow, then a roar, and finally an earsplitting banshee scream. After it got itself tuned up, it vibrated loose from where it was clamped in the vise and made several very quick orbits around my father's head (giving an excellent demonstration of the Doppler effect, I noticed from my remote vantage point). While it was circling, it whipped at least three, well-tied, wraps of battery wire around his neck. Then, throwing dignity to the winds, it flew out the door of the shop with him. After he was gone and the wind of departure let the oily instruction book fall open to the last page, I noticed WARNING: DO NOT CLAMP ENGINE IN A VISE. THIS ENGINE MUST BE SECURELY FASTENED TO A STURDY MOUNT (SEE DIAGRAM "A") WITH THE BOLTS, DOUBLE NUTS, AND LOCK WASHERS PROVIDED BEFORE ANY ATTEMPT IS MADE TO START IT.

I guess dignity is sort of like virginity because the next time we heard from him he was out there in California in the movie business.

Storm Boat Motor

*in which, due to the onset of puberty,
I foolishly expand my compulsion to include machinery*

Back in the early fifties, people still thought that outboard motors should be something that one person could carry down and clamp on the stern of a boat all by himself. Of course, they were beginning to fudge a little. My father had an Evinrude thirty that I believe was the first electric-start outboard motor in the world. It would stagger him pretty good while he was waddling down to the boat with it in the deep sand. It was a silly motor all around. Though it had a little vestigial electric starter on it, it didn't have any generator, so after about two days he had to stagger back through the deep sand with the battery. Fortunately the motor had a real recoil starter hidden under its cover, but you had to open this silly little door to get to the starter rope. Before the gremlins that eat all outboard motors had destroyed it, the situation evolved down to where we left off the foolishness with the battery . . . took the silly little door off and started the engine by hand. In spite of all this, I sort of liked that motor because in my speedy youth, it would trot the old Lyman pretty good and I thought it was hot stuff—at least until I saw my first storm boat motor. I was sixteen years old.

I had gone to this lake with the Lyman to show the girls and everybody else what was what when this guy launched a little plywood monstrosity with a big naked-style antique-looking outboard on the stern. I thought to myself, *Look-a-here at this piece of junk . . . let me blow him out of the water with my streamlined thirty-horse Evinrude Lark.* When he got it in the water, the boat was so down by the stern from the weight of all that cast iron that the sheen of gas and oil from the foot threatened to follow the water in over the top of the transom. The man couldn't get back in the stern to go through the motions of starting this thing for fear of sinking, so he stood in the shallows while he did all his doings and wrapped the rope around the flywheel. Then he scrambled in and quickly pulled the rope before the whole business sank; when the motor fired, he scrambled forward to get to the steering wheel. The old motor started pooting smoke and hopping and jerking violently back and forth and began to almost run a little. The man sat there on the seat and clutched the steering wheel like he expected something to happen, and something did. The damn thing backfired four feet of smoky yellow flame from the front and a gout of blue smoke out the stern and seemed to explode. When the boat cleared the pall of smoke it was already going about sixty (probably an accurate estimate from later experience). That man ran all over the lake with that thing. It bellowed like a bull and left such a sheen on the water that, if it had been these days, the Coast Guard would have sent the C-130. I kept the Lyman up there next to the grass. I didn't know that boats could go that fast. I decided to find out a little more about it.

Well, it was a storm boat motor. They were built by Evinrude for the government during World War Two. The intention was to propel a sacrificial landing craft (called a "storm boat") full of sacrificial men at planing speed on a one-way trip to storm the beach. Somehow, they figured out some other way to sacrifice the men and when the war was over, there were a bunch of these old motors left and they were sold cheap as surplus. Some people made little race cars out of them and some were fool enough to actually put them on boats.

I had found the source. That man had about twenty-five of them, all in their original wood boxes complete with propellers, spare parts, instruction manuals, and carrying (yeah, right) handles. He was ready to let one get away from him too. He showed me how to cut them down to size (they were very long in the foot in the original configuration), re-pitch the propeller (the gear ratio was about one to one—needed more pitch for a little boat), drill two big holes in the muffler to let out the noise . . . and mix the gas (I might be wrong, but it seems to me that it was one quart of fifty-weight motor oil to the gallon) to make the sheen that was always in the water around one of those old motors.

It was a peculiar outboard compared to what we are used to now. I guess it was an offshoot of the old two-cylinder opposed engines of the thirties. A storm boat motor was four-cylinder opposed, two-stroke cycle. It acted more like a two-cylinder engine because both the cylinders on each side fired together. The reason for the four cylinders (I was told) was because the pistons would be too big to cool properly in the center if the motor had only had two cylinders and they were trying to build the biggest two-stroke engine they could. To enhance the spark for starting, there was a doohickey that shorted out the two plugs on the port side, so when it first started, it was actually running like a one-cylinder engine—a real rough-running one-cylinder engine. It had a side-to-side snatch to it that would break the arm of anyone who tried to interfere.

The starting ritual was like this: First, you opened the gas shutoff and the vent on the cap of the gravity-feed gas tank. Then you retarded the spark (necessary if you wanted to stay in the boat with the pull rope), wrapped the rope in the flywheel groove, and hit the primer pump on the carburetor a certain number of strokes according to the temperature of the engine and the air. Then you opened the throttle wide, waited for your knees to quit knocking, and gave a hell of a pull. If you had figured the number of priming strokes right, the engine would start. If it didn't, you could hit the primer again and take a chance on flooding the crankcase, which required all four plugs to come out and be dried off and the flywheel spun enough to clear the gas from the crankcase and cylinders (that's where part of the sheen of gas that accompanied these engines came from). Cranking one of them was a matter of intuition, brute strength, dedication, and reckless desperation.

After the engine started (running on the two starboard cylinders), you had to quickly advance the spark, stand to one side, and hit the wildly gyrating doohickey that let the electricity into the portside plugs. There was no neutral. She was already under way, and you better get your ass under way for the steering wheel so that if the two portside plugs weren't fouled you could outrun the quart of flaming gasoline that belched from the carburetor when those two cylinders went to work. And so you could be in a position to try to steer when the boat hit the water after the initial leap. After that, it was just plain loud stinking joy for a little while. The engine wouldn't run at anything much less than full throttle without fouling the plugs, so you had to let it eat, and eat it did. There were some storm boat motor men who could manipulate the independent spark and throttle enough to get it to go at half speed for a little while in an emergency, but nobody could make one idle. For me, it was wide open all the time—at least until the gas gave out. When that happened, the silence was deafening. The old motor would sit back there stinking and sizzling water and frying oil just daring you to pour some more gas in the tank.

I had a girlfriend back then. She was not the one I married and I soon realized was not made for that kind of duty. On her first boat ride she got kind of disgruntled after I had whipped black, greasy streaks from that stinking gas-soaked starter rope on her yellow bathing suit and naked hide over and over again trying to crank the storm boat motor. I had a feeling that the end of our relationship was near. Finally, we went on a trip down the Suwannee River. I had gotten to be pretty good at running that thing by then and we didn't have any bad trouble until the bar that held the two steering cable pulleys vibrated off the back of the motor (*vibrate* ain't exactly the right word) and the thing kicked all the way over and popped the top board off the transom and came in the boat with us, bellowing like a bull and biting like an alligator. It was hard to get one of the son of a bitches to start and hard to get this one to stop. By the time I finally managed to find a way to stop it without losing my hand, it had gnawed up the whole stern of the boat and was hopping on its flywheel up front after us . My girlfriend and me had to walk about ten miles up the riverbank back to the boat ramp to get the car. The skeeters ate that girl up, too. She gave me up after that—she eventually married a chiropractor and, as far as I know, has never set foot in a boat again.

I kept my storm boat motor for years on a sawhorse out under the lumber shed. I told myself that I was going to build just the perfect boat for it one of these days, but one day I was out there looking for a board when I smelled an old familiar stench. It seems that the termites had finally eaten one of the legs of the sawhorse clean off and pitched that old bastard, carburetor-down, into the dirt. A tiny bit of the ancient essence had dribbled out. I just left her lay. I guess I just ain't the man I used to be. Oh well.

Warning: Safety Devices Are Addictive

in which I become an addict at an early age

I know, because I am seriously addicted to several of them. It all started when I was a teenage race car fan back when the legendary Fangio was showing us how to drive a tiny car very fast on real crooked roads. I was just about a Fangio, but the best I could do to properly equip my car for the races was to install a single Warshawski Bros. lap belt for the driver's seat (Fangio and I took no prisoners). That belt didn't turn my thirty-six-horse Volkswagen into any Maserati but after I gutted the innards out of those two little chrome shotgun barrels that it had for tailpipes, it sure sounded bad.

I soon found that I was addicted to the lap belt. Every time I had to suffer the indignity of riding with my mother, I felt like I was fixing to fall out of the car. I had one date during this time and I carefully hid the seat belt so that the secret of my affectation would remain safe from the hapless girl. I felt so uncomfortable without my belt that I had to take her home early. I have often wondered if my success rate with women (measured alongside the accounts of the accomplishments of my peers) would have been better if I had come along later when seat belts were acceptable.

Somehow or other, I have always worked in dangerous jobs. I started out tripping slabs in a sawmill. If OSHA had been around back in those days, there wouldn't be near as many widows and one-armed men in these parts. Not only did they have saws as high as your head with no hint of a guard, there were miles of flat belts running wide open everywhere. Forklifts and all kinds of other equipment tore around the muddy yard like they were trying to run over you. Logs, boards, and slabs were always falling off rickety conveyers at you, and the noise. Nobody wore any ear protection of any kind. It's a wonder I can hear what little I can. The only thing I ever saw that was as terrifying as that sawmill was the hangar deck of an aircraft carrier during blacked-out night operations. I was so scared at the sawmill when I was a kid that the only injury I suffered was from a grasshopper who crawled into my ear and kicked a hole in my eardrum. It'll never happen again because I always wear my earmuffs when I am around grasshoppers. Early exposure to terror is probably the cause of my present obsession with safety devices.

I am addicted to two sorts of hearing protection. I have some big plastic earmuffs that I wear for short loud jobs (and grasshoppers) and, because the earmuffs make my ears sore, some little plastic sponges that I roll up and stick in my ear holes, where they expand and shut out the noise, when I have to be in a loud situation for a long time. These sponges are the most addictive. Like most addicts, I have become secretive about my habit. I conceal these little sponges in my left pants pocket. I sneak them out of their little plastic container and roll them up while my hand is still in my pocket then it only takes an instant with a quick little Jack Benny gesture to insert them. I began this secrecy when my granddaughter exclaimed at how dirty the little sponges were. They are, too. The nature of their business makes them like that. Even new ones become rapidly discolored. When you roll them up, not only does any tiny little smear of sawmill grease from your fingers get on them, but it is then condensed as the sponge is compressed . . . sort of like the writing on a balloon when the air goes out . . . and becomes black enough to alarm anybody. That's why I started with the secrecy. No need to try to tell me that there are little non-expanding earplugs that are just as effective. Like the mainline drug addict needs the feel of the needle, I need that little secure feeling that I get when those little sponges swell up in my ears. Now I find that I like to wear my little sponges at times when others might think they are inappropriate, like in public places. I have been subtly shamed into not shouting at people while I have my earplugs in. *"Mr. Ben . . . take those damn earplugs out of your ears so you can stop bellowing like that!"*

I overcame one addiction . . . in a way. I used to feel uncomfortable without my safety glasses until my eyesight degenerated so that I had to wear real glasses all the time. Now I have these little removable side guards that I can clip onto the earpieces. I keep them in my pocket with my earplugs when they are not on my glasses. Lately I find that I become alarmed by too much peripheral vision. I imagine that things are passing by when they aren't. I have had several cricks of the neck from turning my head too rapidly to avoid some imaginary missile. I am not embarrassed to wear these guards all the time now. I have nothing to hide . . . except my earplugs.

Not long ago, I dropped my old childhood hammer into the ocean. The new one had a little sticker that read, CAUTION! ALWAYS WEAR EYE PROTECTION WHEN USING THIS TOOL AS CHIPS OF STEEL MAY FLY FROM THE FACE INTO YOUR EYES. I felt pretty smug with that. Oddly enough, I had to go to the patent attorney the next day to see if any of my brilliant ideas had paid off yet and there was a man in the waiting room with a hammer just like mine except that he had the suction cup of one of those little sink-style plumber's friends stuck on the end of it. I had to ask him about it. He said that he had read the caution statement and thought about all the poor fools who would disregard it and get their eyes put out by flying bits of steel. He said that the plumber's friend cup would prevent that from happening. I wondered if it might prevent the user from seeing where the nail was when they struck at it. "I know you are wondering," he said, "how the user will be able to see the nail, but when we get into production, this guard will be made of transparent vinyl instead of this black rubber." My hand independently slipped into my left pant pocket and began rolling up an earplug.

I started getting serious about respiratory safety when I began using modern boat finishes. When I painted a boat out in the yard, I noticed that dragonflies twenty feet up in the air would plummet to earth as if they had been shot when they flew through the fumes. Bugs used to seem attracted to good old regular varnish but the smell of the new stuff would chase all the grasshoppers (for whom I am always prepared) out of the grass and the whiteflies out of the all the gardenia bushes in the yard. I bought the best face mask I could find. A good thing too. The other day, while I was at the Little League ball game, I was trying to find out what my wife was telling me by reading her lips when a foul ball, hit by a six-year-old kid, slipped past me on my blind side, bounced off the steel toe of one of my shoes, and hit me smack in the face. Fortunately I was wearing my twin-canister NIOSH/MSHA-approved organic vapor mask, so it didn't bust my nose.

The Chicken Feed Boat

in which I scratch up the scratch for a store-bought boat

The first Grumman Sport Boat I ever saw was way back in the middle fifties and I only caught the briefest glimpse of it on a trailer on the paved road behind a V8 Ford station wagon. I tried to get a better look but Momma's thirty-six-horse Volkswagen just couldn't catch up no matter how hard I hunched behind the wheel. I was relentless in my pursuit even as a boy (fifteen at the time with a special driver's license that I had had since I was fourteen because we lived so far beyond the school bus run) and it didn't take me long to interrogate around and find out what kind of boat it was. Then I set out to get me one and an outboard motor to go with it. At first I tried to coerce my father into springing for the money by the use of eloquent explanation but he said "We already got the Reynolds so what do we need another aluminum boat for?" "It is so light and easy to handle that y'all wouldn't have had such a mess on that Ochlocknee River trip that time," said me. "I don't have any plans for another Ochlocknee River trip in the near future, so I don't need the ideal boat" was his final statement. With that, I knew I had to get me a job and buy the boat on my own.

I went to work for the "Chicken King of Cairo, Georgia" (that's pronounced *Karo* like the corn syrup that originated in that metropolis). I didn't have to submit my résumé or stand for an interview or anything. The job was unloading boxcars of chicken feed at fifteen bucks a car and if you could do it before the railroad deadline, the job was yours, if you couldn't . . . and particularly if you couldn't pay the demurrage for the extra day (coincidentally, also fifteen dollars), your ass was gone. I was kind of small and unused to hard work but I was smart. I slipped in the side door as a striker for a big black man whose last name will remain anonymous since I don't know what the statute of limitations situation is for some of the crimes that I heard him tell about in the close association we had in the chicken feed cars.

Robert had been a bootlegger during the best years of that business back in Prohibition days. He had a series of stills back in the tributaries of the Ochlocknee River and was so slick that not only did he not get caught but managed to employ a good many folks and expand his business . . . "Had a still on every creek," said he. My family owns a good little bit of the land of the Ochlocknee drainage system. "Hell, boy, we had them all over y'allses place . . . yo granddaddy was my best customer," said Robert. My grandfather was already dead by then so I never got a chance to ask him about it.

Another thing about Robert . . . he was in the train wreck when the shaky trestle over the Ochlocknee River at Hadley Ferry broke down and the sawmill train fell in the river and scalded all those men to death in 1925. He was the fireman in the engine and ought to have been the first one to die but he dove under the water and, though the concussion of the implosion made him bleed out the ears, he was the only survivor of the whole crew . . . had to walk twenty miles to tell the news and nobody believed him because he was just a (. . .) (I ain't going to say that word because my momma taught me not to).

So I tried to help Robert unload that chicken feed for free for a long time. I was too light to handle the damn hand trucks on the steep ramp. I holp (that's an actual word in wide usage in the rural South . . . kind of substituted for "helped" but not in all cases . . . I won't labor over it right now) load and trotted down behind Robert to help stack the bags but I could see that I would never be able to carry my end unless I could get to where I could get down the ramp without letting the load get away from me. I tried half loading but Robert said, "Boy, you kinda getting in my way with all that." One day (this mess went on seven days a week) Robert had to go to Memphis on business and sent his nephew to take his place. The very first thing that happened was that the nephew let the hand truck get loose from him on the ramp and busted open about eight paper bags of feed. I said, "Boy, you kinda getting in my way with all that."

It took me from then until car-moving time at nine o'clock the next morning (about twenty-six hours) to unload that boxcar but I did it . . . fifteen bucks . . . big money. I don't remember what-all I had to do that time, but I finally evolved a way to brake the hand truck with first my shoes, and then two pieces of flat belt that I riveted around the axle and stood on to drag on the ramp to slow the buggy down a little. Pretty soon I was able to ride the truck down the ramp, steering with my "brakes" sort of like a hotshot skateboard kid these days. Robert and I teamed up. He loaded his buggy while I rode mine down and dumped it at the bottom, then I would hurry back up the ramp with the empty buggy and get the next load. After the car was empty, we would double-team stacking the sacks down in the warehouse. Piecework in the face of poverty will make an efficiency expert out of most anybody and Robert and I made some pretty good money . . .

enough for me to order a brand-new Grumman Sport Boat and buy a secondhand, three-horse, two-cylinder Evinrude weedless three.

We both lost our jobs at the same time over oyster shell supplement. At that time, ground oyster shells were either mixed with chicken feed or fed separately. A train car loaded with oyster shell was a bitch. Though the flimsy paper bags were much smaller than a fifty-pound bag of feed, they weighed ninety pounds and the car waiting on the siding was just as full as it could be. It was real hard to even pinch any oyster shell car up to the dock and it was almost impossible to beat the demurrage deadline, no matter how bad we busted our asses. I am afraid that I was the one who feisted up at the "Chicken King" about it and cost us our jobs (which were eagerly taken up by lesser men who had to work late into the night even with carloads of straight laying mash).

I felt guilty and told Robert. "Unloading chicken feed ain't all I know to do," he said and I think he went into the rooster-fighting business with some Cubans down around Miami but that's just a supposition. He is still alive. In fact, he is the one I get my gardening advice from. He told me to go ahead and set out my tomato and pepper plants after the new moon of February 5. "Dang, Robert ain't that mighty early?" said me. "Naw, it's all over. You might have to cover them up with a sheet one or two times but they need to be in the ground with that hot manure," said he. I noticed the last time I passed his place that his were even bigger than mine. I think it might have something to do with all them roosters in those little cages behind his house.

Grumman Sport Boats

Grumman Sport Boats are no longer built because (somebody told me) it was impractical to put flotation high enough up so that a sunk boat would pass the test and stay right-side up with the engine that it was rated for (six horsepower) perched up on that flat-topped transom and five people sitting bolt upright on the seats. I saw one that had plastic doohickeys along the sides in an effort to comply but that was a long time ago. Though mine is an antique (forty-seven years old) it has enough flotation to hold up the engine, people, and the picnic too, of course the people would probably have to get out of the boat. There is a long, useless foredeck with a bunch of some kind of primitive foam bulkheaded up under it (I think it is still in there) and the whole stern thwart (Sport Boats have three regular seats) is boxed in with foam. That's a case where they regulated out a good thing. I don't know but I bet there have been fewer people drowned in Grumman Sport Boats than there have been strangled to death with the prize in boxes of Cracker Jacks. All the people I have ever seen with one of those boats did not look like the kind that normally fool around and drown themselves.

A Grumman Sport Boat is fifteen feet eight inches long by fifty-four inches wide (not counting the damned bush-catching outboard oarlock sockets). The transom is thirty-two inches wide, which separates it completely from a "square stern canoe." It is made with a good tumblehome to the stern, which makes the boat paddle about like a canoe, actually better with only one person than a standard seventeen-foot Grumman canoe. You'll know why canoes have tumblehome after you have paddled one of those straight-sided fiberglass monstrosities of the seventies all day long. It is impossible to pull a tumblehome boat out of a one-piece mold and paddling one that you can pop out will get you right between the shoulder blades from having to reach so far out to clear the rail. Though I have paddled my boat many a mile, such is not the best propulsion method.

A Grumman Sport Boat is a rowboat with few peers. You have to get mighty fancy to beat one with anything that short and wide (why, when I was thirty years old . . .). I like eight-and-a-half-foot oars and my extra-high homemade aluminum oarlocks (don't use bronze). I learned a lot about rowboats trying to improve on that boat all these years. It ain't the shape of the front of the hull and certainly not anything to do with all those rivet stumps sticking out of that extruded T-beam keel that makes the boat row so well, it is the fact that it has almost no rocker to the bottom and a planing boat stern. Despite what I always thought, the stern of a displacement boat does not have to stick up any higher out of the water than necessary to clear the stern wave at the speed you are going to be able to make with the load you intend to carry. The Whitehall transom sits up there so high because the man who was doing the work knew he was going to have a boatload on the way to and from the whorehouse. When I'm pulling in the stern station of my old boat all by myself (no matter where I am going) the transom trims about half an inch in the water at rest which is a "no, no." You can "no, no" all you want to but you better save your breath if you intend to pull up far enough to see how she trims when under way without having to crank your neck (When I was thirty years old . . .).

I finally figured it out. A Grumman Sport Boat hardly pitches at all when rowed hard. The little drag the transom makes when slightly immersed as the boat tries to squat at the beginning of the stroke is offset by its steadying influence. I think that pitching makes the wavelength of the bow and stern wave longer and the amplitude higher than what is normal for a non-pitching boat running at hull speed. The net effect of pitching in a rowboat is to make it act like it has a shorter waterline length than it actually does and is going faster than it actually is. Now, all my rowboats have a good wide transom close to the water but it took a long time to get it right. Which, I wish I could build one for something like the Blackburn Challenge but getting back to the original problem, it costs a lot of money to outrun a Grumman Sport Boat and the folks that are still strong enough to pull hard for that long can't afford the boat. Oh well.

The other obvious thing that makes the boat run so well is that it is sort of light. Mine weighs 135 pounds. There is a lot of erroneous lore about boats and one is that old foolishness about how a heavy rowboat carries its way better and that is supposed to offset the fact that you have to move all that extra displaced water out of that way. If heavy boats rowed better, it would be possible to win races with a lot less money. As for me, I ain't ever had any boat that I wished weighed another pound.

Another lesson I learned from my old chicken feed boat is that boats that are light, narrow, and easily driven at displacement speeds will plane most efficiently too. My old aluminum boat will plane two grown people with a weedless three. I don't know of any other production boat that will do that. With one person and a long tiller extension my boat will run eleven knots with that old fifties engine. The transition from displacement to planing is so subtle that it is impossible, without leaning over the transom, to tell when it happens. There is never any wake. I figured that out too. What happens is that the boat begins to plane before it gets to its hull speed so it never makes enough disturbance in the water to have to climb any bow wave or tear away from any stern wave to get going. I have built a bunch of boats that run that way and I believe that sixteen feet on the water is about the minimum. With boats that are borderline too short (like the Grumman) you have to make sure that you trim by the bow so you get all you can get of hull speed. That leads us into the problem section.

A Grumman Sport Boat is not ideal. It has about the same bow shape at the bottom as an aluminum canoe . . . no deadrise . . . almost flat. That makes it not only wet, but bad to pound. My old boat will slap even the lightest chop hard enough to knock the oxide dust loose to blow back in my eyes (along with the spray). Even at low speed . . . rowing . . . the boat pounds and throws water in a chop. That makes it unpleasant in anything but smooth water. It is dangerous in rough conditions. If you trim it by the bow like you need to do to ease off on the pounding and get any practical displacement speed, it will root into the back of a following sea or one of those big, almost stationary waves that you find at inlets and river mouths on a falling tide. I don't think it would take much misjudgment to root one of them bad enough to broach around and turn over and drown somebody. If you don't trim by the bow, the damn thing will not go to windward if it is even a little bit rough. It will pound so bad that you can't stand it and stick its bow up so high that you won't be able to hold it into the wind. About the only thing you can do when it breezes up is get back in the stern and go downwind. A Grumman Sport Boat ain't no sea boat.

I'll tell you this though. Mine stays in use, the bottom is shiny from pushing through so many lily pads and acres of grass. There is no telling what it would read on the hour meter if it had one. It will go right in the back of a pickup truck and we can snatch it out and be long gone before the bass boat crowd gets through discussing the necessity of being able to go seventy mph (statute) up the river. They won't ever see us when they finally get fired up because we will have dragged old "Chicken Feed" over into some virgin slough somewhere and will already have two or three big redbellies that have never seen a metal flake in their lives. Whooee . . . Dang, let me put this computer down, I already had to pull the boat out of the bushes so I could measure it to set down the facts, might as well just slide her on in the truck . . . might go see if old Robert wants to go, he got them big black wigglers all around under his rooster cages.

The original Chicken Feed Boat

This is my first successful improvement over a Grumman Sport Boat. It has about the same weight and dimensions except it is sixteen feet long on the water. It will plane well with that weedless three and is a good sea boat. It is the pride and joy of its owner who has successfully maintained that all-over varnish job for many years.

This is the best "improved" Sport Boat yet. Though it is the same in all dimensions except length (it is sixteen feet), it has good deadrise in the bow and a hollow forefoot. Notice the good tumblehome in the stern and the big, useless foredeck. There is another myth-dispelling improvement. It is made of wood and is thirty pounds lighter than its aluminum counterpart . . . so there.

Pipe

in which I own up to another addiction acquired at a tender age

I used to smoke a pipe. I started when I was very young (maybe twelve) because of my infatuation with Huckleberry Finn. I was kind of a solitary little wasp, and that pipe was just about like having a dog for a companion . . . a nasty, stinking, nuisance looking for attention all the time, but I kept up the companionship diligently for many many years until I finally realized that the roles had reversed and the damn pipe was sucking on me. I laid her down and though it has been more than twenty years, it still stinks and wants me to stick my finger down in the gurry hole.

I'm not going to talk about all the pipes I sucked on but I remember every one. One (I don't know what the hell kind it was . . . had little holes drilled all around the rim of its fluted bowl to stick a toothpick in, I guess) of especially long duration finally convinced me that I was wasting a lot of time trying to keep my respiratory system polluted and my little finger stinking and smutty so I tried to quit smoking it and as a gesture of sincerity, threw it out of the window of my truck . . . spent half the next night combing the grass alongside the road with my flashlight . . . my new pipe clenched in my teeth trying to scald the already raw sores in my mouth even rawer. . . Jesus.

I remember the first pipe I bought after I joined the Navy (at seventeen). I had thought that all those other men would give me enough companionship to be a substitute, but I had to smoke wretched, puny, ready-rolled cigarettes all through boot camp to keep my habit about half down (which a big, strong, expensive cigar, or if you can't afford that, some Prince Albert in an OCB, is the only thing that approaches the nastiness of a pipe and still doesn't come close). As soon as they sent me to school to learn how to keep company with the second most horrible killing instrument ever on this planet, I strutted my little white-clad self straight to the drugstore and bought a little, short, yellow holed thing that just about burned my lips off before I finally got a hint of crust on that yellow paint. I remember what became of that pipe too.

I was still at the bomb school. I had a little buddy, a shy young fellow sort of like me. I don't ever remember him saying a word all the time I knew him . . . I did all the talking . . . don't even remember his name but I do remember his pipe. It was a short, miniature Sherlock Holmes job and he smoked that mixture 79 (I was always P.A. and had a callus on the inboard side of my right thumb to prove it). The pipe drooped down over his bottom lip so the smoke came out of the bowl straight up along his chin and up his nose to his eyes. One time we were walking back to the barracks smoking our pipes when he blindly stepped into a utility pole hole that they had dug. I mean, he went clear to the bottom and all I could see was the faintest hint of the gleam of his white hat down in there . . . and his pipe, still smoking malignantly, there at the very edge of the hole.

Anyway, we went to a dance where the local girls (those whose parents were negligent enough to let them associate with cursed sailors) came. I couldn't ever remember having seen a girl before in my life and neither could my buddy. We were so stultified by the situation that we just sat on the wood bench and smoked our pipes in terror. The unbelievable happened . . . we won the door prize. I have never won anything before or since (played check poker in a seven-man shop every two weeks for four years and never won . . . what are the odds against that happening again?). The prize was a case of warm Carling's Black Label and we took it and fled. We sat on an abandoned bridge over this little deep swift creek and drank the first beer either of us had ever drunk. . . . That's the operant word too. I dropped my little just-broke-in pipe in the creek. Dogshit.

The last pipe was an aluminum tube Kirsten that one of my boys found washing around in the surf on the seaside of St. George Island in Apalachee Bay in the north Gulf of Mexico. That was back when there was nobody on the island but just every now and then and I have no idea how that pipe got there but it had been washing back and forth . . . rolling over with each wave for so long that the bowl was worn most exquisitely oval and the aluminum tube had the most marvelous patina. The cake in the hole was still perfectly intact and so was the little O-ring plug in the end, but the stem was gone. Even with just my lips on the aluminum, it was the best smoking pipe I ever had so I carved me a stem out of a palmetto root and smoked it the whole time we were camping on the island. At first I thought the reason it was so good was the close association with the sea but even after I got back to the mainland and made me a proper stem, it continued to be a good pipe. Finally the threads that held the wood bowl on the aluminum tube stripped out and I had to put two little pins in so I could hold it on with a rubber band . . . had to keep it fixed, couldn't put it down for another . . . until I finally had put it down for good.

Though I don't think there is anything I ever want to suck out of that nasty little hole again, I still might take it back up. There is a random occurrence of Alzheimer's disease skipping around in my family. My wife says that if it hits me, she is just going to set one of those potty chairs out in the yard next to the hose and plop me down in it and hand me that pipe, a pound can of P.A., and a box of kitchen matches. I bet I'll be able to work that thing after every other capability has been long gone . . . Jesus y'all.

How I Became a Boatbuilder

in which I take a wife, turn professional,
and learn a lot all at the same time

I guess my father started me off. He was a boat fiend and a writer . . . a good writer who wrote books about boats and people who built boats. I read them when I was little and got so enthusiastic that I couldn't help myself. It began a compulsion that has lasted all my life.

It is easy to train eager children. All you have to do is watch them until you see them doing something you want them to do and marvel at it. (It has to be the real thing though, you can't fool yourself into thinking that your children like something just because you want them to, and you can't fool *them* into thinking that you are really marveling when actually, you are a little disappointed). My father had the formula down perfectly.

First, he would write a good book about boats and children and send it off to the publisher. When the check came, he would take off on a long trip to find out something else to write about. I would stay home and read the book and build me a boat so I could be like the kids in the book. After a while, he would come home and marvel at the boat that I had built. He would marvel in earnest too, not because the boat was so wonderful, but just because I had built it. He couldn't build any kind of a boat himself from scratch (could handle a kit fine) and it impressed him to see a ragged-assed little cattywompus thing nailed up out of plain old boards floating in the pond on our place. The reason he couldn't build boats (he was a pretty good house carpenter) was because he couldn't sharpen edged tools, not to save his life. But he could write and he could marvel.

I can remember my first edged tool perfectly. I have it in my tool cabinet beside my big English slick in case I need it. Its little blade is just about worn half in two. They called it a "Christy" knife, and I guess the name was copyrighted. It had one little limber blade that slid back into the steel wire handle when you worked its button with your fingernail. It wasn't much (my apologies to Mr. or Ms. Christy), but it was marvelous in my hands. I was just a little preschool kid when one of my uncles sent it to me for Christmas during World War Two. Momma quickly slipped out the back door with it as soon as she could and dulled it on the brick steps so I wouldn't cut the fool out of myself. Little did she know that I watched the process carefully from the bushes. As soon as she was through and I had my knife and a little privacy, I determinedly ground the edge right back on it on the very same brick. I cut down fifty feet of *Pittisporum* hedge the first day and wore a regular groove in that brick. When my father came home from the war, he just marveled.

I was a filthy-footed, gritty little boy. I stayed so dirty that people in my family wouldn't let me in the house except for occasions special enough to wash me off out on the steps. I used to have to eat my dinner on the steps with my brick. The men who worked on the place used to bring strangers to see me and make me show them my Christy knife. First the visitor would look at it and laugh, then he would feel the little worn blade. I tried to teach my father how to sharpen. He couldn't seem to get the knack, thought it must be the brick. He went to the hardware store and bought the biggest and best double-sided Norton stone they had (twelve inches by three inches—I still have it, worn almost half in two like the knife). It was much quicker than the brick, but the results were the same—I could but he couldn't. I sent him a "Lansky" device just before he died, but I guess he was too old and shaky by then because it didn't work either. If he hadn't discovered X-Acto knives back in the fifties he would have been helpless. I wish he could have seen all these disposable-blade tools they have now.

So, I built a bunch of boats when I was a child by the chopping, carving, and nailing method. I used plain old black tar to caulk them with, and they made me wash off with kerosene before I could come in the house to sleep. The smell of kerosene still makes me feel adventurous even after fifty years.

I took down the whole chicken house for lumber (probably seven or eight hundred board feet of virgin cypress five-quarter by twelves). I chopped stems out of firewood with a five-pound ax (a sharp ax is a useful tool). Every now and then, one of those old waterlogged flat-bottomed boats will fill with methane from the bottom and ooze to the surface of one of the ponds on the place for a little while. My granddaughter will show her little friend. "My granddaddy built that when he was a little boy." "Yeah? . . . But, what *is* it?" It will let out a big poot of pond gas and settle to the bottom for another fifty years. The little girls will stand on the dam and marvel. One of those old boats is the nucleus of a two-acre floating island in the biggest pond. Not long ago, I tried to rob some of the wood off it but it was grown in so tight with willow roots that I couldn't. Besides, an alligator tried to eat me while I was out there.

After I grew up (sort of), I joined the Navy so I could see about some bigger and better boats. Sure as hell, they stationed me in Puerto Rico on shore duty. I was disappointed at first, but my ramblings soon disclosed that I had been dumped right in the middle of the masters of the chopping, carving, and nailing boatbuilding method. When all the other fellas at the naval station jumped in the publico and headed for the museums and art galleries on Luna Street in San Juan, I jumped on my motor scooter and went to the little town on the water right close to the naval station where the masters were.

I had been introduced to this little town by my Mexican roommate when I was a messcook. He was always broke from sending money home to his family in Mexico and didn't have the publico fare to San Juan. He still liked to hang around the museums and art galleries, so he rode on the back of my scooter and showed the way to this bar in a little playa. I sat at the bar and nursed my tiny Corona (that's Puerto Rican Corona . . . different from the high-priced Mexican import so popular with the yuppies) while he tried to talk a little noise to the young girls and their duenas. I soon got bored with that and went out on the patio facing the sea. This bar was built right exactly on the water's edge. Moored fifteen feet from the jukebox, shining in the neon lights, was the prettiest sailboat I ever saw in my then limited life (and I ain't seen too many any prettier since, either). I came back in the daytime.

I was a real young-looking, innocent little fella back then, and the old lady at the bar liked me fine. Soon I had interrogated out the facts about the boat in my pitiful Spanish. It belonged to Julio and he had built it right beside the bar and he was right out there this minute building another one. I went straight to see what was what, and sure enough, there was Julio with some other men sitting on some logs playing dominoes. There was the beautiful skeleton of a boat standing with its sternpost almost in the water on some little posts. I (with my flat-bottomed experience) marveled. Julio was not impressed with me, neither were his friends. I had the feeling that they had seen all the young sailors they wanted to, but I couldn't bring myself to leave. I sort of hung around and looked at the boats and the water and the side wall of the bar, against which they peed. The domino game went on until dark and some beer came from the bar and some little bowls of something that smelled real, real good. I decided to go inside and try to find the source and I did. It was some rice with beans and some kind of gravy on top. I thought that it was the best thing I ever ate in my life, and I vowed to stay in Puerto Rico forever, eat rice and beans, build boats, and learn how to play dominoes.

To make a long story short, I hung around the bar all the time. Finally Julio grudgingly allowed me to step and fetch from the bar and pull and wrassle rollers when they were pulling boats out. (They pulled some very big boats out right beside the bar using nothing but the same little logs that they sat on to play dominoes and a little pushing and pulling, and some discussion.) I earned myself a name because I thought if I showed them how sharp my pocketknife was, they would marvel like the people back home and let me be one of them. They didn't marvel, but they did name me "El Cuchillo," which I took to mean "The Knife." I was so out of touch with everything else but the business beside the bar that I didn't know that Bobby Darrin had just sung that song about the other man with a knife and that it was very popular on the jukebox. Later, amid many chortles, my name was shortened to just "Mack." It was bad timing altogether.

Strong compulsions run deep in my family and I hung on through thick and thin at the bar. Things were pretty slack at the naval station back in the leisurely fifties, particularly in the galley where I was still a messcook. Messcooks aren't real cooks, just some temporary help that other outfits send to help out, usually as a disciplinary measure (they call it "KP" in the Army). My tenure as messcook wasn't because I was bad, just that I was inconvenient. The Navy had spent a lot of money sending me through this big-deal weapons school (where I excelled, if I do say so myself) only to find, when I had to take the physical examination before I entered the swimming phase of the school at the end of the program, that I was color-blind. I asked them what the hell that had to do with swimming, since, as a result of my previous experience as a boatbuilder, I could swim like a fish (pulling a sunk boat, no less). They said that color-blindness made it impossible for me to be what they had trained me to be. I never figured it out and neither did the Navy. Here I knew all this secret crap and couldn't be sequestered with all the other hotshots who knew the same thing so they could keep an eye on me to be sure I wasn't playing into the hands of the Russians. The Navy's solution to this was that I stayed a messcook for longer than anybody else in the world while they tried to figure out what to do and while I went to the doctor once a week to see if my congenital color-blindness was any better or not. My solution was to buy me an old motor scooter (Sears Allstate Vespa) so that I could poot off to the bar where the boats were built between meals at the galley. Meanwhile I attempted to memorize the sequence of the cards in the Ishehara color-blind test.

I got to be such a fixture down at the bar that, every now and then, they would let me debark logs with a dull shovel and maybe scrape bottom paint or unload lumber and logs if they were in a good mood. I watched everything like a hawk and I was sure that I already had all the skill to do it too. All I needed was to understand the method and get to where I could eyeball the shape like Julio.

They didn't have any complicated tools. Most of the cutting was done with an ax and a machete. They used an ax like a slick to back out the inside of planking. They hardly ever sawed anything. Planking was ripped from boards of resinous Caribbean pine by nicking the edge to the line with a machete and then chopping off the blocks between the nicks. Keels and all the other deadwood parts were just plain chopped out of Caribbean pine logs with a regular chopping ax. Sometimes they would use a machete like a drawknife or a scraper to smooth something up. It is easy to get the impression that this was a slipshod business from this description, but it wasn't at all. The boats that Julio built were beautiful. The planking was as smooth and fair as anything ever touched by sandpaper . . . The chopped-out Madeira mahogany frames were beveled to fit the planking better than any tilting arbor bandsaw could have done it (and better than many big-name stateside yachts). They made all the hardware right on the beach out of car springs and other salvaged stuff. Some of it was sent to San Juan to be galvanized, but most of the time it went right on the boat like it came from the charcoal forge after being painted (a forge prepares steel for paint just as well as a sandblaster). Julio could make a perfect mast band in about fifteen minutes if the forge was already hot. They inlet a short piece of chain into the masthead and drove the top band down over it for a place to hook the halyards and shrouds. All the shrouds were three parts of galvanized single-strand wire that they twisted into a cable. There were no turnbuckles or even lanyards. They just drove a spike between the lay of the wire and twisted the shrouds up tight (I guess that's where the term *Spanish windlass* comes from). I have had a good many boats rigged like that since. It is sort of nice to know that water is not freezing in your swaged fitting down there at the dock in January, or that your fifty-dollar emergency stay-end fixing kit ain't still home when you are down around Cuba and one of the nineteen strands of your backstay sticks its tongue out at you. There is something to be said for that kind of hardware. Half an automobile leaf spring with the eye still on the end makes a real trustworthy chainplate.

I watched and learned a lot from Julio and the others, but I never was allowed to really participate and they never got to see how well I could chop and carve and drive nails. I found out later that these men weren't discriminating against me because I was a sailor-boy or foreigner at all. There was just a rigid tradition in their art that young poots like me weren't allowed to touch edged tools to wood. They also believed that derision fostered the development of humility and character. I was just too young for boatbuilding—or dominoes. I should have been glad, because I found out later that I wasn't as good as I thought I was with edged tools and the masters wouldn't have marveled at all the mis-licks I made with the ax and the crossgrain splinters I pulled up with the knife and the machete. There was one thing I could do though, I could pee higher on the wall than any of them.

Nothing lasts forever. After I got off messcooking and made enough rank, I went home on leave and found out that I had become mature enough to be attractive to and attracted by the little Reynolds crew girl that hung around my sister, so I took her back to Puerto Rico with me. We bought one of Julio's oldest boats with her first allotment check ($137.10 got us the Nueva Eva, nineteen feet) and took it around to the naval station and tied it up in the little marina. Every Saturday we would go down there and run rings around all the other boats the naval officers had. One of them hired an architect from St. Croix to take the lines off the Nueva Eva, and he confided in me, "Captain Bridgers don't know it, but there are hundreds of these kinds of boats and all of them will sail like hell. I ought not to take his money, but I will."

I set up building boats in our little house on the Rio Blanco river halfway up the side of El Yunque. I didn't have the ability to find and cut the Madeira ("majaguilla") trees for frames and I didn't know where the keels and planking came from so I ordered plywood (quarter-inch five-ply, marine) through Rasmusen Hardware and glue (Weldwood) and screws (Everdure monel, a wonderful thing) from Defender Industries and started building plywood boats when I wasn't working on secret stuff for the Navy. I sort of had a captive audience. The Navy wouldn't ship a boat for enlisted men like they would a car or household appliances, so the only way those people at the naval station could get a boat was from somebody like Julio or me, and Julio's boats weren't what everybody wanted. We, like so many, were infatuated with plywood boats. It was a mistake. I actually believe that the widespread acceptance of plywood as a boatbuilding material was just as responsible for the notion that wood is not the best material for small boats as the invention of fiberglass and the development of cheap aluminum boats. There just aren't any old plywood boats that have seen much use.

My mother-in-law sent me a book by somebody named Chappelle (I still have it, worn almost half in two) and I marveled. I learned to loft on the front porch of our house. I hope the full-sized lines of that beautiful little Hampton boat are still under a little paint on that concrete slab.

When the time came for me to get out of the Navy, I cashed in my savings and ordered a bunch of tools from Sears and Roebuck to be sent back home so I could set up shop and be a successful boatbuilder. Soon after we got home, fiberglass was just hitting its stride and you could buy an aluminum butt-head skiff (now appropriately called a "honkey drownder") from the discount store for $59.95. I wound up painting houses, working at the trailer factory, furniture factory, and all sorts of things in the early years so I could afford to build boats. Fortunately, there were always enough customers to keep me going—if I could build the boat cheap enough. I remember building a decked, marine plywood, double-ended sixteen-foot duckboat with a steam-bent oval coaming for seventy-five dollars. Years later, a man used it for the plugs (hull and deck) to make a chopper-gun fiberglass version that was pretty popular around here for a while before they relaxed the no-airboat-and-outboard-motor rules during duck season. I have talked to old boatbuilders who were put out of business by aluminum and fiberglass and they said that it wasn't the superiority of the material that ruined the wood boat business but the cheapness. If it hadn't been for the commercial fishermen (who have never liked fiberglass boats, let alone aluminum around here) and a few die-hard discriminating people, the wood boat business would have died completely out in the north Gulf of Mexico in the sixties.

I went through all the stages: plywood (I quit that about '67 except for one or two single-boat lapses) bent-frame carvel, sawed-frame extra-heavy-duty Caribbean-style, and strip-planked boats built from all sorts of lumber. I built one extra-light cold-molded boat from sawed veneer and epoxy when it first came out (a nasty business). Now I mostly build lapstrake boats even lighter than that—and Caribbean-style, natural crook-framed, heart-pine-planked sailing smacks.

Did I ever go back to good old Puerto Rico to see if things were still the same? I am sort of scared to. They might put me back on messcooking and, besides, I still don't know how to play dominoes. What happened to the girl I hauled down there and back? I still got her. Worn about half in two, but she is still ready to get in the boat.

A Note About the Boats of Puerto Rico

The boats of Puerto Rico were inside-ballasted sloops built sort of like the boats of Bermuda, the Bahamas, Cuba, and on down the Caribbean. The frames were chopped from the little Madeira mahogany trees that are becoming so scarce now on the Greater Antilles and Bahamas. Even in the fifties, black mangrove was substituted, particularly for repairs. The boats were very long lasting, although it was sort of like the story about George Washington's ax. Some of them had three new sets of planking and two sets of frames. The deadwood, transoms, and planking of boats that I saw were always made of very dense Caribbean pitch pine (*Pinus elliottii* var. *densa*), and some of those parts seemed very old indeed.

By the time I came along, all of the fishermen used outboard motors, but most of them kept the old sails and rudders for their boats in the house in case of hard times. Though the only sailing Puerto Rican boats that I saw, except for the Nueva Eva, were big schooners on their last legs and a few little builder's jewels like Julio's own little boat, boats were built to sail. Though they weren't usually sailed, they were all built like sailboats. There is deep water all around Puerto Rico and fishing there is an open-sea proposition. Outboard motors probably made the fisherman's life a little easier but it was no place for the cheap, flat-bottomed skiffs that took over the inshore fisheries in a lot of other places with shallow flats and bays.

These boats were all different from each other and from other Caribbean models, but they had some things in common. The keel was straight on the bottom and there was very little drag to the stern. Puerto Rican boats had straight stems with a good bit of rake. The stems had just enough curvature in profile to keep them from looking concave. The rabbet was straight. The forefoot was extremely hollow. The builders went to a lot of trouble to carve and bend the hard-pine garboard strakes into as much distress as the wood could stand so as to accentuate this hollow, indeed, some of the garboard strakes were split trying to do this. The splits were opened up and beveled with the tip of a machete and caulked just like any other seam. The builders tried to build a lot of flare into the bow and the boats always had voluptuous cheeks. One of the advantages of building by eye is that the builder can alter the shape to accommodate the tolerance of the particular boards on the job.

The body of the boat had almost straight deadrise into a pretty hard bilge. Sometimes the floors had a slight bit of hollow as the planking approached the keel, particularly in the garboard strakes, but the floors were never convex. The run was very flat and the deadrise of the transom was either flat or slightly hollow. The old Nueva Eva would lay over and plane on this flat run (one reason for her ability to outrun the modern cruisers and daysailers at the naval station). The wide transoms were heart-shaped with a good rake unlike the transoms of boats from some of the former British colonies.

The rig was an extremely long-boomed jibhead main with a small jib. The boom stuck way out behind the transom and the first reef was just to tie this off with a lanyard. The mainsail was laced to both the boom and the mast and there was no board or club at the peak like in some island boats. The Nueva Eva had way more sail than any other nineteen-foot boat I ever saw (another reason for her success at the naval station). I never measured anything, but her mast was tall and her boom was long. The jib was sort of small. Sometimes, in light wind and a head chop, she would not come about unless we backed this little jib, but the old boat could be easily balanced to self-sail in any forward wind by adjusting the jibsheets. The rudder just lollygagged behind the boat without being lashed when she was trimmed right. I eyeball built a replica of her in 1965 that would do the same thing.

I believe that the longevity of these boats was due to the heart-pine planking and deadwood and the single-sawn Madeira frames (double-sawn frames in open boats don't hold up well in the tropics). Though the bottoms were painted a different color from the rest of the boat, copper bottom paint was not usually used. The bottom paint (usually bright blue) had a distinctive downturn of the boot top up by the stem, which accentuated the hollow forefoot.

The boats were commonly pulled from the water on rollers. When a fisherman came in, everybody on the beach would lend a hand. It was not unusual for a helper, sort of incapacitated by age or drink, to get himself run over by the rollers in the soft coral sand. After she was out, one of the floorboards would be wedged under the rail and there she would sit on the rollers until time to go out again. The people would sit in the bar and admire her; discuss what they would do differently if they were to build themselves one—and eat rice and beans and play dominoes and listen to Bobby Darrin on the jukebox. Dang . . . the good old days.

Volleyball

in which Gasparetti set me up to look like Mortimer Snerd

I don't have any of my own front teeth anymore, except on the bottom. They all went several different ways after the first one but I won't burden you with all that. Anyway, I now have a nine-tooth bridge that, though it looks cute as all get-out, ain't worth a damn except for looks . . . cost more money than any automobile I ever owned. That's vanity for you ain't it?

Like I said, the only thing interesting about the loss of any of those teeth was the first one. My commanding officer knocked it out and I can remember all the circumstances of the thing but not the actual knocking out . . . I think I was knocked out because all I saw was a flash of light and then I was lying down in the back of a pickup on the way to sick bay. I'll have to begin at the beginning.

When I was in the Navy in the late fifties and early sixties . . . too late for Korea and too soon for Vietnam . . . thank goodness, I was assigned to a peculiar little secret outfit that didn't actually have anything to do. We just kind of waited around for the Cold War to get hot and inventoried batteries. There were just exactly the right number of men in our little outfit to play volleyball, but I am getting ahead of myself.

Our commanding officer was very dear to us. He was an old j.g. "mustang," which means that he was old, a lieutenant (junior grade) who had come up through the ranks all the way from the lowest seaman up through chief petty officer (torpedoman on a PT boat during World War Two) and, because of some glitch in the social exclusivity, was promoted from chief to ensign and then j.g. Which, I never understood that . . . seems backward. I would heap rather be a chief than a j.g. I don't give a damn if you do get to go to the officer's club. If you have ever been to the chief's club, you'll know what I mean.

H. I. didn't have a wife so he lived at the BOQ (Bachelor Officer's Quarters to you). The naval station we were stationed at was so small that there were only two other permanent officers batching it up there but, because this place had a big airfield and lots of temporary detachments of aircraft-connected officers from far away, just in there for "operations," the BOQ was a big place with a whole staff of Filippino stewards (another social peculiarity about the Navy that I didn't understand). Just like he was with us, old H. I. was a favorite with those stewards . . . some of whom were about his age . . . and they took good care of him. Everybody did and it was a good thing because H. I. was a hard drinker. He was such a nice guy . . . it is funny how often those two things seem to go together.

H. I. didn't have a car . . . didn't drive. Us single, enlisted men used to have to go by the BOQ in the shop pickup on our way from the barracks to our secret hideout to pick up our commanding officer every morning. The old chief stewards would have him sitting out on the steps, all dressed, shoes shined fit to kill and ready (ready or not) and they would help him into the front seat and we would take him to work every day. Well, not always every day . . . H. I. was very lenient with free time for both us and himself. If you had something you needed to do, and you let him know the day before, he would let you miss muster, and if he had something to do, and didn't show up at the BOQ, he would miss muster too. An old chief steward would be waiting (in his immaculate whites and brilliantly spitshined shoes) on the steps to tell us that Lieutenant Williams sent his regrets but he would not be present for inspection this morning and directed that the chief conduct morning muster instead and for us to carry on . . . which we did.

One of the things that H. I. did that made him apt to miss muster was to hobnob with visiting admirals. He knew everybody of any significance in the Navy. I wish I could remember who-all he knew, but I remember that Hyman Rickover and Elmo Zumwalt were buddies of his. Anyway, the word was, among his superiors (damn near every officer except visiting boy jet jockeys) around the naval station that it didn't pay to fuck with Lieutenant Williams . . . that if you wrote him up, the paperwork just wouldn't go through nearly as smoothly as his automatic "satisfactory" fitness reports all did. Those fitness reports weren't automatic just because of the influence of higher-ups or the protection of his men. H. I. was a good officer and we kept those batteries inventoried, each and every one. Our shop always passed, with flying colors, the rigorous inspections with which such places must contend. If the Russians had tried anything, they would have learned, just like all the other troublemakers, not to fuck with Lieutenant Williams (and his crew).

Those jet jockeys could be a problem for H. I. As I said, he was very old to be a j.g. and he liked to have a little drink at the bars in town (where he was a great favorite among the bartenders and whores) and those hotshot, pimple-faced Navy ensigns and j.g.'s and jarhead second lieutenants some-times attempted to overstep themselves by being wiseassed. Usually the bar-tender or somebody could explain things in time, but sometimes one of the fartfaces was just too stupid to learn any sense. Then everybody would just sort of stand back. H. I. was the nicest kind of guy. He would sip on his drink and smile and agree with his tormenter right up until the point when he decided that he didn't want to be insulted anymore then he would pop the man such a lick that they always had to call somebody to come haul him to the sick bay . . . and, if any of the jet pilot's buddies decided to break bad, H. I would send their asses to the sick bay, too. He was one of those kinds of men with huge hands, big forearms, and big bony elbows . . . came from a long line of loggers in Oregon . . . hit you like a line-drive baseball (and I know what I'm talking about).

How come H. I. knocked my tooth out? Was I a young troublemaker like some fartfaced jet pilot? Well, "yes" and "not exactly." Unfortunately, there is no short answer to that so you will just have to bear with me: John Kennedy was the president then and he got to looking at the troops and de-cided that they were in pitiful physical shape . . . that the peacetime USA military was not a lean, mean, fighting machine anymore but kind of plump and complacent for the most part. Our little shop was probably a pretty good example of the problem. After all, counting batteries ain't all that stren-uous a business and there were one or two pretty fat little fellows among us. Of course, some of us were in pretty good shape . . . like H. I., the Nichol-son twins,[1] Gasparetti, and me, but we all could use a little exercise. Like I said, H. I. took his job seriously and when his commander in chief, the old PT boat man, said for us to shape up, that was all it took.

It was muster every morning for every single one of us from then on. H. I. was standing on the steps of the BOQ straight up and ready to go in his gym shorts. We played volleyball . . . and how. I mean, since we didn't have much to do, H. I. said that we would play volleyball. We started early in the morning (0700) and except for lunch and a few water breaks (no smoking) didn't stop until knocking-off time (1530). We took a minute or two for a battery check every now and then, but the rest of the time . . . no joke . . . we played volleyball. And, you know, if people take on a project like that, ain't long before even a mixed bag of turds like us can get to tumbling sort of smoothly. We were good . . . played by the rules for the most part but there was one thing we did that was sort of outlaw. Not only did we rotate within the teams like you are supposed to do, we rotated men from one side of the net to the other. There were not any actual teams. We strove as individualos (this was a Spanish-speaking country where we were) and after all that practice, we got to where we knew each man's weaknesses and strengths . . . exactly . . . and could extrapolate that intuition to people outside our shop too.

I believe I better interrupt the smooth flow of this narrative to explain a little about that so you won't think we were doing any complicated "brainwashing" or anything. It was more simple than that. Which, what the hell is "psychology" anyway? I had to take it both times I went to college. First was a real university and everybody had to take it. The class was so enormous that it was held in the main auditorium of the place and the professor had to walk around on the stage with a microphone just like Bob Barker . . . even had some "beauties" to hand out the handouts to us as we sat out there in the audience (every seat taken) and took notes on our knees. I didn't learn a damn thing that I didn't already know, which leads me to believe that psychology majors must be mighty ignorant to start with. The next time, I was already "getting on up there" when I decided I wanted to teach science in middle school just to see if I could do it. I had to enroll in this damn education-specific diploma mill so I could supplement my real degree with some gibberish. Damned if I didn't have to take "education psychology" along with "movie projector, slide machine, VCR, and overhead projector 101." What a bunch of nonsense. The damn scrics of psychology professors (you have to take a lot of that to get certified to teach school) were, I believe, the most ridiculously oblivious of their own idiocy of anyone I ever met. I'll tell one college story and then get back to volleyball team. There was another, sort of laid-back, elderly student in the class of young fools who was not eagerly writing down everything this professor said. The petty potentate in charge was concluding about three days of droning on and on about "gifted" (why don't they just say "smart") children. Some of those young teachers-to-be had filled two or three notebooks with all the new words that mean exactly the same thing as old words. He finally wound up his lecture with a question: "Now, given all the cognitive ability that you have acquired from this course and supposing, given the faculties at my disposal, that my wife and I wanted to raise a gifted child of our own, could you lay out a linear set of sub-objectives for me to apply to the accomplishment of the overall inclusive objective of raising a gifted child?" All the other students began to flip back through their notebooks but this old gal shot up her hand about four feet. "Yes," chirped the professor, "Mz. . . . oops, I am afraid I have forgotten your name . . . Freudian slip I guess . . . ha, ha. What would you suggest for the first objective in the overall plan for my wife and I [*sic*] to raise our child as 'gifted'?" "Well," she said (in the gravel voice of a longtime smoker), "perhaps you could get someone else to *father* the child."

Like I said, the psychology wasn't all that complicated at our shop. The language was much simpler for one thing and it didn't take much of that to rattle some of us and there were a couple of us that could be shook without a single word: There was one man who rode his motor scooter to church outside the gate (H. I. gave him a carte-blanche pass . . . see what I'm trying to tell you) about four or five times a week. I went with him once or twice but I got tired of how those people admired and fondled each other so much. That scooter . . . dang, I got to get off the subject one more time.

You know, life would be mighty good if the world was such that a person could get along with just a motor scooter. It would be even better if all you needed was a bicycle, but I am a child of internal combustion and I certainly do love a motor scooter. I am talking about the kind where you sit on the little cushion (Cushman?) with your feet on the little platform in front of you. You know, you can haul a watermelon on one of those. One time I rode my scooter (Sears Allstate Vespa . . . baby blue) all the way to San Juan. What a lovely trip down the little shady road with the hibiscus, frangipani, and all blooming everywhere. It was idyllic until I got close enough to smell the pissy smell of the city. I messed around a little bit in town looking at the sights and then headed on back to the naval station (about thirty miles). About halfway, I passed a little fruit stand and saw an enormous, striped, oblong watermelon (Charleston Gray) just like the ones we used to raise when I was a boy. It was an extravagance, but I couldn't help myself. I put the watermelon crossways on the foot of my scooter and tooled it on down the road with my feet propped up. About ten miles farther on down, I saw a man walking toward me down the middle of the road. As I got closer I realized that he seemed sort of incapacitated in some way or other and appeared not to see me coming so I blew my little buzzer at him. He still didn't get out of the middle of the road and didn't even look at me. I had to dodge around him. As I passed, he deftly kicked that watermelon out from under my feet and it didn't even make one bounce altogether.

Anyway, this other motor scooter man was easy to rattle. He prayed before each serve. If he was the one fixing to serve, all it took to mess him up was a single, well-chosen word. If he was eligible to receive the serve, all you had to do was hit him before he said "Amen." It seems like his Maker would have told him that to every thing there is a season and a time to every purpose under the heaven, don't it?

Another easy mark was a roommate of me and the Nicholson twins. He had the distinction of being the only man at the naval station whose momma came to visit him. She looked just exactly like Nikita Khrushchev . . . warts and all. He was deeply in love with Jackie Kennedy. He had a big picture of her taped inside his locker door and he used to leave it open and lie in his bed and gaze with rapture. We used to, cruelly, prance into our little cubicle after taking a shower and drop our towel before he could slam the door on his locker so Jackie wouldn't be exposed to any lewd display. He never learned. And he never learned how to return a ball after one of us struck the same pose as on that picture either.

He brought me up in front of H. I. on charges of insubordination one time. He had told me to stop laughing about something and I couldn't. I wanted to but it's hard sometimes. Besides, he wasn't but just a second-class petty officer and I was third-class (and gaining on him) so it wasn't such a wide span of authority that had been breached. H. I., nice man that he was, calmly and kindly talked the man out of pushing it . . . didn't tell him that, sometimes, it is possible to make a fool of yourself with too much officialdom.

Another easily rattled (and none of us were all that tough, not even H. I.) man was my best friend. He was almost silent all the time and didn't do much but read when he was off. He would walk down to the little enlisted men's Mariposa and drink one beer and eat one hamburger (just meat and bread . . . no fixings whatsoever and the Mariposa had the best fresh tomatoes). Then he would go back to the barracks or to the library and read.

I better tell you about the library. That old naval station was built in the time of Theodore Roosevelt and I believe it must have been a special project of his. It was a big deal back then when Teddy thought we might need a place to show the Spanish a thing or two about a thing or two. The library was a lovely place. It was an airy concrete building with a wide porch all the way around. There were John Kennedy–style rocking chairs on that porch and, inside the building, there were the most wonderful books. I believe Teddy might have sent an angel down to pick them . . . all the Jack Londons . . . a complete set of Tarzan and all the Hornblowers. Of course they had all the ridiculous James Fenimore Coopers, too, but, at least, they were the originals with the wonderful Howard Pyle illustrations . . . Mark Twain . . . Emerson . . . Nordhoff & Hall . . . John Bartram's *Travels in Georgia and Florida* . . . *The Decline and Fall.* They had the whole set of *Memoirs of Casanova,* which there ain't no modern half-assed pornographic romance novel that can touch that seventy-five pounds of nonstop nookie.

Most of the sailors at that place complained all the time about how they hated the duty and couldn't wait to get back stateside where there was something to do. Jesus, what some dumb-asses. I bet they are all fat and dead by now from excessive TV.

So my buddy, with his little ritual self, though he ate his supper at the Mariposa, used to eat lunch with the rest of us at the galley every day. We always sat at the same tables in the same positions . . . him right across from me. One time, I said something funny while he was drinking his Welch's Concord grape juice, which the galley served by the drum (and from which the cooks and bakers made wine . . . by the drum). He had just taken a big swig when he got tickled and silently, solemnly, he allowed all that grape juice to flow in two, uninterrupted, unaerated, pure purple streams from his nostrils onto his tray. All I had to do to make sure he would not return a serve was to make a gesture sort of like Santa fixing to rise up the chimney.

We beat the pure piss out of VU 8, a little airplane squadron down there in the same fix as us but without H. I. Then we went to San Juan and stomped the shit out of the naval station jarheads up there. We were just about ready to go to the tenth naval district championship when H. I. knocked my tooth out.

The Nicholson twins and I were the tallest men at the shop. H. I. and Gasparetti were hell on the net too, but they just didn't quite have the reach of those boys and me. Anyway, it was a ruthless game, the way we played it . . . that's the way H. I. and all of us wanted it. When I or one of the Nicholson boys got on the net, the whole rest of the crew set him up and we would slap it down some poor joker's throat . . . time after time after time. It was a cold and vicious business. Like a pinball wizard playing the tilt to the hilt, we knew just exactly how long we could keep our hand on the ball without getting called for throwing. That's what went wrong with me on that day. I was on a roll. It was a three-step situation as long as I was on the net. Gasparetti knew just exactly how to set me up and whoever tapped the ball first set up to him and he fed it to me perfectly. H. I. would come up as high as he could but it wasn't quite high enough. I would reach clear over the net, eagle eyes on both sides watching that my belly never touched, and catch the setup and whip it around behind him and usually whap him in the head. H. I. was a man about it though and didn't complain so I got bolder and bolder this one day. Like I said, I was on a roll and every time H. I. would come around, I would nail him. It was beautiful. These days, I would probably earn a nickname sort of like "Sailor Air White" but what happened that day took the wind out of my sails all right. I think I kept my hand on the ball a millisecond too long. When he quit seeing stars, H. I. said quietly, "Holding on a little bit aren't you there sailor?" "I don't think so sir," I replied. Then I did it again. They had to haul me to sick bay in the back of the pickup . . . H. I. holding my head. "Volleyball accident" went on the report. As I said, it don't pay to fuck with Lieutenant Williams.

The Navy gave me a big, surrealistically white tooth stuck on the front of a very pink orthodontic "retainer"-looking thing. I think Mortimer Snerd must have played volleyball while he was in the Navy. Anyway, when I went to pick up H. I. early on the morning we won the Tenth Naval District volleyball championship . . . wearing my new tooth (I think that was the first time I ever saw a hint of a smile from one of those old chief stewards), H. I. said. "Better take that thing out during the tournament, White. Somebody might slap it down your throat for you."

1. I know some old naval expert is going to call me on this business about the Nicholson twins being in the same outfit. Since all the Sullivan brothers were killed on the same ship during World War Two, they don't let brothers, and now, I guess, sisters, serve on the same ship. Rickover made an exception with us geniuses in the spook business on shore duty though.

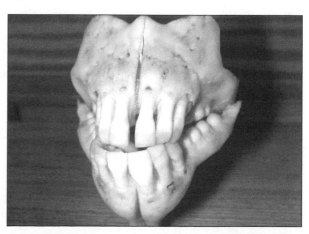

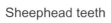

Sheephead teeth

When the Russians Were Coming

in which I unearth a time capsule

All this worrying about Weapons of Mass Destruction and homeland invasions by horrible people bent on destroying our "American way of life" isn't anything new. Hell, I remember when everybody was wringing their hands because we thought the Russians were coming any minute. Back then, we knew how terrible that could be because we had just seen what they would do to a freshly conquered country. We woke up every morning to find out what Dave Garroway thought we needed to do to protect ourselves. Civil defense "czars" explained in patronizing detail all about "fallout" and how to construct bomb shelters of various degrees of complication so we could huddle with our families and breathe filtered air and drink water from jugs and eat out of cans and go to the bathroom in other cans. We were told to stock up on everything we might possibly need to survive for months and . . . to arm ourselves . . . so after the fallout had finished falling out, we could emerge as a powerful militia and listen to the special radio announcements on our battery-powered sets and become disciplined and capable units ready to whip those barbaric Russians' butts for them.

What brought all these memories back to me was that I unearthed a time capsule. Now, don't get overstimulated. It wasn't any poured-concrete Hitler-like buried sarcophagus or even a Saddam-like "spiderhole." It wasn't even buried at all. I'll tell you all about it in a minute but, first, I need to explain a little so you'll understand. My mother was a very resourceful person. When she was young, she and my father ran off to the British Virgin Islands and bought one of those virgin islands for thirty-five dollars (real estate was pretty cheap in the BVI in the thirties) and built a poured concrete house on the very top of this little island by mixing the concrete in a tub with a hoe. They lived there all through the Depression and eked out a living in what to me seemed a perfectly satisfactory situation. When World War Two came, my father went off to fight in the Pacific in the US Navy, the British colonial government took the island away from my parents (belongs to Pusser's rum company now) and my mother came back to the old home place on the Ga.–Fla. (that was before the days of "GA–FL") line and built herself another house. By that, I don't mean she did it like most of these carefully coiffed women for whom "I built a house" means that they harassed a contractor for about five months. Momma built the house herself. Well, that's not exactly true either. It is pitiful how convoluted a story has to be just because one is trying to be scrupulously honest. A long time ago my grandmother had an old house taken down on the home place because they had just invented tractors and had decided to consolidate a bunch of little one-mule fields so as to make the plowing work better (possibly the beginning of "agribusiness") and this old house was in the way. They were just going to burn it up but it was sort of interesting . . . had thirteen-foot ceilings for one thing and, since it was built in the 1830s, all the lumber and molding was hand-planed and the doors and windows were handmade. Placidia (my grandmother . . . anything but) meticulously numbered all the parts of the old house with a blue crayon and the field hands carefully took it apart and stacked all the boards in neat piles and put all the old nails in kegs and it lay there in the woodshed for thirty years until Momma laid claim to it. She hauled it to her house site and put it back together. My oldest sister and I were little children then and I remember our mother sitting on a keg and straightening out the old handmade nails on a stump with a claw hammer. She decided to turn the handmade tongue-and-groove flooring upside down because it was very worn and skinned up on the top side and I remember her planing some of the top lip off the groove edge of each board because, you know, flooring is made to fit tight on top and a little loose on the bottom. When she got the flooring nailed back down she got a big billy goat, ostensibly to mow the yard so rattlesnakes wouldn't get my sister and me, but what happened was that the damn goat got us. He was so mean that he wouldn't let us up on the floor at all so we had to stay out there in the yard with the rattlesnakes. Momma got tired of doing all that planing on that old rock-hard heart longleaf pine so only about a third of the house has the flooring tight. "Poo," she said, "all those cracks will give a place to sweep the dirt." Anyway, I bet anything, if you were to dig a little of that dirt out of those cracks, you would come upon quite a few ossified goat turds. Good thing they aren't seeds or they might sprout some more of those damned billy goats.

So . . . the original house only had two big rooms and no kitchen or bathroom or closet or anything. Momma wanted to build some partitions in there but she didn't have enough money to do it up Martha Stewart–style with everything matching so all the new partition walls were Sheetrock with very few studs. Her master plan was to eventually replace the Sheetrock with vertical board-and-batten paneling to match the rest of the house when my father got out of the Navy and brought home some money but what actually happened was that he got out of the Navy and ran off to California so the Sheetrock stayed where it was. When Dave Garroway got her all hepped up on bomb shelters and self-defense, she partitioned off one of the closets with some more Sheetrock (half-inch Sheetrock instead of three-eighths like the rest of the house because this was supposed to be a serious structure) and made a little hole about like the door of a coon trap to get in and out through. She rigged a little vent fan to blow up into the attic and bored a few holes in the floor to let air in. She figured that when the atomic bombs killed the electricity for the fan, she would just have to make do with convection. She was pretty smart. She figured that where we lived was too far from a strategic epicenter so we would be out of range of the fireball and shock wave and all she would have to deal with would be the fallout. It would have to drift all the way under the house to get sucked up into the vent holes in the floor, and maybe the spiderwebs would catch most of it while she and we children huddled in there and used up the cans and water jugs. Of course, by the time all this got finished, I was in the Navy and my oldest sister had gotten married and moved to Illinois and my baby sister was gone off to college so Momma figured that it was just her and Dave Garroway from then on. After I got out of the Navy, she showed me the coon trap door and said, "That's the door to my bomb shelter." "Looks like the door of a coon trap," said me and I never felt like squirming through there into no telling what kind of a trap.

When she died my little sister inherited the house and immediately started in to rectify some of its deficiencies. One of the first things she did was to completely line the closet where the coon trap door was with aromatic red cedar . . . just paneled over the door to the bomb shelter like it wasn't even there. She even planked the floor with cedar and damn near asphyxiated herself trying to sand it with a belt sander. The fumes were so powerful in there (remember, that little cubicle was thirteen feet tall . . . looked like the inside of a red-brick chimney) that, when she got out her winter woollies, you could see the vapors rising off her like around the gas hole of a car when you fill her up . . . but there were no moth holes in any of her garments. Initially she was a schoolteacher and didn't have the time or money to completely Stewartize the old, drafty outfit in one fell swoop so it was linoleum in the kitchen one year and a cabinet in the bathroom the next. Finally she found out that entertaining adults paid better than entertaining little children and she made enough money that she felt she had a little left over so she got hot on fixing up the old barn. By then, I was going strong in the boat, sawmill, and . . . Yes, Virginia . . . reproduction heart longleaf door, window, and cabinetry business. One of my sons was with me full-time and the other part-time. We built some doors and windows and cabinets and a little furniture and ran her a little new-old flooring and . . . I agreed to build a bookcase to cover up one of the Sheetrock walls. This bookcase was going to be thirteen feet high and fifteen feet long and have twenty-four glass doors (mortised with the tenons going all the way through like is proper . . . by hand) and enough shelves (dovetailed into the uprights . . . by hand) to house all the printings of all the Jane Austen books ever printed. I had just read that one man built the whole interior of the ballroom of the *Titanic* and carried his tools home with him every night, so I figured I was up to the job and I was. I cleared that room completely out and hauled my workbench down there and went to work. I plugged in my little radio and listened to the oldie goldies and the steady chirping of the NPR while I planed and tappety-tapped on my mortising chisel with my good old live oak mallet for days and days. Finally I got to the part where it was time to take down the Sheetrock and put up the paneling that would be the inside of the back of the bookcase.

Wow, what a thing. There was Momma's old bomb shelter exposed like it was in the picture window of a store. There were all her cans of food stacked on boards resting on concrete blocks and her jugs of water (brown glass Clorox jugs). There were glass jars of pickled okra and artichoke hearts and mushrooms and pimientos. There were about fifteen boxes of Kleenex and a bale of toilet paper and, over in a corner, a stack of cartons of cigarettes. No, they weren't the old green Luckies that went to war. The time that this capsule represented was when people were beginning to think about what they already knew . . . that smoking was bad for you . . . these were Viceroys . . . filter-tipped coffin nails. I thought the bathroom facilities were most ingenious. There was a sixteen-inch clay chimney flue sticking up out of the floor with a regular toilet seat fastened to a concrete platform on top. When I raised the lid, there was a galvanized trash can lid under there to seal it off. The hole down into the ground under the house was just exactly as deep as posthole diggers would reach and was bone-dry. The flues went all the way to the bottom. No chance that any fallout would rise up out of there. She had a brand-new, old air mattress and a brand-new, old Davy Crockett sleeping bag neatly rolled up alongside the toilet paper. She had a folding canvas chair and what must have been a complete collection of Reader's Digest condensed books (at least up to 1959) and a for-sure complete set of all the volumes of *The Memoirs of Casanova* stacked in the corner. My oldest sister's Bible was open to the part about Armageddon on a little table by the chair along with a coffee cup and a little kerosene lamp. I figured that one of the Clorox jugs must be full of kerosene. I immediately looked to find the coffee and, yep, there it was, Nescafé, instant . . . ten family-sized jars and there was her radio already tuned to the civil defense station. There weren't any batteries in it, though. There weren't any in her Geiger counter, either. I figured she must have known that they would go bad so she probably kept some outside to grab when the time came to squiggle through the hole. Over in another corner past the potty was Momma's old childhood .22 rifle with a carton of five hundred shells . . . Super X hollow points. I bet she would have given those marauding Russians a fit when it came time to come out of her bomb shelter.

Guess what I did? After I had sat in her chair and read a little Casanova, I walled that thing back up exactly like I found it but with hard pine instead of Sheetrock. We have never figured out what to do with Momma's ashes and they are, now, in a jar in that elaborate bookcase between Jane Austen and the Palliser novels. Maybe I should have built in a little secret removable panel, so, just in case, we could slide her into her fallout shelter. I know she would be glad to get away from Austen and Trollope and back in there with Casanova.

Yaupon, Banana Daiquiris, and O'Rourke

in which I make a new friend and learn
a thing or two about overindulgence

Down here on the north Gulf Coast where I stay there is a little bush that is real common along the shore. The Creek name for it was Yaupon (say *yo-pon*) and they made a very good tea out of the leaves. We did it, too, when we were children and still do for special occasions. Yaupon tea has an extremely high caffeine content and there is something else to it . . . might ought to be a controlled substance. Anyway it has a wonderful flavor but it is a lot of work. The best way to make it is to get little children to pick the young tender leaves (tiny, about the size of a baby's fingernail) and dry them on a piece of paper in the back window of a car parked in the hot sun. It takes a lot to get a little. When the leaves are dry and shriveled up good, make a pot of tea with them and strain out most of the dregs. The leaves are so powerful that you can get two or three boilings before they are completely depleted. I don't know if you can do like I heard some drug-using natives of someplace do and drink the pee of the participants in the first boiling and work that on down the chain of command or not but it might work. I'll let you know if I find out. Anyway, drinking Yaupon tea brings up the cere mony in people and is a very grave occasion. It takes a lot of concentration. Conversation is limited to mumbles.

Back when the fools who "discovered" and explored Florida were at- tempting to bullshit their way through European courts, they described the Yaupon ceremony of the Indians as something akin to an orgy. They, in the erroneous convention of the time, got it all wrong. They said that the tea (which they called "black draught") made the people who drank it vomit so they gave it the scientific name *Ilex* (Yaupon is in the holly family) *vomito- ria.* The tea does not make one vomit but vomiting was probably going on all right. According to one expert (Bert W. Bierer, "Indians and Artifacts in the Southeast," 5552 Sylvan Drive, Columbia, SC 29206) Indians some- times did that at feasts so they could make room for more feast. It is too bad that the fool white people did not confine their activities in the New World to feasts and frolic and recreation like had proven for thousands of years to be the best way to live over here. Vomiting is a strong possibility upon any occasion where one might overindulge in most anything.

Why, when I was eighteen years old, I was in the US Navy stationed at the enormous but mostly abandoned Roosevelt Roads Naval Station in eastern Puerto Rico (completely abandoned now I am told). To people with wild-natured tendencies that place was heaven on earth. The coastline was hundreds of miles of virgin Greater Antilles forest. There were just a few vestiges of civilization scattered around. It was as if the government had big plans for the place but sort of lost enthusiasm after World War Two. The biggest dry dock in the Caribbean is at Roosevelt Roads and I believe the fanciest chief petty officers' club, too. The library was wonderful with a big shady porch to sit on and take the air under the shade of the frangipani trees. The enlisted men's club had the most spectacular view of any place I have ever been in the Caribbean. It was situated on the highest mountain on the base and faced to the east. On a clear day you could see the clouds over St. Thomas and St. Croix. Vieques and Culebra were sitting on the startlingly blue sea like a picture in a fanciful painting. If Columbus could have taken a postcard of that picture home to Isabella, he would not have been vilified quite so bad. Hell, if he had just told the truth . . .

Anyway, the enlisted (that's first-class petty officers and below) men's club's location was the best part about it but the main trouble with it, too. It was miles and miles from the barracks. The naval station had a bus that ran continuously all over the far-flung civilized portions of the base including the enlisted men's club (the officers and chiefs all had cars). It was just a plain old gray school bus and its schedule was sort of intermittent. The civilian driver liked to go home of an evening so participation at the club was difficult. Most single pukes just went to a little beer joint/hamburger emporium right by the barracks or out the gate where there were some other opportunities for entertainment beyond sitting on the porch and looking down the mountain at the view. It was possible to ride in a publico to San Juan and visit the art galleries and museums on Luna Street if payday had just occurred. The enlisted men's club was just not very popular. But it existed just the same. About 1600 (the peacetime Navy knocked off at 1530) the staff arrived up there and opened up the big shuttered windows (no screens or glass . . . no mosquitoes) and scratched around in the ice machine and got ready. There were three civilians who worked there full-time and a ready staff of temporary people for big events like the Fourth of July and such and they took their jobs very seriously. It was hard to find a good job that far from any metropoli. Fajardo was the closest real town and it was just a small fishing and farming village. Working in any capacity at the naval station was a much-valued vocation and these people enjoyed their jobs. They were very friendly and accommodating and I got to know them very well. I never spent much money up there because I was somewhat strapped since I had bought myself a little secondhand motor scooter (Sears Allstate Vespa . . . baby blue with white cheeks) with a note from the Banco Credito. The scooter (gas was twelve cents at the Navy Exchange) was my ticket to ride and ride I did. I think I might be the only person alive who knows Roosevelt Roads . . . every nook and cranny. I made it a ritual to pull that long hill to the enlisted men's club every afternoon and drink one small bottle of Corona (they had two brands of Puerto Rican beer, India and Corona, and they were both very good . . . two sizes, twelve ounces and six ounces). There was something very charming about those tiny bottles and I sat out there on the veranda of the club all by myself and watched the setting of the sun behind me change the way Vieques and Culebra looked minute by minute almost every afternoon. Then, after the sun set behind me and closed like a curtain the spectacle of the islands and the sea for the day, I would coast silently on my scooter down the lonely little road all the way to the flat plain where the airfield was. Then I would ease it into high and pop the clutch and the little two-cycle engine would tune up, the little dim headlight would begin to shine, and I would amble on back to the barracks in the dusk dark.

This ritual went on for quite a while before someone came along for whom such an activity might hold a little charm. He was a Yankee named Lewis and, though he was technically subordinate to me (I was a fast learner in the Navy and moved up the ranks quickly . . . E5 before I was twenty) we became good buddies. I tried to leave him at the barracks but he insisted on finding out where I went every afternoon and he, like me, was a brilliant genius so it didn't take long before he was sitting on the stern of my scooter going up the hill at 1531 every afternoon. I don't know if you have had any Italian scooter experience or not but there is a good bit more to them than the cuteness of their looks might suggest. I think mine had 150 ccs worth of old-time, slow-speed, high-torque, two-stroke punch and though the additional weight of old (eighteen years) Lewis on the stern slowed its ascent a little bit, it took us up there all right. I think it actually did the engine good. It seemed to run better after Lewis . . . might have de-coked the top of the piston and the head a little bit or something. The spark plug certainly never showed any smutty signs after Lewis.

It was a good association. Lewis was a philosopher and knew many things that I didn't know like how labor unions worked and about the politics of coastal New England and subways and economics. Lewis was the first person to explain inflation to me so I could understand it. He thought it was good for the balance of trade between this country and the rest of the world. He explained to me how inflation paid for World War Two. I can't remember exactly what occasion occurred that broke the one-beer ritual of the daily event but one time something happened to cause us to discover the 151-proof banana daiquiri. I think it was all Lewis's doing. We sat there at the bar and drank those delicious things for a long time. The cheerful bartender took a good bit of glee in their preparation for us and gave us a new little parasol for each one. Though the supercooled icy banana soup disguised the taste of the rum pretty good, those things were so powerful you could see fumes rising from the glass like what comes out of the gas hole of the car when you fill 'er up. Lewis and I soaked those daiquiris up like men fresh from crawling out of the desert. Soon we began to notice that the rest of the staff was looking in on us as if we were an item of curiosity. After a while I felt a hint of queasiness in the pit of my stomach rise above the euphoria and the next thing I knew I was on all fours crawling toward where I thought the bathroom was. Lewis wasn't far behind me. He said he was going to visit O'Rourke the friendly Irishman. We fell off the scooter thirty times trying to get back to the barracks . . . broke the clutch lever off . . . Good old Sears and Roebuck had a new one in the mail within a week. I do not like bananas to this day but I still love Yaupon tea. Where did all those children get to?

Note to the editor about the capitalization of the word *Yaupon:* It is an extremity of bigotry to use capital letters for the late-model European given name of the genus of an organism and relegate the thousands-of-years-old original name to a lower case. Linnaeus hadn't ever had a sip of Yaupon tea in his life.

Terrible Torque and the Floorboard Man

in which there is a pitiful tragedy so you might want to skip this one

Just before I went back to Georgia to get married, it got to where I was spending so much time down at the bar where Julio and them built the boats that I became acquainted with other people in the little town. There was a little drugstore there and the owner and his wife were very kind to me. They had one table where they served various meals to a few people. It was almost like being invited for supper to eat there. Since there was only one table, the customers all sat together and, since the town was so small, they all knew one another. Little old lonesome me was attracted to such as that, and the women of Puerto Rico were very nice. I guess the men were, too, but they were so aloof that it was hard to tell. I ate supper there all the time and it got to where the women would give me a little taste off their plates and I learned that Puerto Rican cuisine was a hell of a lot more than just the delicious rice and beans that had become the staple of my diet.

Julio had just finished planking up a most beautiful boat and I had been on messcooking so long by then that I had a little clout with the cooks and bakers who ran the galley, so I was able to wigglework my schedule and I could get on my scooter and show up at the bar most anytime I wanted to. Though I was far too shy to speak the language except in emergencies, I had learned to understand a good little bit of Spanish . . . particularly the language of boats. I think the taciturn Julio and the others might have surreptitiously helped me a little bit by speaking slower and enunciating a little more carefully. Anyway, I had watched the painting man scrape the seams, where the caulking iron had frazzled the edges of the planks on the already fair hull of the new boat, with what looked like a piece of glass from a TV picture tube. There was a tradition of subcontracting in the building of the boat. Julio always set up the deadwood and the few initial frames that served as the molds and he beveled the transom and cut the rabbet in the stem (there was no rabbet on the keel; the heavy, stiff Caribbean pine garboard strakes just bore on a bevel) and he was always elbowing right in the middle of the crowd when the garboard strakes were forced to comply with the notions of his eye but most of the rest of the boat was built by subcontractors who just drifted in when the time came. I learned to listen to the discussion about when who was supposed to arrive and learned a good little bit about the social life of those people, too.

The man who subcontracted to fit the intermediate frames and floors to the already planked hull was very fat and seemingly slow. His work was truly an astonishing thing. There wasn't enough room on the beach by the bar to accumulate the enormous pile of wood that you see around every other boat shop I have ever been in (mine is beginning to cascade), so all the raw material for each job was brought in on Julio's big flatbed truck. You ought to have seen what the frame man had to work with. They backed the truck right up to the boat so El Gordo could climb, snorting and puffing like a bull, up onto the bed with a whole truckload of what looked to be a jumble of gnarled limbs straight out of the forest of Hansel and Gretel. Like so many of the operations of building a plank-on-frame boat by old professionals, all that chaos was carefully ordered and the frame man knew exactly which of the crooks he needed and where it was supposed to fit after he had chopped the bark off and shaped and beveled it by eye using a little hatchet and a chopping block on the stern of the truck. He was so good that he seldom had to adjust either the curve or the bevel after he had tried the futtock for fit. He had a little nickel-plated, all-steel Stanley Yankee push drill in his hip pocket, and after he had drilled the holes through the planking to fasten the frame, he would position it and buck it with a sledgehammer head. I tried my best to detect the signal that summoned one of the others to come drive the nails when he was ready but couldn't. At first I thought it might have been a grunt, but he grunted all the time. It must have been subliminal.

Anyway, that was what it was like down by the beach. Up in the bar and at the drugstore, the social life was even more interesting. I had already committed myself to going back home to Georgia to find out more about that girl who had been writing to me, so my interest in the young girls of that town was like that of a casual observer. You know, respectable (and there weren't any other kind in that place) Spanish people have a rigid set of customs about the courtship of their young girls. Though it is perfectly permissible for girls as young as thirteen to go to the bar where alcohol is drunk and gambling is occurring, they may not go alone. Some old duena has to go with them. Even though the old gal might have been well into her dotage, her eagle eye made sure that there was no hanky-panky to the tune of the jukebox. Nevertheless, love was fallen into and proper liaisons were set up under the rigidity of that system—a system into which came a newcomer.

Not me, Terrible Torque.

Here is what happened to Terrible Torque. I finally got off of messcooking and went to work at the secret shop where I was supposed to be. By then I had taken the test and passed into what they called "third-class petty officer," and even though I was brand new at the shop, I outranked a good many of the old hands including Terrible Torque. I hate to let this out, but you know, intelligence, experience, and ability have nothing to do with the hierarchy of the enlisted men of the Navy. Rank is established simply by taking a little abstract and mostly irrelevant written test. Though I had never actually seen a World War Two steam-driven torpedo and such a thing had nothing whatsoever to do with the job for which I was trained, how that weapon worked was the basis of the tests I took to advance myself through the Navy and a marvelous machine it must have been . . . right up my alley. I'll briefly describe its mode of propulsion. Oxygen and alcohol were injected into a heavy-duty steel flask where they were ignited and burned with an astonishing fury. Water was sprayed into this hellhole and the unbelievably powerful jet of steam that resulted drove a tiny turbine to generate a horsepower more like the result of an explosion than the propulsive efforts of machinery. Though the steam pressure was so high and the vapor so hot that the turbine blades were quickly eroded, the torpedo was a one-shot device and durability was not a factor in its design. I don't remember figures exactly, but the whole engine of the thing wasn't much bigger than a two-gallon bucket and put out many hundreds of horsepower. I was so fascinated that I, a messcook, quickly became the youngest third-class petty officer in the US Navy.

Terrible Torque earned his name because he was sent (not by me, thank goodness) to the battery locker to put a little water in the batteries that we perpetually maintained so, in case the Russians were to break bad, we could whip their asses. There were zillions of bucks' worth of batteries in the battery locker. I know the technology of secret batteries has made great progress since 1959 but I still wouldn't want to let any cats out of the bag, so I will just tell you that one of the ingredients of the plates of some of those batteries was sterling silver. Anyhow, the way you added water to them was to unscrew all the little plastic caps and, using a syringe, fill the cells up exactly like you used to do a car battery before the manufacturers worked that scam called "maintenance-free" in which, if you can figure out how to take the plastic caps off, you can add a little water to maintain one of those to last much longer than its intended life span. So Terrible Torque took all those caps off and filled up all those batteries, and it took most of the day. When he got through he read the checklist, which said, "After all the cells are filled, replace the caps and torque them to 50 inch-pounds using torque wrench Mk 5, Mod 3." Terrible Torque finished the job and came into the little office room and lounge where we hung out most of the time.

"Man, I sure will be glad when I make third class and don't have to do that shitty job anymore," he proclaimed, glaring at me.

"Well, it's over with now. You won't have to do it again for thirty days," said the chief. "I hope you didn't just screw the caps on and not torque them like Gasparetti used to do because I am sure gonna spot-check your young ass."

"Yeah, I torqued them but I couldn't get no fifty foot-pounds on any of them," explained Terrible Torque. It turned out that he had stripped the plastic threads on every single plug on eighteen quadrillion bucks' worth of batteries, which had to be destroyed and disposed of in a ritual that was mind-boggling in its extremity. In case the ridiculousness of this narrative has you confused, there is a big difference between the torque of fifty inch-pounds and fifty *foot*-pounds . . . a terrible difference.

Terrible Torque was a nice young man. The whole thing was the Navy's fault. They ought to have had better sense than to put two different fifties on a torque wrench. Anyway, Torque had gotten conned into having a certain pretty large portion of his paycheck deducted into government bonds. Not only that, but he had committed himself to make exorbitant payments on an enormous gilt Bible and some other publications that were sold by a well-organized cadre of rapacious old chief petty officers. In short, he didn't have the carfare money to go to San Juan to visit the art galleries and museums on Luna Street like all the other single pukes at the shop so he rode on the back of my scooter to the bar on the beach where he sat and listened to the music. It didn't take him long to notice the young girls sitting demurely with their duenas. Old Torque became more mesmerized and more mesmerized. He asked me how it was done to get to talk to one of those girls. "Well," I opined, "probably the first step would be to learn a little Spanish." "Hell, man, I can't do that right now," he wailed, "can't you just teach me one or two words just to get me started." "Well, okay, just go over there to her and say '¿Balle?'" (Ed.: Puerto Rican Spanish is different from Mexican or Castillian Spanish and I ain't sure about how the interrogative form of "dance?" is written). After he had practiced the word and got the inflection of the question right, he gathered his gumption and walked over where the girl who had caught his eye sat with her snoozing grandmother and said his word. With that, she was in his arms and they were dancing to "Just a Closer Walk with Thee."

I can see that this story is fixing to get ponderous if I keep on like this so I'll cut it to the nub. Language proved to be no barrier to Torque and the daughter of the people who owned the drugstore. For one thing, she spoke excellent standard English, for another, true love has no need for speech. It was pure, proper euphoria (the best kind) around that little town. Torque and the girl progressed rapidly through the ritual. Kisses and hand-holding were permitted, but not much. If they got to sighing too loud, the ever-present old duena would wake up and, "no, no, no." Finally an agreement was reached and Torque cashed in his government bonds and bought a plane ticket to take the girl and her grandmother to Miami to meet his parents. I hate to tell you this. I think it is the most pitiful thing I ever heard of. They came right back. It turned out that Terrible Torque's mother and father thought the girl was a little too dark to suit them. The grandmother and the girl got right back on the plane and flew back to Puerto Rico. Torque stayed on to argue and whine for a while but to no avail. The young couple never saw each other again and though the people in the town still tolerated me, they were kind of reserved acting after that. Both Torque and the girl were the saddest-looking kind of people for all the rest of the time I knew them. I think their hearts are still broken to this day.

After something like that, it is hard to concentrate, but I'll try to tell about the floorboard man. I don't know if you know this, but fitting floorboards in a round-bilged boat is some tricky business and, though, I didn't know that, either, I still had my doubts about the floorboard man. He was so old that Julio had to help him into the boat. By then it was complete except for the rigging and the floorboards. The white hull gleamed like a beauty there on the edge of the Caribbean Sea. I don't remember the exact color of that particular boat, but Puerto Rican smacks are always tricked out in bright colors from the rub rail up. This one might have had the sheer strake painted bright yellow with blue rail and cap. I know that the boot top was bright blue and had the distinctive downcurve as the hollow of the forefoot approached the stem that is so characteristic of the boats of that region (and which will still bring tears to my eyes when I see it in a picture or my mind's eye). I have seen a lot of small carvel-planked boats and it might just be nostalgia, but none of them has been as pretty as Julio's. That ain't got nothing to do with the floorboard man. I was just trying to set the scene of what it looked like while he was at work. He must have been much respected because everybody was very helpful. He stood in the boat or sat on the seat and folks handed the wood up to him. Using just a machete and a claw hammer, he chopped the strakes of the floorboard so that they fit around the frames exactly. You know, in a fishing boat, the floorboards have to fit tight or the bait or the fish might get in the bilge and get lost in the rocks of the ballast. He had a little chopping block on the seat beside him to back up the plank as he drove the machete blade into the crossgrain for the frame notches with his hammer, but he cut the beveled curve that fit the planking by holding the board across his knee. I watched carefully as he chopped little notches along the edge and then popped off the chunks between with the machete. He hit close up by the handle and the inertia of the long blade beyond carried the sharp steel through the wood. He had a little triangular file with which he touched up his blade. He had all the floorboards fitted by midafternoon and the men helped him out of the boat and into the bar where, I guess they talked quietly over their tiny Coronas and rice and beans. I wouldn't know though because I couldn't leave the boat. It was such a piece of work.

Displacement Behavior

in which studious cussing is considered an art

There is an animal behavior ritual described by ethologists and named "displacement behavior." Dogs sometimes engage in this ritual. One of the things that can cause it is when a big dog comes into the yard of a little dog. The little dog wants to eat him up for all his presumptuous pissing, but wisdom (if he has any . . . which some little dogs don't) forbids so he "displaces" his displeasure by biting and shaking hell out of something else, something like a pinecone or a rag.

I do something like that too. While I don't bite flat tires and stump-toe roots, I like to cuss them out real good. I guess I would cuss some people if I had the nerve and, if I didn't know about displacement behavior, I would probably think that there was something wrong with me besides timidity. I used to love to cuss ice trays about the best.

I have to stop for a minute right here and set you straight about something or you might not understand the essence of this cussing. Studious cussers like me don't just thoughtlessly use the same nasty word over and over with no regard to the context of the situation like the ignoranti you see all over the place. Despite what devotees of "standard English" would have you to believe, cussing does not always indicate an inability to express oneself because of ignorance of the language. Skillful use of profanity is an ancient expansion of the standard issue of *any* language and I am a serious student of the English usage of that skill. My father started me off quite early with a pretty eloquent profane capability. Also, when I was little, I used to hang around with some pretty hard-cussing field hands and logging crews in the woods and learned a different dialect. When I was sixteen, I took a summer job unloading boxcars full of chicken feed along with some grown men . . . a piecework venture that taught me quite a lot. But the thing that really set me up and made me the eloquent expert that I am today was when I enlisted in the Navy for four years. That is certainly the zenith of the cussing business and, if I do say so myself, I found that I had a natural aptitude for the art and very quickly became one of the best.

It is a good thing that most people don't get to see me in full flower. Despite what one might think, I run with pretty high society and have to control myself. I got to where I could do that because my tolerant and non-foulmouthed young bride asked me not to cuss around her mother. It was hard at first, but then I developed an alertness to inappropriate behavior. I was able to carry that abstinence another step after I noticed that I could read the lips of other drivers as they cussed *me,* so I made a rule never to cuss other people when I can see them. Of course, an ephemeral phosphorescence on a television screen is not a real person and I know that many a ninny or nincompoop TV star's ears would burn if they had the slightest notion . . . and the idiotic chirpers of the radio . . . Saints preserve the bliss of their ignorance.

All that is well and good, but what I really like to cuss is inanimate objects like ice cube trays. They seem to have some kind of diabolical, anthropomorphic talent. I won't go into what-all they do to deserve what they get . . . you know what I am talking about. They, along with loose-battery TV-muting doohickeys, are right up there with a car that wants to cut off all the time and are certain to hear from me. A backlashed baitcasting reel . . . a huge, immovable, dead battery on a log skidder . . . all those things better get ready to cringe. A bonehead computer . . . %$#@*! I feel for anybody on the information superhighway who never learned to cuss. But I sort of strayed away from explaining how all that correlates with displacement behavior.

Now, we have a refrigerator that automatically dumps the ice into a little box so there are no ice trays to cuss anymore. I feel a strong sense of deprivation every time I go in there to get a few cubes for my glass. Sometimes I do drop some of the ice (can't exactly call them cubes . . . maybe "turdletts?") on the floor where they bust into many unrecoverable smithereens that leave little isolated puddles like where a girl puppy might have repeatedly peed. I cuss each and every fragment individually. I know I am cussing the wrong thing . . . I know who dropped that ice . . . that's displacement behavior for you.

Seagull

in which I learn not to be so gullible

When I went home from Puerto Rico to get married, I was able to catch a hop in an old P2V anti-submarine plane to Mayport just across the St. Johns from Jacksonville. She was coming to meet me so I wore my best whites and spitshined my shoes. I had to sit back in some makeshift quarters and my whites got so filthy that after inspecting me, the marine in Mayport almost refused to let me out of the gate. Not only that, but the bomb bay where I rode was unheated and I like to have froze to death. Not only that, but the flight crew played a cruel trick on me. They told me, as the only occupant of the bomb bay, that it was my duty to announce to the forward part of the plane that the bomb bay was "all secure sir" after we got off the ground. I was to lift the lid to this little tube and holler this information down in there as soon as the plane leveled out at cruising altitude. When I finished doing that and looked up, the entire crew including both pilots was standing in the door laughing and slapping their thighs. I thought I saw the world passing by down through that little tube and it seemed to me that it smelled strongly of urine. Oh well . . . one a minute, P. T. said. I guess, now that they have women on aircrews, they have a dishpan welded on that thing to make all opportunities equal.

After we got married, we flew back to Puerto Rico on a regular airliner (Pan American, Lockheed Super Constellation . . . bathroom accommodations not so concise). Jane had a bunch of things that she needed to take, like her clothes and some cooking utensils and stuff, but we had to leave most of her belongings behind so that we could take the outboard motor. It was a wonderful little two-cylinder, three-horse weedless Evinrude (made in Belgium in 1954) that I had worked for a long, long time unloading boxcars of chicken feed to get the money to buy. It turned out that we should have taken the other stuff on the plane with us. The little three was too short in the shaft and too puny in the propeller to do much with the old Nueva Eva. Though it wasn't suited for that duty, it has always been a delight on the little narrow skiffs that I use it on now. Yep, I still got it.

As soon as we got settled down in our little house, I set up building boats in the one-room where we cooked, ate, and slept and started making a little spare change. We saved up and bought a brand-new British Seagull—a five-hp, five-blade wheel, brass gas tank, "Silver Century Plus," made in Poole, Dorset in 1959. Dubbed by its maker "The Best Outboard Motor For The World," that engine showed us what that "Plus" meant the first time we fired it up on the transom of the old Nueva Eva. We were astonished. The old boat cut through the water like a destroyer. We made a bunch of expeditions up rivers, into mangrove swamps and bays where we had never been able to go before because of certain preferences of the boat's for wind sort of coming from the side or behind and certain preferences of ours away from rowing in stifling heat and biting bugs when there was no wind coming from the side or behind. Though we appreciated the extra mobility, we soon found that the real joy of the expedition came when we were able to shut the damn Seagull down. When it was running, it was sort of intrusive. First, it made a lot of noise. A weedeater, chain saw, or even a wretched Jet Ski ain't nothing compared with a British Seagull at full bleat. Second, it made a pall of smoke that seemed to wad up behind the transom of the boat and then curl up and jump on us like some Djinni gone bonkers. There was a certain vibration too. We found that it was necessary to completely break contact with the boat in order to steady our eyes so we could see the sights when the engine was running. We learned to time our levitation to coincide with the gaps in the pall of smoke. I especially hated the carburetor of that Seagull. It had this little tin choke that pivoted into a little cut in the throat of the thing from the outside. You had to choke the damn engine to start it even if it was hot. It would start though and continue to run with the choke closed but it skipped much worse than normal and the resulting violent snatching made it almost impossible to grab the crazily wiggling choke without either getting tangled up with the flywheel or getting the hell burned out of you by the hot engine (the damn thing got hot all the way from the water to the gasoline). Not only that but it slung a large slobber of oily gas out of the gaps in the carburetor all over you while you were trying to catch the choke on the fly. If the engine was cold, not only was it necessary to fight the choke but you had to push down on this little leaky button on top of the float bowl that depressed the float against its will and allowed the carburetor to flood the crankcase with enough gasoline to start the engine (or a DC3).

We were young and excitable though, and hardship was just the predecessor to joy for us. We tried to wear that old Seagull out. I even tried to improve it a little bit and about the only successful one of these experiments was a fuel pump I machined up on Navy time so we could quit having to pour gas into the hot engine every time it ran out. I don't have to tell you that, when we got out of the Navy, we brought the old Seagull (and the Evinrude three and a Wilcox Crittenden thirty-pound yachtsman anchor) home. As soon as I could, I built a copy of the old Nueva Eva. We clamped the Seagull on the stern, spread a little gas around, and commenced exploration of the Gulf of Mexico. Though we could always count on the old Seagull to crank and run, it was sort of like how you can always count on income tax time. Along with the regular disgusting behavior of the thing, we had some interesting mishaps. Once, while we were still in Puerto Rico, it spat out the "sparking plug." I knew something was wrong because the engine began to hit every lick instead of every other lick like it usually did when it was easing along (we never ran it wide open for various reasons). When I looked back to see what was what, I saw the spark plug on the end of the wire swinging back and forth with the violent wiggle of the engine like the tail of a dog who is real glad to see you. Just as the engine blew so much of the gas out of the hole that it no longer had the excess it required to run, the spark plug was flung off the wire and plummeted to the bottom of the clear water. So did I—found it immediately. Back home when that happened, in the muddy Apalachicola River, I could not find the plug. It was a strange-looking, big-thread thing, not commonly available in stores—or at least that is what I thought—so I machined an adapter and ran it on an old Volkswagen plug. Then one day I was messing around in the Western Auto looking for this and that when I saw a British Seagull spark plug. Of course, the box said that it was supposed to go in a Model T Ford. I thought that was pretty appropriate. After we had had the old engine for a long time (seemed like forever) we were coming in the pass between St. George and Dog Island with a fair wind against a falling tide. In those conditions, when the water running out of the bay through the pass encounters the wind blowing in from the sea, the resulting conflict makes for great big, almost stationary waves. I had the old engine running to sort of help us through. When we hit the first of those waves, the boat pitched up and the engine pitched off the stern at the same time. The silence was delightful. We said "too bad" and sailed on through the pass as if nothing had happened but after we were inside, I noticed that the boat didn't seem to be acting quite right. Turns out that the old Seagull was porpoising along behind on the gas line. I had it running again before we went into the river.

The diurnal alternation of the sea-breeze, land-breeze situation is very pronounced in the summertime in the near-shore Gulf of Mexico. The sea breeze begins to pick up just about exactly when the morning starts to get uncomfortably hot and the land breeze comes right after dark. Both of them are pretty predictable and wonderfully welcome. Old-time sailors knew this and, along with the tides, worked it to their advantage. As you know, the phenomenon is caused by convection from whichever surface—sea or land—is hotter at the time. Any wet, rising air condenses as it encounters the coolness of the upper troposphere and that makes thunderstorms and rain . . . out to sea at night and over land during the day. There is nothing more sweet smelling than a land breeze coming out of the wet woods across an island or a boat.

One dead-calm evening, we were coming back from Waccasassa Bay across the Gulf when the fair land breeze made up. We began to smell a hint of the fresh, rained-on woods of the land mixed in with the exhaust of the old Seagull. The sails tightened up, the boat heeled a little and began to sail on the tack she loved so well. I shut the Seagull off. When I pulled the pin and let her slip into Davey Jones' locker, I could see my wife nod just the slightest little bit.

Epilogue

One time I had to buy a part that had vibrated (we say "viberated") off the old Seagull. Of course we had bought the engine from a yacht store in San Juan. But since we did not remember the address of that place I wrote to the address on the gas cap: "British Seagull, Poole, Dorset, England." I am afraid that I explained things too much in that letter. As a result, the part came immediately, and a lady there became a pen pal of mine. She was part owner and main captain of one of the "Little Ships" of Dunkirk. She had a garden in her backyard and we exchanged *Brassica* seeds for many years until she died about 1985. I heard that the "Best Outboard for the World" is now being built by Pakistanis. I give them joy of each and every one.

Monkey Island

in which I leave my young bride for . . . monkeys

After my wife and I got married in January 1961, we rented a little one-room concrete house halfway up El Yunque near Rio Blanco, about twenty miles from the naval station. My mother, though she, like the Navy, didn't approve of us getting married so young (my wife was just seventeen), felt like we needed a car so she shipped an old ragged Volkswagen down there for a wedding present. We did need a car. I had a motor scooter, and while it was an easy ride down the mountain to the Navy, it was a pretty hard pull for that little thing with its .410-gauge tailpipe, coming back with both of us and all the groceries from the navy exchange. We didn't need the Volkswagen for that though. We needed it to sell so we could afford to buy Julio's own precious jewel of a sailboat. You know, if your boat isn't too pretty to walk away from without looking back, you ain't getting all the goody out of life and I can walk away from any automobile.

I think that long haul up the mountain did that scooter good . . . might have burned the smut off the spark plug. It always ran much better after that, particularly after I started hauling plywood on it too . . . which made for a pretty sporty trip, specially that part on the tall bridge across Rio Blanco. Sometimes, when the wind was right, it was hard to decide if it was rolling, flying, or fixing to swim. You can call that sort of thing irresponsible if you want to but I have been trying all the rest of my life to get back to that status. Two boats, no car, and a seventeen-year-old girl on the back of my motor scooter to help me hold the plywood. How can responsibility compete with that?

Well, that exact situation didn't last too long—we sold the old Nueva Eva. Julio's jewel (Rosa, twelve feet) was such a joy that we never used the big boat. I have found that to have been the proof to a pretty good rule. I call it the "rule of joy." Simply put, it says, "The important thing ain't comfort, it's joy." Joy in boats is inverse to their size. When they get big and full of engines, batteries, toilets, stoves, and other comforts, there just ain't as much room for joy. All those things are like a bunch of relatives that vote wrong. Not only can they cancel out the good you are trying to do, they can beat you and there is nothing you can do about it. The little Rosa though . . .

whooo. Memory is sort of selective and I might be forgetting a little misery but if there was any, it was quickly pushed out of that little boat by the joy . . . no room.

The peacetime Navy ain't no (I hope I'm not letting any cat out of the bag) real hard job and we had plenty of time to sail all over the paradise that eastern Puerto Rico was in those days. There were uninhabited islands everywhere. Some of them belonged to the Navy and had the abandoned remains of old World War Two buildings on them. One old rotting-down barracks building looked like nobody had been in it since the guys moved out. There was still a picture of Lana Turner hanging on the wall. Even Vieques and Culebra didn't have hardly anybody on them. Those were so far away that, though we started out once, we never made it all that way. Jane was pregnant by then and the groundswell was so big that, while we did fine on top of the waves, there wasn't any wind down in the bottoms and she didn't like it down there. Finally we turned back after we topped one wave and saw a destroyer that hadn't been there when we were on top of the previous wave. I remember noticing that it was so close that we could see the little clear circles in the windows of the bridge where the spinners were slinging off the water from the spray that was flying from the bow clear across the whole superstructure as the ship tore through the big even swells (there was no water at all coming in our boat, which brings us back to the previous comparison). We never did get around to trying another trip to Vieques and Culebra. We had plenty to do sailing to the many little islands near the shore.

I remember the first one we went to, Cayo Santiago off the coast opposite Humacao. We could see it from where we moored the little Rosa beside the bar in Naguabo Playa. One day, early in all these adventures, we packed our lunch (Gouda cheese, long bread, Clorox jug of water, and two apples), hopped on the scooter, rode to the bar, waded out to the boat, and sailed to that island. It was an interesting-looking thing to flatwoods children like us . . . high, heavily wooded, and rocky. After we got close, we could see a tiny cove with a little coral sand beach. By the time we managed to beat in there, we noticed that there was a metallic clang coming from back in the woods somewhere. There wasn't a regular rhythm to it like machinery but it was happening often and it was loud. It sort of made us worried about landing in the little cove but we had sailed all that way and were itching to scramble all over that island and see what was what. Finally we worked the boat up where it was shallow enough to wade ashore and I took the tiller (majaguilla, dense and hard) so I would have an edge in any negotiations with whoever was making all that noise. As soon as we put the first foot on the beach, a swarm of big monkeys came out of the bushes and trees and started screaming and hopping up and down and gnashing their terrible teeth so loud that no negotiations were possible. We did a little hopping ourselves and ate our bread and cheese in the boat while we sailed around the island.

Though we didn't get to swim in the freshwater pools and take a little nap in the shade, we did find out the source of all the loud banging. Those monkeys must have belonged to somebody because they were eating out of a plain old steel dumpster . . . A monkey had to open the lid and get in, and slam the lid behind him, to get something to eat. We noticed that some of them had short-looking tails for Rhesus monkeys (which is what they were) and assumed that those were the slowest. After a while, the in-monkey would raise the lid and get out of the dumpster or another monkey would raise the lid and get in and chase him out. It took at least two bangs for each monkey to get a little snack. They were eating something that looked just exactly like what we used to call "big-turd" hog feed. One would come out of the dumpster holding as many of those big pellets in his mouth, feet, and hands as he could and still work the lid. As soon as the outgoing monkey hit the ground, the lid would slam and all his friends would jump on him and take his hog feed pellets away. It was kind of comical and we always stopped by there to drift and watch when we passed on our way to the other islands that lay beyond that one. We were always very careful not to drift too close for fear those terrible monkeys would come take *our* hog feed away from *us*.

Although I didn't have to do much, I did have to go to work at the base. I had a friend who worked in the same shop. We had one of those antagonistic friendships that men have where, though they never have anything nice to say to each other, they are still buddies. This guy was from Michigan and came from a long line of dedicated steel-mill- and automobile-factory-working men. Our experiences were so different that we had plenty of interesting things to explain. I had never seen a union or a factory and I was curious and listened to what he said with interest. He had never seen hog feed or a possum so he listened to what I said too. The main difference was that I had read about factories and unions and knew the Jimmy Hoffa news of the time and my buddy's experiences were pretty believable to me. He thought I was pulling his leg with my alligators, armadillos, fifty-pound catfish, and things like that because he was ignorant. He didn't believe the Monkey Island story at all . . . called me a bullshitter.

Finally the ribbing about it got involved with money and a bet was made. To save my dignity, one Saturday I had to leave my wife home and take this joker to see the damn monkeys. I was planning to make a quick trip but it was the time of year when the trade wind is not absolutely reliable like it usually is and it took a long time. It was hot and stormy looking too and by the time we finally got in range of the island, I was beginning to feel like I was earning that twenty. Not only that but, just as we rowed up into the little cove, a hell of a thunderstorm came up. The wind whipped down on us and the rain burned like a bunch of slingshot rocks. Fortunately the cove gave us some protection from the waves but the bottom was rocky and the anchor didn't want to hold. It was shallow so we jumped out to hold the boat until the storm blew by. At least, it was shallow back at my end. Old union man went in, over his head, in a hole. By the time he had scrambled halfway back in the boat, we had drifted to where he could stand up too, but he still wasn't comfortable because it was blowing cold rain like hell . . . felt like it was fixing to hail . . . and he had lost his flip-flops when he fell in the hole.

We held the boat for what seemed like three hours. We squatted in its lee to keep the rain from stinging quite as much of us and to hide from the lightning that was flashing all around. Finally it let up enough so we could talk a little and then we could see the island and the little beach. "Let's get this monkey business over with so I can take that twenty bucks of yours. I think I saw a bar back there where we got in the boat," he said, mincing ashore in his bare feet on the rocky bottom. I was beginning to worry, because I hadn't heard a single clang from the dumpster in all that time. Maybe they had taken the whole monkey crop to the auction just like we used to do hogs. By the time we got anchored and waded up to the beach I was feeling my soggy twenty-dollar-bill for maybe the last time because there were no monkeys anywhere. Usually they would be hopping and screaming by the time we entered the cove. "Where are my damn shower shoes?" demanded the money winner. "They ought to be right here on this beach." With that, I heard the sound of a thousand-monkey fight way back in the woods. "Hear that, union man?" says me. "Them's monkeys and they sound like they are on their way down here to collect their union dues. Let's us get back in the boat while I collect my dues." "I ain't going no goshdurn where until I find my foolish shoes," said he in the traditional language of the enlisted Navy man of that time (a language in which I became very proficient in only four years . . . if I do say so myself).

In spite of all that bravado, he did have to leave without his shoes when all thousand of those monkeys came running down to the beach. I was already in the boat when the first ones appeared from out of the trees and I got to watch the other fella realize he had lost his money and then decide to abandon the search for his shoes. We both pushed the boat off into deeper water and watched the monkeys. They ran out of the woods for ten minutes. Apparently they had been occupied doing something interesting way back in the bushes during the storm and didn't find out that there was something more interesting to do on the beach until just now. I wondered what could have been more important to them than eating us up until I saw the king monkey strut out of the trees. It looked like he had been in some kind of bad monkey fight. He looked like he was mighty proud of those shower shoes he was wearing too.

Monkey Island was featured in the January 2008 issue of Smithsonian.

Triumph

in which my luck holds out once more

Since this story is about an automobile, it might seem like it ought to be about a Triumph car but it ain't. It is about an old VW Bug.

When my wife and I got married we were very young and my mother did not think it was such a good idea so, true to her nature, she became bone-headed and revengeful. Before the house sparrows had eaten the rice in the church parking lot, she had sold my room and had it moved across the highway where it became some guy's pool house. I always wondered what he did with the full-length photo of Marilyn Monroe I had on the inside of my closet door. I have also wondered what happened to all my model airplane stuff. Oh well.

As soon as we got married we went to Puerto Rico to live until I finished my four years in the US Navy. Because I was so young, I had not had time to ascend to the giddy height in the ranks of the enlisted where one is allowed to live in Capehart. Capehart was (is?) the ubiquitous name for little housing projects the Navy maintains on bases all over the world for married enlisted men above the rank of E-5. I guess they call those settlements the same name to fool poor little Navy brats into thinking they are in an "American" home no matter where they are so they will turn out to be normal enough to be ignorant of anything not American. Anyway, the place we found to live was twenty miles from the naval station way out in rural Puerto Rico. Due to the current homeland security situation in this country, I hate to make an un-American statement in print but I would still much rather live in that little concrete house on the side of that mountain in the boondocks of the third world than in any ranch-style, pastel-painted bungalow in any dad-blamed Capehart and we continued to live there after I made E-5 (second-class petty officer in the Navy, buck sergeant in the Army, Air Force, or jarhead corps) and became qualified to live in the official enlisted ghetto.

Though my mother continued to disapprove of our early marriage (and never admitted that she was wrong until she died after we had been married for forty years) she did not remove herself completely from our affairs. After a while down there, Jane became pregnant. We were using a Sears Allstate Vespa motor scooter for transportation and, despite the fact that such a thing is the standard for the pregnant young women of most of the rest of the world, my mother thought someone pregnant with her grandson (as it turned out) should not ride on the back of any motor scooter upon the mountain roads of a primitive country even if it was a commonwealth and actually part of the USA with full citizenship rights for everybody, so she went to Jacksonville and shipped her very own car to Puerto Rico. The peculiarities of my mother have been well documented in my sister's book *Momma Makes Up Her Mind* so I will not elaborate. Look it up for yourself if you need any more information. Anyway this old VW showed up on the docks in San Juan. It was a rusted-out mess. I think it cost me more to catch a publico to get the damn thing than it was worth. The man at the dock was flabbergasted. The battery was hanging, stone dead, through the floorboards on its wires like the result of some successful automotive execution, the clutch cable had rusted and busted, and the gas was rancid. Getting that thing running well enough to go the forty miles back to El Yunque was a real challenge. Fortunately the bystanders at the shipping terminal in San Juan just loved a challenge.

You know, at that, I believe I must deviate from the straightforward style of this narrative and make a statement of ethnic generality. I think Caribbean or other tropical people who live in a more third-world-style situation than all these cell phone talkers and SUV drivers we have here on the mainland are among the most resourceful on the earth. Take Cubans for instance . . . look at all those old American cars they keep running despite the fact that the embargo has deprived them of replacement parts since 1959. I saw how those resourceful Cubans can play a regular old LP record without the benefit of electricity. They just tape a cone of cardboard onto the arm of the same turntable Hemingway left when he bailed out of there in '58, stick a regular stickpin through the apex, drop the point in the groove, and turn the record with one finger and, voilà, Johnny Mathis. If it wasn't for the fool embargo, they could get a new record and listen to the same boogaloo as the rest of us. Those bystanders at the shipping terminal in San Juan had that old VW percolating in jig time. Of course they couldn't do anything about the clutch cable so they had to aim me at the gate and push me off in second gear. They cheered and hooted and slapped their thighs as I rode out of sight grinding my way into third. I was sorry that I was long gone by the time I got fourth and they couldn't see how I synchronated the engine and transmission speed so she just dropped on in as slick as if it had had a working clutch.

So we drove the old VW some but, I guess, to fly in the face of my momma we mostly rode the motor scooter. That VW had two problems I couldn't fix besides the frozen clutch cable. Which, at that, I must make another statement of capability. You know, Jane learned to drive in that car . . . on the side of a mountain. There are women who claim they can't learn to drive a clutch car. Yeah, well, it ain't the feminine mystique, y'all. It is just another example of the hopeless helplessness that has infected the privileged citizenry of this country.

One of the aggravations was that the VW had a completely rotted-out sunroof. Given the other problems, that fact made it less satisfactory than the motor scooter. I solved the sunroof problem temporarily by carrying a little green pram on a homemade roof rack. The trouble with that was that I kept selling the damn pram and that let the rain in again until I could build another one. Because of the moist atmosphere, animals lived in there. We learned to drive down a twisted, really bad mountain road with a large tree frog or a tarantula completely obscuring the vision of one eye.

As Jane rapidly became more and more pregnant, I began to think about the impending ride to the naval station hospital. The other unsolvable problem with Momma's VW was that it had a rusted-out gas tank. By the time her time came, it was leaking so badly that we couldn't leave any gas in it overnight. We slid a dishpan under the car to catch the leak and, if we had to use it, poured the gas out of the pan into the extra-large gas hole and hurried. I figured we were good to go but on the night Jane woke me up and told me that she had timed things and it might be best if we went on, I stepped in the damn dishpan and spilled the gas. We thought about turning the scooter over and pouring its gas into the dishpan but it looked so inviting sitting there on its twin kickstands with its capable little baby-blue self that we just hopped on and rode down the mountain with Mr. Allstate's little dim light showing the way. The only trouble was that they wouldn't let me into the hospital because my foot stank so bad of gasoline and Sam was born without the benefit of my attendance.

In a world filled with logic and reason, that would have been the end of this story but it ain't. Shortly after Sam was born (all went well . . . I mean if a person has the capability of learning to drive a clutch car in the mountains without a clutch . . . functions of the body come naturally) my time in the Navy was up. I was E-5 then and that qualified us to send our belongings back home at Navy expense. We had a beautiful little twelve-foot sailboat so I boxed it up and hauled it to the naval station terminal behind the VW on a borrowed USN trailer. The officious-acting civilian in charge informed me that they did not ship boats. I explained that I did not have a refrigerator, stove, washing machine, dryer, hi-fi, TV, matching living room, dining room, or bedroom suite or any of those things and I was not even going to ship that old car over there. "All I want to ship is this box," I explained. "We don't ship boats. The only vehicles we ship are cars," he explained right back. "Well then, you constipated bastard you," I snapped, "ship *that*."

We had been home in Georgia about three weeks and I was in the middle of my first job, which was painting the inside of a gigantic printing outfit for $1.75 an hour. I found that the Navy had qualified me very well for that. A dollar seventy-five was about right and I knew how to paint exposed pipes. I got a letter saying that my "car" was in Mayport Naval Station right across the St. Johns River from Jacksonville, Florida. I caught the Greyhound and showed up at the base with a good hot battery, a gallon of gas, and a bicycle pump. I knew there were only government workers there so I was on my own just like a Cuban. I was gone in about fifteen minutes. Old Familiar plugged all the way across the bridge and all the way through Jacksonville. I was an expert at changing gears by the synchronation method and the hot battery started it in gear every time at all those stoplights. I filled up with gas on the outskirts of town. It was about to get dark by the time I hit old 90 out in the country. I turned on the lights and, under the influence of the hot battery, at least one of them still worked nearly as good as the little vestigial beam of the Allstate so I propped my heel on the little roller of the gas pedal and let old Rusty rip. About the town of Starke, the battery fell through the floorboards. I like to have run off the road trying to reach around and pull it back up through the hole by the wires (you know, the battery in old VWs was under the starboard side of the rear seat in cars that still had a rear seat) but it was no use. The resulting sparks ignited the gas that was steadily dribbling from the tank and I was scared to stop so the battery ground itself to pieces on the highway. The light dimmed and the engine cut off and I knew I was in a bad fix but about the time we coasted to the top of the hill, the fire went out, the car started coasting fast enough for the generator to begin to percolate a little bit, the old engine gave a poot or two and tuned up, the lights came back on, and we tooled it on home in triumph.

Note:

That's the end of the story but I must say that I took that VW back to Momma the next morning and said, "I appreciate the loan of this car." She said, "You're welcome. You didn't take very good care of it, I see." She took it to Huegel (German . . . about like Cuban) at the shade tree and he put in a clutch cable, new battery wires, installed an outboard motor gas tank under the hood, fastened a piece of tin over the sunroof with sheet-metal screws and tar, and Momma drove the damn thing for five more years.

Prams

*in which I become a successful professional boatbuilder
first shot out of the box*

By the time we were settled down in our tiny house on El Yunque I had
made up my mind to go ahead and be a professional boatbuilder. I ordered
something called *Boatbuilders Handbook* from Weston Farmer's wonderful
Science and Mechanics Magazine and built an eight-foot V-bottomed plywood pram from plans in the book . . . well, sort of like the plans in the
book. This boat was supposed to be for rowing only and had small transoms both bow and stern. Outboard dependence had already become established by then so I modified the design so that it had a big transom at the
stern to float the outboard and the sailor. My wife and I built a bunch of
them and sold them as fast as we could build them for eighty bucks each,
unpainted . . . which suited me just fine. The sailors all wanted to paint
them themselves and I think they stole the paint from the Navy because
there were a lot of gray prams circulating around the big harbor. We had a
captive bunch of customers because it was almost impossible to buy a cheap
boat in Puerto Rico in those days. Even an old Puerto Rican plank-on-frame
boat cost hundreds of dollars.

I think we hit our peak of production, two prams a week, just before our
first son was born. Our normal pace was a pram a week but we usually took
the weekends off to go sailing. When the time for the baby to be born came
close we thought we ought to hang close to the scooter on weekends so we
were able to slap another pram together on those two days. Jane was driving screws with a Yankee screwdriver when the first contraction came.

Which, those prams were built without the benefit of electricity. I ripped
the plywood with a handsaw (you hold the handsaw upside down and walk
forward with it—try it sometime), drilled the holes with a hand drill (which
I still have), and drove the screws with the wonderful Stanley Yankee Spiral
Ratchet Screwdriver (which, in the right hands, will hold its own with any
rechargeable driver drill and will beat it with big screws). I planed the bevels
with the same secondhand block plane I use now. The plywood (five-ply,
quarter-inch, marine—three sheets to two boats) came from Rasmusen
Hardware Co. in St. Croix, which arranged shipment to their branch in

Naguabo on the mailboat. I ordered the screws (#6 by one-inch straight slot, flathead, Everdure monel . . . such a wonderful metal . . . such beautiful little screws) from Defender Industries in New York . . . the Weldwood glue too. The Puerto Rican mahogany for keels, chines, seats, and transom frames came from a little sawmill right down the road and was delivered on a big truck in rough bark-to-bark flitches of variable thickness. I made the transom frames out of the wigglesome edges that I ripped off to get something straight for the keel, chines, and seats. I planed all that with the block plane—made a man out of me—made a pretty nice pram for eighty bucks too, if I do say so myself. I wonder if there are any of them still moseying around down there in that beautiful place. I still have the plans and the old tools and the same woman. Now all I need is a stack of that five-ply plywood, a pile of those mahogany flitches, some of those beautiful little screws, and a bunch of captive customers.

I made enough money doing that to order a bunch of tools from Sears and Roebuck to be sent to Georgia so I could be set up to continue in that profitable business when I got out of the Navy. I figured I could manufacture those prams and one or two other economical boats and make a good living. The baby and my walking papers came about the same time. It was raining like hell the whole trip down the mountain on the scooter to the Navy hospital.

When we got back to the States with our new little son, we found that every discount store in the world had a nested stack of aluminum skiffs ten feet high . . . $59.95. I couldn't build a boat as cheap as that.

I wound up doing a bunch of other stuff . . . painting houses, building cabinets and furniture, working in factories and on tugboats and commercial fishing boats. Hell, I even went to college and became an oceanographer. Taught eighth-grade general science for ten years but I built boats all that time. I built a nineteen-foot sloop while I was carrying twenty quarter hours college work and supervising a night crew at a furniture factory. I finally gave up completely on plywood about 1967 or so and quit trying to compete with factory prices. My two sons were raised in the shavings and helped from the time they were old enough to poke a rivet in a hole. As the years went by, their participation has varied from being full- or part-time partners to being just full-time kibitzers as usual. One of their contributions to the business is an edict that I can't build any more unprofitable boats unless they get first dibs. There was a brief lapse in this policy when the youngest son, then thirty-five, decided to come in with me full-time and try to make a go of the business. We shook all the vacillating prospects out of the bushes by lowering the price and, though we gave some mighty nice presents to some pretty oblivious people (and some who weren't), he was only able to hang on by the skin of his teeth for four years before his shoeless children became social outcasts at school and he had to go back to his schoolteaching job to make a living. I was pretty lonesome in the shop after that but now those shoeless children are sticking rivets in the holes and rolling around in the shavings. Life is a circular thing, ain't it?

Flagrante Delicto

in which I find a surprise on Lover's Lane

It so happens that, because of pure chance, I have seen a good many human copulations in my lifetime in which I was not a participant. I selected these few chronologically:

The first time I saw one was when I was a boy about paperboy age. One night my buddy and I were hurrying on our bicycles down this little dirt road shortcut (appropriately called "Lover's Lane") to the ball field to see if we could catch a fly out in the parking lot, when we came upon this copulating couple in the exact middle of the road. It all happened so fast that there was nothing we could do but run over them, first Malcolm and then me. Though it happened very fast, I remember it exactly . . . as if it was just yesterday.

We came around a corner of the road and there they were right in the middle (the bushes were high and close on each side). The first thing I saw was something very white and big in the road. I couldn't tell what it was until Malcolm ran over it, then it materialized, out of the dark, into a man's hips. As I ran over them, I looked down and saw the whole scene. There was a man on top of a woman. He had his hat (fedora) and shoes (pale-soled with black socks, well pulled up) on but no other clothes that I could see. I couldn't tell what the woman was wearing because all I saw was her legs spraddled out all the way into the bushes on both sides of the narrow road so any shoes would have been hidden. When I ran over them (just like Bing Crosby . . . "Straight up the Middle") one of them said "oomph-oomph" when my tires hit. I couldn't tell which one it was.

Much later my wife, my littlest son (say five), my sister, and one or two others and I were walking on the deserted little strip of beach that separates the ocean from the marsh down west of our old coast house. We were probably looking for crabs and weren't whooping it up, so we didn't alert this couple until we were almost on top of them. The first hint I had of it was when my wife grabbed the little boy, whirled him around, and hustled him back toward the coast house with that stride that means that she means business. All I saw was these two, very large, very white, naked behinds scooting away across the sand in the direction of the marsh. They were on all fours, hands and feet throwing up divots of sand like race horses, the sun so bright on their white buttocks that there seemed to be a halo, kind of like how the sunlight is reflected into the sky from a white beach, as they scurried for the sparse concealment of the marsh grass. We all turned around (I had to help one sister) as quick as we could but we discussed it for quite a while. Fortunately, our son, though he had seen all that had preceded what I had seen, missed the halo part and never understood until years later why we laughed about that walk so much.

Another time, many members of this same crew and some others had gone way down the bay in a canoe, again, crabbing. Among this group was the same son, now thirty-five years old, and his new, little, very blond wife. After they had been gone all morning, my wife began to worry about the hot sun and our daughter-in-law's skin and told me to go get them in the other boat before she got burned to a crisp. I found them wading along three miles down the beach towing the canoe. They had a good many crabs (females, carefully selected to be without external eggs) and were ready to go home. I took the canoe in tow and all of them got in my boat, which was hardly more than a canoe itself, but with a little outboard motor. There was a very high tide, glass calm, like it usually is in the late summer. We were easing right along the edge among the sand spits looking for a few more crabs to make up a mess when my niece, standing on the foredeck with the net, ready to hop overside to catch the crab, spied this strange thing in the water ahead just as we came around the bend. *"What the hell is that?"* she hollered. When we all looked, we barely made out a copulating couple, flat in the water right in front of us, partially disguised by the waves radiating from the rump of the dedicated man. I quickly cut off and tipped the motor but the long, skinny, overloaded boat carried way too well and we slid right across that human sandbar and on down the bay. Luckily the towed canoe didn't hit either of them in the head.

The Time We Almost Lost the Chicken Feed Skiff

in which some bad luck leads to a night we've never forgotten

About 1965 or so, I built an eyeball replica of the old nineteen-foot Nueva Eva sloop we had when I was in the Navy. It was a good boat for us when my sons were little. Though it was an open boat, it would easily carry us and all our camping stuff for long trips in the big water. Like the real Nueva Eva, it had a long straight keel with very little drag (only drew eighteen inches) and would balance to self-sail on the wind. We made many a long voyage of exploration in the open water of the Gulf of Mexico and the bays, rivers, and marshes around here in that old boat . . . trips that were the joy of our youth. We played like we were original discoverers as we sailed into places where there was no sign that we weren't the first. Even in less pristine new ground, we developed the talent of ignoring the beer cans and fishing skiffs out on the flats as we explored ahead . . . little lookouts on the bow hanging by the forestay . . . supper cooking on the coal pot in the sandbox on top of the live well.

Early one spring we were on the eastern tip of St. George Island (where the state park is now . . . FOUR WHEEL DRIVE VEHICLES ONLY ON THE BEACH the sign says). We had the New Nueva Eva anchored in a little sandbar cove and had gone ashore in the skiff to mess around while we waited for the tide to run out enough to dig a few clams . . . you know, there are five kinds of edible clams in Apalachee Bay. One is the regular old *campecheinsis* quahog, the ones the wild people called "female clam." Some of them here are as big as a grapefruit and one of them is a chowder right by herself . . . if you can bring yourself to kill a twelve-year-old girl. Another is the Sun Ray Venus, a very active, well-decorated clam that can dig as fast as you can (depending on who you are). They are sandy inside and considered to be inedible by most people but if you know what you are doing, they are better than the big hard clams. There is also the great seaside cockle whose shells used to be so thick on the seaside of the barrier islands that we built igloos out of them when we were children but now are kept pretty well picked up by eager women who think they need to own every seashell they see. Sunray clams are pretty agile but nothing compared with a live cockle (a seldom-seen thing). Cockles have such a long, prehensile foot that they can climb out of a pretty good-sized bucket . . . may jump out. Cockles are even more full of sand than sunrays but . . . if you know what you are doing, are delicious. You have to watch out if you fry them for fritters though, they'll pop hot grease on you worse than anything I ever saw. Then there are two kinds of clams that Atlantic people call soft clams that live in permanent, deep burrows on the flats. One makes the shells that are called "angel wings." The wild people called them "male clam." There is another male clam too but he is so seldom seen that I can't find any mention in the literature. This is a giant burrowing clam almost as big as the geoduck of the West Coast. Anatomically, they look like the soft clams they have over on the Atlantic side but are much bigger. I think that one reason they are not well known is that they live in a hole about four or five feet deep dug into the roots of the grass of the flats. We planned to enhance the one-pot meal we had simmering in the sandbox with one or two of those kinds of clams . . . hoped for about five sunrays . . . when the tide fell.

While we were waiting, we had walked a long way west up the seaside beach when we saw a long line of black clouds coming down the bay. We picked up both little boys and started trotting back to the boat but were too late. Even though the rain didn't start before we got there, the blow did and was so strong out of the southeast that it blew our aluminum skiff off the beach where we had pulled it up and whipped it out into the bay. I put my boy down and lit out running but by the time I got as close to it as I could get, it was way too far to swim after and was scooting along so fast that I couldn't have caught it if I had been an Olympian so we hurried to the big boat only to find that it was landlocked by the falling tide. We dug a little ditch in the sand and by hauling her down by the halyard and washing with a bucket in the driving rain finally managed to get her out of the hole and into floating water . . . but by then the skiff was long gone and it was late in the afternoon. I might have considered letting the durn thing go because it was getting cold and windy and we would have to sail dead downwind but it was a good skiff that I had unloaded many a boxcar of chicken feed to scratch up the scratch for when I was a boy and was dearly beloved to me (still is). We scrambled in and snatched up every scrap of sail the old boat would stand . . . and she would bear a lot. We boiled off downwind down the bay into the sunset smashing into the backs of the waves and steering fine to avoid yawing enough to jibe or even broach to in the big following sea that was blowing in through the pass between St. George and Dog Island. Straight-up downwind sailing has always been a rare thing with us and it was exhilarating business despite the fact that the skiff was out of sight by now and we knew that we were in for a long cold night.

When it got dark it got real dark. The sky was overcast and the moon wasn't due to rise until some eleven o'clock or so. We just held on downwind and decided to go until I could tell that we were fixing to run up on Porter Bar way-the-hell-and-gone down by East Point where the last light had shown the downwind drift to hit the land. I knew the tide would still be rising when we got there so I figured to just round up in the shallows and wait for daylight or the moon to peek through a gap in the clouds enough to try to look for the skiff. The wind was so steady that I hoped it would be in sight, stranded on the bar just downwind. As usual, once the plan was made, we relaxed as well as we could in the fast-sailing boat (which, it don't pay to act too smug about your yacht when in the presence of a Caribbean sailing smack . . . sailing off the wind in a good breeze). While we were eating our clamless chowder and crackers with cheese I could see a hint of the moon every now and then and by the time the boys were sleeping under their sailbags on the life preservers under the foredeck, the front passed and the sky was clear and the almost still-full moon was shining bright. The wind was even moderating a little bit when I finally saw the skiff, aluminum gleaming in the moonlight, as it slid bow-first down the bay. When we finally caught it (a lost aluminum skiff with only a light outboard motor and a pair of oars for ballast will plane in twenty knots of wind) it was late at night and we were fifteen miles downwind of all our camping stuff. We began the long, long beat up the bay. Those shallow-keel-style sailboats are not built to go dead upwind. The people who normally use them are not frantic about where they think they need to be all the time like most North Americans. The old boat would beat upwind though if it wasn't pinched too close. I learned that it was best to try to make just the least little gain to the tack and keep the boat sailing along at a good clip instead of creeping along and sliding sideways. This one would self sail just right without having to tie the rudder so all I had to do was push the tiller a little while my wife wordlessly reached up from her warm sailcloth nest and backed the forestaysail with her foot for each tack. We sailed all night in the clear air with the water sparkling in the moonlight around us. The next day was wonderfully clear too and they dug sand fleas and caught the delicious pompanos off the seaside and fried them for our lunch while I snoozed in the warm sand. Dang, I believe I'll go try to lose that skiff again.

An Unfortunate Incident

in which sleeping in a state park leads to a headache

Back when I was still sporadically attending college, I had to go to a special marine biology class that was located down in the Keys. They had all these arrangements made that, to me, looked like they were too expensive. My college methods were sort of like my boatbuilding methods . . . outlaw. Some of the textbooks were a little bit overpriced in my opinion so I checked them out of the library. Colleges are pretty slick and I think they get a cut so usually the textbooks are "for reference only." Fortunately, they have some nice chairs in there and it didn't take long for me to cull my way through most of them (good thing marine biologists don't have to take calculus). This story doesn't have anything to do with that though. I was just trying to show how tight I am about unnecessary expenditures in the pursuit of education . . . something that should, in my opinion, be more widely distributed within the public systems of this great nation.

So, they had us all lined up to eat in restaurants and sleep in motels and ride in chartered boats to and from the research grounds. This was winter quarter in the Keys . . . the top of the big-money season for those predacious people down there. Like I've said, I am an experienced beach camper and I'll be damned if I'll sleep in no telling who-all's bed and pay for the privilege when I can crawl into the bushes under the Australian pines with my own good old fragrant sleeping bag and I'll be damned if I'll pay big money to ride in somebody else's Boston Whaler and I'll be damned if I'll sit in a restaurant and pay big money to eat a fish just exactly like the one I saw swimming around the pilings of the patio while I was waiting for the maître d' to find me a table. No sir.

So, me and another poverty-stricken GI Bill drove down there and pulled a little aluminum boat on a trailer behind his VW. It was the middle of the night when we got there and, though I was positive that I could find us a good place to hide when I could see to reconnoiter a little bit, we were tired so we dipped into a little state park that allowed camping. The damn place was absolutely full. I mean, the cars and tents were so close together that you had to wedge between them. The man at the gate said that there was only one other space and boy, it is good that we had a Bug and a tiny boat because when we finally got off the road, we both had to climb out the sun-roof because there wasn't enough room to open the doors. The only place to sleep was under the boat trailer but Bill and I were ready. We crawled under there and went immediately to sleep. About two thirty or so in the middle of the night, I heard something fall into my boat. It sounded exactly like a car battery that had been dropped about twenty feet. I boiled out from under there to see what was what only to find that it wasn't something that had fallen into the boat at all but something that had risen up under the bottom of it. Bill had been sleeping with his head a little too close to the trailer tire and . . . this big old dog . . . right in the ear. Jesus, you ought to have seen the dent.

Sheephead Head Soup

*in which there are the natural histories of two fish and a worm
and . . . yet another recipe*

Back in the midsixties while I was in college, I worked for this mad researcher who was trying to eradicate corn ear worms on the island of St. Croix. He figured, if he could do that, then he would know just what it would take to do it to the whole American continent and corn ear worms are the number one agricultural pest. I won't go all into it, but corn ear worms don't confine themselves to the hairy end of corn but eat tomatoes, tobacco, soybeans, and almost anything else. If it hadn't been for corn ear worms, there would have been no need for all that DDT.

At first I lived with the entomologist who was pushing this project, but his family was due to arrive as soon as the school summer vacation started back in the States so I moved out into a little derelict trailer that was on some land owned by a resident biologist at the experiment station. I wasn't sorry to leave, either. Though he was nice, the man with the grant didn't want to talk about anything but corn ear worms and the only thing he ever ate was peanut butter sandwiches. I moved to where the conversation was interesting and the food was exquisite and I'll get to that here in a minute. There were two of those trailers in an old abandoned mango plantation on top of a high hill. Mine wasn't level but, fortunately, the wall side of the bed was down so I wouldn't roll out. Sleeping for a little time was all I needed to do in there. The only trouble was that I would wake up in the middle of the night and imagine that the damn thing had gotten a flat tire on the low side and was fixing to tumble down the hill into the Caribbean Sea.

The other trailer had been fixed up pretty good. The occupants had leveled it up and hooked up the electricity. The people who rented that one were Manny and Ivan. They were there in St. Croix working on the building boom that they had before those terrorists shot those golfers down at Fountain Valley and put the quietus on tourism in St. Croix, maybe forever. Manny was from St. Martin on the French side and Ivan was from Saba. Back in the sixties, though a man could eke out a living on those islands (and from the sea), there was no way to make any money, so industrious men from all over the Lesser Antilles went someplace to work for as long as they could stand to stay away from home.

Ivan was lonesome. He showed me photographs of his family and his little house and farm. He had a sweet-looking, bashful wife and two sweet-looking, bashful girls and a very small house on the windward side (indeed in the town of Windward Side) of the mountain. You know, Saba is an interesting-looking place. It is an extinct (we hope) volcano and the only level ground is in the bottom of the crater (indeed, the town of Bottom). Ivan's house was jacked up in the front about twelve feet and was clinging to the cliff with the back side. He had a little white picket fence about a foot from the road and about a foot from the front of the house. There was no room for any steps so they had to climb up to the back door from the road. But there was room for his little bashful crew to stand looking over the fence at the camera so Ivan would have something to remember them by while he was working in St. Croix to better their situation. He remembered them, too, I tell you. I think he was weighing the value of this money he was making.

Manny was a different kind of man. Though he had a wife and what looked like about twelve children back on the French side (you know, St. Martin belongs half to France and half to the Netherlands and ain't neither one got much), he also had a girlfriend in Christiansted. I never met the woman, but sometimes Manny would come home to the trailer and take a quick little dip and doll himself up with so much perfume that I don't see how he could keep his eyes open to drive. But he could drive. He had spent some of that money he was supposed to take home to his wife and shoeless children on a car. It was an old Volkswagen and I rode to town with him once. Not only was the perfume just about deadly, but Manny couldn't drive worth a flip. I mean, the man had no notion that a car could be turned over. He didn't pay attention to where he was going or to what the car was doing. He was always wandering from one ditch to the other. If it hadn't been so dangerous, it would have been comical. It was as if he never realized where he was heading until he got there, then, when he felt the tires drop off the pavement he would get very surprised and snatch the wheel, then drive contentedly over on the other side and hit that ditch. And he changed gears the same way. He would start off in first and, when the poor car got to going as fast as it would go in that gear, he would peer down at the accelerator pedal (one of those with the roller for your foot) and mash a little harder, peer at it some more, mash some more, then get a surprised look on his face and begin to peer at the gearshift lever and clutch. Finally he would change gears and act very satisfied with himself until he realized that the car had stopped accelerating again. Damn thing had four gears. It was a trip. My first trip in that car was my last but I don't think Ivan knew any better, because he had never ridden in any other car but Manny's.

Ivan and Manny only worked six days a week (pouring concrete for a new hotel, now empty) but I had to work seven. The completion of my day's work was a borderline business, I tell you. I had to check these little sticky moth traps (you know, corn ear worms are the caterpillars of a moth, *Heliothis zea*) every day and there was one on every square mile of the island. I had this old tore-up, raggedy Ford station wagon that the researcher had leased, and I drove it all over the place full of these horribly sticky traps (I kept a rag hanging out of the gas hole to wipe my hands). If I started before daylight and drove like a bat-out-of-hell and ran through the bushes like a wild hog to change out traps, I could barely get through in time to catch five or six hours' sleep before it was time to haul ass again. I had to eat peanut butter sandwiches on the run.

On Sunday, Manny and Ivan drove in Manny's car to the rocky cliffs on the Fredericksted end of the island and climbed down and caught parrot fish on their handlines. You know, the people of the Caribbean don't fool with reels and rods. They just buy a spool of about twenty-pound monofilament and slip a big lead on the end of the line, tie on a hook, bust open a soldier (a pretty big, very aggressive, terrestrial hermit crab), and let fly. The line spirals off the end of the spool like a spinning reel. The favorite fish of those folks is parrot fish but they'll eat most any snapper, squirrel fish, wrasse, moray eel, grouper, triggerfish, barracuda, tarpon, grunt, angelfish, cowfish . . . most anything but they would rather have a parrot fish and they are expert at catching that particular critter too. A parrot fish is, next to a sheep-head, the most adept of bait stealers. They are set up just like a parrot in the mouth and, if you dive and watch them, they eat like a parrot . . . nibble skillfully at little things and separate out the good part, like the bait, and let the trash (like the hook) fall. "You have to pull just before he bites" is the advice of experts like Ivan and Manny to frustrated newcomers to the sport.

Anyway, they would catch parrot fish and bring them back to the trailer and invite me over for supper on Sunday night. I was delighted to get to go, too, even though that little weekly visit cut me back to about three hours of sleep that night. They had a tiny, travel-trailer-sized propane gas stove and a tiny black-and-white television set and were very proud of both. As soon as they saw me drive up to my little cattywompus outfit in the old sticky car, they would ceremoniously come up and invite me for supper. "We will watch the television set while we cook supper," they always announced.

First, they scaled the parrot fish (very big scales) head and all. Then they gutted him, being very careful to excise the rectum without any waste. Then they would put him into their pot and parboil him (or her or them) on the stove while they washed and cut up the salad and the ingredients of the soup. They did this part of the preparation sitting on their chairs pulled up, along with mine, which I had brought from my trailer, in a semicircle around the TV, which sat on a wire spool in the middle of the tiny living quarters of the little trailer. It was the Ed Sullivan show, and they would marvel at the spectacle of the likes of Topo Gigio, the little Italian rat, various acrobats, and Shari Lewis talking lip-to-lip with Lambchops (at that, Manny would hitch at his britches and pronounce her "A very attractive woman, no?"). I saw the Beatles for the first time with Ivan and Manny, who did not appear to understand the significance of the great event and I am afraid I even dozed off for a few "Yeah, Yeah, Yeahs" myself. There was no TV on St. Martin or Saba back then, so everything on there was a big deal to those poor fellows. Now, I am going to stop right here and tell you something: I can't see the point to all this luxury. I bet you any amount of money that Ivan was just as overjoyed to get back behind his picket fence with his little family as John Lennon was to get back to the hotel with Yoko. Pure joy is about as far as you can go . . . ain't no point in over-accessorizing it.

Anyway, back to the recipe: They always made two dishes for Sunday supper. They sat there on their chairs and carefully picked all the meat off those parrot fish. They had two plastic bowls and they put the meat off the bodies of the fish into one and the skin and the meat of the heads in the other. They even separated the vertebrae (parrot fish have very big bones) and extracted the spinal nerve to put into the head bowl. They didn't waste a thing. There wasn't enough left on the bones to interest a mongoose when they got through picking. They made a salad with the meat of the body of the fish and put the head meat back in the pot with the broth, added some onions and other things to make a soup. I am going to have to interrupt the smooth flow of this narrative again. You just think you know what's gourmet fare if you have never eaten what people like Manny and Ivan have for Sunday supper every week. The salad was variable in its content depending on availability, but onions and lime juice were always in there. Sometimes they would have some little raw green beans and usually a can of garbanzos. Any kind of fresh, raw greens might go in and always plenty of pepper and salt. It really didn't make all that much difference . . . the parrot fish was the best part.

The soup from the head was the next course. Except for the fish, onions were the main thing in there. The rind of the lime that was squeezed for the salad was cut up in there too. I think, sometimes, a red or yellow bell pepper might have been included and maybe some celery or maybe some carrots. Though the ingredients of the two dishes were similar, the results were completely different. But both of them were absolutely delicious. I always went home and slept like I had been bitten by a tsetse fly.

Now, I am from the Deep South (born and raised in a brier patch about two miles north of the Florida line). These people down here are fried fish fiends. They'll bake a flounder every now and then and grill the steaks of a big fish like a cobio (cobia, ling), but what they really like to do is to shake the salted and peppered fillets in cornmeal and fry them in deep peanut oil. If you put the fillets in, skin-side down, the vaporization of the water will bubble the skin away from the meat and the fillets will turn over all by themselves when the time comes. If done right it ain't half bad either, and the first time I went to Sunday supper, I couldn't believe what Manny and Ivan were doing. I thought that the hardworking, po fellas were doing their fish that way because they just couldn't afford any frying oil (any store-bought anything was very expensive in St. Croix). I certainly learned my lesson. They did it like that because that's the best way to do it.

Sheephead Head Soup

You need at least one sheephead head. Sheepheads are just about the equivalent of parrot fish around here. They both eat little things that they find living on rocks or pilings or boats . . . things like barnacles, little mussels, oyster spat, little shrimp, crabs, worms, and amphipods. They, like parrot fish, have strong muscles in their heads that enable them not only to bite hard, but to wiggle their jaw from side to side to separate the good from the bad. They have the most human-looking teeth of any fish and, inside their mouths, they have little nubbin teeth all over their palate that they use to grind up hard shells and fishhooks. Sheepheads are very good fish no matter how you cook them, but like parrot fish, they have very big bones and the boneless part of the fillet winds up mighty small considering the extent of what's left. Anyone who throws away the backbone of a sheephead is extravagantly wasteful and anybody who throws away the head is crazy. Cut out the gills and simmer the whole head in salty water (I use seawater, but that depends on where you live). I like to put a lime rind in there, too, with a whole onion and some peppercorns. There is no need to try to scale the head because, unlike parrot fish, it is impossible; besides, the skin comes off very easily after the head is poached.

After you get the head simmered for about an hour, let it cool enough so you can hitch your little chrome-plated steel chair with the thin vinyl cushion right up close to the TV and you and your roommate can watch the show while you pick out the meat. You'll be astonished at what you get. The head of a fish is not actually a solid skull but many small, barely attached plates of bone separated by discrete muscles. The eyeball muscles are even easy to get out and there is a jelly around the eyeball itself that is very good. The cooking solidifies the lens of the eye until it is about like a dried lentil and too hard to eat, but the rest enhances the soup most excellently. The jaws and teeth, when cleaned, dried, and put back together, are an interesting ornament. My sister has a set on the windowsill of the pantry and even the prissiest of passersby cannot escape a double take. Family members all exclaim, "Jesus, that looks exactly like your momma after Dr. Gravely scraped off the pyorrhea."

After you get it all picked out, put the meat back in the pot with the onions (leeks will work fine), lime rinds, and whatever else you have scratched up. (Ain't nothing wrong with a little cauliflower and some celery either. I like to season with red and black pepper and that hot Hungarian paprika—can't go wrong). Stew it for long enough to cook the onions down (don't hurt to fry them in a little olive oil to hurry up the process) and then dip yourself up a little bowl. You'll see. Don't eat it all, though.

Cold sheephead head soup is a marvelous thing. It jells into the most wonderful consommé. It kind of stratifies before it solidifies and the pepper settles to the bottom. If you can get it out in one piece, it is best to turn it over so you can see exactly where to cut . . . might be a scale on the bottom.

Sheepheads

The actual accepted common name is sheepshead but people who live where sheepshead live call them "sheepheads." You know how your momma told you not to cross your eyes because they might stick that way? I think if you say "sheepshead" too much, you might develop a bad lisp.

Anyway, sheepheads are good-sized (two or three pounds on the average) bream-shaped saltwater fish with alternating black and white vertical stripes. Sheepheads have a mighty sheepish-looking face. They usually hang around in small groups of two or three but sometimes there will be twenty or so hiding out in a hole or under the pilings of a dock. Though they will wander along the seaside beach right in the surf looking for mole crabs and *Donax* (the genus of little bivalves that tourists call "coquinas"), they like to hang out around objects like stumps and rocks. They love oyster bars and will hang around a big stingaree while he is digging so as to steal a snack. I have seen sheepheads biting barnacles off big horse conchs and *Busycon* conchs. They don't work very hard at anything and are very fat . . . absolutely delicious. Sheepheads are highly prized by expert inshore fishermen like me. They would be extinct if they weren't so hard to catch.

You are really beginning to approach becoming as capable as your ignorant ancestors when you can catch a sheephead. I won't go into how hard it is to do with a hook and line. There are some people who can actually do it but they keep their own counsel. I have caught one or two like that but I ain't got the patience to sit there and snatch and cuss for hours and hours. I throw the cast net over them. They are very alert and fast, but, if the conditions are right, they can be caught. What you have to do is catch them when the water is cloudy enough that you can barely see them and they can't see you throw. The water has to be deep, too, or they'll dart when the net hits the water and run out from under it. They dart a distance that is inverse to the depth of the water. If it is shallow, they'll run clean away, if it is medium-deep, they'll probably run just outside the drop of the leads. If it is deep, they'll just give a little twitch and let the net settle, most satisfactorily, over them. Sheepheads don't act like most fish when they realize that something has got them. They don't tear around inside the net like crazy, they just bristle up and stick right where they are. (Black drum do that same thing. I once caught one of those, in an eight-foot net, that must have weighed thirty pounds.) With that, I am going to let you in on my little secret. When the tide runs out, sheepheads congregate in deep holes and wait. If you know where the holes are and can get back in there . . . and manage not to get hung up (takes a lot of boggy research) . . . you can hit the jackpot. Dang, I wish Ivan and Manny could come for supper.

Panty Hose

*in which, though there is no real profanity, the story evokes
graphic images in the imagination and may be unsuitable
for young people or adults of a prissy nature*

I think Lyndon Johnson was still president when the mini skirt and the panty hose came into fashion for some women. I remember those inventions because they became the subject of some curiosity for me when I was in college. Other feminine decorations of the time were white lipstick, big hair, and white cowboy boots but those are beyond the scope of this study.

There was a very short time while mini skirts were at the height of their popularity when women still wore individual stockings held up by cloth belts with little dangling straps that had buttons and wire clips on the ends. Each wire clip retained a little pucker of the stocking material in encapsulation around the little button. This union tied the stockings to the little straps and so to a little elastic belt on the woman. Though it sounds complicated in words, the combination was simple, reliable, and easy to handle. I always thought of it as the Marlene Dietrich rig and remember it fondly. There was quite a bit of bare skin between the little dangling straps above the tops of the stockings and, as the mini skirts became shorter, this nakedness was often exposed to plain sight. It was a nifty time in the evolution of fashion. The daring of some of the young ladies at the college where I studied was astonishing. Lots of the little skirts were too short to touch the chair when these people sat down. An attentive listener could catch the chirp of flesh on Formica as seats were taken at the beginning of class and a careful observer could occasionally see an ephemeral bit of fog condensed on some of the polished chair bottoms as we rose at the completion of the lecture, sort of like the fabled "green flash" that sometimes follows sundown in some places. Though I have looked for it all my long life, I have never seen the green flash. I have seen the ephemeral fog . . . but it's been a long time.

This condition of dress (the mini skirt without the panty hose) lasted for just the briefest time. The intriguing peculiarities of the combination were completely ruined by the unbelievable popularity of the panty hose. I will always remember the horror of my first encounter with this garment. As I was trudging to class up the stairs of the building where I was forced to take

French in order to better communicate with the other herpetologists of the world, I happened to glance upward and there was this young person in a mini skirt on the stairs above me. Before I was able to politely avert my eyes, I observed a deformity of the crotch the likes of which I had never seen before. There was not only a horrible asymmetry to it, but the whole business was stretched way out of shape and was twitching inhumanly far below its proper place. It worried me so badly that I was unable to concentrate on my French recitation and received several patronizing corrections from the teenage graduate student the college had foisted off on us in lieu of a certified teacher.

Further research revealed the facts of the matter, but in no way removed the horror. I found out that what I had seen was the cursed panty hose in its primitive form. I found that the sight of the crotch of one of these garments . . . stretched wide . . . several inches below the hem of a mini skirt . . . alternating its wrinkles as it twitched cattywompusly with each step became only too common. I can't imagine even Marlene enslaving the most pitiful wretch by the use of such a tool. I even found out the reason for the asymmetrical appearance when I found a pair of the hideous things hanging, abandoned, in a bush in the fire lane that serves as my driveway. By careful poking with a stick, I discovered that these trouser-hose were just a pair of ordinary stockings sewn together with an overlap where they met and a gap in the top to get in or out of. The overlap was what made things look lopsided and deformed. I was not relieved by the discovery.

Now the damn things are everywhere and I still don't understand the reason for their popularity. Not only are they unattractive but they must be impractical because, if someone tears up one leg of a pair, the whole thing is done for, whereas old-fashioned stockings may be replaced one at a time as they are destroyed. One of my sisters, whose job requires the wearing of some kind of stocking or other (a social injustice that ought to be looked into), has a ragged old car with springs sticking out of the seat and old license tags covering the rusty holes in the floor. This car eats up stockings. For a while she wore the disgusting panty hose to work. She drives that old car because she is a little tight with her money. She discovered that damaged panty hose could be fitted with a new leg by cutting the old one off and stuffing the good half of another ruined pair down through the hole. This meant that she had to wear a double layer of the wretched britches part, but at least she had two presentable legs for a little while. The trouble with this system was that the right leg was the one that was consistently eaten by the car . . . Not to be thwarted, my parsimonious sister just put the two left halves together with one foot heading to work and the other heading back home. She just gave one of them half a twist as she put it on. It made a wrinkle up her leg that looked sort of like the lateral line on a flounder but it passed for a stocking. She finally resolved the whole mess by getting a letter from her good doctor saying that she shouldn't wear that kind of crap for health reasons. I am glad that she did because, not only are panty hose unattractive, impractical, and, judging from the specimen in the bush in my drive . . . unhygienic, they are also dangerous.

A friend of mine who had put off his foreign language requirement until he was ready to defend his doctoral dissertation found that the only way he could make it all the way from French class to the graduate school on time was to ride a bicycle. One day he was wheeling through the crowded sidewalks of the student union with his ocarina to his lips and an acquaintance on the handlebars. This girl had on the uniform of the day . . . mini skirt and sagging panty hose. Somehow the sagging part of the panty hose just touched the spinning front tire of the bicycle and, before you could say "Jackie Robinson," had made about eighteen wraps all the way around. After the poor girl's ankles were quickly tied tightly to the front forks down by the axle by the twisted panty hose, the bicycle stopped and pitched them both headfirst into a big concrete flower pot with a scraggly juniper bush in it. My friend was able to climb out, but the poor girl was completely immobilized by the hard twisted nylon rope that used to be her panty hose and used to be, partially at least, pulled up but were now pulled all the way down and twisted greasily around and around the axle and cinched tightly into the flesh of her ankles. All she could do was to cling, sullenly, to the rim of the concrete flower pot while my friend carefully tried to cut this hard nylon thong in those close quarters with a tiny scalpel from his dissecting kit. To make matters worse, a well-meaning passerby mistook what he was seeing for some kind of assault or other and began an attempt at rescue. My friend said that it was very hard to do an operation much more delicate than excising the rectum of an oyster while this fella was beating him over the head with the ceramic ocarina. By the time it was all over, the poor girl's toes were purple and her naked rump had been ogled by hundreds of people and my friend had bumps all over his head.

Harmless though the mini skirt, white lipstick, big hairdo, and white cowboy boots were, they now only exist in vestigial form whereas the dangerous panty hose are everywhere. They dangle perpetually from the teeth of giant front-end loaders at landfills all over the world. Panty hose by-products are surfacing. Precious babies cuddle teddy bears stuffed with the disgusting things. In the newspaper, home economists smugly proclaim that the best way to preserve the delicate crop of sweet Vidalia onions is to suspend them in the kitchen in a pair of worn-out panty hose. I, for one, do not find the lumpy suspensions such a sweet sight. One old man I knew kept a big white oak snake in a pair hanging in his fig tree to keep the birds away while the figs were getting ready. The poor snake spent all his time climbing from one leg to the other. "Would have kept Jesus away from the second coming" was what his wife had to say. Convenience stores all over the country are routinely robbed by scum made unrecognizable by panty hose pulled down over their heads. I saw a video of one such robbery where the man had his head in one leg while the other hung down his back sort of like a skanky bridal veil. As I watched the video, I was puzzled by a white spot on the back of his neck. That was how I was introduced to the "cotton crotch panel." My own mother used the ruins of the miserable panty hose to strap wild epiphytic orchids to trees in her yard as part of a lifetime of futile attempts to move them to the high pine woods from the river swamp where they naturally lived. I always thought that the sight of a pair of torn-up panty hose (the point of junction of the two legs stuffed with the moss that formed the substrate for the attachment rhizomes of the plant and the legs tied around the tree in a hideous sort of amplexus) distracted the eyes of the observer from the beauty of the orchid . . . but not my mother. She thought that she had found a very practical way to recycle the terrible things and used them for that purpose until she died . . . I can still see the expressions on the faces of our visitors as they stared, pop-eyed, at the orchid experiment. I believe my mother's legendary hardheadedness explains her association with the awful things. I will not speculate on the reason for the inexplicable popularity of panty hose with so many others.

Some things have changed since my college days. Now my friend is the world's authority on the bowels of pelecypods. He doesn't know what happened to the girl, the bicycle, or his ocarina. The crab apple bush in my driveway that was unfortunate enough to catch the discarded pair of panty hose that I first examined with the stick is now, in spite of its contamination, grown into a healthy tree. If I am careful of the thorns I can push the branches apart and see the cursed things still hanging from the little dead snag where they caught so many years ago. They still look the same . . . as good as new. The orchid experiment is over and all evidence of it is . . . I hope . . . gone from the pine trees on the hill. The juniper bush in the concrete pot never recovered and was replaced by a pyrecantha about the time Richard Nixon took over. Now women everywhere wear dresses with enough cloth in them to make draperies for a whole funeral home. I guess they do it for the mystery effect. Ain't no mystery to me what they have on up under all that and it can stay there, too.

Stylettes

in which we find that the race does not always go to the swift

A long time ago I went to various colleges and universities off and on just to see if it was possible to learn stuff that way (which it was but there was a lot of static noise filling in the vast spaces between gems of wisdom). I had to do it on the cheap because I was still building boats and working at various jobs to pay the damn tuition and buy the overpriced textbooks . . . unless they had them at the library. When I was doing my undergraduate work in biology and chemistry and all, sometimes I slept in my sleeping bag behind the boxwood hedge in front of the Conradi Building, which was the main biological edifice at FSU in Florida's capital city. Nobody ever noticed that there was a homeless man there. It was a very convenient place to camp. Some times somebody would throw a beer bottle back in there amongst me but I never actually got hit. A roosting Joeree crapped on me a time or two but the bathrooms in the building were very nice and I became pretty good buddies with the building custodian with whom I sometimes sucked up a pitcher of draft beer at the "Long Branch" (Yes Virginia, there was a Miss Kitty) right across the street. I even made a little money cooking breakfast for the late-night drunks at a little greasy spoon within twenty yards of my hideout, which visiting dignitaries sometimes frequented while they were down there by the university trying to eyeball some chicks. I even got a fair-sized tip from some of them while the euphoria was still on them but you know at three thirty in the morning, that's fading fast. I hate to see a state legislator or other elected official trying to cut up a link-style sausage with the wrong side of a knife, don't you?

All that doesn't have anything to do with the story, though. I was just trying to set the scene. So, I finally finagled my way into the marine biology graduate school. I wanted to be an oceanographer like Jacques Cousteau with my own *Calypso* and a PBY (that's the beautiful Catalina flying boat of World War Two) and a whole bunch of young people listening to every word I said as if I was a Florida state legislator or guest lecturer hot on the town. Of course nothing ever turns out to be exactly as planned. I did turn out to be an oceanographer but my *Calypso* is a little skiffboat and my PBY must have leaked and sunk. I do have a batch of young people but they don't pay any attention to anything I say even when I am wearing my tiny black wool bathing suit. I learned a lot in graduate school, though. One time this other graduate student and I wound up on a shrimp boat. I think he was fixing to write a "paper" and get it published so it would become a reference in the "literature" for thousands of the papers of other marine biologists. He was that kind of person. Me, on the other hand, I just wanted to see what-all came up in the net. This was a deep-water vessel we were on and they were going way out around the Florida Middle Ground, which is a peculiar anomaly in the middle of the Gulf of Mexico where the Gulf Loop Current circles around after it comes up through the Yucatan Channel. Somehow the loop keeps the water there more tropical than one would expect from its latitude and there are many peculiar creatures who live there. The water of the Middle Ground is not deep enough for those real deep-water peculiarities with lanterns and things on their heads but there are many tropical species and . . . sometimes the shrimp called "royal reds," which are great big red shrimp worth about three times what normal shrimp are worth. It takes determination and a specially rigged boat to drag the Middle Ground. Because of its tropical nature, there is a lot of coral there to tear up the nets and some government entity dumped a lot of trash and bombs and stuff there, too. There is at least one pile of concrete culverts that I heard has spiny lobsters as big as a Clumber spaniel living in them. I wouldn't know about that but I do know about Captain Junior.

Junior had about five shrimp boats and a reckless but tightwad nature. He hired some of the most derelict deckhands I ever saw. I think he got some of them straight out of jail. One way to tell a Junior boat was that it never came in until it was time to pay off. I guess he was afraid his crew would skip out so the boats always anchored off during the day when they were working the bay (you know, shrimp boats in the Gulf drag at night and snooze during the day) instead of coming in to port. Old Junior used to love to go offshore to try to drag up some royal reds and kept one of his boats rigged to do that. Junior and my mother were good friends. Momma used to have a party every now and then and he would come and bring a little something to make it special. I mean, one wedding party Momma threw had bulldozer lobsters. I don't know if you know that species of animal but they don't look anything like any other kind of lobster. They look more like a big isopod (you know, a roly-poly or pill bug) but they are genuine decapod crustaceans like all lobsters and are extremely good to eat. They don't have any claws or thorax hardly . . . all tail and most wonderfully flavored. You only get to eat bulldozers if you are good buddies with an offshore shrimper.

Anyway, one of the professors at the marine biology school was talking about the aloof attitude of the few shrimpers who would fish the Middle Ground and how biologically significant the bycatch would be and how valuable a trip on such a boat would be to any graduate student who could finagle him- or herself on board for a trip. "I know one of them offshore shrimpers," I recklessly chirped. "I bet I can get him to take me and maybe some other people, too." Well, instantly (even though I had explained the primitivity and social peculiarities of shrimp boat society) I had a bunch of volunteers so I went to see Captain Junior and worked a con. To make a long story short, finally the volunteers dwindled down to me and this one other guy who was the most serious and dedicated of the graduate students. All the others were studying marine biology mostly for the ambience, I guess. There were at least three girls who declared that they were majoring in "delphinology" (the study of dolphins . . .) and there were some clownfish aficionados and a few sea turtle experts and such but this other guy and I were a good bit older and had more universal interests. So I conned the two of us on with Junior for a trip to the Middle Ground as unpaid hands.

It was an easy ride out there. It was just us and the captain and a deckhand who appeared to be a refugee from some kind of special-ed class. He was a little too honest in the face . . . you know what I am talking about? He was very shy and did not do too much talking. Of course Junior told a lot of stories, which was his nature. He told about the time he came across a bale of marijuana that had been floating out there so long that it had goose barnacles on the down side. He grappled it on board and, when he finished his trip, turned the soggy bale in to the sheriff. The next trip, he heard his deckhand (not this open-faced kid) complaining that his last nickel bag stank like something dead and had a barnacle in it. Junior decided that if the sheriff was going to sell them floaters he might as well bypass the middle man so the next time he found one he spread it out on top of the deckhouse and dried it out and sacked it up and passed it out among his no-account crew for distribution on the halves-share method and made three thousand bucks. "Of course, Charlie over there wouldn't have anything to do with nothing like that."

Finally we got to the Middle Ground and began to drag. I won't go into what it was like but it was pitiful. The deep trawling killed everything in the net but a few shrimp. There were all sorts of dead animals in each trawl and a few very big shrimp but overall the trip was a real bust . . . didn't even find a floating bale. The graduate student spent the whole time preserving specimens in jars of formaldehyde and explaining the mysteries of biology to everybody including me. The deckhand showed him a shrimp and said, "That's a pretty big bug right there ain't it?" "Well, actually bugs are arthropods with sucking mouthparts," the graduate student pontificated. "Like mosquitoes?" the deckhand asked. "No," the graduate student explained. "Actually mosquitoes don't suck. Their mouthparts are twin, barbed stylettes that slide back and forth beside each other and penetrate into the integument of the animal from whom they are seeking blood, and when the stylettes penetrate a blood vessel, even as small as a capillary, the blood flows between the perfectly mated surfaces of the two stylettes by capillary action and is drawn into the esophagus in that manner." "Both my sisters are stylettes," proclaimed the deckhand. "They are twins, too . . . been fixing hair ever since they got out of high school."

Epilogue

The deckhand was drafted to Vietnam and became a helicopter medic and is now a vascular surgeon at the Mayo Clinic in Jacksonville. The graduate student got his PhD and wrote a bunch of papers about blood chemistry in *Limulus* (the genus of horseshoe crabs). I went back into the skiffboat business. Captain Junior died at a ripe old age . . . still shrimping. The two stylettes own a whole chain of beauty parlors covering three North Florida counties. You have probably seen them . . . you know, La La's Beauty Shoppe . . . remember they were identical twins.

The Jimmy of the Hole

*in which I realize the value of acting like
the most formidable-looking arthropod*

By late summer crabs have already finished their reproductive doings. They do it all summer long. The males hang out up in tidal creeks and pools in the marsh. They like it where there is a pretty good current running and, indeed, bury themselves when nothing is moving. If you wade up a creek at either low or high slack water or even a good bit before or after, you would swear that there are no crabs in there at all . . . unless you step on one and then, you'll "swear" all right . . . between the wails and whimpers. I have always been interested in anything to do with blue crabs (*Calinectes sapidus* . . . "beautiful swimmer"). I like everything about them. I like their outlook on life and I'll explain that, too, directly. Anyway, when I started going to college, one of the first things I did was to try to lie and connive and manipulate around all I could to circumvent what they called "basic studies" so I could get to where the valuable knowledge was disseminated. I found out that there was this one professor who had degenerated down or graduated up the echelon to the point where he did not deign to teach basic studies. You had to be in graduate school to find out what he knew and he knew plenty. He had been born and raised on the Chesapeake (Tangier Island) and made a lifetime specialty of the denizens of bays and marshes. Though he was a grumpy and, in most social situations, uncommunicative man, he was the world's expert on blue crabs and very famous in the field of the genetics of many other sea creatures. I don't remember how I managed to get into graduate school before I finished silly psychology, ridiculous "humanities," or absolutely unnecessary English (certainly not any foreign language and absolutely no PE) but I did. I was a good bit older than the kids in college and, though I had not fully matriculated, I was not ignorant so I guess people just made some erroneous assumptions. I jimmied my way into graduate school and the first class I took was estuarine science (the study of all things connected with a place where fresh and salt water mix). Needless to say, this old Chesapeake denizen was the head booger of that section. I quickly found out that he was not overwhelmingly eager to take an eager young (?) student under his wing and quickly explain everything he knew (boats for one thing). You had to go through the ritual. His method was to stand up behind a podium and read his doctoral dissertation from when he had been in graduate school back in the late thirties. I remember a little of it . . . something to do with the genetics of pelecypods. I think he was the first person to look at the chromosomes of a clam under a microscope. Altogether it would have been a waste of time (and hard-earned money) but he had to pad it out to fill out a whole quarter's worth of time and could be sidetracked by a cleverly worded question. It didn't take me long to find out what I wanted to know. I know most of you have read Robert Warren's *Beautiful Swimmer* but if you haven't, I advise you to. It is a good book and in there is about a tenth of what that old man knew about crabs.

Grown male crabs don't wander all over the place. They fight for the best location. Competition in the little creeks of the marsh between the male crabs is a terrible (horrible) thing. Because of that, there are way fewer male blue crabs in the world than there are females. Not only do the bigger crabs chase the littler ones back out on the flats, they kill and eat them every chance they get. The little ones are relentless, though, and so the big ones get bigger and fatter. My professor said that there were no bigger blue crabs anywhere than in the Chesapeake Bay. The whole time I was associated with him I tried to prove him wrong. One time I was wading up a little creek running into the bay (Apalachee Bay in the Gulf of Mexico . . . almost as big as the Chesapeake and not as confined and polluted . . . yet) down between the St. Marks and Aucilla Rivers. I had my cast net all made up so if I saw some mullet I could try to catch them. The tide was running out and when I came around a bend, I saw a crab so big it looked like his wingspan was two feet. Even though he was standing by an oyster bar, I threw the net. I caught the crab and about fifty sharp oysters, which I gingerly had to pick out of the net without cutting too many holes in it. As soon as I got him out (he bit me through the thumbnail so bad that it has a deformity that causes a perennial split to this day) I put him in the bucket and trotted straight to the old man's office and poured him out on the desk. It is funny how old men get hardheaded and refuse to acknowledge that things are not exactly as they thought. He never admitted that that was the biggest crab he ever saw but it was the biggest one I ever saw. Do you think I have him in a jar of formaldehyde waiting for universal recognition by the big crab committee? Hell no. I ate him. Crabs are one of those things like mullet and (judging from the antics of the Japanese) tuna that are better when they are big. I am not interested in any world records but I am interested in eating a big Jimmycrab anytime I can.

The best time is in the late summer but I hate to bother them when they are in a tender social situation. When the current starts running to suit him, the biggest male crab around comes out of his hiding place and places himself strategically at the narrowest place in the creek. He likes to stay close to a deep hole so, if something more dangerous than he is comes along, he can dart into the deep water and bury himself, but until that happens he stands there with his arms outstretched facing the incoming traffic. His needs are few. If a fish or little Jimmy comes along, he'll swat with both claws and maybe catch him and, if so, he'll hide and eat him. If a little virgin female crab comes up the creek . . . Think about that for a minute. Here he is, one of the most formidable and certainly the most intimidating looking of the arthropods, standing there looking like . . . well, I have to tell you that I have adopted the ways of the blue crab. I think it is attitude that gets one by in this world. If you act timid, little dogs will bite you on the ass. If you play meek, you will not inherit the earth but will be putty in the hands of people possibly less capable than you are. My advice is to stand up and act like the Jimmy of the hole. You don't have to actually engage in any hideous slaughter or be the object of hideous slaughter but if you act like a crab, people will give a little thought before they impose their wishes upon you. Back when I first got out of the Navy and started looking for something to do to enable the boatbuilding business, I discovered that there was a trend for house trailer manufacturers to come down here from Indiana because down here there were no unions. For some reason, there was a boom in the demand for trailers and the factories that they threw up all over the place couldn't meet that demand. These canny Indianans soon discovered that the usual slow pace of the normal Georgia workingman, though it came cheap, was not exactly what they wanted at that particular booming time. They instituted a system of piecework that, for extremely hard work and some skill, would pay a man pretty good. It was a vicious way to run a factory. All these men were in direct competition all the time. Some of them, like Jimmy of the hole, were very dangerous. I couldn't resist, though, so I crabbed my way right in there among them. Though I do not like to fight and hate like hell to get my teeth knocked out, I know exactly how to play Jimmy. In a confrontational situation, I sashayed myself into the middle of the narrowest place and spread my arms out as wide as I could. If some fool made like he was going to approach, I would make a hard slashing feint with my two-foot-long twenty-ounce straight-claw hammer. Though my act was so effective that I never had to go to Jimmy's next step, I was ready. I already had my hiding place picked out and was ready to scurry to the side. I was going to get back to how powerful the reproductive instinct must be in crabs but I need to tell you exactly how effective my masquerade actually is. Another thing I used to do to make a little boatbuilding money was to drive a semi truck to New York City (yes, Virginia) and unload a whole load of South Florida produce. Like the piecework at the trailer factory, it paid pretty good. Nobody is going to load fifty thousand pounds of ripe tomatoes (or, heaven forbid . . . strawberries) onto a truck driven by somebody who don't know how to act like a Jimmy crab. Anyway, though it paid good, it was money earned. I used to drive up in one trip, unload, and drive to New Jersey and pull off at the horrible Jersey City truck stop just across the river. There I would eat the best five tomatoes of the whole load, lock myself in the cab, idle up the engine and turn on the air conditioner (or the heater) and sleep like a dead man. After my nap, I would cash my check, buy fuel and a little snack, and deadhead on back. One time I was coming out of the building after paying for my fuel. As I crossed the parking lot, three men (or boys . . . hard to tell sometimes) acted like they wanted to corner me. They all had baseball gloves and bats and when I first saw them I thought they might be coming home from practice . . . but it was three thirty in the morning. I did just like a big Jimmy and it took them so aback that I was able to take it to step two and, by the time they recovered from the initial shock, I had scurried sideways and was in my tractor and had already changed three gears and they had to scurry sideways to keep from getting run over but I did run over one baseball glove. I think it was a first baseman's snag. You know the kind that look like they have been mashed flat. Of course I only saw it in my rearview mirror.

It is a brave little virgin girl crab who will come up the creek into the arms of such as the Jimmy of the hole but they'll do it. It is in the nature of virgin girls of most any species to take risks. He'll greet her with great kindness and, terrible arms still outstretched, will help her into the embrace of his six walking legs. Then he'll stand there as before and if a fish comes along (or little Jimmy . . . God help his young ass) he'll catch him and sidle off to his hiding place. He'll give her a little snack, too. It is the kindest kind of copulation. After the real business is tended to, he'll turn her back over and around so she is facing forward and he'll guard her (and feed her) until she is hard enough to take care of herself. It is a dear little ritual and that's the reason I don't bother the old Jimmies until all that is finished with in the fall. Then, old man, look out . . . you just thought you were the Jimmy of the hole.

Eating Blue Crabs

in which Maine lobsters take a backseat

The good old fierce blue crab is a good thing to eat. Some of us prefer them to the astonishingly expensive Maine lobster or the equally delicious Caribbean spiny lobster. They are way harder to get out of the shell than either of those and even harder to eat than the very trendy Dungeness crab (which most people just call "crab legs" since nobody has ever seen the body of one) or the Alaska king crab, the biggest arthropod on earth. Any yuppie-scum drinker of Mexican beer and follower of current trends in food fads can eat one of those but it takes determination to get the goody out of a blue crab. It can be done, however. I think the difficulty of getting at a delicacy is directly proportional to its value. Take the peanut and the bean for example. Both of them are legumes but the bean is borne up in the air in a tender pod that even a baby can shell out while the peanut is formed under the gritty ground inside a hard shell that takes accurate incision by the incisors to get to. That's why shelled peanuts cost more than pinto beans. A blue crab is like a peanut . . . well, more like a hickory nut.

Cooking them is easy. The only tricky part is to make sure they are all still alive when you do it. One bad crab in the batch is a dangerous thing. Though properly prepared crabmeat will keep for a long time when refrigerated, a dead, raw crab quickly degenerates into as deadly a seafood snack as there is. If it doesn't kill you outright, it will give you a case of the scours that you will remember for the rest of your life. Do not leave live crabs in stale water or in the bottom of a bucket for very long. The commercial folks now use something that looks like a plastic laundry basket . . . well perforated. The old standby was a wood produce box with cracks between the slats. An aerated live box works well but crabs are high-energy animals and need a lot of oxygen and stagnant water in a bucket just will not do. They make out better in the fresh air. The absolute best way to keep crabs alive until you get ready to cook them is to let them run around in the bilgewater of a boat but they hide and are very happy to take their revenge at any opportunity. You know, I don't think there are very many animals more intimidating for their size than a blue crab . . . maybe a pygmy rattlesnake.

The way to cook live crabs is to boil some seawater in a big pot and, when it is boiling real good, put the crabs in there. Make sure they are not sandy. Also make sure you stand back pretty far because though they die as soon as they get in the hot water good, they do not go easy into that good night and will throw scalding water all over you. I guess it is cruel to throw anything alive into boiling water but I can't think of a more humane way to kill a gallant warrior. The best way to do it is with a steamer basket where you put them all in there at the same time but I never had a rig like that and besides they crawl out and run around on the floor and try to bite you so I put them in individually with some kitchen grabbers. We used to boil them in a crab net in a foot tub on the beach when we were children (crab nets used to be made of real string instead of monofilament). Either way, let the water boil up good for at least five minutes after they are all in there and then turn off the fire and let them soak for a little while. That'll help make the meat turn loose of the shell. You can steam them and put seasoning on them in the Cajun or Chesapeake manner but we don't fool with all that. It doesn't improve on the end result all that much and stains the fingers and burns the lips.

Cleaning crabs is best done standing in the sea. Eating crabs is best done standing in the sea. It sort of turns into a communal operation involving many different species. Little fish come running when you begin to clean and eat crabs . . . they nibble at your toes. Other crabs come running, too, and it is best to be wary enough so that they don't nibble at your toes. As soon as both your hands become involved with the cleaning operation horseflies come zooming in for a little nibble and if there is no wind, no-see-ums will get in your hair and bite the bejesus out of you. You know how no-see-ums work don't you? They dab a little drop of concentrated hydrochloric acid on your skin and then lick up what gets dissolved. That's why they hurt so instantaneously and why it lasts so long. They don't just inject you with some enzyme, they burn about a half-a-square-millimeter hole in you about half a millimeter deep and the acid keeps working down in there even after you have rubbed the no-see-um to bloody death.

Anyway the way to clean crabs is to pull up the abdomen flap (might have to use a claw to get started) and use it to pull the carapace off the body of the crab. Then clean out everything that is not meat or shell. Pay careful attention to that cavity behind the teeth. I always break the front out of the shell with my thumb to facilitate the cleaning of that place. That stuff in there is what the crab last ate and sometimes it is not good to re-eat that. There are many things under the carapace that are very good but it is best to know what you are doing. I covered that subject at length in "A Few Recipes of the Reynolds Crew" so I won't repeat it here. Just clean the damn crab and don't forget to pull off the dead man's fingers.

Getting the meat out is not as hard as an ignorant person might imagine. You can just stand there in the water and use teeth and fingers and do pretty good but to do it like the pros do, you need two implements. One is a little knife. The best is what they call a "crab knife" and is all stainless steel with a short, not very sharp blade and a heavy handle. There are ladies down here who can pick out a dozen crabs a minute and, if you are real serious about learning the tricks of the trade, the best thing you could do would be to go to a crab house and very politely ask if you can watch for a little while. Don't stay too long because you'll quickly wear out your welcome by inhibiting the normal conversation that occurs in such places. You'll see that the first thing they do is pull off the claws and break the body of the crab into two pieces. They then cut all the legs and the two swimmers off a little way back into the body of the crab so the most proximal joint is completely removed. They then cut the shell off around where the swimmers were. The big swimmer muscle (called the "lump") is the biggest piece of meat in the crab and is all in an undivided hole in the back of the body. A little examination will show that all the leg holes are divided so that the lift-up muscle is separated from the pull-down muscle by a partition of shell but there is no partition in the lump cavity. Once the lump is out, the women (there are no male crab pickers . . . men are unacceptable in that select society because they are too stupid to know any good conversation. You know, southern men are carefully selected for stupidity as a qualification for breeding purposes. That explains a lot). Well, anyway getting those little leg-wiggling muscles out is way too complicated for a southern man to explain in words. Perhaps a woman could watch the operation in the crab house and figure it out but I just eat that part shell and all. The claws are picked out by some other women and the way they do it is to whap the claw very skillfully with the metal handle of the crab knife. They hit it just the right hard so nothing is squashed and no juice flies too far and they do it at exactly the right place . . . in the joint. When the claw has had its joints busted they pull the meat from each section by the distal end of the muscle. The muscles of crabs turn loose of the shell in the cooking and there are no tendons so the meat is actually just lying in there but there is a little fin of "cartilage" in the middle of the pinching muscle. The picker flicks the muscle off that fin very expertly with her knife. They are so skillful with the rap of the handle of the knife that the little finger of meat that was in the nonmovable jaw of the claw comes out with the muscle, too. If you are a pro, all you need is the crab knife but if you are an amateur you need a pair of very rusty household-style slip-joint pliers.

The best thing to do is to eat the crabs right after you cook them. They are all right in the refrigerator (I guess) for maybe twenty-four hours but if you think you might need to take them home or something, it is best to boil the cleaned bodies and claws up one more time before you put them in the refrigerator. That way they will be sterile from the cleaning in the ocean. Not only that, but the oxygen will be removed from the water in the interstices of the shell and the meat will stay fresh longer.

If you fool around and poison yourself with crabmeat (or bad oysters or any other rotten seafood) you'll need some reading material that is good for intermittent use. You don't want it to be such that exclusive concentration is required to understand it and you don't want it to be something that you have to remember in the intervals between bouts of reading. Newspapers would be all right except for how awkward they are in confined places during spasms resembling tetanus. The *Reader's Digest* will work but laughter is not the best medicine. I suggest anthologies of poetry or Peter Spectre's *Mariner's Book of Days*. *The New Yorker* is okay if all you do is look at the cartoons and read the poems but stay off the editorials and stories. You ain't going to be able to participate in any of the "Goings on About Town" so skip that. I think the best thing to read when in extremis is an old *Messing About in Boats*. A little Hugh Ware maybe.

Robb's momma eating crabs.

Piecework

in which I see teamwork . . . at work

Like I said, I worked for a while at a trailer factory slapping together "mobile homes." It was a piecework, pre-OSHA, completely unregulated, violent business. For a little while, it was possible for a workingman to make some kind of big money around here . . . if he was quick and aggressive. People fought each other every day in that hellhole, trying to get the job done in the middle of all those other people trying to get their jobs done. If you got in the way, you just got run over. They hospitalized about two or three a week until things finally got adjusted to an equilibrium, then it dropped down to one a week.

They paid eighty bucks to put the wretched framework of the roof on one of those junkpiles and that money was split between two very bad jokers. They had teamed up and run off the rest of the crew that used to do the job and were slapping the top on six trailers a day right by themselves . . . that's 240 bucks a day . . . each. Down here in South Georgia where a man could get fifteen bucks to unload a whole boxcar of Portland cement in ninety-pound paper bags, that was good money. These two men were so intense that if it hadn't been a two-man job, one of them would have killed the other one (and that's what he would have had to do) so he could get the whole 480.

The way they worked was, one man worked off an aluminum ladder and the other threw the flimsy rafter trusses up on top of the trailer while the first man, hopping the ladder down the line, sort of straightened them up and stapled them to the little rinky-dink wall plate, first one side and then hopping around the stern, the other, with a giant air-powered staple gun. When the gun gave out of staples, the floor man quickly grabbed the loaded spare gun and threw it up to the ladder man who unplugged the air hose and dropped the empty gun. The new gun was plugged to the hose and the slapping-on of the roof proceeded with hardly a pause. After the last trailer rolled by, they would double-team shooting together the wretched, little, flimsy trusses for the next day.

That pair dominated the hellish scene for a while. For example, if somebody else was trying to load one of those cheap-junk hot-water heaters (paid twenty bucks, wired, plumbed, and still holding forty psi of air at the end of the line) in the door and got in the way of the ladder for even a second, the bastard on the ladder would shoot him with a staple.

Some said it served him right when he stapled his penis to his leg. He didn't do it on purpose to show how bad he was . . . it was an accident. When he was changing guns, he clamped the fresh one between his legs while he plugged the hose on with one hand and held the truss straight with the other. Somehow or other, something hit the trigger at exactly the wrong time and *bam* . . . shot himself right through the dick with a three-inch, cement-coated, divergent-chisel-pointed staple. The damn thing went all the way through that member, the muscles of his thigh, and about an inch into his femur where, I guess, those chisel points diverged.

I was the one who was elected to take him to the doctor. He wouldn't let me try to pull the staple out with the pliers. He wouldn't even let me help him down off the ladder. We had to get him down with a forklift and load him onto the flatbed of my truck on a pallet for the ride to the doctor's office. He said he couldn't let that one leg down to walk and didn't feel like hopping. He also said I hit every bump in the road. The old doctor had had a lot of experience with people like that in similar situations and treated him right there in the parking lot of his office. Doc, very matter-of-factly, reached way down in that indentation in the denim and grabbed the top of the staple with his Vise Grips and with a strong twist and a couple of hard jerks . . . You have to give that man credit though. He was tough . . . rode back with me in the truck and was back up on that ladder before they moved that same trailer. He did change the way he plugged in the gun from then on.

The other guy on that team was sort of comical. Still, if you got in his way, he was dangerous . . . in a comical sort of way. He lived in Hahira (say *hay-hyra*) way the hell and gone out in the woods about sixty miles from the trailer factory. This man, we'll call him "Ferrol," had this big, one-cylinder BSA "Star" motorcycle that he rode back and forth to Hahira every day. When they got the six roofs slapped on the trailers for the day, he and his tough buddy would go to The Ship Ahoy drive-in and drink beer, try to put the make on the rough girls that hung around there, and beat up on anybody that interfered until way late in the middle of the night. Then old Dick would head home to his woman and Ferrol would get on his motorcycle and ride all the way to Hahira, on a long, empty, barely paved, narrow little road, to make sure nobody was moving in on *his* woman.

He was thumping it home one night on his one-cylinder, way out in the middle of nowhere, when he felt like he needed to go to the bathroom, so he stopped. He left his motorcycle idling on its kickstand, pulled down his britches, and squatted in the grass on the shoulder of the road. He said that he couldn't do nothing because the grass was tickling, so he, britches down, hopped out onto the pavement where the grass was a little thinner. With that, unbelievable as it may seem to one who knows that road, another motorcycle came over the hill and ran over him and broke his leg. The other fella tumbled down the road quite a way with his motorcycle and broke his leg too. It turns out (not surprisingly) that they knew each other and, hollering in the dark, worked out a plan. The other guy had to drag himself back to where Ferrol's motorcycle was still idling beside the road and Ferrol had to abandon his britches. They helped each other up onto the single seat of the BSA and rode off. The other guy had to work the gears with his one good leg and Ferrol had to work the brake with his good (fortunately opposite) leg all the way back, fifty miles, to the hospital. They barely got him fixed up in time for work. That was the first time I ever saw a man in a paper hospital gown punch a time clock. Thank God he wasn't the ladder man.

Pleistocene Creek

in which I almost give it all up and quit the boatbuilding business for good

I have a cousin, a little younger than I am, from whom I was inseparable until I joined the Navy. We even invented our own language in which we were both named "Old Eeen." We did a lot of wild things together when we were boys and his folks said that I was the one who always instigated the worst of those things. After I got out of the Navy, I continued to try to push up some kind of insurrection in the Old Eeen.

One of the things we did when we were boys was to try to live off the "fat of the land" back in the Ochlocknee River swamp like we were some of the wild people of long ago. The land back there, though isolated and wild enough, wasn't as fat to two little new-boys as it had been to the long-gone old hands who had left their sign along the banks of the river. We did manage to live like wild things for weeks at the time but we were some hard-bitten, filthy, and very hungry little boogers when we finally made the decision to give it up and walk the five miles out to see if there were any cinnamon rolls in the pantry.

I got out of the Navy just before President Kennedy got shot. On that day I had just finished restoring an old bandsaw and I cried on the freshly polished table . . . rusted it up. Not only that, but I found that the Old Eeen had grown up. I was anxious to go wild again but the Old Eeen was always remodeling the bathroom or hanging Venetian blinds or fooling with his car or some other civilized domestic chore. I missed him but that didn't keep me out of the bushes, swamps, and wild coastline around where we live. On one of my explorations, I found Pleistocene Creek.

I was down there at the coast messing around in the marshes and rocky shallows where, if you can ignore the contrails of the jets heading to cursed Tallahassee, it is possible to imagine that nothing has changed since the old days. I noticed that in some of the little marsh creeks, even on the rising tide, the water seemed to be running out and it seemed to be a little bit fresh tasting. I wondered if some of those little streams might actually be distributaries of undiscovered rivers that flowed from the abundant limestone cave-springs that, when the sea level was lower, were home to the people of the Pleistocene . . . the hunters of the mighty mastodon and the long-haired mammoth, eaters of the colossal *Megatherion* and giant bison, savage com-petition for the great bears and terrible cats whose bones are found around the ancient fireplaces, wonderfully preserved in the cave-springs ever since the ice-age time. Those are the same springs that made the short little rivers that still bear the names that the people gave them so many thousands of years ago. After the ice melted back about where it is now and the sea came back, the water table rose and filled the caves. The people lived along the banks of the old rivers and spoke the ancient names. These were the cheer-ful catchers of the lowly oyster, pinfish, blue crab, mullet, scallop, and Semi-nole killifish, the durable parts of which show up in the kitchen middens from only a thousand years ago. These were the same happy folks who were run off by worried fools like us who roar thoughtlessly around in high-pow-ered machines and don't even know the name of the place where we are or see what it is like . . . people who would starve to death like ignorant pilgrims if they were set down, naked, in the middle of all that.

Late one fall, I took my lightest little boat way back in the marsh and let myself become stranded by a low spring tide when the north wind blew the water even farther away from the land. Tasting the trickles, I dragged the boat through the little marsh creeks all through the mud and over the rocks and oyster bars looking for a stream running fresh water. It was hard work. When it got to be dark, I squatted in the low-tide mud and savagely ate my raw pelecypod snack and lay my skeeter- and no-see-um-bitten self down in the bottom of my tiny boat where it was grounded solid in the mud of the creek that I was working my way up right then. Before daylight I was awakened by the wind singing in the trees—trees that weren't there when I went to sleep.

I found out that the wind had shifted around to the southeast, the tide had turned, and the combination had done, in just a few hours, what I had been trying to do, off and on, for a long, long time. I was drifting in my tiny boat, spinning slowly in the current, of a small, limestone-banked river so far from highways, boat landings, and houses and so hard to get to that it was easy to convince myself that I was the first person to see it since the wild people. After it got to be daylight, I could see what it was like—a concise, deep little river maybe thirty feet wide. The solution-hole-riddled limestone banks were almost vertical and there was a layer of black loam overhanging the rock walls. The woods on either side were higher than anything I had seen along this section of coast. There was an overstory of cabbage palm, red cedar, and live oak trees. Except for scattered palmettos, a few Yaupon bushes and leaves, the ground was shaded bare. I could see taller trees farther back from the river that might have been ash, tulip poplar, swamp hickory (*H. aquatica*), *Magnolia grandiflora,* red bay, and laurel oak. Some places on the bank and little ponds off the river were lower than the rest and there were short, big bald-cypress trees and tupelo. There was a generations-old osprey nest in a cypress snag right on the edge of the creek. It was easy to see potsherds sticking out of the dirt along the bank and on the bottom in the shallow nooks of the river. I saw two shell middens that looked untouched since the last person had dumped the last basket of shells a thousand years ago. Though I longed to start looking further I knew better. Those things didn't belong to me and besides, the tide was already getting ready to go out. I paddled with it, looking at the landmarks as best I could, and went to get the Old Eeen.

Things in the modern world are always more complicated than they ought to be and it was a long time before I could get back to that place. My wife and I had two little boys by then so I was working all week at a paying job and the boatbuilding business took all my weekends. I guess I sort of joined the Old Eeen in the real world for a while. I didn't have time to paddle for days, sleeping in the bottom of the boat at night, just to get to the memorized spot to go into the marsh. One of the outboard skiffs that has become so indispensable to me now would get me down the coast to the go-in place but that wouldn't have suited my romantic notions so I put it off until I had the time to paddle all that long, long way. Neither me nor the Old Eeen had time to do things right anymore. That wonderful place was just as safe from us as it was from the TV football fans for a long time.

Finally I managed to shake loose one January when I got laid off at the furniture factory where I was working at that time. I called the Old Eeen. He was just getting ready to paint the house and fix the gutters but I browbeat him into putting it off for a little while since it was so cold. On the way down in the car, I told him about that place for the first time. I painted a pretty picture too. Then I said "Eeen . . . we could go wild again. We could stay wild this time. Nobody in the world knows about that place but me. It ain't on the quadrangles and you can't even see it from an airplane. Even if they knew, nobody will drag a boat all that way just to get to a little creek . . . too far from the TV. You could just not show up in your classroom on Monday morning. The doings of the world would get along just fine without either one of us. Your wife could get along just fine without you and, Lord knows, mine's (Ed.: Don't mess with accurate dialogue) would soar like an eagle if she could drop this old heavy load. We could go back there and just set this damn skiffboat adrift. This norther would take it to Cuba. Somebody would be delighted to find it washed up. We could dug us out a canoe and live off the fat of the land forever. Wouldn't ever have to worry about no insurance or nothing." The Old Eeen sat silently over there on his side trying act like he was looking out the fogged-up window. "We could be real savages too, like the unconquered Calusas," I went on. "We could paddle swiftly but silently out of the marsh in our canoe . . . keep our heads down out of sight behind the grass . . . then we could swoop down on those fishing boats out on the flats, slip up behind them before they knew what was happening and knock them in the head with a lighter'd knot. We could drink all the beer out of their icebox and smoke up their cigars and then send their boat on off to Cuba too. Nobody would ever know . . . 'lost at sea.'" The Old Eeen's eyes darted around a little bit but he still sat there silently. Finally, he reached in his pocket and got him a cigar and gave me one too. After he got it lit and smoking good, he said, "Eeen, what if there were some women in that boat?" "Well," I said, "if they were plump with pulchritude and cheerful looking, we could take them back to the creek and indoctrinate them into our ways and smoke up their Kents. If they were mean and bossy looking, we would just knock them in the head too." "I ain't too crazy about that," he said, looking worried. "Maybe we could tell in advance. You got your knobblers, ain't you, Eeen? We could spy on them from the marsh grass and just pass up any boat with mean-looking women in it. I wouldn't want to knock no woman in the head." "Naw Eeen," I scolded. "You cain't have no knobblers back in the naked wild woods. Hell, you cain't even have no matches." "Yeah, but we could light them Viceroys with a coal when we got back to our fire," said the Old Eeen, eagerly smoking hard on his cigar.

Things don't always turn out right, even with the best of plans. Like I said, this creek was a long, long way down the coast from the nearest road. After we had launched the skiffboat at the closest possible place, we had to hurry so we would have time to pole in and take a brief look at that wonderful little place and then make the long, long trip back to the boat ramp before nightfall because that sort of country is not navigable in the dark.

While we were tearing along in the calm, shallow water in the outboard skiff in the north-wind lee of the marsh, I hit a perverse conch (*Busycon perversa*) shell with the foot of the motor and sheared the pin in the propeller. It was freezing cold, so even though the water was shallow enough to get out on the flats to pull the wheel, I decided to lean over the stern to do it. After I got the propeller off, damned if the engine didn't tilt down and flip me over the transom, out of the boat, flat on my back in the cold, cold water. Not only did I get saturated wet, but I disjointed my right middle finger (never did get completely well and sometimes makes people think that I am attempting some sort of communication) and dropped the durn propeller nut and we couldn't find it to save our lives. We had to turn around right there and row all those miles back to the boat ramp. If the Old Eeen hadn't had on two pair of britches I would have froze to death.

Epilogue

I can't remember if the Old Eeen and I ever managed to get back to that little creek. When my sons got old enough to be interested in that kind of thing, my family went back and carefully camped on the ancient bank right where I knew the old people had last slept a thousand years ago. After it was dark, it seems like we heard their spirits out in the woods. Next day, my oldest son and I swam all the way to the little spring that was the headwaters for most of the little river. The clear water bubbled up through big-grained white sand and thousands of salamander larvae and eggs. The banks were thick with poison ivy and other terrible bushes and vines. It was the wildest little place I ever saw. Sometimes we talk about going back, but the boys are grown men now, just about in the same fix as the Old Eeen. I haven't been back there in twenty years. I am sure that the population explosion around here since then has not let even that spot go undiscovered by the damned go-anywhere airboats, Jet Skis, "go Devils," and other such joyriding travesties that are so popular among the ignorant and thoughtless. Both my children and the Old Eeen's are long grown up. He is still a schoolteacher—has all Christmas vacation off. He finished digging a pond in his yard and sold his backhoe and I noticed that his house was all painted up and the roof looks sort of new—well maintained. I am just as no-count as I ever was. We are both so old now that the dilemma about what to do with the women has solved itself. We'll just knock them all in the head. What the hell did I do with my phone number book?

Along the Road

in which traveling the same road over and over creates keen observers

Traveling for long distances on the same road over and over again brings out a peculiar kind of keenness in the eyes of the observer and a peculiar kind of sharpness to the conversation if there is more than one observer. We have spent a lifetime riding the same road from the home place to the coast and back. Keeping our eyes open and talking about what we see made the trip fun years ago and still does.

When my sisters and I were little, we used to ride a hundred miles to the coast every chance we got with our mother in a pickup truck. Us children always rode in the back (danger, danger). There was a Burma Shave series in this one little field: DINAH DOESN'T on the first sign then TREAT HIM RIGHT and BUT IF HE'D SHAVE and finally DINAH MIGHT. We, in our juvenile ecstasy, thought that was the wittiest thing anybody could have ever put on some little signs and always stood up to read the whole thing as loud as we could. Once when we were shouting the message into the thirty-five miles an hour's worth of wind coming over the cab of the truck, my big sister got hit in the mouth by a yellow jacket who stung her on the back of her tongue. By the time we got to Sopchoppy, it was swollen up so big that she couldn't get it all back in her mouth and Momma had to let her ride in front so people who were following us wouldn't stare at her so. Fortunately, she didn't suffer respiratory arrest and die, but after that we memorized the signs with our mouths shut and ducked back down in the bed as each sign passed to do our hollering.

Now my wife (also a participant in that foolishness in the back of the truck) and I drive that same old hundred miles to the same old coast for the same old reason. The Burma Shave field is now chip-and-saw-sized planted pines and the whole world is different. Even though it is different, it's still the same. There is a woman, who lives just past the place where we hollered into the wind, who decorates her yard according to the season and when we pass her place, it is as if our whole lives are flashing by (at sixty miles per hour, now, not thirty-five like back then). She never takes in any of the decorations when the season is gone. There is one thing that nobody, except keen observers with years of experience, could ever recognize. It looks like an aluminum-foil-covered plywood comma on a stick growing from an enormous fire ant bed. Beside that is another thing that used to be an orange plastic bag full of leaves and grass clippings with a pumpkin face to celebrate some long-gone Halloween, but now has squatted and erupted so that it looks like the Wicked Witch right after Dorothy threw the water. Behind that, there is a small field of varicolored Easter crosses, some flat where they rotted off at the ground and some no longer crossed where they deteriorated at the duct tape. A plastic Santa tilts crazily among them, a dirt dauber nest nestled under his nose. A two-year-old Easter bunny looks like a mildewed boat cushion washed up by a hurricane, his ears like straps flat on the ground. Valentine hearts droop and sag in an out-of-sequence demonstration of durability differences (helium balloons don't hold up long) and whim of location among the other decorations. Real five-year-old Easter eggs decorate partially straightened rusty coat hangers stuck up in the ground. American flags flap in a sequence of shreds from all the fence posts on the place . . . Veterans Day, Memorial Day, Fourth of July . . . which one? which year? "What," you ask, "is that aluminum-foil-covered comma-looking thing?" Why, Halley's Comet, of course.

Islands

in which I reveal yet another obsession

I love islands and have ever since I was a little boy. I think it is a natural human instinct that, if not stultified by the maturation process, is apt to persist right on up into old age. I used to build islands when I was a child. Down at our old coast house there was this little dark-water marsh creek that ran across the beach every time it had been raining much. I used to ditch and dam until I forced it to divide into two distributaries as it crossed the wide, white sand . . . made an island for myself. Pretty soon my expeditions of exploration on my property would have it completely covered with my tracks. Man can't do much better than that to mark what he owns.

You can occupy ready-made islands too. When my boys were little, because of my persistence in the boatbuilding business, we were real poor and couldn't afford to go to resorts and theme parks and stuff like that, so we went on long expeditions to islands either in the new Nueva Eva or in a car with a little boat on top. First we would go to the surveyor's office and pore over the quadrangles to find islands that were not on regular maps, then we would load up our camping junk and head out. I ain't going to tell you where all of those islands are so when my grandchildren start looking for them, they won't find all of y'all covering them up like wasps on the nest in the late summer. But I will tell you about one good place.

Right off the defunct (thank goodness) Cross Florida Barge Canal south of Yankeetown and north of Crystal River are some of the most charming little islands in the world. Some of them aren't much bigger than a car but are high and dry and rocky with pretty deep water (ain't much water anywhere down there) right up to the bank so you can tie up like to a dock. The first time we went there was in the summer and we had forgotten our shoes. We wanted to walk all over and around every one of those zillion little islands but they were rocky and sharp (a lot like the Bahamas). Finally we sat down and wove us some shoes out of palmetto fronds—good shoes too—nothing better for wading as the water and sand can just run out the bottom. When a hole gets worn in the heel or the ball of the foot, it's just the work of a minute to re-cap that place. We ate good too. There was a stone crab under every rock. There were plenty of oysters, clams, and blue crabs, and the fishing was very good right off the bank. There were some running peas growing on the beach, looked just about like regular field peas with pale blue flowers. We could have stayed down there forever if it hadn't been for school and boatbuilding . . . insurance payments, electric bills, taxes, and Santa Claus.

The only thing wrong with that place was that every night, a whole scad of very impertinent coons would swim over from the mainland and rampage all over every single one of those islands. As the sun went down, you could see them coming . . . hundreds of little intense faces heading our way . . . kind of intimidating to those who know coons. They were so brave that I believe that if you didn't keep the tent door zipped up, they would pull you out of the bed and feel you all over with their little busy hands looking for something edible. At any rate, we could hardly sleep for all of them chewing and squabbling out there—had to catch a little catch-up snooze after the sun came up and they swam back—ears sticking up in profile against the glare of the rising sun.

When I was towing fuel oil and gasoline into the little tank farm in Yankeetown or the big power plant at Crystal River . . . had to pass right by our little place and I would get homesick. Sometimes I could even see the coons early in the morning or late in the afternoon and one night, I swung the old carbon arc searchlight around and illuminated one of the little islands and the sight of all those little bright-eyed faces just about snatched a knot in my heart . . . Dang.

The island I live on now ain't much more than that, actually much less stable . . . just a sandbar out in the Gulf of Mexico about three and a half miles from the mainland. Every time we have much of a storm, the sea washes clear across and shifts the island's position relative to our house . . . kind of keeps a man from getting too big for his britches. Lots of the other houses over here (some regular big-deal outfits too) have had the island move right on out of the yard and leave them standing temporarily in the breakers of the open ocean . . . temporarily not because the island came back again, but because the sea does not go easy on such a thing as a house, no matter what kind of big-deal outfit it was. For some reason our little shanty, which we knew was temporary when we throwed it up, still has some sand piled up around it (knock wood). As a matter of fact, some of those other people's land has washed down here with us and our once tiny lot is now pretty big . . . won't gloat though because it might be gone tomorrow or the county will find out about it and raise the taxes.

One time, a house over here wound up in the water and it was a temporary situation of the other kind. Before the whole house was bashed into smithereens and strewed all up and down the beach, some kind of eddy or other put the sand right back where it was—but not before the surf tore off the big-deal, elaborate steps. It was sort of mystifying to the owner who spent the whole time all this was going on in federal prison for some impropriety involving large sums of money. When he came back, there was his house, seemingly just as before except that the fancy steps were completely gone. He couldn't get into his house. I am afraid I watched him through the binoculars as he tried to climb one piling after the other as if the next one was going to be easier. Finally he trudged off down the sand bed that these fools over here call a road and borrowed (stole) a ladder from another house. Normally this would be the end of the story but it gets worse. I heard (I don't communicate with little jerks like that unless I want to carry it to fruition) that he was skulking around over on the mainland somewhere and found his steps on another house. They must have drifted ashore after the storm and someone decided to claim them as flotsam. The little criminal thought the man had come to the island and stolen those steps off of his house. Anyway, this little fool got hopping mad and made some threats or something to the man with the steps. The funny thing was that the man he was threatening was the prosecutor of the county and got little criminal's parole revoked and sent his ass to Walla Walla, Washington. The house still ain't got no steps and somebody re-stole the ladder. No telling what will happen next. There will be plenty of time though. I heard twenty years.

One batch of our grandchildren is big enough to take care of themselves at the coast now and like we used to be, they are long gone right after breakfast and not likely to come back until no-telling-when. We just had the spring tides of the full moon. The main low was about nine o'clock PM. The children did not show up when it got dark. My wife and I set off across the wide flats following the yellow brick road to the moon. We thought we saw some coons marauding in their intent, busy way out on the wet sand down by the mouth of the big marsh creek. When we got closer, we recognized the three children acting just exactly like coons. They were on all fours, butts sticking way up and digging furiously. They didn't even see us as we walked close enough to see what they were doing. The light of the full moon revealed that they were busily maintaining moat creeks of sparkling water around each of their three islands. We were able to slip away without being seen. Ain't no telling when they came in but I bet it was after the tide rose and took their property away from them.

The Giant Catfish of Mobile

in which I meet an astonishing transvestite . . . and cook breakfast

I used to work on tugboats in order to make enough money to stay in the boatbuilding business. It worked out pretty good. I would tug for twenty days and then had ten days off to build on the boat. I used to cheat a little and figure out what I was going to do on the boat while I was on the tug. I carved half models and drew plans, developed the panels for V-bottomed plywood boats, and even did my lofting out on the barge so I could carry the patterns for the molds home folded up in my suitcase.

The tugboat I mostly worked on was a captive deal. I could quit anytime I wanted to and come back and get on when I got ready. They had a terrible run. There was this one little Gulf Coast town where there was a tradition of small, locally owned seagoing tugs that contracted to haul petroleum barges across the Gulf from the giant refineries in Mississippi Sound, Louisiana, and Texas to the power plants and tank farms down on the Florida peninsula. These little boats (all under ninety feet) ran all the time, and were so trustworthy that they just about had a monopoly on the petroleum contracts beyond the eastern terminus of the Gulf Intracoastal Waterway at Dog Island. Because the boats were so little and diligent, the captains had a hard scrabble to try to keep a crew on there during the winter, particularly after it got to where folks didn't have to work to eat. Though it is not legendary for roughness like, say, Cape Horn, the shallow Gulf of Mexico is a rough little piece of water some of the time. I can remember some trips when we were trying to come back from someplace like Crystal River with two empty barges on the towline in a norther when we hammered on the same spot for forty-eight hours. When I got to where I needed a little cash, all I would have to do was show up with my suitcase and a big grin about Christmastime. I know how to cook, splice big lines and wires, and fix junk machinery. I advise anybody who wants an easy job on a tugboat to learn to do those things. If you can do that, you always got a ticket to ride—at least in a non-union situation in the wintertime among desperate people.

This story ain't got nothing to do with all that though. I was cooking on there one time about 1971 when we had to go in for a crankshaft job. Most of those little old boats had two engines. This one had sixteen-cylinder 99

Caterpillars but some of the boats ran GM, EMD (Electro Motive Division of General Motors, still two-cycle) railroad locomotive engines and quite a few still had the old Atlas or Enterprise heavy-duty, direct-reversible (that's where you had to shut the engine down, rotate the camshaft drive gear a little bit, and crank it back up running backward to get reverse) engines. The engineers on those boats could do most any kind of overhaul work on one engine while the other was running so we didn't have to stop and hurt our reputation. We replaced pistons, liners, and connecting rod bearings, did cylinder head jobs, turbocharger bearings, rebuilt and calibrated injector pumps and injectors, rodded-out oil coolers, fixed pumps, generators, all kinds of junk—all that at sea—rocking and rolling down in the unbelievable din and heat of the engine room, dancing cheek-to-cheek with each other and the two engines, one scattered and sliding all over the place and the other one thundering loud and scorching hot. We did that so we could keep running, which was the only way a small operation could beat out the fierce competition from Louisiana. We could do all that at sea but we had to go to the hill to take the top of an engine off the base to change out a crankshaft and main bearings. We called ahead to the yard though and had everything set up so we wouldn't cool off too much while we were out of fix.

I was having a little trouble with this old second engineer on there. He didn't like me and I didn't like him. Though it was against the rules to let personal differences interfere with the work of the vessel, we both pushed it pretty good. Every morning I would get up about four o'clock and cook breakfast for six men (three at one sitting, captain, engineer, deckhand, and then they would relieve the other three and I would feed them). It was a ritual on there that they had the same thing for breakfast every morning. I would put two strips of bacon for each man in the pan and, while those were trying out, I would make the biscuits in an iron frying pan . . . seven biscuits . . . six catheads around the rim and one hexagon in the middle . . . buttermilk biscuits, shortened with bacon grease. After I had put the frying pan in the oven and put on a pot of grits, the bacon would have shrunk up enough so I could put in the sausages. Those and the eggs were the only variable allowed in the breakfast ritual. The sausages could be either link-style or patty-style and the eggs were cooked to order as the men came and got their coffee and sat down. I always thought it was a fairly good breakfast back before they discovered cholesterol. It was also a pretty nice sociable occasion until this fool got the ass.

At first he started complaining that I was overcooking the bacon. I even tried to take his two strips out a little early but then he whined, "This bacon done got cold. This must be left over from yestiddy." Then, "These is some soupy damn grits. You cain't cook a goddamn biscuit neither." The eggs were never right. "This what you call over easy? These damn eggs is plum leathery." He would eat it all, though, and wipe up the grease out of his plate with his last biscuit. I put up with all that complaining until we got tied up beside the dry dock for the crankshaft job on the port engine. One morning, since nobody was on watch, we were all crowded in the galley eating breakfast and he announced, "I cain't eat this. This ain't fit for a dog." With that, I stomped over there and snatched his breakfast out from under his big red nose and, with one fluid motion, opened the starboard-side galley door and flung the complete contents of his plate up against the side of the rusty floating dry dock where they slid down into the nasty water of the Alabama River. The yard men were already welding on another old junk boat in the dry dock and in that ghastly flicker, I saw the sausages, eggs, and the palette of grits slide out of sight beneath the slick from the bacon grease and the fuel and oil that is always around places like that. The two biscuits were left floating in the scum.

After I got through washing the dishes and pots and pans (and listening to a few impotent threats), I went out on deck to see the morning. I noticed that there was only one biscuit floating in the bacon grease. I wondered about that. I was thinking to myself, *Theoretically, identical biscuits should do the same thing under identical conditions,* when I saw this enormous pair of pale gray lips rise up, solemnly, under the remaining biscuit. There was a long, slow, deliberate, loud suction noise and the biscuit gradually began to spin in a counterclockwise direction. A vortex slowly formed and the biscuit was sucked down into those lips. I was mesmerized.

I knew where two more biscuits were.[1] Our "old captain" (we had two captains on at the time, the other one was the "little captain") didn't have any teeth. Oh, he had this set of cheap choppers that were used only for display, but he couldn't eat with them. Us cooks always saved out two of the biscuits (one of the catheads and the hexagon) so he could mash them up in his bowl with his fork and some buttermilk. Since he had his teeth in this morning so he could effectively negotiate with the dignitaries of the crankshaft job, I decided to flip one of his biscuits over the side to see if I couldn't get a better look at those toilet-seat-sized lips. It worked real good. I saw not only the lips but clotted, slimy whiskers as fat around as somebody's fingers, two opaque, milky-blind eyes, and a hint of the body of an enormous catfish. I dashed for the captain's last biscuit and my handline.

To make a long story short, hooking him was easy but I couldn't stop him from going back under the dry dock and cutting me off. I tried again, but when I saw my hook stuck in his lip and scars from other hooks, I felt bad and quit trying to catch him. One old man who was trying to braze up some of the worst of the notches in the propeller of the boat on the dry dock with a huge acetylene torch said that catfish had been living under that dry dock for all the thirty years he had been working there and that nobody could catch him. "Too much steel on the bottom, besides, he is big enough to eat a grown man." "That a fact?" chirped me.

It was boring on the boat in the shipyard. I wandered around all through the old place looking at all the artifacts left over from when they used to work on wood boats (there was a gigantic shipsaw all grown up in the bushes for one thing) and messed around in the river with the little aluminum skiff we kept on the roof, and even went up to the causeway one night with the deckhand to this little bar. There the deckhand met an amazingly extroverted woman who was so charming that he decided to go to her house as a guest. After they drove off through the tunnel to Mobile in her Mustang, I trudged it on back to the boat. About three o'clock in the morning, I heard somebody stomping onto the eerily quiet boat and went to see. There was the deckhand washing up for bed. "What happened to your woman?" I asked. "That wasn't no goddamn woman," he replied, disgustedly. "Had to leave my goddamn shoes and my money," he lamented. "You don't never want to walk home through no goddamn tunnel without no shoes," he concluded.

Fortunately, I didn't have to do that. I was able to catch the bus right out there on the causeway when I got tired of all that and walked off the job one more time.

[1] I know damn well that there will be some biscuit-counting nitpickers among you gracious readers so I'll explain the situation so you can rest easy. On some crews there were people who, like me, did not eat biscuits. The reason I don't eat them is that I believe the invention of the biscuit heralds the day of the beginning of the decline of mankind into the wretched state we are in now. A biscuit is an abstraction, sort of like car insurance. Civilization is an abstraction, sort of like cars. On this crew, Junior (the other captain) did not eat biscuits either. He didn't even eat breakfast. He always came down in the middle of the night (made his engineer steer) and ate up all the leftovers from supper. He could eat half a gallon of black-eyed peas and two ham hocks . . . bones and all. When I had to cook for other crews in other biscuit situations, I made eight biscuits in the pan and the middle one turned out to be octagonal . . . So there, damn your eyes.

Seasick

in which a case of mal de mer leads to a promotion

I have seen a lot of seasickness in my day. I have participated in a good little bit of it, too, but this will deal mostly with the seasickness of others.

My first observation of the effects of this terrible ailment was when my father decided that he wanted to go to Europe and write. He was an imaginative man and I imagine that he imagined that he was something like a Hemingway. Unfortunately for the romance of the excursion he was unable to play the part of that man in Spain who had the dysfunction that kept him from consummating anything of a family nature. My father had to take all of us trailing along behind him when he went to the bars and bistros in search of the wormwood stuff that will poison you eventually if you drink too much. I am afraid we children sort of killed the mood when we crowded around to see if it actually did cloud up when poured in water like it said in the book and to see if he showed any early signs of approaching death after he drank it.

It was on the voyage over that I saw my first seasick person. We went on the USS *Constitution* and it was a rough trip. My father took some home movies on board of the ship. One scene is of me and this unidentified other little kid sloshing from one side of the swimming pool to the other. Another scene is of me playing Ping-Pong with some of the crew. The ball looks like it has a lot of English on it, but it ain't the ball, it's the table. It was so rough that they had to shut down the shuffleboard on the promenade deck because the pucks caroming off the bulkheads kept tripping up the few promenaders.

That first seasick person I saw was my oldest sister, and boy, it was pitiful. When she found that she was the only young girl in first class, she got ready to cut a wide swath through the old men, middle-aged men, and boys in both the passengers and crew. She rummaged her suitcase and had her bathing suit on before we cleared the Verrazano Narrows Bridge. By the time the crew got the deck lines stowed, she wasn't looking so hot anymore. I never saw that much skin so pale before in my life. She stayed out of sight until we docked in Naples.

I saw that same ailment again very soon on that first day out. I conned my way right back through second class to the stern so I could look over the taffrail at the wide white wake. It was amazing to me how the ship was straightening out so much water. I was fascinated by the roils of turbulence kicked up by the propellers so far down under the counter. I turned to one of several other people who were also looking down over the stern to comment. When I spoke, the man turned. I noticed his lips were sort of pursing and unpursing in a peculiar way and that his eyes were rolled back so that they were looking at something inside his head. He had blue lines radiating out from his nose across his cheeks and lips kind of like a baboon. He didn't look like he was interested in talking about the interactions of the ship and the water so I decided to discontinue my attempt at conversation.

When my wife and I were young, we had a little twelve-foot Caribbean sailboat. We decided to sail with a young friend to Vieques Island in it. We had the steady, strong trade wind to reach both ways and we set out. We had both had a lot of experience sailing around the coast of Puerto Rico in boats like that, and were confident. Everything went fine until we got out into the open ocean. There the waves were pretty high and very far apart. There was no danger in it but the little boat stayed becalmed in the trough about half the time. Then she would rise up to where the wind was and sail for a little while, then drop back down into the bottom and stop and drift until the next wave came. I got seasick as anything. We hadn't been married long enough to be completely over shyness about our inabilities, so I sort of hid my condition behind the sail when I could. Later after we got so that we communicated better, my wife said that she had gotten seasick, too, and that she had hidden behind the sail just like me. Many years later, I saw the friend again. He said. "Remember that time we tried to sail to Vieques in that little boat? I bet you never knew I was seasicker than anything. Had to hide behind the sail so youse guys wouldn't find out." "Why," says me, "I thought you were a seasoned sailor like us." Now that I think about it, we must have been chasing that little sail all over that boat.

Some seasick people aren't so passive. One time I worked on what they call a "head boat" cutting bait. A head boat is one of those boats that will take you out deep-sea fishing if you show up on time and buy a ticket. There is no need to make special arrangements like you do on a charter boat. The way the people who worked on there were paid was that the crew's share of the ticket money was split up according to a formula. If the bait boy or anybody else on the crew couldn't do their job, they would have to forfeit their share, even if they were incapacitated for just a short time. There was this one son of a bitch who tried to provoke seasickness in the other crew members. If there were a bunch of people on there, he would wait until all the bait was cut and we were on the way back, rolling with the following sea breeze. Then he would make his sandwich . . . big piece of bread, a can of mustard sardines, extra mustard, and a big slice of onion. That, in itself, usually was not enough to cut the victim loose from his share . . . not even the first watery squirt of mustard from the squeeze bottle. It was when he drank that yellow juice from the sardine can that got them. I saw more than one resolute man fall under that spell just before the money was made. Once, he did it three times on three trips to the same silent little man. I don't know why the fella kept coming back, but he did. He cut up bait all day long rolling at anchor and then he'd fall for the damned "money sandwich" just before we went into the river. The last time it happened, the little man watched the construction of the sandwich and, just as the money man was fixing to tip the can to drink the juice, "You drink that and I'll feed you that sandwich, can and all," said the little silent man. The man drank the juice anyway . . . fool.

Years went by and I never got too far away from boats and ships. I worked, off and on, for thirty years on this little seagoing tug that towed two barges across the Gulf of Mexico from someplace like Chalmette, Louisiana, to Yankeetown, Florida. This particular tug was a legendary roller. When it was built, the plans called for ninety-five feet, but the company that owned the boat found out that the dry dock in Mobile that they always used could only handle eighty-five so they left out the middle. That must have been where all the steady was. One legendary trip, the damn thing rolled so bad that it rolled one deckhand out of the lower berth and another out of the top. Then she snapped back the other way and rolled the top man into the bottom bunk as he fell. The bottom man slid down the ladder into the bathroom, which was a good thing. Both of them were so seasick that they just lay where they wound up. The engineer washed the bottom man off with the hose.

I had my worst experience with seasickness on board of that same little cut-down tug. I was cooking on there one winter. I got the job not because I was such a good cook, but because it was winter. Even the little Gulf of Mexico can get sort of rough, and it is hard to keep a whole crew on a rollish little thing like that in the wintertime. One morning I was holding on to the stove with one hand and the frying pan with the other, watching those sausages turn themselves over and over, when the notion struck me that the sight of those sausages rolling around in that grease was the most nauseating thing I had ever seen in my life. I took the frying pan with me to the lee door but I lurched wrong and sloshed some of the grease out onto the steel deck. Then I stepped in it and down I went. I helped that damn sausage grease spread completely all over the whole galley. They promoted me to engineer that same morning.

There are a lot of things that people say will cure seasickness. I have heard that all you have to do is stand up straight and look at the horizon. Yeah right. Some people say that a little hair of the dog will do it. Just jump in the ocean. That might work good if you are in a rowboat in the bay, but what you gonna do if you are fifty miles out in January and in the company of unsympathetic people? My mother (who was never seasick) always said, "Well, you just keep on doing your job, that will take your mind off it and it will soon go away." It used to infuriate me to hear that. I even went so far as to take her out thirty miles in my old surplus motor whaleboat (a roller with few equals) to take a video of flying fish. When it got dark and breezed up, I put her beam to and opened my can of mustard sardines and broke out the bread and cut the onion. When I tipped up the can, she said. "Damn, that is a good-looking sandwich . . . Save me a little of that juice."

Tugboat *J.R. Ferguson*

Snowmobile Suits

in which I discover that Yankees know a thing or two about comfort

I know it doesn't make much sense for a man who lives in Florida but one of my favorite garments is a snowmobile suit. It gets cold around here. When I was in the Navy, I used to travel all over to places like Keflavic, Iceland, and Great Lakes, Illinois, but the coldest I ever was in my life was while I was standing in my whites beside the runway in Mayport, Florida, waiting to hitch a ride to Guantanamo Bay, Cuba. It was breezing up from the north so that my bell-bottoms were whipping my shanks and that cold wind clear from Alberta, Canada, was cutting through that thin cotton jumper and freezing my ribs like the coils of the evaporator of a freezer locker. I didn't know what a snowmobile suit was back then but I do now.

The first one I ever saw belonged to Jimmy-of-the-Ferg. The old Ferg (*J. R. Ferguson,* Apalachicola, Florida) was a little (eighty-five-foot) undersized, seagoing tug that I worked on for intervals of various lengths for almost thirty years. Its main business was towing fuel oil and gasoline barges across the Gulf of Mexico from refineries down around the Mississippi Delta to little tank farms all up and down the peninsula of Florida for various small-time oil companies back when there was such a thing. Jimmy was the full-time deckhand all the time I was on again, off again at whatever job they had open at the time I needed to work. Jimmy, like the boat, seemed to be too small for the job . . . what we used to call "banty Irish" around here. I don't know if there is a separate race of the Irish that produced people like Jimmy and his family (none much over five feet tall and Jimmy the littlest one) but the gene distribution systems of modern society have pretty much mixed us all up down here so that ain't none of us much of a pure strain of anything anymore. I reckon anthropologists will have to take up a grant to go to Ireland and dig up a bunch of DNA to find out the facts of the matter.

I guess, now that I have brought up Jimmy's family, I'll have to go all into that before I can finally get back to his snowmobile suit. It is impossible to work, even off and on, with a man for thirty years . . . particularly on the small crew of a tugboat, always under way, in the isolation of being at sea . . . without finding out all sorts of things. Jimmy was raised in the woods of North Florida in a situation that might be impossible for some to understand. His

father had a short-log, cross-load, Brown-Loader pulpwood truck with
which he followed the federally privileged saw-log crews in the Apalachicola
National Forest making a hand-to-mouth living getting tops, lightning
strikes, knock-downs, and bug kills. Jimmy and them didn't actually have a
real house that they lived in for any length of time and were so far from any
school bus route that I don't think any of them hardly ever went to school.
They might have lived in and around and under that log truck more than
any other place. While their daddy was working in the log-woods, Jimmy's
momma took the children (a slew of them, all tiny, like a family of baby
quail running through the bushes) out into the woods to grunt worms.

That's an interesting business. What the worm grunters do is to go to a
place that they find by intuition and drive a big lighter'd (I think that's a
contraction of *lighter wood* . . . kindling little known outside the coastal plain
of the Southeast until fancy mail-order clothing stores up around Maine
started selling it in tiny, expensive bundles called "Georgia Fatwood") pine
stob into the ground. Then they rub the resinous butt of the stob with a
leaf out of the spring from a big truck or a short section of antique small-
gauge railroad track left over from the little trains of the great clear-cut of the
turn of the last century, in a special way so that it vibrates the ground violently enough to make your feet itch if you stand too close. The vibrations
either irritate or excite the wonderful, big, pale, valuable (fifteen cents each,
retail, when this century turned up) "pond worms" so that they crawl from
their deep (over six feet according to grave diggers I have talked to) burrows
to the surface where they gleam pale and iridescent in their slime. When the
time comes, the person doing the grunting makes the signal and all the children who have been sitting quietly on their buckets hop up and scurry
around gathering the produce before they can worm their way back into
the ground.

Pond worms are the ace bait of piney woods fishermen . . . they are big
enough to be cast without split shot (best done with a cane pole) so they sink
naturally while they wiggle in their slow voluptuous way. There are few bass
and no bream or catfish that can stand to lie by and watch that provocative
descent.

Jimmy was used to the primitive life and not self-conscious about his notions. When we changed crews on the old Ferg, he brought his whole outfit in a little paper sack. The only clothes he brought were what he was
walking in. When it was hot, he wore nothing but a miniature, short-legged

pair of overalls . . . no underwear, no shirt . . . just them. He washed his overalls in a white plastic bucket back on the stern of the boat and dried them on one of the turbocharger exhaust feeds (big old V-style Caterpillars have two, one for each side) of one of the engines while he pranced around as naked as a jaybird on deck and in the engine room (the captains would-n't let him in the galley or the wheelhouse like that). In the wintertime, he wore his snowmobile suit and never washed it for the whole twenty days of his shift.

I forgot to tell you what he had in his paper sack. That was his shore out-fit for the few times when we stayed anywhere long enough to go ashore . . . and for going home after his twenty days were up. Jimmy was some kind of little stud when we hit the hill and when the first haze of land ap-peared on the horizon he would start getting ready. If it was night you would find him hopping up and down under your elbow trying to see the radar so he would have plenty of time to get his sack. All he had in there was a comb (no wiggletail water), his toothbrush (no toothpaste), a razor (no soap or aftershave), and a little roll of money (no billfold . . . no driving license . . . no shoes . . . no shirt . . . no underwear . . . no deodorant . . . no rubber). Even though he wasn't all dolled up, he was a welcome little man anyplace he went.

Before I get back to that snowmobile suit, I better tell you what he looked like so you can warn your daughters, granddaughters, wives (and grand-mothers, by now) when you hear the rumble of powerful engines coming up the bay. Though he was a tiny little man, he had some big features . . . like his feet. Jimmy's feet (always bare) were big in every way . . . long, wide, and thick. His toes were huge and well spraddled . . . with thick, dark toe-nails and long black hairs on the knuckles. They were impervious to the el-ements. He was an amazingly strong, agile, and muscular little man (one of his brothers was real dangerous and I hope he's still in jail) and he had a big head and wide face with big strong white teeth. His hands matched his feet. His disposition was cheerful and his attitude was willing. He was the best deckhand I ever saw, one of those intuitive kind so precious to a wheelman . . . could catch a line on the bit with the most uncanny precision . . . han-dle the worst-looking, fishhook bristle barge-wire cable as quick as anything. After Jimmy made up the bridle of the towline to the bow of the barge, he would come back to the boat on the hawser, hand over hand like a monkey to save the aggravation of backing down in the close, swift water of the mouth of the river to get him. As soon as the captain saw that Jimmy had the wires of the bridle made up back there on the barge, they just hooked up the throttle and never looked back. Sure enough, pretty soon Jimmy would bring them a cup of hot coffee to drink while he sat in the wheelhouse door and leaned back against the forward jamb to watch the land fall away once again.

His snowmobile suit must have been made for a child. At the beginning of his shift, it was dark blue and you could still see Snoopy embroidered on the pocket but as the twenty days dragged by, it got shiny and very dirty with rust stains and patches of grease from the barge winches. It got kind of rank inside too, about like a squirrel's nest. Jimmy said that it always got to worrying him around crew-change time because it got so strong that when he took it off to go to get in bed, it would get off its hook and try to get in there with him. He said that he could barely fight it off on the last few days. "If I had to go another day, it would get me."

You would think that Jimmy's snowmobile suit would never be clean again but somebody, maybe his momma (maybe yo momma . . .) somehow scrubbed it and patched up the holes with neat, intricate, varicolored patches and it came back clean and ready for the duty after Jimmy's ten days off.

Which, it was the perfect thing for that kind of duty. Sometimes it is rough in the shallow Gulf in the wintertime. We towed two barges, the front one on the longline, "eye on the bit," and the other behind it on a long intermediate hawser with two wire bridles. Like I said, the various companies that owned the Ferg were small and poor (one "Oil Well Co." had signs at its gas stations that looked like miniature drill derricks) and these old barges were in rough shape. They had to keep the cargo part (the whole middle of the barge) welded up good enough so that the refinery would okay to load but the flotation tanks in the ends ("rakes") of both barges were in such bad shape that on a long, rough trip (damn near all of them in the wintertime) some of the stobs would get pounded out of the rust holes in the bottom and that end of the barge would sink down about level with the water (a fuel oil barge will sink lower than a gasoline barge and we drug one of them halfway across the Gulf on the bottom about the time of Hurricane Camille). It was usually the end that was acting like the bow that this happened to and the damned thing would try to dive to the bottom in the rough seas. The only thing for it was to head them up and run back with the boat to put the deckhand on the barge with a long air hose to hook to the rusty old reciprocating pump kept tied to a rusty cleat near the expected problem. After Jimmy was on the barge, we would try to stand by within the range of that hose while he pumped out the rake and climbed down in there to find the leak and re-stob the hole, which sometimes took two spruce "Paul Bunyan" two-by-fours side by side chopped to fit with an ax . . . sometimes took all night long too . . . sometimes while it was raining sleet.

That kind of duty is hard on both the man and his clothes and is dangerous, what with the waves that had pounded the stob out in the first place breaking over the bow of the sunk barge like that. When I had to do it, I always got soaking wet, damn near froze and scared to death. Jimmy would get wet too, but that "Hollofil" insulation, tough nylon housing, and lady's underwear liner of his snowmobile suit wouldn't hold the water and he stayed warm and light enough to do the acrobatics that it took to get back on the boat after he got the barge back up on top. I envied him that garment, I tell you, but this was before the Wal-Marts and Kmarts and them came down here and stocked inappropriate Yankee goods like tire chains, walleye lures, windshield scrapers, ice fishing augers, and snowmobile suits.

One year, after the old Ferg was long gone, I let a man con me into delivering the boat I built for him all the way up to that little cutoff section of Michigan they call the "UP." He was a nice man and I was well compensated so I had a solid hundred-dollar bill in my pocket with which I was supposed to pay for motel rooms and restaurants. I am too shy to do that so I planned to sleep in my old Valiant (God rest its good soul) and eat groceries from the grocery store and snack on a big sack of green peanuts my wife gave me for the trip. I vowed to keep that hundred-dollar bill until I got up there to what surely must be snowmobile suit country. It worked like a charm too. I bought such a snowmobile suit as has never been seen down here. The only thing wrong with it is (I still got it) that it must have been made for Godzilla. I am a pretty good-sized man (make three or four of Jimmy if you just considered the size) but my snowmobile suit just swallows me. I have walked around with the britches legs rolled up so much that the liner is worn out down to the fuzz all down around the bottom. Its crotch hangs so low that I have to make two or three hauls to reach the bottom tallywhacker of the zipper . . . the sleeves almost drag the ground. When I turn around to go in another direction, it takes several steps for the damn thing to catch up. I am scared to death I might wear it too long but it is very warm.

After Kmarts and them metastasized all the way down here and put all the little family outfits out of business, I bought my wife a little well-fitted snowmobile suit, too, so we could sit out at night in the cold at our house on the island with the big doors open after the front had passed and look out through the clear air at the stars and the yellow brick road of the moonlight sparkling on the water while we listened to *Prairie Home Companion* on the radio on a Saturday night (that's living large ain't it?). It is a cozy little business. Sometimes I can imagine that I hear the old Ferg rumbling by. I unroll my britches legs so the cuffs won't catch any cracker crumbs and only wad up one sleeve at the time to find my hand so I can sip on my cup. When it gets too hot for that we wash our snowmobile suits and put them in one of those wonderful, cheap plastic boxes (surely, along with the white plastic bucket, one of the best inventions of the twentieth century) until the next winter. My snowmobile suit is so big that it takes up a whole box by itself.

We keep everything in those boxes. They keep the salt and wet out and consolidate our junk into easily identified, neat, perfectly nested stacks in the corners of the house. We write what's in the box on there with a stank Magic Marker so we never have to rummage to get the quilt or the tent or the bottom-job junk or the spare well pump or any of those kinds of things . . . we just grab the right box and go. This spring we decided to sail our tiny boat down to a little uninhabited island (Marsh Island in Apalachee Bay) to spend the night of the full moon lying in our sleeping bag looking at the silhouettes of the migrating birds through our binoculars as they crossed its bright face. We have a big homemade, warm-weather sleeping bag that we keep in the same-sized box as our snowmobile suits. You guessed it. Somebody grabbed the wrong box and when we got to where we were going, all we had was my old big snowmobile suit. Even though it was dead calm, no motor and a long way back to the house, there was no real calamity. We just both got in there and lined up our knobblers with the full moon. It was actually better than a real sleeping bag. We could stick our binoculars down in the sleeves to keep the dew off and with our feet down in separate leg holes, there was no toenail scratching or anything. The place was so remote that there were no other out-of-place fools to get alarmed and dial 911 on their cellular phones about them two heads.

When the old Ferg rusted out and became obsolete about the same time around 1981 or so and was cut up for scrap down in the delta someplace, most of the members of the crew were old enough to draw Social Security and still strong enough to scratch up a little extra with fishing and crabbing to keep a little salt in the box. I thought I saw Jimmy driving a half-loaded pulpwood truck on State Road 65 in Liberty County but I couldn't catch him with the damn old car I had at the time (hadda had my Valiant, I'da blowed that wood out of the bunks). Ain't no telling where that little booger is but I bet he is warm.

Jimmy of the Ferg.

King Tut

*with whom I prove the disclaimer that
none of these stories could possibly be true*

A little after that biscuit-catfish incident—maybe 1979—the tug was waiting our turn to lock out of the Mississippi River going west when I read in the newspaper that King Tut with all his raiments and accoutrements was on display across the river at the Sugar Bowl. I could see right where he was from where we were tied up to some bushes. They were having some kind of trouble with the lock and we had been tied up to the same bushes for so long that the paperboy had put us on his route and we had started running a trotline alongside the barges. One night, I was up in the wheelhouse trying to get away from the company when I heard the lock talking on the radio. There were so many boats tied up along the river that there were some thirty lockings ahead of us. I had plenty of time to swim the river and go see King Tut.

I took off all my clothes and shoes, put them into a white plastic bucket, clenched a sock with my collection of Susan B. Anthony dollars in my teeth, and climbed down the tires into the river. Pushing my white bucket in front of me, I started swimming. I have had a little experience with that old swift river and ain't stupid, so I didn't delude myself that I could swim straight across to the dome. I figured I would need a little hiding place to put on my clothes anyway, so some less exposed downriver landing would be just fine. I was in no hurry to get back to the boat, so I planned to pull out of the river someplace down by the Huey P. Long bridge, wipe off a little bit with my rag, put on my clothes and shoes, and stroll back to the dome. I got messed up though.

Just about the time I got to the middle of the river and began to adjust my estimate of a landing site because I was making such good time, a damn tanker (EXXON PASCAGOULA . . . MONROVIA, LIBERIA) that had been anchored upriver of us, waiting to get to the dock, decided that it was time to go, hauled anchor, swung broadside the river, and came down on me. I had to skeedaddle sideways like a crab to get out of the way. While I was trying to make up my mind if I wanted to swim downriver, contrary to my notions, around the stern or try upriver around the bow, we drifted so far that I wound up way the hell-and-gone down below the Tenneco refinery at Chalmette. The bank was steep and rooty and when I finally got myself hauled out, I was worn out from the decision-making process and didn't have my plastic bucket anymore.

I started searching in the dark through the horrendous mess of trash along the bank for something to wear. Finally I settled on a plastic shower curtain, which I identified by feeling the snap-on rings. I was able to use these rings, cleverly, to attach the shower curtain around me sort of like a toga. I figured, once I got up to the light and managed to scrape some of the mud off me, I wouldn't look too peculiar for New Orleans where people are used to a little peculiarity. I still had my Susans. I would just trot up the river bank to the phone booth, just outside the refinery gate, call a cab, and go see King Tut.

I found a little, more or less, clear water puddled in the asphalt of the road and splashed around in it like a bird until I couldn't feel too much grit anywhere. Then I started moseying back to town. I thought I cut a pretty fine figure in my outfit, swinging my sock full of dollars as I strutted up the road. My notions were reinforced when a car came up from behind me and blew the horn in appreciation as they passed. "Good old New Orleans, " I said to myself, "what a fine place." After two or three other cars had admired me that same way, some of the occupants shouting gleefully in appreciation, I decided I was so attractive that maybe I could stick out my thumb and eliminate the phone booth/taxicab step altogether.

It worked like a charm. A car full of happy people stopped to pick me up right away. Only after the inside lights of the car came on when the door opened did I notice that my shower curtain was one of those transparent jobs. Like I said, people in New Orleans are used to things like that. Lucky for me, they were on their way to see King Tut, too.

The Sailor's Grave

in which someone gets his comeuppance and deserves it

We built a dock on the Crooked River at a place called "the Sailor's Grave." We used to go fishing and swimming down there when we were children and, though it was called that then, we never wondered about the name. Not too long ago, I finally got curious and asked some old folks about it. They said that someone had buried a sailor there around the turn of the century. The sailor was some kind of Yankee from off one of the lumber ships and had worked for Captain Charlie's daddy. Got shot. Of course, that was so long ago that Charlie was just a little baby when it happened.

Captain Charlie is dead now. He lived to be nearly a hundred years old and was on the city commission until the day he died. Even long after his opinion had no bearing whatsoever on the subject at hand, they kept on electing him because everybody said, "We won't have to worry about no hanky-panky as long as Charlie is on the board." He was the most respectable little man you ever saw. He never drank a drop or cussed a bad word or darked the door of a church or did a mean thing in his life. We all just loved him. I worked for him when I was a boy and I'll give you an example of how nice he was. One time we went to this old widow's house because she was having trouble with her well. These wells around here all pump sulfur water (salt water, sometimes after a hurricane) and it eats up the pump and the casing and all the plumbing. The worst culprit is the foot valve because it stays down in the water all the time where the hydrogen sulfide corrodes the valve seat so it won't seal and the pump loses prime. Well, me and Captain Charlie had to pull up the black plastic pipe with the foot valve on the end of it out of this woman's well. We just about had it when the hose-clamp holding the pipe onto the nipple on top of the foot valve got snagged and snatched loose and let the foot valve fall back in the well. We listened to the long *whooooop* of the air and the *ploop* when it hit the bottom and Captain Charlie just said, "Well, if that ain't the doggone dickens." Took us all afternoon to fish that foot valve out of the well and, even though the yellow flies were eating us up the whole time, those were the strongest words to come from Captain Charles Franklin. When we went to the back door to tell the old gal her water was back on, she said in the whiny voice of the entitled, "Well, Captain Charlie, what do I owe you?" "Not a thing, Mrs. Cook. Just glad I was able to fix it for you."

Charlie's momma was a tiny little woman (Charlie was no giant himself) and so pretty, they say, that you couldn't take your eyes off her. There is a picture hanging in the vestibule of the City Hall. In the old photograph, she and a bunch of other women are at a bandage-making party like they had during World War One. There she is, peeking around the biggest pile of bandages, just beaming with a great big smile among all those prissy-looking sisters sitting at that table with their little piles. You can see what they mean about how pretty she was. They say she was sweet too, just like Charlie . . . do anything for anybody. She caught the typhoid fever from trying to nurse the colored people in Sumatra during the epidemic of 1921. They said that she was so dear, lying in her coffin, that it was almost impossible to shut the lid on her.

Charlie's daddy was another story. He owned one of the two sawmills at the mouth of the river. He was a mean old man. Even though the sawmill business during the clear-cut of the virgin forest of the coastal plain made him and a bunch of other people rich, he paid the lowest possible wages to his help. They said he would start the new men off in the mill low and tell them that he would raise them up to where they could have a place to live and something to eat after they proved themselves but then that raise would never come. Pretty soon, they would be working full-time just to keep credit at the store. They say that not only did he own the store and the biggest sawmill, he had a controlling interest in the other sawmill, owned the logging operation and the timber lease, and there just wasn't any other place to go. If the hands tried to run off before their store bill was paid, Charlie's daddy would send the law after them. They had to stay and work for nothing.[1] It was a tough time back then. Some said that if a man got killed on the job (which wasn't any kind of a rare thing in the sawmills and logging operations of the turn of the century) and didn't have any family to come get him, Old Man Franklin would just have him rolled off the log ramp into the river.

So this Yankee sailor came here on one of the lumber ships and stayed. They say he was one of those brazen-acting men who treats you like he knows you when he don't. Wasn't scared of anything, not even Charlie's daddy, and somehow that appealed to the old man so he kind of hired or contracted with the sailor to do some meanness or other between the sawmill and the logging crews in the woods. The Yankee man was back and forth all the time raising hell and beating up on people and gambling and terrorizing the whole world around here. The law, what there was of it, kind of overlooked him. Then, all of a sudden, he came drifting down the river deader'n hell and all swole up. They said he had been shot in the head and they buried him right on the bank where he washed up. Called the place "the Sailor's Grave" from then on. Though there was a lot of speculation, the law never did accuse anybody of shooting that man. I don't know if you know it or not, but Florida was just as wild as the territories of the West back then.

In spite of his daddy Captain Charlie grew up to be the kind man I knew, got married, and had three daughters. They were all nice shy girls . . . stayed home. Finally, when she was about thirty-five years old, the youngest one married this out-of-town man. Everybody said, "Captain Charlie, how come you let that happen?" The man didn't seem like the type to be Charlie's son-in-law. He drifted in, kind of like a derelict. Slept in his old car. He had some kind of pension from the Vietnam War. When he got his check, he would go to the Shanghai (actual name "Shangrila," a little like the magic island) and drink that pension up by the second or third of the month, then he would go to work. He did freelance boat-bottom jobs . . . worked at all the marine railways and travel-lifts all around here. He was the toughest man I ever saw. He had one of those big heavy-duty twenty-amp grinders and he would get up under a boat and sand all day long. One of my buddies and I watched him grind all the gelcoat off a forty-five-foot fiberglass sailboat right down to the woven roving without putting that grinder down a single time . . . didn't wear a mask, earplugs, gloves, shirt, goggles, hat, or anything. I said, "How can he stand that?" "Tough," said my buddy. "Do that all day and drink whiskey all night . . . smokes cigarettes and chews tobacco at the same time. Take five licks to kill him with an ax. If we had had another one like him, we wouldn't have lost that war."

He got to be a fiberglass bump specialist and no wonder. That's a nasty job. It is expensive to get somebody to do it right if you can get it done at all. What happens is that fiberglass boats grow big bumps on the bottom. Fiberglass is not exactly waterproof and one of the juices in it is hygroscopic and attracts water into the layers of plastic and glass by osmosis. The water just keeps on soaking in trying to dilute the attracting juice and the solution is so bound up that the water can't get loose to get back out again. Hydraulic pressure is powerful so the layers de-laminate and the boat grows a bump everywhere that is happening. If those bumps grow enough, they will bust and cause a leak in the hull of the boat. People pay big money to get those bumps ground off and the bottom puttied back up, sanded fair with the terrible, torturous longboard, and painted with epoxy, which is waterproof enough to, sort of, slow the bump garden down. This tough vet with the big grinder would make short work of that nasty job. Made enough money to spend most of his time at the Shangrila even after he married Charlie's youngest daughter.

He went home long enough so he and Charlie's daughter had a child. She was a smart and pretty little girl. Charlie said that she put him in mind of his own momma. We used to see her down around Captain Charlie's dock when she heard that he was coming in. Charlie had a snapper boat. She loved him even when he smelled like fish and diesel fuel and old man. He was about the most successful red snapper captain in the Gulf. Captain Charlie could even catch them when they were getting scarce and the price was up. He quit though . . . tried to get the rest of them to quit too. Said, "It would be a shame to catch them down to where there were so few left that they couldn't find each other to breed back up . . . just because they are five dollars a pound."

Well, Charlie got feeble pretty quick after he quit fishing. Couldn't hear a thing and half of what he said was irrelevant. He still got around though. His granddaughter had a job up at the IGA, checking out. Charlie and his two old-maid daughters didn't live but about half a mile from there and he would walk to the grocery store to see her at least once a day, rain or shine. Charlie's granddaughter was just a small, pretty little girl until she got to be about fifteen or sixteen then, God knows . . . whoo Jesus. It is hard to describe it. It was sort of like the progression of a ripeness, a natural thing. She didn't have to get dolled up or practice any particular motion of the lips or wiggle of the head or posture this way and that to show off first one little piece of cute and then another. She didn't even have to learn any contemporary chirp to show that she was some kind of something. She seemed to shine like the light on her was special like it is when the sun comes out after a dark thunderstorm. Everybody noticed the progression but her. She kept on scanning groceries all through it. She had no idea why all those old men would just stop and forget what it was they had on their list and stand there leaning on the buggy, blocking the road. The word *stunning* ain't applicable every time it is used but she surely was an amazing thing. She was sweet too, just like Charlie and his Momma. Maybe there is a gene that passes through the generations in a zigzag. Pretty soon she was the favorite checkout girl of the old people and black folks, not to mention young men and boys, especially checkout boys. Sometimes her line would be full and all the others would be empty. One time I saw her not only root through the pocketbook for the proper food stamps and write out the check for this shaky old lady, but enter the amount in the little checkbook ledger for her, figure her balance, and then, when she found out that there was enough money in the bank, write the check for the light bill. Even though she was always busy with such as that, she didn't hold up the progress of the business. She was quick and accurate . . . even the scanning machine seemed to jump up and take notice, and there was always a checkout boy standing by. They would put the groceries in the car and hurry right back.

But then this horrible man started showing up in her line. He came in on a scallop boat. Every now and then . . . unpredictably . . . bay scallops will thicken up offshore and there is big money to be made for anybody who can keep a piece of junk shrimp boat[2] running until it is over. Sometimes they make over ten thousand bucks per boat trip . . . three or four trips a week . . . attracts all kinds of people. You can hardly find a place to park your car in town when the scallops are here. This man had a tattoo of a snake's tail down his arm (*Elaphe guttata,* red rat snake . . . a beautiful snake and a good tattoo too). Except for not being a Yankee, he was just like the sailor of 1901, presumptuous, mean, and nasty. He would say, "This snake done crawled up my sleeve." With that, he would pull open his shirt and there the tattoo continued down his chest. Then he would grab himself and say, "Goddamn, I got him by the head now. I think he wants to come out and play with little Fluffy." Nasty son of a bitch would do that to anybody even Charlie's sweet granddaughter. Wouldn't leave her alone. She was too shy to tell her daddy and it was a long time before he found out, but then . . . That's another indescribable thing. I'll just say her daddy took that job on like he did the bottom of a boat. He beat three or four thousand dollars' worth of dents in the cars in the parking lot with that snake. They had to send the Life Flight helicopter down from Tallahassee.

The snake man didn't learn his lesson, though. As soon as he got out of the hospital, he was right back at the IGA. Had a leather sap in his hip pocket. A lot of people hung around up there to see . . . and it didn't take long . . . except that it didn't happen at the grocery store and nobody saw. Snake man floated up in the river not far from the old Sailor's Grave. They did an autopsy and determined that he had been shot in the head with some strange kind of .32. The bullet was a jacketed soft-point like a rifle bullet. Most .32s are either just all-lead revolver bullets or full-metal-cased like out of a .32 automatic. They didn't understand it. The penetration was about like a pistol but the bullet looked like what would have come out of a rifle. They arrested the bottom job man right away. Kept him in jail long enough to temporarily purify him from alcohol, but the grand jury wouldn't indict him. Everybody said "Unh-hunh."

Some things never change but some things change quick. While his son-in-law was in jail, Old Captain Charlie had a bad stroke and died. After they got him in the ground, his oldest old-maid daughter sent me word that he had told her about some things that he wanted me to have, so I went around to the house. She gave me a paper bag with his good slicker suit, his old belt, a nearly worn-out Queen fish knife, and some old pictures of people in my family that he had been keeping. When I got home, after I had looked at the pictures, I took the old slicker suit out to hold up and look at. It was a cute little thing . . . looked just like Charlie and brought tears to my eyes. Something heavy was in the pocket, a big old revolver, what they call a cowboy pistol.[3] Said on the seven-and-a-half-inch barrel, 32 WCF. That stands for 32/20 Winchester Center Fire, an old rifle cartridge from the 1870s . . . back in the days when a man liked to get the bullets for both his rifle and revolver out of the same box. It had the initials CWF engraved on the butt strap. I figure they must have been his daddy's initials because Captain Charlie was Charles C. for Collins, his mother's maiden name.

1. That system is called "peonage" and is against the law now. Not too long ago, shade tobacco farmers in North Florida were working people like that. While I was listening to the radio to try to find out about the Apollo moon mission where we almost lost those men, I heard that the federal government had just convicted a Gadsden County man of peonage.

2. Scallops are caught by an ordinary shrimp boat. It has to be big enough to work well offshore and haul a big load. They stay out and drag until they have a regular mountain of the little bivalves piled on deck. Because of their littoral habits, bay scallops are able to survive out of water for a pretty long time but even with that, no time is wasted. There have been some desperate bilgewater and engine room doings to try to keep the boats running in the face of all that possible decay and possible money. After the scallops finally pick up and leave (or get picked up and hauled off) the shrimpers have the money and time to fix the old boats up right . . . then they go back to regular old starvation shrimping, like always.

Captain Charlie refused to drag for shrimp. Said, "It is a shame to tear up all that bottom and kill all those little fish just for a few bugs, no matter what they are bringing." He was right. The bycatch ratio always averages worse than ten to one and that is just for the vertebrates that are killed by the trawl. The net always comes up completely full of things that used to be alive. There is no commercial fishery so persistently destructive as the fleet of shrimp boats that desperately scour the whole continental shelf for half a pound of shrimp an hour so ignorant gourmets can smugly show off their love of consumption at any price. You know, St. Peter is gonna smite their asses for enabling such a pitiful waste.

3. The real name for a cowboy revolver is "Colt Single Action Army." Some delighted red man lifted one right out of George Armstrong Custer's hand before it had time to cool off. The first ones came in the same three calibers as the old 1873 Winchester rifle, "the gun that won the West." The barrel inscription for each was: 32WCF, 38WCF, and Frontier Six Shooter . . . didn't have to put the caliber on that one . . . everybody knew it was the man . . . 44/40 Winchester Center Fire. That's the one that went "Rootey-Toot-Toot" when Frankie shot old Johnny down. The first number is the intended diameter of the bore in inches and the second number is the number of grains (an archaic measure of weight not equivalent to anything . . . kind of like a drachma) of black powder loaded into the cartridge case. By modern standards, even "the man" was puny. That's why Frankie had to shoot three times to stop old Johnny from wiggling. Don't tell that to all the dead people you meet when you get to Hell. Might make them feel bad . . . Po old Johnny, wouldn't want to insult him in front of all those shrimp-eating gourmets.

The Slave's Recipe

*in which I do a little more tugging, get involved in a criminal conspiracy,
and get locked up for murder . . . and learn a new recipe . . .
and satisfy a lifelong curiosity . . . a long story*

I have a recipe for peach cobbler that a man from Estiffanulga gave me about 1982. He was a slave. It wasn't 1860 or anything and the man wasn't even black but he was a sure-enough slave. I met him while the little tug I was working on was towing barges of gasoline and fuel oil out of the huge refinery at Pascagoula in Mississippi Sound. We towed two barges through the Alabama WPA ditch and the Wimico wiggles down the Jackson River to its confluence with the mighty Apalachicola. When we got there, we met the *Roulette,* a homemade paddle-wheel pushboat that could sometimes, eventually, push one of our barges all the way up through the locks into Lake Seminole and on up the Chattahoochee as far as Columbus, Georgia. We would tow the other barge across the Gulf and then up the pretty little Withlacoochee River to the tank farm in Yankeetown between Cedar Key and Crystal River.

Roulette was an unusual boat, made by a mean old man specially to navigate the powerful and crooked Apalachicola. It was just a low, steel flatboat covered by a screen porch. There was a little shaky wheelhouse on the tin roof of the porch so the wheelman could see over the barge and an old wore-out EMD railroad locomotive engine sitting naked, on deck, right in the middle, that drove the reduction gears for the two side wheels through two enormous greasy roller chains running off each end of a semi truck rear axle. That axle was the key to the whole thing. The boat was steered (powerfully, I'll give him that) by working the air brakes on each end of the axle, first one side and then the other, with little rocker valves located all over the boat. There was even one steering valve beside the rusty, dangerous looking, LP gas stove up under the wheelhouse so the old man who was captain, owner and inventor of the thing could steer while he was cooking his dinner. He was so mean that most of the time, he couldn't get anybody to stay on there with him to cook, make up barges, pour oil in the old engine, grease the chains, change the carbons in the searchlight and fix the roof and screen wire, but towards the last, he had this man from Estiffanulga working as a slave on there.

This was back before insurance companies outlawed towing on the short line in inshore waters. Short tow is the cheapest and easiest way to handle a barge. You ain't always breaking all those cables and knocking all those big scabs of rust off the boat and the barge trying to make up to the stern to push. The boat can run a real short crew because all they had to do to work the barge was to take in or let out on the towline to suit the conditions of the sea or the river. Some inshore boats ran, at least some of the time, with only two men . . . one in the wheelhouse and one to work the engines, barges, cook, and catch a little snooze when he could before his turn in the wheelhouse. Even some little seagoing tugs like us had to do that when it was too cold and rough to attract a crew, but it was tough. Towing on the short line in narrow and shallow water is dangerous. Lots of tugs were run over or tripped upside down and towed under by the barges after they messed up and ran aground right there in front of the tow. Though the few pushboats, like *Roulette* (there never was another one of those), that worked the Apalachicola River had to make up astern of the barge and push because the river is so swift and tricky that running aground is the usual business, they could get by with short crews since they could push up and take a nap anytime they wanted to and only had to work the barge once per trip. Which, that business was a little tricky in this situation.

As soon as we got a lull in the barge-transferring operation with the *Roulette,* the slave would swarm on board of our boat to swap porno magazines. Deckhands get tired of looking at the same old naked gals all the time. I guess that's a pretty good rule about relationships with women in general, even real ones. If you don't love them, before long you get tired of looking at them even when they are naked. There wasn't much opportunity for conversation during the normal barge transfer. We would idle as slowly upstream as we could and still stay between the banks with both barges (sometimes three) on the short line while the *Roulette* tried to catch up and make up to the after barge . . . sort of like the copulation attempts of a string of ducks. As soon as he got the wires over the bits, the enslaved deckhand would run up the barges, monkeying from one to the other on the intermediate towlines and their wire bridles, and come on us, hand over hand down the hawser like an orangutan with his magazines clenched in his teeth. While all these acrobatics were going on, the *Roulette's* captain screamed and hollered back there about how he wanted to get tightened up to his tow and turned loose. Once or twice, the deckhand had to swim back and got his new sweethearts wet when the old man got so mad he boiled out of his wheelhouse onto the barge and himself threw off the intermediate towline between the two barges. Once the slave traded a magazine whose theme was devoted to very buxom (some could even be called fat) redheaded, naked ladies with freckles and I was able to satisfy a curiosity that I have had since childhood.

One trip, when the river was low, we had to tie up to the *Roulette* long enough to visit a little. The reason that happened was because when it got dry in the fall, there wasn't enough water for a full barge to go all the way to Columbus even with that old wigglesome *Roulette* hunting the deep water. We would tie up alongside and pump half (or whatever the old turd thought he could handle) the gasoline out of one of our barges into the empty one that they had brought back. It usually took about four or five hours. The slave deckhand from the other boat would stay in our galley and eat up the leftovers, drink coffee, and try to read all the porno magazines (hundreds . . . some from back in the forties . . . ghastly stuff) that were stored under the galley seats while he gossiped with the cook—me (I alternated among cooking, decking, engineering, and in the wheelhouse depending on the season and how pissed off they were about the last time I quit). He told me his story and gave me the recipe, which I cooked up for dessert that night and made a big hit with our gourmet crew.

He got to be a slave because he had run off from the state mental hospital and the word was out. That hundred or so miles on the river below the Jim Woodruff dam is just like one small town. All he would have had to do would have been to stop hiding in the swamp long enough for some sister's brother to catch a little glimpse and it would be back to Chattahoochee for him. The reason he got committed was that he had a certain attractiveness and willingness to fornicate frequently around the neighborhood. Then he would slap his thigh, laugh loudly about it, and defend himself capably when confronted by the family of the willing girl. He had simply messed with the wrong people and got into a situation of local legal manipulation that was beyond him. Bad as it was, it wasn't as bad as it could have been. Some of these old daddies will shoot a man for that. I know it may sound callous and opinion has no place in a story like this, but it might not be such a bad thing. Some girls go through a little spell where they don't seem to be able to use their own good sense and are liable to get pregnant before they are ready. If a man has to think about old daddy (or old granddaddy) and that .30/30, he might pay a little more attention to what he is doing. Wouldn't be so many women who can't take good care of their children and maybe not so many people in places like Chattahoochee—like this man. He wasn't a bad person, just a reckless young fool. All he needed was something to make him think—like he had now.

As a fugitive from the mental hospital, he was hanging around the empty barge we left tied to the black gum (*Nyssa aquatica* . . . "tupelo" to real native Floridians) trees where the *Roulette* came to swap and he followed the pushboat upriver. At that time, the old captain was working the boat all by his mean-assed self and he had to tie up to the bushes every night to eat his supper and take his little nap. His evening ritual was that he would steer with his air valve by the stove while he cooked supper to get as many miles as he could in the few days when the dam's electricity gates were open and the river was navigable. The poor hard-bitten, hungry fugitive ran through the bushes (*strolled* would be a more appropriate word, old *Roulette* wasn't no real bank washer) and smelled the cooking. After the old man pushed up for the night, the escapee slipped on board and ate up the scraps and left a few little coon turds around the deck so the old man would misblame the theft.

Before long he caught the man coming for his supper and blackmailed him into being a nonpaid hand. With two people running the boat, watch and watch, the old *Roulette* managed to run twenty-four hours a day during the short times that the river was navigable, and things worked pretty good for everybody but the slave. I would have busybodied in and done something about it if I had thought it was the right thing to do, but the state hospital wasn't near as nice a place as the *Roulette*. Shoot, in those days, it wasn't even as good as Tate's Hell swamp, and I'm not so sure it's any better now.

Finally we rusted out so bad that the company had to put our old boat in dry dock over in Mobile to half sole the bottom one more time. What we had been doing was driving wood stobs in the rusty holes. When the old (just about in as bad shape as our boat) floating dry dock they had in Mobile finally got enough water pumped out so the old boat's bottom was visible, all those stobs sticking out of all that rust put me in mind of some old World War Two mine that you used to see in the movies. We stayed in the dry dock for a long time. The crew hung around in the galley all the time and got on my nerves and I had to take a plate once or twice. (It was a tradition on there that if a man complained about the food, the cook could snatch up his plate and substitute a paper plate, a can of Vienna sausages, and a stalk of old roachy saltines). I went to town a couple of times and I walked up and down the riverbank, but I soon got tired of all the nastiness of Mobile and took my sockful of change and caught the bus back home.

I have been doing things like that off and on for most of my life. I worked on that same old boat a bunch of separate times for many years. I don't remember exactly what I did after I quit while they were in dry dock in Mobile. I think I drove the bus for the senior citizens' center for the summer and worked on the boat in the shop (I always have a boat in my shop, no matter what) in my off time. Anyway, when the winter came, I figured the old tug would finally be back on the job and shorthanded because of the mean conditions of the Yankeetown run when it was cold and rough. I sort of got along with the old captain who had been on there ever since the boat had been built in 1948, and even though he would get pretty pissed when I walked off, he would put me back on if I showed up grinning . . . in January. He was kind of comical about it. He would shuffle around and around in the bedroom slippers he wore all the time to try to stave off his terrible gout and work his false teeth first one cockeyed way and then the other. Finally, after he had jammed his hands down in all his pockets and snatched them back out again like he had felt something hot down in there, he would stammer his same old speech about how he ought to be ashamed of himself for encouraging sorryness, "But goddamn people are so goddamn spoiled with the government handouts (not that you got to have none of that money, you sorry-assed bastard you) that you just couldn't get nobody that would work no goddamn more."

I got on as engineer this time. I was overjoyed about it. My old nemesis hadn't quit. He was a lifer with the company, just like the old captain, but my being on there put him on one of the other crews and I didn't have to associate with the mean son of a bitch. This little tug tried to keep three complete crews—captain, engineer, and cook-deckhand. They worked twenty days on and ten days off. On the boat, it was four hours on and four off, and, except for big deals like sinking barges and bad weather, there was only one crew on duty at the time. It was possible to completely avoid somebody on another crew if you wanted to. I turned the mattress over and settled right back in again.

Some things were different. First, though we were still on the Yankee-town run, we were towing straight out of the refinery at Chalmette, just below New Orleans. While the boat was in dry dock, the company had leased a Louisiana delta boat (commonly called "Coon Ass" boats for some bastardization of one name for French-speaking south Louisianans, which circuitous etymological trail has long been lost. If you decide to add that to your vocabulary, watch yourself because there is another branch of French speakers in that state who call themselves "Creoles" and neither group likes to be confused with the other and nobody down there likes the English to overstep themselves). The delta boat was to take on the intracoastal work. The New Orleans boat was experienced with big, swift, crooked rivers and they soon shooed the old *Roulette* off the Apalachicola and started taking the gas to Bainbridge and Columbus and St. Marks all in the same trip, in a route just like a potato chip truck. As soon as that happened, the old turd that owned the *Roulette* promptly went bankrupt and got a job abusing people at the state hospital in Chattahoochee. The slave hit the river swamp again.

On my first ten days off I went down there to see if I could find out what it would take to buy that old *Roulette* from the court. I found out that the boat was sunk up in a slough just off the Jackson River and would probably go pretty cheap. I borrowed a skiffboat and went to see what kind of shape the machinery was in. When I got there, I was in for a surprise.

First, only most of the hull was sunk. All the guts and the screen wire part were still sticking up above the surface (at least at that stage of the river). I wandered around looking at the junk and thinking how I could have the damn thing back to running in about two days if I could get a big pump down there, when I noticed a little pig tied by one leg to the stove. I poked around a little and found a dry box of matches and a small stash of porno magazines and I knew what was up. I left in the skiff like I was going back to Apalach, then I slipped back on the bank and caught the ex-slave feeding crawfish and fish heads to his pig.

I spent the night on there with him and we caught some stumpknockers (that's a river bream) and one speckled perch (that's "black crappie" to some) to go with his palm cabbage for supper. We got to talking about his prospects. Though the wreck of the *Roulette* was a good camp for him, it was sort of exposed to traffic in the river, and the wheelman of every tugboat that came by felt obligated to study it intensely with the carbon-arc light (a very intense light). He said that fishermen were starting to come displace him on weekends to stay in the screen wire and run trotlines and drink beer. "Wouldn't leave a full can behind for nothing," said the ex-slave. He was wondering about the prospects of getting on with us. "Y'all still got all them magazines under the seat in the galley? Reckon I'd get caught?" he wondered. "Yeah, we still got every single one and you probably would get caught but nobody would pay any attention to it. Everybody looks at those magazines," says me. "Naw, goddammit, I mean do you think somebody would find out who I was and send me back to Chattahoochee? Ain't no telling what that old asshole would do to me if I got locked up in there with him." We talked about the isolation of the tank farm in Yankeetown and how we never had much communication with any boat in the Gulf and, after I told him a thing or two about New Orleans, he decided to take a chance.

He went to Chalmette and got on with one of the other crews as cook. I wanted to warn him about that mean engineer but there was hardly any opportunity. Besides, I figured, if he could deal with the captain of the *Roulette,* he wouldn't have any trouble with the second engineer of our boat. But it was a complicated situation, and the way things turned out it would probably have been best if he had known how it was on there.

The old captain had a cataract operation that turned out not to be very satisfactory because of some disorder of the retina of both eyes. He was pretty close to his retirement time when all this happened and he knew he had to keep plugging until then. I don't know how he worked it, but he managed to keep his license even though he could barely see the bow of the barge. The mean engineer had been with him all that time. When the captain got so that he couldn't see, he and the engineer just sort of swapped jobs. When I was on the crew with them, I handled the boat in the refinery and at Yankeetown and didn't tell anybody. When I wasn't on there, the engineer knocked down the pilings at the refinery and Yankeetown and rooted up the trees along the river. I ought to give the devil his due. He was a pretty good wheelman. He wasn't the ace that I am or the old captain when he could still see, but he could, in his slow and sloppy way, get the barge to the dock. He didn't have a license and it would have been hell to pay if he had hit anything, but as the old captain had said, "What the fuck they going to do, pull my license and take my goddamn Cadillac? Hell, I'm seventy years old. I got thirty dollars, I'll catch the goddamn bus just like you with yo sorry ass. Just go live with my daughter—at least she can cook." I said, "Look out now. Don't be complaining about the cooking. You would starve to death before you could work that first Vienna sausage out of the can as blind as you are and you never would get them saltines gummed open."

The whole criminal conspiracy would have worked fine except for one thing. The engineer was one of those damned aggressive, dangerous sodomites like you find in jails. That's how the fugitive managed to get hired so easy. There are supposed to be three men on each crew. Because of the engineer, there was usually a vacancy on that one. Mostly, that was no problem because the short towline method required a minimum of decking and both the captain and engineer were old hands at it. After the engineer ran off each new deckhand, the boat just ran shorthanded until another desperate fool like me or the fugitive showed up.

When our crew went to relieve the old captain's crew including the new cook-deckhand from his very first trip the boat was waiting to lock out of the Mississippi into the Gulf. There were a bunch of New Orleans policemen in the galley talking to the old captain and the new cook-deckhand and drinking coffee. All the business was tended to already, and the crew change out went normally except that the mean engineer was not there to be relieved. The old captain and the ex-slave got in the old raggedy company car that we had come in and drove away. The way the locking was going, it looked like I might have time to set the valves on one engine before our turn came so I didn't get into any of the discussions but went straight down to the engine room to try to do something during that rare time when the engines weren't running. As it turned out, we had to go in the lock before I got all the valve covers back on and I had to start the engine and just let the oil run down.

By the time I got it all wiped up and washed off (never a drop in the bilge) and had a chance to come up, we were already through the lock and it was time to put the barges on the towline (barges have to be made up to push in the locks no matter what kind of hotshot short-tow man you think you are). Turned out that all the hullabaloo with the law was because the old captain's engineer had disappeared while they were tied up in Chalmette at the refinery. Couldn't find him anywhere. One theory was that he might have gone ashore and got messed up. I doubted that. The mean-assed bastard never went ashore. I always thought it was because he was afraid somebody might decide to find out just how much there was to him with all his big talk.

As it turned out, later, there wasn't quite enough. We found out that his body washed up in the bushes along the bank of one of the distributaries down in the delta. He had been cut wide open (right through the belt) with a real sharp knife. The way we found out about it was that the Coast Guard sent a helicopter to intercept us way out in the middle of the Gulf. They said on the radio that they wanted "the deckhand." They let this man down on a quarter-inch cable in a bosun's chair to pick up the suspect. It was hard to communicate with him after he got down because of the racket of the helicopter and the feeling from that machine gun they had up there looking right down our noses. I was volunteered to go with him since I was the closest thing to a "deckhand" they had.

It took a long time in New Orleans, what with my crew and alibi still on the boat plugging for Yankeetown. I don't want to issue no sweeping prejudicial statement, but it's not good to get locked up in New Orleans even if you aren't the right man. I was lucky and able to stay single because of my age and the ferocity of my response to proposals, which was taken as comical by the old hands in the jail.

I finally got turned loose when my momma called up some people she knew down in the parish. Everybody apologized and went on and on about how they didn't know I was a friend of Mr. this and Miss that. By the time they finally got hot on the trail of the fugitive from Estiffanulga, he was hid out back in Tate's Hell swamp. I don't guess he would have stood a chance if they could have sent a real delta SWAT team up there, but those regular old Florida good-ole-boy refugees from the big-screen TV and the can of beer couldn't get far enough from the four-wheel drive and the metal-flake bass boat to find him.

The embarrassment of the Coast Guard fiasco where they picked up a man from the wrong crew and the frequentness of a dead asshole floating up in the Mississippi River sort of cooled the pursuit after a while. I got transferred onto the old captain's crew and took over in the wheelhouse just about like the dead engineer. It was a good winter overall, sort of calm some trips. The old captain, without the burden of his regular engineer, hired a good man for the engine room and took over as the unofficial cook-deckhand. I couldn't help teasing him a little because his reactions were so comical, but I only got my plate taken once or twice. Actually, he was a pretty good cook, even made lasagna. About the only thing I could think of to complain about was how often we had that damn peach cobbler recipe that the slave had given us. Even though I was engineer, I had to make a few lemon meringue pies just to break the monotony. You know, a hint of diesel fuel don't hurt a pie all that much. Two men from South Carolina bought the *Roulette* from the court, put it about halfway back together, and skirted around in the shallow water next to the woods between Apalach and Tarpon Springs to take it around the peninsula through the Keys. They were trying to get to the Dismal Swamp canal where they thought they would get rich pushing in that shallow water. The whole thing was a desperate, low-budget operation. When they got to the Keys they messed up and went through, under the bridge, at channel five and into the Atlantic. I guess they were thinking that they would just ride the Gulf Stream up to the Carolinas like the big ships do and save fuel, but the waves started batting the back sides of the paddle wheels and stripped the pinion out of the differential in the truck axle and the whole mess washed up on a pretty coral reef and tore up hundreds of years of work by the tiny commensal polyps. Four or five agencies of the government tried to fine them to help pay for the salvage operation but those fools didn't have anything to pay a fine with.

Things got to running so smooth on our old boat that it got boring. Some of the crew even went together and bought a damn TV. Fortunately we were out of range on most of the Yankeetown run but it finally got so that the most exciting thing on there was trying to find the place to drive another stob in the bottom. When I finally got tired of standing up there in the wheelhouse listening to all those people with cartoon-character voices on the radio and decided to jump ship again, the old blind, toothless captain still had about seven or eight months to go to get his pension. I was itching to go (had complete, full-sized patterns for a set of molds for a sailboat under my mattress), but I couldn't leave the old man in such a fix as that. What he needed was a good reliable wheelman who didn't communicate with the authorities too much. Soon as crew change came, I went to Apalach and borrowed the same skiffboat as the other time and headed up the river.

It was spring by then and the mighty Apalachicola was high and swift from all the rain. It took me a long time to get up beyond the mouth of the Jackson River, because I had to stop to dump the water out of that silly-assed aluminum butt-head skiff (or honkey drownder) a bunch of times. It had metal-fatigued and split all along the bottom of the transom and the duct tape was coming loose. Once I had to take the spark plugs out of the 9.9 when I waited too long and the boat sank and immersed the engine. It was dark and cold when I finally came to the place where we used to tie up the *Roulette*'s empty barge. It didn't take me long to smell smoke and slip up on my man so I could back up to his fire while we cut us a deal.

The last time I saw him was in New Orleans. He was driving the captain's old Cadillac convertible down the street, just as bold as brass. He had two very fat freckle-faced, redheaded ladies in the backseat holding up those little celluloid whirligig propellers like we used to give children at parties a long time ago. I couldn't tell if they were coming from a party or if it was just getting started.

Here is the slave's recipe:

Peach Cobbler

While you preheat the oven, put the frying pan on top of the stove and melt one whole stalk of butter in it (I said butter, not yellow-colored Crisco . . . which during World War Two they packaged the coloring stuff separately . . . ain't got it the right color yet). While the butter is melting, open two cans of peaches and drink the juice out of one can. Pour the rest—peaches and syrup—in with the butter and turn off the fire. Broadcast a whole handful of flour, more or less evenly, on top of the butter and peaches, then sprinkle a whole handful of sugar on top of that. Poke it around a little bit but don't stir. Put the frying pan in the oven and look at the porno magazines until the sugar gets good and brown. It'll make you fat if you don't look out . . . but it won't make you redheaded and freckled all over.

Working Skiffs of Franklin County, Florida

in which a traditional working boat hauls a house

All the coast of the Big Bend of Florida (Apalachee Bay) is and always has been a very productive fishing ground. Each section has developed its own kind of boat to suit its particular situation. Over to the east of Franklin County all the way around to Crystal River, the coastline is mostly deeply indented marshland best suited to small skiffboats. I don't want to raise any hackles but I believe Wakulla County is where the biggest and best mullet in the world grow and the fishermen of that county traditionally worked that resource most skillfully out of small skiffs less than sixteen feet long (like the Wakulla Beach Model Bow Skiff). Over here in Franklin County where I live, the bay is more open and the shoreline is more sandy and, though mullet are plentiful and much sought after, the main inshore fishery is for oysters and crabs. I know my opinion is of no real significance, but I have eaten a lot of oysters and the ones called "Apalachicola" are the best I have ever eaten. Chesapeake oysters (is there still such a thing?) are too fresh to suit me. In that bay, they used to drag them with sailboats because the law said that no internal combustion could be used. I don't know what happened to that idea but it was a good one. The way technology is these days, any fishery that is not strictly regulated is in immediate danger of extinction and we certainly can't count on the fishermen to regulate themselves. The best example I can think of is the amazingly cheap, and effective, nylon monofilament gill net. When they invented that thing, man, it was Katie bar the door but Katie was asleep at the switch. Ingenious fishermen overfished all species of inshore fish so bad that it finally became apparent to enough plain, ordinary people that serious environmental damage was being done, so they rose up (with a lot of big-money support from powerful sportfishing magazines and such) and amended the constitution of the state of Florida to outlaw gill nets of any kind. That was overkill and eliminated the traditional profession of thousands of people, which a little timely regulation by the Florida Fisheries Commission would have prevented.

I didn't mean to get onto that sore subject. I was just going to explain the fishing boats of Franklin County when I started this. There are two main kinds. Oyster skiffs and crab skiffs. I don't know the ancient history of them but when I came along, they had become more or less standardized to a design by a Mr. Joe Lolly over in Eastpoint, halfway between Carrabelle and Apalachicola. Mr. Joe was a very skillful boatbuilder with many years' experience building everything from big round-bottomed offshore red snapper (another fishery ruined by tardy regulation) boats to little skiffs. His oyster and crab boats were so well adapted to the conditions of the work and the bay that they quickly set the standard. The first ones were all cypress-built. They were some twenty feet long, maybe seven feet wide, and chine-built. Although they had a shallow V bottom in the bow they were mostly flat-bottomed boats. You know, there are flat-bottomed boats and then there are other flat-bottomed boats. I don't want to cause anybody to start snorting through his nose and stomping around in a fury but I think the Atkins were the champions as drawers of plans for flat-bottomed skiffs. They had that magic touch of being able to make a sow's ear look like a silk purse and so did Joe Lolly. You could tell a Lolly skiff from one of the many imitations with just a glance. I don't think you could have walked around with all sorts of sophisticated measuring devices and have found very much actual difference but there certainly was something about them. For one thing a cypress Lolly skiff would last thirty years, which is saying a lot about a working skiff down here. One of the things he did that is hard to do (and I am here to tell you) was he could twist a good flare to the bow and then take it to a tumblehome stern on a two-plank-sided boat. One way to fudge a little of the difficulty out of that is to put too much rake to the stem of the boat but that wastes lumber. It is a shame to cut the end off a twenty-foot board for the chine plank just to make the job go easier and, besides, it wastes waterline length to rake the stem too much.

That little V at the forefoot was another thing. You know, if you pull a good flare into the bow of a flat-sided boat, it not only makes an abruptness to the sheer up there but the side planks pick up off the baseline at the bottom, too. If you were to turn the boat over and plank it flat-bottomed like that, there would be way too much rocker in the bottom forward and the boat would pound real bad and throw water straight out in front of it like a johnboat or one of these big fiberglass johnboats called "Carolina Skiffs," which are so popular in smooth-water situations these days. The V that Mr. Lolly built into the bottom forward not only kept the waterline length as long as possible (an important thing for a load-carrying boat or any other planing boat for that matter . . . you know, it has to walk before it can run) but made for a dry boat that did not pound too much. Of course with a loaded oyster skiff, pounding was not a problem.

Even though the V kept the bottom of the boat in the water pretty good forward, the keel line still curved up a little bit right at the forefoot. Mr. Lolly put a little wedge of wood down there to not only take the scuffing of beaching the boat but give a toehold to help the boat hold up into the wind a little bit better. They still do that around here . . . call it a "toe." Nobody would think of building a plywood oyster or crab skiff without a cypress toe. It wouldn't take but one or two times of beaching on the pile of oyster shells at the shucking house before the plywood of the forefoot would be gone. Yep, the working skiffs of Franklin County are plywood now.

During Joe Lolly's lifetime (he died sometime in the late seventies . . . still building skiffs) it got hard to get good cypress so he did like most everybody else and switched to plywood. It was still easy to identify a Lolly skiff, though. He went up to twenty-three feet with plywood (two twelve-foot sheets scarfed together) but he kept his flare and all the tumblehome he could twist into the plywood without over-stressing it and had the same little V forward and the necessary toe.

I believe this is the place to explain the difference between a crab skiff and an oyster skiff. They had the same hull. I think that was dictated by the possible methods of construction and the mean chop of this bay up here. An oyster skiff was laid out with very wide side decks flush with the gunwales of the boat so the man (and I mean that) could stand there and work the tongs. Mechanical harvesting has never been successful around here. Oyster tongs look like two long-tined steel rakes with twenty-foot handles hooked together like scissors. The man stands on the gunwales of the boat and works the handles so that the rakes dig around in the oysters down on the bottom and break them loose and let the little ones fall through the tines. It is very hard work and there is an art to it, too. After a little while of working the long handles of the tongs, a good man will pull up about ten pounds of big oysters, mostly separated from empty shells and shorts. He'll dump them on the culling board and take him a little break while he knocks off the ones that are too little and the empty shells and sacks the big oysters up in a burlap bag ("croker sack" in the South). When he is ready to take up the tongs again, he dumps the culls back in the bay and climbs up on the side of the boat and goes back to work and work it is, too . . . make a man out of anybody. I don't think it is good to provoke an oysterman beyond his tolerance so I never have.

An oyster skiff is worked off the bow so the man can pull his anchor (the favorite is an automobile flywheel) and move to an unworked part of the bar. It has a little square house way back on the stern where he can sit and steer on his way back with such a load (hopefully) that the boat is borderline with the freeboard and throwing water like a destroyer. The little house serves two purposes. One, obviously, is to give the man a little shelter while he is bringing in the load but the other is to give a little aft windage to the anchored skiff so it won't sail back and forth and make him lose his place on the bottom.

The favorite engine of oystermen used to be the old heavy-duty OMC two-cylinder forty-hp tiller-steered rope-cranked engine. They were good old stuff and would sometimes hold up for two or even three years in that rough service. The tiller-steered version with the pull rope was never popular with recreational boaters because it was so hard to pull the big pistons through compression with a rope. I had to grab the rope with both hands and brace one foot against the transom to start one but an eighty-year-old oysterman can start one with just a flick of the wrist.

I used to stop on the causeway leading to the old swing bridge across the river into Apalach and watch the oyster skiffs coming in. Sometimes they would be so loaded that they weren't actually planing but the man would be sitting in his little house, looking out of his little square window, bringing home the bacon with the handles of the tongs sticking out over the bow. I would meet him at the dock and buy a whole bag . . . $7.50 right off the boat. Good money and good oysters. You know, it takes a good bit of skill to shuck oysters while you are driving a car but I could do it and, though I do not advocate distraction when driving, I advise anybody to do that. Take old SR 65 off 98, just east of Eastpoint, and head up north on that. You won't see any other cars at all.

Crab skiffs are different from oyster skiffs in that they had narrow side decks and a house in front. At first they were just open boats with no house and some of them are still like that. Crabs and crab traps aren't as heavy as oysters so the boats ran drier. After a while, crabs got sort of scarce in inshore water and people started putting a little shelter up on the bow and a steering wheel and electric start and all on them when they had to set out farther. Maybe it is that crabbing won't make enough of a man out of somebody so that starting the engine manually is just a flick of the wrist. I don't know.

Though I have never done any tonging (that's a clannish and territorial business, not kind to interlopers) I have run crab traps and, to my notion, it is hard work. I have noticed that a lot of the men eliminate the battery with an engine that still has a magneto and start it by hand.

The way crab trapping works is that a man saves up enough money to buy a bunch of traps (or makes them himself). He baits them all and loads them in the boat as many as he can carry and still get behind the steering wheel. Then he goes out and sets them where he thinks there will be some crabs at that time of year. The next day he comes back with only one baited trap in the boat. He idles up alongside the float of the first trap in the string, pulls the engine in neutral, hooks the warp, and pulls the trap out of the shallow water hand over hand. When he gets it on board, he kicks the new trap off the bridge deck, between the motor compartment and the belly of the boat, and heads for the next trap in the line. While he is going, he empties the crabs out of the trap, baits it, and gets it ready. After he has enough experience, he knows how to set the wheel to compensate for the wind and tide so the boat runs just about at the next trap while he does his doings and, about the time he gets through, it is time to idle up and pull the next trap. You can tell how much experience a crabber has by noticing how close together his buoys are. A good man can work a lot of traps in just a little while and make some good money, too. It is a tough way to make a living, particularly in the wintertime, but sometimes stone crabs get in the traps, then, and that is a welcome bonus . . . kind of helps compensate for all them chapped cracks in a man's hands.

So, before Joe Lolly died, he had a young apprentice named Bobby Shiver. Bobby was a house carpenter and weekend preacher, a hard worker . . . very skillful and cheerful. That's why Mr. Lolly picked him from among the many applicants for the job when he got to where he needed a little help to throw a twelve-foot sheet of three-quarter-inch plywood up on the sawhorses (the boats were three-quarter inch on the bottom and half an inch on the sides . . . carefully picked over Douglas fir marine). When Mr. Lolly died, Bobby Shiver started building the boats himself. He changed the model a little bit by eliminating the antiquated-looking tumblehome and keeping the same flare all the way back but the boats were built the same way. They had a heavy-duty two-by pine transom with the boards splined together. Bobby would cull through all the two-by-twelves at the lumberyard to pick the best stuff for that. The boats were very heavily framed with cypress sawn frames.

The floors were at least eight inches high and were notched for the rough two-by-six keelson and two other longitudinal two-by-sixes. There were (are) limber holes big enough to pass the trash that is associated with the duty. The floorboards are just regular low-quality pine plywood meant to be replaced often. Most of the fishermen don't even bother to paint the floorboards.

Why, one might ask, does old frivolous, opinionated Robb White know so much about those workingmen's boats? Well, I owned one, that's why. We bought this little sandy plot of land over here on Dog Island as a speculation, back when I was making a little money in some kind of distraction or other as a hedge in case we were to lose the old coast house, and when we did, we were forced to build a little something over here so we would have a some shade. Fortunately, this was back before the damn government got in cahoots with big-time development and regulated the code so that a person had to be a multimillionaire to comply and we got the plans for this little shanty approved. We had to have some way to haul the whole house over to the island and needed a boat made to carry a heavy load economically.

I got Bobby Shiver to build that boat for us, unpainted. I started to fiberglass it with epoxy to try to preserve the plywood but decided to just use it to haul the materials for the house over to the island and then sell the boat while it was still in good shape. I did prime it with the two-part epoxy called "Gluvit," which is about the best primer for plywood I've ever found. Though it has a quick-evaporating solvent, it is a pretty good sealer. Because of the solvent, it is not such a pain in the ass to get smooth as solventless epoxy and it is flexible enough to stand a little swelling and shrinking, so it suppresses the checking of the plywood pretty good. I painted the boat with regular oil-based marine paint and, since we had bought one of the tiny World War Two apartments in Lanark to work out of and planned to keep the boat in the water all the time at the little Lanark Boat Club basin (a friendly outfit . . . I have been a member off and on since the early sixties) I painted the bottom with that old Trinidad, which is a vinyl-based copper bottom paint that was (is?) the best thing for the conditions of this bay and we hauled her to Carrabelle and slid her off and commenced construction.

Gill Net

in which the white plastic bucket earns its distinction
as the one good invention of the last century

Two people, I know, didn't have to wait for the Florida net ban amendment to take effect to stop gill-netting. One is an old buddy and ex-employee of mine who told me what happened. When he worked for me, his most notable adventure was when he decided to cut the top out of a fifty-five-gallon drum that used to have lacquer thinner in it . . . with a cutting torch. Everything went fine until he pushed the little lever and blew that oxygen down in the drum. Later, in the hospital, he said that it didn't stay in there very long. Later still, he said that it was a minor calamity next to his last trip as a commercial fisherman.

The other fella is Mrs. Sinclair's son. He sort of plays at working. He used to have a crop duster, then he had a bulldozer, then a boat dealership, then a snapper boat, and finally a fancy bird-dog net boat, a big house in a small Gulf Coast fishing village, and my old employee for a flunky. Some people say that Mrs. Sinclair partially subsidizes his businesses. I only know that when he had the bulldozer, he didn't like to get on it before about eleven o'clock in the morning.

After the lacquer thinner drum blew up, my old buddy was never quite the same. He never was the most agile thinker in the first place but he didn't have that crazy look to him like he does now. He is still the most loyal and willing helper in the world. He will eagerly do anything for you but they say you have to tell him exactly what you want these days. He doesn't show much initiative anymore. He was the perfect partner for Mrs. Sinclair's son at the time of this gill-net incident.

My buddy (Buddy) and Mrs. Sinclair's son (Sonny) lived at this little fishing town down at the coast. They called themselves commercial fishermen but they were the only commercial fishermen in town with a two-hundred-thousand-dollar house and a 250-horsepower outboard motor on the net skiff however Sonny bought a lot of beer and they were hail-fellows-well-met down there for a while. That job with Sonny was working out so well that I thought I would probably never see old Buddy again but I did. After about a year or so of that commercial fishing, Buddy showed back up at the sawmill to see if we needed a little help on the logging crew. He said he needed him a safe job.

He told me that Sonny had decided to go out fishing one night in the fall when the mullet were with roe and the Japanese were with money. It was pretty choppy on the four-mile trip out there to the offshore bar where the mullet were supposed to be spawning . . . choppy and dark. Sonny was proud of that 250-horsepower and that brand-new, all-marine-plywood, bird dog tunnel boat, so he and Buddy pounded out onto the flats and struck a thousand feet of brand-new monofilament gill net. It was so dark that they didn't notice a little water in the bottom of the boat until after they finished racing around running out the net. When they slowed, the bow settled and the boat sank right out from under them leaving them in the water with nothing but a white plastic bucket, a sheen of gas, and a line of little floats stretching a thousand feet into the dark.

I guess I better leave those boys in that fix and explain a little or y'all won't be able to understand what is happening. The invention of the "bird dog" net boat along with the development of the cheap nylon monofilament gill net is the thing most responsible for the net ban amendment to the Florida Constitution. Such a rig is so cheap and efficient that any fool can catch too many fish. Doctors, lawyers, politicians, and people like Sonny even got into it with super-long nets and overpowered boats, just for the hell of it. The highly evolved bird dog skiff has the engine mounted way up in the front in a well with a tunnel leading aft. That way, the tilt of the engine can be adjusted and it will run with just the least bit of the foot in the water so that the net can be run inshore of a school of fish (usually mullet) in very shallow water. With the motor in the front, the propeller can run at actual water level instead of in the depression created by the passage of the boat. Also, with the engine up front, out of the way, there is room on the stern for a big net platform so the net can be run out around the school at planing speed. The basic boat of the normal commercial gill-netter was just a cheap, flat-bottomed plywood skiff with about forty-hp worth of engine steered by the handle. Hotshot rigs were bigger with huge engines steered from a silly bow pulpit and a ridiculous steering wheel. Though such an arrangement makes for a crank steering boat at slow speed and much inefficiency at high speed, there has never been anything more efficient at catching fish. Such rigs radically changed the ecology of inshore Florida waters before the net ban and, even now, years after gill nets have been outlawed, some species seem to have been displaced from their usual place in the food chain. Now that gill nets have been removed from their particular sort of destruction, shrimp boats are the most ecologically destructive thing in the Gulf. I hear that the bycatch (the ratio of "trash fish" to saleable stuff) is above twenty-seven to one and that does not include invertebrates. Desperate shrimpers who will haul all night for a little box of what used to be called "bait" aren't the only bad thing left either. Arrogant, big-deal, high-tech sportfishermen with their "box full" attitude are doing the same thing to offshore species that gill nets did to in-shore fish. I think the only solution to the problem of overfishing is to tax hell out of horsepower. A man can't do much damage in a low-powered boat and if someone wants to top it the knob, let him finance the construction of a school with his boat registration taxes.

Now, back at the ranch with the desperadoes, what had happened was that the engine well up in the bow that holds the motor and keeps the water out was built for about forty horsepower. On the trip out there, it had suc-cumbed to the pounding and the weight and thrust of that 250-horsepower and had come unnailed and hopped completely off its big hole in the bot-tom of the boat. When they stopped, the bow came down and kept on going down. Sonny and Buddy didn't know all that at the time, all they knew was that they were in a hell of a fix. They swam around in the sheen of gasoline and oil, hanging on to the white plastic bucket, looking at the little floats dis-appearing into the dark and having an earnest discussion for a long time, be-fore they noticed the specially painted camouflage transom of the boat barely above the surface a short distance away.

It turns out that the boat was hanging, bow-down, by the air pocket under the net platform nailed across the transom. The net was tangled up in the en-gine controls and steering wheel on the fancy stainless-steel bow pulpit that Sonny had had custom-made in Jacksonville. When the pull of the net slacked off after the boat stopped, the air under the net platform had pulled the stern up, but the platform was not airtight, and the bubbles told the tale.

Just as Buddy and Sonny got to the barely floating transom of the boat with their white bucket, swimming through the sheen of gasoline . . . it sank. Only desperate work with the bucket managed to bail enough air into the cavity to bring it back up. Sonny and Buddy spent the night working hard to keep it in sight. They gnawed and tore the hem off Sonny's PARTY NAKED T-shirt and tried to caulk the worst air leaks by poking the shreds into the crack with the car key (their only tool). Air is harder to caulk in than water is to caulk out though and they spent most of their time dipping air under the net platform with the bucket . . . all night long.

As they were doing this, and talking about it, the outgoing tide working on the thousand feet of net pulled the boat miles and miles out into the shallow Gulf. Sonny and Buddy didn't have any wives back at the house to be worrying about them so nobody called the Marine Patrol or the Coast Guard. They were on their own out there in the middle of the Gulf in the middle of the night but they weren't completely alone. A thousand feet of gill net doesn't stay empty very long. All night, it caught Spanish mackerel, ladyfish, hardtails, and big pogies.

The air dipping had become routine by three in the morning. Buddy and Sonny were tired, waterlogged, and disgusted. Even though their faces were burned by the continuously renewed sheen of gas from the vent of the custom-made aluminum fuel tank and they knew that they had no loved ones back on the hill to call the authorities, they were hopeful. At least, the water was warm. They were talking about how many fishing boats were fixing to come out first thing in the morning and looking at Sonny's genuine Rolex Oyster to see how long they had to wait when something forcefully pulled the transom of the boat way down under the water. That was the end of the optimism.

Finally the transom of the boat barely reappeared some distance away and the air dipping became really frantic. Conversation was at a minimum. In spite of the warmth of the water, their teeth began to chatter. About every now and then, the same thing would happen. The boat would give a little twitch like the cork on the fishing line of a cane pole and then be snatched violently from them and submerged beyond the reach of their feet. Sometimes a big belch of gaseous air would climb, from the depths, up their naked legs as the boat was pulled sideways. Buddy and Sonny would go through the horrors and spin around like freaked-out water ballerinas for a few minutes desperately looking to see if the boat was going to come up again. When it came, they would beat the water into a froth trying to get to it before it sank. Then they would bail air like . . . well, like their lives depended on it . . . not just to keep enough air in it to keep it afloat like before, but all the air they possibly could so that it might have enough to emerge the next time. When they had some spare time, they frantically dove trying to find the place where the net was attached to the boat eighteen feet beneath the surface, or the "Rambo" knife stuck between the frames in the rail way up (now down) in the front of the boat. Buddy said that Sonny told him to swim out to the first float and pull up the net and try to gnaw them loose while he stayed with the boat and dipped air . . . told me, "You know, I ain't never refused to do what the boss told me to do before but I said, 'I tell you what Sonny, you better be the one to go out there and let me stay here with the boat . . . My teeth are chattering too bad to gnaw.'" He said that the resulting hard feelings didn't make a bit of difference. "Couldn'ta got no worse than it already was nohow" was what he said.

Finally morning came . . . a beautiful early-fall morning . . . blue sky, wind out of the north, light chop on the sea. They couldn't see land but they *could* see the sharks that had been cutting the fish out of the net, and there were plenty of them. After the sun came up, a little school of hardtails (blue runners, the preferred bait for big fish) took to hiding around the boat. Buddy and Sonny were exhausted but not so bad that they couldn't scramble frantically around to the other side from the sharks that would, every now and then, come to look at the hardtails. Buddy told me he sure didn't like it when those hardtails would get scared and come running to take refuge all among his legs. They frantically scanned the horizon looking for the fishing boats that were sure to come. Around noon they had to scan the *whole* horizon because they didn't know which direction to look anymore. The sun cooked the gas-burned skin on their faces and made them even more miserable, if there is such a thing as misery in the face of terror. By three o'clock they were in such bad shape that they didn't notice the helicopter until the down-blast hit them.

Somehow, the Coast Guard had had some place to go in a helicopter that just accidentally took them right over this calamity. In minutes the cable was let out with the little seat on it and Sonny established his rights as boss and his ass in it. Buddy, though, for once, showed a little initiative and established himself on top of Sonny and up they went.

Epilogue

The Marine Patrol went out and found the net from the loran numbers. They called the sea-tow people, who pulled up the boat by the net and surmised the details of the problem: There were over a hundred shark holes in the net. Sonny wound up with a pretty good-sized bill from them and also from the hospital where he was treated for exposure and gasoline burns in the eyes. Buddy got on the bus and came home to his momma. Neither of them ever went gill-netting again.

The Canned Ham Incident

in which I do not participate so Hurrah for the other side

I guess it was about 1985 when I heard this story from a permanent resident of this island. Given that I was not an eyewitness, some of the accuracy may be in doubt, but it ain't the kind of thing that is normally embellished too much and the details are all too bizarre to invent—all highly technical stuff, so if you ain't into that, better skip on. This is a long, long story . . . takes about three hours, what with kibitzing, to tell it right but I'll try to cut it to the very bone.

There was a preacher from Missouri, or someplace like that, who got some supporters to outfit a missionary project and he built a big pirate-ship-looking thing to sail down the Mississippi to the Caribbean to save the heathens down there. He had already made it down the Mississippi and east as far as he could go and still stay out of the open ocean. Though I was not a participant in the actual incident in question, I did see the ship docked in Carrabelle at the eastern terminus of the north Gulf Intracoastal Waterway where he was fueling up to head outside for the first time across the gulf of the northeastern bend of Florida. You know, just that he had come all that way says something for the man and his ship. Errol Flynn would have been right at home on that thing. It looked like the boat was almost fifty feet long but it was hard to tell where the actual boat stopped and the decorative part started. It had all sorts of filigree and dolphin strikers and chicken beaks and stuff up by the head and some sort of balcony and extra transom and windows back by the stern enclosing the enormous head of what would normally have been an outboard rudder. The kitchen was way up in the forecastle . . . on deck with full standing room and a regular-sized cast-iron combination LP and wood-burning range. The living quarters were in the poop and had the rudderhead protruding up through the roof with a twenty-some-odd-foot tiller way up there seven or eight feet off the deck. It was worked by hauling tackles to a homemade spoked wheel, at least seven feet tall, mounted on a preaching pulpit in front of the forward bay windows of the living quarters. The well-lit cabin must have been a delightful place with all those windows and all those Bibles and hymnals and prayer books in shelves lining the walls, their spines gleaming with gold. There were two huge masts that looked just like pressure-treated utility poles with varnish on them. I noticed an ingenious use of semi truck mudflaps as chafing gear for the gigantic yards that were lashed to the masts and secured at the ends by braces and the sheets that would normally be made up to the clew corners of the sails. The preacher was even kind enough to take me below to show me the stores and the engine room. I noticed hundreds of canned hams stored under a grating in the dry and spotless bilge and boxes of spaghetti in racks along the sides of the hull. Big agricultural liquid tanks gleamed palely up in the bow. There were cardboard boxes of even more Bibles, prayer books, and hymnals secured with big rope netting. The immaculate engine room had a little Perkins diesel engine . . . heat-exchanger-cooled, three-to-one "Velvet Drive" gear, one-and-three-eighth-inch stainless shaft, patent, "never-drip" hard-seal well-pump-style stuffing box. There were at least two fuel filters and a sediment bowl. A big old polished bronze and glass raw water strainer glistened like jewelry in the fluorescent lights. I was able to catch a glimpse of the dull but expensive gleam of no-telling-how-many genuine Rolls batteries under the stainless-steel expanded metal of the engine room deck. There was a paper towel holder handy to the dipstick. Bounty paper towels—there was nothing second-rate down there. Errol might have fit in pretty good on deck, but you could tell, that preacher wouldn't have let him penetrate ever so slightly into that engine room with his slap-dash self. I even felt a little out of place, but I was glad to get a chance to marvel at it.

I liked his engine room and agreed with him about his mission. Somebody needed to do something about all those heathens down in the Caribbean islands. I told that preacher that I thought the way to do it would be to clench a Bible, hymnal, or prayer book in his teeth and swing over onto the heathen yacht on a halyard with a canned ham under his arm. I hope I don't give the impression that I am making fun of the man. His boat might have been something of a show and I guess that is what he thought it would take to accomplish his mission. It was obvious that he knew exactly what he was doing, so far, and I'm sure he knew exactly how to deal with heathens without me. Unfortunately, I had to come back to our shop in Georgia to try to build a boat for a man and was unable to supervise the crossing of the open water of the northeastern Gulf of Mexico . . . too bad.

The way I heard it from my islander buddy, the preacher listened to the droning, on and on, of the National Weather Service and looked at the

weather fax until it looked like it would be good for a while and then motored out the pass between St. George and Dog Islands into the open Gulf,
heading for where the Intracoastal Waterway resumed at Anclote Key about
a hundred miles away. He was planning to motor the whole way like he had
been doing so far and save his sails for "the trades." He listened to the radio
too long though and missed the tide in the pass and by the time that little
4-108 had pushed that behemoth out past all that water coming in, it was
getting late. Later he told my buddy, one of Dog Island's hard-bitten permanent residents, that he was counting on the land breeze to give him a
nice lee of the island and the shoals east of there to make it an easy cruise.
It probably would have been a nice trip in a more predictable season of the
year. After the preacher got outside the pass in the nice easy swells of the big
water, he activated the autopilot and went into his house and got a chair and
his bedroom slippers and sat there watching his great big wheel turning
ever-so-slightly in tune to the flux gate and watched the Floridians turn on
all those electric lights that they use to demonstrate their dominion over nature. I guess he was thinking about opening up one of them canned hams
when the wind started breezing up from the south a little like it does around
here when a cold front whips a little farther down than expected and begins to draw the weather in from the Gulf. By the time he got the chair and
the bedroom slippers secured, it was blowing pretty good. Too bad it was-
n't the expected land breeze and there wasn't any lee. The preacher said that
it was blowing about fifty with fifteen- to twenty-foot swells. The data buoy
anchored eighty miles out in the Gulf said eighteen with gusts to twenty-
two and four- to six-foot waves, but you know, things are real variable in
the Gulf of Mexico.

About midnight or so my buddy, the permanent resident of the island,
was coming home across the bay. I guess I better explain that situation. This
island where I live most of the time has no bridge or public transportation
to it. Because of that and certain other characteristics (like intermittent electricity) there are only a few people who live here all the time. Most of the
folks over here just come on weekends when the weather is good and the
FSU "Noles" ain't playing. It takes a special person to be able to handle this
place. So, this friend of mine was coming back to the island in his motor
whaleboat from checking in at the Tiki Bar (a little bar right on the river with
roaches in the palm-thatched cabanas—to enhance the ambience) on the
mainland, which he sometimes visited for a little while, when he noticed

eleven very bright flares from somewhere around the shoals east of the island. He knew that a vessel was in distress—big-time, from the quantity and quality of those flares—so he headed to the rescue and found the preacher and his boat washed up sideways on the sandbar (called "Dog Island Reef" on the charts). Turned out that, while he was skirting the windward side of the shoals watching his GPS and loran and radar wondering when the land breeze would start up, the beam sea began rolling those telephone poles around in the holes until they wallowed the wedges out and then they really went to flopping. Before long, the yards had snatched enough slack in the lines securing them so that they were trying to sweep all that tophamper off the deck. There was nothing the preacher could do but hold on to the wheel and try to give the autopilot and that little Perkins all the help he could while he dodged those spars. He would have probably managed to slide by the shoals if one of the canned hams hadn't hopped over and popped the nipple off the "state-of-the art" plastic (I ain't gonna mention no names but I am a bronze-age man myself) raw water intake through-the-hull fitting to the engine. After that it didn't take long to boil all the coolant out of the heat exchanger. The preacher was too busy to notice until the engine ran hot and seized and the whole mess washed sideways up on the bar. The preacher dove for his emergency cabinet and all those (not-out-of-date) SOLAS-approved flares. Would have shot an even dozen but he dropped one while he was sideskipping the sweep of the main yard. My buddy says he was amazed at the spectacle of just eleven of those things. Said, "You know, them little shotgun-shell flares like go in the plastic pistol, just ain't in it with the real thing."

When my buddy got there, the big boat was lying over on its side with its bottom to the breakers in about four or five feet of water. My buddy eased the whaleboat around to the lee side and tried to hold a conversation with the preacher about what he wanted to do. Turned out that he should have just told him to hop on board if he wanted to go back to Carrabelle because the man refused to abandon all those Bibles. While they were trying to shift the Good Books from one boat to the other in the surf, that one-inch fitting in the bottom of the big boat was equalizing the inside water level with the outside water level (both well above the batteries), which killed all three radios (single-sideband, VHF, and CB) and left only the meaningless drone of the dry-cell-powered weather radio. The wind shift from the cold front came, the tide turned and took the wreck off the reef where it sank down to where the spars and part of the preacher were all that were sticking out.

It took a while for the preacher to convince himself that it was all right now to give up the good fight and get out of that cold water. Unbeknownst to both of them, during the decision-making process, the whaleboat was winding up six hundred feet of half-inch nylon line with its propeller. My buddy finally figured it out when a big inflatable boat appeared, coming rapidly up from astern. The cold, the Tiki Bar, and the frustration of trying to be subtle with this preacher had dimmed his wits and, at first, he thought this thing was just coming to see how things were going when, in fact, it wanted to dive under the stern of the whaleboat, explode, and wrap all up in the wheel in a knot as hard as a truck tire. He and the preacher spent a long time trying to cut the damn thing loose but they were frustrated by the coldness of the water, by the toughness of the fabric of the top-notch dinghy, and by a five-horse British Seagull outboard motor that was also wrapped around the wheel and shaft of the whaleboat. By the time they gave up on trying to clear the propeller, the Seagull was all they could get loose. Too bad the "stopped lark's head" the preacher had tied around the mast of the ship to make up the whaleboat didn't hold like that knot around the propeller and they had been drifting rapidly toward the Florida Middle Ground all this time. They tried the old trusty 12H Danforth that had held the whaleboat so faithfully for so many years in the rough anchorage at Dog Island but it wouldn't find the bottom with the line that they had close to hand. Of course they had the six-hundred-foot dinghy painter spooled up between the wheel and the strut but that was unavailable. My buddy estimated that they would end up somewhere down around Fort Myers if they were really lucky. If they were just sort of lucky and the wind came on around more east like it usually did, it would be the Keys or Cuba. If they weren't lucky, they might get to work with the heathens after all. Hard to predict on the first day of a four- or five-day norther.

My buddy finally brought all his faculties to bear on the problem and decided to try to get the Seagull running. The muffler was gone, the shaft was bent in a U, two of the five propeller blades were busted off (all on the same side, wouldn't you know), and the whole steering handle/throttle control arrangement was gone. Not only that, but it looked like something had been snatched out of the carburetor by the throttle cable. Only after they had taken the foot off and straightened the little square tubing thing that the Seagull factory uses for a shaft between the head and the foot, and beat the housing back into some kind of shape that would allow a little strained rotation, did they discover that the crankshaft was bent so that the flywheel was jammed against the magneto stator plate. (Y'all following all this? Might better read back over it or the rest ain't going to make a bit of sense.) They finally straightened it out so that it could wobble almost clear by driving screwdrivers up under the rim of the flywheel and prying against the stator plate and the face of the core of the coil.

My buddy had five gallons of gas that he was carrying to the island for his generator but there wasn't any oil. He was very proud of the integrity of the whaleboat's own 4-108 and felt that the display of gallon jugs of Delo 400 was undignified in a good boat. They had to break the antenna off the weather radio to use as a straw to suck the black oil out of the dipstick hole of the whaleboat's engine with their lips. My buddy, an old mariner for real, said that that sucking business was the closest he ever came to being seasick in his life but he had to do it. Luckily, the preacher was up to the job, too, so they took turns sucking on the antenna. They mixed the oil with the gas a little at a time in a cutoff bleach-jug bailer and poured it in the Seagull's squashed gas tank. Then they tried to crank it while it was clamped onto one of the interior bulkheads of the whaleboat . . . no spark . . . so they turned it upside down and poured gas all up under the flywheel to try to flush out some of the water from the points and coil and all. When they pulled the rope after that, the old Sea Gull fired right off . . . literally . . . Those SOLAS flares were puny compared with the fireball that came out from under the flywheel of that Seagull.

So there it was running, wide open (the thing that had been jerked out of the carburetor by the throttle cable turned out to have been the throttle itself) in a pool of flaming gasoline. My buddy said it was hard not to back up to the fire for a little while in that cold wind in his wet clothes. Finally, the out-of-balance of the wobbling flywheel, the bent shaft, the broke propeller, and the nature of the Seagull itself combined to vibrate the clamps loose and the whole bellowing mess fell off the bulkhead into the fire where the oxygen finally burned up enough to shut it down. Of course, the impact knocked some of the paper towel (not Bounty) stuffing out of the holes in the gas tank and added more gas to the fire, which increased the draft so that my buddy and the preacher had to dance around quite a bit to avoid the flames that were whipped every whichaway by the increasing north wind. Unfortunately, they had chosen the bulkhead that the fire extinguisher was mounted on for their mechanicking. Luckily those old surplus whaleboats are made out of fire-retardant resin or their gooses would have been cooked. Finally, all the wasted gas burned up and they were able to proceed to step two—after they had sucked some more oil out of the dipstick hole with their lips.

I'm going to try to cut this thing down as best I can but there is only so much that can be left out . . . What finally happened is that they nailed the cut-bait board to the stern of the double-ended, thick fiberglass whaleboat so that it wobbled sort of cattywompus off to one side and clamped the Seagull to it and tied it off to the towing bit to help the nails hold a little longer between renailing and motored off into the cold wind. It was a slow trip, but they didn't get bored. They found that they had a steady job sucking oil out of the crankcase of the whaleboat's engine. They were mixing gas by instinct and scared to death that they might starve the Seagull of oil and gall the liner and rings and maybe even seize the already over-stressed crankshaft, and then, considering the way the wind had veered, it would be the heathens of Africa for sure, so they sucked hard. The colder it got, the thicker the oil became. When they cranked the diesel to warm the oil up a little so it would be easier to suck, the dipstick hole pooted little droplets of black oil right in their faces, but that was an insignificant thing in the face of the rest of all this. Finally, in the desperate scramble to transport the open container of precious mix and pour it into the out-of-reach gas tank of the crazily wiggling Seagull, one of them bumped into the whaleboat's gearshift, and instead of instantly choking the engine down against the fouled propeller, the old whaleboat began to motor ahead. It turns out that all the pitching and rolling from the rough seas had unwiggled the Avon from the wheel, unwound the six hundred feet of line, and they were under way, upwind in a forty-horsepower motor whaleboat built just exactly for that kind of duty. They hooked all forty of them horses up, pried the baitboard off the stern, let all that foolishness go to the bottom, and headed for Dog Island. They got there just in time for the arrival of the eleven AM private ferry. "Man, what happened to y'all's faces?" said the wit that met them trudging up the dock.

Epilogue (I'll cut this to the bone too)

They went back and refloated the *Heathen's Revenge* with two water beds inflated in the hold by a scuba tank and sold it and divided up the revenue in an agreeable fashion. The preacher went back to Missouri and my buddy went back to the Tiki Bar.

The Motor Whaleboats of Dog Island

in which I explain temporarily abandoning skiffs for a big boat

Note: This is not a regular story. I include it just to satisfy any curiosity that might be aroused by the boat in "The Canned Ham Incident."

Lore

My wife and I live over here on Dog Island in the northeastern Gulf of Mexico. It's a sand barrier island about seven miles long and almost a mile wide in one or two places. The mainland is about three and a half miles across a shallow bay and about fifteen or twenty feet deep. There is no bridge over here so people have to get back and forth in their own boats, wait for the private ferry, or hope that the grass airstrip isn't too wet to fly into or out of in their little airplanes. Most of the houses on the island belong to people who only come every now and then, but there are some ten or eleven places that are inhabited by hard-bitten permanent residents. Because of the situation, some of these people own old twenty-six-foot Navy-surplus motor whaleboats . . . mainly permanent residents who have to go to work on the mainland.

One reason that the old whaleboats are so popular is that they are cheap to own and run. All of them were bought surplus from the Navy for from $450 to $4,500. They will go about fourteen nautical miles to the gallon of fuel and require very little maintenance. Some of them have changed hands several times but most of them have been in service more or less continuously for years. It isn't unusual to hear some kid ask his parent at the public boat ramp on the mainland, "Dad, what is that old boat?" "Why, son, that's one of them Dog Island Trawlers, they can go in a hurricane," is the approximate reply.

Ain't all that far-fetched. When hurricanes come, and they have been coming often around here these last twenty years, someone will miss the last ferry from the island and one of the permanent residents will haul them to the mainland in a motor whaleboat. During one such storm, a friend of mine was trying to help out some people who had holed up in the little harbor on Dog Island and were dragging anchor, when he wrapped up a drifting inflatable dinghy into the wheel. The whaleboat was disabled while too far to swim to land, and my poor friend had to spend the night of the hurricane anchored out, had to wrap himself up in a blue tarpaulin in an attempt to keep warm. Luckily, his big old anchor held because the boat he was trying to help wound up way up in the trees.

Description

The fiberglass twenty-six-foot Navy motor whaleboat is the latest of a long evolution of tenders for the ships of the Navy. I guess the name comes from the double-ended boats back in Queequeg's days. Real whaleboats are made to easily work well from ships, and probably fit the role of ship's boats just fine. I don't know when they first installed engines in them, but the result was notable enough to change the name to "motor" whaleboat. During World War Two motor whaleboats had a little four-cylinder gas engine and were steered with a bronze tiller. There is a good scene of one of that model in the movie *South Pacific*. One that I saw was strip-planked from mahogany. Some of the early fiberglass boats were powered by four-cylinder Buda diesel engines cooled by a keel cooler recessed into the hull . . . a very good rig. Now they are all made of fiberglass, and for the last thirty-some-odd years have had a four-cylinder Perkins diesel engine (marinized by Westerbeke). These boats are about twenty-six feet long and eight wide and weigh about five or six thousand pounds. They are built heavy-duty.

The manual says that. There is one genuine dog-eared Navy-published motor whaleboat manual in circulation among the Dog Islanders. Most people have forgotten to whom it belongs but it belongs to me. It was soaking in the flashlight cubbyhole (along with the flashlight and a package of condoms) of my whaleboat when I hauled it from Jacksonville back in '80. The Navy motor whaleboat is unsinkable, self-righting, fire-retardant, fitted with a collision bulkhead forward, and will haul twenty-six men (fourteen in extreme weather). Sounds like a pretty good boat don't it? The new (since the early sixties) boats are built of thick fiberglass and have seats and bulkheads built into the heavy liner. The engine sits about in the center of the boat under a fiberglass take-apart box. The engine bay is separated from the forward and aft compartments by bulkheads almost as high as the sheer of the boat. Starboard and just aft of the engine is a little console with a big bronze steering wheel sticking up on a vertical shaft and some instruments (usually defunct in surplus boats). The wheelman (coxswain to you) stands on one of the ten-gallon monel fuel tanks and braces his back on an aluminum backrest mounted to the after bulkhead while he steers the boat. There is a standard, two-handle Morse control to deal with the throttle and the shift. The seats are neat. They are molded into the sides of the liner and run smoothly all around the whole boat and have hatches for access to storage compartments underneath. The bilge of the forward compartment is covered by a cast-aluminum grating (diamond plate in some). The stuffing box for the one-and-three-eighth-inch bronze shaft (usually bent, but easily straightened) is covered by a removable fiberglass floorboard. There is a big Wilcox Crittenden piston-style bronze bilge pump mounted on the after side of the aft bulkhead, which pumps the sump at the heel of the keel. The bilge is continuous, and there is supposed to be a bronze centrifugal bilge pump, belt-driven from the engine and low enough to be self-priming, though I have never actually seen one that worked.

Some Common Problems

Most of these old boats aren't running when you get them. Mine was not only not running, but was full of water with the engine oil floating on top. I imagine that the reason that they are surplused out is because they quit running. My friend, though, bought the $450 jewel because the hull was busted by some accident on board the ship or in the surplus yard where I have seen forklift holes in other boats. When he got it home after various trailer mishaps (never underestimate the determination of a whaleboat to destroy a trailer when it has to suffer the indignity of land travel) he climbed up into his prize next morning and during his inspection, pushed a button and the horn blew loud enough to wake the dead. "Wow," he thought. "Must have some batteries in it somewhere. Wonder what this button does?" damn thing fired right up. Took him so long to figure out how to shut it off that the day tank was boiling over and the raw water pump impeller was ruined. All he did was put in a new impeller, patch the busted place in the hull, paint over the gray, run it for ten years . . . and act smug.

That impeller is usually the reason the old boats aren't running when you get them. The raw water pump is a little miniature Sherwood, driven off the camshaft in front of the engine. The, usually rotten, hose to it is in a bad place and has usually been left alone for too long. Whaleboats are not normally left in the water by the Navy, but hung in big davits on board ship (mine was starboard aft on the USS *Saratoga* all through the Vietnam war). Every time the boat was launched, the little Sherwood had to run dry for a while. Though the engine has a heat exchanger and freshwater coolant, evidence shows that most of them ran hot a lot and need a piston ring and crankshaft job. If the block is not busted, the original engine can be repaired with readily obtainable Perkins parts. The cylinders are even replaceable. Lots of parts can be scrounged up from places other than "marine" to save money. Those little Perkins diesels were, at one time, used on the refrigeration units on semi trucks, and lots of Thermo-King places have new-old-stock parts that they are eager to unload.

The transmission in late boats is a big heavy-duty Paragon hydraulic rig set up to run two to one. They all leak transmission fluid out the rear seal where the coupling makes up. The rusty sealing surface is one problem, but the real thing is that the coupling flange that forms the sealing surface fits onto splines on the output shaft of the transmission. This output shaft is part of the big reduction gear. The damn transmission is practically bullet-proof except for these splines. Even the manual warns that "Repeated operation of the transmission from forward to reverse at full throttle will cause excessive wear." Wow, I reckon so. I can't imagine doing it all that much, but maybe someone did. What happens is that the loose splines from that kind of treatment allow the flange to wobble in the seal and make it leak. It has to be fixed or else the damn thing will dribble about a quart of automatic transmission fluid an hour into the bilge and that ain't right. Oil thickeners don't seem to help a bit. The best fix is a new output gear, flange, and seal for a bunch of money. One of us glued the flange to the splines with this epoxy J. B. Weld to try to keep it from wobbling, but got it on there crooked so that it wobbled and leaked worse than ever. He has one of those old horizontal heavy-duty Yanmar single-cylinder engines that is beginning to look pretty good.

Other than Minor Mechanical Problems, Any Other Imperfections in These Jewels?

A motor whaleboat will roll with the most vicious snap I ever saw, and I have seen aplenty. Back when the dew was still on the lily after we had resurrected our whaleboat my wife and I went to the Bahamas in it and had to ride a nasty little beam chop all the way in the Gulf, then a regular Gulf Stream thing all day across. I tell you, our behinds were sore just from clenching onto the seat. As one Dog Islander said, "Damn thing will roll the dipstick out of the hole."

They'll also throw water on you. A motor whaleboat has a blunt stem and convex entry to the bow that, to my knowledge, has no rival for throwing water to windward. A semi-V aluminum boat comes close, but they aren't as determined. The exclamation, "Wow, what a nifty boat!" quickly becomes "Hey man, you need to put some kind of shelter on this thing" when we get out of the river.

To give the devil his due though, there is nothing I ever saw that will go straight into it or straight away from it like a motor whaleboat. They've got enough horsepower and a big-enough wheel to maintain speed to windward in mighty rough weather and the stern is shaped just right for a following sea. One of us routinely unloads lumber, septic tanks, and things like that on the seaside in the surf by pushing up on the bar and holding the boat straight, stern to the breakers, with the rudder and engine while a rusty backhoe takes the septic tank off. Try that in your outboard powered deep V.

My friend, the wit, here on Dog Island put the performance of the Navy motor whaleboat this way. "They can stand a hell of a lot more than you can."

Another thing they will do is wash sand. Our local wit says that they can go anywhere if they can just get a little water to the wheel. After Hurricane Kate, two of them washed a deep-draft forty-five-foot sailboat off the dry land. Made up alongside each other heading in opposite directions, one whaleboat washed toward the beach and the other washed the sand that was stirred up out away from the operation. Before long, both whaleboats were completely landlocked in a seven- or eight-foot hole, which they moved slowly toward the beached sailboat. After two days of twenty-four-hour wide-open washing, they had the sailboat upright in the hole with them. Two days later they had accomplished a salvage job that had a low bid of eighteen thousand dollars with barely a hint of what had happened left on the beach.

When I bought mine, I hauled it gleefully home, fixed it up, and it has served me well for a long time. Now, mostly, it hangs on its mooring up there in the harbor while I gallivant back and forth in these little skiffs and sailboats that I love so much, but I know that if I need to, I can take a battery up there and fire up my motor whaleboat and do what I need to do.

If you want to look into buying one of those old whaleboats, the phone number is 800-GOVT-BUY.

Po Boy Bahama Trip

in which we change from messers to cruisers

I bought the motor whaleboat (came off the port side stern of USS *Saratoga*, CV 60 down in Mayport, Florida) back when I thought we would need something other than a little skiff to get back and forth to the island where we live. I have since realized that maintaining the mooring and feeding the barnacles and all ain't worth the few trips we made when it was too rough for the skiff. What it amounts to is that if it is too rough for the skiff, it is just too rough no matter what kind of boat is throwing water on me. I still have the whaleboat . . . just as good as new, sitting flat on the ground out in the yard of the shop. I go out there every now and then and fire it up just to listen to the old 1957 Mercedes marine engine (636 . . . same thing as used to be in a ThermoKing semi truck refrigerating unit). I did it just the other day and when I scrambled aboard, I noticed a very big imported fire ant nest built all up around the wheel, so when I had her warmed up good (an oversized keel cooler works pretty good in air when the engine isn't actually working too hard) I pulled her in gear and scattered those ants out a little bit. When I shut down and went back in the shop, they were all swarming out and around gathering up their little pale, naked babies. I had to pussyfoot quite spry. Though I hate them like sin for being so indiscriminate with their biting, I felt kind of bad.

After I hauled the old boat back from Mayport behind my log truck, when I won the sealed bid (I think it cost me $750 in about '84), I tried to fix the old Perkins-Westerbeke (4-107) that was in there but it had run so hot that, after pricing the parts, I decided it wasn't worth fooling with and I had this old Mercedes that had come out of a tour boat at Six Flags Over Georgia when that early-model theme park converted to electric boats about '80 so I adapted it to the old *Paragon* transmission (two-to-one reduction turning an 18/14 three-blade wheel) of the whaleboat.

We had the old whaleboat working pretty good by that summer and our son Wes had a little Cape Dory 25. He had left Dog Island and was on his way across the Gulf before I frantically got finished up with the obligations of the shop. Finally we loaded up all the junk that we had been accumulating, loaded the whaleboat onto its trailer, and hooked it up behind the log truck and headed for Stuart. The trip down there was uneventful . . . good tires had a lot to do with that. We launched the boat at a little freshwater public boat ramp just above the first lock on the east end of the Okeechobee WPA ditch, put the truck and trailer in a mini warehouse in Stuart, caught a taxi back, cranked up and locked through into the St. Lucie River, and found Wes anchored just below the lock right between the bridges of I-95 and the Florida Turnpike.

He had eaten up a bunch of groceries on the eight days he had been gone, so we moved down the creek to downtown Stuart and anchored along with a bunch of other boats near a little park upstream of the first drawbridge and walked to the grocery store. When we got back, there was a little derelict-looking fiberglass sailboat alongside the whaleboat but nobody was there. We found out by gossiping with some people who lived on boats there that that little boat was swinging on about five hundred feet of black polypropylene line and was apt to come alongside any boat within a thousand-foot circle and had been doing it for years. "Well, why don't one of y'all shorten up on it a little bit?" asked me. "We like it like that . . . kind of like having a big front yard with an automatic lawn mower," they explained. "Adios," said me. "Vaya con Dios," they replied.

The highway bridge and railway bridge are very close together right there in downtown Stuart and the bridge operators liked to play with people by opening one and not the other, or closing both of them to catch some little underpowered vessel (like Wes) between them so they can see how good he is at keeping a tight circle in strong current. We managed to evade their pranks though and got out into the bay. I do not know east coast inlets and since we were going to have to leave in the dark (moonrise too late) so we would come on the banks in sure daylight, we decided to go all the way south to Lake Worth, which they say is the most predictable. A departure from there would give a good shot to hit West End, Grand Bahama, with a little help from the Gulf Stream. The old whaleboat didn't care with its steady seven knots, no matter what, but Wes had a pretty puny little outboard and didn't want to burn much gas so he needed to sail.

We took our sweet time going down behind the barrier islands with all the condominiums on them and looking at all the people barbecuing and riding around on their lawn mowers and blowing leaves back and forth into one an other's yards with those cursed yowling leaf blowers. We found and finally caught a few mangrove snappers (gray snappers), which are smart and hard to catch, but my wife is smart too and an expert with long experience so we ate well. Our first anchorage was at Hobe Sound so close to the railroad track that the trains woke us up. The second day we made it to the upper section of Lake Worth behind Munyon Island where we dug some pretty good quahogs and made us a chowder. Wes took the skiff to someplace in Riviera Beach and bought a little ice and a six-pack of beer so we could whoop it up a little bit before the iceless, beerless places we were fixing to get to soon.

I'll have to stop and tell about the skiff now I guess. That was back when I was thinking that the best tender for the Bahamas was something sacrificial. I had bought this rough-looking fourteen-foot fiberglass boat (Larsen, actually a pretty good boat, still running over on Dog Island) and cobbled together a very bad-looking, mixed-up old 9.9/15 Evinrude/Johnson. We were planning to use the cargo boom to turn this skiff upside down on the bow of the whaleboat for the trip across. If I had known what I know now, I would have towed it like I have for all the other trips and I would have taken something much lighter and easier on gas and better rowing for when the gas gave out. It worked okay though but was a lot of extra work and cramped us all up in the tiny little shelter house in the stern for supper while we were anchored up behind Peanut Island the next day getting ready to go when it got good and dark.

When the time came, we eased on out by the Coast Guard station. We could feel a pretty good little sea breeze blowing into the inlet and the tide was rushing out too and I had a feeling. We went first in the whaleboat with Wes, close-hauled, about a hundred yards behind. As I expected, we encountered the first of a series of very big, almost stationary waves. The old whaleboat would have been able to bully its way through but I knew that Wes would never get out with the wrong wind and little help from his engine so I wheeled around and headed back in. I remember Wes's face as we passed him without explanation. It didn't take him long to figure it out though and he did a neat jibe right in the narrow channel and we went back to Peanut Island to wait for the tide to slack off a little and the land breeze to pick up. I almost decided to stay another day because it looked borderline for getting to the check-in place before the price goes up (never check into the Bahamas after closing time . . . normally it is just a driver's license and a little money but if they have to make a special trip, it is a pain in the ass and big money) but the weather was right and we were getting tired of

South Florida so as soon as we could, we moseyed on out.

We could still see the lights of the condominiums when it began to get day though we were in the middle of the Gulf Stream. After the sun rose, the water was so blue that it looked like it would stain a white shirt. I have tried to take a picture of that, but never was able to come close. I believe there is only one way to find out what it really looks like. After morning came, the wind slacked off completely and we took Wes in tow and eased on across the smooth, incredible-looking blue sea. I didn't have any navigation instrument except for my compass but I have had a good bit of experience and the speed of a motor whaleboat and the Gulf Stream is predictable and pretty soon we saw the radio mast of the old Jack Tar Marina on West End, Grand Bahama. We checked in in the nick of time too. There was a woman in a ridiculous bathing suit trying to check in ahead of Wes and me and if that hadn't griped the ass of the official so that he sent her back to her boat for "the captain," we would have run into overtime. Never gripe the ass of a Bahamian official. They have a good bit of autonomy and can run up your bill pretty stiff.

There is an anchorage-looking place right there at West End right off the Jack Tar golf course and I dove in with the anchor (never anchor anyplace in the Keys or Bahamas without making sure you are onto something). I was hoping to find some squirrel fish holes so I could rig up the reliable Bahama moor with two anchors set on tight lines either side of the bow so that when the wind or current shifts, the anchors won't become unwiggled and turn you loose, but there was nothing on the bottom at all but a thin layer of white sand over solid, smooth limestone. I finally found a little rock sticking up about a foot and by chopping with the fluke of my Herreschoff/Luke, I managed to cut a recess deep enough to hold a shackled bight of chain. By the time I finally got hooked up good enough to suit me, it was dark and my wife had caught a triggerfish (a feat). We pulled Wes in on the towline and cooked up some supper. Sure enough, during the night a thunderstorm came up from the southwest and we were pitching pretty good all night. Not only that, but I was still a little worried about my rig to the rock so I had to leave the engine running so I could maybe keep us off the rocks of the golf course if something were to come aloose down there.

The next morning, as soon as it was day, I jumped in and took a look. The chain had deepened the groove pretty good and probably would have cut that rock loose if it had been snatched on for two or three more hours.

It was calm as glass again and Wes and I swam all around the rim of the golf course marveling at all the big slabs of fiberglass among the rocks of the beach. One piece was the whole deck of about a thirty-five-foot fiberglass sailboat, complete with big shiny winches. The trouble was that it was upside down and we couldn't get to the fastenings. A little tugging with the whaleboat fixed that though and we salvaged them and a bunch of more good hardware. We also salvaged about ten feet of one-and-three-eighth-inch bronze shaft with a lump on the end of it that might have once been a propeller. In a little pocket in the rocks, I found the contents of what must have been a cardboard box of all kinds of jib hanks, little bronze shackles, bronze rings, and clevis pins . . . some poor person's little treasures. There were about ten marine engines and enough lead ballast keels to have been a lifetime supply for a pretty good yard . . . big, busted marine batteries were scattered all over the place. It was a sad business how all those people's cruising dreams came to grief on that lee shore when the anchor dragged in that treacherous trap.

We have begun to be able to recognize places like that and salvaging in the Bahamas has become a ritual with us. One true treasure trove is South Riding Rocks right on the edge of the Great Bahama Bank south of Bimini. I guess people come across the stream on their way to Andros and beyond and anchor up for a little rest before heading on across all that way on the bank. Either that, or big deal sportfishermen down from Bimini working the Gulf Stream anchor up there for a little snort and a nap. What happens is the bottom is just like I described and though it is possible to swim around for a while and find a couple of squirrel fish holes right for the Bahama moor, it ain't easy. Right there on the edge of the abyss like that is a dangerous place when it breezes up. There are so many engines and batteries among those rocks (a nightmare of a place to be shipwrecked too) that it is pitiful. When we went there, it was dead calm and we were in our old sailboat, which does not have the room for salvaged junk that the whaleboat did but we dove up such a rick of five-eighth-inch stainless-steel, solid-back, half-oval straps that I still have a lifetime supply. I also have a wonderful monel ladder that I rigged to fold up on the transom of my sailboat to swim from. In holes in the face of the wall of rock that rises from the depths of the Florida Straits to form the Grand Bank (and such as these "Riding Rocks") there were spiny lobsters so big that if we succeeded in tickling them out of the hole, we couldn't handle them in the net. There were parrot fish that weighed ten pounds and while we were swimming out over the drop-off with our snorkels just to see what it felt like to look down and down and down in the perfectly clear water, I looked over at my wife and swimming alongside of her, just like a good dog at heel, was a barracuda at least as long as she was. We just sort of eased back to the rocks and he eased on back with us. We stayed anchored up there as long as it was calm and never did get to see all we wanted to. That same great barracuda took up residence right alongside the rudder and ate scraps. I know my credibility ain't all it should be, but I have a movie of him eating a big plop of dehydrated mashed potatoes. I was surprised that he didn't spit them back out like I had done.

Another interesting thing was that there were quite a few barn owls living in the cavities of the exposed rocks (there are about four or five house-sized and house-high, solid, soilless, pitted limestone rocks that comprise "South Riding Rocks" and you ride the rode there at your peril). There is a legend of the Chickcharnie on Andros . . . supposed to be a great big mythical barn-owl-style spirit and indeed, in rock caves on Andros, there are the remains of extra-big barn owls left from when the Bahamas were much bigger when so much of the sea was tied up in the ice caps of the poles and glaciers of North America and Europe during the last ice age. On the biggest of the Riding Rocks, there is a little poured-concrete lighthouse that, according to the cruising guide, is supposed to be working but when we took Wes's little dog there to go to the bathroom (he does not like to go to the bathroom on the boat . . . a true hardship for him on the long run) there was a rusted-out acetylene cylinder that looked like it had last been serviced when the British still ran the place. Long shots of the white excrement of some big bird streaked the cylinder and the inside walls of the little den and . . . there were owl pellets of an extraordinary size littering the floor. Bird feathers and bones and lightfoot Sally crab scraps were the main ingredients.

I kind of went off on a tangent there on another boat and left the old whaleboat at the anchorage at the golf course. We didn't stay long after we had dived up all we absolutely needed. We found out that there is a big pipe that empties into that place from Jack Tar and it might be best to keep that in mind if you decide to go there and do a little diving. Next, we went to the north a little bit to Wood Key, which we had found by messing around in the skiff. It was a shallow anchorage just barely deep enough for Wes and us (both two and a half feet) but well sheltered and plenty of squirrel fish holes for the anchors (I used the big Luke and a small, antique Northhill

. . . Wes had two Bruces). Good fishing too. Every afternoon the snappers would drive the shiners into the shallows along the beach and all you had to do was be prepared. It was still dead calm and we needed a little wind for Wes to save gas (an outboard motor burns a lot of gas pushing a sailboat) on our planned trip to the back side of Abaco. We caught fish and cooked them on the beach on a little fire to save propane on the only stove we had, which was just a rusty steel camping rig running on disposable propane cylinders. It was actually pretty idyllic. The town of West End was temptingly close and I am afraid we ran over there quite a bit in the skiff for a little taste of expensive beer (beer is very expensive in the Bahamas . . . don't think about smuggling any . . . Bahamian justice is astonishingly swift and sure).

Which, it is time to digress a little bit. I don't know what the problem with beer is in the Bahamas. Everything is high, but beer is like gold. They even have their own little brewery but that doesn't help the situation. All beer costs the same . . . German, Canadian, British, Dutch, American . . . probably four bucks a bottle by now. These sailboat tourists who ride the inflatable to town and sit in the bar and guzzle the little drinks with the plastic palm trees sticking out of the top are often approached by the owner of the bar to see if they have any extra beer to sell and help out with the tab. Watch out . . . that's just like when somebody calls on the phone and tells you that they have found a big unclaimed bank account with your name on it and they just need a little ready cash to help you claim it. I know a man who sold a case of beer one time. They towed his boat to Nassau and had the auction in one day. Then the bank charged his card a two-hundred-dollar fee just to let him have enough cash to catch the mail boat back to the place where he had left his wife. Then when he got there, she was drinking with the bartender (who most likely was the one who tattled on him for half the auction proceeds) and she wasn't ready to catch the plane yet. It was a messy business all around. The Bahamians have a saying . . . "You make no trouble, there'll be no trouble." They got another saying too . . . "Let's don't waste no time."

Just before we got to feeling like we knew little Wood Key too good . . . the same big stingray came by at the same time each day and ate our scrap fish bones . . . a good wind sprang up and we took off across the Little Bahama Bank for the go-in place to the bight of Abaco. We made it all the way to Mangrove Key just in time to take Albert (the dog) ashore to try to find a piece of dirt to use for a bathroom. We anchored up in shallow water (deep sand bottom for a change) beside a brand-new-looking airplane that was sitting on its wheels on the flats just like somebody normally parked it there. During the night, some people came in a skiff from Grand Bahama and started taking the engine out of it. I heard a little cussing and carrying on and after a while, somebody came over to us and asked me if I had a hacksaw they could borrow. One does not go cruising in the Bahamas without a hacksaw, so I did . . . and a bunch of extra blades (good ones too, not "El-Cheapo" brand) so I loaned it out with one extra blade. When I woke up in the morning, they were gone and so was the engine of the airplane. There was a white plastic bucket sitting on the wing and I thought I saw my hacksaw hanging on the rim. Come to find that the bucket was full to the brim with gasoline and there was no blade in the hacksaw . . . a pretty good trade if you ask me as gas was three dollars a gallon then. Of course, I have worried that I might have been aiding and abetting something or other but those people were polite to me and that engine was certainly going to ruin in that environment.

We made it to the tricky entrance to the completely unpopulated west side of Abaco in plenty of time to dive the anchors and catch a few fish for supper (that's about when we discovered the excellent taste of queen angelfish). We stayed there one night and then went to Cave Key the next day. At first, we anchored in a little cove on the west side but it was rocky there and no good place to cook on the beach, so after exploring in the skiff we found another little, very shallow bay that had not only a little beachy islet, but some big mangrove marls with plenty of those big fiddler-crab-looking land crabs. We moseyed right on down there. The feeble Bahama tide was falling and Wes managed to get in over the little limestone ledge that lay in the entrance to this charming place but the whaleboat hung up right in the middle of its keel. We tried everything short of dynamite but she was stuck . . . balanced on the rock. We just rigged our little mosquito net and spread out our sleeping bags and went to sleep. Next day, the tide did not rise high enough to turn us loose but we had slept good and were right where we wanted to be so we just went hunting for land crabs (which are delicious and the preferred crustacean food of people wherever they occur). The only place I ever saw better hunting for them was at old Roosevelt Roads Naval Station, Puerto Rico, which must have been the biggest unpopulated area of the Greater Antilles back in my day. We stayed hung up like that for three or four days while we rampaged all up and down Cave Key in the skiff and even walked all the way across the uninhabited island through the unbe-lievably thick woods. Even after we finally floated loose, we stayed. There was a little cove on the tiny island (about as big as a riding rock) at the entrance to our bay where a rock bar stuck out. There were a jillion ignorant snap-pers around that place and my wife caught them and we cooked them on the beach in a little rat-trap wire grill. We squatted like savages and ate them with our canned beans. Little stupid-acting sharks (bull sharks and lemon sharks mostly . . . both aggravating and dangerous) came as far in to the lit-tle cove as they could to try to take the snappers off my wife's handline and to eat the scraps after we had had our lunch. There are plenty of sharks in the Bahamas and the danger isn't that one will come along and eat you while you are swimming, but that they might not have sense enough to know who they are looking at while you are wading around and sometimes act like they might want to bite you on the foot. It is impossible to catch more than one or two fish most places before they come and make you have to move. Unlike some people, I think sharks are inedible and it ain't because I am prissy because I will eat a stingaree and love small barracudas and bonefish. I just ain't crazy about shark. I wish I did like them though because it is so neat the way you can just cut them crossways into steaks right through their cartilagenous bones.

We hung around that place for so long that it got to be hard to find land crabs without a long walk through the marls and mosquitoes. We would have moved on down the bight to Basin Harbor Key except that there was no wind for Wes and his dignity did not allow needless towing. Finally a lit-tle breeze sprang up and we eased on down the line. On the way to Basin Harbor, we saw the only porpoise (that's what we call bottlenose dolphins) we saw in the Bahamas on that trip. I don't know why, but they are sort of scarce down there compared with Florida. I wonder if the Bahamians shoot them and eat them. When we got to Basin Harbor, we anchored up in a pretty little hole behind a tiny, very high island. It was a different kind of place from the marls of Cave Key. Though there were some pretty good wet-foot flatwoods with pigeons nesting in the bushes (never break the game laws of the Bahamas . . . which are simple, only real Bahamians can hunt), we became fascinated by the extensive bonefish flats between Basin Harbor Key and the back side of the big island of Abaco. It is hard to catch bone-fish on a handline and we soon got tired of trying so we became fascinated with the sheer rock cliffs of the west side of the Key.

There the water was twenty or so feet deep right up to the island and the rock of the base of the Key was riddled with big solution holes and big rocks that had broken off and formed a regular labyrinth all along the high cliffs. We swam all along there until we knew the topography as well as downtown. There were umpteen thousand snappers looking out of every hole and crevice and some of them were very large. Even the mangrove snappers were very big, but those big-toothed Cubera snappers were intimidating. They are a bad-looking fish anyway, but those looking out of the holes up under Basin Harbor Key were something else. I didn't like the way they examined us as we swam by. They looked like they were thinking about darting out and grabbing you by the hand with those terrible teeth and snatching you back into the hole. My wife, for once, was stumped in the snapper-catching business because, even though she could perch like a goat on the cliff face with her handline and entice one out of the hole with a busted-out soldier crab (which are little land-dwelling hermit crabs) or a little Sally lightfoot, once the fish was hooked, she couldn't keep him from swimming back under the rock and cutting her off. We ate some small barracudas (it's not good to eat big barracudas or snappers . . . they are the ones that will nail you with the ciguatera poisoning) that we caught around the flats and a few errant snappers but mostly we lived on triggerfish and land crabs in that place.

After a while, a little breeze sprang up and we moseyed on down toward the south end of the bight. Wes wanted to sail around to the populated side so he could visit the boatbuilding metropolises on the outlying islands of Hope Town and Man of War and the schoolteacher summer was evaporating from under us so we didn't stay anywhere else for any length of time. I remember we stopped at the ruins at Norman Castle on the big island to see a freshwater well where there had been a lumber-loading operation. The woods were small, second-growth Caribbean pine (*P. elliottii* var. *densa*) with small cabbage palms and saw palmettos and had just been burned . . . looked like home. There were a bunch of poor-looking dogs messing around the place and we didn't need any water anyway so we moseyed on down the line to Joe Downer Key.

I would love to stay there for a long time. There was a long, long sand beach with open, shady woods of the invasive but attractive casuarina trees (which have displaced most of the native beach trees of damn near every tropical place in the world). Behind this sand beach, were the great marls of Abaco . . . , certainly one of the wildest places I know of and one of the last places for the breeding of pitifully endangered great flamingos. I believe that if I could have stayed there wandering the vast expanse of the marls, I could have put myself in the mood so that I would have imagined that I saw Maturin's little skiff pulled up on the beach but we had to move on so we could see the tourist traps of the other side of the main island.

I forget where else we visited in the bight but we never saw a sign of another soul. Finally we wound up at the nice little town of Sandy Point at the south tip of Abaco. We anchored on the shallow flats off the busy little harbor and rowed ashore in the skiff to buy a little drop or two of gas for the outboard (had been out and rowing for most of the trip, a standard business with us) and maybe three expensive cold bottles of beer. There was a low-pressure area that hung around breezing it up for a few days so we hung around too. We found out that the reason the little harbor was so busy was that it was the time of the run of the "passing jacks," which were small scombrid fish which looked just about like the blue runners that are such fine big-fish bait. Passing jacks are a good-eating little fish and blue runners ("hardtails" around here) ain't half bad either.

Anyway, these folks were certainly working to get the most out of the run. They were using Abaco-built plywood outboard skiffs about fourteen feet long and of an excellent model. They ran out around the end of the island into the deep water where the jacks were passing and handlined them into the boat like fury. When they had a good load, they hurried back to where the refrigeration was and dumped the load to be cleaned and frozen and took off to go back fishing . . . all very interesting. We tried to buy a few of the little jacks to see what they were like but the people would have none of it. They gave them to us . . . already cleaned. That's really an excellent little fish. I wonder where they go to be sold.

On the next to the last night of our stay at Sandy Point, a celebration started on the beach with fireworks. Wes and I decided to go see what was up and found out that it was July 14 . . . Bahama Independence Day. Folks were sitting on white plastic buckets drinking cold beer and playing cards and dominoes. The fireworks were being set off by a herd of little children. The Bahamas haven't been independent for too long, and those people are still glad enough to be free that they take their celebration seriously. Wes and I were the only ones nursing those Disney World–priced beers. Every now and then, one of the domino players would holler to the kids and give them a little passing jack money to buy more bottle rockets. After a while, the kids got kind of bored with such plain excitement now that the Roman candles and real firecrackers were all gone and started lighting the bottle rockets and sticking them down the hole headfirst. The bottle soon got smutty and the result was just a feeble flicker and a little smoke for a while as the propellant burned and then a little poot out the mouth, which sent the kids into an ecstasy of hooting and prancing around on the sand. Finally a very drunk domino player got up off his bucket and purchased a whole handful of bottle rockets and staggered down through the soft sand and, as he passed them out to the kids, demanded, "Now, don't crowd around the bottle so. Stand away so everyone can see the beauty of it." It was a beautiful night and a wonderful celebration.

Soon it calmed down enough so we felt like we could get into one of the seaside passes into the bays of the exposed east side of Great Abaco, so we set off. The weather was still unsettled, and I wished that we could just mosey back to Joe Downer or maybe even Basin Harbor. Tourist traps hold no fascination for me, but Wes was convinced that real boatbuilders were really building boats on those barrier islands. From the excellent Abaco-built skiffs of Sandy Point, there was no doubt that he was right, so we eased on out around Hole in the Wall Point where all the passing jack catchers were hard at work. Sure enough, it started breezing up out of the southeast. I thought about going back to Sandy Point, but it was a fair wind and not too bad looking yet. By the time we were passing Cherokee, it was blowing about twenty or so and getting late. I was just about to decide to haul off and lie-to, idling into the wind and not chance any of the hard-to-see passes to the inside, but it would be a long aggravating night so we went up to where the channel through the bar north of Lynyard Key was supposed to be. Big waves were breaking all the way across the bar but it was easy to see the deep water of the channel and unlike Florida, there was no tide to push up a bunch of stationary breakers so we decided to go in. I went first in the powerful (and thick-skinned) whaleboat to see what it was like and there was nothing to it. We anchored up in the lee of Lynyard Key in a little cove after dark.

It was still stormy, but the high rocks gave us a nice shelter from the still-rising wind. I wished that there was enough light to do the right thing about the anchors, but there wasn't so I put out the big Luke/Herreshoff on salvaged British chain and backed down until it hung up on something. I hate to do that because of the damage to the bottom, but I couldn't think of anything else. Wes hung off our stern and we ate a little snack and turned in.

In the middle of the night, I heard Wes hollering about something and rose up to see us all dragging toward the key. The wind had backed around and built up to about thirty and unhooked the Luke. I dove for the glow-plug button while Jane got the chain and the Luke. I tell you, it was a near thing but we got away again. We idled all the rest of the night into a nasty chop and thirty or better knots of wind. I held her by looking at the silhouette of Lynyard Key against the sky.

Somehow, in the night, Wes's tiny dinghy chafed off its painter and got clean away. It seems like it ought to have gone ashore on the key but it wasn't there. There was nothing for it but to ease on down the line and hope to catch up with it. We checked all the baysides of all the barrier islands we passed with no luck. We guessed that it must have blown out the pass into the big water but when we got to a little hole at Elbow Key, there it was tied up behind one of the cruising boats anchored there. We anchored up right in there with them and Wes went to negotiate an arrangement. The people were very nice and gave Wes back his boat but there was a daughter who thought she ought to go with the deal so we had to skeedaddle out of there.

Though we never saw any boats actually being built, we saw some of the exquisite racing sailboats that are such a sport in the races among the islands and I thought I caught a whiff of fiberglass resin. I still don't know where the skiffs of Sandy Point were built . . . guess it was on the big island somewhere.

Anyway, to get this thing over with, we joined a regular parade of cruising sailboats heading north along the well-marked route. Which, as an aside, we have done a lot of whaleboat cruising and there ain't no sailboat that will stay with a motor whaleboat on a day-to-day basis . . . that seven knots all day long no matter what is what does it. I don't remember much of that cruising except that we had a fair wind and made good time . . . Wes to hull speed all the time. I do remember that we anchored up in one little, very pretty bay at the north end of Great Guana Key. There was a nice sandy beach with some miniature palm trees just back of the berm. Unlike the Keys of the other side, the woods were sort of open and we wandered around all in there. For some reason, the whole place was littered with towels and underwear and things like that. It was a puzzle to us until we went back to the bay to try to catch a little something for supper and found a colossal cruise ship shaped just like a barge with a cruise ship edifice tacked on top anchored right in the tiny bay beside us. There had been a trawler cruiser there when we anchored but he was gone. We soon found out why. By suppertime, the whole bay was dooked up by all the flushing going on on the cruise ship. Too bad it was too dark to run away (never run a boat in the dark in the Bahamas) because we could hardly sleep from listening to all the yelps and squeals of all the cruise ship patrons who were running through the bushes strewing their drawers and towels. I was glad to get away from there.

The farther north we went, the scarcer the cruising boats got. I guess they were not actually cruising boats but rental jobs from towns like Marsh Harbor, Hope Town, and Man of War. There were no regular tourist traps north of the elbow so the traffic wasn't quite so bad and we finally got to catch us a little snack and snork a little snorkel as we cruised on back. The best place we stopped was behind Angel Fish Point where there is a bight that separates Great Abaco from Little Abaco. If we had had a little dinghy gas (or a good little sailboat like we have now) we would have done a lot of messing around there, but as it was, we only stayed one or two days in that fascinating place. If I had it to do again, I would anchor up in that bight and stay all summer long but now I have become so infatuated with the far reaches of Andros that I bet I'll never go back.

We anchored by the airplane the night after we left the angelfish and then good little old Wood Key in time for the charge of the snappers. Our old stingaree was glad to see us. Finally a little breeze came up and it was fair so we headed out for Florida. Soon the wind died completely and it was a surrealistic trip in the sparkling night across the stream in the flat-calm water . . . Wes coming along on the slack towline. Everybody was asleep except for me and the easy-working engine. It seems that half my life has been like that and it ain't a bad thing. I listened to the radio and watched the ships riding the stream all the way across. When day came, it was navigation by condominium . . . checked in with the customs at Rybovitch-Spencer boatyard in West Palm. The lady couldn't believe we hadn't brought anything back to declare but I told her, "Ain't got nothing, cain't get nothing." I pulled the whaleboat onto the trailer with the log truck winch at the freshwater boat ramp at Indiantown where the divorcée Wallace Simpson was a waitress before she took up with the king of England and Wes sailed off down the old familiar Okeechobee Waterway where my father's book *The Lion's Paw* played out.

Epilogue
The whaleboat was pretty good for that sort of thing. We had enough fuel on board for the whole trip (14.2 mpg) and though we sometimes got chased back into the cramped little wheelhouse by a driving rain, it was very

pleasant snoozing up there on the bow under the mosquito net. All that deck room under the shade was wonderful during the day . . . ain't no better place to cook when it is hot than on the engine box of an open boat. The big acrylic shade over the whole bow of the boat had a drain in the middle and we caught way more water than we needed. I had decked the whole forward two-thirds of the boat over so that the deck self-drained through two big scupper holes just aft of the engine. We could reach down under the deck into a bunch of shallow compartments through deck plates and we had enough food and junk under there to go to Tierra del Fuego. I even had a complete spare fuel injection system and a spare starter and alternator . . . bunch of glow plugs and extra fuel filters and such but the old Mercedes never missed a lick (actually, has never missed a lick since it was built). If I had to design a boat to do that better, I would cut the draft to less than two feet and make the damn wheelhouse long enough to lie down flat in to get out of the rain. The only real problems we had on the whole trip were that I got a crick in my neck from sleeping in the fetal position and old Albert had a hard time finding a place to suit him. I didn't keep up with the expense of the trip but I know it cost less than staying home . . . no phone bill . . . no electric bill . . . no beer bill.

Vehiculosis

in which a peculiarly virulent local strain of a common disease affects the temper of many Dog Islanders

The island in the north Gulf of Mexico where I live has a grumpy sort of social situation. When you read about neighboring islands in the paper, they are having a neighborly time at the chili cookout listening to Tom T. Hall or something like that but when you read about this island, the story is always about some unpleasantness among the citizens. It is tempting to think that the teeming masses of the other islands are able to calm themselves by going to all the bars, bistros, and low dives they have but these old grumps over here, where there are no public facilities at all, can't do that so they get mean. That's not what it is, though. What is wrong is that they are infected with a peculiarly virulent local strain of a common disease that frustrates them and keeps them so furious all the time.

Vehiculosis is probably the most widespread disease in the US. Surely it ranks right up there with herpes and some of the fungus infections. In its chronic form, the usual symptoms of the disease are sort of like a parasitic infestation where the host is not harmed so much that he or she can't continue to produce that which the parasite needs. In the case of vehiculosis, those things are gasoline and money. Sometimes an acute attack of vehiculosis results in an isolated outbreak of "road rage" where some arrogant jerk tries to run over another arrogant jerk with his or her car but usually, the sufferer blends in so homogeneously with the rest of the diseased population that it is hard to tell that things are as bad as they really are because everyone is equally sick. Over here, the common chronic malaise gives way to an astonishingly violent, acute attack that, while the sufferer is too puny to do much on his or her own, makes him apt to join gangs and do things that make the paper.

Why this island instead of some of the others? Well, it is just as simple as it can be: There is no bridge. If a person wants a car over here (and most all do . . . it's a symptom of their infection) he or she has to pay big money to get it here . . . or back . . . so here it stays. The island is not but about half a mile wide and when the waves break on the seaside, spray is thrown up into the air, the water evaporates, and the liberated salt crystals blow, sparkling with malevolence, all the way across the island and up under the hood. The first thing a new visitor to the island sees when she or he steps off the private ferry (the whole island is private property, including the ferry) is a bunch of vehicles . . . way too many vehicles considering the paucity of roads. There are some pretty good-looking cars, trucks, and utility vehicles belonging to sports rusting in the sand bed near the ferry dock, but most of them are the worst-looking junkers anywhere . . . some have squatted into such intimate contact with the sand that there is no doubt that their rolling days are over. Others have rusted half in two . . . Ugly stains seep from under them like body fluids from some horrendous massacre. No gated community in any of the other places where these people live would allow such a hideous mess. Some of the junkers have been spray-painted with names and slogans that in another ghetto setting might seem to be gang-related. Such a sight, in any other place, would make most folks turn tail and run and some newcomers no doubt take a worried look at the departing ferry. No need to worry, the gangsters of this "hood" will not jump on you and beat you up. They are too debilitated by their disease.

Some of them are apt to become furious though . . . make no mistake. Road rage is caused when people get frustrated because they can't do what they want to do with their cars. It usually happens in traffic when folks are late to work or can't get home to watch what they want to on the television set. On this island it happens because they can't get the damn car to crank. It is almost easy to sympathize with them. Here they are . . . rode all the way from Atlanta or Tallahassee or some other god-awful place . . . had a miserable, wet trip on the crowded ferry where they had to associate with their sworn enemies, be associated on by huge, pedigreed, inbred dogs, smell other people's stinking gas cans, listen to unsolicited opinions, and then, when they finally get to their beloved getaway island, the car won't crank and they can't get away from the ferry dock. All their iceboxes, clothes boxes, grocery bags, gas cans, plastic jugs of store-bought drinking water and other beverages . . . all the junk that they need to conduct their lives in the manner to which they are accustomed is sitting there in the hot sun in the middle of the road . . . the ferry is gone and the car won't crank.

Even after their sworn enemy patronizingly tries to jump it off, the damn thing still won't crank. They can't call Mr. Goodwrench or a tow truck or a cab or anything. They helplessly have to accept a, smugly offered, ride to the house in a car without electrical, brake, or exhaust systems and they have to sit with one hip in the lap of someone they despise because the car is stuffed absolutely full of junk, other people, and big, wet, sandy, demonstratively dangerous, sexually deviant, or at least sloppily affectionate dogs. After they get to the house, they spend the whole weekend begging rides or walking back and forth to the ferry dock trying to get the car to work (and maybe the well pump, stove, satellite dish, phone, and air conditioner, too, but all that is beyond the scope of this study).

Benign mainland vehiculosis with the AC and the stereo doing their soothing best is not as apt to bring on such a fury as a whole weekend of carrying car batteries and gasoline back and forth down a deep sand road in the blazing sun with the yellow flies, green heads. and dog flies around the shanks, ankles, and toes, mosquitoes on the neck, hands, and arms. and the no-see-ums up the nose. Even if they get the damn car running, things are liable to go wrong again. I don't think there is any other place where one can see a woman, dressed fit to kill . . . in high-heeled shoes . . . trying to dig a behemoth SUV out of the sand with a Frisbee. This is a good place to study the outer limits of the range of the symptoms of acute, frustration-induced, infectious vehiculosis.

One of the characteristics of this disease is that all that fury must be directed at something other than the thing that is the true cause. Those wretched people can't just slosh that five gallons of gas in the driver's-side window and toss in the battery to make a spark . . . they must find some surrogate. Though there have been a few instances of feeble physical attacks by islanders, such a thing is not likely because they have already whipped themselves by the time the road rage strikes. The only kinds of things they can do are accusations of misuse of island equipment or threats to turn one another's dogs in to the dog catcher . . . like what you read about in the paper.

Mullet and Casting Nets

in which a flock of serious bicyclers, out sightseeing,
see more than they expected to

Mullet are wonderful fish. They live together in a complicated social system that is as impossible for us to understand as anything. The doings of lots of species of social animals like monkeys, birds, and bees have been pretty well figured out but about the only thing we know about mullet is that they are much smarter than it seems like any fish ought to be . . . way too smart for a common man to catch. One of the delights of the longtime residents of Florida (be careful of the use of that word *native* now; all of y'all don't qualify) is watching people who don't know any better throw lures and bait at a school of high-jumping mullet. Usually the newcomers run around, exclaim excitedly, and put backlashes on their reels as they cast into the mullet school with no more effect than a slight interruption of the business of the fish as they allow the lure and line to pass and some amusement for spectators who think they know something. It looks like the fish examine the lure as it passes through the school. It is as if they think it is funny too. Mullet, like porpoises and dolphins, are too smart to bite silly-looking lures and little pieces of inferior food with hooks in them and strings attached. I guess it is because they are capable enough to get anything they want anytime they want and they like it just exactly like they like it. Mullet can be caught on a hook and line but only in fresh water where they go when they get ready and then only by special people who know exactly what they are doing. One lady told me that the fresh water makes them crazy. Crazy or not, no mullets are ever caught by the common fools you see all over the place.

Which, I have been trying all my life. When I was a little boy, my father bet me a new automobile that I couldn't catch a mullet in salt water with a fishing rod on a single hook. I beat the water of the Gulf of Mexico into a froth with all sorts of various rigs and never caught a single one. Just before he died, forty years later, I finally foul-hooked[1] one by pure accident. Wow, what an experience. That mullet fought like a bonefish and jumped like a tarpon . . . tore the line off my reel like he (actually she) weighed fifteen pounds but when I finally got her in, she was only about two and a half. I had to sit down in the bottom of the boat until my knees got strong again.

When I wrote my father about it, he gave me joy of my fishing, but reminded me that foul-hooked fish didn't qualify for an automobile.

After years of frustration with fooling around, I sort of gave up the project but only the hook-and-line part. I still itched to catch the elusive fish. Mullet are very good to eat. As a matter of fact, there is no fish that compares to fresh mullet. Sure there are other fish that are just as good, but mullet are something else. They are (I guess) strictly vegetarian. Whatever they are, they have a good fat content in the meat and that fat, while delicious, rapidly changes to the normal, ordinary flavor of mullet that has made them an eagerly anticipated major part of the diet of southerners within range of the Gulf Coast for no telling how long. But real fresh mullet, killed near the frying pan, before oxygen has worked on the fat or the lysosomes in the cells have had a chance to affect the meat, is another thing entirely. There aren't too many people who know what I am talking about. Certainly the smugly ignorant people who frequent tourist joints and "mullet tosses" and such have no idea.

Mullet have, probably because of that high fat content, the ability to keep without refrigeration for a comparatively long time, for southern fish. They can be caught in seines and gill nets by expert people who have worked hard to learn how to outfox the cunning fish and the folks who do that just throw them into a box, without ice, and haul them to the fish house when they get through fishing They know that ice won't help a bit to delay the change that occurs so rapidly after the fish are dead. Though, after a hard, hard day's fishing, they might take a few out of the boat box home for supper, normally they sell the whole load and take the casting net to some little secret hole at dusk and get them a few fresh. It's not an easy thing to do unless you know what you are doing but it sure is worth it. There just ain't a fish like a mullet that has to be killed so he will hold still to be scaled and then mealed up and fried right then.

A casting net . . . now, that's another wonderful thing. They are used all over the world and have been since no-telling-how-long . . . surely since biblical times. The fishing disciples of Jesus fished with casting nets. The New Testament says that they "cast their nets upon the water" and the Hebrew word used is the word that means "casting net." Certainly the round net that is thrown by one person has fed the multitudes for thousands of years.

Casting nets are circular nets that can be thrown to land flat on the top of the water where there are fish or shrimp. The bottom fringe of the net is weighted so that it sinks and traps the fish against the bottom. In deep water a good net can even hem them up before the net hits the bottom. There are little lines ("brails") that lead from the weighted rim ("lead line") up through a grommet ("horn," for the material that it was made from for centuries). These brails come through the horn and are attached to a long line (as long as forty feet in the hands of an expert), the bitter end of which is looped around the wrist of the person throwing the net. After the net settles out over the fish, the person pulls this line, the brails gather the weights toward the center of the net, a pocket is formed all around the rim of the net, and the fish are caught and drawn in. There are little casting nets that you can buy in the discount store that can be flipped out a little way to catch a few baitfish by anybody after a little practice. All you have to do is catch the lead line in your teeth and flip the rest out like a discus ("Frisbee"). The little net will fly into a flat circle like a cheerleader's mini skirt and small, stupid fish can be caught in it. Mullet laugh at such as that though. About the biggest net that can be thrown by that simple method is six feet, radius. A school of mullet can discuss which direction to run, reach agreement, and be long gone outside such a little thing as that. To catch the wonderful mullet, the net has to be at least eight feet in radius (twelve is better), it has to be thrown more than twenty feet (forty is better), and it has to be heavily weighted so it will sink to the bottom before the fish can swim out from under it. You can't just flip such a thing with one tooth and two fingers. It takes an extremely complicated arrangement of the net all over the body and arms just to get ready to throw. The draping of a big casting net is so all-encompassing that there is no way to even shrug at a horsefly after you get ready. You have to make a simple decision when one bites . . . either let him eat or unload the damn net. The various arrangements of a big net are so complicated and impossible to explain in words[2] and pictures that the knowledge just about has to be handed down from ancestor to offspring. It is hard not to think that the whole business wasn't handed down entire, like creation, from Heaven above. A little ethnic research could probably figure out which method came from whose Heaven. Me, I use the Panacea throw myself.

After you finally get to where you can throw the big net and figure out mullet, things still aren't exactly hunky-dory all the time. There are horror stories about people who, while blind-casting off a bridge or pier, caught something that they couldn't handle and were dragged off into the water before they could get loose from the line around their hand. I, myself, once caught so many fish in one cast from a slowly moving barge that I couldn't pull them up on deck and had to hop a long way down the side before another man finally came and helped me pull them in. I had my sharp knife in my hand by then though and if he hadn't hurried up I was prepared to leave that net with those fish. Another time, I was fishing on a popular Florida barrier island down at the state park end. The road, though very close to the bayside beach, is separated from it by a long, virtually impassable, though very narrow, salt marsh. Because of this and because the bay is real shallow for a long way out from the beach, it is unapproachable by most people. There are miles and miles of this narrow beach without a single human track. The intelligent mullet are as plentiful on that side as silly human beings are on the spectacular beaches of the sea side of the island. I went to great pains to put myself there at just the right stage of the tide to catch some with my big net. I already had two nice ones sticking out of my bathing suit pockets when a whole flock of serious bicyclers in their black unisex tights wheeled by down the road on the other side of the marsh. Since I was standing there in the shallow water, looking so fine with my great big net draped so picturesquely all over myself (poised to throw, just like an old Poseidon in a big, dirty, purple bathing suit and T-shirt covered with mud and rotten sea grass) they all stopped and leaned on their bicycles to watch me throw. Now, in a shallow-water situation like that, it is very hard to catch mullet. They can see the net coming and run out from under it. Only an intuitive expert like me can guess the direction that the fish will run and figure the proper lead. Only years and years of practice and perfect physical tone can make it possible to throw the net far enough and accurately enough to reach the wary fish. It helps to have the ability to look incompetent so the mullet will think that you are just another damn fool and not a prime example of the most destructive predator ever to infest the planet . . . hence the purple bathing suit. I always clutch my net as close to me as I can so the fish can't see how big it is (or the state of my physical development). I put on a special expression to my face that I carefully practiced in front of a mirror under the supervision of my granddaughter to conceal my intelligence. In spite of the way I looked, I was filled with confidence and neither the bicyclers nor I had long to wait. I saw an arrogant little school of mullet moseying along at the absolute maximum casting net range. Two of them jumped[3] to have a look at me to see if I was anything to worry about or not. I know what they said when they got back, "Look at that old fool with them skinny legs . . . ain't nothing to worry about there," because they kept coming. I tensed up all the muscles I was going to need and relaxed the other two. All eyes upon me, I threw the big net with all my strength and skill. It flew true and wide to the end of forty feet of line and fell on top of the school in a perfect twenty-four-foot circle. I could only see one or two of the outfoxed fish make it out from under before the leads hit the bottom. My bathing suit, with those two three-pound mullet in the pockets, hit the bottom at exactly the same time in a perfect demonstration of Galileo's delightful experiment. It seems that the net had got hung up on the little drawstring where I had burned the unravels into a knob at the end and not only untied it as I threw but snatched it out of the top hem entirely. I saw it, still hung in the net, gleaming palely, right there in the water forty feet away. Except for a certain coolness about the loins, it was the first sign I had that something had gone wrong. I saw the string, glanced at all that bare skin where my bathing suit used to be, at the bathing suit and the two mullet down around my feet, at the popeyed bicyclers, and then at the net full of mullet already nosing around the edge fixing to dig out. I did what I had to do, spectacle or not. I expected to see the bicyclers still staring when I got all the mullet properly wrapped up but they were long gone. I guess, after looking at all those fit young buttocks squirming inside those shiny pants all day, the sight of one old naked poot scrambling around in the water was poor entertainment. It was very hard to get back to the boat holding the net full of fish and my bathing suit up too . . . almost as hard as it was to put that limp little string back in the hem.

A LITTLE MORE ABOUT MULLET

The black mullet, *Mugil cephalus* (a lesser subspecies called "striped mullet" occurs in the Atlantic and the south Gulf) of North Florida, is a large minnow-looking schooling fish with big tough scales, a tadpole (Lester Maddox) face, and no lateral line. Mullets are herbivorous . . . except for poor old dwindling sea turtles and manatees, they are about the only major vertebrate to eat the plants of the shallow seas of the world. Mullet are a most excellent food fish, either fried, baked, salted, or smoked. Their roe is a delicacy. Even the big male gonads ("white roe") are esteemed by a lot of people. Asians just love such as that. While big mullet mostly live in salt water along the north coast of the Gulf of Mexico, they also range far up rivers. Where these rivers have been dammed up, some populations of them have become landlocked. In fresh water they seem to eat vegetable matter mostly from vascular plants and may, during a crazy spell, eat a little worm sometimes. In salt water it looks like they eat algal mat and sand off the bottom and somehow grind diatoms and other small plants off the individual grains of sand. They have a little fusiform muscular gizzard that, when fried, is a great delicacy among people who know. Mullet congregate in big schools along seaside beaches to spawn in the fall and despite the fact that they have the biggest roe (hence reproductive potential) for their body weight of most any fish, they recently became relatively scarce because this group spawning behavior makes them easy to catch in modern long, cheap, nylon monofilament gill nets (which catch by entangling the fish by the gills) struck out from fast outboard motor boats. This, in conjunction with a great explosion in popularity of their roe among the Japanese, caused an overfishing of both mullet and an incidental bycatch of other species that contributed to a statewide vote that caused a change to the Florida Constitution called the "net ban amendment." Now that gill nets are illegal and the prolific (and high-priced . . . for once) mullet are coming back, casting nets, which are not outlawed by the amendment, are, once again, popular among commercial fishermen.

Salt mullet and salt roe were staples of the diet of southerners before refrigeration. Folks used to travel to the coast in the fall after the crops were in with their big boiling pot and wagonloads of firewood. One old-timer told me the trip was so slow that the children would often walk back home to sleep after the first day's travel. They would camp on the beach, expand the gene pool, boil seawater for salt, and catch and trade for mullet. They had a grand old time. I wish I could go.

Most anyone can learn to throw a casting net with proper instruction and a lot of work. Though only a few can catch enough fish to make it worth all the trouble, there are people who can feed a big family and all the neighbors, year-round, with a casting net. It happened all the time during the Depression.

Casting nets have been found intact in Egyptian tombs closed before 1000 BC. Antiquity seems to be associated with the use of the net even now. Though it is best to start when you are still a child before your enthusiasm dries up, a person's ability with it seems to peak at about seventy-eight years of age.

1. "Foul hooked" is what you call it when you hook a fish someplace besides the mouth. Even mullet can sometimes be foul-hooked with a weighted treble hook thrown by a casting rod.

2. How to throw a casting net . . . explained in words as best I can and I am pretty good: First, coil the line in your left hand, if you are right-handed. (If you are left-handed, change all this around. I, myself, am right-handed and it is a good thing for the mullet since I live in the Northern Hemisphere and a left-handed person can, theoretically, throw the net better because when they throw, the net doesn't have to spiral clockwise contrary to the Coriolis Effect.) Grab the horn in that hand so it is sticking up between the left thumb and forefinger with the coils of line. Then gather what you have to of the net in the same hand so when you pull up to your shoulder what you got with that hand, the bottom part with the lead line on it is touching the ground when it comes tight. Then, making a loop of furled net to go with the loops of line already in your left hand, catch the net about pant-pocket-high, still with the left hand. What you have then is all the line, the horn, and about a coil or two (depending on the size of the net and the size of you) of furled net all hanging in one hand with the lead line on the ground.

Then, lifting the weights ("leads") off the ground, raise all you got in your hand up to your left shoulder and, with your right hand, catch the lead line where it is hanging down your front and flip about a foot-length bight of it over your left shoulder, keeping the leads in a natural arrangement so that the part that is on top is the part that goes down to the part of the net, outside, away from your body (got that?). Then reach down with your right hand and catch the outside lead line again and flip some over your right shoulder and upper arm. Do this again and again (don't let it twist as you flip) until you have about half the lead hanging from your left hand and half over your right shoulder (it helps to look in the mirror until you learn how many flips it takes). Notice, while you are doing this, whether any of the brail lines are tangled up with the leads. If they are, drop the whole shebang, straighten it out, and start all over. After you get to be an expert, you can just continue flipping and backflipping net until it gets straightened out.

If everything seems right (yeah, right) then ease your right hand up under the outer portion of the part of the net you have over your right shoulder and catch (palm-up) the bunch of the net that is coming out of your left hand, going around your neck to your right shoulder with your right hand next to your left hand (see . . . simple). Carefully (no, gingerly) shrug your right shoulder and let the right-shoulder part of the net cascade off. It is important that you don't lose the bight from your left shoulder. If you do, or if anything slips out of either hand, you will have to start all over again. After that, you should have half the lead weights hanging from your right hand and half from your left hand except for the little bit that is still across your left shoulder. Both hands should be close together holding the net up by your left shoulder. Now carefully turn loose with your left hand only that part of the net that goes to the right-hand leads, not any of the part that goes to the leads that are hanging from your left hand. That will give you enough slack to lower your right hand with half the net hanging from it as far as you can without pulling any net from your shoulder. As you do this, carefully disentangle your right thumb and forefinger completely from under the net while still holding the right-hand bunch of net with the other three fingers. Reach around the outside of the net with the thumb and forefinger (hold your mouth still . . . you ain't feeding no baby) and grab one of the leads as far down as you can. Make sure that none of your fingers is sticking through any of the meshes of the net so when you throw, none of the inertia of the heavy leads will be lost while the monofilament strips the hide off your knuckles. Swing your whole body back to the left until you feel all the leads begin to pull and then, beginning with your right thumb and forefinger, using everything you got, throw the net from left to right in a strong sweeping motion. The sequence of release is the trick. Let the net progressively come out of your hands starting with the left part, then the part held in the last three fingers of your right hand. Hold on to the single lead that is between your right thumb and forefinger until last. It is possible to manipulate the final shape and place where net will hit the water in a miraculous fashion with those two fingers. If it turns out right, the sweep will begin to open the leads that are hanging from your right hand while you are still holding that part of the net, then the opening will progress to the leads that are over your left shoulder, which will smooth the transition between the spreading of the two halves of the net. After the bight of net comes off your shoulder its inertia will take up the leads hanging from your left hand. They will, in turn, take the opening net forcefully from the three fingers of your right hand and, as the net spirals out in a perfectly flat circle twenty-four feet in diameter, you can guide it with the single lead that you are still holding in between your right thumb and forefinger, which fingers and lead will wind up low down close to the water and far to the left. As the wonderful net flies, it will pull all forty feet of line from your left hand and fall in a beautiful big circle, near leads hitting the water first, right on top of the horrified fish. You can feel them hitting the net. Which feeling is one of the most exciting of vindications but take your time . . . better let the net catch them. You won't catch a one without that net. With it, you might catch enough to feed the inaugural ball of the next governor of Florida. After you gather the leads, you can slap that horsefly that has been chewing on you all this time.

3. Mullet jump for no apparent reason. They don't knife through the surface on the way out and back in like most predatory fish, but sort of flip up and flop back in a very insolent manner. I think they do it so they can look around in the air to see what's what. Most of the time, they rotate while they are up there, as if to scan the whole world, before they flop back on their sides. They seem to do it every single time you make a miscast or get your toes tangled up in the net and have to hop and stagger or flop.

Sources:

WHERE TO FIND A NET

Memphis Net and Twine Company, P.O. Box 8331, Memphis Tennessee 38108, or memphisnet.net. These folks have a complete line of English-style casting nets up to twelve feet in radius. There are two kinds of big nets: the "English style" with brails like the little nets in stores and "Spanish style" with a pocket made into the net down by the lead line and no brails. Though there are strong prejudices, the basic difference is that the Spanish net will outcatch the English net in shallow water (whoopee, I can hear the squawks right now) but the English net is easier to get trash like crabs and oyster shells out of and is easier to load up if the brails ain't all tangled up with the leads. You can get an excellent English net from Memphis Net and Twine but I have never seen a Spanish net that wasn't homemade. Their catalog also has an interesting history of cast nets and an offer of an instruction book and a video (probably "handed down") showing how to load and throw. I haven't seen it so I don't know what method it teaches.

A GOOD BOOK ABOUT IT

Ed Greene, Greene Publishing Co., Tallahassee, Florida, has a little picture book describing what I call the Panacea method (use of which name will, I'm sure, infuriate folks from Apalachicola, Carrabelle, East Point, Steinhatchee, Cedar Key, St. Marks, Sopchoppy, the Atlantic Ocean, and Asia).

WHERE TO SEE A CASTING NET THROWN

If you drive along the Gulf Coast Highway (US 98) at daybreak or dusk-dark you might see somebody standing, patiently, out in the shallow water. If you to stop the car and be patient for a little while too, you might see something interesting. If it is a stupid-looking old man in a filthy purple bathing suit, prepare yourself.

WHERE TO SEE MULLET IN THEIR NATURAL HABITAT

Wakulla Springs State Park below Tallahassee is the best place. They have a glass-bottomed boat. You can take a ride with the other tourists and look down into the beautiful clear water of the biggest single spring in the world and see big mullet swimming around all over the place. Those mullet are in fresh water and so they might be a little crazy but they ain't so crazy that they can't see you up there in that boat. They say, "Look a there at them fools in that tub. They act like they don't even know we looking right up their britches legs. Look at that one with all them little dimples on her thighs. That's how you tell the ones that are full of roe."

Hem-Em-Up Creek

in which the location of a honey hole is not revealed

You know, watching the behavior of animals is just about my favorite form of biology. I just love to try to figure out what they are doing and how they are going to do it and human beings are just about as interesting as insects. One time I watched a woman, dressed fit to kill, on her way to a party over here on this island get stuck in the deep sand of the road in an SUV big enough to haul a ton of hog feed. Though the only road on the island passes right in front (?) of our house, we do not have a car. Not only that, but we do not participate in the antics of those islanders who are infected with the disease of vehiculosis. It is unfortunate that the worst sand bed on the island is right in front of my house . . . well, it is unfortunate for the poor fools who get stuck there but sort of entertaining for me. At first this woman in the evening dress tried to dig out this monster, which was sunk to the axles in the deep sand with first one, then the other, high-heeled shoe. Then she tried a Frisbee for a while . . . had to hike her evening gown up quite high to get enough freedom of motion to get down to where the sand was. Finally she realized the futility of her struggle and put on her high-heeled shoes and strutted (?) off down the deep sand of the road to the party for some help. In no time at all, the whole road was full of well-dressed, drunken, pot-gutted gallants with their all-terrain vehicles jockeying for position like a herd of male beetles attempting to gain ground on a possible copulation. It soon got too dark to see anything and we got tired of the revving of engines and the stink of exhaust and went to sleep. At least one of those male beetles must have been a fairly capable tumble bug because when we woke up that SUV was gone.

I know I have to get off this jag pretty quick so I'll cut to the nub: the thing we witnessed while raking the last of the mayonnaise out of the bowl with the spoon. Here came a Ford pickup truck with three stooges and two fine-young-things. Two of the stooges and one of the fine-young-things were in the back with the icebox full of beer and the head stooge (Moe?) and another fine-young-thing were in the front. When the truck got to the sand bed, it started slowing down and hunching like all pickup trucks do before they stop and stick. As usual, the stooge in the front thought that horse-

326

power would overcome sand and floored it and, as usual, sand overcame horsepower and he stuck it to the frame . . . all four wheels. During the ensuing stomping around and discussion, the personalities of the participants became apparent to us casual observers. First, the two women displayed the characteristic response of fine-young-things who have been trained, like me, not to participate in antics of this sort. They stood on the sidelines while sand was dug and hopelessness materialized. The three dorks were identifiable by the way they approached the problem. One was quite along in age for the company he was in. He had bushy gray hair and a stylish way of acting . . . sort of like he might have been *somebody* in another situation, but here he was too drunk to know which way to cut the wheel so as to "Straighten the hell up, goddammit." One of the other jokers had on a pith helmet and was dressed all in khaki . . . most exquisite thin stuff . . . very finely sewn, I know because I found one of those shirts washing around in the surf and, after I got the barnacles picked off, they left the most stylish-looking little holes and, when I wore it in public, people mistook *me* for somebody. Anyway, this khaki-clad man was so drunk that I was afraid he was fixing to have a stroke out there in the blazing sun. The other one was the only person in the whole crew who appeared to be worth a shit. He dug furiously under the wheels and we dubbed him "Digger."

I got to get back to the boat part. There was a hell of a lot of carrying on that I am going to leave out. So what finally happened was these two women decided that they needed to go back to the house. They stared at our wretched-looking outfit and then, thank goodness, down the seaside at our neighbor's place. Though it was much farther away, they decided that that must be the best place to seek assistance so the whole crew trudged down the deep sand of the road (binoculars are the true tool of animal behaviorists . . . that's "ethologists" in the jargon). Poor little drunk Khaki brought up the rear and should have had a drink of water. There was some standing around and a lot of head wiggling and finally the man of the house trudged off with this whole mess of people down his little path to the bayside where his boat was anchored (he ain't got no car neither) and hauled them off down to the east to their house. Later, when we went in the boat down that way to the harbor to get the mail, we saw old Digger walking down to the beach from a house that wasn't all that far away. He was carrying a car battery and, when we got back, the truck was gone. The pitiful thing of this was that, while we were down at the harbor, we saw both those fine-young-things posing for a photograph on the bow of a Bayliner. They sure looked fine in their designer sunglasses with those long, diaphanous split skirts on over their bathing suits.

So, before all this happened, we went to "Hem-Em-Up-Creek." That's a wonderful place but it is far down to the west and to hit it right you usually have to leave before daylight so we left before daylight. You know, with that, I must digress but I'll be short with it. Fishing ain't what you got, it's what you know and that statement requires no elaboration. We were running kind of late because I had worn out the original aluminum propeller on the damn unreliable four-stroke Evinrude fifteen and I had bought a very expensive stainless-steel prop from a yard sale for twenty bucks but it was too low a pitch so I used much valuable time squatting in the water with my two hammers to get it right, but I got it. It doesn't even cavitate in hard turns quite as bad as the original. I am very delighted. We got there (I am letting out quite a few of my secrets but I ain't about to publish the location of Hem-Em-Up Creek . . . you're on your own) just as the sun was burning off the dawn haze. As soon as we poled silently up to the mouth of the creek, I could see mullet swirling in the shallow water up in there. This little place is a short, blind creek that goes a little way back into the marsh and stops. I don't know what is so attractive about it but somehow big mullet just love the place. Of course, they are all over up and down the flats down around there but they don't go up into any of the other little creeks. I have gradually found out a thing or two about the behavior of big mullet (the finest of the fine). What I think is that they are smart enough to know that they are too big to be caught by an osprey so they are brazen about shallow water. They frolic in a most insolent manner up there by the marsh grass knowing that they are perfectly immune from porpoises (I refuse to call bottlenose porpoises "dolphins"). They are immune from cast nets, too. When you come along, ready to throw, they know who you are and what you can do and have the uncanny ability to stay most frustratingly just out of range. They jump and look at you in a most patronizing way. It'll provoke a dedicated predator like me, I tell you. If you crowd them too much, they'll swim up into the marsh grass (*Spartina*) where they know damn well that the net can't get to the bottom. If you can't help yourself and throw anyway, they won't panic but will saunter around until they find a place where the leads are held up by the grass and wiggle out from under. They are so confident that they won't even go very far but will look you, once, straight in the eye before going on about their business.

I can catch a whole boatload of what they call "dappers," little mullet about twelve to fourteen inches long and very good, but a big mullet is an extremity of delight, not only for the coup of catching the fish, but because they are the best eating. Small mullet are softer of flesh and not as fat as big mullet. An eighteen-inch mullet is as strong as a workingman's arm and almost as hard as a piece of wood. Fried up correctly, they hardly absorb any oil at all and are most exquisitely delicious . . . the gourmet fare of knowledgeable southerners everywhere, especially children and other primitive people. Big mullet command a much higher price than small fish. Back in the pre net-ban days, specialists around here used a big-mesh gill net to select out the big fish for the high-priced market.

At that, I believe I better explain the Net Ban Amendment to the Florida Constitution but, as politics is not my favorite subject, I'll be brief. In the midnineties some sportfishermen got organized and, by use of big-circulation, slick-paper magazines, were able to circulate a petition banning gill-net fishing and any other fishing with any kind of big net in inshore waters of the state. The popularity of their project was helped by the arrogance of some commercial fishermen who would strike a thousand feet of gill net around a place where people were trying to fish with a hook and line and catch everything in the circle. The old law permitted the netters to legally catch way more fish than the pole-fishing limit and such behavior not only seriously depleted the stocks of inshore fish of all species but aggravated the common folks into signing the petition in cahoots with big-deal hotshots who wash the banks of every waterway in Florida with the enormous wakes of their extravagance. The amendment passed overwhelmingly (just like similar works in Texas and Louisiana had done before) and inshore nets were restricted to five hundred square feet and had to be small-enough mesh so that they did not qualify as "entanglement nets" according to the law. There has been a lot of furor since then but the net result is that inshore fisheries of the state have improved dramatically. Mullet, once the staple of the diet of a lot of people, have recovered to prehistoric plentitude. I met a sixteen-year-old boy who had played hooky from school during the fall spawning run of the year of 2000 and caught fifteen hundred bucks' worth in one day with a cast net. He didn't even use a boat but drove from creek to creek in an old rusty Datsun pickup truck. He told me that his granddaddy had taught him how to do it.

Since the net ban has been so successful, I am waiting for the people to smite the poor old commercial fishermen the final blow and outlaw shrimping. A five-hundred-horsepower shrimp boat scouring the bottom all night long is the most biologically destructive implement imaginable. The gourmet appetite of people like the ones I saw get stuck in the sand drives the market so that the price is so high that it is profitable for a boat to work all night and catch and kill thousands of pounds of "trash" for a few pounds of bugs. Shrimp are very low on the food chain so they renew mighty quickly. Despite that, none of these shrimpers is making much money. There are just too many of them working the resource so that a fancy woman on the east coast can drive her SUV all the way across the peninsula to "pick up some jumbos" that she heard about over on the Gulf side.

I know that being a gourmet is a mortal sin but, like the east coast woman (I know her) with the extravagant tastes, I just can't help myself when the big mullet finally arrive at the creeks and marshes of the panhandle of the state of Florida so my wife and I stepped silently out of the boat and carefully placed the anchor on the sand at the mouth of the creek . . . our eyes riveted on the swirls of the fish within. I slowly took the big cast net out of its box and carefully arranged it in the elaborate arrangement that precedes the Panacea throw, which is the best way to throw a heavy net while wading about thigh-deep. No words were spoken as my wife positioned herself at the mouth of Hem-Em-Up Creek and I slipped down the beach to creep in through the marsh grass to the blind end. We had done this before and I knew that they might be in the deep water of the head hole and I might make a good throw. When I got through the grass to the hole, I could see no sign of the fish on the surface but the water was pretty deep and I knew they were in the creek somewhere so I threw anyway. Boy, it was perfect. The big heavy net spiraled out and almost completely covered the surface of the hole. The strike of the leads on the water sounded like somebody had dropped fifteen car batteries in the early-morning calm. But all I caught was about fifteen hermit crabs, which had to be laboriously taken out of the net because even that little abstract weight will interfere with the precision of the spread of the next throw. I waded down the creek toward where my wife was trying to block the entrance. I saw the fish in the shallows of the middle section of the creek but they were too far away yet. I slipped up into the marsh grass and hurried as stealthily as I could down to where I thought I was in range and threw out onto the shallows where I had seen some big swirls.

When the net hit, I saw three big fish erupt from the water. Though they were inside the net, they were so powerful that they were able to lift the leads from the bottom and no-telling-how-many ran for their freedom. There was no arrogant sauntering to this escape, I could hear the grunting of their bones as they swam as fast as they could for the mouth of Hem-Em-Up Creek. Like the boys in the wonderful movie *O Brother, Where Art Thou,* I know just what they said: "We in a tight spot." My wife made the same motions as a hockey goalie but the mullet had the situation figured out and ran past her and between her legs . . . some jumping where the water was too shallow to swim. There were a few who were intimidated by her and swam back up the creek toward me, but I had three in the net and couldn't get ready so they went back up beyond me. After I got the three out (a tricky business) and into the bag, I made the arrangements and went up after them. They were nowhere to be seen and this is a blind creek. I have a little song I sing to myself as I quiver with readiness in a situation like that: "Just give me a little sign, girl . . ." I couldn't figure it out until I saw a hint of a shimmer . . . "hup, my baby," in a little pocket of marsh grass along the bank. I knew that, if I threw on that, the leads wouldn't be able to compress the grass enough to get to the bottom and they would get out so I decided to flush them out like quail. When they ran, they were like bullets in the water. I could see the whiteness of the vacuum from the cavitation of their tails in their wakes. Trying to lead them as much as I could within the range of a possible throw, I let fly. The big net soared up and away but I could see that they would be out from under it before it hit. My wife feinted to the east and splashed to the west before them and, miraculously, they turned and swam back toward me just in time to hear the complete circle of the splash of the leads all around them. They did not panic at all but swam within the net looking for a hole. I would like to lie to you and tell you that their intelligent, deliberate efforts were not in vain but we took home six big, fine mullet and had a primitive feast.

There is a lesson to this story: If those three mullet had kept running the first time they could have gotten past my wife and been free with the twenty-five or so others, so what we did was to aid natural selection in increasing the intelligence of the survivors of that species. Like I said, fishing (and escaping) ain't what you got, it's what you know and it is too bad that the ability to hem-em-up is no more significant in the master plan than the ability to pose on the foredeck of a Bayliner.

Blue Goose Bar and Other Stories

in which we watch a daring rescue

I know this place is not unique, that there are other places with traps set up to entangle those inexpert at the art of inshore navigation, but there are certainly a bunch of places around here that regularly see what seems like more than their share of tragedy. One such is now called (by us) Blue Goose Bar. The whole bayside of this island is sort of treacherous but, if you hold off a reasonable distance, you can safely coast the complete length without mishap . . . if you know enough to dodge Blue Goose Bar. We used to call it "Rubber Bushing Bar" because, though we knew enough to dodge it, I cut it a little too short one time in the old twenty-three-foot crab boat that we hauled this whole house over here with and stripped the rubber bushing out of the prop. I guess those things were an improvement over shear pins . . . for the makers and reconditioners of propellers. Another shear pin replacement was the scored down shaft between the head and the foot that OMC used for a while. That way the shaft wrung off when you hit and the engine acted just exactly like it had a sheared pin, only it couldn't be fixed until next week back on the mainland. I won't go on and on about advancements in maritime technology because this is a treatise on local navigational hazards.

The Carrabelle River where the only boat ramp giving access to this part of Apalachee Bay for twenty miles lies is a real trap in itself. It is mind-boggling how many people put in there and boogie out the river with all the passengers and crew staring straight ahead without a thought that it might be a good idea to look back so they could see what where they will have to go back to looks like. Then they come over to the island and cook themselves and eat out of plastic bags and drink out of aluminum cans all day long until the afternoon thunderstorms build up and come marching down the bay. All of a sudden the wind is whipping the chips from their lips and blowing the foam off the cans and sand onto the towels and it is time to go. Actually, it is too late. The daddy of the crew will announce, "Well, it's a good thing I went ahead and put 500 horses on this baby instead of the 350 that Bayliner certified as the minimum ain't it?" Of course, by then, it is so rough that twenty-five would have done just as much good as the behemoth deep V wallows in the trough while all those people stare in confusion at the shoreline as if they had never seen it before.

I'll give them this. The mouth of the river is so hard to see that our neighbors down the beach haven't been able to head straight to it in the twenty-five years we have been watching. They always head too far to the east and, when they finally see something that looks like the river, cut about forty-five degrees and head for that and, then when they get close enough to see that it still ain't right, cut back about twenty-five degrees and finally wander into the channel leading through the spoil bank into the river . . . if they are lucky. Sometimes the thing they see that they want to go to is on the other side of a spoil bank and, through the binoculars, from three miles away, it is possible to see the boat come to an abrupt halt and, after the sporty rooster tail from astern finally diminishes, it is possible to see the boat lying on one or the other facets of its deep V at whatever deadrise the manufacturer had decided was the best compromise between stability and soft ride in a moderate chop. It is too far to hear the ensuing discussion, but it ain't long before Harry shows up with his big towboat and lines are waded out and the boat is hauled off. There is one seldom-noted advantage to the V-hull form, they drag a lot better than a flat-bottomed boat . . . leave a trail just like somebody had been out there with a mule and a middlebuster.

The trap to the situation is that the mouth of river is almost invisible in the daytime. At night you can see the ranges and the little blinking of the nuns and cans but, during the day, it is just another wooded shore with no apparent structure or opening. But to the east, old Highway 98 comes close enough to the water so that you can see houses and the highway department outfit and two motels and to the west, there are the houses of Carrabelle beach and the bridge across the river is visible through a notch in the trees where a marsh is. That marsh and all the structures to the west lie behind about a mile and a half width of flats so shallow that, when the tide is out, it is easy to see what looks like fifty or sixty mules have been out there with middlebusters. To the east, the motels and the highway department structures lie behind Lanark Bar, which is mostly out of water but, in some channel-looking places, has an oyster bottom about eighteen inches deep at high tide. That's pretty bad, but the real trap is what we call Gloria's Spoil Bank, which lies directly off the mouth of the river for about two miles parallel to the shore and is only marked by two day beacons that are illogically marked as if they were green and on the wrong side of the channel for someone looking up the river. You see, this is where the Intracoastal is backward from the river . . . a trap if ever there was one. Gloria ain't the only one to pile up on that bank but I believe she has done it the most. She has one of those kinds of sailboats with the bedroom in the back and the cockpit in the middle. I guess such a configuration is a good thing, but it makes the boat look large by the ass and down by the bow and I don't care if the bed *is* king-sized, I couldn't sleep knowing I was in the middle of such ugliness. Anyway, though Gloria lives right there in town, she apparently has never gotten those two green markers straight in her head, and she is a common sight sitting out there, high and dry, waiting on the next high tide at something like three in the morning and, sometimes, is so enraptured by the comforts of the aft cabin, even though it has quite a list, that she will miss the tide and spend the whole next day out there. That spoil bank is a real trap because it is, even at most low tides, deep enough for most small motorboats to clear by several inches. Sometimes one can hear the bleat of an engine that has had all the blades gnawed off the hub of the propeller by the rocks (limestone and flint blasted from the old stone ridge that blocked deep-water access to the river until WPA days) but, most times, the boats tear right across with their captains and crews standing behind the windshield staring straight ahead, completely oblivious to the possibility of calamity. The captain will explain to the children, "Red, right returning, remember. We are returning into the river now so what side do we keep the greens?" "Left!" the children will chirp in unison. "Right!" the captain will congratulate them and they'll go on with no clue that the green was associated with the Intracoastal system and that they were "Wrong!" and that the foot of the engine passed between two blocks of stone with only three-eighths of an inch to spare all the way around. Then one day, they'll come in on a spring low tide. "Now, crew, see that green day beacon up there? Which side do we pass on?" "Blammety- blam-blam— yow-yow-yow" the engine will answer as they cross treacherous Gloria's bar leaving five thousand dollars' worth of scrap aluminum behind.

One dark and stormy night, we were hived up in our dark little house on the island with the seaside doors closed and the bayside open looking at the spectacular lightning over the mainland some five miles away. As is often the case at night in summer, when the land cools from the rain, the convection of the heat of the water draws thunderstorms off the land into the bay and that was what was happening. The thunder from the almost continuous lightning was getting worse and worse as the storms gathered themselves and walked out to us. We were just about to get ready to get ready to batten down when, in the ghastly glare of the lightning, we saw a little sail coming down the bay with the wind from the west. "I hope he knows what he is doing," we said as we dove for our binoculars (two pairs, wouldn't you know). There was, indeed, a little dark-hulled sailboat tearing along in the strong wind with nothing but the working jib up. The seas were so big that the little boat (maybe twenty-six feet) seemed about to broach as it piled onto the backs of the breaking waves. He was headed straight for Rubber-Bushing-Bar. Though I don't normally interfere in non-life-threatening foul-ups, I got my flashlight and fumbled for my little handheld VHF (standard, six watts . . . a good one) and attempted to call him. I guess he was tied up with something else because he didn't answer . . . surfed up on the bar until the boat was lying with the mast perfectly horizontal. Even as shallow as that, the waves were still breaking completely over the hull. In the flashes of lightning, we could see the man scrambling around trying to set an anchor. Despite the fact that he was hard aground, I think he was a seaman . . . which, ain't no shame in running aground. It is only shameful if you act like you don't have a brain in your head and require taxpayer-funded assistance. When someone reflects properly on the possibilities and still messes up, that's seamanship. When a person just drives straight into oblivion, that's stupidity. It's like the old thespian symbol of grins and grimaces. Tragedy versus comedy and this was tragedy.

That bar juts most unexpectedly out into the bay for about a mile and a half. There is a prominent point to the west of it that would be where an observant person would expect a bar to be. It is normal, knowing the Gulf, to think you were in the clear after rounding that point. After he got his anchor walked out (into breaking seas, now) as far as he could, he made up to his sheet winch through the bow fairlead and tried to pull her off forward, but it was too far and against too much weather. Finally, we heard him on the VHF. I explained to him that there was nothing we could do until the thunderstorms passed and then not much with our little fourteen-foot skiff but that I did have a good pair of 12H Danforths and six hundred feet of line and I would be down there at the high tide of the morning and help him get off. With that, I heard another boat call him. Unbeknownst to us, one cove up to the west, there was a small spud barge and its little tug anchored up waiting for a fair chance to go into the river. The little pushboat (you know the kind . . . tiny little things with about a 6-71 semi truck engine swinging about three feet of wheel) unhooked from the barge and valiantly made her way around the point yawing every whichaway in the following sea. Talk about seamanship . . . he backed the boat in with the surf and drifted a line in to the stranded seaman. During that operation, the tug captain drifted sideways so, after he got made up, he didn't know where the deep water was in the dark and we stood out there on the porch in the now driving rain with the lightning flashing all around and, by lining up his lights with lights farther down the island, gave him a heading over the VHF while he hauled the Blue Goose off the bar.

Epilogue: Maritime Rescue by Golf Cart

This is not a real epilogue and is quite long so it might be best to knock the dottle out of your pipe.

After I had written the preceding part, we ate our supper (fried mullet with tartar sauce and coleslaw) and listened to *Prairie Home Companion* on the old Radio Direction Finder (it was a quiet week in Lake Wobegon) and went to bed. What had prompted me to write the other part of this was a regular ripsnorter of a thunderstorm that lasted maybe three hours. One of these thunderstorms wrung the impeller off my little wind machine so I don't know how hard it blew, but it was a regular house wiggler . . . say seventy or so out of the due west which is a little obliquely onshore to the bayside. I tried to step outside for a second to take a picture of our little skiff in the raging surf of the bayside shallows but the damn wind was flapping my lips so bad that I couldn't concentrate on my little despicable camera enough to see which hole to look into. Anyway, it brought back some memories. Thunderstorms like that aren't uncommon at all and there are a bunch of people who have memories like mine. We discovered one that very night.

About three thirty in the morning, we were rudely awakened by a jet airplane (Harrier!) flying slowly and loudly along the sea side of the island shining a light so bright that the reflection from the beach illuminated the whole place (including the airplane) like bright daylight. You know, something like that will get a person right out of bed particularly since our house is so high that I could see the top of the wing of the plane and the starboard strobe passing not more than a hundred feet from our seaside porch on the second pass. I had to step back behind the doorjamb so the two pilots couldn't see how naked I was. As I stepped back out on the porch to try to look down the seaside beach to see what had made them turn around, I was almost spotted by a helicopter following close behind. About half a mile down the beach, the helicopter dropped a very bright phosphorous flare. I'll cut the details to the nub. While I was snatching on my clothes (bathing suit and awful T-shirt . . . a gift from the sea) and hunting for my binoculars and flashlight in the dark house, a golf cart bounced down the wretched road going in the direction of the flare. I slipped out of the house and sneaked down through the sea oats toward the eerie glare of the burning phosphorous. The flare was in the surf of the seaside and went completely underwater as each wave broke over it . . . gives a surrealistic look to the seascape. I kept sort of hid as I made my way down alongside the road peering with my binoculars. I saw the lights of the returning golf cart and squatted down behind a dune (I don't believe in declaring myself until I know a good bit about any situation in which I am fixing to participate) and watched the golf cart pass within ten feet of me. There were two men, one woman, and a girl child, all talking loudly, in the golf cart. After it passed, there was just me, a few ghost crabs, the flare, and the surf beating on the seaside. Then I heard the unmistakable sound of wire halyards ding-a-ling-ing against an aluminum mast. I trotted in the direction of the sound and, sure enough, there was about a thirty-three-foot sailboat stranded on the seaside bar, bow in but still a little broadside to the waves coming from the west. Spray was beating all the way across the boat as it wallowed in the breakers. I put my binoculars into a little clump of sea oats and waded out to the boat. Though the water was only about waist-deep, there was a deep hole washed out around the hull and the boat was standing almost upright. I slipped into the hole and wet my flashlight. I hollered, "Anybody home!" and beat on the hull but nobody answered. After I waded carefully ashore sliding my feet for stingrays, I saw a few tracks on the hard sand where it looked like about three people (one child-sized) had stood around for a little while and then gotten into a golf cart. On my way back to the house along the seaside beach, I spotted the flotsam from the wreck . . . three life jackets (one child-sized), one little tiny oar, and some polyurethane foam.

When daylight arrived, here came the Towboat US and a man of about my age jumped off into the surf with a line and swam and waded to the boat and, through a feat of remarkable agility and strength, managed to catch hold of one of the wildly gyrating stanchions about six feet above the water and haul and scramble himself aboard. He made up his line and the towboat commenced to pull. I went down there and waded out to see if I could be of any help. I talked to the man on the sailboat who turned out to be the captain. Here is what happened. This man had been hired by another man to bring this sailboat around to a repair outfit in Carrabelle from a little fenced-in community about twenty-five miles to the east. He brought his wife and granddaughter along for the ride. They got a late start because the boat drew six feet and they had to wait for the late-afternoon high tide to get out of the canal. By the time they had weathered the storm and reached the island, it was dark. It is the new of the moon so it was very dark. The man intended to coast all the way along the island and go in at the pass but got fooled by the looks of the beach and ran aground. He is not the first one to do that. There is a very abrupt drop-off to the sea side and the on-coming waves don't break until they are almost on the beach. The dunes are a variable distance from the beach so it is hard to tell how close you actually are. If you ride along looking at a bottom machine, it reads better than twelve feet until you hit. Many people have made a Gulf crossing only to come to grief on the seaside of this island.

After three hours of wiggling and hauling, the towboat managed to pull this boat off and take him into Carrabelle.

Those folks were lucky they had a wind blowing sort of off the beach. One of the best ways to see the shoddy practices of modern fiberglass boat-builders is to examine the scraps scattered up and down the shore after one of these seventy- or eighty-knot thunderstorms. Later, I heard that the harrier and the helicopter weren't even looking for those folks at all but for another boat that was in an even worse fix from the thunderstorm. The situation we witnessed was strictly a private operation conducted by cell phone.

Old Coast House

in which a midnight trick results in a restless night in a sandy bed

We hurried back to the coast to see how wet our house got during that last tropical storm. It rained a lot and the roof leaks and we always have to go dry out the house so it won't mildew. I don't know if you paid close attention to Dave Carnell's article about antifreeze killing any fungus but he is right. Moldy wood can be completely restored with antifreeze. One of the doors is right under a place on the porch where the roof has a bad hole in it and the rain runs down the door and it mildews on the inside . . . or at least it used to mildew on the inside. Alcohol will kill mildew on fabrics, too, but it isn't a permanent fix like antifreeze.

Anyway, we certainly were lucky (again). The old house was still there. I feel sorry for those folks down in Pine Island Sound where Port Charlotte and Punta Gorda are. I know some of those people had a lot of money but those up there where most of the damage happened were just regular working folks who didn't need to be put into such a bad fix.

After any kind of bad storm the Coast Guard always flies the beach . . . looking for wrecks and dead people, I guess. While we were sitting in the seaside doorway watching the sunrise and eating our breakfast, here came the C-130 flying down the beach so slow and low that we could see the pilots' faces and smell the exhaust (I think they burn diesel fuel). Later we went in the Rescue Minor all the way around the island to look at the sea turtle nests to see how many had gotten washed up by the surf (only one out of about thirty . . . so far . . . Kate and Opal got them all) and saw a lot of wreckage from busted-up boats. I hope they were just some that got loose from the mooring somewhere and not somebody who got caught out. Of course this storm never got much above fifty knots' worth of steady wind and passed by pretty quick but there are plenty of boats that can't stand even a little of that kind of thing. Some of the wreckage was from what I believe was the worst-built plywood boat I have ever seen. The cabin roof was made out of half-inch pine plywood with an edging just nailed into the end grain of the plywood with galvanized finish nails. No telling what kind of junk the hull was but we didn't get to see that . . . probably down there where the C-130 went.

When we got back, I got my big binoculars and in the clear air that follows such events was able to scan the shore of the mainland pretty good. Our old coast house is exactly where the sun sets from us at this time of year and, though it is about ten miles away, I can easily see it with binoculars and, just for old times' sake, I look for it every now and then to see if I can recapture my childhood and see a bunch of children marauding the flats over there. This time, I could plainly see that there was a large sailboat on the beach right in front of the old derelict place. We don't usually go over there because the beach erosion and the decrepit nature of the old house makes me feel sad but, even though the old familiar beach is all built up with these tall plywood mansions with vinyl siding and fake chimneys and spires like some kind of monastery, it is still familiar so we do make an occasional excursion to our old stomping grounds. Of course this whole part of the country was and is our stomping grounds. So, Jane and I got in the Rescue Minor and struck a beeline in the calm, muddy water for the old familiar tree line where the log house is. There used to be one of the biggest sand dunes on the coast (Royal Bluff on the charts) just to the east of the house and we children used to inhabit it like it was a fortress. We had little trails all through the low, stunted live oak trees that capped it and pretended that we were Indians who were shooting the white people who strolled down the beach or came by in boats. The bluff has just about eroded into the sea now. Some fool has built a house right on top of it, which is fixing to slide down to join the sand in the shallows before long. One time some of us kids set a trap up there. The highway (US 98 . . . the coastal highway) runs in a cut through the back of the dune so there is a high hill on both sides of the highway. We set up a fishing line across the road and carefully folded about five or six rolls of toilet paper like an accordion in the middle of the road and taped them to the fishing line so, when we hauled it in, the paper would unfold and rise straight up about twenty feet like a great white barrier across the highway. This was about 1954 or so and there was hardly any traffic in the middle of the night along there (bumper-to-bumper now anytime) so we had to squat in the bushes and slap skeeters for a long time before somebody finally came along. Boy, did it ever work spectacularly. The car was a '49 Ford and when that great white wall sprang up in the headlights, they ran off the road into the sand bed at the base of the dune. We saw four great big college football players come piling out of the car. Needless to say we (I was about twelve years old) cut and ran down our little trails for the house and jumped in the bed and pretended to be asleep. Pretty soon here came the college boys up our drive to get somebody to help them get unstuck and my father and one of my uncles had to get the chain and go down there with the car and pull them out. We were too petrified to get out of the bed even though it was sandy as hell in there. Somehow, not a word was ever said about that incident and it is almost as if it never happened. You know, I don't even know what those football players told the men of the coast house about how they wound up in the ditch. They might have tried to lie out of it (hard to do considering all that stray toilet paper) but, if they told the truth, it wouldn't look too good that they got buffaloed like that.

So we idled up to the familiar anchorage in front of the old house and set the marvelous Bahama moor (even though it was dead calm and only about eight inches deep) and went looking around. I do not trespass on other people's property so we didn't visit the old dilapidated house but I did examine the sailboat that was on the hill right in front. It was a documented vessel from New Orleans, a fiberglass sailboat about thirty-five feet long . . . one of those that is built for accommodations more than speed . . . short-masted and big-bellied . . . high, center-cockpit-style. The most interesting thing was the propeller. It was big and two-bladed and controllable-pitch . . . SABB was cast in the stern tube casting. I don't loot other people's stuff or I would have been severely tempted to go get my tool box out of the boat. Of course, that thing must have weighed seventy-five pounds, and I don't have any use for such, but it was certainly admirable.

We walked up the beach to the west like we have done thirty jillion times in the past. We saw mullet jumping in the shallows that were absolutely uncatchable to us when that was where we lived. The same old stone crabs were under the same old pieces of concrete rubble where the Steyermans had that miraculous boat house that had a poured-concrete slip dug back into the bank. Beach erosion from a hurricane got that thing back when we were just kids and I bet we have pulled umpteen thousand stone crabs out from under the chunks. We didn't bother them this time though because the tide was falling and we sure didn't want to get stranded even if the flats were familiar . . . besides, we didn't have but one roll of toilet paper . . . so we strolled on back just in time to haul off and go back home. Luckily I didn't have any sad dreams or get waked up by any jet airplanes that night.

The Wreck of the *Daily Bread*

in which Rosalie keeps a secret

The latch on the screen door of our house was salvaged from the wreck of the *Daily Bread*. It is a solid brass miniature of a real lockset with a miniature key and tiny knobs. I have never seen anything like it in my life. It was made to be mortised into the stile of the door and I did that on our screen door but on the *Daily Bread* it was just screwed onto the plywood like a rim-lock. My four-year-old granddaughter likes it a lot and has become fascinated by its story, so here it is . . . all we know at this time anyway.

The *Daily Bread* was a small shrimp boat from the east coast of Florida. The type originated to work the lagoons inside all those islands over there. They are cheap-built, plywood, shallow-draft, single-rigged shrimp boats that make a scratch-by living trawling for shrimp, usually bait, in the shallow water. The *Daily Bread*–type hulls must have all been built by one outfit because they are more or less alike . . . shallow deadrise, low-sided, chine-built, narrow boats about thirty-five feet long . . . sort of good looking for something shot together out of plywood with staples and doo-get-around. The distinguishing feature of all of them is a round stern built of plywood bent at just about the radius that half-inch plywood can stand. They have a wheelhouse way up forward and are set up with various kinds of inboard engines right behind the wheelhouse with a long shaft to leave room in the stern to work the net and cull the haul. I imagine that they were sold sort of semi-finished to be fitted out by the people who used them, because there seems to be quite a variation in the "finishing" touches. The floorboards of this one were fiberglassed in place to keep the shrimp and trash out of the bilge and there was no access under there except for a little hatch over the stuffing box and a hand hole to grease the pillow block . . . a disposable rig if there ever was one.

Apparently there were a bunch of these boats that were run by some sanctified people, because I have seen them all over the place with names like *God's Mercy*, the *Daily Bread*, *Lord's Blessin'*, *Shall Return* . . . names like that. The religious folks must have used these sacrificial lambs until it was about time for them to return to their Maker and then sold them cheap because their rotten-chined, de-laminated carcasses are scattered all over the Intracoastal Waterway from Savannah to the Keys. The one our door latch came off of made it all the way across the peninsula and the Gulf of Mexico before it was finally called home.

One dark and stormy night in early November the *Daily Bread* was wrecked on the seaside of Dog Island off the panhandle of Florida. It didn't take long for the ravages of nature and man to clean up the spot where it happened. We know what we know because of diligent research by my granddaughter Rosalie. As I said, she has become attached to the story and for a long time all she wanted to do was to walk up and down the beach looking for any kind of little piece of wood or plastic that she could imagine had been part of the wreck. Once she came home with a little plastic icebox latch and explained to us that this was part of the icebox of the *Daily Bread* . . . then she told us the story of how that part of the *Daily Bread* came to be just a piece of trash on the beach. I tried to tease her and tell her that the thing she had found was actually part of the breadbox. "No," she snapped, "it was the icebox and it is too wet to keep bread in there with the hot dogs. I'm going back to see if I can find the breadbox right now."

Before she could get away though, the meter reader (a permanent resident on the island) dropped by for a glass of iced tea and she knew he had been on the island the night when the *Daily Bread* went on the beach so she decided to stay and see if she could find out any more about the wreck. "Well," he said, "he spent the night in Rex's bunkhouse. Old Rex wouldn't even give him a sheet or a blanket and it was cold too after the front come through. All he had was a towel that Susan let him have. If he hadn'ta had that, he would have froze to death. Next morning, they carried him to the mainland and he called his momma to come and get him." "What did he look like?" my granddaughter wanted to know. "Well, he was a nice-looking young boy to be so redheaded and freckle-faced. Wasn't no real sanctified person neither. I had a beer or two with him over to the Shangrila while he was waiting on his momma. Come from over there around New Smyrna Beach or someplace like that. She had a seashell shop over there . . . you know . . . sold them little seashells to the Yankees and all. She the one bought the boat for the boy. He had heard that you could make a little money shrimping over here in the fall and spring. He had been working for the Jesus people over there and knew that there wasn't no money to be made there so he borrowed some money from his momma and bought this old boat. I remember the name of it . . . it was called the *Daily Bread*. All them boats had names like that: *Daily Bread, David's Stone, Lord's Blessin', Ten Commandments, Arc of the Convent, God's Mercy* . . . names like that. You don't see many of them over around here because they are built too shitty . . . whup, 'scuse me. They wasn't seaworthy enough to cross the Gulf unless it was real calm. You know, them kind ain't no actual sea boat when they new . . . work them little holes of water between the bridges over on that side. This old Gulf can get sort of rough. Remember that time me and Bingey brung that big aluminum sportfisherman over from Fort Myers for Dr. Patronis when that front come through? Shit, we pitched and rolled around knocking on the same spot for two solid days. We would have tried to head in behind Atsena Otie to wait it out but the seas had pounded all the sense out of the loran and the compass was pointing at the engine all the time and we were scared to go in there among them rocks with all those squalls of rain. Had to change fuel filters three times from all the mud got stirred up out of the bottom of the tanks. Couldn't fix nothing to eat but Vienna sausages and crackers and Bingey couldn't even eat those. This *Daily Bread* boy was lucky to wind up standing on both feet on this beach after he missed the pass and homed in on Rex's security light . . . had a been a month later and a real front passed, he woulda been swimming around out in the Middle Ground with a bunch of little pieces of plywood. I don't know what the hell he thought he was up to with that mess. Sho couldn'ta amortized his investment working this bay here. We ain't got no real shrimp no mo either and he sho wouldn't have been able to go outside and drag for scallops like all these other desperadoes. Them shallow-water boats from over there had them old gas engines into them too. Hell . . . whoo, gracious, there I go again . . . ain't used to talking to children . . . anyway, it would take six hundred bucks' worth of gas to bring one from over there to here even if they cut through the WPA ditch from Stuart to Fort Myers. That old boat had a big-assed Cadillac car engine into it . . . old quadrajet carburetor . . . five hundred cubit inches . . . made to drink gas . . . run the wheel off the automatic transmission too. Probably slipped about one revolution out of five from the torque converter pulling in low gear like it had to do. Rex pulled it out with his backhoe after the boat wrecked. It was kinda sandy but it hadn't never actually been submerged . . . run good, sold it over to Panacea, got four hundred bucks for it . . . engine and transmission. He got the wheel and the shaft too. Had to dig up the deck with the bucket to get that. I got the winch and the cable . . . old wo-out hand winch, but it had about three hundred feet of new three-eighths, seven-by-nineteen stainless wire on it. I give it to Wayne to put on his piling rig. That wreck had the cutest little door latch on the wheelhouse. I was gonna get it but it had them damn square hole screws holding it on the plywood. I tried to prise it off with my pocketknife and couldn't do it and by the time I got back with my little thing, somebody else had done already took it off. It was cute too. I wanted it bad enough to walk all that way back just to try to get it. Can I get another glass of this tea please, Jane . . . put a little more sugar into it too, please'm."

After he was gone Rosalie said, "Good thing you had your little thing in your pocket Pop Pop. I sure am glad he didn't notice that the door latch of the *Daily Bread* was on our door aren't you? Let's not invite him back anymore. Did you notice how big and sandy his feet were? Where is New Smyrna Beach?"

Still looking for the bread box.

Birthday Bomb

in which a birthday present proves hard to get rid of

My wife found a bomb on her birthday last year. Usually she gets a fishing reel or an outboard motor or a chain saw or something like that but I must have forgot because all she got was this bomb. It was on the seaside of the island rolling around in the surf. We both tried to read all the badly spelled, stenciled writing on it, but none of it made any sense even after we had put a foot on it to stop the rolling. There was no question that it was a bomb though and unexploded. There were a bunch of children messing around including our own grandchildren, so we carried it up the beach and hid it in some very thick Yaupon bushes and went in the skiff to look for the authorities.

It wasn't hard to find them either because it was calm and a Saturday and they were out in force checking to see if all the paperwork was straight on all the boats in the bay and if the registration numbers were spaced out right and all. We eased up alongside a pair of them and told them about the bomb and made an appointment to meet them to show them where it was. We hung around all the rest of that day and all the next day and they never showed up so we figured they didn't really want to fool with the bomb anyway, or perhaps the history of certain credibility problems had preceded me or something.

I knew another of the authorities (notice that I am not directly identifying the organization to which "the authorities" are attached) personally and decided to just wait until I chanced to see him out counting PFDs and checking to see if the ESPD (efficient sound producing device . . . a plastic whistle) had been stomped on. I figured that the bomb was in a safe place hidden in the bush far from anyplace where anybody would want to go so I waited. It turned out to be almost a year before I saw my man out on the water (it was sort of rough that year . . . no weather for the authorities). I eased up alongside his big fenders and requested a courtesy check.

After he got over the shock of that, I told him about the bomb. Now, this man is the right kind of lawman. If you don't do right, he will get you . . . kind of legendary around here, and I knew the bomb was as good as gone. I told him exactly where it was and marked the spot on his chart while he filled out the report. He didn't know what a Yaupon bush was (cassein, the caffeine-bearing beach holly so dear to the real Florida natives) so I offered to lead him right there and show him. We took off toward the island but his boat was much faster than ours and he got there first. We met him coming back. He stopped and told us that there was no way that he could get in there where the bomb was and that he had called the bomb disposal people about two hundred miles away and told them to await the confirmation call. I said that I would be glad to wade in and get the bomb and bring it out to him but he said that he didn't want any civilians to go anywhere near the thing but he did need confirmation that it was still there and how long had it been since I had last seen it?

"About a year," said me.

"Are you sure it is still there?" said he.

"Ought to be," said me. "I'll be glad to take you to get a little peep if you want me to. You can run up in the shallows and pull off them shiny shoes and roll up your britches legs and I'll show you exactly where it is."

"Oh, no," he exclaimed. "We'll just have to accept your confirmation. You go confirm that the bomb is still there and call the reporting number on the telephone and they'll dispatch the disposal technicians."

"Ain't got no phone," I said.

"Dogshit," I think he said but I'm not positive. "Well, when you confirm, you can give me a signal from the beach." All this time, we were drifting ashore and by the time all the arrangements were made, we were in about fourteen inches of water and only about a hundred feet from the bush where the bomb was but I declined to offer any more suggestions that might simplify the situation and waded in and peeked at the bomb and waded back out and told him all about it and he took off for the mainland, running about half a mile ahead of his wake (it don't pay to try to outrun the authorities).

About six hours later, five men (including my man of authority) arrived in a junk car belonging to one of the island residents (no road or car ferry to the island). They had a big special-looking box and I took them down to show them the bomb. They peered at it through the bushes like it was a rattlesnake, then made all us civilians (me and the man who drove the car) go hide behind the dune. The authority man came with us voluntarily . . . getting sand in his shiny shoes involuntarily. After a while, we heard some cussing and arguing and finally, the bomb men came struggling up through the soft sand with the nose of the bomb sticking down in the special box and the tail sticking out the top. They loaded it into the old rusty car and took it away on the rough island road. I was surprised that it didn't bounce out or fall through the floorboards and get run over. We listened for an explosion and watched the authority boat cross the bay but there was no mushroom cloud.

Three days later, there was a short article in the paper, "Authorities Find Unexploded Bomb on Area Island." The only thing I regret about it is that I forgot to tell them that the bomb was my wife's birthday present.

A Tough Weekend

*in which we fly in the face of conventional weather advice
and live to tell about it*

Sometimes the weather down here can be the damnedest thing. Here it
is the middle of July and the jet stream is dipping so far down that the National Oceanic and Atmospheric Administration says that a cold front (!) is
forecast to stall out just south of the fall line where the piedmont turns to
the coastal plain and all the rivers and creeks have to take a little fall . . . a
weather-making place. A cold front is a pretty good weather maker in its
usual season during the relatively dry wintertime but, man, in the summer
when the temperature is nearly a hundred and the humidity is too, a little
differential of twenty degrees is something else. It doesn't blow a five-day
norther like in the wintertime but usually just jacks up the regular southwest
wind into blowing very hard out of the due west and with serious storms
training along just ahead of the front, one right behind the other. Before we
came down, they were talking about hail and flooding and tornadoes all
along just north of us where the front was. Such a thing as that makes for a
doubtful seagoing situation but the daddy of five of our grandchildren had
a little time off so they fed all the cats and hamsters and came down. Boy, it
was a rough trip over in the old Rescue Minor but we were all used to it so
it wasn't nothing but a thing (two of them fell asleep) and we got here about
lunchtime and ate a little something out of the ice chest and headed east to
Tyson Harbor, which would give us the only chance of a lee. I hoped I would
be able to catch some mullet to feed all those gourmets but rough conditions
make it hard to see them. Which, you know, when I first started fishing
with a cast net, an old man (commercial fisherman . . . didn't know he was
the last of the Mohicans) told me that there were two things you had to
learn to be able to catch fish with a cast net: "You have to learn how to throw
it and then you have to learn how to throw it on the fish." Those are simple rules but I think you have to work at it for about fifty years before you
get any significant compliance with those two rules. It has been tough trying to catch something to eat this year. You have to be able to see them before they see you and, when it is rough, you can't do that but just in a rare
chance. We anchored up in the lee of a little beach in the harbor and they

all piled out to swim and I took the net and went looking. Right there the water is very deep real close in and it is a good place to throw if you can ever see where they are. Just as soon as I got made up, I saw one jump. I could tell by the horrified expression on his face that he had no idea that anybody was anywhere around and the net followed him back down before he could tell everybody else to run. I caught six real nice ones by the short-snatch method. That is, when I feel the first fish hit the bag, I snatch the net up short and haul it in before it ever gets to the bottom. You miss a few fish that way but six Tyson Harbor mullet are plenty for a crew like this. Harbor mullet aren't as big as marsh mullet (say eighteen versus twenty-two inches) but by this time of the year they are as fat as possible and hard as a piece of wood . . . most excellent. You know, there are some gourmet children in this crew. The littlest one (Rebecca Jane, six years old but only forty-five pounds) will damn near eat her weight in fish and still have room for the field peas and a Dixie Doodle and the Chinese . . . whoo, y'all . . . a Jewish or Italian mother would love to have a crew of them around the table.

It stormed all afternoon but after supper the tide started to fall and the wind died down some. That's one meteorological phenomenon I am not sure I understand. It might be that all that water heading out to sea drags the wind with it or maybe there is a net loss of heat with the loss of water or something but it usually calms off a little inshore when the tide runs out. Sometimes when the conditions are right it fogs up, too. Maybe it is the coolness of all those flats getting exposed but whatever it is, this is the week of dark nights and the low tide was at 10:30 PM—a very low spring tide— so it fell quick and the wind did, too. Children love a low tide on the flats. They call it "when the islands come out" because all the little bars turn into islands and there are plenty of them to lay personal claim to and the children of a five-child family are very possessive. Of course they like to have visitors to their property so invitations are being continually offered and, since there is plenty of land to go around and no debtors' prisons or starving serfs or happy-go-lucky natives to exploit, empire building is not possible so all is polite out there on the flats about sunset. Running from island to island is risky business, though. Not only might someone step on a crab or a perverse *Busycon* conch . . . I have to stop right here and explain one of the silliest aspects of marine biology. I believe there are people in that business who, after the rigors of the field trips of graduate school, spend all the rest of their lives in air-conditioned "laboratories" looking at dead animals and smelling formaldehyde and arguing about the proper Latin names of those stinking animals. Take formaldehyde for an example. Though they deal mostly with dead things, marine biologists do not like to be put in the same class with undertakers. They don't call their preservative "formaldehyde." It is "formalin." It is the same stuff, though, and I don't like it. One time, this girl (plenty of them in "marine biology") was on the little FSU research vessel while they were sampling the benthic (bottom) fauna out on the Florida Middle Ground, which is a peculiar shallow place in the middle of the Gulf of Mexico with an environment much more tropical than the rest of the waters of that latitude. They were pickling all these animals they dragged up in jars with "formalin" siphoned from a drum down in the hold of the boat. To do that, they had to lead the tube down below the bottom of the drum and hold the jar down in the bilges. Apparently this degree-bearing scientist did not understand gravity (who does?) or something because she siphoned fifty-five gallons of formaldehyde into the bilges of the boat and they had to cut the trip short and sleep on deck all the way back in because, even after extended bilge pumping and flushing, nobody could stay below for more than fifteen minutes without running the risk of becoming embalmed. It was a rough trip, too, and I saw them getting off the boat. They were very disgruntled looking and probably vowed to stay in the lab from then on and argue about the name of the perverse *Busycon* conch (which is not actually a conch at all, it's a whelk) but they get big enough for those who are not so picky about classification to call it a conch if they want to. What makes them so perverse is that they spiral the wrong way. If you hold a regular conch (or whelk) by the nose with the hole looking up, the opening is on the right side, but a perverse *Busycon*'s opening is on the left side. I don't remember the sequence of all the various ways they have agreed (?) on the name but the species name of this animal has gone from *sinestris* to *perversa* and back at least sixteen or twenty times. I think biologists need to put the thesaurus back on the shelf and go trot around on the flats a little bit. Then they would know that what a left-handed conch does when the tide goes out is bury himself deep in the sand with nothing but his little sharp nose sticking up just below the surface and, if you are running around and step on that thing, it'll cut a perfect little cylindrical core out of the bottom of your foot and it'll hurt like hell and be slow to heal, too. I bet I stepped on a hundred of them before I learned not to run around out on the flats. Caution must be self-taught, though, and no adult can explain the dangers to a child who is ready to go. Rebecca Jane got stingareed in the heel. When I saw her stop and holler, I hoped it was a *Busycon* (say *bew-see-conn*) but, when Rosalie (the oldest, nine years old) put her on her back and headed for the house, I knew it was something bad. Jane had the hot water ready as soon as she got here. What you have to do is soak your foot in water hot enough to denature the poisonous protein of the living encapsulating sheath of the spine without actually cooking the tissues of the foot. It ain't a pleasant thing to have to do but works miraculously. In fifteen minutes a pain unlike any other you ever experienced will be completely gone and the wound will heal up without infection or any other trouble. That's a tough call for a little kid but old Rebecca Jane was a man about it. You know, a man just has to do what she has to do.

She was perfectly all right in a little while . . . well enough to play a game of chess before going to bed. Chess is a good game for children. They like the rigidity of the rules and the personalities of the little characters and . . . they love the warlike tendencies of the game. They like to bring somebody to his or her knees is what. One would think that real young children couldn't master all the complications but he would be wrong. Though a four-year-old might get crossed up with the movements of the horse from time to time, it is not that she doesn't know how the thing moves, it is that she is not mature enough to understand that she can't get away with trying to fool somebody with the same trick over and over again. I mean, if you play with a little kid, you are liable to notice that one of the baby's pawns has somehow sidestepped and opened a hole for the dread castle, and not know when or how that happened or what to do about it so you just play on. You have been outfoxed is what and while you are thinking about whether or not to make an accusation, a damn horse will, in some inexplicable manner, take your queen or a queen will, in movements at least as inexplicable as those of a horse, box in your king in a totally unexpected checkmate. My advice is to pay attention to what you are doing. Playing chess with babies is a lot like running with stingarees. It is easy to underestimate them so they are dangerous and might put you in hot water.

It breezed back up for real during the night and got stormy, too. We listened to the weather radio and they were trying to hedge their bets about how that front was going to stall out and, by morning, the wind had lost all its south and was blowing out of the west a steady thirty knots (a west wind in the Gulf turns into a northeaster as it goes up the East Coast). This thing turned into the bad northeaster of the middle of July 2004. The weather service said that it was blowing up to sixty in squalls out to sea and there was "torrential rain" and hail in some of the storms over the land and they predicted that it would get worse all day and most of the night as the front passed. This was Sunday morning. Daddy is a band director for a little school with a very proud little band and they were in the middle of band camp, which is the most important practice period of marching musicians, and he had to get back. We were thinking that we would wait to see if there was a chance that it would lie down a little bit when the tide went out just before sunset but it sure didn't look good. The children have all learned enough to watch the weather and they were making educated assessments of the situation, too. The eight-year-old Chinese boy looked out at the dirty-looking waves and gray whitecaps rolling down the bayside and the Rescue Minor pitching at the two anchors of its Bahama moor and said, "Is that a good boat?" "Sure, boy," Rebecca Jane chimed up, "Pop Pop built that boat," as if that laid the question to rest. You know, I would get the big head if it hadn't reached its elastic limit when I was about ten years old. Anyway, while we were watching, a big thunderstorm formed over the mainland to the west with tendrils of rain blowing out at about sixty degrees from vertical on their way to the ground and lightning flashing almost continuously. We noticed that it was so far away that we couldn't hear the thunder and then, all of a sudden, the wind dropped off completely because the storm was drawing the air into itself. We trotted for the boat. The children were so quick that I didn't have time to get both anchors before they were piling in over the side and putting on their life preservers. We hauled it for the mainland. At first there was a little residual round-topped sea but it didn't impede the progress one bit. I hardly ever run the Rescue Minor wide open and I was curious to see if I could detect any black in the exhaust but, though there was a little cloud, I believe it was condensation of hot exhaust water vapor in the saturated atmosphere. I couldn't see any black. I think I am going to pitch the wheel up another inch. Anyway, as we went in the river, big cold raindrops about the size of gummy bears started to pelt the big Bimini top. We idled on in all huddled in a wad. Fortunately the lightning stayed inshore but the wind did not. I nosed up and they hopped out and ran for the car while Jane poled us back off and we idled out the river trying to put on our slickey suits. Boy was it ever a rough trip. We couldn't see either the mainland or the island and didn't know the exact condition of the wind shift as the storm moved through but we knew it had shifted because of the confused state of the violent chop. Jane leaned over and hollered in my ear, "CONFUSED SEA." You know, blind navigation by looking at waves is sort of tricky but anybody can learn how to do it if you know which way the wind is blowing. You have to remember that waves refract toward any land they come close enough to so that their turbulence touches bottom. They curve around so they break on every shore. On the lee end of the island when it is real rough blowing right down the length of the island, they'll curve all the way around to where the bayside and seaside waves meet each other head-on. That's a confused sea for real. I started to get the GPS or the compass out of the box but decided to hold just about what I thought was right in all that confusion and finally a little gap in the rain showed me the island and I knew I was right and we came on in. The lightning started striking as soon as we got both anchors set and we just abandoned the boat. We had left the house wide open and the rain had blown all the way through and the chess men were all lying in puddles under the furniture and all the children's salty clothes were plastered against the seaside screen. They weren't salty anymore so it wasn't all bad.

Memorial Day 2005

in which we skirt around the white trash bash and
revisit one of the good old beaches from the good old days

Normally I wouldn't expose myself to the bedlam of Memorial Day at the coast for anything if I didn't feel like I needed to protect our little shanty against burglary by alcohol-crazed, teenage fartfaces. One would think that this little isolated island would be immune from such but it isn't.

The worst trouble with Memorial Day weekend now is that there has been established the remarkable fad of what they call "the White Trash Bash." Somehow three years ago a rumor got started that there would be a drunken orgy in Shipping Cove on the bayside of Dog Island on the Sunday before Memorial Day. It was a call to action that had an amazing (to me) response. There must be an enormous segment of the population around here that delights in being identified as white trash because there was a parade of boats down the bay to the west that was mind-boggling. All the boat ramps for forty miles were so tied up that some of these trash (which, I am afraid included some people I know) said that it took all morning to get launched and then a three-mile walk back from where they finally found a place to park the truck and trailer. Down at Shipping Cove the two-mile bayside beach was so crowded that there wasn't any room for new arrivals to pull up on the sand to join the orgy and they had to mill around out in the bay for an hour or so before they could put in just long enough to discharge their cargo of females eager to pull off their bathing suit tops and males eager to drop their oversized baggy shorts. That was just the first year. The second year was even worse . . . over a thousand boats the local newspaper reported. This year . . . there was a boat parade past our house that started early Saturday morning and lasted until late Sunday night. I tried to quantify it a little bit and one count was twenty-six boats passing in the view out the door of the house at the same time. That view from my vantage point covers about a mile and a half of bay . . . say thirty mph average for twelve hours. That's a lot of boats. Every boat was dangerously overloaded with potential revelers. That's a lot of trash. Do you think we went down there to revel in all that? Hell no. We ain't no kind of trash. We did peer with the binoculars though and there was one great big white boat down there that we could see sticking up above the trees.

Last year the melee got so out of hand that the Marine Patrol (now the FWC and the only entity of the law in attendance that year) was unable to exert any influence whatsoever . . . got outrun by some trash in something like a Cigarette for one thing. Guess who that big white boat anchored up down there was? The US Coast Guard cutter *Sea Hawk*. They stayed the whole weekend and, though they failed to discourage the steady stream of trash, I bet the sight of the loom of all that white and the display of artillery and the reputation of "zero tolerance . . . board and seize" made some of those party-naked animals feel uncomfortable. After dark we were able to see the sweep of a powerful carbon arc light searching the beach from time to time. I don't know what effect that had on the proceedings but I believe it might have been significant.

There was a steady parade of island boats hauling island children (and trashy adults) back and forth from down there, too. I guess they must have had a designated trash driver or the Coast Guard would have got them for "alcohol impaired." They had a big inflatable boat alongside the cutter for that purpose (I presumed). Of course I don't see how they could manage to single out one boat for a "safety check" among the hordes of demonstrably impaired operators. We saw one man (trying to anchor his boat in the bay by his house) fall headfirst over the side when he failed to get the second leg clear of the gunwale after giving the anchor a mighty heave. It took him a long time to come to the surface, too, and the load of drunk children he had just landed did not notice that he was drowning. I was fixing to go down and drag his corpse out and lay him down on the beach and stomp him in the belly to see if I could resuscitate him a little bit but he finally surfaced and wallowed to the beach where he collapsed in the sand. There was a lot of mighty heaving going on. I believe the Coast Guard would have been able to issue a good many citations for "a sheen upon or an emulsion beneath." All in all, I think the presence of the *Sea Hawk* at the 2005 Memorial Day Weekend White Trash Bash was good. For one thing, if anybody had any sense down there, the sight of the US flag flying on a good-looking military vessel ought to have been a reminder of the actual significance of the holiday.

Late on Sunday afternoon, a little golf cart went tooling by on the seaside beach carrying two large sheriffs. I guess the Coast Guard had run out of jurisdiction on the melee on the beach and some property owner down there had become disgruntled with people peeing under his house and puking on his white sand and had called in for some land-based reinforcements. If I had been in charge, I would have sent in the jarheads. I believe the sheriffs did good though. There were rumors of rapes and other assaults from down there last year. Nothing has surfaced about any violence after this year's event yet. Now all we have to do is pick up all that trash.

Do you think we spent the whole weekend supervising nincompoopery from a distance? Hell, no. Jane and I put one-quarter of a new roof on our house. We did it in the early morning before the crowd got tuned up. I hope all that knocking with the big hammer and sawing with the Skilsaw didn't break into anybody's morning-after reverie but you know, a man just has to do what he has to do. Hurricane season commences right after Memorial Day and we need to fix this old raggedy roof so we just let her rip. Of course it gets mighty hot mighty early up on the roof so we had to knock off and do a little fishing so we wouldn't have to go to the mainland and brave the cauldron of wakes in the river and the frantic fury at every possible landing place just to go to the grocery store to buy some hot dogs. We had to pass the *Sea Hawk* and Shipping Cove on our way to St. George Island but we stayed out far enough that the cutter did not feel that its homeland security was in danger of being violated. The smoke from the vast mass of boats along the beach looked like somebody was burning off the sea oats but we managed to pass without being run over by any white trash. It was a pretty day, calm and clear for one thing and still early, so we ran all the way to Rattlesnake Cove on the bayside of St. George.

You know, most of our end of St. George Island belongs to the state. That's where we used to go when we were children and it hasn't changed at all except that now there is a road running down the backbone of the dunes of the island but it is separated from the bayside by a continuous marsh at least seven miles long and you can't see the road from the bay-side beach. Only at the easternmost point is the bayside beach accessible without wading in high marsh grass (*Disticylus* mostly . . . the kind that looks like a real sharp knitting needle on the end and loves to slide up the leg of a bathing suit and stick you in the rump) with the biggest and most insolent cotton-mouthed moccasins I have ever seen anywhere. There has been some research that hints that moccasins are diversifying on these barrier islands into niches that moccasins don't normally occupy kind of like the finches of the Galapagos. They are certainly the most common snake on Gulf Islands and they live in the high dunes and deep woods as well as along the beach and in marshes. I think that not only can they swim well enough to go wherever they want to in the Gulf, their eggs hatch inside them (ovoviviparous) so they don't have to find something besides pure, hot sand to bury their eggs in. There are plenty of rattlesnakes on these islands, too. They can swim just as well as a moccasin . . . float real high in the water . . . and are also ovoviviparous but they are not as common as moccasins. I'll tell you, the sight of a big rattlesnake on the white sand is a sight to see and the sight of a big, arrogant moccasin all ready to bite you in thick marsh grass will make you think twice about where all you think you need to go, too. Anyway, it is a long walk from any access point to that isolated beach and Jane and I nosed up in the Rescue Minor and anchored and walked for miles just like we used to do when we were children without seeing any evidence of a human footprint or any other sign. It might have been 1952 . . . back before white trash got rich enough to afford boats called "Scarabs" and rolled their own cigarettes out of ungummed OCB papers and Bugler or Prince Albert tobacco. You know what a scarab is? It is a dung beetle. You know what the scarab said to the goat? "Hand me down some of them ready-rolls."

It is a good ten miles to Rattlesnake Cove and the whole bayside of St. George is very shallow flats . . . much shallower and wider than on the bayside of Dog Island. What is happening is that the bay is silting in more up there because of the proximity of the big Apalachicola River (second only to the Mississippi of Gulf rivers). The water is fresher up there, too, and Rattlesnake Cove is the beginning of the oyster beds for which the big bay is so famous. Oysters only thrive where there is a good bit of fresh water. Back in the old days, estuaries like Chesapeake Bay (and our bay . . . second in size only to the Chesapeake on the East Coast) were just right. Even after the towns got big, oysters did real well. You know, oysters are filter feeders and strain plankton out of the water they pump through their shells all the time the tide is high enough to cover them up. They don't ingest sand but they are indiscriminate about plankton . . . just love *Escherichia coli* (the fecal bacteria). Hepatitis germs don't bother them a bit. What killed the Chesapeake oysters and what is killing this bay is fertilizer and pesticide runoff from farm fields and golf courses. Oysters flourish on the living contingent of human excrement. If you believe the Environmental Protection Agency has all this crap under control, you just go ahead and eat all the raw oysters you want to. You know, Atlanta is on the upper end of one of the tributaries of the Apalachicola and there is enough toilet paper hanging in the willow trees along the river for five miles below the city to recycle into a whole run of the *New York Times* . . . twice a day. The oysters of Rattlesnake Cove were perfectly safe from Jane and me but there was a time . . .

The mullet weren't safe, though. There is something about St. George Island that promotes or tolerates stupidity. It might be all the white trash that hang out in those bars and low dives and boutiques down west of Rattlesnake Cove. You can see the condos lining the seaside beach from the state boat ramp in the cove. I think the occupants of condos must self-select for stupidity. For one thing, why in hell would somebody want to pay half a million bucks for just part of a building? I mean you can't even hide behind your little fence of bushes. If you are sitting out on your miniature veranda sipping the Chardonnay and scintillating you can hear the suction of your neighbor's lips on his or her glass of Chardonnay barely a yard below your feet and hear their scintillating. Of course, if they are drunk children, you won't find out any information. "*Your dad,* is just so *totally* . . . you know what I am saying?" Some modern girls just use their voices as ornaments and couldn't talk their way out of a wet paper bag.

Anyway, what I am trying to say is that the stupidity that is rampant over there (and rampaging in Shipping Cove, too) permits certain animals to breed and prosper when, in a less stupid situation, they would be removed from the ecosystem and their genes would be smacked out with their bloody guts like the three hundred stupid St. George horseflies Jane killed with her blue flyswatter as we tooled down the virgin beach toward Rattlesnake Cove. We stopped and scooped up half a bucket of stupid (but delicious) crabs, too. Over on Dog Island, you have to be mighty quick to catch one but, on St. George, they don't run . . . just stand their ground and wave their arms. You know, women love to catch crabs . . . even stupid women love to try. That's why the crabs of St. George are so easy. Chardonnay sipping in the middle of the day does not fine-tune the hunter-gatherer instincts as well as a desperate search for something to eat and those crabs have been getting away with scaring those women over there off for too long. About twenty of them learned today that there is one kind of woman and then there is another kind of woman. Of course it did not do their race any good in the grand scheme of things.

Dog Island mullet are so smart that they can not only size up a man (or a woman . . . a woman taught me how to throw) with a net but can, somehow, communicate the specifications to other mullet who are out of sight.

All of a sudden no mullet will allow me within 42.5 feet unless they are in grass where they know the net will be propped up and they can make a leisurely exit. The only hard part about catching the fish of Rattlesnake Cove was waiting until they got clear of all those oysters so I wouldn't cut up my net. It was easy money, though. I caught three in one throw in water so shallow that they weren't completely submerged. Another thing about St. George mullet is that they have the biggest gizzards I ever saw. One of the fish I caught was about twenty-two inches long and had a gizzard as big as a golf ball . . . a real delicacy with a sip of Chardonnay.

While we were messing around exploring the little islands around Rattlesnake Cove, we saw some people launch a big, fiberglass Tremblay bird dog net boat at the most excellent state park boat ramp. Toward the end of the gill-net era in Florida, Mr. Tremblay started manufacturing net boats out of fiberglass. That was when gill-netting was such a fad that politicians used to do it as a status symbol to show their constituents that they knew how to get their hands dirty doing a man's work. Of course a Tremblay boat was way too expensive for anybody who *had* to work and anybody who had one was just a playboy like these people who have the new status symbol, the Hewes flats boat, like what Randy Wayne White (no relation) popularized in his flats-fishing-guide-based detective books. You won't see any bonefishing guides running a Hewes down in the Bahamas. So these people took off in the big Tremblay in pursuit, we assumed, of mullet. We fooled around a little longer racking up stupid horseflies and wandering the beach (found one of those plastic yard chairs that, except for a few barnacles, was good as new) and when we finally got ready to go back and cook the crabs and mullet, we passed the people in the Tremblay not far from the boat ramp. They had made a strike along a run of marsh grass (*Spartina alternifolia* called "mullet grass" around here) with a net that looked to be about the legal five hundred square feet of mesh too small to gill big mullet. The mullet that inhabit the shallows where spartina grows are always very big and smart. They are smart enough to know that they are big enough to be osprey- and moccasin-proof is what. They were about Tremblay-proof, too. There were two very fat couples of middle-aged people chasing the fish. I bet one man weighed 300 pounds and the other weighed 250 and nobody was very tall. The two women were very roly-poly. The mullet were hemmed up along the bank in the grass and were making runs at the net and jumping out. The people were scrambling around on hands and knees trying to catch them in the grass and up alongside the net. It was very comical. If it had been Dog Island mullet they wouldn't have caught a one but they had two or three in a sack.

We eased on back to the east along the deserted beach and crossed the pass (East Pass) between the two islands. It was the lull between the land breeze and the sea breeze and it would have been dead calm except for the wakes rolling in every direction from the melee just around the west point of Dog Island. I was surprised that the *Sea Hawk* wasn't rolling. The haze of smoke from all the idling outboard motors was so thick we couldn't see the beach at all. When we got home, the wind made up from the west a little bit and we could hear the unmistakable sound of a highly amplified Jimmy Buffett drifting down on the polluted air. I think it was a recording. You know, he is the guru of the drunker-than-hell-at-the-beach movement but I believe, if he had actually been in attendance at that party, even he would have had to make a few changes in latitude.

So what finally put the quietus on that foolishness down there in Shipping Cove? Was it the *Sea Hawk*? Was it the two sheriffs? Was it the FWC? Was it that little helicopter that flew over surveying the scene about two thirty in the morning of Memorial Day itself? It was none of the above. It was a thunderstorm from the west about four AM blowing a hard-driving rain at twenty-five knots (sustained) with gusts to thirty-eight. It was sure pleasant lying in the bed under our new section of roof knowing that it was well nailed down.

Pompano

in which a windfall saves us from hotdogs

Me and Jane were coming back from getting skunked all morning long one day this fall. I mean, though fish are very plentiful and the mullet are at their most prime in the fall, the water clears up about like the air and they can not only see the boat and the menacing look of the man standing in the bow looking down but see him throw and the net hit the water and the net itself as it sinks. Mullet are so smart that they don't even get in a hurry, they just leisurely swim exactly far enough to form a perfect circle the size of the net as it lies empty on the bottom. That vacancy doesn't last long, though. They are not afraid of anything after the net is thrown and quickly close back in. They only move aside enough to allow the, now harmless, net to pass as it is pulled back up. They seem to be inspecting it to note where the holes are so if one of them is a little slow next time, he can get out. They act like they know not only the net but the person throwing it. They say, "Here comes old Twenty-Five Feet. He is pretty bad but do you remember old Thirty-Five Feet? Now, that was a dangerous man. I am glad he died."

Anyway, here we were heading home in the Rescue Minor to cook the hot dogs and I was fiddling with the GPS to see what speed I was running when something hit me in the back so hard that it knocked the wind out of me. I thought the engine had slung a piston at me or something but it was a real big pompano and he ricocheted off me and hit the underside of the Bimini top and fell right smack in Jane's lap. Do you think she threw up her hands and hollered *EEEK!*? I know I have described her accurately enough in past stories so you know damn well she grabbed that wildly flapping (and certainly surprised) big old fish and put the clamps on him with both legs and both hands. He tried his best but there ain't no getting away from Jane when she is hungry and we took him home and ate him. Whew, I had forgotten how delicious a pompano is.

Pompano are about the best eating of the jack family of fish to my notion. I used to think the other best one is the little hardtail, which they call blue runners down on the Atlantic side. They are the preferred bait for these people who run out to the Gulf Stream and drift for sailfish. Which, I'll tell you my opinion of catch-and-release right now. I don't believe in it. What the hell does somebody want to put some fish through a hell of an ordeal for if he doesn't have any use for the animal? Stuff him? Phooey on that, too. I have heard that you can have a fish you caught and turned loose stuffed by proxy. Taxidermists don't stuff sailfish anymore anyway. They might actually skin a bream or a bass or something just for the hell of it but there are so many stuffed sailfish that they work it differently with that species. If you actually bring in the poor old dead thing you caught they might ooh and aah a little bit and ask you if you want the fish mounted looking to the left or to the right. After the knee-jerk nincompoop finally makes up his mind about that the taxidermist tells him that he has a special "visitor's rate" for people who flew down just to catch a fish and he can accelerate the process to one day for a little extra money so the man can take his stuffed fish home with him and not have to wait the usual three months. After the customer leaves, the fish stuffer drags the dead fish out the back door to the dumpster (pew) and opens up his storage building and gets out a big cardboard box marked SAILFISH-LEFT-MADE IN CHINA and writes up the bill. Anyway, a little, live hardtail on a hook down in the startling blue of the Gulf Stream is mighty tempting to sailfish and one on the plate is, to me, too. They weigh less than a pound on the average but that's just fine. They fry up fine and bake and smoke good. I love them but a pompano . . . goodness.

There is another little very good-eating jack they catch down off the east end of Abaco around what they call the hole in the wall which is a hole in a bulwark-looking buttress of rock sticking out into the deep water. The people of Sandy Point call these little fish "passing jacks" because they are migratory and just passing by. When that migration happens the whole town turns out to see if they can diminish the quantity that get to pass. They fish out of good-looking little fifteen-foot plywood boats that are (I was told) built around in Marsh Harbor. They handline the little passing jacks over the side as fast as they can and haul them back to the icehouse as fast as they can. They gave us some back in the old whaleboat cruising days and, boy, they were delicious. The passing of the jacks comes at variable times but it is sometime around July 14, Bahamian Independence Day. I advise anybody to go to Sandy Point to participate in that celebration. You don't even have to have a boat. Just go to the east coast of Florida around West Palm and ask around for where the Grand Bahama mail boat docks these days. They'll take you over there for a small fee and you can connect to another mail boat and eventually go anywhere you want to in the Bahamas. Mail boats ain't nothing but regular shrimp boats that aren't rigged for shrimping. They haul groceries and stuff in addition to mail and people. You can meet some very nice and interesting people on a Bahamian mail boat.

There is another eatable jack called amberjack. They get very big and I don't like them all that good but one time my mother and father were about to starve to death down in the British Virgin Islands because they were ignorant (that's the only way to starve down there) when Momma finally caught a fish. They were out in the bay of the little island where they lived. I better tell you a little bit about that. My father was a struggling writer when they first got married and they ran off down there to escape the Depression. They heard that you could live real cheap and be something like a Bwana. They bought a tiny island called Marina Cay for thirty-five dollars and a twelve-foot sailboat, which they used to haul Portland cement and water from Road Town, Tortola, to mix with a hoe and build a tiny poured-concrete house on top of the little rocky island. They said it was a hard job but they did it. When World War Two came, they went back to the States and my father went into the US Navy (he was the oldest ensign in the history of the service) and the British colonial government disallowed the purchase of the island and took their property away from them and now Marina Cay belongs to Pusser's rum and is a resort. The little concrete house is "The Robb White Bar." Jesus.

Anyway, Momma was out there in the little cove of Marina Cay in the twelve-foot sailboat (named "Jalopy") and not catching anything when she looked down in the clear water and saw about thirty enormous fish just lying on the bottom. That's why she wasn't catching anything. Those big amberjacks had already cleaned everything else out of that hole and were taking their little after-lunch nap. They wouldn't bite any bait either so Momma put a naked hook on her handline and let it down and peered carefully enough through the crystal-clear water to guide it so that it was under the jaw of one of those fish. Then she snatched. She said the whole event was very entertaining but she finally got him in the boat and killed him by beating him over the head with the tiller. They ate all they could hold but there was still a lot left (he was as big as a grown person) and they didn't have any refrigeration so they took him to Road Town and tried to sell him to Maurice Titley who ran the store but he said, "We don't eat dem things." I agree with him but a lot of hotshot offshore fishermen down here think they are delicious and catch them with live bait . . . usually pinfish (*Lagodon rhomboides*), which are a lot better to eat than an amberjack to my notion. I would just skip the offshore part of the process if I was them. The best offshore fish to my notion are triggerfish but I was on the subject of pompano when I started all this wandering around in the past.

When I was just a baby, my father was assigned to the naval air station in Pensacola for a little while and Momma caught pompano casting off the beach. I better explain my father's assignment a little. Because my father was a writer with several books in print by then (*Run Masked, The Nub, In Privateer's Bay,* and *The Smuggler's Sloop,* which won the *New York Times* book award . . . find one of those old collector's items on the eBay if you can) the Navy decided that he should be assigned to the propaganda section and that's what he did all through the war. He was only in the States long enough to glorify the naval and marine aviators and then they sent him all over the Pacific. Though he was a noncombatant (he did have a carbine and S&W revolver along with his typewriter) he was in almost every conflict they had over there. They flew him all over the place . . . usually in a big old PBY Catalina (a beautiful airplane to my notion) but in little Piper Cubs, R4Ds (C47s in the Army Air Corps . . . DC3s in civilian life), and carrier-based planes, too. He was sunk on a jeep carrier (*Gambier Bay* or *Notoma Bay* . . . he was on both of them but I forgot which was sunk) by a suicide pilot. He was on submarines and he was on PT boats in the Solomons and lived in the mountains with the coast-watchers who radioed ahead when they saw Japanese ships coming up the "Slot." He was at Leyte Gulf, Midway, hideous Guadalcanal, Iwo Jima . . . all them places. He missed Hiroshima and Nagasaki but he was on the tiny atoll of Enewetok (say *any-wee-tock*) where he lived in a tent and built a windmill-powered air pump for his aquarium. When I was in the Navy they blew Enewetok up with a hydrogen bomb. My father was disgusted about that but he loved the Navy and wrote about it all his life. Too bad he didn't live long enough to get with this *JAG* television program. He also wrote about legal stuff (wrote a lot of the old Perry Mason scripts) so that would have been right down his alley.

Anyway, when he was writing about pilot training in Pensacola, Momma used to take me to Pensacola beach and let me eat sand while she caught pompano in the surf. She dug these little sand fleas (*Emerita* spp.) for bait and pulled the pompanos in and let me stick my finger in their mouths (pompano don't have any teeth at all) and feel their eyes. I remember the whole business . . . especially after we got home to the tiny apartment where we lived and ate the pompanos. They were much smaller than the one Jane caught. I think I could eat a whole one when I was two years old and so could any of my grandchildren but Jane and I had a good bit left over from that big one she caught. We had the rest for breakfast with a little homemade tartar sauce. It is pitiful to have to be poor and not get to go to Red Lobster.

Oh yeah, my mother and father didn't remain ignorant down there on Marina Cay (say *key*) for long. They caught lobsters (spiny lobsters . . . *langousta* in Spanish, crawfish in the Keys). You know, the lobsters you get at Red Lobster are the same kind. I read an article about how they are caught for that restaurant chain. Most of them come from the Caribbean coast of Central America and are caught by Mosquito Indians who will dive two hundred feet with scuba gear to try to satisfy the insatiable tastes of all these landlocked gourmets. The article says decompression sickness (the bends) is the most common disease among the young men down there. They keep on doing it until they don't have any legs to swim with anymore. You know, all you have to do to cause a lot of misery and deplete hell out of a natural resource is to turn a vast population of eager consumers onto a new gourmet fad.

Equinoxes, Crock-Pots, and "Searching the Sky"

in which high-tech takes a backseat to the sense of smell

We had some changes here around the equinox. It ain't actually the "First Day of Fall" like so many newsmen, secure in their regional smugness, love to say it is. It is just that time in September when a straight line drawn from the center of the earth to the center of the sun intersects the equator and there are the same number of hours of daylight as darkness all over the world . . . even down in the Southern Hemisphere where their newsmen smugly proclaim "Today is the First Day of Spring." I wouldn't want to cast aspersions at anybody but a person is a fool who will stand in front of a television camera in Tallahassee, Florida, with his credentials emblazoned right there on the screen and say something like that on such a day. No matter what they say, fall is a long way away in September and the corn is knee-high on the last week in March around here. The changes that made this time remarkable were we had a thick foggy spell and the GPS bit the dust.

About the time of the equinox, it's hard to get to our house on the island before dark. I don't like to run in a skiff when I can't see. Dark is difficult but fog is bad and I believe the combination is dangerous. Fog is not as common here as it is in some places but when it comes, it is just as thick. It is not my navigation that worries me, it is the navigation of others . . . might get run over in my skiffboat by some joker with his nose glued to the GPS watching his course and speed and CMG and all when he ought to cut that speed, switch off those wheelhouse lights, and stick his head out the window to find out if he can see or hear anything. When we finally get gratefully settled down up there in our house, it's not uncommon to hear, from somewhere out in the fog, the awful yelp of some powerboat that has wandered from his virtual "highway" and slid way up on a real sandbar.

Enough of that. We were easing along somewhere out the mouth of the river in the thick fog on the Friday evening after the equinox, eyes peeled, ears wide open, GPS lying on the grocery box SEARCHING THE SKY when I realized that it ought to be nagging me MESSAGE: PLEASE PRESS "PAGE" so that I would have to stop paying attention to the world and call up the notice APPROACHING RIVER #1. Though it was long since time for the little devil to be percolating up the vital data and telling me the ETA, it was still

SEARCHING THE SKY. To make a long story short, the damn thing was still peering just as myopically as we were when we got to the island. Fortunately, I still had my old compass in the boat box and was able to feel around in the floorboards and find the recess where it used to sit and I was pretty sure that the island was still in the same direction that it used to be. Though relying on the GPS to lead us by the hand had caused me not to start navigating until I wasn't positive about the actual position of the WAYPOINT of departure. I knew the set of the tide, though, and believed I could hit the seven-mile-wide island, so we poked on as usual. I figured that as soon as I could see something besides the water dripping off the end of my wife's pigtail, we would try to recognize it and decide whether to go up or down the beach to the house. Fortunately, I didn't have to do that because about the time the ETA was due, I smelled my neighbor's Crock-Pot and was able to hit it right dead on the money.

Epilogue

My rocket scientist niece, who gave me the GPS in the first place, explained the phenomenon to me. It seems that there was some manipulation of the rigamarole by other rocket scientists (I don't remember exactly what it was because I have trouble paying attention to that kind of information) which had caused all the GPSs in the world to become, instead of the brilliant little geniuses that they had been, as stupid as any loose-battery TV remote control. She said that there was a way to straighten it out. I don't know about that because I couldn't fix it by boiling it in our Crock-Pot all day long on Saturday. Don't misunderstand . . . despite this temporary disgruntlement, I know that high-tech will continue to escalate with me. I'll probably have to buy a bigger pot to boil this computer shortly after the solstice which, as you know ain't the "First Day of Winter" but just that particular inclination of the axis of the earth so that the North Pole is leaning away from the sun as far as it can and the daylight is as short as it gets . . . at least in this hemisphere. I give you joy of your independence from the stooges of this world.

Loons

in which I give up veterinary practice

I know there are some of you gentle readers who want to know what somebody from way the hell and gone down here is doing writing about the national bird of the Far North. Well, I have to tell you something. Loons are not just denizens of northern lakes and little glacier potholes up in their "true home." They spend about half their time down here. Like "snowbirds" they come for the winter and mostly stay out in the bay but sometimes you can see (or hear) them around freshwater rivers and lakes.

Loons usually show up around Thanksgiving and they all come at once. All of a sudden they'll be all over the place. They are very intelligent-acting birds and soon learn who is who and will get pretty tame in the right situation. I guess they are territorial because you never see more than two in the same vicinity and they sort of hang around the same place. There was one old loon who stayed down by Jam Box Point (named that because somebody left a big black tape player sitting on the beach and it stayed there for years). Usually loons stay in the water all the time but some of them will drag out on the beach. Loons can't walk because they are built like diving ducks with their legs too far aft so they have to push with their feet and slide on their chests and will flap if they get in hurry. Anyway when he wasn't out fishing, this loon sat (lay) on the beach beside the jam box for three or four winters before he finally got too old to make the trip back south. I would think that some animal got him while he was up in the true home of the loon but I don't think animals mess with loons all that much.

One time my granddaughter and I were tooling it down the bay and we saw a loon sitting on the beach. He (I can't tell the difference) was picking at something on his elbow and I thought he might be tangled in some fishing line or something so we stopped and I ran around and headed him off before he could get to the water. Man, I tell you what, that loon speared me in the forearm so deep that I believe his beak was better than halfway through me. Scared the punk out of both of us and I hurried home and doctored it with hydrogen peroxide and pine oil in case his beak was nasty but there was no infection at all. I left him alone and he stayed all winter and left with the rest of them. I don't know what ailed his elbow but he was welcome to tend to it himself.

They leave just like they come . . . in unison. I am sure they communicate all up and down the coast with a relay of their cries. There is no set time. I guess it is the weather that gives them the cue. Might be March or they might hang around until April. One day they'll all be gone. I wish they would take these damn cormorants with them.

There is one kind of pitiful thing about these loons. Some of them realize that they are too old to fly back and stay down here. After the others leave, the lonesome old birds stop hollering like they have been doing all winter. Eventually they die and, when their old bodies wash up on the beach, they are as light as a feather, just skin and bones. I always wonder what old Yankees who are familiar with the North Woods think when they wake up in the middle of the night and hear a loon. They probably think they are dreaming that they are back in their true home.

Why Willets Hate Humans

in which I try to see the world through the eyes of willets

Willets are those big sandpipers that run along the beach and holler with a voice that is just as pleasant as the shriek of a prepuberty girl when the natural tendency to call attention to herself first erupts but before the realization *why* she wants to call attention to herself emerges. I don't know what the hell willets are trying to do with all that fuss but they do it every time they fly up when somebody comes along the beach. You would think they were scared to death from the volume of the shriek but they don't seem to fly as far as they would if they actually thought you were a serious threat. I think they are cussing you for being on *their* beach in the first place. They'll certainly cuss you if you go anywhere within half a mile of their nest or even where they are thinking about building a nest. Not only will they verbally abuse you, they'll dive-bomb you screaming like a banshee the whole time and only peel off at the last second. A mad willet will give one of the best demonstrations of the Doppler effect I ever saw. They don't actually build nests. All they do is squiggle their butts around in the sand to make a depression deep enough so their eggs won't roll down into the water. They nest up in the sea oats but not far from the water's edge. I think they nest so close to the beach as an act of belligerence so they'll have an excuse to scream at people walking by and dive on little children and scare them.

I can sort of understand their anti-human feelings. Human beings cause willets (and other sandpipers) a lot of extra work. Sandpipers walk along the beach at the water's edge and, as the thin sheet of the wave recedes, they trot out and probe the sand with their tender beaks while the individual sand grains are still in a state of suspension. They do not ram their beaks down into hard sand. They can feel (I assume) the little burrowing worms and shrimp that live there. You know, when you walk along a sandy beach at low tide there are a lot of little open holes with, sometimes, a little water welling up. Sometimes there will be tiny dark cylindrical objects about the size of short sections of 0.7-millimeter pencil lead in the water that is welling up. Those holes are the burrows of a small filter-feeding burrowing shrimp who makes his living filtering plankton out of the waves like *Donax*. Those little cylindrical objects are the excrement of those shrimp. Those little shrimp turds sometimes get washed into a wad in some little pool and will stick to the bottoms of your feet most marvelously. Willets eat a lot of those little shrimp. All that is neither here nor there. I was fixing to explain how the slow-wittedness of willets makes it so that people cause them extra work. You know, that is sort of a universal rule in the behavior of animals of all sorts. If one of them is less smart than another and gets to feeling put-upon by the smarter animal, the stupid one is apt to become sullen and mean. Wild hogs are like that. They know they aren't as smart as the human beings who feel the need to intrude into their territory and, stupidity notwithstanding, they feel like they might want to eat these humans' smart asses up and sometimes do. I even believe that this theory can be applied within the ranks of human beings. When they get put-upon, stupid people get sullen and mean, too. Willets can't eat our smart asses up so they do what they can.

What happens is that, when the willets (and other sandpipers) are feeding along the edge, here will come a crew of gamboling humans with no apparent purpose to their smart-assed lives at all. When they get too close, the sandpipers fly away from the people down the beach a little way (and the willets scream at them) and go back to work on worms and shrimp. Pretty soon, here come the damn people, again, and the birds have to get up and fly down the beach a little farther. As this repetition progresses, other small flocks of sandpipers are overtaken and the flock of birds that is preceding the flock of people gets bigger and bigger until finally the birds stupidly look around at how big the flock has become and some of them (the smartest ones . . . still not MENSA level) say to themselves, "Hell, man, look at all these damn birds. I think I'll fly around these people and work my way back the other way." So they fly out to sea a little way and circle around the people and light back on the beach behind them and continue with their lunch . . . until the people remember that they better turn around and go get *their* lunch and then the cycle has to resume all over again. That's why they hate you and scream at you so.

Facilities

in which the white plastic bucket enters the picture once again

On the way to our house on this little sandbar island out in Apalachee Bay off the Big Bend of North Florida, I got into a discussion with some of my grandchildren about how people go to the bathroom on boats and ships. They were at the age when curiosity is in full bloom and we spent the whole trip discussing the history, variety, and social significance of that subject, not only as it applies to maritime situations but . . . you know, one thing leads to another.

Even though I am getting on up there, my curiosity and childish enthusiasm for subjects like that have not been completely satisfied nor exhausted yet, and I was able to join in the discussions not only as a widely experienced expert but as a willing participant in the speculation. I told the children that in the old sailing days folks had to come up on deck and climb out alongside the bowsprit and hang on for dear life to use the "head." Immediately they wanted to know why that exact location was chosen. It seemed to them that someplace back in the stern of the ship would be better and I had to explain that all the high muckety-mucks lived back there and they didn't want any troop of ordinary scum marching through their quarters to go to the bathroom. But, the children pointed out, anything that happened up in the front would make its way back to the rear anyway, and besides, what if it was real rough and raining? I explained that a man just had to do what he had to do and if it was real rough and raining real hard when he had to do it, he would find out how bad he really had to do it. The children had been on my old junky sailboat and had marveled at the little bitty potty in the tiny room so small that there was no room for an extra roll of toilet paper. Once when we were sailing, close-hauled, to the island, their father had to go into that little room and he stayed for a mighty long time and the children (they were much younger then) broached the subject of how the bathroom seemed to be upwind of all the rest of the boat. I had to fall off a little bit to quiet the discussion some. We all decided that the forward head was a bad idea and that blindly following in the steps of tradition was, too.

The youngest girl, now five, told us that one of her earliest memories was one time Na-Na held her suspended over the side of the skiff when she got caught short on the way over to the island. She wasn't even a year old at that time but she made up her mind then that there must be a better way.

I reminded them about the glorious white plastic bucket trick we often use on the skiffboat; how people, when in proper company, could use the white plastic bucket anywhere that suited them on any boat. We agreed that this would work fine when out of sight of the land or boats or binoculars or low-flying helicopters. Of course, we all knew that already, because we are all familiar with that application of the white plastic bucket and had discovered that, if the bucket is too big or the child is too small, the arrangement is liable to be treacherous. Nevertheless, we decided that a white plastic bucket was better than a built-in head up in the front of the boat. We discussed the possibility of using kitty litter in the bucket so, if we were in a place where it would be bad to just dump it over the side, we could wait and maybe, as a conservation measure, do a little scooping like is done behind the doings of a cat. But we decided that it would be better to just take the contaminated kitty litter to land and find a place that looked like it could stand a little fertilizer and dump the bucket there.

One of us (eight-year-old girl) said that if you did it long enough, the sequential dumping of the bucket would create a chronological record sort of like the layers of sediment in an archaeological dig and someone might become intrigued and say, "Look here . . . in 2005, this person was eating frozen black-eyed peas."

"Rosalie, how would they find out something like that after years and years had gone by? That's ridiculous," exclaimed the seven-year-old boy.

"Nope, ain't ridiculous," was the instant rebuttal. "They would just use a DNA test." Indeed, I read in a book Walter Cronkite wrote that, from an archaeological dig in Edenton, North Carolina, there is a collection of pottery pieces that they glued back together. Apparently when the poor old slaves broke a dish, they threw it into the privy so their owners wouldn't find out about it and punish them. I thought about introducing that strain but I was overridden before I could get started.

The topic of maritime facilities was still hot. The facilities of cruise ships, naval vessels, and commercial boats and ships of all kinds came up. I told them about a little seagoing tug I worked on that had two bathrooms and how the downstairs bathroom emptied into a one-elbow pipe that evacuated right through the side about at the average waterline and how, when it was real rough, air and water would spout from the toilet like a whale and how we stuffed a mop in there to stop that. I told them that the upstairs toilet flushed down a pipe that went down the wall in the cook's (my) room right beside the bed and, "No," I proclaimed, "it did not leak but it would wake you up all through the night when the old captain's prostate gland was acting up."

I declined to explain the dynamics of the prostate gland but I did tell about how holding tanks were invented to prevent the over-stressing of confined environments by pipes like that and told them how, one time in the Bahamas, we were anchored up in a pretty little cove when a colossal cruise ship came in. Immediately, even before the fleet of inflatable Zodiac boats had begun to ferry the patrons to explore the "unspoiled" island, the little bay became so polluted that strands of toilet paper threatened to come on board with the anchor line as we pulled up to get away from there.

I also told them of my adventure in the bathroom of a destroyer when I was in the Navy and we crossed the equator and I stayed in the bathroom for hours flushing all the toilets to see if I could tell when the water started circulating clockwise instead of counterclockwise (the data was ambiguous).

The children became curious about airplanes and "what if?" I explained that, except in certain cases, airplanes hauled the contents of the potty with them until they landed at a big city with a proper pump mounted on a proper truck with a proper tank and a proper hose. I was properly gratified that they now knew what a holding tank was but I also knew it was inevitable that they would want to know about "certain cases" and they did. I explained how when I was in the Navy, there were anti-submarine airplanes that did not have a real toilet.

"Well," they needed to know, "what did y'all do?"

"We did without" was my quick reply.

"But . . . ?"

"Well, we could always crack the bomb bay doors a little bit," I said with a wink.

All this conversation took place on the car part of the trip and that wasn't over, yet, so the next subject was an inquiry into the history of land-based facilities. I warmed to the subject immediately and explained that when I was a little boy I went to a three-room schoolhouse that only had three teachers but six grades. I explained all the logistics of that and padded it out with the details of education of long ago: Like how one teacher taught the first and second graders in her room and another taught the third and fourth graders in her room and the other teacher taught fifth and sixth in her room, and how they had separate morning recesses and how some of the big girls would come read to the little children during their recess while the big boys worked in the corn and cotton field that they had for educational reasons and how very pleasant it was in that school and how I think I learned most everything worth learning at school there. I also explained that they had the kitchen in another building and how the ladies in there would pass our lunches out the window and we would sit around under the trees and eat and feed the jaybirds crumbs and chicken bones . . . and how, if it was raining real hard, we would have to crowd into the little kitchen. I also explained how we had to wash our own dishes under the careful scrutiny of the lunchroom ladies. I explained how we had to carry wood for the classroom heaters and the kitchen stove, too. I began to get the feeling that some of my grandchildren were beginning to get bored with the long car ride and since I didn't have a DVD player in the car, I pulled out my hole card. I heard Maurice Sendak explain how he did not believe in boring children with tame stories and that's why he has been so successful at his work. I already knew that so I explained the intricate social implications of another little building they had at that school—a four-hole privy—and the interest perked up immediately and I knew I could finish the trip without any whining from the peanut gallery in the backseat.

An Analog Mind Stuck in a Digital World

*in which I finally, in the twilight of my life, figure out
what the hell is wrong with me and effect a complete cure*

I was starting to think that I was going to turn out to be one of those disgruntled old men who snaps at everybody. I wasn't paying attention to what the people in my family were saying anymore. It was getting to where my own opinions were taking on far more importance than at any other time since I started trying to get over puberty. I listened to a radio show on NPR where they explained that cheerfulness was healthy. As soon as I started on my cheerfulness program to regain my youth, I noticed that my grandchildren stopped playing with me. It took a trip into the bathroom to explain why. We had all taught the children not to play with people with such a leer as the one I saw in the mirror in there. I let my face fall into the normal wattles and wrinkles that it has accumulated over the years. Everybody seemed relieved except me. I decided to stop drinking.

I am not a hard drinker, mind you. I'm not the type to try to suck the bottom out of the bottle and then raise hell all over the place, but I do like to clutch my old trusty glass and prop up my feet on time every evening. It seems that the older I get, the more important this little ritual becomes. Since the search for the reason why I was getting to be so disagreeable hadn't turned up anything else yet, I decided that maybe, at this late stage in my life, I was deluding myself about my little habit. Maybe, I told myself, it is a big habit and it is ruining your life. I stopped completely for a long time. It was a help in some ways. I found that I could tie enough flies to keep ahead of the ones I popped off my line or hung up in the top limbs of trees because of the time I saved when my feet weren't propped up, but I remained just as grumpy as ever. It began to interfere with the exercise of my authority, sort of like with the boy who cried "Wolf." The grandchildren began to ignore instructions that I issued in my best stern voice. I realized that it was because I always sound like that now. It is hard to pay attention when an old man grumbles because you are standing on his belly in hard shoes when the way he sounds is the same as when you are standing on his belly not in hard shoes. Luckily, just as I was reaching the end of my rope, I discovered the real reason and was able to correct the problem.

It was the damn clocks. All of our clocks were the new digital style and they were all over the place. The radio had one, the car had one (actually two, one on its aftermarket radio and this crazy damned thing on the dashboard that came with it when it was new . . . I guess) and there was one on each of the bedside tables where my wife and I sleep. There were two in my shop: one on the radio in there and one on the time clock where my employee used to punch his card before he punched out because I was getting so hard to get along with. Everywhere you looked, they were smugly displaying numerals . . . digits . . . 11:11 . . . things like that . . . 1:23 . . . for Christ's sake . . . 12:21 . . . as if that had some significance.

I was waiting in line at the post office to try to buy some stamps because the machine in the lobby refused to respond to some pretty hard licks and strong language. In the line, a nice old lady was trying to find out what time it was from a nice young girl ahead of me. "Ten fifty nine," was the reply. The old lady seemed a little hard of hearing and asked again. "TEN FIFTY-NINE," was the reply. She still didn't understand. "IT'S TEN FIFTY-NINE," hollered the girl. "Why don't you just say it's almost eleven o'clock," I suggested. "Well, it is now," said the girl. "Eleven zero zero." I looked at my watch, an old self-winding Bulova that has been keeping perfect time for years and years. I saw that it was not quite eleven yet. The long hand was almost there but not quite. I took issue with the girl about the precise way in which she was mistaken. She smugly pointed at the satellite adjusted electronic clock on the machine on the postmaster's counter . . . 11:00:41 . . . 42 . . . 43 . . . official government time. I was embarrassed.

Confrontations like that were not the cause of my irritable nature, but a result of it. There used to be a time when I was almost obsequious with such young women and accepted whatever time they said with good cheer. It was just the digital nature of the information that was getting to me. The poisonous seeds of digital irritation were being planted every night and manured and watered all day long every time I saw one of those damned clocks.

I always wake up two or three times each night to see what time it is. It is an old habit left over from years of standing watches on boats at sea. I half wake up, look at the clock, and then roll over and mumble to myself, "Hot dog, it ain't but about ten o'clock, let me snuggle back down here right this minute." Or, "Goody, goody, I still got about an hour and a half before the alarm goes off, let me droop back off till then." Or, "Still got a little more than half an hour, oh joy, I thought it was later than that, think I'll snooze just a short little snort or two more." Then one of the children kicked the last of the old Baby Bens off the stool and busted the smithereens out of it so badly that even I couldn't get them to goagulate back in there again.

We bought a digital clock radio. At first, I thought that the thing that was irritating me was the ridiculous, cartoon-character-sounding voice of the announcer of the radio station first thing every morning. I soon learned to circumvent that and then I thought it was the backhoe-in-reverse sound of the electronic alarm that was grating on my last nerve. So I went to the store and made the poor harassed-seeming clerk plug in all the clock radios they had until I found one that just made a loud buzzing sound like a seventeen-year-old-cicada in a beer can, which, for some reason, did not irritate me too bad. I put the other radio on my wife's side so she could see what time it was on her own clock without having to crawl all over me to get a myopic glimpse at mine. That was another sign of the degeneration of my good nature, that this now irritated me after all those years.

Time (5:55) to bring this to a close. The truth dawned on me one night when I woke up, looked at the clock, and flew off into a rage right there in the bed. "3:21? What you mean, 3:21 you damn fool you? What kind of countdown is that? You with that dead-looking battery hanging out on that little wire. You think you so modern . . . you got a face like a 1950 Mercury." Luckily my wife got me calmed back down before I electrocuted myself. The trouble was that I don't have enough sense, in the middle of the night, to figure out what "4:44" means. I have to wake completely up and do the fool arithmetic. I have always hated arithmetic. The only way I got through school was by memorizing, estimating, and my momma's politicking. The mere sight of digits like 2:02 reminds me of past failure and, in the middle of the night, kills the joy of the time left.

I unplugged every one of the blinking things and had a yard sale. I was able to make enough money off it to buy an old Big Ben and a Baby Ben, two old surplus schoolhouse clocks, a roll of black plastic tape to cover up both the 11:11s and 10:01s in the car, and still had enough left to get my old Bulova cleaned. Now all I have to do is keep my mouth closed in the post office and that's not nearly as much trouble as it was. If I could just find some good store-bought flies everything would be all right. "Just look at these hooks . . . wire big enough to make glasses frames with. How in the world is a man supposed to get a thing like that to float? Seems like for all that money they could make one that didn't have the hook sticking out to the side like a dog raising his leg. Holy mackerel child, get off my belly with those big clodhop cowboy boots, you gonna make me spill my drink."

Naked Machining

in which I pull off my socks, put on my glasses and
engage in one of my obsessions in the middle of the night

It is pitiful to be in the grip of so many obsessions that I have had to let go of some of them (model airplanes for one) in order to pay proper attention to others. One of the obsessions most persistent is making little things out of metal. I think I owe the blame for that to the wonderful writer Nevil Shute. When I was a boy, I read a very good book that he wrote called *Trustee from the Toolroom* about a man who made miniature machines in his little shop and then wrote articles about the projects for a magazine for enthusiasts of that sort of thing. Somehow (and I won't spoil it for you if you have never read it) he got in a fix where he had to go halfway around the world. Miniature machining wasn't all that lucrative a business so he had to do his traveling on the cheap in little boats. It was a good book for an impressionable kid looking for obsessions. I had an acetylene welder and a metal lathe by the time I was twelve.

One of the advantages of machining metal is that you can stop anytime you want to, go do something else, and come back and take up exactly (well within 0.0001 inch if you are like me) where you left off. One time, I was cutting Acme threads on a piece of one-and-three-eighth-inch bronze propeller shaft (Tobin bronze . . . good stuff) and watching the tool pare off a long spiral of bright gold like some kind of beautiful Christmas decoration when the time came for my breakfast so I switched off the lathe, ate my breakfast, and took off sailing to the Bahamas with my wife for about eighty days. When we got back, I went in there and switched the lathe on and it commenced paring off the same Christmas decoration just exactly like before. The only way you could tell that the interrupting interval had occurred was that the previous part of the spiral was slightly darker than the new shaving.

I do my machining anytime I get a chance, like when I have to wait for the epoxy to set up and all, but I do most of my machine work in the middle of the night. I am kind of intermittent with my sleeping habits. I would think it came from standing watches on tugboats all those years but I have been like this ever since I was a child. The schedule of my nocturnal machinations has varied through the years but, now, it seems like I wake up at two twenty-two every night. The older I get the less delighted I am with the prospect of wasting my time lying around in the bed trying to go back to sleep. I guess I think about when I am lying in my deathbed thinking . . . "Hell man, you should have got up and gone and done something . . . now don't you wish you had all that wasted time back?"

So I hop right up and pull off my socks, put on my glasses, and trot right in there and switch on the machine. Next thing I know, I smell coffee. It is kind of a nice way to start the morning. Metal-cutting machinery runs quietly so the tranquility isn't destroyed and my wife in the other part of the house (my shop actually used to be the living room of our little concrete house before the boys moved out) can snooze right through it all. I made the whole drive-belt tensioning rig for the Rescue Minor standing naked at my milling machine in the middle of the night. Well, that isn't actually true, I sit on a stool when I am just working in one axis. I only have to stand up when I get on two or three knobs at the same time. Which, I have done so much milling that I can freehand-carve a Herreshoff cleat with nothing but a straight half-inch end mill (if you believe that, send me a quarter).

I'll work a milling machine while I am naked but I wear an apron when I am running the lathe. Those long shavings come off the piece like they are a snake looking for something to bite. They have a diabolical twisting motion to them and are hotter than hell, too. I don't like to get approached by them. The chips from a milling machine come off in a more benign manner and just pile up on the bed and don't chase after you so I work it naked all the time. I always intend to set the feed and go put on my clothes so as to be ready for the day but, sometimes, I get sleepy from all the tranquility of the work and want to go back to bed so, if that happens, all I have to do is switch off the machine, trot in to the bedroom, take off my glasses, pull on my socks, and I am asleep before any time is wasted at all.

I know y'all are wondering about the socks. Well, the floor ain't all that clean in there in the shop and my feet get dirty and unnecessary foot washing is a waste of time so I put on socks to protect the sheets from getting dirty. I know some of you are nitpickers and want to know if I go to bed at regular bedtime with dirty feet. Hell no, damn your eyes. I take a bath just like anybody else and scrub my feet until they are as clean as Martha Stewart's. Even at that, I have to wear socks to bed to cover up my toenails so as not to shred the sheets or claw scratches on my wife. You see, bogging around and stomping oysters at the coast is very hard on toenails. They get ragged and serrated and dangerous. They'll make short work of even 50 percent polyester sheets and when I dream that I have made fun of one of these fools enough to offend him and he is in hot pursuit with his tire iron, I instinctively break into a hard run, even when I am lying asleep in the bed. My wife is a light sleeper and very quick but, if I didn't have my socks on . . .

Ain't this thing ever going to end? Now you want to know why I don't just wear my socks in the shop. Hell, man, have you ever walked around in metal shavings in your socks. The shavings will work their way into the fabric and hang up on the barbs and only come out in the bed and my wife doesn't like them. Fortunately, because of my coastal and other habits the bottoms my feet are as tough as those old-style flat belts that they used to run farm machinery with so shavings don't bother me (when they are on the floor). There is no need to question the wisdom of my methods. I know exactly (believe me) what I am doing.

So now you want to know what I made last night don't you? A beryllium copper oyster knife . . . kind of marvelous.

Hook-and-Line Fishing

in which, again, a fish is "caught" without hook, line, or net

Hook-and-line fishing is sort of like sex. Sometimes it pays off but mostly people just do it for recreation and they do a lot more of it when they are young and ignorant than they do when they are old and smart. Me, I don't waste my time in fruitless endeavors anymore unless the circumstances are so tempting that I just can't help myself. Say, something like a herd of bluefish chasing the pogies slap up on the beach will make me trot for my pole all right or a big cobio circling a mooring float. Nobody but a crazy person would throw a hundred-dollar cast net on a school of blues or a big cobio. You know, bluefish are pretty good if you do them right and do it immediately. I love smoked bluefish. They don't keep well, though and don't freeze worth a flip.

A cobio on the other hand is a delicacy right out of the freezer and the knowledge that there is a fifty-pound one of those lying frozen in there will make one sort of self-satisfied. Before I got so epoxified, I used to build boats outside and my bandsaw was set up right there under the shade tree. I would take the huge carcass of the cobio out of the freezer unwrap the visqueen and saw off some steaks and wrap him back up and put him back in and the ants would carry off the fish sawdust. I always started my steaking at the tail and the steaks just got bigger and bigger as I progressed up the carcass.

I don't usually grill fish steaks (or any other kind). I am a frying-pan man, myself. I am too stingy to stand there and watch all that gravy drip onto the coals. I fry the steaks in a little butter or olive oil and then make onion and mushroom gravy with a little wine. I have a big old cast-iron commercial-style frying pan and a big, rusty gas hotplate that I scavenged from the dumpster. Which, as an aside, you know the modern throwaway style people these days have just about eliminated yard sales from my itinerary. The little granddaughter who is currently employed as an apprentice at the shop got to be two years old this year and all two-year-old children need a sliding board so we went to Lowes and cursed Wal-Mart looking but the damn things were so cheap-made and high-priced that I just couldn't bring myself to do it.

I decided to make her one out of galvanized tin. You know, the lubricious nature of zinc has long been exploited by people like me. My first sawmill was just a long wood table covered with galvanized tin with a bandsaw in the middle. I could just chop out a cant with a broadax and pop a chalk line down the middle and push it through by hand. It worked wonderfully. If you bust a cant right down the middle like that, the two pieces will bow apart as the tension is relieved. Then you can turn the cants so they sit on the table like the rocker of a rocking chair and rock right along cutting out planking. The curve of the boards is exactly like what you would get if you sawed a lapstrake plank out of a big, wide board and the grain runs along the sweep, too, so cutting the gains in the ends is easy and the little rolling, tapered rabbet doesn't try to split off on you and the plank is quarter-sawn so it has maximum stability. That early, primitive sawmill setup is how I lucked into finding out how to build such good boats without having to spend big money and devastate vast acreages of public land.

Whew, y'all, am I getting worse and worse or what? Anyway, my wife and I were passing by the dumpster one afternoon and she spied a sliding board somebody had discarded. Not only was it far superior to anything Wal-Mart had for sale, it was attached to a most excellent swing set. We already have a swing hanging from a live oak limb twenty feet off the ground. I don't like swing sets because they aren't high enough to get any good swinging and the damn little seats are way too narrow for my big ass but I do like free steel tubing. I bet I have pumped more automotive, farm, and industrial machinery exhaust through a swing set than anybody.

My wife had an old rusty B 18 Volvo that I bought for a hundred dollars back about 1968. It was such a bargain because none of the local yahoos at the used-car auction could figure out how to make it run. You know, those little original Volvos that were first imported into the US in the fifties looked sort of like a miniature '48 Ford. They had two SU (short for "satisfactory/unsatisfactory") looking carburetors that are just plain inscrutable to the ignorant and it doesn't take but just a little mis-fiddling to disable them. Because it was so rusty, I knew this car hadn't belonged to any southerner and must have come down with some Yankee. It wasn't just the rust that suggested that. Real southerners do not like small cars. Of course I am not a pure-blood southerner so I guess that accounts for a wider range of tolerance and a potential automotive bargain does not escape close scrutiny no matter how outlaw it might be. It needed a little work but it was easy to do . . . mostly it was just the carburetors all messed up. After I got it running, I welded up a swing-set exhaust system that pooted out the side right in front of the port-side rear tire. Though it had a cherry bomb muffler welded into the system, the whole run was so short that it was very loud. I don't know if you know this or not but a B 18 Volvo was a sleeping bomb for real. An MG or a TR3 or a 356 Porsche wouldn't stay with one and most American cars wouldn't either.

This was the time when four-lane roads and streets were just beginning to appear down in Tallahassee and those people down there are ridiculously competitive. I think Tallahassee thinks it is the LA of the South. Anyway, you ought to have seen the shocked expressions on the faces of the yahoos in the fast lane when the hellish bleat of that eighteen hundred ccs worth of exhaust assaulted them straight down the ear hole as the old Volvo walked off and left them. It finally rusted half in two . . . the car, not the exhaust system. I would lament the passing of the old car (it is back behind the shop in "junker grove" with every other car we ever owned) but my Diesel Dodge has taken its place. It is just as ratty looking and I didn't put *any* muffler in the exhaust system at all. It is straight pipe right from the turbocharger. Though I have to change five old heavy-duty transmission gears and am a little slow on the get-off, if I can get through the first three, ain't an SUV in Thomasville that will stay with it. Of course I have to run in the fast lane because the noise comes out on the starboard side but that just enhances the ambience of the situation. Here this little woman is sitting alongside talking on the cell phone saying, "What is this old man doing in the fast lane in that old piece of junk?" Then the light will change and she'll shower down on the big, shiny Escalation and gain three car lengths on me before I can get in fourth gear . . . then, though, by God . . . I'll drown out the volume on that cell phone. I would go down to Tallahassee and smoke them off the road down there but I am working on the Guinness Book world record for *not* going to Tallahassee. I ain't been back since I "graduated" from FSU in 1969.

Anyway, to get back to hook-and-line fishing, just barely in time to legitimize this tome, I was sitting on the sofa looking out the door at the sunrise on the seaside this morning when I noticed a little fish activity in the calm water. The ospreys had just started their morning foray for breakfast and I could tell that they were ready to get it, too. They always act mighty anxious early in the morning and none of them are sitting around on the nest or standing on limbs or anything. They are all out and about as soon as it is bright enough to see. This morning (and last night) was beautifully clear and calm and it was easy to see fish. There were little pockets of pogies dimpling the water all the way to the horizon and the ospreys were working on them.

One time we were coming to the coast down Highway 98 in my old convertible Cadillac (yes, Virginia) with one of my sons and his girlfriend. The road goes right along the beach down at St. Teresa and the ospreys take advantage of the updraft, caused when the sea breeze hits the trees of the beach, to gain a little altitude to fly back to the nest with their heavy catch. Eagles harass ospreys and steal their fish all the time and that day we saw an eagle attack an osprey that was carrying a big pogy and the stoop of the eagle scared the osprey and he dropped the pogy. The eagle tried to catch the falling fish but couldn't do it. They don't really care if they catch the stolen goods in the air or not. They'll stand right there in the middle of the road and eat him. Anyway, we were so fascinated at the drama of all this that I just slowed to a stop in the middle of the highway and damned if the pogy didn't fall right into that girl's lap. Luckily she was built for the duty and luckily, the eagle pulled out of his dive just in time but we felt his wind and smelled him (kind of strong smelling). So, this morning I was watching the ospreys and pogies when I saw some kind of big fish jump clear out of the water right in the middle of one of the schools of bait. I felt the old hook-and-line twitch and started to go get my pole. Then I saw another fish jump and recognized him either for a very big Spanish mackerel or a small kingfish (a very big mackerel, indeed). Instead of grabbing my rod, I went and got my computer and sat back down and wrote this story. I ain't crazy about mackerel no matter what their ethnic origin or aristocratic rank is. If they had been bluefish it might have been another story and, if I had seen even a hint of cobio, I would be down there right now and y'all wouldn't know anything about the traditional swing-set exhaust system.

Oh yeah, the sliding board was most excellent. It has a stainless-steel sliding surface and steel rails and all. I had to build a jackleg ladder to hold up the high end but it works well. I think I can elevate it in stages as the child grows . . . might give it five speeds like my old Dodge. Of course the swing-set aspect of the scavenging won't work for an exhaust system on the truck because it needs about four-inch pipe . . . Maybe one of these old raggedy Mercedes. A turbocharged diesel engine suffers a lot of horsepower loss from exhaust back pressure. I wonder what a Mercedes sounds like with straight pipes? I wonder how fast one is? I wonder which side would be best to poot out of?

Toughies in the Back

*in which I explore a lake too pretty to believe
in a boat too pretty to walk away from*

I have been working on the doodads of this radical departure in the shop so intensely that I have been getting up in the middle of the night to go in there (my wife and I have a tiny apartment attached to the shop) and stand at the lathe in my wrapper robe. It has been so hot this December (eighty-eight degrees on Pearl Harbor day, which I remember perfectly what I was doing when FDR told us about that horror . . . lying in my bassinette snoozing and drooling) that sometimes I do my machining, buck naked, at two thirty in the morning . . . have to adroitly hop back every now and then. That inability to sleep is one of the time-saving benefits of getting to be old. Boy, I wish I had discovered that back before I decided to give up sex to save time.

Anyway, I had to go to my granddaughter's ballet show (they sure do have some young ballerinas around here . . . some hardly walking age . . . maybe ballet is just another, poorly disguised, form of day care). While I was in the bathroom shaving off the whiskers that such a compulsive boat-building weakness fertilizes, I happened to look myself dead in the eyes. They looked like two piss holes in the snow. "Man, you need to go fishing," I told myself.

Just the day before I had been talking to my old friend who runs the bait store just up the road. You know, a bait store man has to keep pretty early hours and that is convenient to old people. "Been doing anything good," I asked. "Well, yeah, I went to Lake Talquin and caught my limit of twenty speckled perch [black crappie, *Pomoxis nigromaculatus*] and they weighed thirty-seven pounds," he said. "Dang," I said.

I was in the middle of machining the fixture to adapt a SHURflo, diaphragm, all-plastic, self-priming, most exquisitely reliable, electric saltwater pump so that it would run, non-electrically, directly off the camshaft of the little Kubota tractor engine of the Rescue Minor to cool the engine oil and wet the exhaust. I had already machined the double-flanged outside part of the adapter, complete with the press-fit bearings and the boss that keyed the thing exactly concentric to the camshaft connection of the engine, and had figured out how I was going to do the shaft, but I knew that it wouldn't be good for my quality of life to continue on that project right then.

I was sitting in the parking lot of the bait store in my old Mercedes with the skiff behind when Charlie showed up at four thirty on Pearl Harbor day. I made him dip minnows while he was still eating his sausage biscuit. I had forgotten to rummage all under the floor mats for some change so I had to get him to put it on the tab, them and two cans of sardines and Vienna sausages. The whole transaction didn't take but a minute or two and I was on the road, heading west . . . minnows sloshing in the back . . . almost full moon shining right straight ahead . . . dead calm, perfectly clear, warm, summer-like morning.

It started out as an idyllic trip to Lake Talquin down the little country roads that I know so well . . . not enough light to see the trash that gripes my ass so bad and too early for the horrendous traffic that is taking over almost everyplace within commuting distance of any metropolis in the world, I guess. I remember one time I pushed my old souped-up Cushman motor scooter seven miles down one of these roads without meeting a single car to give me a ride and now I can't get out of my driveway without a ten-minute wait. Well, all right I heard all those yelps of disbelief about the souped-up Cushman from those who have not yet learned to believe everything I say. I'll lay that doubt to rest with just two words . . . *nitrous oxide.* It would outrun a thirty-six-horsepower Volkswagen for a little while. The reason I was pushing it was because the end of the half of the connecting rod that was still attached to the crankshaft had beat a big hole out the side of the crankcase. I'm certainly glad the piston didn't come up through the seat.

Back to the me and the minnows sloshing in the back of my old station wagon. The only town on the way to Lake Talquin is little old Havana, which ain't much, just a little bigger than Coon Bottom, which doesn't even have a store anymore. The county, where Havana is, used to be the shade tobacco capital of the universe. They grew thousands of acres of very pampered tobacco under vast muslin shades. Hundreds of people worked constantly under there picking off bud worms (actually corn ear worms, *Heliothis zea,* the most destructive agricultural insect in this country) and the huge, surrealistically bizarre-looking tobacco hornworms (which take three stomps to kill) and breaking off the tips of the plants and popping off suckers to force the tobacco to make the biggest, best leaves to be used as the wrapper for cigars. It seems like it wouldn't be such bad work under the shade like that, but I tell you it was terrible. For one thing, muslin ain't much of a shade material but it will certainly cut off the breeze. For another thing, tobacco is, I believe, the meanest vegetable to have to fool with I know . . . worse than okra. It'll put an itch on you that won't quit.

That tobacco labor was a peonage situation. The black folks who did the work never could manage to get paid up with the rent, the bill at the store, the car loan, the kerosene tab . . . never saw any money. If they didn't show up for work, here came the sheriff. Finally, about 1960, the federal government shut that system down and sent the shade tobacco business to the Dominican Republic along with many of the few white people who owned the whole county. Big old antebellum houses fell to ruin and Gadsden County became one of the poorest in Florida. The tobacco fields (some of the best farmland in the state) went over to tomatoes and pole beans and the field hands went Hispanic. I don't know, but it doesn't look like the wages situation in the field is much better than it was. At least, the hideous urban infection of Tallahassee has brought in a little money as politicians, bureaucrats, and their support yuppies metastasize out through the countryside like the spread of an infestation of German roaches. Some things are bound to get better while others get worse, I guess.

Fortunately, as I passed through Havana, it was impossible for me to see all the "Shoppes" that now occupy the little former fertilizer and hardware stores that sold what it took to raise shade tobacco . . . and the little grocery stores and general-merchandise places where the poor peons could never catch up on the bill. I have a talent for ignoring things that I don't like, but about first daylight, it became impossible to ignore the bumper-to-bumper parade of behemoth SUVs wallowing into the rising sun in the oncoming lane. They were all driven by intense little women, cheeks gleaming like polished apples, eye shadow like coons, lips shining like taillights in the glare, heads wiggling like hand puppets to the tune of the cell phone clamped to the side of every head. They say that women can't get a foothold in the management of this country but it seems to me that they damn sure do run the state of Florida . . . over the phone. I think I saw the one who decided one presidential election for us.

Except for me, the only people heading west away from the metropolis were field hands packed in the back of pickup trucks going to pick tomatoes (and this December 7 . . . I told you it has been a hot winter) and school

ROBB WHITE

buses. I could see the tomatoes gleaming on the healthy bushes in the fields and the children waiting in little groups by the driveways of trailer parks. Most people hate to follow a school bus and some do ridiculous things in order to get past, but I like to watch the children get on. It is a cheerful sort of camaraderie and makes a hopeful start to the day. I ignored the trash alongside the road and refused to look at the women tapping impatiently on their steering wheels in the other lane . . . the bus strobe made a bad sight intolerable.

Pretty soon I had progressed so far west that I was out of commuting range of Florida's capital city and into the sharply divided hills that signify the presence of a big river. The Ochlocknee is the second biggest river running through the panhandle of Florida (the Apalachicola is much, much bigger) and was the first one around here to be dammed up by the Army Corps of Engineers to generate electricity. Back in the twenties when the dam and Lake Talquin (which was named after little old Tallahassee, smaller then than Thomasville, Georgia is now, and its twin, Quincy, county seat of Gadsden County) were built, the generators produced all the electricity the people needed.

Anyway, it is real hilly around the river. The Ochlocknee runs through our old home place just north of the state line and it is hilly there, too, and as wild as anyplace on this planet. My cousins and I had a hard time staying away from the river when we were children . . . especially me. As you can probably tell, I skipped a lot of school to mess around back there and, when I see the land change into something that looks like river to me, I still get excited, thinking I am skipping some unpleasantness . . . like I had some unpleasantness to skip nowadays.

I skipped myself down to the boat ramp. There wasn't a soul there except for a great blue heron and a big old gray horse standing right in the middle of the ramp. The horse was taking a leak . . . you know how they do . . . a real delight for children. He didn't act like he wanted to move when I backed down to launch in the foam. The heron moved but it was easy to tell that he didn't like it one bit. Despite all obstacles, it was only the work of a minute (practice makes perfect) and my skiff was floating like a beauty in the shallow water (you know, if your boat ain't too pretty to walk away from without turning for another look, you ain't getting all the good out of life) and my old car was parked in the shade of a big swamp chestnut oak and I was on my way. I got all the way out on the lake and was admiring the scenery when I remembered the bucket of minnows still in the back of the car.

I have to admit something to you or I won't be able to live with myself. After I got the minnows, I sat there in the middle of Lake Talquin, without a hint of civilization showing anywhere, either on the water or the virgin woods of the bank, and called the fishing license hotline maintained by the state of Florida . . . on my cell phone. I expected lightning to strike me out of the clear blue sky as I explained to the woman (probably one of those that I passed) all my particulars and read her my credit card number. Jesus, y'all. Since I don't normally fish the public fresh waters of the state of Florida, I only have a saltwater license and those people weren't awake when I finally made up my mind. I had to do it. When you go around acting like me, you know you damn sure better be in compliance.

Lake Talquin is, I believe, the prettiest lake around here. Early in the morning of a weekday, it is hard to see any sign of civilization. Somebody has taken good care of the shoreline and it appears to be virgin woods. The whole shore is very steep, almost impossible to climb with your shoes on. Enormous oaks, ashes, poplars, hickories, beeches, magnolias, and the biggest Walker pines anywhere grow all along the high banks and there are big black gums and cypress trees on the little bit of low, level land. The shade keeps the ground almost bare except for the leaves and acorns.

The sun was rising beautifully in the clear air as I finally, face as red as those women's lips, put up the phone and started my engine. I even hated to do that . . . wished for my little felucca but there wasn't a breath of wind anywhere on the lake. Talquin is about fourteen miles long and maybe two wide if you measure up into the convolutions of the shoreline and there were a bunch of places I wanted to go see, so I set out. I had to go slow because, when they built the lake, they left all the trees still standing; then they died and rotted off about flush with the average waterline and the stumps have been preserved just as solid as if they were brand new. Some of those old stumps are so big and flat that you can prance around on them and throw the cast net for shad minnows. But you damn sure better know where you are throwing because the whole bottom of the lake is covered with tops and limbs and even two or three airplanes and the water is not clear enough to see how you are tangled up so you have to get in there and feel it aloose and the average depth is fifteen feet.

I didn't have to throw for no shad minnows though. I had two dozen store-bought minnows swimming around in the medicinally poisonous blue water from the bait store. I don't know how they raise those things and don't want to but they have selectively bred them so that they are as far removed from a wild animal as a chicken. You can't hardly kill one of them for one thing. I like to hook them in the mouth and up through the top of the head. That way they'll stay on the hook when you throw and the hook will ride point-up. You can't hook any kind of real minnow like that or he'll die on you and speckled perch are sight feeders . . . won't mess with a dead minnow. You can hook one of these poor little "toughies" through both eyes and he or she will still pull hard enough on your line that you can feel him and they aren't but about an inch and three-quarters long. They got some bait store worms that don't look exactly right either, probably inbred. You know, earthworms are set up both ways, so they might even be self-bred. I don't normally buy bait, but this was a special situation.

I know the previous paragraph might be repulsive to some but, when you think about it, the inability to bait your own hook is a dysfunction, just like the inability to provide your own food directly from the source . . . and nothing to be proud of. I would rather be a shad minnow than a toughie and I would rather be a heron than a chicken. If I had to be a bird though, I wish I could be an eagle. That is one government project that turned out fine. There are plenty of eagles around here and I saw two working Lake Talquin. An osprey is also a fine bird to my notion, but they have to jump in the water in sort of an undignified way to catch a fish while an eagle flies down and snatches the fish right straight out without even getting his feathers wet. Don't you know that's a horrible experience for the fish. Here he is swimming along minding his own business, and the next thing, the talons are clear through him and he is on his way in a completely different, and absolutely hopeless, situation. When I was young, there weren't any eagles around here and I formed a misimpression. For one thing, they hardly ever soar like buzzards, they beat their wings quickly and powerfully all the time . . . none of that lazy work like herons and certainly none of the sloppy flapping like a crow. They aren't so big looking either. Except for the way they act, they would be hard to tell from an osprey. They are built different, though. An osprey is very light but . . . they had an eagle at the Junior Museum down in Tallahassee back when I was teaching. He was kind of tame and would sit on the arm of the man doing the explaining. "Mr. White, would you let that bird stand on your arm like that?" one of the kids in my class provoked. "Why certainly," I replied thinking I was perfectly safe. With that, the man handed me that big old eagle. Fortunately he gave me the thick towel first but even then, I could feel the power of the eagle's grip on my forearm . . . and the weight . . . and I hoped he wasn't looking at me like it looked like he was. An eagle is as dense as a turkey. God help a poor fish within sight of that eagle eye and within reach of that hellish grip . . . or anywhere near me when I am in my eagle mood with my cast net.

I moseyed slowly down the shoreline in the brilliant sun. I have never seen so many squirrels in my life. It has been a very good year for acorns and hickory nuts. When I stopped to drift, I could hear the big (pigeon-egg-sized) swamp-chestnut-oak acorns hitting the leaves. The thrashing and chattering of the squirrels was so loud that I had to stay pretty far out on the lake to get any tranquility. I had put in at the upstream end of the lake and the old riverbed runs right along that north (Gadsden County side) bank so there was enough current to drift pretty good and that is what I mostly did. I even drifted up on a good many deer eating the swamp chestnut acorns.

It was just the loveliest kind of a day. I finally got to the mouth of the Little River and crunk the motor and eased up at a dead idle. The little river was so narrow in places that the squirrels could jump across on the enormous trees that grew on the mountainous banks. I tied up at one spectacular place and got out and climbed up. It was too steep to do with shoes but fortunately, I didn't have any. When I got to the top, I tried to take a picture with my disposable camera, but while I was peering through the little hole, I got a case of the blind staggers and dropped the damn thing as I was clawing at a palmetto bush to save myself. It bounced all the way down and floated most marvelously. It took me so long to get back down that it was long gone . . . brand new too.

When I got back in the boat, it was so hot and still that I had to take off my hat, but the overhanging trees gave so much shade that I didn't need it. I would have taken a little dip but I have never seen such alligators in my life (another successful government project). They were insolent too and I know enough about them to know that they are dangerous as hell so I stayed in the boat. You know, alligators eat a heap more Floridians than sharks but even with that, they ain't getting the job done. Alligators are normally holed up by December, but these enormous things were on every log and flat place on the banks of the river. I felt like William Bartram on the St. Johns (*Travels Through Georgia and Florida*) before the Revolution . . . wished I had brought my never-miss old .25/35 just to lay my hand on every now and then. I did have my old single-shot S&W .22 (which has missed once or twice but that was back in the ignorance of my youth) and my miss-aplenty slingshot with some extremely excellent taconite pellets that Dennis Bradley sent me, but those alligators and squirrels and deer were perfectly safe from this terrible terrestrial predator. I was fishing that day.

I finally saw some other fishermen and stopped to talk awhile. They were regulars down there . . . I believe illegally catching speckled perch to sell . . . nice men, sons of the shade tobacco hands. They said that they had done pretty good yesterday but that it was slow today. They liked the looks of the skiff and were glad to get the two dozen toughies I gave them and they gave me two turnips to eat with my sardines and Vienna sausages . . . a good combination for real.

I didn't wet a single hook and was back on the road by eleven o'clock and back at the lathe by twelve thirty. Although I felt reinvigorated, my eyes haven't improved all that much. I might have to give up that naked machining at two-thirty in the morning or . . . maybe take up sex again. It don't take all that long. Damn I wish I hadn't made that phone call. I guess I'll just have to go back to the lake to amortize my investment. Hell, I might as well go right now. I done ruint the day writing this. I wonder if Charlie will spot me some minnows one more time. I still ain't been to town to liquefy none of my assets. Shoot, I'll just take my throw net, I ain't got time to fool with Charlie and that way, I won't have to haul minnows trying to slosh out in the back. When I get time, I am going to try to find the ones that sloshed out last time . . . might still be alive . . . toughies you know.

Wild Rice Canoe

in which my mother eats wild rice and I forget to read some fine print

I was lying in the bed the other night trying to think up something to worry about when a thought struck me so hard that I didn't get another wink of sleep all night long. I had lost a boat. Sometimes (rarely) I go to some enormous shopping center to get something I can't get from these little merchants I normally do business with and I just stupidly get out of the car and, completely oblivious to the geography of the damn place, trot in and start looking for wide-toed shoes or something, and when I finally get through and come out into the real world I can't remember where in hell I parked the car . . . have no idea . . . not a clue. I can soon figure out the east and west of the place but I can't remember on what side of the hundred-acre parking lot (absolutely full of SUVs so big you can't see over them even if you hop as high as you can) I left the car. Anyway, I just have to wander a search pattern like the Coast Guard does when they are looking for some lost boater out in the middle of the ocean. Fortunately my car is easy to recognize when I finally actually see it and I am soon gone but this lost boat was last seen so long ago that I had no idea where it was within miles and miles of possibilities. I better explain.

Back in the early seventies we were real poor. My wife was working for minimum wage as a teacher's aide, and that only four hours a day, and all our other income came from my various half-assed endeavors. We had some kind of a sea boat or other all that time, but nothing I could just leave down at the pond in case I was wandering along and saw a fish acting hungry out there, I could get my handline out of my pocket and, quick, catch a grasshopper and push off in the boat and go catch him. I had built a series of small plywood boats but, if I neglected them as I am wont to do, they always rotted down in short order.

I had a long standing prejudice against the El-Cheapo aluminum buttheads that I might have possibly afforded, not only because they were what put me out of the plywood boat business, but because my mother had one of the first ones of the damn things ever made and it wasn't worth a flip. Not only couldn't it be paddled or rowed with any efficiency, it hung up on lily pads and grass worse than anything. I don't know if it was the exposed rivets or the runners on the bottom or just that all that flat bottom sucked to the lily pads like suction cups but it was damn near immovable in any weeds at all. One time my sister and I were out in it in the middle of our old, big swampy pond shooting bullfrogs (you shoot them with a .22 short . . . hollow-point . . . and somehow, the hydraulic shock just stultifies them and they keep sitting right where they were until you pick them up and put them in the sack). Anyway, I shot myself through the forearm with a pistol. The hollow point penetrated all the way through and there was a plug of meat as big as a Vienna sausage hanging out on the output side. We were terrified and horrified. I sat there holding my arm while she tried to pole the boat to the hill so we could go to the hospital with this horrendous wound but she was too little and weak to overcome the suction of the lily pads. I started to get up and take up the pole but she just jumped over the side in the shallow water and took up the painter and towed me (sitting like Cleopatra on her barge) rapidly to the bank. When we got to the doctor (good old Dr. Charley Watt . . . the man who discovered what to do when you get rattlesnake-bit) the piece of meat had retracted back into the hole so he swabbed out both sides as best he could with something like gentian violet and put two Band-Aids on there and sent me home. "What do you think I ought to do about being careful with it and all?" I asked as I walked out of his office. "Don't shoot yourself anymore" was his medical advice.

So, was that butt-headed pain in the ass the boat I lost? Hell no, I know exactly where that son of a bitch is and it is welcome to stay there, too. The boat I lost was the wild rice canoe my mother and I sort of went together and bought. My mother was funny about how generous she was to poor old me. One time I was whining about how I hated the particular old wore-out outboard motor I was running at that time and she said, "Bingey . . . you need a *new* outboard motor and I am going to buy you one so I won't have to raise any orphan children when you break down and drift to Africa." The next day she called to tell me to go to Bellamy's boat shop and pick up my brand new 1967 Evinrude "Sportster" (twenty-five hp). Whew, it was pretty . . . first fifty-to-one mix I ever owned and ran so smooth and started first pull every time. I loved it. The payment book came in the mail the next day.

So, you can see how I might have been sort of skeptical when she said, "Bingey, I have been reading about this promotion where we can get a brand-new Grumman seventeen-foot standard canoe with box tops from Uncle Ben's wild rice. I love wild rice so I will eat the rice and give you the box tops." I was going to read the fine print but never got around to it before I got to Albany (that's Albany, Georgia . . . not the capital of anything, yet) with a fistful of box tops to pick up my canoe. As it turned out, that canoe cost me a bunch of money. While we were loading it, I asked the dealer what it would have cost without the box tops and he said, "Same thing." Oh well. Before I get back to the canoe, my mother was truly an unusual woman. If you want to find out more, I plug my sister's book *Momma Makes Up Her Mind,* by Bailey White.

We used the canoe for a long time off and on but it wasn't all that good of a pond boat . . . too big and too much windage for stealthy fishing Finally I got around to building a better boat and just left it hidden around one of the ponds on the old place so, if I was to shoot a duck in the middle of the wintertime, I could keep from having to swim to get him. The present trouble was that I couldn't remember which pond it was anymore. I like to hide boats and an aluminum boat doesn't mind lying for years under a pile of sticks and leaves, either. Somehow it enhances the appearance of the boat as the mildew covers up the shiny metal. In the proper environment (like down around a pond) lichens will grow on aluminum, too. The last time I remember the wild rice canoe was one time my oldest son and his cousin and I went a long way up the Ochlocknee River on a fly-rod-fishing expedition. We took our lunch in an icebox and I had a jackleg rig sticking out on the port side to run an outboard motor and had an Evinrude weedless four-horsepower on there and we were tooling it down the narrow, stumpy, log-jammed river like we knew what we were doing. We came to a place where a fallen tree caused us to swerve over into the willows and, somehow, a dry willow stick went so far up my son's nostril that he turned us over. It was instantaneous, too. When the boat flipped, the engine passed me and caught me by the sleeve with the throttle lever and went to running wide open. Amazingly, it kept on running for quite a few revolutions after all of it but the propeller was under the water, but when all the air got sucked out of the cowling and the first pure mouthful of water went into the crankcase, it locked up and never ran right again. The flywheel turned sort of stiff. I think the hydraulic shock bent one of the connecting rods or something, kind of like what happens to a bullfrog when a hollow-point shot stultifies him. I cannibalized the engine for parts. So, how did we three fly-rod fishermen get back down the river? We found the paddles but not the fly rods or my tackle box. The cousin caught the icebox and saved the sandwiches.

I know we brought the canoe back from that expedition and I was pretty sure it was hidden around one of the ponds on our place but I was worried that it might be one of the ponds on the part of the place that got inherited by one of my mother's siblings and was sold off. I decided to go looking on our part first and Jane and I set off the morning after I had dreamed about the boat. It was a wonderfully warm early-January day and the woods were beautiful. We walked all the way around Chef's pond without finding the boat. Chef's pond is named that because it was down behind Chef's house. Chef was the cook at the big house back when my mother's family was still sorta rich. (Did you know that my great-great-grandfather invented shoe polish?) Chef was an educated man and, though he was the son of people who were slaves before the Civil War, put five daughters through college and they were the ones who taught me not to make any reckless assumptions about people without finding out the facts first. I remember when Chef's pond was built. It is in a deep and very beautiful little valley and the way they built it was to drag the bottom of the valley with a dirt pan behind a bulldozer. They made a little road up out of the valley to the downstream end and dumped the clay there. After about a week or two of hauling dirt with the pan, they had a dam and old Chef's pond has been a mighty good one ever since. My mother built a dock on the dam and most any child can stand on that dock and catch bream and bass with a cane pole. One time this little kid was visiting my grandson. They were both about two years old and we decided to go down there and fish off the dock. This little kid was pure Italian (mother Sicilian . . . daddy from the peninsula) and had the blackest hair and eyes I ever saw and was very cute and intelligent. My grandson had a plastic bag of small, soft plastic octopuses and he insisted that we use them for bait. He and the other kid sat there on the end of the dock fishing with their cane poles for a long time. Finally the Italian kid said, "I don't think we are going to catch anything on these octopuses." That expression has become part of the family and that's what Jane said after we had circumnavigated Chef's pond and poked every pile of sticks and leaves we came to.

I knew we were just starting the search. The other likely pond was the big old Swampy pond . . . some seventy acres. It is called "the Mitchell pond" for the people of the original land grant for the place in 1836. The Mitchell pond has been almost dry for about ten years and I couldn't remember when the last time I had the old canoe out in that pond but I shoot ducks there some and I might have hidden it someplace around just in case. We started looking. Because the edge of the pond has been out of its natural swampy state for so long, it is very thick and briery around there and it was tough going but we finally found it. The only way we did it was that we were standing there trying to decide which way to go next when we heard the unmistakable sound of a big hickory nut hitting an aluminum boat. Boy, it was hid good. The original pile of limbs and leaves that I covered the boat with had contributed to the fecundity of the situation and that had favored the spot with a very dense growth of high dog fennels as hard to see over as a sea of SUVs and we couldn't see the canoe until we tripped over it. It was all grown up with roots and vines and very hard to turn over, but when we did, there was a perfect bamboo pole right where I had last left it maybe twenty years ago. There was also a pack rat den (pack rats and white-footed deer mice build similar nests in the woods; the way to tell which is which is that pack rats do not use the bathroom in the house) under there and two enormous fire ant nests in the flotation compartments in the ends. We dragged it back and put it in the truck and took it to Chef's pond and went fishing. Did we fish out of the old forgotten wild rice canoe? Hell no. An aluminum canoe ain't worth a flip for fishing, particularly if there is any wind at all. We fished off Momma's old rickety dock and Jane caught about a three-pound bass and I caught three little shellcrackers, which we had for supper. So why did we go to all the trouble to resurrect the old thing? Because five of my grandchildren live up there in Chef's old house and they come down to the pond all the time and need them a boat that doesn't have to be taken care of too much. I left it half sunk in the pond to drive out the fire ants. I hope I can remember where in case they ate all the flotation and it sinks to the bottom and is lost for real.

Freshwater Fishing

in which I introduce an old friend who is a bad joker

I just read that hook-and-line fishing story and realized that I had made a grievous error so I am writing my own rebuttal. I forgot to say that hook-and-line fishing is not my thing in *salt* water. You can't catch freshwater fish with a cast net so I always use a hook and line there. Well, Jane is the one who mostly catches the fish. It is funny how much better women are than men at fishing and it isn't just patience, either. A woman taught me how to fish and I am pretty durn good, if I do say so myself but I had to learn. Jane just came by it naturally. What it is is that she just knows where a fish is and what kind of mood he (or she) is in. She won't hesitate to drop her worm in the worst weed patch in the pond, either, and has a miraculous ability to pull (lead) a big fish through the bushes like he was trying to help her. Because of that tendency, she is always getting hung up in limbs and snags and stuff but, unlike a man, she does not get frustrated and hysterical, but just wiggles and fools around until the worm helps her get loose. We have been to Chef's pond two successive days and caught our supper on both days. The pond is in that wonderful state when the fish are biting and the cursed *Hydrilla* (a noxious weed introduced into the US by aquarium fanciers) still hasn't completely covered the pond for the whole summer.

Ten big bream are just what we need for supper and my breakfast the next day (which a big, old, cold bream beats hell out of a bowl of Froot Loops). Because it is not blowing like the dickens for a change, we have been using the old Grumman wild rice canoe. A canoe ain't bad for a fishing boat when the wind is not strong enough to send it planing sideways right in the middle of where the fish are every time you lay down the paddle and pick up your fishing pole. You have to be very careful when you lay the paddle down and not stomp around on the aluminum either. I have proven time and again that fish cannot be caught out of any aluminum boat containing a two-year-old child but, without the child, it can be done. On the first day we went, Jane caught nine big bream and I caught two little ones and one of them was too small to keep. We have two species of eating-sized bream in that pond. One is the regular old blue bream that is ubiquitous all over the country and the other is the shellcracker, which is a smaller fish than a bluegill but with a bigger mouth and, to me, the best eating of all bream.

Down here bream get big. The biggest blue bream are in Lake Miccosu-kee, which is a natural lake and ancestral home of the long-gone Miccosu-kee Indians. There have been some four-pound bream pulled out of that lake. I know a lot of you know what it is like to catch a big bluegill and can imagine what a four-pounder would do to the old Zebco. I don't think there is any fish that fights harder for his size than a bluegill. I have never caught even a two-pound one but I can imagine. What he'll do to the Zebco is chew up the line so bad where it goes around the pins that you'll have to change it after (if) you get the fish in the boat. There are bream beds on Miccosukee so big that fifty boats group up on one bed. I don't participate in social gatherings of that nature but I had an old friend who was down-right fiendish about fishing a bream bed in company with all sorts of other people. There are women who fish bream beds but it is an all-day proposi-tion and most women don't like to have to pee out of a boat with a bunch of other boats close by so they usually fish off the dam or something while the old man goes out and anchors on the bed and pees over the side. All the other fishermen act like nothing unusual is happening when one of them does that but this old booger friend of mine had a nasty streak in him and he rigged up this rig with an automotive electric fuel pump pulling water out of the live box and pumping it up his britches leg through a carburetor hose and he would stand up to pee and just keep on peeing a hard, steady three-eighth-inch-diameter stream as long as he wanted to. The other fishermen would try not to notice but couldn't help looking a little nervous. You know how human nature is . . . particularly here in the South . . . people don't like to acknowledge any human abnormality by staring at it. Wheelchair people are almost invisible around here.

I went to an auction where they were selling off a whole farm's worth of equipment after a different old man had died and this same old booger was there with a little dog leash with an empty collar dangling on the end of it. The leash was rigidly arranged so it looked like the man was following an in-visible little dog and this dog was very willful and kept going up under women's dresses. "Get your ass out from under there," the old booger would scold and snatch the little collar back hard enough to flip the woman's skirt up pretty high, and then he had the gall to keep going on . . . apologize to the woman then cuss the dog some more. He was a nasty man.

This story started out about bream fishing so I'd better get back on track.

You can catch them with a cane pole and a lot of people like that method but Jane and I like to fish off the bank a lot and, unless you stay in the same place and watch your cork all day long a cane pole is unsuitable. All our ponds are grown up around the sides with big trees and bushes, and a cane pole will drive you crazy trying to burrow through the undergrowth. I have an ancient Zebco 33 that I bought from that same nasty old booger back when he was running the bait store forty years ago. It is sort of like George Washington's ax. I have swapped out guts and covers so many times that I don't know if there are any original parts to it but I still like it. You know, in my opinion, most men over-accessorize themselves when it comes to fishing tackle. Some of them have a tackle box worth a thousand bucks with all those expensive baits and all. Mine ain't worth but about two hundred dollars and most of that is the pistol. Me, I am a wild worm man and so is Jane. I don't give a damn how much money you spend, you can't have a better bait than a wild worm big enough to cast without any weight at all. He'll (actually it's a he/she hermaphrodite) sink slowly and wiggle enticingly all the way down. I don't know the species of these naturally occurring worms down here but they are very dark-colored and kind of iridescent like a hologram and, in the right conditions, get big. One right condition is in a pile of old junk-mail catalogs. Because of the nature of this business, we get a world of them and I pile them up out in the yard in a likely place and the worms get in there and eat their way through the paper. Back in the old Sears and Roebuck catalog days (which I hated to see the end of . . . Wal-Mart ain't in it with Sears and Roebuck in their heyday), anytime I wanted to go fishing, all I would have to do was sweep the leaves off my Sears catalog and flip through the pages and put the worms in my Prince Albert can (which I hated to see the end of, too). Usually the lingerie section would have the biggest worms and it isn't because of any nasty connotation or anything . . . they just had a lot of slick pages in that section and worms love that clay-coated paper. They really love a stack of *Cruising Worlds*. Anyway, when you uncover one of those worms, he doesn't just lie there in acquiescence like a night crawler or pond worm but goes to flipping and twisting like an alligator on a hook. They don't like to be stuck with a fishhook, either. I don't care how high-tech a man gets with his equipment, you can't beat a wild wiggler fighting the hook as he slowly thrashes all the way to the bottom . . . ain't too many fish that can stand to watch that happen right in front of their noses for very long. Bass will come running from fifteen feet away if the water is clear

enough for him to see. Which, that brings up a peculiarity that I have noticed. Both largemouth bass and bream are in the same family and, with bass,
it is the female that gets to be the biggest whereas with bream, it's the male.

So, believe me, it ain't the equipment that brings in the bacon, y'all, it's
the technique. As I said, my equipment is an old Zebco and a cheap, short
rod, four-pound line and a package of fishhooks, and a pocketknife . . . and
a few wigglers. Jane's is about the same except she doesn't own the rod. She
just uses one of the children's "Mickey Mouse" Zebco rigs. I don't know
when Zebco started but it might have been thirty years ago that they began
to make that little cheap one-piece rig with Mickey printed on the cover. It
is all plastic and the rod is so short that it only has two guides on it. The little reel comes with six-pound line and it has no drag so I always get in there
and kill the anti-reverse. You know, it is a lot better to *give* the fish line than
it is for him to have to take it. If you give slack, the fish will stop fighting,
but if he feels the resistance of the drag he'll tear off into the bushes and lily
pads and hang you up. If he is heading in the wrong direction, Jane
backpedals on the handle and gives slack line until he stops and starts heading in the right direction . . . then she catches him. Except for the nostalgia
of it, I would use a Mickey Mouse (or Goofy . . . same thing) Zebco. Of
course I would take that six-pound line off there and put on four-pound
line. No fish likes to see anything but the worm and that brings up my
axiom: You can catch big fish with light line and a little hook but you can't
catch little fish with heavy line and a big hook. When you are looking for
something to eat, you have to have your equipment suit the situation. Another tip is to hook your worm in the nose. If you do like the kid in *McElligot's Pool* and hook him in the middle, the bream will grab him by the head
and run off with him until he breaks off where the hook is. Fish (especially
bream) are keen observers of everything and are omnivorous in their habits
and are never really hungry so they are picky eaters and have sense enough
to know that a worm won't go down very good backward because they have
those little bristles leaning back like little barbs so they always grab him by
the head. Make sure the point of the hook is sticking out good and make
sure the hook is so small as to be practically invisible. I like a #10, fine-wire
blue Mustad (the oldest manufacturer of metal objects still in business in the
world) Aberdeen-pattern hook, myself, for bass and bream. But there is one
time when such a little hook is inappropriate and that fact was once again
proven yesterday.

Jane spied a slight quiver to the water in the middle of a lily pad patch about as big around as a kitchen table and flipped her worm over there even though she knew he/she was going to land right in the middle of all those lily pads and a big wad of *Hydrilla,* too. The worm lay there on top of the lily pad for a while and then crawled off the edge and a little bream about as big as child's hand grabbed him by the head and tried to drag him down to the bottom. Jane coaxed him out around the lily pad stems into the *Hydrilla* and started dragging a big mess of it to the boat. All that grass was too heavy to lift into the boat to untangle the little fish so she reached over the side. As soon as she got the little fish untangled, he started to swim off and a bass as big as a beagle dog hit him just as soon as he got clear of Jane's hand. Whew, it sounded like somebody had dropped a car battery in the water and Jane snatched her hand back and just managed to catch Mickey Mouse before he went overboard. The bass ran all the way out in the middle of the pond before Jane could manage to catch the whirling handle and feed him enough slack to stop him from taking line but he already had a lot. We decided to let him have plenty of time to maybe eat that little bream good enough to get to the tiny hook but he didn't make another move so Jane sat back on him in an attempt to snatch the hook out of the little fish's mouth and maybe hook him in the lip and it appeared to work. He pulled and Jane pulled and fed line and I paddled to try to keep up a little bit. Finally he spat out the little bream and went on about his business. The hook was still all the way in the little bream's mouth. We know where he (she) hangs out, though, so as soon as the spawning season is for sure over (January and February and part of March down here . . . usually completely over in April . . . but this has been a funny year) we will set up and go catch her. We'll put eight-pound line on the Mickey Mouse Zebco and a big hook and I'll catch another little bream and we'll hook him through the lip with plenty of hook sticking out and make a special trip. I thought I heard some skeptical remarks about credibility issues from the peanut gallery so, if I am going to have to prove something I may as well pile it on. Last week my seven-year-old, intensely determined grandson caught a very big bass on a little plastic octopus with a Mickey Mouse Zebco . . . with four-pound line and a #10 hook. The fish had to live in the bathtub until Daddy got home to cook him. Oddly enough, big bass are very good eating. A baked ten-pound bass stuffed with onions and celery and red bell peppers is a real crowd pleaser around here and my grandmother made catching them a special project all her life. Of course they didn't have plastic octopuses in those days so she climbed a tree and shot them with a .25/35 Winchester.

That is my boat and those little children without PFDs are my grandchildren. That's my pond and that PFD business is my business. That's your worm though if you want him. I know he is dirty, but you can wipe your hands on your shirt after you get him on your hook.

Bullnecks

in which the chicken feed boat carries . . . well . . . duck feed

I had to reactivate the old real Grumman Sport Boat this fall. It is in its original configuration and in its original location after a long, long hiatus. There it sits down at our big swampy pond in the little creek that connects the north and south ends through the "divide." Back when my family first came here in 1886 they attempted to raise rice in that pond and set a bunch of people to work ditching and built a dam across the narrow part between the north and south ends of the pond. It didn't work. All those natural weeds choked out the rice. The old, original (?) weedless (?) Evinrude Lightwin is on the stern. That boat and that engine have stayed down there in the weather so much that most of the paint has weathered off the engine. In a torrential rain, the boat will fill up and sink down so the head of the engine is barely above water but there is enough flotation in the stern seat to save it.

The reason it is down there ready to go like that is because we have been baiting up bullnecks (ringnecked ducks). You can't see a ring on their neck . . . it's on their bill . . . but they have a big, thick, short neck ("bullnecks"). They are very small diving ducks that fly like a bullet. To me there is no flying thing as spectacular as a flight of bullnecks. We harbor them on the big old swampy pond or did before it went dry. Now the old pond is full again and full of all the weeds and stuff that grew there during the drought. It is an ideal duck habitat and the wood ducks (we call them "summer ducks" because they are here year-round) are thick as fleas down there but the bullnecks who spend the summers up north were late this year. Summer ducks are dabblers and will get out of the water and walk around in the woods and eat acorns and things so they aren't as vulnerable to corn baiting as bullnecks. They stay down there around our pond all the time but bullnecks love corn and if you bait up a good-sized lake, they'll flock in there and get shot by the dozens. Somehow duck hunters have some kind of agreement with the government that allows the ones with plenty of money to get away with murder. It is illegal to pour corn in the water and then shoot the ducks that come to eat it but it is not illegal to drain a big pond and plant corn in it, and then, just before duck season, run a combine through the whole field, harvest the corn and just let it pour out of the corn picker onto the ground, then flood the pond (or pump it full). Some of these rich people around here have an eight-inch well and an irrigation pump running off an 8V92 Detroit diesel engine . . . five hundred hp . . . will fill a pond in a hurry. We think that is a travesty.

Jane and I had been spreading two hundred pounds of corn a week in the old pond using the old chicken feed boat and that three-hp engine. I was afraid that the bullnecks would have forgotten about their old refuge during the five years the pond has been dry and it looked like they had because they weren't coming to the deep holes we had spread the corn in (bullnecks can dive forty feet deep) during the week before opening day of duck season. We saw a few canvasbacks and I heard some mallards over there in the north end in Summer Duck City but no bullnecks. It cooled off for opening day (November 19) though and I was down in the woods hunting deer when daylight came and I heard the duck hunters open up down on Lake Iamonia (about seven miles away as the duck flies). It didn't take long for them to kill or run off the few ducks that were lingering around where their preseason corn used to be (the officials at public lakes are very diligent). I heard a few summer ducks fly over me on their way to our pond but not many. Our rich neighbor has a little (maybe fifteen-acre) duck pond but it is no competition for our seventy (plus or minus) acres of ideal habitat and I didn't hear a single shot from over there. I know those people were out there in their blinds with their L.L. Beans on and I know they were disappointed when they came back to the "lodge" empty-handed. Hell, some of them had probably flown all the way down from no-telling-where in the Learjet for opening day. The trouble was that their corn was in water too deep for wood ducks to reach and the bullnecks were still up north.

Then, the second week of duck season, I saw all that weather on the Weather Channel coming across up north and I said, "Jane, let's go get some more corn . . . bullnecks are coming." We hurried to the corn store and loaded up the trunk of the Kia until the springs squatted to the axle (I am not sure it has any springs . . . drives about like a go-cart). We poled the heavy loaded Grumman out to where it wasn't too weedy for the little three to run and moseyed out to the deep part. You know, that's one thing I have discovered. A heavily loaded boat will run in lily pads better than a light boat. I think it is because it pushes the lily pads aside instead of trying to run over them and getting them sucked onto the bottom, dragging on all those

Grumman rivets sticking out all along the keel. If Grumman made airplanes like they do boats they wouldn't be able to fly. Flat-bottomed boats ain't worth a flip in weeds. We baited three deep, clear holes. I unzipped the string and held the fifty-pound sack on my lap and let the corn dribble over the transom into the prop wash of the old engine. The pond is very clear and I could see the yellow corn swirling as it sank. You know, the objective is not to feed the durn ducks but just to give them a little outlet for their cravings. All ducks are greedy but I think bullnecks are the most craven of all. They live for the moment and I think that, if they can find a kernel of corn every now and then, they'll stay and eat natural food instead of flying off to get shot gobbling some real bait. That's the theory anyway.

We did the last baiting job on Wednesday and then the cold weather came down here and we had a delightful day and night of steady winter rain. Like in the old Ray Charles song it felt like it was raining all over the world. It has been a very dry fall (which is usual down here). I shot one deer that was standing in the fire lane and when he fell, it puffed up a cloud of dust. I had to dust him off like you beat a rug before I skinned him. I shot some more deer during and after the rain (the limit is twelve in Georgia and I aim to get them all . . . all these children ate the seven I killed last year by the middle of the summer). I had deer hanging all over the screen porch where I store scrap (?) wood that week. I didn't go anywhere near the pond but while I was hunting I thought I heard the whistle of bullnecks high in the sky and hoped they had found our offering. Then, early on the second Saturday of duck season, I was down in the woods when legal day came and I heard what sounded like a war down at Lake Iamonia. It only lasted about thirty seconds, though. There were a few scattered shots after the initial barrage then I heard three shots from the rich folks' pond and, then, I heard a thousand wings. I hurried down to where I could see the pond and got Momma's tiny binoculars (genuine Zeiss . . . my mother's retirement present from many years working for the Red Cross) out of my pocket and watched them land. You know, bullnecks don't just fly in and flop like mallards. They make a real production of landing on the water. For one thing, they always make a circuit or two of the whole situation to see what's what. Bullnecks fly about a hundred mph and they bank in unison in a spectacular way. Their wings whistle most marvelously the whole time. The landing of all those bullnecks was some dramatic stuff, I tell you. They hit the water doing about fifty . . . turned thirty acres white. I was mesmerized.

One year the rich man passed over our pond in his Learjet and noticed those ducks. Then, about daylight every morning, that same jet flew very low over the pond and scared the ducks off. Do you think I was dismayed and perplexed and helpless? Hell no, I had gone to school with his pilot and all I had to do was go to the airport and have a few words with him when he landed . . . haven't seen that jet over our place again. You want to know what I said? "Which seat you sit in?" I asked and when he told me he sat in the left seat, I said, "Well, if you fly over that pond and notice a little flash of light from down there you better swap seats in a hurry."

Eating Ducks

in which you will learn the English notion about how to eat gamebirds

So, one might want to know, will I eat a wild duck? Shoot yes. I love them and a bullneck is my favorite. They have very dark meat kind of like a jacksnipe and it is very gamy and flavorful . . . makes my wings want to whistle. I don't break the game laws especially not on migratory birds. Those ducks belong to everybody in the country. My grandfather had an understanding with the game warden. He told him that he would not allow any game laws to be broken on our place if the warden would not come aggravating people all the time. Though we have been through dozens of game wardens (a tough and dangerous job if there ever was one) since then I have always had an agreement with them, too. They know we bait those ducks on that big pond and sometimes they slip down there just to see what it looked like back in the good old days. I do not shoot baited ducks or any other kind of baited animal. I think corn hunters are the sorriest kinds of "sportsmen." Well, maybe not *the* sorriest. Those Florida road hunters who sit in the little swivel chair on top of the dog box in the pickup truck alongside the road and drink beer and talk on the CB while they wait for some poor dog-tired deer to stagger out into the highway are the actual sorriest. I shoot my ducks at one of our other ponds or in the Black Hole (which I'll explain sometime) where the only bait is what comes naturally. I always wait until the last day of the season so, when they fly off, they won't go somewhere else and get crippled. I am not greedy. I just need a little taste. A lot of times what I get is a poor cripple where some yahoo didn't know the range of a durn shotgun.

You know, the British have some unusual notions about how to eat gamebirds. They like them "well hung." My grandfather's people came over here after the industrial revolution starved them off their cottage looms in Liverpool and they brought their peculiar epicurean notions with them and I inherited some of them. A bullneck is a delicious bird and the wound around the shot is the most delicious part. You have to watch these durn modern iron shot, though . . . break a tooth. I'll eat a wood duck, too, and I have even eaten a mallard (you can buy them at the grocery store) and once, when I was a boy, a black duck (which are actually brown . . . taste about like a mallard) but bullnecks are my favorite waterfowl. Oops, I forgot jacksnipes. That is a most exquisitely gamy and flavorful little morsel right there . . . worth about thirty bucks each considering how many shotgun shells it takes for me to finally hit one of the little zigzag bullets. I never got to eat any jacksnipes until after my mother died. Every time I would come in with my shotgun (my grandfather's Model 12, sixteen-gauge) my mother would come hobbling out (killed a mule with a motorcycle when she was sixteen years old) and say, "All I need is one of those bullnecks. You can hang him and those jacksnipes out on the porch for me. They'll be ready in four or five days as warm as it is."

Ducks, Slingshots, and Winter Camping

in which, although I do not break game laws,
I become an accessory after the fact

After I wrote that story about baiting up the bullnecks, I kept on thinking about ducks. I like ducks. I like their attitude. They just live for the moment and don't worry about anything. They take it as it comes sort of like the ninety-five-year-old man who married the seventeen-year-old girl. When the doctor tried to warn him of the health risk in that situation, he said, "Well, if it kills her, it kills her." Anyway, ducks think they can fly away from anything and don't have sense enough to notice that old Charley and Bessy fell from the sky while they were leaving. They just fly happily to another place and eat a little more corn. You know, I have tried to pattern my life sort of like that . . . working pretty good so far.

When I was young, I used to hunt summer ducks back in the Ochlocknee River swamp. What it is back there is a little meandering river that has meandered all out through the woods and left a bunch of little oxbow ponds completely isolated from the main river. It is a long way back in there and no good road and the river itself is only navigable in a boat when it is pretty high and the fall is usually so dry that it is just a trickle . . . hard to get to . . . unless you are a duck . . . or me. I used to drag a tin canoe (yes, Virginia) back there and camp and kill ducks. The reason I wanted the canoe was because the water in those cutoff holes is cold and deep and I have never shot a duck in my life that didn't fall in cold and deep water. Before the parallel evolution that caused errant geniuses all over the world to simultaneously invent the tin canoe the day after tin was invented, I used to have to pull off all my clothes and swim for the durn duck. Whooee, not only was the water cold, there are some kind of little animals or plants in the weeds that bite hell out of you. Of course while you are floundering around out there getting the duck you are too numb to notice but after you have put your clothes back on (kind of hard to do without a towel) you start itching all over. It was aggravating having to drag the tin canoe that four or five miles through the woods but it wasn't nearly as aggravating as swimming for those ducks was and, besides, I always left the canoe and the next season it would still be there . . . if I could find it. You know, all those landmarks look the same

417

back in a place like that but it is easy to find your way out. You just walk up-hill for a while and pretty soon you'll come to something recognizable but lateral searches are kind of confusing. I have swum for a duck a lot of times I tell you.

Another duck story is about that terrible old booger I used to mess around with. He was outrageous. He was the original owner of the bait store where I get most of my speckled perch lore. I could write a whole book about him but nobody would believe it. One time I took him with me to St. Marks where the federal wildlife refuge is. That's another government project that failed to do what it was supposed to do. Back in the thirties the government took over about fifty miles of the marshy coast around the St. Marks River. That was a good thing because that place was one of the most wonderful wildlife habitats in the world . . . as good as Aransas Pass in Texas. Then they ran the CCC boys and the WPA in there and ruined it. What they did was build a bunch of dikes to separate the fresh water from the salt. A lot of the ducks started bypassing the place and the geese completely changed their flyway and have never come back. I don't understand government projects at all. Now they say they need billions to "restore" the Everglades. What the hell are they going to do with the money? Three or four of these big Komatsu excavators would be all it would take to dig a bunch of holes in those dikes they built and let the water run out into those cane fields and that would be that. In the St. Marks Refuge, one of the imported alien grass species they introduced to "improve" that place has gotten out of hand so they are having to herbicide the whole freshwater side and start all over. Jesus. Just send Mr. Komatsu down one of the "hiking trails" and dig a hole in the levee and let the ocean back in there with that grass and see how it likes living in a salt marsh.

I sort of got off the subject of my old buddy and the ducks but I haven't forgotten. We launched the boat (old Lone Star semi-V aluminum with an old five-hp Johnson pump-prime-style engine) at the boat ramp by the old Spanish Fort (San Marcos De Apalachee) and started easing down the river to go fishing on the oyster bars out by the mouth where there were plenty of redfish and sheepheads. As soon as we got going good, the old man noticed these little ducks (lesser scaups . . . oh, Lordy . . . I have to interrupt again but this isn't a rant at least).

When Wes was a boy, we were fishing in the bay out from our old coast house in the winter with his cousin. We were catching these little white trout (similar to a speckled trout but without specks . . . "speckless trout" we called them). There were these little, tiny ducks flying by. Sometimes they would light in the water and mess around diving down into the grass beds. "What kind of little, tiny ducks are those?" asked the cousin. "I don't know, 'less 'ey're scaups," answered Wes.

So, the scaups were flushing ahead of the boat and flying a little way and setting back down . . . just living for the moment. As that cycle repeated itself they became more and more habituated . . . probably said to themselves, "Here them sombitches come again. Ain't nothing to them though. We are perfectly safe in this federally protected refuge. We'll stay here a little longer and eat some more of these periwinkles off this grass . . . ain't they delicious?" Finally they let us get so close that, as they took off, that old booger stood up in the bow of the boat, reached in his pocket, pulled out a tiny slingshot, and killed one in the air with a piece of lead he had cut off an automobile wheel weight with a pair of electrician's pliers Fortunately there was no federal game warden hiding in the needle rushes and we were able to retrieve the little duck and hide him without getting locked up and, fortunately, the old man was so disgusted with how tiny he was that I was able to convince him not to do that anymore. You know, he is the same one who rigged up the electric fuel pump to supply a three-eighth-inch hose of water up his britches leg so he could stand up in the boat at the crowded speckled perch hole and pee for ten minutes in front of all those people.

As another aside, my grandson and Jane were forced to make a slingshot while they were stranded at his school waiting for some complication to become resolved. They didn't have any materials or tools except for some big rubber bands, which prompted the idea in the first place. They broke and gnawed a little crotch out of a pecan limb they found in the schoolyard and used his shoelaces to tie with and made a pouch out of a piece of used duct tape I had been using to keep the radio antenna pulled down on Jane's car so it would quit hanging up on bushes in the woods all the time. It is one of those nonretractable stainless-steel wires that comes out at a rakish angle above the door . . . catches on limbs and stuff when you forget and back up. It is so strong that it will eventually break the limb loose and spring back and hit the top of the car and make a very startling noise. You know, jackleggery is a wonderful thing for the evolution of technology. That duct tape is a much better slingshot bucket than leather. I am glad they didn't have a pair of electrician's pliers or the wheels would be out of balance. Even at that, I bet there isn't a single scaup left at that schoolyard.

We used to go camping down at the coast all the time when the boys were little. Hell, we used to keep them out of school in the wintertime if the weather was too good for school. That was back when it was possible to learn some of the essentials they taught in schools from other sources so, if you missed a day or two, it wasn't quite so catastrophic as it is now that they have to learn soccer and ballet and "computer science" and all, too. We always went to the coast if one of them was sick. Lying in the warm sun on a little palm-and-cedar island is the best way in the world to cure the school flu. Now sick children have to go to school so they won't miss the next in the sequence of computerized math games. I'll control myself now and finish the story.

There is nothing in the world like lying in your sleeping bag on a little high spot in the marsh on a cold, perfectly clear, absolutely calm winter night so far from any civilization that you can't see the glow in the sky of any man-made light. One of my favorite places is east of Econfina Creek (there are two Econfina Creeks, this is the one east of St. Marks). It is far enough from Tallahassee that you can't see that light and far enough from Perry that you can't see that either. The coast is a little higher there and there are plenty of places to camp. There is even a little cedar-and-palm island about a mile offshore out on the flats but I like to be closer to the marsh so I can listen to the ducks. Boy, they love to whoop it up at night. They are like a bunch of cooped-up businessmen turned aloose at a wild convention. Mostly they'll be redheads but I have seen all sorts of ducks down at the coast. We even have a few European widgeons show up around here. You know, if you can fly a hundred miles an hour and only live for the moment so you don't have to check any baggage you can take off anytime you want to and the whole world is yours. Dang.

Jet Ski Slingshot

*in which a marine-grade instrument for administering
corporal punishment is recommended*

I read a good little bit of what I call "sensible boat literature" and in the "Opinions" section, there has been some mention of rudeness on the water and what to do about it. I don't think there is any conventional solution. I think that way because I tried it for years and years with no success whatsoever. The whole trouble is that rudeness is not against the law and, even if it was, the movers and shakers have lots of more important things to do than fool around with litterbugs and people who will run you out of the channel or wash you up on the spoil bank with their wake. One of those important things is to perform "safety checks."

I don't think there are but two things to do about rudeness on the water: One is to move to someplace with extremely shallow water and lots of oyster shells and rocks. Of course down here in the Big Bend of Florida where I stay there is still an occasional airboat but you can hear them four miles away and get ready for the other thing . . .

Which . . . corporal punishment is not quite as simple as abdication. Each case is slightly different. One time, I was sitting on the beach on the bayside of a little island watching the sunset and drinking a carefully hoarded can of cheap beer when a party boat came hauling ass into the little cove I was in and anchored just about the time the land breeze made up as the sun went down. In a minute, the breeze brought me some loud Rolling Stones and three big Styrofoam cups, three little potato chip bags, and three identical cardboard boxes with little oil slicks around them. Many years of parenthood, schoolteaching, and grandparenthood have taught me how to control my temper, nevertheless I calculated that it was time to take action. I swam out to that boat and swarmed over the transom like in an old Howard Pyle picture. Though I was able to break the plastic fitting that held a six-foot-long fiberglass antenna, I was unable to snatch but about eight feet of slack in the tough wire that conveyed the transmissions . . . and it was a sixteen-foot boat. I did manage to clip two of the party animals pretty good around the hips and thighs before they could crowd into the safe zone but one of them got off scot-free.

Jet Ski nincompoops are vulnerable to being shot by things like BB guns.

Of course, a standard El-Cheapo child's toy is too inaccurate and weak to do much good unless you are real close but a good pellet gun will get them quite a distance away. Neither thing is marine-grade equipment though. Fortunately, because of many years of childhood devilry, I am an expert with an ordinary slingshot. Not only is a slingshot marine-grade equipment but it shoots hard and, in the right hands, accurately and is easy to hide after the shot. One of the reasons for my early success with that implement is an abundance of iron ore rocks, which are found in the clay soil of this region. In the thousands of years that these little pellets have lain embedded in the basic clay the pH has partially reduced the ore back to its element and these little round rocks are quite dense . . . just right . . . not heavy enough to penetrate human skin, usually, but they hit hard. I never go to the coast without a pocketful and my slingshot. Why, just the other morning, I scored a double. I was sailing slowly out of the river with the dying land breeze in my little boat, well out of the channel, when an enormous sportfisherman pulling a huge wake and stifling pall of black, oily smoke from a pair of diesel engines severely overloaded with wheel tried to wash me up on the spoil bank. Following close behind this monster playing skip-dee-doo with the stern wave was a Jet Ski. He elevated his stern just as he jumped across right in front of me . . . I was so quick that I was able to nail him and shoot at the sport on the flying bridge, too, then hide my slingshot without discovery. Unfortunately, although I got the Jet Ski artist right in the middle, I missed the far shot at the boat driver. I always shoot just by instinct and it might have been that I was distracted by the sight of a woman standing beside him who had both bare hips either side of (I assume) a hidden string. Anyway, I hit the moon instead of the driver. Damn . . . but she was guilty by association.

Getting caught is rare. People who do things that are mindless do it because they are mindless people. Once I shot the same man five times in the backside, side of the head, and neck with mud snails (ran out of iron ore rocks . . . it was a bad trip) as he sat on the rock jetty, fishing in the manmade shrimp boat cut through a barrier island, drinking beer and eating potato chips and throwing the cans and trash into the water. He thought that horseflies were biting him (as indeed they were but he was too stupid to notice that). Mud snails are not as dense as iron ore rocks and this man was too dense to suit me so I shot him in the love handle with a lead sinker that I found on the ground in the other litter. He was quite overweight and out of shape and it took him fifteen minutes of clawing and squirming around before he was able to scramble back up onto the slick granite rocks of the jetty. I heard him proclaim to his companion (who had been sitting in the truck drinking beer and eating out of plastic bags and throwing the cans and trash out the window), "I ain't never gonna come back to this son-of-a-bitch place . . . something bit the pluperfect shit out of me down there . . . bit me right through my shirt. Just look-a-here at this here son-of-a-bitch whelp on my side right here." "I bet your shirt wasn't pulled down." she replied through a mouth full of half-masticated yellow cheese turdules. I was even called over to witness the injury. "Dang." I said, "A horsefly did that? You ought to have stayed home and watched the TV."

See what I am trying to tell you? If I had gone to the courthouse and demanded that the man-in-charge send somebody out there to arrest this fool for littering, it would have come to nothing good. Though the man I shot will never change his ways, he might not sit quite so complacently, surrounded by his trash, on the rocks at the pass again . . . might take my advice and stay home to watch wrestling and infomercials on the TV with the AC where nothing will bite him except them chips and all that beer.

How to Make a Jet Ski Slingshot

Contrary to popular hype (as usual) the best slingshot rubbers are not surgical rubber tubing but ordinary big, flat rubber bands (the translucent latex kind like they tie up bunches of turnips with). I like three to the side but I like to shoot hard . . . two will work fine. Tie the ends to the crotch and the bucket with sections of good polyester jogging shoelace with a lark's head knot lubricated with lemon-fresh Joy through the rubber bands. For deliberate, very accurate long-range work, it is best if the shoelaces to the bucket are sort of long so as to allow full extension of the arms (some six feet according to Leonardo) when the rubbers run out of elasticity. All that length is just to improve the muscle memory for accurate alignment of the arms with the flight of the projectile. There is no need to stretch the rubber anywhere near that far . . . two or three feet is plenty to accelerate a little rock to hull speed. For quick, out-of-pocket, rapid-fire work, it is best if everything is kept as compact as possible to avoid the possibility of you standing there in the face of the shot fool with your best Charlie Chaplin look and eighteen inches of rubber and a slingshot bucket (Yankees, coastal westerners, and South Floridians call it a "pouch" I am told) hanging out of your pocket. The crotch should be small, too. I like dogwood best but it is not universal in distribution and I once had a crab apple crotch that I liked almost as well. Use it until it is polished all over from the tough skin of your hands.

Learning to Shoot

That's the trick. Ain't no point to it if you can't hit. The best stance is to hold the slingshot sideways. That arranges the tendons and thews of the arms and hands most naturally and helps prevent the terrible "slingshot elbow" syndrome. For rapid-fire work, you can hold a supply of rocks in your mouth like Demosthenes. That'll help with the Charlie Chaplin look. The best target is the target at hand. I am afraid that in my formative years, I did some terrible things. Our mailbox and the weather vane looked like beaten silver and the cats around here developed an uncanny alertness that, contrary to conventional wisdom, appeared to be passed on to their off-spring. I got to where I could hit a running squirrel either on the ground or in the tree some one out of ten shots, which doesn't seem too good until you remember that I could shoot all ten of those shots at the same squirrel before he could squirrel around to the other side of the trunk of the tree. My sisters and I used to skin them and boil them up in a can in the fetal position . . . head, tail, and all (except foots) . . . a little pepper and salt, maybe an onion to season the broth. Once, when I was about ten, I hit a flying crow with a bunkie marble hard enough to knock him out. I kept him as a pet until I realized that his personality was so objectionable that he was not actually a pleasant companion so I took him to school and sold him to a classmate who kept him for almost thirty years. He has a wife who acts exactly like that crow and cost a lot more.

I don't hold out all that much hope for the restoration of dignity and logic upon the waters of the world. I think it is going to take a good stiff ice age to reinstitute a little selective stress on us humans so we won't have enough environmental slack to coddle up such an overload of stupid people with their ridiculous excesses. But until then, I know a place that is too shallow and rocky for anybody but a fool like me . . . but just in case . . .

The Time My Buddy
Almost Lost the Outboard Motor

in which a drowned outboard motor responds to CPR

I have a buddy who has been a paraplegic since the late sixties. He has full use of his arms and a good little bit of the rest of him too . . . like his head. After he got out of the hospital and got to where he could make that wheelchair do a little bit of what he wanted it to and got his business percolating up a little money, he decided to rig up a boat to suit him. He bought one of those wide butt-head aluminum skiffs and a twenty-horse outboard. He built some good floorboards and a fold-up ramp in the bow sort of like a landing craft. With that rig, he could push his boat off the trailer, flop his ramp down and roll over the bow and back to the stern, and run the engine right from his wheelchair—and he could push up to the bank get out just as easily. It was a good working rig and everything would have been fine except Buddy is sort of a reckless and careless person by nature.

One time he and his wife decided to go way up into the wilds of some of the dead lakes. Those are places where a lot of the rivers around here sort of lose their way in thickets and swamps after they get out of the hills and into the flatwoods. The fishing is very good back in there because the people are usually pretty scarce so places like that are attractive to folks like him and me. It is possible to get stranded in all those creeks and sloughs and lose your way and feed a lot of mosquitoes before you can get back out. There is a legend about a man named Tate who got tangled up in some of that kind of country between the Ochlocknee and Apalachicola Rivers in the panhandle of Florida. Like a lot of those kinds of places it is hard to tell which river system "Tate's Hell swamp" is actually associated with. Might be "Whiskey George Creek" for all I know. Anyway, this old Tate went back in there around the turn of the last century for some reason or other and couldn't figure out which way was the right way and stayed lost back in there for about a year (exact dates and duration depend on who is telling the story). When old Tate finally came staggering out, his hair as white as snow where it had been black as smut before, and he was skinny and et up by skeeters and had scratches all over his shanks . . . no shoes, no hat . . . clothes in rags. When they said, "Damn . . . Tate, where you been all this time?" He answered,

"I've been in Hell boys," and keeled over and died.

Well, it didn't happen to Buddy quite as bad as that . . . but he did get himself in a bunch of trouble back in there. He and his wife were about twelve miles back in the wilds in his excellent rig. He had just checked the gas to make sure he hadn't burned more than half of it and they were thinking about heading back to the semi-civilization of the boat ramp because they already had a mess of those big old stumpknockers and redbellies when all of a sudden, the drone of the engine ceased so abruptly that the silence was deafening. He said it went, "Moom, moom, moom, moom, moop . . ." The boat finally eased to a stop and they could hear the crickets, cicadas, and frogs singing their afternoon song . . . birds in the bushes . . . bream popping the bugs on the surface of the water and the little diminishing wavelets of their passage slapping on the steel gas tank of the outboard motor where it was floating upside down about a quarter of a mile back.

So Buddy got his paddle and sculled back there to find out what he could. I don't know if it is a regional thing or what, but freshwater fishermen (some professional) around here used to scull over the bow of the boat. Some of them used a special little short paddle and rested the shank of it up their forearm while they zigged and zagged the blade in the water and some of them (like me) use a full-length paddle and sort of hold the shaft between their neck and collarbone. You can hold a boat pretty well against the current (or a little breeze) while you dangle your worm in one little likely spot after another but it is another almost lost art now that most fishermen (some professional) have degenerated down so completely to those electric trolling motors. I guess it is too undignified for a man who professes to need a sport utility vehicle that costs more than a college education to be seen propelling a boat without the benefit of machinery. About the only vestige of the old lore left is that they run those motors over the bow while they fish. Some of them even have a little remote-control thing like for a TV, which if it is like the one I have for my shop radio is liable to ignore the command to steer this way or that and run you up into the bushes. I heard a fishing newsman on the radio say that there are some new ones that respond to voice command. I wonder how they react to profanity.

I got off the track there for a little minute and left Buddy and his wife in that terrible fix way back in the swamp where old Tate roosted with the moccasins and alligators. I told you that he was smart and one of the smartest things he ever did was to pay attention to one of my tirades about how stupid it is to trust an outboard motor so he had his oars. Too bad I neglected to rant about how you need to make a little ritual twist on the clamp screws every time you think about it and not trust any little nylon cord hooked up to an eyebolt to hold twenty horses when they hop off the transom and take off on their own.

It was easy for Buddy to find his motor with that big red buoy marking the spot. When they got back where the gas tank was floating, they discovered that it was still hooked up down there. That's unusual, too, because I have found out that most outboard engine problems are because those little half-assed clip-on gas hose things ain't but about half clipped on or else have clipped the O-ring about half in two and are letting air in the line so what the engine is getting is about half air. Enough of that, too. They tried to pull the engine up with the gas hose but could tell that it would pull off before they could get it high enough to grab it. Then they spent about half an hour trying to hook it with the anchor but, when Tate's mosquitoes started finding out the good news, they realized that it was time to get serious with this retrieval project or else get those oars and start trying to pull that unmanageable, butt-head tub back to the ramp. Buddy got out of his wheelchair, climbed over the side, took a deep breath, and followed the hose down to the engine. Luckily the water was shallow enough so that he could press his butt down in the mud and barely lift the engine up high enough for his wife to grab. It took two or three frantic tries and he was so stuck in the mud after each attempt that he almost drowned trying to scramble loose so he could come up for a breath of air but they finally got the heavy engine back in the boat.

Now, Buddy is a good, old-style intuitive mechanic . . . meaning that he don't have to have the book or any set ritual to get started doing what he has to do. The skeeters were eating them both up when he got back in the boat, it was getting dark, and he couldn't see what to do to get this engine running so he decided to just clamp it on the stern and make one try to start it without even taking the spark plugs out. But when he tried to pull the rope, the engine was locked up from all that water it had swallowed when it hopped off the transom running like that. Buddy said that by then, he was wiping those mosquitoes off by the bloody handful so he just pulled on the rope steadily, as hard as he could, and gradually he got a little and then a little more as the water in the cylinders leaked past the rings. Finally he had struggled both cylinders through a couple of compression strokes and it got to feeling sort of normal and he pulled it a bunch of times like you have to do a chain saw and squeezed the gas line bulb and worked the choke and all for a long time while his wife wiped the skeeters off both of them. He wound up having to cut the gas line near the engine end and used the fuel bulb to squirt gas into the venturi of the carburetor while he pulled and finally the engine backfired a gout of flaming gas into his lap and acted like it wanted to run so he gnawed the one-shot, plastic hose clamp off the titty of the connector fitting, hooked her back up, and cranked up and headed for home. Unfortunately, in accordance with their luck, they had squirted too much gas around the outfit back there and gave out a good bit short of the ramp and had to row anyway.

When he told me about it later on, we went and had a look at the engine (freshwater immersion leaves an engine as good as new). We figured that spark-plug-in purging operation wouldn't have worked if the engine had had points. Us old die-hard square-nut mechanics can say what we want to, but electronic ignition is a good thing. It is a cop-out not to like it because we don't understand that little "module" like we do points, condensers, and spark coils. What I understand about those is that they are, all three, treacherous . . . them and the wires and the plugs. I would certainly rather carry an extra module (even if I don't understand it) than a flywheel puller. Buddy said, "Hell, if it hadda had fuel injection, it might have beat us back to the ramp."

Land Breeze

*in which the most insidious of human accomplishments
ain't in it with the joy of the land breeze*

You know, I read all the Hornblower books when I was a boy. C. S. Forrester was a good writer and gave me a strong feeling for the delights of the land breeze that took my hero away from the impotence of being landbound on half pay and put him where he was in control. You don't have to have a seventy-four-gun ship of the line and be on the way to "The Far Side of the World" (oops, that was Patrick O'Brian) to appreciate a land breeze and you don't even have to have a sailboat but that's how it is best. There are few joys better than to have that delicious-smelling, startlingly cool, wonderfully fair wind come to fill the sails and take you out of a miserable, helpless fix. Sailing away is one part of it but coasting along is just fine, too. It is hard to go to bed when your watch is up while the land breeze is blowing. Reading Hornblower books and some of my other doings are responsible for how I turned out to be not able to properly appreciate modern society as we know it. I'll spare you all but one example. Air-conditioning is, I believe, the most insidious of human accomplishments. I'll try to explain why I think that as briefly as I can.

It is hotter than hell in South Georgia in the summertime. During a cold winter and during a wet and stormy spring, it is hard to imagine that the summer is really all that bad. But it is. It is hot during the middle of the day and the nights are hot, too. The old farmer's saying is that the first time you have to throw off the covers is when you plant peanuts. We used to raise peanuts back when I was young. It is a tricky business . . . and, like tobacco, well regulated by the government. Peanuts are a low-growing, running-style vine and after one or two (usually just one) passes with the cultivators, they close up the rows and are best left alone. Peanuts are legumes and make their own nitrogen. They like sandy, impoverished soil like old worn-out cotton land and, because of that, there aren't that many weeds that can outgrow peanuts except for other legumes like beggar lice and coffee weed and cursed *Crotolaria* (a taxpayer-funded government introduction like kudzu and Johnson grass). There used to be a breed of solemn stoics who would wade all around in their peanuts and pull coffee weeds all summer long but my family never subscribed to that horrendous masochism. We went to the coast after the peanuts were laid by and let the damn beggar lice do their worst while the peanuts did what they could.

It is cooler at the coast than it is up inland. The sun is just as hot down there, but the water doesn't heat the air like the land does. I don't guess the wild people of long ago had it so bad back when there were all those trees to shade the dirt but now that we have pushed up the trees to make all these peanut fields and interstates and shopping malls, the sun has a lot more baldness to cook. When such a place as a hundred-acre parking lot with all those egg-frying-hot cars gets to cooking good, there is a paper-airplane-flying thermal coming off it that is spectacular. I wonder how long a paper airplane can last up on the roof of a hospital before it rots away.

Anyway, it isn't so uncomfortably hot at the coast but, as I said before, the best pursuit of mankind is not comfort but joy and there is nothing like the joy of a land breeze after a hot summer day. What usually happens on the hottest days, when the sun shines down from a perfectly clear sky from about six in the morning to eight thirty at night, is that the land gets so hot that the plants droop and all the animals have to take shelter. Doodlebugs dig deeper into the sand and ants go in the hole. Snakes and lizards hunt the shade. All that hot air rushing up into the sky is a buzzard's delight. Once I saw an osprey carrying a big mullet by the head. The fish was so big that the bird could hardly keep him out of the water. Times were tough, though, because it had been a windy day and, when it is rough, ospreys have a hard time seeing fish so the bird didn't want to let go. She flapped as hard as she (I guess . . . ain't much difference except size) could toward the land with the tail of the fish tipping the waves. She was headed straight for the parking lot of the St. Teresa boat ramp and, when she got there, her troubles were over. She soared up into the sky like that mullet was a pinfish and effortlessly gained enough altitude to easily make it to her ancient nest where her two already-fledged-out babies were jumping up and down in anticipation. "That's how you do it, y'all," I bet she told them.

We don't have any air conditioner at our coast house. The house is built such that we can open it up twelve feet on both the bayside and seaside. The wind can blow right through the place and it is not uncommon to find all the paper plates and napkins from supper stuck to the seaside screen. My mother used to sleep right in the middle of the place on a mattress on the floor to get the goody out of the land breeze and it was not uncommon to find her sheet stuck to the screen wire in the morning. One night, an off-shore thunderstorm came up and drew such a land breeze through the place that I thought I better close the windward side just to keep the old raggedy furniture in the house. Momma was lying there clutching her wildly flapping sheet with fingers, teeth, and toes. The flying tails were popping her flanks like little whips. "You ain't about to close up are you?" she demanded when I began to batten down.

We have a bunch of old rusty fans at the coast house for the rare times when there is no breeze. The Chinese have been making some pretty good-looking retro-style fans and we bought some of them for an amazingly cheap price at Big Lots (you ought to have felt the heat from the parking lot) but they ain't in it with the real thing. A regular old box fan is pretty good. They blew harder back when they had metal blades but the new plastic ones don't blow flakes of rust in the bed with you. I talked to a shrimper who had trawled up a box fan and he said that when he got home, he rinsed it off and let it dry and plugged it in and it ran fine but only on high . . . sort of out of balance from the barnacles. My favorite fan of all time was a rusty old tall-style Vornado we had at the old coast house. It had the most wonderful sound to it. One time I was trudging down the hall in the biology building at FSU when I was overcome by an amazing feeling of nostalgia. It turned out that they had set up a Vornado fan exactly like the old coast house fan to blow the ether fumes out of the fruit fly lab. If the fumes had been gin, it would have been perfect. What finally happened to the old coast house Vornado was interesting. First the sheet-metal Kort nozzle rusted off it, that and the screen that was supposed to keep little children from sticking their fingers in there. The blades were made out of some primitive, very good plastic and held up fine. The stand was made out of thick-enough pipe so it continued to support the motor. Of course the switch defected first and we just hot-wired it. It ran for years in its naked stage and would take a towel away from a small child in a second and leave him (or her) standing there in naked confusion. Nakedness gets nakedness—ain't that appropriate? Anyway, what killed it was when the armature core swole up so that it starting hitting the field coils. It started knocking and then it threw sparks and locked up and went to stinking. My favorite fan now is the old Hunter Zephiar. If the Chinese ever copy that exactly they'll have something a hell of a lot better than these nickel-plated cuties with no visible pitch to the blades. They can leave off all that excessive wire to the guard, too. How the hell is a child going to learn about machinery if she (or he) can't stick her finger in the fan. How in hell is a child going to learn about combustion if they can't play with matches and only have access to "childproof" butane lighters. My son says that impotent warnings . . . verbal instructions that carry no consequences because of excesses of safeguards . . . are responsible for the way children routinely ignore what people tell them. "Do Not Allow Body Parts to Contact Moving Fan Blades" doesn't teach anybody anything. When I was four years old my mother taught me how to open a box of matches and extract one, close the box, and strike the match, first try . . . with my toes. Jesus, y'all no wonder all these kids want to do is play video games and abuse substances.

My nearest neighbors at the coast aren't quite as rich as those multimillionaires down there on the west end of the island but they are rich enough to maintain an air conditioner in this destructive environment. Of course they have to change it out at least once a year (only an extravagant fool puts central-heat-and-air in a coast house). Despite the way their air conditioner sounds as it approaches change-out time, the neighbor's window unit ain't but about fifteen thousand BTUs and maintaining that level of comfort is not as bad a strain on the family budget as, say, keeping an SUV fed. The logistics of the change-out are sort of aggravating . . . transportation of the new unit and disposal of the old being the main thing. Because of experience (and the desire for instant gratification of the comfort zone) it doesn't take them long to get the thing in the window and plugged in, but one time, back when they were less experienced, they brought one over that had the wrong kind of 220-volt plug on it. I thought they were fixing to have a heatstroke over there cussing and fuming. Because of my childhood experiences, I would have hot-wired it, but they had to go all the way back to the mainland and contract with a certified electrician who told them that they had to "upgrade" the service to handle the draw of the heat strip in the new machine. Because of certain problems of inaccessibility with this island, it took all summer and they never did discover the land breeze because they went home and stayed home until the "upgrade" was complete and, then, when they came back on the Fourth, a shrimp boat anchored on the electric cable to the island and uprooted the whole shebang and they never did get any comfort.

The pitiful thing is that they (and a bunch of other like-minded people) love to come to the coast. They sit out on their deck and watch one of the prettiest sunsets you ever saw. It has usually just rained on the mainland and there are cumulus clouds reaching all the way to the stratosphere. Many times there is spectacular lightning in the tops of the clouds as the sun goes down and the convection collapses. Because the woods are wet from the rain, there are usually layers of haze close to the horizon that magnify the setting sun and, sometimes, make two or three sunsets to watch as it passes through the layers. Despite the sunset, it usually hasn't cooled off all that much and, usually because of the instant collapse of convection as the land cools from evaporation of the fresh rain, the sea breeze that makes the daytime tolerable dies immediately. As soon as the rim of the sun disappears below the jagged line of trees on the mainland, our neighbors quit the deck and scurry inside to watch the TV, rattle ice, and unwrap supper. The air conditioner is running wide open and they have no idea when the land breeze makes up. You can see it coming across the bay in the twilight. The reflections of the light from the clouds begin to sparkle as the ripples come toward us. Then there is that deliciously cold goose-bump breeze and the smell of fresh-rained-on piney woods. The spectacle of the lightning in the dark makes it hard to go to bed. What joy . . . damn near as good as sailing.

Embarrassment

in which I become tempted to search for lost treasure . . . well almost

Well, it wasn't me . . . this time . . . it was somebody else. I learned a long time ago to make sure I do anything that might turn out to be embarrassing when I am hid out. Unfortunately there are a lot of people who haven't learned this trick and so make fools of themselves right in plain view of heartless observers . . . like me. Two of these three incidents I am fixing to relate happened because of the same storm and the other ridiculous situation was created by the cause of that storm. I'll explain.

What happened while we were at the coast this last time was that a tropical depression came across the south part of the peninsula of Florida. The counterclockwise rotation around this thing caused a perfect reversal of the flow of weather that we have had all year where storms were drawn to the northeast off the Gulf of Mexico inland right through my stomping grounds and all the way up the whole East Coast of the US all the way to Canada . . . all year long. I don't know about y'all up there, but it has begun to be sort of tiresome down here. This new phenomenon drew the weather off the land for a change and, for the first time, it cleared up and the pressure went up and it got as pretty as all get-out. Poor cooped-up desperadoes bailed out of the house (or the office) and hooked up the boat and hauled it to the coast even though it was a Wednesday.

We were already at the coast but had been cooped up in the house all week dashing out for a brief sortie with every little lull. Of course we got wet a lot but we bore it with dignity and there is nothing wrong with being wet if you know how to be dignified about it. The first undignified situation involved this big (thirty-five-foot?) house-style sailboat . . . you know the kind . . . big and wide with a raised deck about three feet above the real sheer of the boat and windows all around and a cockpit sitting on top of all that about seven feet above the water. Though this thing had a little short mast and a roller-furled jib, the jib was furled and the mast only had halyards slapping the aluminum. The boat was under way with the engine when it hove into view coming into our cove. I quickly grabbed the knobblers and examined the state of seamanship on board. Two fenders were deployed on the port side and three to starboard and there were two (not one but *two*) barbecue things on the taffrail. The cockpit was so full of people that it was impossible to make a head count. Not only were they jammed in there as tight as possible, they were listening to some music so they were bobbing and waving their heads so you couldn't tell which was which but I believe there were between nine and eleven people. It was easy to see the captain because he had on a Greek fisherman's hat (wool, in Florida, in August) and was standing behind a tubular stainless-steel wheel big enough to steer a destroyer with. Which was a good thing because he needed it to hold him up when he ran hard onto "Nissan Propeller/Blue Goose Bar." Fortunately, the bar shoals up real abruptly and is just a hard sandbar so the boat did not slide very far up on there and he, aided by the strong rising tide current and that big steering wheel and powerful engine, was able to wiggle off. He backed her off a little way and set what looked like about a twenty-pound, welded-steel imitation of a Simpson Lawrence plough anchor on about fifty feet of bright yellow five-eighth-inch line of some kind. With that, several of the women in the crew trotted forward to the prow of this vessel and pulled off their shirts and shorts, revealing that they had already put on their bathing suits in readiness for the cruise, and dove into the murky yellow water that had just recently run out of the Carrabelle River. They splashed around in there whooping and squealing so loud that I was discomfited from thinking about all the little sharks that had been making such a nuisance of themselves while we were trying to fish in that very place earlier that morning. Finally they smelled the cooking going on at both the barbecues and scrambled up the high sides of the vessel on a little dangerous-looking ladder made out of aluminum tubing and polyethylene steps held on by sheet-metal screws (I told you I have some good binoculars, didn't I?). While all this was going on, an enormous, brand-new SUV as big as an EMT ambulance (you thought I was going to say "UPS truck" didn't you?) came down the sand bed these nincompoops over here call a road and parked in the narrows just past our house and a little family got out. They left all the doors and tailgate open so the unfamiliarly hot sun wouldn't make the genuine leather seat covers so hot that they would get their fannies burned when they got back in. Anyway, these folks walked down to the bayside beach to look at all the wonders. They walked way on to the west and saw many things and picked up a bunch of shells. There was a little boy who found a large, dead horseshoe crab that he was determined to keep despite what looked like earnest entreaties from his parents and what I took to be a much older brother. I know just exactly how the kid felt. Every little boy needs a dead horseshoe crab to decorate his room with. I had several when I was a little boy. When the cat came by the door of my room, she always went through the motions of trying to bury something even though there was nothing to bury and no dirt to bury it in. Anyway, while this young family was exploring down the beach and these folks on the sailboat were cooking their "baby back ribs" (steer clear of that culinary delight unless you want that baby fat back on *your* ribs), I spied an extremely black little cloud coming very rapidly down the bay from the east . . . absolutely backward from the normal procession of such things, not only this year but almost always. What had happened was that the rapid upper-level circulation from the storm far to the south had whipped the Atlantic sea breeze clear across the peninsula from somewhere over around Jacksonville. The heat from the sun on the land got it ready and when it hit the warm waters of the Gulf, it intensified most miraculously. Jane and I jumped for the doors and barely got them closed before the buffeting of the wind took hold. When we got all battened down, we peered out the window to see if the folks in the sailboat or the little family had noticed what was coming. The storm was so finite that, though it was shaking our house on its pilings and rattling the windows in the frames, there was no sign of anything but bright sun where they were . . . unless they looked up. The first ones to be made aware were the little family. You could see them jump when the stinging sand struck them. Then they looked around and all pointed at the rapidly advancing wall of rain and the willy-waw waves coming rapidly across the bay (I believe it was moving better than twenty-five mph). They started to trot into the hard wind (better than forty . . . you'll have to trust me). The little boy refused to drop his horseshoe crab and the extra drag was such that his momma was about to pull his other arm out of joint trying to haul him along. Finally she picked him up with the old straddle-leg hip carry that comes so naturally to those who carry children and began to run but he was so big and that horseshoe crab was beating her on the legs so bad that she dropped him and rearranged her hold so that he was held horizontally with the horseshoe crab hanging out to the side in the clear. Even at that, she wasn't making much time against the wind and the rain and even more wind was fixing to hit them for real. I thought the daddy and the big boy were going to abandon this kid and woman because they were stroking it on for the truck but, finally, they came back and took up some of the burden. The daddy took the kid and the other kid took the horseshoe crab and the whole crew scurried for the car. Unfortunately, they had about three-quarters of a mile to go and when they got there the car was so full of water that I could see it cascading out over the door sills. As they drove off, I could see the kid crying and carrying on through the still-open hatchback. The big kid had dropped his horseshoe crab.

That sight was so enthralling that I completely forgot the sailboat. When I finally turned my attention to it, it was raining so hard that I couldn't see anything at all. I knew this storm would be gone soon, so I got all poised to catch a glimpse when the first hint of a clearing came. I fully expected this mess to be washed up sideways on Nissan Propeller Bar but through the haze left by the retreating rain, I could see it still anchored where it had been. It was tacking back and forth like all get-out and I thought I could see smoke coming from the barbecue grills but it wasn't them (both the covers were gone and so were the baby back ribs and the fire was out). It was the engine. The captain had cranked up and was standing there like Odysseus at his big wheel trying to hold his behemoth against the wind. Because of those fenders, I had underestimated his seamanship. Not only was he able to keep the anchor from dragging on that short line, he had sense enough not to run forward too far in the driving rain and get the line in the wheel. The embarrassing part was that it did not calm off after the storm, hardly at all, but blew such a norther that his anchorage was no longer tenable and he had to take his whole party back to the mainland to get something to eat. "Could be worse," Jane said.

So, we decided to leave the next morning. It was still blowing a good steady twenty out of the north but Rescue Minor has proven to do all right in such a mean situation and I knew we could put on the slickey suits and idle across. The mainland gives a slight lee in a norther when you get close enough and that's a help. I tell you what I think. I believe if you coddle yourself all the time, when something bad comes along, you won't have had any practice and might make a fool of yourself. I'll just interject a little example right here that has nothing to do with this story but is a good illustration. A lot of people over here were used to riding the ferry and kept an old car (only a crazy person would keep a good car over here in this place) to get back and forth from the ferry dock but, somehow, the powers-that-be over here had pissed off the man who owned and ran the privately operated ferry and he just plain told them to go to hell. Then the folks who took up the slack charge sixty bucks each way so, soon, there were a bunch of people crossing by boat who have no business doing that. One crew habitually pulled the boat up on the beach and tied it to a bush on the bayside opposite their house over on the seaside. One time a norther came (which puts the surf on the bayside and the lee on the seaside). These people did not realize that there was anything wrong until they came down the bunny trail with all their luggage ready to leave. There was the Boston Whaler still pulled up on the beach and tied to the bush but the beach had incorporated it into the scheme of things and the only part of the stern that was visible was the very rear corner of the outboard motor sticking up about three inches out of the smooth sand that covered the whole stern of the boat. They had a big black Labrador retriever and he took it upon himself to mark that little corner of projecting plastic as his property. The tide was out and stayed out for a long time. A strong norther does that to this bay. They had et up all the food and drunk up all the bottled water, sodas, and beer.

Which, that phenomenon of how a strong and prolonged north wind can overpower the influence of the moon and sun on the predictable ebb and flow of the tides is interesting to me. Sometimes a norther coincides with a regular, extra-low spring tide caused by the new moon or a full moon and then it is something else. You reckon I better stop right here and explain the tides like I used to do back when I taught eighth-grade science? I can do it quick (a help around eighth graders) so I will. The gravity of the sun and moon pull the waters of the earth wopsided. Because the moon is closer to us than the sun, its influence is the strongest but when they team up (like when the moon is on the same side of the earth as the sun) we get a new-moon spring tide. We also have spring tides when the moon is on the opposite side of us from the sun during the full moon. A full-moon spring tide is what I call a two-lump tide and though the lows and highs aren't quite as extreme as the one-lump new-moon tide, the two lumps pull the water thin between them and the tides are more extreme than if the moon and sun are running, say, ninety degrees to each other and sort of canceling each other out. Whew . . . sorry about that. Anyway, though Apalachee Bay ain't no Bay of Fundy, the tides can do some pretty sporty things in this shallow water. Some ace oceanographer back in slide rule days sat down with his charts and put his graduate students to work and they calculated that the average declination of the near-shore Gulf of Mexico is about a foot to the mile. That means that, if the flats are beginning to be exposed, and the tide falls another foot, there is a mile of new ground to be explored. Of course, it takes more than a foot drop to get the water off the steep slope of the beach and a tide drop of two feet from the beach-forming average ain't all that common but it happens.

There is a story around St. Marks about a man who was trying to get home from a fishing expedition in a little skiff when an unexpected norther came along and blew all the water out of the bay. If the average declination of the bottom is a foot to the mile for the whole Gulf, St. Marks is about three inches. This man was no fool and knew exactly what was happening and tried his best to skirt around the edge and stay in the water so he could get back to the river and go home. But finally the rapidly thinning sheet of water stranded him way out on the flats far from home. He knew he was in a fix. The norther was blowing about twenty-five all the way from Saskatchewan. His little model bow skiff was too heavy to drag so he put out his anchor and started walking to the north . . . into the wind . . . toward the out-of-sight beach so far away and so far from home. Finally he came to a little rockpile and, since he was about to freeze to death in the cold wind, he squatted down behind it for a little while. He saw some oysters growing on the rocks and took out his pocketknife to open a few to help keep him going. Where he pried the first oyster off the rock he saw the unmistakable gleam of gold. He fell to with a passion. All the rocks were pure gold. He marked the place carefully in his mind and ate enough oysters to hold him for a while and headed off, dead upwind so he would know that the gold was downwind in a norther from where he wound up (most northers have a little east in them and he knew that . . . this wasn't any half-assed nincompoop from Dog Island). Anyway, he finally got home in terrible shape but he never could find that solid gold rockpile again. He did find his boat anchored about six miles out on the flats and was able to go back to tonging oysters for a living.

So that brings us to close this misery. Jane and I headed up into the nasty chop toward the mainland (had to rig the damn bilge pump halfway across and it ingested a paper towel and almost burned up before I finally became aware that the water wasn't running out the clear vinyl hose). We hauled the Rescue Minor out on the trailer, washed the caterpillar doo doo off the windshield of the old junk Mercedes where I park it under my private shade tree a long walk from the boat ramp (why is it that a man or woman will go jogging or walking to stay in shape and hunt the closest parking place to the Krispy Kreme?) and headed back to the shop to see if anything had been accomplished. It is an interesting contrast to ride in an automobile with the windows rolled up after a week or two in a skiff in terrible weather. We were just getting used to it when we passed the St. Teresa boat ramp. That is a wonderful little place. The ramp is inshore of Alligator Point and that little bay is wonderfully sheltered especially from a norther but it is very shallow. When we passed, there were two men standing beside a camouflage-painted aluminum butt-head skiff stranded about half a mile from the ramp. It was easy to see that they wanted to take out and go back to Crawfordville to watch a little TV. They were actually scratching their heads. Me, I would have wasted no time but would have unscrewed that motor and headed for the truck. Of course, in the tradition of this area, the damn motor was too big for one man to carry but I wouldn't have had such a thing.

Oh yeah, I know the exact palm tree where the man of the rockpile walked ashore and I know how to figure the tides and northers, too. Of course I wouldn't want to make a fool of myself freezing to death out there on the flats . . . but I could take my tent.

Naked Woman Inlet

in which there is no rest for the weary

I hate a man who, because of his own ignorant adherence to sloppiness and thrift, will endanger my people or my property. I'll give you a couple of examples out of many. One time we sailed across the Gulf to a little inlet called Pass-A-Grille which is just above Tampa Bay and is the farthest south we ever make landfall to cut off the Big Bend of Florida. Usually we head for Steinhatchee or Cedar Key or Anclote Key off Tarpon Springs. There is no real advantage to making a lot of extra deep-water miles, instead of coasting from Cedar Key on down the peninsula to get into the Atlantic on our way to the Bahamas, but Pass-A-Grille is a good anchorage to stop off while we are coasting down or up. I am not a deep-water man like Bert Dow unless I have to be. I don't like to sit out there holding the tiller for days and days until I get a crick in my neck and the butt rash. I like to pick my weather and make my crossings quickly and under ideal circumstances. I have been known to swing at anchor for a long time in some sheltered spot until conditions get to where they suit me for a crossing of the Gulf Stream. One time we stayed anchored up at Peanut Island where the Lake Worth inlet of West Palm Beach makes the shortest passage to Grand Bahama for long enough to get to know most of the homeless people who lived in a little park on the mainland because we kept walking to the grocery store to get yet another bag of ice. The man who invents an efficient way to make ice on a sailboat will have won the hearts of many of the self-indulgent among the sailing community.

The reason we sailed straight across to Pass-A-Grille (which has a big, old very pink hotel for a landmark) was because our son had just gotten married and was taking his bride for her very first cruise and on previous trips he had discovered this little restaurant there that had become a tradition for him. The deprivations of a long sailboat trip sort of set one up for a heady participation in the hedonism of everyday life. If you have been in the Bahamas all summer and are trying to come back in time to teach school and running long days in the hot August sun with no wind and the exhaust of the old nine point nine hanging right with you all the time and eating out of cans that have already been passed over time and time again, a meatball

441

sandwich in an Italian restaurant in the shadow of a big old very pink hotel is a memorable event. That's what Wes wanted to introduce his girl to . . . pure delight as a start of a lifetime of good memories of joy in relief from deprivation. Of course the only voyaging they had done so far was a calm crossing from Dog Island to Steinhatchee and after one night in the river there, a fair wind to ease down to Pass-A-Grille where they anchored up in "Naked Woman Inlet." I don't know the real name for the place but it is a little bay just south of Pass-A-Grille pass separated from the Gulf by a narrow spit of land that must be a public park because it doesn't have fifteen condos towering to the sky . . . yet. One trip while we were anchored up in there I was sitting the cockpit drinking my cup of coffee and eating a few cold, fried pinfish about sunup when I saw a very active naked woman walking along the bayside beach of the little park. She examined every seashell she saw and had a plastic bag for all the trash she picked up. I thought she was a very admirable person. This time my youngest son of the meatball sandwich planned to anchor up at Naked Woman Inlet and motor across the little pass to the town in his very cute and seaworthy tiny dinghy and partake of that memorable delight every evening while they waited for Jane and me.

So we finally showed up after a hell of a rough trip across. I would have instantly made another plan but I knew the thrill of the meatball sandwich was giving out so we kept on plugging. The old Morgan 30 (designed, I am told on credible authority, by Charlie Hunt . . . a good-sailing old boat) has that old-fashioned roller reefing of the mainsail where the sail rolls up on the boom. There is a little worm gear in the gooseneck and you can just go up there by the mast and wind a little bit on the crank and feed a little on the halyard until you get it where you want it . . . in theory. When they invented that kind of reefing, it was all the rage but soon fell into disfavor for various reasons like how winding a sail with a belly sewn into it onto a cylinder spoiled the shape of the airfoil because the leech and luff get tighter and tighter and the belly of the sail gets slacker and slacker as you roll it up and the battens put a strain on everything as they roll up in a spiral around the boom. Regular old-style reef points are much better but, with the rolling boom rig, if you walk along and sort of arrange the sail as it rolls up and take the battens out when their time comes it works pretty good. Especially when you haven't quite gotten around to allotting the money out of the hedonistic side of the family budget to fix something that ain't broke.

When it started breezing up about thirty knots dead out of the wrong, we lashed the tiller in the hove-to position and both worked to reef the main down until it was just enough to keep a little heel on the boat. The jib had long since gone below. That "motor sailing" when very close-hauled with only the main in rough conditions beats the dickens out of beating to windward in very rough conditions with a tiny jib, a reefed main, and without any motor. The steady thumping of the old two-cylinder Volvo down there laboring on our behalf will make a man feel mighty fond. I am going to get the dear little antiquity out of the dinette pretty soon and plop her back under the cockpit where she belongs.

I can't remember how long it took to get to Pass-A-Grille (the Spanish named most of the coastal features of Florida and I guess they knew what they were doing) but it was a long, long time before we could see the lights of the peninsula and another long, long time before we could see the navigation lights of the pass. You know, Floridians certainly do love the electric light . . . the higher and brighter the better. They especially like strobe lights on tall towers. I remember back when such things were navigation features and were shown on charts and new ones were mentioned in "notice to mariners" bulletins. If the federal government were to map every strobe-lit cell phone tower in Florida, they would have to stop the war in Iraq in order to have enough people to do the job.

Wouldn't you know it, as soon as we got to where we were looking for the sea buoy, it calmed down to a rolling slick. Somehow we made some sense of all that glitter and eased on in the pass about three thirty in the morning. We were barely able to pick out Wes's little Cape Dory 25 (except for a lot of weather helm, a good little boat) and we staggered around and put out the trusty Bahama moor with our two 12H Danforths (which, when properly done, will hold a boat pretty good) and went in the hole like two ghost crabs that have seen the dog coming. We were dead asleep in thirty seconds and, in what seemed like another thirty seconds, I felt something hit one of the anchor lines and I came topside ready to fight. Here this big pale drooptailed, cheap-junk inboard boat was hung up on my anchor line. Somehow a little thunderstorm or something had caused a slight breezing up and this two-story junkpile had dragged its anchor. I think I better describe the boat by some more specific means than just derogatory adjectives. I have surveyed such boats for insurance purposes. There are plenty of them . . . particularly in South Florida. The way to identify them is by how they look . . . truncated. From the high bow back they look sort of like a sportfisherman except they cut off the whole stern of the thing and there is no place to fish. If they had about thirty feet of stern added on, they might look like a real boat. When they cut off the stern, they forgot to put the transom back. I guess they call that "swim-platform-style" but they run so bow-high that it looks like, if the people lounging back there were to turn loose of the piña colada it would slide right out the back. Another characteristic of them is the factory model name. The first part is always some word evocative of coastal Mexico or something a little Hawaiian or Tahitian or at least Californian and the second part is the length of the boat. I think the one that hung up on us was a "Margarita 35." They aren't designed to do anything but run up and down the Intracoastal dragging big wakes and looking pretentious until they decide which popular party spot they will spend the night at by listening to the constant chatter of like-minded people on the VHF (which is always turned all the way as loud as it'll go) up there where the man of the hour steers this thing with the bimbo of the minute beside him adding to the ambience of the scene by a prominent display of her well-oiled self. They are all steered from a "command center" that looks like something a cadre of NASA engineers working closely with the people who designed the dashboard of the push-button transmission era of Chrysler products would agree was appropriate. And all this is way up on top of the roof of a very tall cabin. Of course, most of this cabin is disguised to look like a very tall hull but it isn't actually built for hull duty. I guess they have a little actual material in the bottom of the boat to keep the engines from falling through but the topsides are nothing but what looks like a thin coat of paint on either side of some kind of yellowish tan foam with big voids in it. Even if one of these boats just sits at the marina all the time, it'll rapidly deteriorate and a bad storm will turn one of them into about five miles of trash in just a few minutes.

So, in the middle of the night, I paid off on the one of my anchor lines and pulled up on the other one until I could get hold of the other boat's line and pulled his anchor and unhooked it from my line and let it go. I have learned a long time ago not to confront fools with their folly. It serves no useful purpose unless you bring it to complete fruition and eliminate him (or her . . . at least 50 percent . . . but they are not usually boat captains . . . female boat captains are always very competent) from the ecosystem entirely. It is better to pull a half-assed anchor and get it loose from you than it is to try to explain to some skinny-legged old fart with a gold nugget as big as a kumquat hanging around his neck that a thirty-dollar anchor from

Waste Marine won't hold a boat as wide as a two-car garage and as tall as a McDonald's arch on twenty feet of line even if it does have five feet of white rubber-coated chain on it.

It blew pretty good for a falling tide until daylight and, when the sun came up down there at Naked Woman Inlet, it was sort of like it had come up behind a mountain range. Because of the height of the structures on the mainland I couldn't actually watch it clear the horizon but I did sit out there in the cockpit and drink my coffee and look around at the morning. Though I didn't see the naked woman, I did see my party boat high and dry almost to the sea buoy.

Twice

in which things seem to be repeating themselves

Jane and I are at the coast, right now, but just barely. It was, as usual for this summer, a rough trip. Not only in the boat but the car, too. The adenoidal, artificial midwesterner on the weather radio called for 30 percent rain chance in the afternoon on the day we came. My only running Mercedes had declared itself to have a bad front wheel bearing and the parts hadn't come yet so there we were in the old truck pulling the Rescue Minor when Jane said, "The sky looks mighty black down the road."

"Naw, Jane, it ain't but 30 percent chance of rain and that in the afternoon, and even if that is a thunderstorm, it won't be nothing to it because it isn't but eleven thirty in the morning," I declared as we drove on. About ten minutes later, the whole bottom fell out. The wind was blowing so hard I was afraid the durn lightweight Rescue Minor on its lightweight trailer was going to blow into a jackknife out of the road. The windshield wipers were absolutely ineffectual and the old rotted-out door gaskets were letting in so much water that a mist was blowing all the way across inside the cab. One time, I had been in such a situation and pulled over into a parking place beside a busy street in town. Another person pulled into the parking place behind me and we were both waiting until we could see where we were going again when another car rear-ended the car behind me. The irate driver of the car that did the rear-end job jumped out in the pouring rain and hollered in the window of the car he hit. "What in the hell did you stop in the middle of the road for!" "I ain't in the damn road, fool," declared a man who was so big that it looked like three people got out of the car in the blur of my rearview mirror. The first guy shut up like the widemouthed frog in the old joke. It was so comical that, even though I had something important to do, I hung around in case the police needed an eyewitness. Of course, the man in error was not as big a fool as the man in the right was a big man so everything calmed right down even before the rain slowed down enough for the geography of the situation to be seen.

Fortunately, just as I reached the decision that we were fixing to have to stop, I barely saw the gravel driveway of the little public park at Newport (that's Newport, Florida . . . not where the *WoodenBoat* show is) and pulled in. I knew the Rescue Minor was filling up with water at an alarming rate so I got out in the driving rain to rig up the bilge pump . . . had to do it twice. As soon as I got one foot on the trailer fender and the other over the rail, a stroke of lightning hit something across the road so loud that it made my ears ring. You know how they say lightning doesn't strike the same place twice? Don't you believe it. Many a time I have seen lighting strike from exactly the same place to exactly the same other place and use exactly the same pathway not just twice but four or five times. Of course the one that put me back in the truck only struck twice.

Wouldn't you know it, as soon as I got my nerve up and rigged the pump, it slacked off some. I looked around pretty good then took off my clothes and wrung them out and put them back on and we started on our way again. It was still raining pretty hard and the windshield had gotten to that stage where the fog cannot be wiped off and we didn't have any Coca-Cola (which will stop that) but the road is hardly ever traveled and I could see pretty good if Jane kept wiping the inside while the windshield wipers worked on the outside and we drove for about another hour before we finally ran out from under it. I could see the bilge pump cycling over the side about every ten minutes. When we got to where we could see the ocean, we could tell which way the storm was moving and realized that we better get moving, too. The storm was moving to the west (which is unusual) just like us. We figured that if we hauled ass and didn't waste a second, we might barely be able to beat it to the island and we did. Just as soon as we got unloaded and anchored up right, here it came down the bay about twenty-five knots, and just as black as before. We went through the same storm twice and I would like to tell you that the second time was better than the first but dammit if the neighbor's little aluminum boat didn't drag anchor down and hang up on my inshore line. When that happens, and it happens often, a boat will slide along the line until it gets to my boat and then it'll try to gnaw chunks out of it so I trotted down in the hard driving rain to unhook him. What he had was one of those little rubber-coated navy anchors like you buy at Wal-Mart. It might have weighed four pounds and wouldn't hold a Chihuahua dog. As soon as I got back in the house and was wringing out my clothes for the second time, damned if the wind didn't switch exactly 180 degrees and the little boat came dragging back to where it came from and I had to go back and unhook it again. It is funny how lucky some people are. That little boat has been dragging up and down the bay here all summer long and we haven't had enough south in the wind to take it to the mainland, where it will eagerly be claimed as salvage, yet. The owner stays gone all the time. I'll keep an eye on it and, if it looks like it might be fixing to come over on me again, I'll take some of my own ground tackle down there and anchor his damn boat for him. That way I won't have to do it but twice this trip.

This doesn't have anything to do with boats but it won't take long. My grandfather was a very modest man (maybe that's where I got it from) but he was a pretty good shot with a shotgun. One time he was telling some people how he had had a pretty good day bird hunting: "I killed four birds on the covey rise." What he meant was that he had shot four bobwhite quail when the dog flushed the birds and the covey erupted into the air and flew off to find a place to hide . . . a real feat especially since he shot a double-barreled shotgun and had to reload both barrels before the birds got out of range. Because of his modesty and perfect credibility, there were no expressions of doubt but the people couldn't think of anything to say. My grandfather continued . . . "I wouldn't have told you but . . . I did it twice."

Bobwhite Quail

Bobwhite quail are little birds that spend most of their time walking around on the ground sort of like chickens but they can fly about like a bullet. They stay in little family groups all winter long and only split up to pair off in the late spring. "Bob White" is what they say to one another during that time. Little boys used to get my goat with too much of that "Bob White" business when I was a little boy and some of them overstepped themselves. Though quail look like little chickens (especially on the plate) they are as smart as all get-out and cannot normally be killed without a good bird dog and a real good bird dog is worth about ten thousand bucks so quail hunting ain't for everybody. Their main talent is the ability to hide and the fortitude to stay hidden until the last possible second. One time I was mowing the pecan grove with my tractor when I flushed a daddy quail and all his brood (the father raises the chicks). Baby quail can fly when they are no larger than a bumblebee. Anyway they flew out into the part that I had already mowed and I was fortunate enough to see exactly where they landed so I shut off the tractor and sat and watched. They stayed hidden for about twenty minutes and I could not see a single one until they gradually started to go on about their business. When I started the tractor and started mowing, again, they flew out into the part that hadn't been mowed and I would have worried that I might mow them but I don't believe you could run over a baby quail with a motocross motorcycle, let alone a two-cylinder John Deere, so I kept on. When I shut down to walk home to eat my lunch, I flushed them again and the little chicks flew right to the tractor and hid under the mower. I slipped back as quietly as I could and started the tractor and raised the mower (420 John Deere's had a hydraulic lift three-point hitch) to see if I could find them in the short grass. After I had pulled up out of the way, even after close scrutiny from the advantageous height of the tractor seat, I couldn't see them so I figured that they had run out into the tall grass on one side of the mower and were hidden there so I got off the tractor to go flush them so I could find out how far they had had to go to feel safe. Damned if they weren't still hidden exactly where the mower had been and they only flew when I almost stepped on one of them. They flew exactly where their daddy was calling.

When I, with my shotgun (but without my dog . . . I ain't got no spare ten grand), finally get too close to the hidden covey that I think I know where is, I will almost step on one before the whole family erupts from the bushes with such a roar that, despite the fact I knew it was going to happen, it'll put a good bit of stress on the anal sphincter and I certainly won't be able to pull myself together well enough to hit one of the little flying bombs . . . let alone two . . . and then another two . . . and do it twice.

Floor Sander

in which I am forced to trade a performance of the Dixie Chicks
singing my song for a dip in cold water

This is a sequel to the story I wrote about how a little aluminum boat dragged anchor down on the old Rescue Minor twice in the same storm when the wind reversed 180 degrees as is common in the Gulf of Mexico in the summertime. When the wind does that it'll play havoc with most any kind of single anchor. With a Danforth, it'll cause the line to tie itself to that little square plate and pull the anchor just as neatly as anything and then the boat will skate to leeward with the anchor planing along on top of the water behind it and making a pretty good rooster tail. I have seen that happen a bunch of times down here at this island. I don't know why these people don't have sense enough to notice that my boats are the ones that do not usually (knock wood) suffer calamities of that sort and come by here and either examine my rig when the tide is out or come to the house and humbly ask for a little advice but they don't so one of those 180-degrees switcheroos will cause a pretty good little boat parade down the bay. Fortunately, in this bay, we are the next to the last house to the west and the bad weather usually winds up coming from that direction so all those boats to the east do not usually cause us any trouble but I am very alert to any hint of breezing up out of the east. The other night, I was snoozing in the bed dreaming that the Dixie Chicks were singing a song with very ribald lyrics that I had made up especially for them when I became aware that a deliciously cold wind was blowing through the east window of the bedroom hard enough to flap the sheets against my flanks. At first I thought it was just applause for me and the Dixie Chicks but then I realized that the wind had switched into that dread direction and I hopped out of the bed and grabbed my binoculars. It is amazing how well you can see at night with a pretty good pair of 6x50 knobblers and it didn't take long to see that same little aluminum boat dragging down the bay. I already knew it was coming because it does it all the time and, herewith, I offer you an axiom: No rubber-covered anchor will hold anything in twenty-five knots of wind. Anyway, here this little boat came making about five feet with each hop of the bow as the waves passed under and it was coming right exactly down the beach to hit my boat. I sat in the doorway until it got close enough and trotted down and pulled both anchors of the Rescue Minor and stood there in the rough water and dodged the little aluminum boat until it was safely past. Then I reanchored my boat and squirted off with the hose and dried off and got back in bed. Jane said, "Did it go past." "Yep, all gone," I replied and then, "Jane, do you know how to send a song to the Dixie Chicks?" "You could probably find out on the Internet . . . now go to sleep." Which I was able to do in short order.

That little boat has been dragging up and down the beach all summer long. Usually the wind is slightly onshore of the bayside and it just wallows around in the surf when it breezes up and the waves splash over the sides and fill it with enough sand and water to finally stop it for the time being. But by morning of the Dixie Chick dream (I have forgotten the lyrics . . . dang) it was long gone. I guess there came a little more south in the wind than usual, which took it out into deep water where it drifted (probably at about four knots from my experience) off to no telling where. Not only did it have plenty of wind but the tide was falling and that makes a good two or three knots of current down the bay to the pass so maybe the thing was making six? Anyway, it was gone beyond the range of my big (20x100) binoculars when daylight came.

Despite the fact that I believe that the results of poor seamanship belong to the poor seaman, I sort of hated to see that happen. The man who has that boat is running kind of a low-budget operation over here on this island sort of like us. Usually, like most of the people over here, he stays gone all the time and only uses the little boat (fourteen-foot aluminum semi-V) every now and then. I don't know why he doesn't pull it up on the beach in front of his house and tie it to the pilings but there are a lot of things I don't understand about how people do on this place . . . like how somebody will build a house and then burn the scraps (including PVC pipe, insulated wire, arsenic-salt-treated lumber, scrap asphalt shingles, vinyl siding trimmings, and no telling what-all) right there in the yard where the well is drawing water from a rain-water lens that floats on the salt water only about ten feet under the sand . . . then they'll pump that poison up and put it in the bathtub with their grandchildren. I don't actually know why most of these people have a house over here. There is one we watched get built about three houses down to the east from us that, except for the initial frolic after the construction, has never been used. The box for the brand-new refrigerator is still full of other packing materials under the house . . . eleven years old. It doesn't make any sense.

But maybe it does. Maybe these people were trying to get "grandfathered in" on some perceived future restriction on coastal construction and the house is just "investment property." Oh well.

Anyway, this man of the little aluminum boat happened to be here this time. I think he is trying to get his "investment" ready to sell. The taxes have gone up mighty high now that the "forgotten coast" has been remembered. A few days before we saw him lugging a floor sander up his steps. You know, on an island with logistics as difficult as this one, such a thing as the arrival of a floor sander is a noteworthy event. I don't know how he got it to his house. Usually people come initially on the big private boat (belongs to one of my old buddies, an old fishing boat captain with a good bit of wit but very little sympathy for frivolity of any kind) and I guess the aluminum-boat/floor-sander man came with him and then hired one of the hard-bitten permanent residents to haul the sander down the sand bed road to his house. It costs sixty bucks to ride my buddy's boat (each way) and such a luxurious mode of transportation is sort of out-of-budget for someone who is willing to sand his own floor so he could have brought it in the little skiff . . . but how did he get himself here in the first place? His boat has been dragging around over here all summer. I guess I don't know every bit of the man's business . . . yet. This guy sanded for three days steady. We could tell because, when he emptied the bag, the dust blew about two miles down the island to the east . . . fortunately for us. The morning the boat got away was a Saturday and we had noticed that the forty-five-minute cycle of the renewal of the dust storm had ceased late Friday afternoon. We figured he was through and was going to take the sander back to the mainland in time to check it in to the Rent-All-Center before the noon deadline on Saturday so he wouldn't have to pay the extra rate for Sunday. I don't know how he got it over here but I do know how he planned to get it back because about nine o'clock in the morning I saw him standing down on the beach beside the sander looking for his boat. To someone who doesn't know too much seamanship, it probably looked like a pretty good day to haul the sander back to the mainland. The east-southeast wind (at least twenty-five knots) was making a lee about half a mile out from the bayside of the island and, if you ignored those white streaks, it looked sort of calm and the trees down by his house had cut the wind off of him so the extra sandpaper he must have been taking back for the refund wasn't trying to blow away . . . but the boat was gone. He looked up and down the beach (no idea of which direction the wind was blowing) for a little while and then went back in the house and got his binoculars and came back and looked some more and then went back inside. In a little while, here came one of the permanent residents in his old rusty car heading west past our house with this man of the sander in the passenger seat. I guess they went down there as far west as the road (?) went and peered out at the wide expanse of water to see if they could see the boat. Say it had been making only two knots for that six hours, that's twelve miles and the end of the island is only three miles from our house.

In a little while the man was back on the beach (barely in time to pull the floor sander beyond the reach of the rapidly rising tide) messing with a little Jet Ski that he keeps under his house on a dolly with fat plastic tires. I have seen him drag it to the water one other time and it was a job of work and he had to have a little help to get it back under the house. This time he couldn't get it to start so back in the house he went and pretty soon, here came the old rusty car again. You know, any permanent resident of this place is working on the borderline of being a desperado and any financial windfall is appreciated. I saw the permanent resident carry the battery of the old rusty car down and jump off the Jet Ski and I believe I saw some money change hands. Jesus this is pitiful, y'all, but I don't know what I could have done to make it any better. I have a lifetime rule that I don't participate in foolishness and I must abide by it. Once you let up on your rules, you'll be a helpless wreck and your children will hate you and your dog will take up with somebody else. I watched this man load the floor sander on the Jet Ski and head out into the bay where it was blowing, probably about thirty by then. I could see the permanent resident peering from the bushes. Pretty soon the idling Jet Ski began to wiggle around a little bit and then it came out from under the lee of the middle point of the island and dumped both the man and the floor sander in the bay. Fortunately it did not cut off or that man might have followed his boat down to that never-never-land where it went. I wonder if he had sprung for the "damage waiver" that covers accidental damage to a rented item and only costs 5 percent of the rent.

You know, hindsight is a useful tool. Too bad it is unavailable until it is too late. If that man had been determined to put that floor sander in the water, he could have saved his boat. I bet that boat wouldn't have dragged a big, old five-hp floor sander very far.

Bruzzwully or Separating the Men from the Boys

in which there was ferocity both within and without

One of these horizontal-driving-rain, continuous-lightning-style thunderstorms we have here in the north Gulf of Mexico of an early summer morning (about two thirty usually) will certainly separate the men from the boys. When I was a boy, me and Bruzzwully (another boy) were the ones who had to go down and find the skiff, wherever it had drug anchor to, while the men stayed at the house and discussed the relative merits of the Northhill versus the Danforth and such high-minded subjects as that over breakfast and coffee. While they were doing that, Bruzzwully and I took the motor off, laid it on the hard beach, and dug the sand out of the boat.

We just got back from our annual big-deal family doings at the coast house on July third and it was about two weeks of ferocity, both within and without. Old loudmouthed Republicans and Democrats squared off inside . . . I must stray from the subject at hand for a little minute before I can tell you about the fury outside. Why don't these fools realize that it ain't the Republicans or the Democrats who run this country . . . that all this messing around, swapping parties and such to get another angle on the manipulation is just that . . . manipulation and both we and they are the ones getting manipulated. We ought to quit arguing about first one smokescreen after another and start refusing to participate . . . quit buying all this gas would be a good start. Anyway, we stayed outside with the boats and children all we could but, I tell you what: this horrendous four-year drought is finally broken. There was hardly any time at all when there wasn't a thunderstorm that had just passed us going ashore on the mainland and another just in the offing . . . fixing to chase us in where the discussion was going on. I always took the tiller with me so I could enforce a little peace and quiet in there while the lightning and thunder crashed all around.

Once, lightning struck the house. Dang. We were all sitting in the lee-side doorway under the porch roof watching the fury when there was a hell of a bang, a very bright flash, and a long-lasting fireball up in the peak of the rafters (equilateral hip roof, no ceiling). My grandson Will came running out of the little room with the fuse box in it hollering "I see some fire." Sure enough, when I went in there, there was a smutty place on the box. I wished for Dave Carnell but there was nothing to worry about. All that had happened was that it had arced across the breaker that fed the wire to the overhead light . . . the one in the peak of the rafters with the long-burned-out, inaccessible bulb.

I had thought about the lightning possibility when we built this house. I mean, it was the highest point within half a mile . . . just sits there on the naked sand like a challenge to the elements . . . sort of like a boat does out on the water. We hauled the whole thing over here with a skiff and carried it up the beach, one board at the time . . . towed the pilings and dragged them up with a come-along. By the time we got to the roof-building stage, there in the blazing-hot summer sun, the little structure was beginning to assume some significance so I decided to do all I could to keep from losing it. I knew that one day, a real hurricane was going to wipe this island perfectly clean again like it did in 1899 and I couldn't do anything about that but the thing that got my attention at the time we were struggling with the construction was these thunderstorms. While we were cowering in terror (terror is a good way to ward off hubris) under the blue polyethylene with the lumber, I was thinking about what I could do to make the house less provocative.

I made a sharp-pointed bronze lightning rod sticking out the peak of the roof and connected it to a Faraday's cage of copper pipe on the rafters running down the pilings to ground out into the water table. It was a lot of trouble and expense but I believe that we would have had more trouble than one smutty breaker that day if we hadn't done all that.

What I think happened was that (according to theory) the electrons of the ground were attracted to the thunderstorm and ran up the copper to crowd onto the sharp tip of the lightning rod and there wasn't enough room so one of them got squeezed off. The presence of his little negativity ionized one molecule of air and made it conductive enough to attract another electron and another and another until a conductive pathway, a "leader," was formed all the way up and the flow of electrons along it discharged the ground around our house. Because of that, the lightning didn't actually strike our house but the discharge current was so powerful that it seemed like it . . . we all smelled the ozone. I have been close to one or two real lightning strikes and ain't no little array of copper or stack of sticks will come out of that scot-free.

I believe that such discharges have happened at that house many times without being powerful enough to cause an arc at the confluence of the cage and the lightning rod at the peak of the roof, but I have found an inexplicably thrown breaker from time to time.

I think it was a good thing in a way. Certainly silenced the Democrats and Republicans . . . might have made them suspect that there might be something more powerful than . . . well, Republicans and Democrats.

Wow, I was going to tell you about men and boys and dragging anchors wasn't I? Anyway, while I am so far off track, I'll just tell you what I do when I get caught out in a boat in a thunderstorm . . . won't take long. I cower in the bottom in terror. If it is a sailboat, I take the mast down and cower under the sail . . . unless it is a big sailboat with an aluminum mast, then I ground all the stays and shrouds with old welding leads that were discarded when the insulation wore off enough so that they started leaking to ground. You can get them at any welding supply place for the scrap copper price. The ground wires have the most excellent clamps and make good automotive jumper cables but the electrode clamp will grab a sailboat stay. I just frazzle up the other end of the wire and let it lollygag in the water. I have a pointed rod on top of the mast too. I don't know if it protects the boat from lightning but it helps to keep the cormorants off.

If I am in an outboard skiff when the storm comes, I cower as far forward, away from the engine, as I can get. One of my friends saw an outboard skiff that was struck by lightning. All the damage was right back aft around the engine . . . three-inch holes in the transom at both clamps for one thing. Don't keep the gas tank back there. That's one reason why you always see me steering with a piece of PVC pipe between me and the tiller of the outboard. Sometimes, when properly provoked, lightning can strike out of a clear blue sky . . . and no, I ain't going to sit up at any silly "Console" with a ridiculous steering wheel connected to the engine with all kinds of wires and cables.

So (finally), it was a rough week or two down there and we got to see a lot of anchor dragging and the results. It didn't happen to any of our boats because we have gradually punished ourselves enough to finally evolve a rig that works in our specific situation. What happens is that, in the interval between thunderstorms (especially between about eight at night and around two in the morning) it calms almost completely off. The boats just drift around every which way with the tide and the slight breeze. You can look down the bay and see them heading in all different directions and then look in a little while and they'll all be heading in another different direction. Other people become complacent within the shield of their ignorance, but we know that what is happening down on the bottom is that the line is wrapping around and around whichever part of the anchor is sticking up out of the sand . . . the little tipping pad on a Danforth or the other fluke on a Northhill or fisherman or the whole thing for people who are fool enough to use a little navy anchor or a mushroom plunket. You guessed it. When the instant 70 (one man with a wind machine registered 115 before his little whirligig wrung off) knots' worth of blowing sand comes off the beach, there is a regular parade of big money dragging down the bay to blow sideways up on a lee beach, dig in, and tip the weather rail down (these deep V's are the champions) so that the breakers can fill the boat up with sand, perfectly flush with the rest of the beach . . . the fancy upholstered furniture and fishing rods and such stick up out of the flat sand in a real cute, Salvador Dalí–looking way. That is only cute if it ain't my boat.

Which, it wasn't . . . not this time anyway. What we do is set two anchors in the "Bahama moor." I used to use two old 5H Danforths, which will hold like an old piano frame (good) in hard sand but I hate the way they clank around in the boat and how they always want to bite you, so now I use two little Chinese Bruces (Simpson Lawrence . . . good and dirt cheap . . . will ride in a bucket). On my tiniest boats, I use the cute little one-kilogram ones and on the skiff, a pair of the two-kilos. We set the two anchors straight opposite each other and try to anticipate what the wind will do so the boat won't lie up alongside one of the painters (I just can't call twenty feet of five-sixteenth-inch line a "rode"). It doesn't really matter though. The boat sits so stationary that there is no chafe and if it comes a blow, it will wiggle across right away. We always anchor near the beach, both for the convenience of it and so these behemoths won't be able to drag down on us when it starts to snort in the middle of the night and make me have to get up and go down there in the driving rain and push somebody's goddamn "Reel Tight" back out into the bay to go on her real slack way.

So, we didn't have any problem other than a lot of bailing (how is it that one inch of rain can put a foot of water in a skiff?) but we saw some pitiful perplexity after the Republicans and Democrats of the other houses finally dragged themselves out of the bed around eleven o'clock in the morning.

Uh-oh, that brings up another puzzle of conventional human behavior and I'll just have to comment: Why in hell do all these people come to the coast to sit around all day and drink beer and talk? Jesus, life is short. It seems like they could save themselves the driving time and just stay home to do that. That way they wouldn't be cluttering up the highways with their damn Exhibitions and the water with their . . . well . . . damn exhibitions. This island is a hard place to get to. If you ain't got a boat, it costs sixty bucks, minimum, one way just to get here and if you do have a boat like most of these people got, it costs way more than that and I think our little shanty is the only house on the island without a satellite dish. I just don't understand it. They can't be trying to "get away from it all" because they all have two or three phones in their bags, chirping like diabolical insects, and a pager biting them on the belly like a tick. It is just another case of excessive slack in the natural selection process. We need another ice age.

So, we watched (I don't participate in non-life-threatening misery) the Bingeys and Bruzzwullys of the other houses digging the sand out of their boats almost every day. Sometimes, the boat would be so big and they would have gotten so late a start that they wouldn't be able to get through in one tide and would have to do it twice. The way the scenario usually worked was that, when the household of the lost boat finally emerged from their stupor, the inhabitants would go down and gather on the beach in their nightgowns and towel-style bathrobes and stare at the place where the boat used to be. Then one of them would be delegated to go get the binoculars and they would argue about which way to look (no idea of the prevailing wind direction of the current set of storms . . . I guess the Democrats were the ones wanting to look to the left). They would try to ignore our little docile fleet right there where it always is as they scanned up and down the beach. Finally the women would go back to the house and some of the men and boys would split into two groups and start walking. Some of the more hung-over-looking men would go back into the house with the women. Usually one group of walkers would find the boat and walk back to the house to describe the calamity. Sometimes, if the boat was on the mainland, they wouldn't. There is a man with an airplane who specializes in projects of that sort. If the house was close enough to us, we could hear the people wailing about the news and blaming each other. The airplane man charges a lot of money. If the boat was found washed up on the island, some of the men might head out to reconnoiter the extent of the calamity but usually, the coffee would be made and the Froot Loops would be in the bowl so the men would go back inside and a little group of boys . . . usually two, looking like Bruzzwully and me but with oversized, long bathing suits, would trudge off down the beach with a bucket and little plastic shovels, though I saw one hard working kid (reminded me of old Bruzzwully) dig one out with a Frisbee . . . a most excellent tool.

Hurricanes

in which you can see why I have a healthy respect for hurricanes

Though I haven't been killed yet, I live down here in hurricane country and have been reminded of that two or three times (so far) this year. I have seen quite a few hurricanes and have had some close calls. The first direct hit I went through was in 1961 while I was in the Navy at Roosevelt Roads, Puerto Rico. There were only a few of us on the naval station (which closed this year in retaliation, they say, for the citizens of Vieques Island protesting the use of their island as a bombing range) and we all huddled in the heavy-duty poured-concrete galley. I don't remember the name of the thing but it blew like blazes and killed a bunch of people. We all marveled as the eye passed directly over us and the bright sun shined down. I, for one, wanted to go out and look around but they wouldn't let us.

Another one was soon after I got out of the Navy. I had a nineteen-foot homemade sailboat in a little marina down at Lanark. I went down to se-cure it and strung lines all the way across the little basin and hauled my boat out in the middle and was fixing to leave and go back to Georgia when the marina operator said I couldn't leave the boat like that so I stupidly decided to stay and make sure it was all right. I sat in my car all night long and it blew and rained like all get-out. It rained and blew so hard that I couldn't even see the boat at all, let alone get out and do anything about it. Fortunately it rained full of water and sank to the bottom (it was an open boat with rock ballast), which was the best thing that could have happened because the storm surge came and all the other boats in the marina broke loose and pulled pilings and turned loose a bunch of floating docks and tore each other all up. One of them got on top of my boat and chafed the mast a little bit but mine was the only boat in there that didn't get messed up real bad. A funny thing happened, though. When the storm surge went down, the wind reversed out of the north and blew the water out to sea and it was low tide so the rails of the boat were above water and I was able to bail her out and all was well (puzzled hell out of all the other people who had boats piled up in a jumble on various banks). I had an aluminum skiff on a trailer behind my car (a Rambler station wagon with reclining seats, vacuum windshield wipers, flathead engine, and six-volt electrical system . . . a late-model car at that time). I never wrote any "love letters to Rambler" (like you used to see in old *National Geographic* ads) and when I got ready to go try to find a way through all the limbs and junk so I could go back to Georgia and tell my family I was all right the damned car wouldn't even move. At first I thought that something must have gotten hung up under the trailer but, when I went back to look, I discovered that the boat was absolutely full of rainwater. I knew I had taken the drain plug out (I didn't forget things like that when I was younger) so I was perplexed. I knew the boat wasn't full of trash or anything (I was very neat when I was younger) so I couldn't think what could have possibly stopped up the hole so watertight that the boat was brimful three hours after the rain had stopped. It was a tiny dead bird (myrtle warbler) stuck in the hole headfirst. Anyway, when the water ran out, that puny Rambler was able to go a little bit and I rambled on back to Georgia.

Another time I was working on the tugboat when Hurricane Frederick hit down around Mobile (just like this damned Ivan). We had loaded two gasoline barges in the Chevron (now Exxon) refinery at Pascagoula. There was certainly no way we could cut and run so we just pushed out and anchored on the bayside of Horn Island. It was rough but we were in no danger . . . had to help the anchor from time to time with the engines and a lot of salt water blew through the door gaskets and we had to wash the whole boat, inside and out. The main thing for us (nothing compared with everybody else down there) was that the hurricane destroyed the Dauphin Island Bridge and blocked the channel into the Intracoastal so we had to tow outside all the way to Yankeetown instead of easing down halfway in the creek. There wasn't anything new to that experience though and it had calmed off pretty good . . . perfectly slick by the time we made Yankeetown two days later. It usually calms off pretty good after a hurricane. I guess the atmosphere gets tired, too.

Another interesting thing happened during that hurricane. An empty petroleum barge got loose from another boat and blew way down Mississippi sound and eventually ran aground on one of the islands and two shrimp boats hauled it off and claimed it for salvage. It made a big hullabaloo in the courts for a long time down there. I can't remember who finally prevailed. I can tell you this, though, I would much rather keep up with loaded barges than empties at times like that. In thirty-five or forty knots of wind a boat pushing two empties has to crab up so high that a lot of places in the Intracoastal aren't wide enough and they just have to push up on something. You'll just have to wait for a lull to go under some bridges. Sometimes a thunderstorm will catch one in some tight place like Navarre or Perdido or downtown Fort Walton and some of those fancy docks are liable to get involved with the pushing-up process. Floridians love a fancy dock just like seagulls, cormorants, and pelicans do. You don't see many fancy docks down on the canals of the Mississippi Delta. The people down there have lived with tugboats long enough to have learned some sense. I was on tugs for a long time, off and on, and we were lucky enough not to have to push up any docks but we did have to run over a Hobie Cat once. Didn't kill anybody, though.

I used to survey boats for insurance companies and had plenty of work after hurricanes. In the early days of fiberglass (what I call the "woven roving era") the boats would be in pretty good shape if they hadn't filled up with water. The main expense was getting them off the hill and fixing all those bent rudders, shafts, and propellers and puttying up a little gelcoat . . . spray on some Awlgrip and the boat was better than new. Now that they have invented the "foam-cored" process it is a different story. I have been watching this year's devastation and I can just imagine the situation. Popular modern big boats are about equivalent to house trailers. That's why they are so popular . . . cheap . . . and a hurricane loves them both equally. You ought to see the trash on the beach after a hurricane. What you find are chunks of foam with a skin of fiberglass about as thick as a three-by-five card on both sides. Because of the bluntness of the way I describe boats made like that, I have decided not to do any more insurance surveys. I mean, my assessment of a wrecked boat is exactly the same as it would have been if the thing was brand new . . . a piece of crap.

Kate back about '85 showed me that lesson. Though it went ashore thirty miles to the west of us, we were long gone. The storm surge was such that the whole island was under water (and high surf) around our house. When we got down there, it was easy to see the power of such a thing. There had been a wide expanse (two building lots deep) of high dunes seaside of our house but they were completely gone. There was no vegetation at all within half a mile of us. The house was just standing there on its pilings on sand as flat and smooth as poured concrete. We were still building on it (still are . . . I guess . . . might be gone) and the building permit that I had nailed to the piling in its little vinyl pouch about eye-high was half buried. All the sand from those seaside dunes had washed under the house. The only things we lost were two sawhorses and a little pile of lumber and all those sea oats, dwarf live oaks, Yaupon (*Ilex vomitoria*) bushes, and the little beach bushes like beach lavender (a lovely little thing). We actually gained a little acreage on the bayside and all the plants eventually grew back but the seaside dunes never did and now we have both seaside and bayside frontage. After the hurricane, I had to dig up the well pump but, when I rinsed it out, it ran fine. Modern electrical insulation is a marvelous thing. The winter after Kate, a shrimp boat friend of mine dragged up a cheap plastic box fan. He said that he rinsed it out and it ran fine after he scraped the barnacles off the blades so it was back in balance. The lesson was in all the plastic strewed all over the place from all the boats that were destroyed. We are waiting for this Ivan to do his worst right now. The highway in front of the shop is full of people pulling their boats north and other people hauling plywood south.

During Hurricane Opal they fooled me. I stayed over on the island thinking that it was going ashore much farther to the west than it did (I was already beginning to get old and reckless . . .). During Kate a bunch of boats got loose up in Tyson Harbor on Dog Island and cut loose and tore up a bunch of more boats. Tyson Harbor is as good a hurricane hole as there is around here if people only knew how to tie up, anchor, or moor a boat but they don't so it ain't. I had, not only my old Morgan 30, but a twenty-six-foot motor whaleboat down there. I pushed the whaleboat up close to the marsh and set out the Bahama moor with a thirty-five-pound high-tensile Danforth and a fifty-pound Herreshoff copy (Luke). I was hoping that I was too far in for it to get hit and I hoped I had figured the wind right but the sailboat draws too much water to get it upwind and close in so I had to leave it on its mooring. My plan was to go down there when things got bad with my buddy who had a running (?) car and watch as best I could with binoculars and a powerful (million-candlepower) jackalight he had. If I saw some damn piled-high-and-deep cheap piece of junk heading for my sailboat, I was going to swim out and climb in the whaleboat, crank up, cast off, and do a little pushing. I don't know if you know them old surplus Navy whaleboats or not but the rule is that they can go through more than you can and I have proven that to be true. They are heavy-duty, self-righting, unsinkable, self-bailing (engine-driven, self-priming centrifugal pump), and fire-resistant. They are powerful (swing an eighteen-inch wheel) and have a very big rudder. I knew I had what I needed for the duty but I was wrong . . . again. The old whaleboat was perfectly all right after the storm but the Morgan was long gone. When I found it on the mainland about nine o'clock in the morning it had already been completely looted. They even took the air cleaner off the engine and the kitchen table and tried to saw the propeller off the shaft. The only thing they didn't take was the mooring line . . . inch and a half polydac (polypropylene and Dacron blend . . . will float), which was hanging from the chock and cut off as clean as a whistle exactly at propeller height. I wondered how that scenario had played out down at the harbor while I was cringing up there in our reinforced bedroom with the waves washing completely across the island under the house and old "Take Apart" tied to the pilings full of water. If I hadn't had to bail her out and put the engine on and all the junk back in I would have caught those looters and God help their miserable asses if I had. That's a terrible kind of person in my opinion. Seeing what happens after hurricanes where all these human predators converge to take advantage of people who are in a bad fix is the sort of thing that makes me such a social skeptic. I think there are a lot of people who operate in the digitorectal mode . . . if they aren't plain-out evil.

This photograph was taken the day after the hurricane of 1899. The ships are on the beach of Shipping Cove on the bayside of Dog Island, Apalachee Bay, Florida. The camera is facing southwest. The bare-looking land in the background is the west end of the island, which is now heavily forested and was the day before this picture too. Most of the ships and schooners are from the Baltic and were here loading longleaf pine lumber and cants from two sawmills in Carrabelle. The bark at left is Russian but the three-master, bow out, is the *President James A. Garfield,* which probably hauled up the east coast. There is a little tug working on the square-rigger that is listing so badly in the background. It might have been successful, but there is a lot of old wreckage that gets washed up out of the sand from time to time by these lesser hurricanes and such. Altogether twelve ships were lost during the storm of 1899 but none of the crew. There weren't so many helpless people on the water back then. The place where our little house is is about a mile and a half behind the photographer . . . waiting its turn. That was what they call the "hundred-year storm" and as I write it is the hurricane season of 2001 . . . overdue. Oh well, it was good while it lasted.

Salvage Job

in which, during a hurricane, some intercoasters lost their dinghy
and their dignity, neither of which was ever recovered

We have a lot of hurricanes flit by our neck of the woods up in the north-eastern Gulf of Mexico. The reason nobody hears a bunch of news about it is because not too many people live up here and the insurance companies don't have to pay for all the uprooting in the swamps and marshes along our coastline like they do when one of the storms cleans up a little new ground down in South Florida or up the Atlantic seaboard. About 1990 one of them (I don't remember the names of all of my relatives, let alone hurricanes) whipped right through here and laid low a bunch of vegetation and put a few boats very high (for Florida) on the hill. One of those boats belonged to a friend of mine over on Dog Island.

It wasn't because of sloppy seamanship that this happened. My friend is more apt to rig too much than too little in preparation for such an event. He is the one who provided us with the mooring from which our old raggedy 1967 Morgan 30 swings while it serves its main function as a bathroom for the cormorants. We helped him set his mooring and he helped us set ours and it was a brilliantly executed big deal all around. He knew the people in Tallahassee who run the concrete outfit and he built a mold out of heavily reinforced plywood that would allow them to cast a cube of concrete four feet wide on every side. He provided them with a bunch of iron including a big eye standing up from the bottom of the box. Then, when the mixer trucks returned with the leftovers from a pour, instead of just rinsing the drum out in the scrap pile, they poured it in my friend's box and threw in the iron with it. When it was full, they called him up and he came and took the box apart and they loaded the block onto his little heavy-duty trailer and he hauled it to Carrabelle behind his old 220D Mercedes . . . all fifty-five horsepower worth . . . and the first block scaled out to fifty-six hundred pounds on the truck scales. Ain't but a hundred pounds to the horse and I have seen a horse do a heap more than that.

All that was just the preamble to the real genius work. There this thing sat on the trailer at the boat ramp. As Eddie Murphy said in one movie, "You dropped the gun when you busted the window. What the hell you gonna do now?" Well, we had a big flat-bottomed aluminum butt-head skiff that I salvaged from the scrap yard where somebody took it after a tree fell on it. It was only the work of minutes to beat it back into workable condition with a sledgehammer and some boards, a little Alcoa "gutter seal" (wonderful stuff) on the cracks, and it was ready for this new rough service. We gingerly loaded the concrete block into the aluminum boat with the travel lift. It took several tries to find the place where the two inches of freeboard wound up even all the way around.

It was a slow trip to the island towing the skiff behind the whaleboat (surplus twenty-six-foot Navy motor whaleboat . . . a common vessel in these parts) because if we went too fast, my son Wes, back there behind the block, couldn't keep up with the bailing. But, eventually, we got to the harbor of the island where we were going to plant this monster.

Which, I better explain that place. Tyson Harbor of Dog Island (right at the northeastern terminus of the Gulf Intracoastal Waterway) is one of the best little storm refuges on this coast for vessels drawing less than six feet. You can find a place in there that is sheltered from a chop in any direction. There are two good holes: One, called "The Outer Anchorage," is my favorite and the favorite of small bay shrimpers. It has a hard sand bottom and is deep right up to the east beach . . . plus, it is out of range of the sound and sight of the people fooling around the private ferry dock and the "Yacht Club." The inner anchorage is more sheltered but, in addition to being up there among everybody, it has two other problems. One is that there are some boats moored up in there and the cormorants use them for a bathroom and they stink (like all get-out and that's what you have to do when the wind shifts to put you downwind of one of them). The other problem is that the bottom is about five feet of the soupiest, stinking, anaerobic, black mud I ever saw. About the only way to get hooked into something solid is to let out about a hundred feet of chain with a big Bruce, Luke/Herreshoff, or plow (forget Danforths and those new, lightweight aluminum clankers) then back down for about half a mile. Most people (including me) don't do that but just hang in the mud kind of temporarily. You ought to hear the hue and cry among the overnighters when it breezes up for a little snort of thunderstorm. "Roscoe . . . Roscoe . . . ROSCOE!" Anyway, that bottom in the inner anchorage of Tyson Harbor has put a lot of people to a lot of trouble and that's why we were out there drifting with the skiff and the whaleboat with this huge block of concrete saying, "What the hell we gonna do now?"

Well, we didn't say that. We knew just what we were going to do . . . had a plan. Wes pulled the drain plug on the skiff and slithered out over the side and swam over to where we were spectating in the whaleboat. Boy you ought to have seen the mud boil up when that overloaded sixteen-foot skiff (seven feet wide) hit the bottom. Wes had to feel his way to the eye to put the chain through. We positioned the whaleboat over the block and pulled the chain all the way around the midships section and hooked it up as tight as we could get it so that, when the tide rose, the whaleboat would lift the block high enough so we could drag the skiff out from under . . . we figured. It took about three tides and a lot of fooling around (boy that skiff was sucked down in that mud like a stingaree) before that plan was brought to fruition but we finally got it. It was easy to see just where to put the next block in the bottom of the skiff too . . . and where we needed a little more gutter seal.

Oh yeah, I know you want to know how we managed to unhook the chain after we got the skiff pulled out. We cut the link that was shackled to the hook with a hacksaw, didn't even have to saw it all the way through and that hook skipped four or five times before it finally sank. We tied the next one.

We set a total of seven of those big moorings over there for various people. We got so good at it that it became a routine operation. We started hauling the skiff to Tallahassee on the trailer so the concrete people could load the block directly into its dent with their forklift to save the travel-lift fee. But we had to launch it at the boat ramp with that two inches of potential freeboard, a ticklish, frantic-bailing business. We even put a big electric bilge pump and battery (buoyed by a crab trap float) in there so Wes could ride up front with us and tell jokes. You know, he is a public school band director and I don't know what it is with that hardworking bunch but they are a major repository of jokes in this country.

All right, now, finally to the meat of this salvage operation. Our buddy had this forty-five-foot sloop hanging on one of those blocks down there in the inner harbor for the convenience of cormorants. The boat was a Starrett, a big-deal racing boat that drew so much water that it could only get in there on a high spring tide. It had worn an irregular circular ditch in the mud around the mooring, kind of like an inverse, submarine Stonehenge with the irregularities marking the lineup of various seasonal events. I understand that the hull was designed for Starrett by Charlie Hunt and laid up by Charlie Morgan down in St. Pete. It was a hell of a thing, had a steel reinforcement built all the way around the middle to keep the shrouds from pulling the plastic out of shape like an old rustic hitching up his galluses when his overalls get to swinging too clear. Some fiberglass boats get so slack on the lee side that the lower shrouds chafe the lifelines and the turnbuckles rattle in the chainplates and if you try to tighten up so they won't do that, you can't close the doors in the kitchen and the mast acts like it wants to come through the overhead. One time my buddy and a friend set out for Fort Meyers ahead of a norther (a surefire way to go south in the Gulf) in the Starrett. When it whipped up around thirty-five or so, they decided to take in the main and just run with the working jib (you could make a circus tent out of the Genoa) only to find that the halyard was jammed and they couldn't do a damn thing with it . . . or the boat either, except to go south. It was a quick trip to Myers, might be a sailing record. They had to rework the goose-neck when they got there. I'll venture another aside here. One thing that jams halyards is those woven polyester rigs. What happens is that the place where the line goes through the masthead sheave chafes enough so that the outer sleeve of the line bunches up into a wad that won't pass through the groove and the harder you pull on the luff of the sail, the worse it gets. If you are going to have to have high-tech on your sailboat (like braided Dacron and built-in masthead sheaves) I recommend wire. It has a bad little ting-a-ling to it on an aluminum mast but you can usually get the sail off the boat. And, continuing with this, I like the luff hitched to something running on a monel track instead of a groove in the aluminum too. But what I really like is grapevine hoops.

So, when the hurricane came, here this monster was swinging on that enormous concrete block sunk five feet into the mud. Not only was it made up with my friend's notion of a proper mooring (one-inch chain swiveled to a Norwegian float as big as the carcass of a bloated walrus and then one-inch nylon to another section of chain through a hose to the bit, a good holding rig) but, when he heard about the storm, he dove a two-inch polydac line through the eye of the mooring and up either side of the forestay and around the mast of the boat, rigged slack, just for insurance. The Starrett tended to tack back and forth on the line and he didn't want it to get loose.

But get loose it did. A mature but ignorant cruising couple in one of those big top-heavy living-room-style Intracoastal motorboats (indeed named *Intercoaster*) pulled in there to take shelter from the storm and let down some kind of inadequate, well-advertised, toy ground tackle and, when it started breezing up for the hurricane, they began to drag all over the harbor with the wind shift. They tried to keep straight with the engine but the top hamper was too much and they couldn't handle it and wound up tangled with the Starrett's mooring lines and gnawed all that loose with the futile thrashing of the prop and the whole mess sailed immediately up onto the east beach of the harbor. The *Intercoaster's* dragging anchor finally found something to hold on to when it got to the sand of the beach and they were able to drive back to deep water (and mud) when the wind moderated but before the storm surge went down. All they lost was their dinghy and dignity, neither of which was ever recovered.

So, next morning, in the brilliant sunlight that follows the wild fury of a hurricane in the night, there was the Starrett about three hundred feet up on the beach, lying on its side with its enormous mast sticking up all the way to the trees and its enormous keel sticking about six feet down in the sand and a few people standing around marveling. It was a puzzle. The people from the *Intercoaster* were very nice and assured my friend that they and the insurance company would put the boat back in the water immediately. Estimates (astonishing) were gotten and a lot of phoning went on and the crux of the matter was that the insurance company declared the event an "Act of God," which was not covered under their policy. The *Intercoaster* pulled out and left the salvage problem to our friend. He is, by nature, undaunted by problems though.

He had told me that he thought that it was impossible to stick a motor whaleboat. He declared that he could wash his way all the way through the island from the bayside to the seaside if he could just get a little water to the wheel. So he backed her in as close to the big sloop as he could get (and still get a little water to the wheel), ran a line to the bit of the sailboat, and started washing. It worked like a charm. The old fifty-horse Westerbeke (Perkins 4-107) was made to put out twenty-four hours a day for years and years and it went right to work. After a while, the whaleboat had washed a very deep channel into the beach in the direction of the stranded Starrett, but then the sand that had been washed out began to bank up in front of the boat and he had to reposition and wash it out farther into the harbor so he could continue to get a little water to the wheel. What he needed was another whaleboat. Fortunately, we had such a thing (though powered by a forty-horse engine . . . 1957, four-cylinder, 636 Mercedes just like in a Thermo King semi truck refrigeration unit) and it was built for just this sort of duty too. I took the line from the bow of the Starrett and my friend made up alongside of me heading in the opposite direction. We set a few anchors and I turned the thermostat down to "freeze 50,000 lbs. of chickens" and the little Mercedes tuned up to match the bleat of the old Perkins. The situation finally evolved down to where all we had to do was to take up and let out on a few lines, check the oil every now and then, and wiggle the tiller to direct the wash (which was too powerful to stand up in). The paired whaleboats ran, wide open, twenty-four hours a day for six days . . . cleaned the carbon off the valves pretty good and polished the bronze of the propellers and rudders pretty good too. It was a boring operation altogether and all I can remember about it was that, finally, the Starrett . . . dwarfing both whaleboats . . . slid down off the bank into the hole we had made and we, gradually, washed the channel deep enough to drag it at least a hundred yards all the way out to the mud.

The story ain't over yet. About three years later, you couldn't see a sign of all that carrying on when another hurricane came and, somehow, my Morgan got loose (the mooring lines were cut right at the waterline . . . my friend and I both have all-chain with a nylon snubber now) and went on the beach all the way over on the mainland where it was looted completely clean of everything but some of the larger parts of the engine and remnants of the mooring line and we had to do it all again. You know, that goes right back to my original main philosophy. I feel just like a cormorant does about a big boat. Abstract wandering in search of comfort is not the best goal of humanity. The worthy pursuit is a direct jump for joy. Joy like a tiny sailboat way back in the shallows of an inaccessible wilderness, pulled way up into the bushes so nobody can see it and a little primitive camp beneath the cedar trees. I mean, are we better off with our insurance policies and our Web pages and our air conditioners, TVs and recliners and worries about what to do about the cormorants than the primitive people of long ago messing around their little hovels and gardens and smoked fish (and canoes!) . . . their little wild children playing with the fire (and canoes) and nobody caring one whit about what the hurricane might take away from them or what the cormorants are up to? I think some of the complications of modern life are just compensations to take up the slack of not having intestinal parasites. You know, taxes and insurance are a lot like hookworms and tapeworms and an automobile is worse than a wolf in the bushes.

Hurricane Dennis

in which an alligator visits Dog Island but doesn't stay

I guess y'all know we live in the middle of downtown Hurricane City. We have had a lot of them hit all around us down at the coast. I can't remember their names but the last direct hit by a category five (must have been, but I don't think they were into the numerical scale back then) completely cleaned Dog Island of everything . . . turned it into a shoal. There is no tree on the island older than 107 years. We are long past due for what the experts call "The Hundred Year Storm." I can't understand what ails the government and insurance companies. I bet anything that there are a lot of insurance companies that would love to change their "coverage" to uncover any structure within twenty miles of the coast from about Texas to Virginia including all of Florida. The building of these big-deal luxury houses and condominiums on shifting sand is just asking for it. I am not real superstitious but I believe objects of great ostentation standing on the beach fly right straight in the face of whoever is in charge of hurricanes. It didn't used to be this way. People built little "camps" down at the coast because they knew that they were subject to obliteration at any time from June till December and the taking of that risk endeared the little weather-beaten structures to the people and their insignificance might have appeased the mighty wrath of the gods. There are some shaky little outfits still standing after many, many years while evidence of the complete destruction of some mighty fancy digs is scattered all up and down the coast in the wake of that Dennis who went ashore a hundred miles to the west of Dog Island.

Which, I have a suggestion for the National Weather Service: Quit naming these damn things all these little cute names like "Dennis." Nobody takes a name like that seriously. Name the son of a bitch "Hitler" or "Typhoid Mary" or something with a little real menace to it. That might alert some that something truly bad is coming. They missed hell out of the prediction for the storm surge of this Dennis and a lot of people refused to leave the coast. I'll give you two examples: One man stayed in his beach house on Alligator Point about ten miles to the east of Dog Island and that infuriated the storm surge god to the point that he gave him an extra ten feet on top of a high spring tide and twenty-five feet worth of waves built up from about forty-eight hours of about a forty-five-knot onshore wind. When the incoming seas got to breaking over his hot tub on the deck and bashing in his sliding glass doors on Sunday morning he realized that his code-certified structure was not going to be up to the duty and he mighta-shoulda-oughta evacuated so he dialed 911 on his cell phone but it was too late. Fortunately, although many of the houses on Alligator Point were damaged beyond logical (or legal) repair and a bunch of them are just plain gone, his stood on its skinny legs through the storm and, when things calmed down, the sheriff (there are some long-suffering law enforcement "personnel" along this coast) came and waded through the water hole where the road had washed out and tried to get this man out of his house but there was nothing at all to do it with. Everything on the ground (and a lot of the ground, itself) had been washed across into the bay and here this man was up there fifteen feet in the air and no ladder, no steps, no nothing. I can't remember what kinds of piling shinnying and all went on (maybe tied the bedsheets into a rope) but the sheriff finally rescued the man and took him to the hurricane shelter.

There is a little camper park right on the beach in Lanark Village named "Ho Hum Trailer Park." Ho hum is right, too. It has been there ever since I was a child and they don't whoop it up all that much down there. I heard that all of those prudent people hooked up and hauled ass days before the storm, except for this one old gal in her Winnebago. The sheriff came back a bunch of times and told her she needed to crank up but she said she still had a few more things she needed to do and "not to worry." Yeah, right. Dennis washed that Winnebago sideways through the trailer park and clear across Highway 98 and way up into the woods almost out of sight. A road-clearing crew came along and piled up all those refrigerators, mattresses, washing machines, floor lamps, tree limbs, sofas, TVs, microwaves, recliners, barbecue grills, plastic shower enclosures . . . I'll stop listing items but there was a hair dryer hanging in a very high limb right over the highway and I saw a box fan sitting on a pile of a whole houseful of wall-to-wall carpet. The fan appeared to be running but I believe it was just the wind. It was like that along US 98 all the way from St. Marks to Apalachicola. I guess two days of strong onshore wind can pile up a lot of water in a shallow bight like Apalachee Bay. Anyway the road crew heard this weak little voice crying in the wilderness and found this old gal back there wedged in among a bunch of pine trees in her Winnebago waving her arm out a busted window and wailing plaintively so they drove the backhoe back in there and dug her out and took her to the hurricane shelter.

When we got to the coast on the day after the storm we had to circum-navigate a bunch of debris and flooded roads and lawmen looking for loot-ers. We must not have looked like looters pulling the Rescue Minor through all that trash with the old raggedy Dodge so they let us through. When we got to the little marina where we pay a yearly fee to launch and park it looked as if nothing had happened even though the rest of Carrabelle looked, well, like it had just been through a hurricane with a ten-foot storm surge. All over town there were boats sitting on docks and boats sitting on other boats on docks and docks sitting on boats and everything all up in the yards of con-dominiums and trash and wreckage washed up all over the place but our lit-tle marina ("Dockside" on Timber Island) was perfectly normal. All the boats were in their slips and the trash had been raked up and the lawn sprinklers were trying to rinse the salt out of the grass and all was well. The only thing we noticed that gave any hint of a hurricane was that the two dockside fuel tanks were way up in the yard tied to palm trees . . . and the man who owns the place looked very tired and stiff and sore. He said he had been swim-ming around all of hurricane day and night making sure that boats stayed tied and centered so that they would come back down between the pilings in their slips and tethering his fuel tanks so they wouldn't spill anything in the water or float off. He also picked up a man's car with the big forklift he uses to put boats in dry storage and took it to higher ground so it wouldn't get flooded. That just goes to show you what one person can do. The contrast between this man's outfit and all that across the river was startling. I wonder what will happen to boat insurance rates after all these hurricanes and the pre-diction for how this is just the beginning of maybe ten more years of this?

It was a rough crossing in the Rescue Minor and I believe we might have been the first people to cross to Dog Island. The storm surge hadn't gone down and the tide was very high. We glanced at our little shanty to make sure it was still mostly there and then made a quick trip in the lee (still blow-ing about twenty-five or thirty dead onshore) of the island up to the harbor to check on the old Morgan swinging on its chain made up to a four-thou-sand-pound-block of concrete and steel scrap. It has no choice but sink or swim. It was completely unscathed and not a drop of water in the bilge even though we found out that there had been some eighteen inches of rain on the island. That is a testimony for an old woven roving-style fiberglass sail-boat. It was very clean, too.

We went home and inspected everything and opened up so the wind could begin to dry the old house out from where three days of rain had blown through all the considerable cracks in the poor little wretched thing. Our house is in one of three "overwash areas" on Dog Island. In storms of consequence the waves on the seaside break over the dunes and wash clear across the island to the bayside. We have been over here when that happened and it is strange looking. It isn't as if the waves break clear across the island. When the waves break on the seaside dunes the water settles down into a sheet of varying depth and runs just like a river. The depth of the water determines what happens. If it is a little storm (like a tropical storm) all it does is comb out the sea oats a little bit and salt the well. If it is a bigger storm, the seaside dunes get eroded some and that sand washes across and settles out on the island. Sand never washes very far out into the bayside because, as soon as the flow hits the more or less stationary water of the flats, it slows down and drops all the sand it was carrying the way a river makes a bar and hence a delta where it meets the sea. If it is something like, say, a category two or three hurricane that comes ashore just to the west of us like Kate and Opal did, there will be significant beach erosion and some of the seaside dunes will be washed completely across the island to the bayside and the accretion on the lee side will make big lobes of white sand sticking out onto the flats for many feet everywhere the overwash occurred. The bayside beach will be very steep, almost cliff-like, for a little while after a hurricane. The place where the water ran will be completely flat and all vegetation will be buried under the new sand. That's what happened this time. There is evidence on the island that the storm surge was even higher than Hurricane Kate, which came ashore just sixty miles to the west of us as a category three in '85. That coupled with the enormous waves coming right from the open sea wreaked havoc on the whole seaside of the island. Some dunes that were maybe seventy years old are completely gone and the oldest dunes on the island (which are, incidentally, the highest dunes on the Gulf of Mexico) had their faces washed so severely that property that was worth a bunch of money the day before is, now, too narrow to be developed. A lot of houses went in or were damaged beyond repair. There are septic tanks on the beach everywhere. As The Nature Conservancy owns all the interior of the island including the road that forms the boundary for possible move-backs and which used to be hundreds of feet from the sea, a lot of people lost all possibility of building again. Because of an article in *Money* magazine claiming that

Dog Island was the best real estate investment in Florida, there was a mini boom over here and investors bought every piece of land that was for sale. You ought to have seen the parade of Learjets flying slowly down the seaside on Monday July 11. I never knew one of those things could fly low and slow like that but they sure smoke under those conditions. I guess some investors were checking out their bottom line. A bunch of people lost a bunch of money on the seaside of Dog Island on July 10, 2005, but one lucky little outfit in an overwash area gained about five feet of altitude and maybe thirty feet more bayside yard. Of course our little shanty is now standing on a perfectly flat plain of pure white sand with the steps going down into it like something Salvador Dalí would have painted but it is still mostly all there. I even know the vegetation is still under that sand and in only weeks, the sea oats will come back up and begin to build the dunes again. Not only that but when we went down to the west to see what had happened at the biggest of the overwash areas, we found a whole palm tree, roots and all, floating in the bay.

We dragged it home with the Rescue Minor, which tows most excellently . . . You know what makes a good towboat? You have to make up the towline ahead of the rudder or ahead of the outboard so it will steer. The rudderhead of the Rescue Minor is what we tow from and it probably wouldn't work well on a normal boat but that peculiar Atkin arrangement of the rudder in that tunnel makes it steer about like there was no towline. Anyway we dragged the palm tree home and wrassled it up into our yard and planted it . . . Ho, y'all, are we Floridians now or what? Anyway, the big westernmost overwash area is about half a mile of water at high tide now. It remains to be seen if it will heal itself or continue to deepen as the tide washes through and make a permanent new cut . . . East Dog Island and West Dog Island might be the new situation. I sort of hope it comes back, not so these islanders can continue to drive the full length of the road on their joyrides holding their hands in a cylindrical formation like they love to do but because the part that washed out is a favorite nesting place for seabirds including the now scarce least terns. The other overwash area besides the new cut and ours is also a least tern nesting beach and the little birds had vacated it once the vegetation grew back after Opal because they like to lay their eggs directly on bare sand. A hurricane is not all bad . . . I bet it didn't bother the real Floridians of long ago too much at all. I bet they just dragged their Winnebagos to high ground. The least terns were already moved in down there in the brand-clean sand only two days after the storm surge from Dennis went down. The only real nonhuman tragedy was that we lost ten sea turtle nests. Jane and I lost our Northern Hydraulics (might have been "Horrible Freight") sixty-five-dollar well pump, which was buried under three feet of sand . . . a submerged pump.

While we were sitting up in our house looking at the sunset and listening to the generator working on the freezer, we saw a great big alligator come moseying down the middle of the island from the west. He sure looked peculiar on all that white sand. He sashayed himself right under our house and slid into the bay right where we had the Rescue Minor anchored in a new little cove we gained from the overwash. I guess he came from Alligator Point. I wonder what he thought? "I ain't crazy about all this sand," he probably said to himself. "I'm just going to keep on walking and swimming until I find me some weeds." You know, there really are plenty of alligators on Alligator Point. When the "discoverers" of America finally quit naming every discovery after some petty potentate or sanctified survivor of the inquisition they used a good bit of logic with the names. Alligator Point for one . . . Dog Island, too. You ought to see all the damn dogs over here . . . need more alligators.

So, I mentioned that we have actually witnessed the overwash of a storm surge under our house. Does that mean that we are reckless with these hurricanes and are liable to inflict some rescuer with a cell phone call? Hell no. I'll play tickledy bender with a tropical storm and, if I can determine to *my* satisfaction that a category two is going ashore far enough away that my experience says it won't overpower my facilities, I might stay down here but when I see something down to 936 millibars and a predicted track just west of here, I am long gone. I don't go to any "hurricane shelter" though. I'll be damned if I want to sleep on a gym floor near any woman talking baby talk to a Pomeranian. I move a hundred miles inland . . . up to the concrete shop and hive up and listen to National Weather Service on the weather radio. I have noticed that in addition to the artificial German and the adenoidal computerized midwesterner they now have a bogus California (South Florida . . . same thing) woman with a sinus infection.

A Rude Awakening

in which we dig up toilets and nearly get stuck with a skunk

It is the middle of February and the word is that winter has finally arrived in Northland, USA. They say they had a lot of snow all the way up the East Coast . . . enough to shut down NYC. I don't know how much it takes to do that but a light dusting will stultify Atlanta. I hate to keep sounding so mean but somebody has to chronicle the facts as they actually are instead of over-elaborating every dadblamed thing. Like on the TV for instance, Jane likes to watch the medical announcements . . . the endless discussion about these meaningless, contradictory "studies" they are always doing so she might find out what will prevent old age. I watched (and listened) enough this week to know that TV medicos don't know batshit, southerners can't drive worth a flip, and Cheney just plain shot that old man.

One thing I learned first hand without the vicarious extravagance of the TV was that all my tirades and instructional essays have not taught some yahoos over here on this island how to anchor a damn boat. Some of us islanders managed to be here to make another trash pickup with the volunteers from The Nature Conservancy. What happened was that during all these hurricanes about ten houses got bashed into smithereens on the seaside of the island and everything (including the kitchen sink) washed over the dunes into The Nature Conservancy's woods. It was the most hideous mess you ever saw. I sure don't understand how a family can just abandon a whole houseful of everything and leave it tottering on the brink for years and years after the county condemns it and cuts off the electricity. I mean, the refrigerator is full of petrified (long past putrefied) stuff, the curtains are still in the windows, the soap still in the soap dish, the Christmas decorations still hung up. The phone still on the wall . . . everything . . . mayonnaise, ketchup, pickles, condoms, romance novels, pillows . . . septic tanks, drain field pipes . . . everything. We dug up sixteen toilets. One of them was still associated with its little blue rug with the semicircle cut out and a matching terry-cloth (who was this "Terry"?) lid cover with a fat little fish picture on it. After I got that all dug up, I set it up on a little hill overlooking the scene for a joke. About an hour later I looked over and there was a tired Nature Conservancy volunteer sitting there taking her shoes off to dump out the sand. I was a little slow with my camera but I probably couldn't have gotten a model release signed anyway. To bring this lament to a close, there have been three pickup projects and those Nature Conservancy people hauled a pure mountain of rubbish to the place where the island's landing craft can get to it. There have been a few islanders like Jane and me working, too, but not many. Most of them drive by in their SUVs and glare at us for clogging up the road with the trash trailer while they talk on the cell phone. It kind of makes an old man like me feel mean.

So we picked up trash all day Saturday. It was a perfect day for that. It was warm and there was just enough wind to make it possible to wear long sleeves so you wouldn't get the old sun-damaged skin so cut up picking pantyhose (remember the foxed-up woman who got stuck on the way to the party?) and telephone cords out of bramble bushes. It was also pretty foggy so the sun wasn't hot and the fog wet the wings of the relentless mosquitoes who have bred up in all the water-filled refrigerators lying on their backs (the compressor makes them self-righting) scattered all through the woods. When we shook the bushes trying to untangle a whole built-in vacuum cleaner system, we could see the mosquitoes launch themselves at us and fall short of the mark. I stomped eleven jillion of them into blotches on the white sand just out of spite and gained one or two skeptical looks from volunteers who caught me speaking to those helpless mosquitoes as I took my revenge on their whole tribe. "Yeah, you little bastard, you, take this . . . and that cell phone, too."

We were tired when we got home so we listened to *Prairie Home Companion* and drank a glass of box-style red wine (our TV-prescribed medicine) and went to bed early. It was a silent foggy night. You could barely hear the seaside surf and that was it. That was it until about one thirty in the morning when a yowling norther hit with a vengeance. The weatherman/woman (both of them) had assured us that the cold front whipping down from the frozen wheat fields of Alberta was going to stop way before it got to the coast and we were going to continue to have clear, warm days with a light southeast wind, "Bay and inland waters a light chop, patchy fog dense at times." Yeah, right. I ought to have known better. I saw those high cirrus and altocumulus clouds up there looking sort of parallel about sunset. We could have switched Garrison off and rigged the running lights and run for it but that glass of red had settled into our old tired bones and we just went to bed. When it hit, it was a single thirty-minute gust about forty-five knots that started the screen wire whistling and the joints of the house creaking. I leapt from my bed with my binoculars and five-cell flashlight and peered through the racing fog at the Rescue Minor pitching in the shallows to the twin lines of the good old Bahama moor. I knew those two little Chinese Bruces (was that Bruce Lee?) were digging down like a pair of *Busycon* conchs. I tried to see how the neighbor boats were doing but the fog was too thick and I knew the norther was set in to blow dead onshore all night long and they couldn't possibly drag down the beach to us so I went back to bed and slept like a person who knows that life is good.

One of the things that has happened as I have gotten older is that I can remember a few dreams when I wake up. When I was young, I used to have the most entertaining dreams but they evaporated into noncondensable vapor before morning. Now I can't remember real things that happen during the day but I can remember some really unreal things I dreamed at night. As the wind of the norther settled down to a steady twenty-five and the old house settled down to ride it out I dreamed about a skunk. In the dream, Jane and I had driven back through the bushes at the head of the big swampy pond on the old home place in the old rusted-out green VW we had in Puerto Rico to look at a flat tire on the tractor I had to abandon back in there. I wanted to see if the bead of the tubeless tire was still sealed to the rim good enough to pump up or not. While we were digging around trying to make that determination, a very large and fat skunk got in the backseat of the car and refused to get out when we got ready to go. We tried all sorts of things short of getting on his (or her . . . couldn't tell) nerves too bad but the skunk would not get out. We decided to drive out of there to get away from the mosquitoes and also in hopes that the skunk would not like it when the car cranked up and began to move but that didn't work. Though we left both doors open the whole way, the skunk continued to sit like a fat little person in the backseat with his dirty little belly poking out. When we got up to "The Drive" (a road through the whole place that my great-great-grandfather had hired ex-slaves to build, by hand, in 1890) I decided to see if I could gently take the skunk out with my hands but, as soon as I grabbed him around the belly, he glommed onto both my arms and hands with all four feet most tenaciously and I couldn't turn him loose. Jane had to drive with me in the passenger seat holding the skunk on my lap. His hair was very bristly and though he did not smell like a skunk, he did not smell good either . . . sort of like an otter or a wet dog. We drove to Thomasville for some reason with me holding the skunk and stopped at the big printing plant I had painted the whole inside of for $1.75 an hour just after I got out of the Navy in '63. We went in and there were all these machines working and steam in the air and all. A woman came to greet us and I handed her the skunk who went willingly and grabbed the woman just like he had grabbed me. "Run Jane!" I hollered and we bolted for the door with the woman right behind us. There was no way we could beat her to the car and get turned around so we ran through the parking lot gradually outrunning the poor woman with the skunk. We hopped over some busted curbing and I picked up some chunks of cement and started throwing them at the woman. That's when Jane woke me up because I was running and thrashing in the bed and I didn't have on my socks.

By then it was almost day but still very foggy and colder than hell. I know I don't have any right to speak about cold so I would like to solicit a second opinion from some of y'all old seasoned Yankees who used to walk to school barefoot in the snow. When you are on your next snowbird expedition down there by Mickey's house, drop off for an hour or two in North Florida and stand on a north-facing beach when it is blowing fog about twenty-five knots and thirty-eight degrees and tell me if it seems a bit chilly to you or not. You know, despite the way I try to act like an ignorant provincial, I have been to a lot of cold places. I have been to Keflavic, Iceland, y'all, but the coldest I have ever been in my life was standing on the taxi strip in Mayport, Florida, when I was in the Navy with the britches legs of my whites whipping around my shanks in a norther just like this one while I was waiting to get on a P2V to go back to Puerto Rico after Jane and I had plighted our troth. Anyway, while we were lying there glad to be in our warm bed up in the drafty old thermostat-less house at Dog Island I could tell that the tide was out by the sound so I said, "I believe the specks are going to be safe from the neighbors this morning," and rolled over to see if I could catch another little snooze without any interference by any damn skunks. The next thing I dreamed was that I smelled coffee.

That norther had beached every boat in the bay except ours. I trotted down for a quick reconnaissance before the fog lifted and one of the boats was anchored with one of those plastic-coated ten-pound sheet-metal anchors with five feet of plastic-coated chain and only ten feet of brand-new half-inch nylon line. All that ground tackle was so brand new it still had the price stickers on it. The line had little tags in the lay of the strands so the mariner could tell how much he had let out. That's how I knew he had anchored on ten feet. There was forty feet still in the original West Marine hank lying in the bottom of the boat. If he had let all that out, that factory-made-up brand-new rig might have held but, in order to do that, he would have needed swinging room. That would have meant that he would have been up to his armpits in that fifty-eight-degree water when he waded in and such a feat is not in the nature of these people. It ain't in my nature, either. That's why I love the close-in and stationary aspects of the Bahama moor.

The reason I made the remark about the speckled trout (squeteague, spotted weakfish) being safe was that when they arrived, late the afternoon before the norther, they had sat in the boat drinking beer and examining their fishing tackle and listening to the VHF turned up as loud as it would go as is the normal thing for big-deal mariners around here. The volume of the radio was so loud that they had to talk louder so they could communicate all the wealth of knowledge they had about speckled trout fishing, maritime lore, seamanship, golf, women (I didn't hear anything about skunks), and how much they were looking forward to getting an early start first thing in the morning.

Well, first thing in the morning, they all came trotting down from their house about the time the fog thinned enough for me to see them with the binoculars. There were about ten of those fishermen and they were all dressed in identical black jumpsuits with identical logos across the back like they were some kind of "Team Diawa" or something. Diawa, schmiawa. That norther had the water blown off at least two hundred yards and the boat was lying on one side of its deep V with all the water and sand it could hold banked up against the down side of the cockpit where the engine controls were. Not only that, but I was able to notice that the switch was pulled on top of the transformer pole to their house. You know, there is a high-test link connecting the top high-tension wire to the transformer terminal. When the electricity is turned on, that link is hooked up but when they cut you off, they just pull it loose with the long fiberglass pole and it dangles and is easy to see. Nonpayment of the electric bill is one way to get the link pulled. Another way is to have some apparent electrical problem like a rusted-out meter base or burned-up main breaker . . . all too common in an environment where salt spray blows constantly. If the meter reader can look into the meter box and see naked fuses or fire or smoke or evidence of fire or smoke, he'll throw the link on you. Electricity is the only "energy source" for heat, toi-

let, running water, and other comforts over here. Cell phones appeared upon
ten of the twenty ears of "Team Diawa" and pretty soon, here came a vehicle down the road. I recognized it immediately. Rescue was at hand. There
is this guy over here who makes his living off just such a predicament as
that. I won't bore you with the details but I bet they involved a long time and
a lot of money. I wouldn't know anyway because Jane and I strolled down
the beach with our bucket and my new homemade and most excellent alu-
minum-bronze oyster knife. The sun came out and we sat down on the creek
bank and shucked out over a pint of now red-tide-free oysters and, when we
walked back home to make the stew, those fishermen and their boat were
gone. There was a two-hundred-yard long pure ditch leading from the beach
to the water where (I guess) the Sea Tow boat dragged that big deep V . . .
probably cost fifty cents an inch.

Bluefish and Hardtails

in which feeding the multitude is a good excuse for many adventures

Jane and I hit the jackpot this morning. We have been working on the roof trying to fix where those four hurricanes wore out all the nail holes in the old corrugated asphalt roof ("Onduline" French stuff . . . cheap . . . very popular on third-world structures like chicken houses in Georgia) that has been on our coast house ever since it was built. It is good stuff and ours is easily the oldest roof on this island and has proven itself to be hundred-mph proof two or three times but it is old and brittle and all that wiggling from all those storms skirting first one side of us and then the other has worn out the nail holes and, where it used to leak pretty bad, now it just pours in a bad rain. We are putting another roof on here one sheet at the time. To do that, we have to take the old sheet off and that is easier said than done. The nails have grown to the wood with rust sort of like how an iron rod driven in the ground grows to the dirt. It takes three pullings to get them out. I had to make a special rig to do it and, even with that, it takes such a lurch on the handle that I almost fall off the roof three times for every durn nail, and there are about fifty pounds of them up there. It really is a pain in the neck. Fortunately, it is such a pain in the neck and I am so old and decrepit now that I am ready to knock off about nine thirty when it gets hot. Of course Jane is still young and spry but, since she can't do it all by herself, she has to stop, too, so we quit and go on an adventure.

This morning we decided to run all the way around the island to see what's what. It is always an interesting trip. The island is in a continuous state of change and I have been trying to figure it out for many years. A lot of the bayside is pretty much stable. There are places where it has been eroding for a long time and other places (like where our house is . . . knock wood) where it seems unchanged since we were children. The ends of the island and the seaside are what is in a dynamic state. It averages out to bad beach erosion all along the whole seaside of the island and accretion at the ends particularly down to the east. Every time there is a significant meteorological event, some houses go in and get strewed down the seaside beach to the east by the prevailing longshore current. When we built our house, there were two building lots between us and the seaside. Now we own to the high-water mark on the seaside beach and those lots are down (I guess) at the east end. Since real estate prices have gone up so much, people who bought property over here on this sandbar and forgot about it are finding out, when it occurs to them to cash in, that it just ain't there anymore. One man sent the surveyor to stake his investment out for the Realtor and the stakes showing the depth of the lot were about two feet apart where mean high water had crept in through the years. That's some mean high water ain't it? That man was probably counting on that little wad of money for something he needed. Now all he has is a bill from the surveyor. I wonder if he paid his last year's taxes? Anyway, that's your real estate investment lesson for this story. I think the legal term is *Caveat Emptor.*

So we went riding in the Rescue Minor down the bayside to the east and then around the end and back up the seaside to west and on around and back to the house. I was standing up looking through my Polaroid glasses at the fish on the flats and there were plenty to see. For one thing, this (early June . . . actually D-Day) is the season of the cow-nosed rays down here. Dog Island is a mecca for rays of most every kind but the astonishing pilgrimage of the cownoses is something. There are usually some of them here all year round but this is the time when they breed, I guess. They swim in formations just like geese or military aircraft. They vary in size within the population but all of them in each formation are the same size. They fly leisurely through the water as if they are purposefully going somewhere special but one group of them will pass purposefully by another group heading in the opposite direction. I guess they, like all nonhuman creatures, know exactly what they are doing but it sure does seem like one crowd would tell the other ones, "Hey, y'all . . . ain't nothing going on back there where we came from . . . might as well turn around and go with us," but they don't. They just keep on moseying up and down the bay. I think their strolling is social in nature and cownose rays are perfectly satisfied to be in the company of their peers no matter how foolish their mission might seem to outsiders. You know, people are sort of like that. I think it is a sign of success when a species can afford to engage in illogical behavior. I don't think cownose rays are the only ones. "The characteristic human trait is not awareness but conformity" (Michael Crichton, *The Lost World*). Swim on cownoses.

We tooled it on down the bay in a light chop. I have been varying my running speed up and down to see what I like. All last year, I ran about 12.5 since that has always been my favorite outboard skiff speed but the Rescue

Minor planes out to what I call wakeless at a lot less than that and 10.5 was the speed I liked at first. That's what I have gone back to, too. I think it is something about the syncopation of the three cylinders. Anyway 10.5 is very soothing to me even though the boat actually gets its best gas mileage at 15.5. Oh well, a man has to indulge himself every now and then. That little sip of extra fuel is sort of like a little sip of Madeira after supper. You go your way cownoses and I'll go mine.

Cownoses bear their babies live earlier in the spring (I guess) because there were a lot of groups of very small rays. I wonder if they are all siblings. Stingarees birth their babies live, too . . . all ready to put you in terrible misery. I don't know if stingarees are social in nature or not but they seem to be sort of grouped up. Maybe a litter of cow-nosed rays are all born at the same time and stay together until breeding time. Maybe they are strutting their stuff like people do . . . in groups. Maybe each group is a bunch of sisters checking out the bunches of brothers. I have seen stingarees breeding (bunch of little males bunched up around one big female right at the edge) but never cownoses. Stingarees are bottom fish and cownoses swim along in the water like spotted rays. Individuals from groups might become attracted to each other in passing and swim off into the blue depths of the pass or something to consummate a little conversation. Hell, I don't know . . . Anyway, there were plenty of cow-nosed rays swimming in diamond-shaped formations tranquilly along in all directions. They barely shied aside as the Rescue Minor eased on by. They, next to great barracudas, are the most fearless of fish. Sharks, even big sharks, will run from a boat.

Though we didn't see any this trip, in the clear water that is typical of the summer, there are sometimes spotted rays around here. They get huge (say ten feet wingspan) and swim on the flats like cow-nosed rays. They don't swim in groups but they are easy to see. They are black on top with white spots. Sometimes they'll be in water so shallow that their wingtips will stick up at each leisurely stroke. They'll run from a boat (make a wake that will break on the beach) but they'll let you get pretty close. They also jump way out of the water and come down with such a splash that it is a marvel to see. A jumping porpoise (we call "dolphins" porpoises) ain't in it with a big spotted ray and I have never seen a little one. They are something else. I have heard they'll bite a hook but I wouldn't know. I have lost my rig to a good many inexplicable things, though. Cownoses will bite a hook for sure. I don't know if they are good to eat or not, though. Stingarees would feed you if you were starving but the meat is gummy and peculiar tasting. I am not fond of sharks either. You know I and all my family are gourmets . . . ain't crazy about any of the elasmobranchs.

To get to the meat of this story (finally), when we got all the way around the east end (noting many mullet, sheepheads, and redfish in the clear water) we tooled it all the way down the seaside looking at the rubble from the houses that went in due to the four hurricanes and current bar formation (no bars parallel to the beach like is the usual summer situation, yet). We stayed out far enough from the beach not to bother the mullet that we could see like they were in an aquarium as the gentle waves peaked up and carried the fish, too. In the right light, a fish is surrealistically displayed when that happens. I have always wanted to take a picture. We scared balao (half beaks, pronounced *bally-hoo* . . . real good bait), which skittered off with their whole body completely clear of the water and swimming with just the lower tip of their tail like a flying fish getting up enough speed to take off. If balao had long pectoral fins they could fly, too. Jane thinks the word *skeedaddle* was invented just for them. Eventually we got all the way around to the west end of the island. For the last two years there have been none of the prominent bars that usually form along there making deep coves, one right behind the other all along the seaside of the end of the island. That's a wonderful thing. A child can stand on one of those bars and fish with a fishing pole in the cove and catch almost anything. When we were children we used to catch pinfish, sheepheads, flounders, speckled trout (squeteague), pompano, redfish, whiting, and . . . bluefish in there. This time there was one prominent bar making a protected cove right on the seaside end of the island. We eased the Rescue Minor over the bar in the surf (much to the amazement of some fishermen fishing out in the pass) and anchored in the cove. We saw mullet everywhere but the water was real clear and they wouldn't let me get within fifty feet. They just insolently crossed the bar from the lagoon to the sea and waited for me to wade by and crossed back behind me. I was hoping for a sheephead, which is a little bit stupider than a mullet, but the water was too clear for them, too. As I was wading out the bar (about thigh-deep) looking so intensely into the lagoon with my Polaroid sunglasses that it was about to give me a headache, I saw some good-sized fish easing in within easy range of the net. "Cain't be mullet . . . too stupid . . . must be black drum," I said. "Oh well," I concluded as I let the old net (two years old . . . many holes tied up) fly. I caught seven fish but, by the time I could get them to the boat, there were only two left in the net. Bluefish will bite out of a net, you know, and big bluefish will bite an unnecessarily big hole it seems to me.

While I was gone with the net, Jane waded out to the mouth where the outwash from the waves that break over the bar goes back to sea. That is always a good place to fish. For one thing, the outwash (called "undertow" by ignorant people and "rip current" by the NOAA and official lifeguards) will carry your bait way out, unless you have a big lead sinker on it, and that is real good because it keeps the bait acting like something to eat and also keeps the bait off the bottom so the durn inedible hardhead catfish won't get hooked. I'll give you this little fishing tip. If you find one of those outwash places, put a live shrimp on your hook and let him drift out. If he makes it a hundred feet I would be surprised. What you'll usually catch is a skipjack (ladyfish . . . ten-pounder) and she'll show you what it means when somebody says a fish will fight. She'll jump ten feet in the air and pull so hard you'll think you caught the biggest fish in the ocean. If you are standing in the surf, she'll swim around and around you and between your legs and tie you up like ZaSu Pitts on the railroad tracks in an old Western movie. When you get her in, you'll be surprised at what a little fish did all that. I have never seen a ten-pounder . . . three is more like it but one of them will pull like fifteen and run like a bullet. They are fun. Well, one of them is fun but they get to be a pain in the neck after a while what with live shrimp at twenty-five cents a pop.

Jane didn't have any live shrimp but she did have some jigs and little pieces of fresh cut-up pinfish, which is pretty good. I watched her and she fished for a while and then went back to the boat and sat in the shade of the Bimini top. I figured she had gotten tired of being tied up by skipjacks but when I got back with my torn-up net and two bluefish I found that she had just lost her jig. We both surmised that it was bluefish and we were right. I'll tell you what I, a southerner, know about bluefish, the national bird of the Yankee saltwater fisherman, in a minute but first I need to tell you about hardtails.

There were a lot of small pogies in the lagoon and they were getting washed out the opening by the current and a bunch of various kinds of fish were eating them as they emerged into the deep blue water of the pass. We could see Spanish mackerel, skipjacks, and bluefish jumping clear of the water as they gobbled the pogies and we knew there were even bigger fish like jack crevalle below. In my youth, such a thing as that would get me very excited thinking of tarpon and other real big fish like cobio and I would have lost all my tackle to the toothy things like all them bluefish and Spanish mackerel. I have changed these days, though. I don't need to bother with any tarpon anymore. "Jane," I said, "reckon there are any hardtails down under all this commotion?" With that, she picked up her pole and tied on the last jig and flipped it out. It was gone in one bite. I had a little piece of wire, though, so we rigged up a hook on the wire with a piece of cut bait and tried again. I tried to let it get down under the mess of gobbling on the surface. Hardtails are peculiar in their feeding habits. I don't think they catch pogies. I think they lurk under the melee and eat half pogies that bluefish have bitten in two. If you can get the bait down to them, you can catch them. I caught one hardtail before something big took my hook, wire and all. A hardtail has always been one of my favorite fish ever since I was a child. They come in the bay in the early summer and only stay for a few weeks and then they are gone. One must make hay while the sun shines. I used to go out in the Reynolds and fish all by myself when I was young. The first time I got into the hardtails, I guess I was about ten years old. I had an old fly rod but I used it like a cane pole. I don't remember the exact rig but I feel sure it was just a naked hook with some kind of bait on it. Back in those days shrimp were very cheap so that might have been what I had. Anyway, I was inexperienced and hardly ever caught anything out of the boat but damn catfish. Mostly I lost my bait to pinfish because I, like so many other ignorant people, still thought you have to have a big hook to catch big fish. Anyway, something grabbed my bait and headed for Yucatan. I thought it must have been a submarine. Finally I caught the mystery fish and he was only about a pound. He was a little man, though, and I quickly caught some more. When I got back to the house, I had about thirty of those hardtails. Nobody knew what they were except my momma. "Hardtails!" she hollered running for her knife. She and I cleaned all of them and fed the multitude and all those people remembered what they were after that. There are few better eating fish than hardtails. What they are in the book is "blue runners" and are one of the favorite baits of billfisherman. They are little jacks like jack crevalle and amberjacks but much smaller and much better to eat. The name *hardtail* comes from how they have ridges of enlarged scales down either side of the caudal peduncle making a thwartships hard fin. You fillet them off the backbone, fry the fillets, and hold them by that little hard handle to eat them. They have thin skin that doesn't shrink up so the fillets fry up flat.

They are also extremely good smoked. You can smoke the little fillets until they are dried out like jerky. Whoo, y'all. Be careful not to founder yourself. Each one of those little shriveled-up fillets will reconstitute itself into half a pound of meat in your belly.

My correspondence with various Yankees has alerted me to the fact that bluefish are very common up the Atlantic coast and are sought after by fishermen. Some of these fishermen tell me, when they are trying to catch the very high-class striped bass (we have them here, too, but they are freshwater fish and live in rivers . . . we never catch them in the bay) they actually catch mostly bluefish. There are so many of them that they call them special names for how big they are like they do various sizes of quahogs (the littlest class of those are "cherrystones"). I don't remember all the various classes of bluefish but the littlest ones are called "snapper" blues and are very little. We don't have snapper blues down here. As a matter of fact, bluefish are an intermittent thing here with no predictable regularity. Sometime ten years will pass by without us seeing any bluefish at all but, when they come, they dominate the situation because they are very big and plentiful. They are always exactly the same size (siblings?). The ones this year are all eighteen inches long. That's a pretty good-sized bluefish. We fried one and the hardtail for lunch and baked the other bluefish for supper. Bluefish are pretty good if you eat them while they are still very fresh but they ain't much (to a gourmet like me) after they have been refrigerated for one day and are inedible if you freeze them. They are like mullet that way. I have smoked bluefish and they are all right but they lose quality rapidly.

It is not the quality of the meat that makes bluefish memorable to us. It is the memory of them. I'll quickly flip out three stories for you. One time, my cousin and I went camping back in the wild coast to the east of St. Marks in a great, big aluminum butt-head skiff I had for a while. It was in the fall of the year and we hoped to catch a bunch of redfish (red drum) to freeze and feed the multitude with. We had a big old icebox and were well set up to catch a boatload (which is possible if you know what you're doing but we didn't). The boat was big enough to sleep in and that was what we were doing. We anchored out on the flats beyond no-see-um range and ate our Vienna sausages and apples and went to bed. I decided to suspend a little pinfish over the side on my booger pole, which was a boat rod with a Penn #109 reel and about ten-pound-test line. I had a little piece of wire and a cork to keep the pinfish off the bottom away from the catfish. We went to sleep lying in the bottom of the boat. About two thirty in the morning, something started taking line off the Penn. I could hear the loud clicker echoing through the aluminum of the boat right in my ear. I woke up but my cousin didn't. I caught a big bluefish (maybe another eighteen-incher). I could see other fish tearing up the water all around the boat so I got my casting rod and baited up and started pulling in these big blues one right after the other. I was so ignorant that I thought we could fill the icebox and feed the multitude with those inedible-after-two-days bluefish so I punted my cousin in the side of the ribs, hard enough to make his lips flap with the breath I knocked out of him, but he still didn't wake up. I kept on catching blues, one right behind the other. It was so exciting that I started missing the icebox with them and I am afraid some of them wound up in the bottom of the boat with my cousin and I am afraid one of them bit a notch out of his ear sort of like how you mark a hog except that the missing piece was perfectly semicircular. Man, it was a bloody mess when the pogies finally moved on taking those blues with them. That incident might account for some of my prejudice against eating big bluefish. I know some of you readers come from the inland parts of this country (or possibly other countries) or the West Coast and have not had much bluefish experience so I'll just tell you. A bluefish is set up in the mouth with big triangular teeth so sharp and close together that they cut clean. To people who know bluefish, the common awe associated with the name *piranha* loses a little significance. There aren't any twenty-nine-inch piranhas.

One year we had a plague of really big bluefish (all exactly twenty-nine inches long . . . a terrible thing to contemplate). They were not only inedible but the very thought of them in the water with you sort of inhibited the joy of swimming. Bluefish are frenzy feeders and just about indiscriminate in their tastes when in a feeding frenzy. They'll strike an aluminum can and bite landing nets, gaffs and paddles, and the feet of outboard motors. Thousands of fishermen are badly bitten by bluefish every year up north (I am told). I have no doubt they'll bite anything they perceive needs to be bitten.

So, back when we finally finished this house over here on Dog Island we sold the twenty-three-foot plywood crab boat and fixed up a twenty-six-foot surplus Navy motor whaleboat. We were deluding ourselves that we needed a big boat for everyday transportation. It was sort of convenient to have the boat tied to our dock way up the Carrabelle River. We could just drive down in a naked car and transfer the junk to the boat and crank up (after we had transferred the battery . . . a battery left unsupervised around here is a goner for sure) and ride to the island in any kind of weather at all. We even had a little wheelhouse aft so I could steer with the tiller since we didn't have a wheel in our wheelhouse. It was very cozy and we came year-round every Friday night. I say night because the trip from upriver was so far that we often didn't get to the house before eleven PM. Since we were making a fetish of the naked car, in the summertime we did not fool with a dinghy (a dinghy left unsupervised around here is a goner) and swam to and from where we anchored the whaleboat. Some nights it would be absolutely pitch dark when we got to the anchorage. I had two little bicycle reflectors lined up, one on a stake on the beach and one on a piling of the house so I could figure out exactly where to drop the anchor (big fifty-pound Luke/Herreshoff fisherman). You know, pitch dark is not an unusual thing to us. There used to be plenty of places around here far enough from town lights that it would be as dark as the natural sky would let it be. On a moonless night, it was literally impossible to see your hand in front of your face if there was enough overcast so the little illumination of the stars was shaded out. On a clear night, you could see the Milky Way arching across the sky clear from the distant tree line of the mainland in the east all the way to the horizon in the west. I don't know what it is with a Floridian but they sure do love to leave the lights on. Maybe they are scared somebody will steal their battery. Anyway, that darkness is fast becoming a thing of the past. On an overcast dark night over here now, not only are the security lights of paranoid fools visible (not only on the mainland but over on the island, too) but you can easily see the loom of Tallahassee reflected on the clouds. Pretty soon *dark* will be an imaginary word.

So, the whaleboat days were an adventure. We hauled our stuff in these plastic boxes which are the boon of boat people (and lots of others) and pulled them along behind us as we swam in from the anchorage on our backs. We tried not to think about sharks and things as we swam in what we hoped was the right direction in the pitch dark. We were very glad to open the house and finally eat our supper and go to bed in our cozy little outfit. I wonder if any of these new people with the big fancy plywood, flakeboard, and vinyl-siding monstrosities enjoy their arrival as much? One time we were fixing to go on an adventure in the whaleboat early in the morning so we dog-paddled out carrying our fishing rods and pushing our icebox. As soon as we got close to the whaleboat, a bunch of grown mullet swam from it to us. At first I thought they were something else and might be dangerous but then I realized that they were just mullet and started to relax but then they got all between our legs like they were trying to hide from something. We began to feel a little edgy and got to feeling real edgy when great big huge bluefish came running from the whaleboat and started biting those big (eighteen-inch) mullet half in two all around us. The water instantly turned bloody and an oil slick formed fifty feet wide from the fat in the mullet. Jane and I made the last twenty feet to the whaleboat pretty quick and I believe we hold the world's record for climbing up the high sides of one of those estimable vessels. After that we started to bring a skiff for a dinghy and it wasn't long before it dawned on us that a skiff was all we needed. It simplified things a lot. Like I've said, before, a big boat is a real pain in the ass.

I almost concluded this epistle before I told you the story about how we came to know the exact size of those bluefish that were biting the big mullet half in two among us. The day before we were fishing on the seaside in this truly tiny boat we keep in the house especially for that purpose. It was barely big enough to hold us and always took at least two or three tries to paddle out through the surf. We were dedicated hook-and-line fishermen then and we did what we had to do even if we capsized and swamped five times in the surf. So we were out there early in the morning fishing in that thing when Jane hooked something big with a live pinfish on a hook with a wire leader. We didn't know what it was and the only thing that kept it from taking all her line was that the boat was so little he could tow us with less effort than it took to break the line. And that is exactly what he did. The big fish resolutely towed us to the east against the longshore current for so long that the sea breeze made up and the surf did, too. Jane is a possessive type of person and not apt to let something she owns get away from her if she can help it (will fool around trying to fix old tore-up worthless junk way longer than is practical for one thing . . . things like Dollar Store reading glasses) so she held on. Finally she wore this big fish down so she could get close enough to see him. We didn't know bluefish got that big and, looking straight down on him like that, we couldn't tell what he was but it was a moot point. We did not have a gaff or a landing net or anything. Nevertheless, Jane was not willing to listen to reason and let *her* fish go so the only thing we could think of to do was to try to land him on the beach through the surf. Naturally she drew him up as close as possible so she could supervise his activities as we tried to surf in and, naturally, we capsized and all washed up in a wad . . . boat, us, fishing tackle . . . and that damn dangerous bluefish. He tried to bite us half in two but Jane clipped him in the ribs so hard that his lips flapped and punted him up on the sand and we took him home and tried to eat him. He was too big to bake so we cut him up and smoked him. He was all right, I guess. I don't actually remember. I do remember that those twenty-nine-inch bluefish were a scourge all summer long. We couldn't catch anything else. They even ate up all the crabs.

Photo Op

in which a mystery is solved thanks to my trusty 20x100 knobblers

The other day I had to get down off the roof of our little coast house because the breathless August day had just gotten too durn hot for my core temperature but while I was still up there I had observed two boats doing something peculiar even for the Gulf of Mexico in August. One was following alongside and slightly behind the other in exactly the position of a good dog when you tell him to "heel." The two boats were moving right along, too, but every now and then they would both stop and come side by side and there would be some activity among the good-sized crews of both vessels and, after about fifteen minutes, they would take off again in the same formation. Both boats were identical . . . even the same color, sort of a burnt orange to the sides and light fiberglass "whiter shade of pale" on deck. They were ordinary-looking high-sided deep-V runabouts about twenty-two feet long with identical dark-colored twin outboard engines of a large size . . . two-cycle from the sound and smoke they made while they were idling during the times the boats were sitting still. Both boats appeared to be brand new and were very shiny. The only difference between them was that during the time they were running, one of them had a man standing on top of the miniature "T top" that is so popular nowadays. I wondered how he managed to maintain footing up there on the slick fiberglass.

So I came down off the roof and, after I had cooled off with a shot of cold well water in our outside shower, got my knobblers and took a better look at those twin boats and their doings. What I saw was a photo session. I guess the boats belonged to some manufacturer and they were setting up for their advertising campaign. The man on top of one of the boats was the photographer and there was a little stand up there against which he braced his back and to which he attached himself with a little strap. Sometimes he had what looked like a thirty-five-millimeter single-lens reflex camera but which could well have been a high-class digital job. After the two boats had stopped and rafted up together (fenders carefully deployed despite the flat, glass-calm conditions) he would climb down and swap the still camera for what might have been a big video rig just like TV field crews use. Then he would climb back up there, strap himself in, and, after a little scrambling around by the people in the boat, the action would start again. I didn't see the ACTION clap-board but it was probably there. I don't know if either Steven Spielberg or Opie Taylor was in charge but it was a regular production.

All this was going on so far from our house that I couldn't figure out every single detail well enough to suit my insatiable curiosity so I carefully unpacked my 20x100 binoculars from their hermetically sealed, childproof case. With them I could see what was up with the squirming around in the two boats during the times when they were sitting still. When the two boats stopped, two young women whom I had not noticed before, and who were sitting in a carefully choreographed array on the front of the boat that was the object of the photo session, would climb down into the cockpit and redo their makeup and rearrange their clothing while the men in charge plugged various wires into computers and video equipment so as to be ready to view the results of the last shoot when the photographer finally finished gingerly climbing down off the roof. The whole crew of men would huddle in a wad watching this marvel of the photographic art until finally they would reach a consensus and start all over again. Every now and then one of the men would go get the two ornamental females and bring them over to show them something on the screen. I guess he was saying something like "It would look more sexy if you was to take this little string and shove it" or something like that. Anyway this business went on for two or three days and gradually most of the ritual became boring to me and I would have quit watching altogether but there was a peculiarity that I couldn't exactly figure out.

This photo session began very early in the morning. Just at sunup both these boats would come blasting out of the river. I assumed that they were looking for that fine early light that makes any boat look so good (?) on the water. The photographer would scramble up to his perch and the two boats would run around and turn and bank like birds or Blue Angels or some-thing. Sometimes one or more of the men would pose on the stern holding one of the fishing poles that were always arrayed in the rod holders on the tiny roof of the boat that was the object of the photo shoot. The peculiarity of this early-morning "shoot" was that the two women were not in evidence. I guess the point to it was that early-morning fishing is for he-men only. That was not interesting to me but about ten o'clock or so . . . time to get off the roof . . . the chase boat would leave the object boat and run back into Carrabelle and come back with the two women. Since it was not the boat that they had to be in to get their pictures taken, I was puzzled as to why they didn't send the boat the women would wind up in. But early one morning I noticed both boats stop just outside the river and a man jump in the water. The 20x100s revealed him scrubbing the Carrabelle scum off the waterline of the object boat with a rag and a spray bottle of some kind so I guess they sent the other boat to get the women so they wouldn't have to do that twice. The transfer operation was very awkward looking. I guess the women wanted to swap boats without assuming any position that would be unbecoming to their garb but it took a long time of many aborted attempts and a lot of chirping. Maybe they were paying these gals by the posed hour and didn't want them just standing around off camera on the company dime while the he-man part was going on. Or . . . maybe those two flowers of femininity just didn't like to get up at no five o'clock in the morning. Since I don't have a TV or read fishing or boating magazines I don't reckon I'll ever get to see the results of all that fooling around. Oh well.

Red Tides, Old Logbooks, and New Orleans

in which Dennis leaves a legacy to haunt our bay

We had a "red tide" after all the rain from Hurricane Dennis. I expected it. A red tide is when something happens that causes what they call an "algal bloom," which means that so much sewage and other kinds of fertilizer wash off the land into the ocean that some species of algae thrive beyond what is normal and the population gets so high that the result of its metabolism kills off animals. Red tides have always happened around here but are getting more and more common due to increased nutrients in the water (I guess). You know, down at the single-cell level, particularly in marine organisms, the plant/animal line of demarcation gets sort of indistinct. There are plants that swim around and animals that make their own oxygen from sunlight and it takes a lot of pedant work to draw the line. Me, I don't fool with all that. I work it like I do with people . . . take them one at a time. The "culprit" of the Florida red tide is a little dinoflagellate. I wrote his name down in one of my old logbooks and though I shuffled through them for two hours, I'll be damned if I can find that obscure notation. They have probably changed the name since then anyway.

I started keeping logbooks when I was a little boy. My hero was this old bird ornithologist named Herbert Stoddard. He wasn't just a bird-watcher, he was a universal what they called a "naturalist" back in the olden days. He knew everything about the natural world and I thought he was wonderful. He had a little polished leather book that he kept in his shirt pocket all the time. The reason it was polished was that he took it out and wrote down not only every bird he saw but every change in the wind, every insect, every twitch of any squirrel tail, every oak gall, the barometric pressure . . . everything . . . and the continual friction of the leather against the cloth of his shirt pocket brought the former to a high state of shine . . . somewhat like the toe of the shoe of a jarhead. Inside this little leather cover was a regular three-by-five-inch ring-topped notebook that looked like it came from the dime store. He had a little pencil in there, too, which he sharpened (with a very large and extremely sharp pocketknife) to a needle point and he wrote in tiny letters so neat that it was astonishing. The whole thing was most admirable and I tried to emulate that in my boyish way but my methods had not been perfected quite yet. My dime store notebooks soon became wet from sweat and though my pocketknife was sharp, my octagonal tapering skills were, as yet, imperfect. Which, as an aside, that's how I judge a man's ability to work wood . . . watch him sharpen a pencil with a knife . . . his knife. Anyway, I finally found out that the little notebook was not dime store quality but was a special waterproof item and the pencil was not a #2 but was drafting lead hard. Even after I got myself properly equipped, I was still not able to do as well because my handwriting is pitiful and I am dyslexic and a drafting pencil doesn't erase off wet waterproof paper worth a toot but I have kept a sloppy log for many years. Of course I can't afford little "Rite-in-the-Rain" books so I have to use what I find on the close-out shelf at the Dollar Store (equivalent to the dime stores of my youth) so my logs are a conglomeration of a hodgepodge like my mechanic tools. Ain't nothing wrong with that. I mean what's the point to having matching wrenches? If your seven-sixteenth-inch looks exactly like your twelve-millimeter it makes you waste time sliding on your back in the gritty dirt trying to get the universal joint yoke a-dammit-loose. I thought the name of that little dinoflagellate was in my Harry Potter notebook but I don't guess so . . . might be in my hibiscus flower notebook but I ain't going to look for it anymore. I get too engrossed in ancient and obsolete information. I just read the fuel consumption figures for the old Take Apart skiff during a trip to Andros as a dinghy behind the old Morgan. It had an eight-horsepower Nissan (made by Tohatsu and now also called a Mercury) two-cycle. Boy, it burned a world of gas down there.

All that, like the scientific name of the dinoflagellate that caused the ruinous red tide of '93, is neither here nor there but just decoration sort of like the hibiscus flower on my Dollar Store notebook. I was just trying to explain red tide to you. When this dinoflagellate, which is always present in the plankton of Gulf waters, smelled the exact combination it needed to thrive out of control, thrive it did. In a week after the flood, the water was so full of the little plant/animals that evaporation from the surface carried enough of their substance to irritate the respiratory systems of the people down at the coast and fish and other organisms in the water began to be poisoned by the products of the metabolism of these single-celled . . . ? Whoa, I got to get this plant/animal crap straightened out so that I may revert to a sensible way of referring to them. Dinoflagellates are real peculiar little things. Though they are one-celled like an amoeba or a bacteria they appear to be a big-deal creature. They are sort of egg-shaped and have a spiral groove wrapping around their whole body. In that groove is a strand of muscle-like stuff called a "flagella," which is about the same thing as a bundle of the same molecules that can contract and expand by chemical means and move a bunch of cells that form a muscle. This thing is just the chemical fibers, though, and its movement is similar to what happens when you pull on one strand of a knitted sock. It bunches up the other fibers and the only way to straighten it out is to pull somewhere else. The net movement of the flagella is just a wiggle in its groove, which makes the cell spiral. At the place where this flagella is attached there is another filament just like it except that it resides in a longitudinal groove and its wiggle creates a forward motion so the little animal/plant swims forward as it spirals around and around. Maybe it does that so the sun can shine on all sides so it can photosynthesize like a plant. I don't know. The trouble with it is that it metabolizes like an animal. It consumes oxygen and makes waste products that are toxic to other animals, unlike a plant, which makes pure oxygen and water as its waste products. In the natural system those two kingdoms sort complement each other. We animals need the products of those plants and, though they can do perfectly well without us animals, they do real well with our help . . . hence agriculture, golf courses, mown lawns, and hog parlors.

In the olden days, back before people began to run amok because they couldn't do what comes naturally anymore due to the pressing need for hedonistic abstractions of all sorts, primitive agriculture was relatively benign. Folks raised what they needed to live the good life and sat on the porch of an evening and shelled ladyfinger peas and butter beans. Late-model life has changed all that. Now it takes two-hundred-bushel-to-the-acre corn to break even. To do that requires so much fertilizer and diesel fuel and chemicals and money that the result of their agribusiness (!) is a profit of a dime an acre so they have to fertilize a lot of land to feed the SUV and run the pool pump and keep Chuck E. Cheese happy. Of an evening most modern people play video games and watch TV and of a weekend, they play golf and mow the lawn. Their butter beans come frozen out of a plastic bag and they ain't ever seen a ladyfinger pea. All would be fine except that the result of all this excess is an excess of fertilizer to rinse out of the field and golf course and lawn when a hurricane brings a flood of rain. The fertilizer (along with the manure from the sewage "lagoon" at the hog "parlor") washes down the river into the bay and causes a bloom of algae of all kinds including those dinoflagellates whose waste products are toxic to fish and certain select other organisms, both plants and animals.

Dinoflagellates would be the perfect primitive animal swimming along in a spiral path through the water by virtue of alternate rhythmic contractions of the molecules of their flagellae except for one thing . . . they have chlorophyll like the leaves of a plant. The populations of most animals in the ocean's plankton are kept in check by oxygen. If they get too thick they use up too much oxygen and have to die back and an equilibrium wobbles back into balance. It works in a similar way with plant plankton. If they get too thick they shade out the light needed for photosynthesis and have to die back to clear the water so the equilibrium straightens back out. Because of their plant/animal metabolism capability these dinoflagellates can make their own oxygen if they can get enough light and if they can't they don't need it so there is no easy equilibrium. In the presence of fertilizer they get thick enough to kill not only animals but plants with their toxic waste.

After the great March Storm of '93, there was a dinoflagellate bloom that killed every hardhead catfish in Apalachee Bay. Not only that but the toxicity killed lots of species of filter feeders (animals that make their living filtering plankton out of the water . . . clams are filter feeders). Sand fleas (mole crabs) disappeared from the seaside and all the filter-feeding worms of the bayside died. There was considerable mortality of other creatures, too. The nearshore turtle grass beds were damaged by the shade from the soupy water and even to this day, some of the old equilibriums have not leveled out. Hardhead catfish (the males raise the babies in their mouths and almost starve to death in the process) have come back and sand fleas but those tube worms that make a sand and trash tube that looks like a child's notion of a periscope are just now, thirteen years later, beginning to be common on the flats again. It was a real big deal around here.

So when Jane and I came easing across after that awful Katrina to see what had happened to Dog Island we were horrified to see dead mullet and other fish littering the bayside beach. We set out the Bahama moor and trotted to the seaside and it was even worse. There were dead and bloated fish from offshore all in the weed line from where Katrina's storm surge (maybe four feet) had left them. We saw sharks, groupers (one at least twenty pounds), Key West grunts, puff fish, triggerfish, pogies, and even remoras. I hurried down to the water's edge to look for sand fleas and they were all right. So were the crabs. I guess it was a red tide but it might have been oxygen deprivation.

You know, there is a "dead zone" in the summertime down around the Mississippi Delta. In a bad year in August and September there is almost five thousand square miles of ocean that is so anoxic that no animals live there. It is caused (the NOAA says) by excess nutrients and organic material coming out of the Mississippi. What happens (they say) is that so much stuff accumulates on the bottom that its decomposition uses up all the oxygen in the water. Maybe all that rain (some eighteen inches on the average) from Hurricane Dennis did that same thing with the Apalachicola and Ochlocknee Rivers. Any fish or other oxygen-breathing animal that was caught out of swimming range of water with oxygen in it died. That accounts for the multispecies nature of this kill. The poisonous excrement of specific plankton is toxic to specific animals like that dinoflagellate was to catfish but oxygen starvation hits everybody.

There were no dead bluefish or Spanish mackerel in the weed line on Dog Island and they had been plentiful last week. I think they were able to leave in time. There were no corporate executives in the Super Dome, either. New Orleans might very well have been the poorest sizable city in this country. People there live in a more primitive situation than in most urban areas. It is hard for working people to get ahead down there with Old Man River. I heard one man sitting on the I-10 overpass right downtown say, "Man I just live from paycheck to paycheck. I don't have the money to rent a car." I don't think there is anything wrong with that and it is a good thing I feel like that because that's how I have lived my whole life. I don't think it is necessary for somebody to mow five acres of grass and play eighteen holes of golf and drive the SUV and talk on the phone all the time to be somebody. It is tough sometimes but it is okay. Some of those check-to-check people are going to die from this, though, but I guess that's the way it is. I think a lot of them will not die and New Orleans will resume where it left off. What I want to know out of this horrible story is what the Army Corps of Engineers is going to do with all that toxic water their failed structures let into the city?

Key West Grunts

That's a wonderful fish. They get to be maybe two pounds and used to be so common offshore that anybody with a capable boat could go out there and get all he wanted. Because of that, certain unscrupulous charter boat people took to lying to ignorant patrons and (though when caught these fish grunt louder than any Duroc hog) calling them "snappers." A Key West grunt looks a lot like a snapper. They have big mouths and insolent expressions on their faces like most snappers (look a Cubera snapper in the face sometime . . .). They also have big scales and are colored a little like a mangrove snapper but they are grunts. Grits and grunts used to be an alternative staple of the diet of people down at the coast . . . alternative to grits and mullets. The most amazing thing about Key West grunts ("Yankee snappers") is that the color of the inside of their mouths is a very bright vermilion orange. They come up on the hook out of the clear water with their mouths open, too. It is a sight to see. Grunts are very good eating. They have big bones and not too many of them and they scale easy. The skin is thin so it doesn't shrivel up and curl up the fillets too bad in the pan, either. But the best thing is that most offshore fishermen pass them up along with triggerfish, which are another real good eating fish. These hotshots are after big game like groupers and amberjacks, which are okay but nowhere near as good as a grunt or a triggerfish. Anyway, there are plenty of grunts offshore and you don't have to go out any farther than it takes to get to the blue water. The grunt zone begins about exactly when you get out of sight of land. We used to go out there all the time in a little sailboat . . . cleaned the grunts on the seat on the way back and threw the heads and guts to the sharks that followed us back in with the sea breeze. It was wonderful. I hope they didn't all get killed by this red tide. I may have to ease out there for old times' sake in the Rescue Minor. It has been a long time since I saw the blue water and the spotted porpoise. I sure did see a lot of Key West grunts, though. Dang.

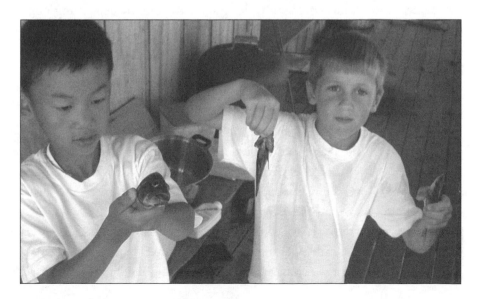

Pleistocene Creek Revisited

in which the role of Riverkeepers is examined

A good friend of mine lives over on the Mississippi coast that Katrina and those floating casinos scraped down to bare dirt. He has sort of been wandering around to escape having to look at all that destruction full-time and he wandered our way. I felt so sorry for him that I offered to take him to the little river I call "Pleistocene Creek" hoping that it would make him feel better to see something that has survived untouched since the last ice age, and I hoped like anything that it was still untouched but it has been twenty-five years since my last trip back in there. I had been trying to avoid the place so I wouldn't have to find that it has a damn flakeboard-and-vinyl-siding-style condominium looming over the habitat of the mastodon and the naked savage. I have to tell you I was scared to death when we rolled the Rescue Minor off the trailer at the nearest boat ramp.

One reason I was scared was that we found the boat ramp had been significantly improved by the government. Back in the old days it was just a little cut in the bank where somebody could back a trailer down to launch a little boat. It had to be a little boat because about five feet out from the edge was a gigantic submerged (at high tide) rock that the boat had to clear or be dragged over. (Not only was the rock gone but the ramp was concrete and two trailers wide, which is a useless thing since the rapidly expanding population of yahoos down here can't back a trailer well enough to occupy only one side while they fiddlefart around with all the stuff they should have done before they backed down so cattywompus that they block all further launchings on both sides of the ramp until they finally get ready to launch and leave. I am trying to avoid becoming an old, dried-up malcontent so I won't have to live the rest of my life in an impotent rage but it is kind of hard to do when you have to launch a boat. Degeneration of boat ramp etiquette is just one branch off the basic stem of all my pet peeves . . . the incompetence, stupidity, and thoughtlessness that runs rampant in American society today . . . brought on, I believe by an excess of the easy life.

Fortunately we didn't have a bit of trouble at the ramp. Launching took us fifteen seconds on only one side of the boat ramp. The boat was already untied from the trailer, our junk was all arranged, the engine had been tried to see if it had what it needed to percolate, and the trailer roller axles were greased so the boat rolled immediately off and my buddy led it with the painter around the end of the dock the government had built so that yahoos could tie their boat up and unconsciously continue to block the ramp even after the boat was off the trailer. Phooey on a dock. I like to pull up on the bank to get in. The trouble is most boaters don't want to get their Sperry Topsiders wet. Me, I leave my Sperry Topsiders in the car and go barefoot in the boat unless it is January, then I wear my white rubber boots like all working boat people do. You know, it takes a particular talent to ride a bicycle with white rubber boots.

So I was scared to death as we idled out the river dodging the rocks that the government had not removed quite yet. Now, I ain't about to tell you exactly where that was but I will set the scene. It is somewhere between Dickerson Bay (Panacea) and Crystal River. That's a long stretch of coast and most all of it is rocky and shallow. Before the invention of the cell phone, it was a regular yahoo trap. Many of them got themselves in a fix of extremis after they knocked the foot clean off the engine on a rock. There is a significant amount of aluminum on the bottom of that coast. I wasn't scared of the rocks. The water is clear enough so I could see anything that was within six inches of the surface far enough away to dodge it. I stood up on the seat and eased along the coast in the bright sun and sparkling water of a perfect fall day toward the secret go-in place that I hoped I remembered right after all these years. This is all classic salt marsh down here, that's an ephemeral situation at best, and we have had about ten hurricanes whip through that exact place since I was last there. I have to tell you that we wandered around in the marsh for most of the morning trying to figure out where the hell we were. I shut down and stood on top of the engine box a bunch of times trying to get my bearings. Fortunately it was only two days past the full moon and we had a two-tide day (one high and one low in twenty-four hours) so the tide was rising and apt to do that all day long. It doesn't pay to get up in a marsh on a falling spring tide around here no matter what kind of shallow-draft boat you have. You are liable to get yourself in a fix that you can't talk yourself out of on a cell phone unless you know somebody with a helicopter.

Finally things started looking familiar to me and I noticed where the current of the rising tide seemed to have found itself a channel and I eased on farther into the marsh toward the distant trees. My buddy broke out his camera and took some pictures as the landscape changed. I got more and more worried as I realized that we would soon be in that wonderful little place.

What I was worried about wasn't hitting a rock but that we would find trash and vandalism and evidence of fartfaces and yahoos defacing a place that ought to be looked at and left absolutely alone. I was even worried that the government might have decided that they needed to do a little improvement project in there like they had done with the boat ramp.

Trash is one of my favorite gripes. I mean, all this trash along the road and washed up on the beach is a good indicator of how sorry and thoughtless the average American has become. I bet you don't see that in Iceland or Monaco or Switzerland. It is easy to see how the trash-throwing tradition starts around here. The city our shop is near does not run school buses. The children have to walk to school or get their parents to take them (few bicycles among them). Before they start home, a lot of them stop off at the vending machine emporium and buy themselves a little snack or two. You can see some of them walking home along the sidewalks in one of the prettiest little towns in Georgia . . . gnawing open plastic wrappers, eating the contents, and throwing the trash on the ground without any more thought than a baby uses when he wipes his nose on his sleeve. There are Snicker bar wrappers blowing down every street and sidewalk in town. I know some of the kids don't do that but I am afraid they are a dwindling minority and there is no hope that the thoughtless majority will ever grow up to be anything but shitepokes. It is possible that they will attain the American dream and drive the SUV but you know damn well they'll throw trash out of the electric window (if the fuse isn't blown) and you know damn well they'll never park between the lines or notice what they are backing into.

The same week as our Pleistocene Creek trip, I was invited to "speak" at the semi-annual meeting of the Apalachicola Bay and Riverkeepers but they didn't want me there as a dignitary to add a little gravity to the serious work of the organization. One or two of them had read my wretched book and thought what I remembered from sixty years ago about the river and the bay they are trying to protect might be entertaining.

I don't know if I told them anything they didn't already know but I learned a lot from the Riverkeepers. One thing I learned was that they are, finally, after many years of fighting, hopeful that they can make a little headway in the struggle to stop the Army Corps of Engineers from dredging the Apalachicola River. Let me give you a little background here: The

Apalachicola River is the second biggest river draining into the Gulf of Mexico. It is a sight to see and may very well be the most unspoiled river in the Northern Hemisphere south of the Artic Circle. It is the result of the confluence of its two main tributaries, the Chattahoochee and the Flint, which used to come together right at the corner where the Florida–Georgia line takes a jog to the north. In 1957, the Army Corps of Engineers closed the gates on a dam they had built on the state line and flooded 37,500 acres of woods to create Lake Seminole (that's 376 miles of shoreline . . . 30 miles up the Chattahoochee and 35 up the Flint). The little Thomasville Boat Club (I rode with Chester Bellamy) made the last trip down the Flint River from Bainbridge before the gates were closed. That was a beautiful place and it still is. The Apalachicola below the dam is fortunate not to have any big towns or industrial complexes to pollute it. It is supposed to be navigable (it is wide, swift, and used to be deep . . . most places) and was maintained in that condition by the corps for a long time. Bainbridge and Columbus up in Georgia are inland ports. You can lock through the Jim Woodruff dam at Lake Seminole and a lot of barges of fertilizer and petroleum used to do that. But Atlanta has grown into a regular megalopolis since 1957 and all those urbanites have to wash all those SUVs and water all that yard and golf course grass so there isn't much water coming down the Chattahoochee anymore . . . lot of sewage and trash, though. Somehow the city of Atlanta and surrounds have managed to litigate and procrastinate themselves through and around many of the government environmental protections. There are so many introduced noxious weeds in Seminole (the weediest lake I ever saw) that I hope most of that North Georgia runoff gets "biodegraded" before it trickles through the dam to feed the dwindling Apalachicola. The ridiculous part, now, is that the Corps of Engineers has continued to dredge that river even though the little bit of water that escapes from Atlanta isn't enough to float a barge more than a few days out of the year and people long ago decided that if they needed reliable transportation of commodities, they better work it through trucks, trains, and pipelines. Not only that, but even with good water the Apalachicola and Chattahoochee are some of the hardest rivers to negotiate with a tug I ever saw, even with only one barge, and the Flint . . . whooee . . . you know, flint rock is hard on a barge bottom or a towboat wheel. There aren't very many wheelmen left who can push up to Bainbridge or Columbus even in the rare times when there is enough water. What I am saying is that there has only been an intermittent trickle of commercial traffic on that system for years . . . no excuse for all that dredging and fooling around.

Eighty percent of the oysters harvested in Florida come from water that is fed by the Apalachicola River. Most of the citizens in Franklin County live by oysters. The men rake and the women shuck and all of them work hard for their money and are proud and independent people and their children want to grow up to be just like them. There is no mechanical harvesting in Florida. They do it by hand and have somehow managed to scratch a living out of the bottom of the bay for a mighty long time. The only machinery involved is an outboard motor and you can buy a beat-up outboard motor mighty cheap down there these days because all those people are literally starving, since the bay has been closed to oystering for most of the summer and fall. It is a minor disaster compared with the tsunami, Katrina, and the Pakistan earthquake but it probably feels about the same to the people it happened to.

So is the situation so hopeless that I am in complete despair? Nope. When my buddy and I idled into the shade of the ancient trees of Pleistocene Creek, it was exactly like I remembered if from twenty-five years ago. There was no trash . . . no chain saw work, no archaeological digs, no government improvements, and nobody at all. The tears came in my eyes. I shut off the engine and we sat in the boat and looked around for a long time then left it just like we found it. When we got out in the bay, we saw a man and his wife working crab traps in their white rubber boots. I asked them how it was going. "Pretty good," said the woman, "these crabs have fattened up all summer from eating all these dead fish. You know that red tide ain't hurt them a'tall." So there is hope. Apalachee Bay is not irreversibly damaged like they say the Chesapeake is and, below Lake Seminole, the river will be much better if they can get the fool dredging stopped. I think there are enough people who have the sense to become aware that maybe some of this pollution can be stopped in time. There is a rumor that the FDEP has realized that they are permitting a useless and destructive project and that there are more and more people who are aware of that. If that is true, all these Riverkeepers have to do is curtail some of this agricultural and golf course runoff and get the US Supreme Court to stop Atlanta from squandering and crapping up everybody's water.

They might be able to do it, too. There were two hundred people at that meeting and that in Eastpoint, which is a tiny little oystering community on the point east of the river. They were meeting in the Eastpoint volunteer fire department building . . . a mighty fine place built all by volunteers. I didn't see any fire truck but I bet those volunteers are building that somewhere, too. Some of those Riverkeepers had on their white rubber boots and I think there were one or two politicians there (not in white rubber boots). I don't know for sure but I bet somebody up there in Tallahassee is going to have to shake a leg pretty quick.

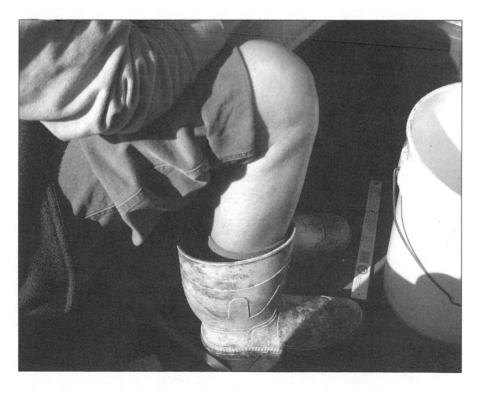

Boat Ramp Antics

in which, due to my great skill at hiding, I remain a spectator

You know, I don't do things that I don't like to do if I can help it. I'm good at it too. I haven't been to Tallahassee since 1969. I wish I could figure out a way to stay away from boat ramps. Our boat is small and light so I used to be able to just find a thin place in the bushes to put in but now the banks are all bought up and guarded by rottweilers. We have to go to the boat ramp. We are quick, though. My wife and I have a little carefully choreographed ritual that, unless we bump heads, works like clockwork. The only thing wrong with it is how self-conscious I feel right there in front of all those people, not only the ones at the boat ramp but those sitting at the tables on the veranda of the Tiki Bar, staring out from under the palm fronds of the old roachy cabanas that shade their tables.

Because the boat ramp is the only public access to the water that leads to our house, I have go there to pick up my relatives who like to cast off the chains of their megalomania every now and then and come to the coast and marvel at all the necessities of life that we ain't got. In the wintertime I have to visit the boat ramp at least twice a week and in the summer, Lord knows, sometimes it is twice a day. Pretty often they are not quite ready when I get there and I have to wait while they go into the Tiki Bar to use the bathroom. I don't stay there in the middle of the launching melee while I wait. I paddle out into the eddy of a tied-up shrimp boat and try to blend into the landscape. I also try to avert my eyes from the doings at the boat ramp but it is impossible. Along with the regulars of the Tiki Bar, I have seen some terrible things.

One time, I was supposed to pick up my yuppie niece. Despite the fact that she has to drive all the way from north of Atlanta, she is usually on time. I asked her how she did it. "I drive like hell." Well, she finally blew a piston out the tailpipe or something and was late. I hung around, following the shade of a shrimp boat, and watched the launchings. The road was full all the way up around the bend with about three million bucks' worth of big-deal boats on trailers waiting their turn. The invisible people sat in their idling sport utility vehicles with the blacked-out windows rolled up and the AC blowing. Then the turn came for the biggest outboard-powered boat I

510

ever saw to launch. The man backed down onto the ramp okay. His nice-looking wife got out and held the rope while he used the inertia-launch method by backing down the ramp and dragging his brakes. The behemoth didn't come off the trailer like it was supposed to so he got out and checked that the tie-downs were loose while his wife stood there holding the rope and other hopeful launchers began to get out of their air-conditioning so they could stand around supervising and consulting. The patrons of the Tiki Bar manned the rail. The man got back into the car and must have decided that it was time to launch her for sure. He backed down the ramp about thirty miles per hour and when he locked the brakes, the whole business slid down into the river . . . all except for his wife, who had sense enough to drop the line. The boat, trailer, and all were swept downriver around the end of the little dock by the outgoing tide. This jackknifed the man's truck all the way into the water except for the very top of the roof and the hood ornament. He had to climb out the window. As he got out, a dead puff fish got in. All the other hopeful launchers abandoned their rigs and wandered off in the direction of the Tiki Bar. Luckily, about then, I saw my niece waving from the other side of the river and picked her up, illegally, at the Coast Guard dock.

Another time, I was stuck at the boat ramp all morning. I had, stupidly, bragged about one of my abilities and got myself obligated to restuff the stuffing box on this lady's sailboat there in her slip right beside the boat ramp so she could save the haul-out fee. I thought she was going to hang around and hand me tools and cool glasses of lemonade while I was head-down in the bilges under the cockpit and fuel tank, but no. I ended up stupidly agreeing to lend her my skiff so she could go back to the island and wait for me to call her on the VHF when I was through. I sure am glad I'm not a sexist anymore and am able to put everyone on an equal footing.

My stuffing-box-fixing method is simple and quick. First I get in the water, swim down, and cram a paper towel into the crack between the shaft and the rubber of the shaft bearing with an oyster knife After I get out of the water, I go down in the boat and scramble back behind the engine with the stuffing and the hook clenched in my teeth and a pair of rusty Channel Lock pliers in each hand. This particular job went so smooth that I was through before the woman got out of sight in the no-wake zone. I had to wait to tell her until she got to the VHF at her house, though.

Back while I was in the water, this man launched a big deep-V outboard boat. The launch must not have gone too well because I could hear a good little bit of loud cussing coming down to me through my snorkel. By the time I got through diving in the water and started diving in the engine room, he was trying to run his battery down cranking on his engine. After I got the stuffing stuffed and was sitting in the shade of the Bimini top trying, unsuccessfully, to call up my ride, he was taking the battery out of his truck. I tried to hide in the shallow cockpit while he ran that battery down too. His wife or girlfriend, a nice-looking young lady, was sitting on the icebox on the dock while this man was cussing and fuming and squirting gasoline all over himself. The truck, still on the boat ramp, was running, wide open, trying to recharge the boat battery. Though it was late and the launchings had slowed down, some people came and politely waited for the man to clear out. By that time, I had abandoned the boat I was on and hopes of a call on the VHF to get away from all that gas and electrical sparks and potential violence. Finally the young lady managed to draw his attention to the people waiting to launch their boat. Though he screamed at her, he did move his truck just enough so that they could get by. Then he tied his boat up with a bad-looking tangle of line to the end of the little dock while he continued as before, cussing, cranking, squirting gas, and drawing big dangerous-sounding sparks with the jumper cables. While I was sneaking back to the VHF sort of like you do when you are trying to slip up on a squirrel, keeping things between you and the quarry and only moving when he is looking in the other direction, the man and his boat somehow came loose from the dock and began to drift down the river. The man was so busy with his crazy mechanic work that he didn't notice until he was out of reach. The little vestigial paddle that is required by law didn't do a bit of good against the current and he continued toward the mouth of the river. After the sound of his voice had diminished to just the hint of a furious chirp every now and then, the lady stood up from the icebox, opened the lid, got out a grape drink in an aluminum can, and plopped herself back down and drank it. I could see her tongue turn blue. Next time I came topside from a VHF attempt, she, the icebox, the truck, and the trailer were gone. When the beneficiary of the stuffing-box job finally came and got me, we snuck out another of the distributaries of the river and I don't know what ever became of that man. I kept expecting to see a ball of fire ascend above the tree line.

The latest event was just the other day. Spring is the best sailing weather around here and there is sometimes a sailboat in the line with all the mega-monsters and metal-flakes at the boat ramp. I had to hang around while my son went to the grocery store for us. I lurked in the shadows while this nice-looking couple launched a small fiberglass cabin sailboat. As usual, there is a power line astride this boat ramp but these people were savvy enough not to electrocute themselves and, after launching, they led the boat down the bank toward the Tiki Bar, out of danger, though not out of view, to raise the mast. They were savvy enough to know about electricity but they didn't notice that something like a turnbuckle clevis pin had vibrated out on the road and when they pulled the mast up with the forestay, it just kept coming. It crashed down on top of one of the cabanas of the Tiki Bar knocking the props out from under the thatching, which fell onto the occupants of the table (drinking beer at nine thirty in the morning . . . serves them right). By the time the beer drinkers had managed to root out from under all that trash and were hopping around trying to slap the huge, insolent Florida roaches (called "palmetto bugs" by the prissy, but the actual, accepted common name is "Walker's Enormous, Stinking Cockroach") off before they could hide inside their clothes, the citronella candle had set the palmetto fronds on fire. Only quick work with a bucket by me and a little Spanish-speaking boy who was crabbing off the shrimp boat dock saved the whole shebang from going up in smoke. He told me later that it is not good to let the roof of the cabana fall into the fire.

Dead Man's Boat

in which I reveal two morals

I have never been more reverent for people after they are dead than I was when they were alive. I mean, it just don't make any sense to me to overlook the facts of the matter. Might as well not hold back on a good story just because the person it is about ain't around to enjoy it.

About 1989 I built a boat for an old, old friend of mine and he was just about on his last legs when he ordered this boat. He already had three of my boats and though he was so decrepit that he wasn't able to use any of them when he ordered this one, he didn't think he was quite through yet. What he wanted this time was a tiny pirogue. He said that he was going to get his granddaughters to take him down to his pond and lay him out in the bottom of it (he specified that it have no thwarts), cover him with his wool afghan, and push him out away from the bank to drift in the sun every now and then when the weather was fine for what he was sure was his last winter in Georgia. I dropped everything and went to work, but in spite of that, I was too late.

I had invented this way to make these little extra-light model bow pirogues a long time ago and they were hot sellers among high-card duck hunters who owned swampland down in south Louisiana. The way they were built was that the whole bottom of the boat was made out of two wide poplar (tulip poplar, *Liriodendron tulipfera*) boards, which were carved so that they were kind of thick along the edges in the wide part of the boat to form sort of a chine to fasten the sides to but were tapered thin at the ends so that they could be pulled up to the stems to form a hollow entry and fine place at the stern to ease loose of the water. The bottom board of the sides fastened along the bottom planking chine-style in the middle and then rolled around so that the forward and aft of the boat became lapstrake with rebates where the planks joined the stem and sternpost. Though there were only two topside planks to the side, the flexibility of the poplar allowed me to get a good flare and made a pretty good looking little pirogue (if I do say so myself). I built them in two versions—"standard" and "extra-light." A twelve-foot, standard one some three feet wide only weighed thirty pounds or so and the lightest one that same size only weighed nineteen—but then the sides weren't but about nine inches high in the middle. You can say that such a thing is too little to be useful if you want to, but down where the pirogue is (or used to be) the true tool, it ain't uncommon for two big men to stand up in one littler than that and each shoot a twelve-gauge shotgun out the same side (at baited ducks on the water before legal daylight, most likely). Of course, the water is so shallow most places that if they had to step out for a minute to catch their balance, they would hardly get their cowboy boots wet.

So my old friend had always wanted to figure out why he needed one of those little boats and it is too bad that he was dead before he finally got his chance. When I heard that he had what was certainly his final stroke, I went to the family and told them that they needed to feel no obligation to me for the almost finished little boat but they assured me that there was nothing that the old man would want better than for them to take it. They said that when he finished dying, they would dress up the littlest of the great-grand-daughters and let her take his ashes out into the pond in it and let him fly. I went out on the side porch where they had him lying in a hospital bed to see if I couldn't get one last rise out of him but even my little statuette of the Venus of Willendorf failed to move him and I knew I needed to hurry back to the shop and get to work.

Everything would have turned out all right except for his youngest son. He has three sons, whom I knew well because they were in my cabin at the Y camp three summers in a row. All three of them were wild for adventures in the woods, creeks, and swamps around the camp and my cabin of boys always came back more muddy and scratched-up than all the others and were sometimes late for supper. Two of those boys have slowed down enough to function fine in the regular world but the youngest turned out to be one of those people who is just too enthusiastic to adapt well. He has been wrapped up to the eyeballs in more wild schemes and reckless jobs than any-body I know, most of them somehow involving paint.

One time he had a job painting the inside of the pipes leading water to the turbines under Boulder Dam in Colorado. He told me all about it. He had to crawl about a mile through this eighteen-inch pipe dragging his paint, a big electric hotplate, a long extension cord, and an air hose. Once he got to the place where he left off last time, he cooked his paint on the hotplate until it was blistering hot and lay on his back while he daubed all around the inside of the pipe. As he worked, he had to rearrange his air hose to blow enough air on him so that he could continue to live and he had to backtrack to drag the hose and extension cord out of his way. He said that the whole business was a pain in the ass but that he made enough money in some four or five months to buy a good used Corvette and make a trip way down into Mexico almost to Nicaragua where it was stolen along with all his belongings—he had to hitchhike back to Panacea. But like the old song, "It was worth it for the time that I had," he said. After that job, he painted television and water towers and even had a job spraying logos on blimps. He was a regular paint man and when his father died, he was in the newly discovered polyurethane varnish business (now he buys surplus Navy paint and sells it to boatyards all up and down the East Coast out of his sailboat).

His family always had plenty of confidence in him and supported every one of his adventurous notions so they insisted that I varnish the little pirogue with his product. I had been epoxifying my boats for quite a while by then but was still using automotive clear-coat acrylic lacquer to protect the epoxy from the sun (which works pretty good). The son had told me of the wonders of this polyurethane and though talk is cheap, I was anxious to try it out, and since these people were perfectly willing to take the burden of proof on themselves, I sprayed the little boat. It went out and flowed into itself so well that I was astonished. The spray gun worked better too. The recommended viscosity would have made a mess of a lacquer job, but though it stayed liquid so long that it absorbed the overspray most miraculously, there were no curtains, runs, or orange-peel. If it could stand the weather like it was supposed to, it would certainly be the trick for protecting solventless epoxy.

After the solvent flashed out, I laid on another coat. There was no sign of any tendency to curtain, so I turned up the heat and let her rip again. After the solvent of the third coat had evaporated, I measured a miraculously uniform wet-film thickness of between five or six mils all over the whole boat and, considering the circumstances, decided to stop right there. Wow, it shined like a diamond in a goat's ass.

The next morning it was still gleaming in there. We had just had a good rain to cut down the pollen (chased the old man's barbecuing wake inside) and my dust machine had worked good. Except for one or two bug turds, I had a perfect varnish job. The coating was still soft enough for me to pick out the turds and swipe the place with my wet finger. I called the family and told them that I probably wouldn't be able to deliver the boat until the next morning and they said that that would be fine because they were having such a good time remembering the old man that they were in no hurry. "Might as well come eat some of these Apalachicola oysters with us while you are waiting." I went too and stayed mighty late because I met another old man who had served on board of a patrol boat as engineer for the old man during World War One and we got to talking. He was an amateur machinist and was just about to finish up a little Stuart Turner 5A steam engine that he had been working on for over a year. I told him that I had just the boat for it waiting for the varnish to get dry.

I can see that this story is fixing to get out of hand so I'll cut it short. Next morning the damn pirogue was still sticky and the wake was about ready to disperse so I gingerly took it to the pond and spread out a piece of plastic on the bottom for the little girl (about four years old) in her pinafore. She set the urn in front of her on the sticky bottom of the boat and took up the double paddle. Though she had only had a little pirogue experience, it had sprung up a good breeze of fair wind and she set off for the middle of the pond to the cheers of all the old man's relatives and friends. We could see her busily strewing ashes on all sides. The whole operation looked a little like dervish work but she got it done. We all ran around to the lee side of the pond for her triumphant arrival. From the looks of the boat and her, I don't think but about half of the old man made it to the water. It took me five gallons of acetone to get him and that varnish off the boat.

There are two morals to this story: One is never to trust the compatibility of two wonder substances until you do the experiments, and the other is don't wait until you are dead to do your messing.

Super Bowl Quickie

in which more boat ramp antics are disclosed

It has been so cold this winter that I haven't been to the coast but once since Thanksgiving. It has been in the twenties or teens every morning and never warms up enough to thaw out my birdbath and I have been having to keep the hose dribbling so y'all's robins can get them a little sip.

It ain't natural for me not to go to the coast all the time. It is part of my business . . . I could call it "research and development" and take the traveling expenses and the Vienna sausages off my income tax if I had any income to tax but actually, going to the coast is just something I do because I love to do it. I think there is something about the water rushing down the hull of the boat that keeps me from becoming too satisfied with the present state of my opinions. You know, the way wind and water treats a boat is one of the most complex real things in this world and there's nothing like frequent exposure to mysterious reality to ward off the complacency of old age.

Which, I finally solved another mystery. You know how Swiss Army Knives always have a corkscrew? Even the ones that are so rudimentary that they don't have a Phillips screwdriver or the little tweezers have a corkscrew. I couldn't imagine those mountain soldiers hauling bottles of wine on every camping trip. I lay awake at night worrying about that for fifty years before I finally figured it out. That corkscrew ain't for wine at all. It is there so they can get the first Vienna sausage out of the can . . . works best on the middle one.

So, it was the day of the Super Bowl. I woke up very early and trotted out the door to see what was what like I do first thing every morning and, by golly, it was warm and calm and the sky was brilliantly clear. I had spent the whole day Saturday running hollow-and-round tulip poplar strips for the big-deal inboard boat I am building. I don't normally build strip-planked boats anymore and back when I did, I beveled and tapered the strips instead of bead-and-cove because they lay better on the boat and you can keep away from the cheap shot of having the strips run out at the sheer fore and aft. I started out beveling this boat like that but by the time I got planked up parallel to the sheer, I could tell that if I kept on with all that planing, old Arthur would set himself down for an extended visit with some of these syndromes in my hands and elbows, so, since all the tapering was done and I could finish the boat with parallel-sided strips, I set up my junk and began what certainly must be the most boring boatbuilding-related job of all. I stood around feeding the shaper all day Saturday and until daylight on Super Bowl Sunday, but I couldn't stand it anymore when the sun came up so I loaded the felucca *Little Bullet* in the back of the truck and my Jane in the front and boogied to the coast. I didn't want to waste time driving all over the world or fishing, I just wanted to sail and not stop until the time was up so we headed for the closest salty water . . . good old downtown St. Marks, my old tug's home port.

I know the South is kind of recently populated by invaders from across the water compared with places up the coast (my own hometown, Beachton, Georgia . . . 1832) but St. Marks is the legacy of the horrendous Spanish . . . inhabited by "civilization" since something like 1550. At the confluence of the St. Marks and Wakulla Rivers, there is an old pile of dirt that they have dolled up and say is the remains of an old Spanish fort (Fort San Marcos de Apalachce). If I had been a conquistador, that's where I would have built my fort, too. That's also where Wakulla County built the public boat ramp but we'll get back to that.

There is another little bit of history about St. Marks. Back during the Civil War, the Yankees sent a ship into these shallow waters with a bunch of troops to take Tallahassee. That was not a real smart thing because, to this day, Tallahassee ain't worth doodley-squat but the stupidest thing they did was to set those poor foot soldiers ashore on the east side of the St. Marks River at the first high ground they came to . . . and leave them. They didn't know it but that was the only dry place there was. Those poor midwesterners and New Yorkers and all struggled and bogged (you can't just pick your foot up, you have to wiggle it aloose first) through the swamps all the way to what they call "Natural Bridge," the first place where the St. Marks River goes underground and comes back up as is so common with the rivers of this karst region. When they finally got there, they were so worn out that they got whipped by a ragtag Confederate force of leftover old men and boys. I know just what they said as they hauled their sad asses back down the river through the swamps and no-see-ums, yellow flies, mosquitoes, guinea wasps, dog flies, moccasins, alligators, and leeches, "These son of a bitches can have this son-of-a-bitching place."

I figured that all the government-related hotshots from Tallahassee would be home . . . plop on the sofa, eating chips and drinking Corona beer, getting all hyped up for the ball game. Usually if the FSU football team ("Noles") are playing in town, the coast is deserted even at yuppie hotspots like St. Marks and I figured that this would be at least as good as a Nole weekend but boy was I ever wrong. They were lined up at the boat ramp like the news reporters at the airport in Tallahassee after that woman took it upon herself to decide who the next president should be. I could tell that there was some irritation and a possibility of boat ramp rage in that situation since the tide was very low and the ramp was still in the same piss-poor condition it has always been in . . . ready to catch some fool in the old trailer-wheels-dropped-over-the-end trap, so we put the little wheels in the rudder gudgeons on the *Little Bullet* and rolled it down the bunny trail and launched it through the bushes. When we came sailing back down the river, we saw a furious man with about a twenty-foot metal-flake bass boat (half on and half off the trailer) about halfway up the ramp. There was such a motor on the stern that it looked like he had a whole car bolted to the transom. What I think had happened was that when he launched the boat, all that motor worked with the steepness of the ramp and the low water so that the stern hit bottom before the boat was all the way off the trailer and then when he foolishly tried to pull out from under it, it refused to come off and he dragged its stern (outboard motor foot and all) about halfway up the corrugated concrete ramp . . . left a pretty good streak of metal flakes. I ain't sure if that is exactly what happened because the river is very narrow right there and I was trying to hide behind the close-hauled sail so I could act like I hadn't noticed how he was fixing to either pull the bow eye out of the boat, break the cable, burn up the winch motor, or boil his Diehard to death before he got that monster back on the trailer at that angle. I was also a little afraid that something might not hold and the whole shebang might back down on us. It was a day full of mishaps. A little way downriver from the ramp, I had to cut one tack short to avoid two very fat women standing in the low-tide mud looking disconsolately at a dead Jet Ski. I thought I smelled burned paint . . . mud in the water intake?

It was close-hauled, back and forth all the way out to the lighthouse, but there was a good little breeze and that's all the little boat needs to go. I like to beat to windward anyway, it is sort of like doing a good day's work and getting paid. Not only was the wind blowing straight up the river but the dark night's spring tide was rising against us, too, so we cleverly freed her up a little bit to scoot across the channel and did our close work back in the eddies and slacks behind the oyster bars and spoil banks. The old St. Marks is an interestingly structured little piece of water and if you know where you are, there are a lot of places you can go out of the main channel . . . which was a good thing. I have never seen so many big-deal outboard motor boats. There were a few inboard boats (one with the loudest reciprocating engine I have ever heard in my life) but gracious what some outboard rigs. The air in the channel was kind of tan looking from all the exhaust.

The most noticeable thing of the whole trip was all those boats going up and down the river, wide open, in that smoke cloud. We saw the same boat (twin, 250-hp two-stroke Evinrudes . . . 500 hp on about a twenty-one-foot boat) make seven trips by us just running up and down the river. I bet that man and woman burned seventy-five bucks' worth of gas and spread out two gallons of oil doing that. Fortunately, the farther down the river toward the lighthouse we got, the more water there was and we could stay farther away from the channel but there is one series of transverse bars that have no cut-through and we had to get right out there with them. I ain't fool enough to think for a minute that people like that have enough sense to know the sailboat right-of-way rule or would dodge us if they did, so we had to luff up in a little eddy behind a bar and wait a fair chance. While we were doing that, two young fartfaces in a boat that cost more than a brand-new airplane came tearing by. I don't know what it is about the roaring of engines that makes people think that other people who are not sitting right in the middle of screaming machinery can't hear every word they are bellowing at the top of their lungs. "I wouldn't *have* no goddamn sailboat," one of the fartfaces hollered to the other one as they roared past us. Later, we saw where they had decided to go on the wrong side of a day beacon and didn't have much motorboat either. Years ago, I used to dive that river during the slack of the tide to see what kinds of prehistoric artifacts were in the deep holes scoured out by the tidal currents at the ends of the limestone bars around the mouth of the river. Even then, there was a lot of aluminum on the bottom. Now I bet you could make a little recycling money just from busted outboard motor foots. Luckily, these fartfaces were running Suzukis and can get them some new foots. I wonder if there is such a thing as stupidity insurance?

Anybody with sense enough stays in the marked channel of rivers like the St. Marks, but as soon as we found a little water, Jane and I sailed out into the marsh away from all that carrying on. We kept on tacking up the creeks until the muffling effect of the spartina grass had completely eliminated any hint of the foolishness back on the river. I wondered how our sail looked sliding along above the grass. Pretty soon we came to a little palm-and-cedar-tree island (what we call a "hammock" down here). I already knew what it would be like because we have camped on many of those little things and there is no better place. Not only do the cedar trees (*Juniperus silicicola*, southern coastal aromatic red cedar) shade out all undergrowth and cut the wind off you, they carpet the ground with their needles about a foot thick. After a long, hard day's sailing and marauding, ain't no bliss like a sleeping bag on that . . . especially in the wintertime. Usually there are ducks and loons all around in the marsh and lying awake listening to them all talking their own language is sort of like listening to the late-night AM radio when they quit fooling with the commercials and just play that old-style jazz and blues. We should have stayed . . . After all, this month is our fortieth anniversary but I just can't help myself. That boat in the shop is just plain gnawing on me. Besides, the anniversary is already past . . . we gave each other a pair of white rubber boots . . . so we took out the dagger board, trailed the rudder, and ran back up the river with the fast water of the tide. It took some time before we realized that all the motorboats were gone. We surmised that they had all gone back to haul out and go home to watch the game and I think that is what happened. You ought to have seen the melee at the boat ramp. Luckily we had a fair wind so we could get through all of that milling around and cussing but unfortunately, all the exhaust followed us up the river to the hole in the bushes where the bunny trail was. We put the wheels on and trundled back to the parking lot without getting involved in that fury and frustration. I still don't know what happened at the Super Bowl. I imagine that it was sort of like a combination of the battles of the boat ramp and Natural Bridge. If I was a spectator by nature, I believe I would rather sit on one of the upwind park benches and watch the boat ramp than stay inside with the TV on such a fine day. So what did I do while the Super Bowl was on . . . stood around with my ear grubs in and ran the rest of those strips.

Girl Scouts

in which the wild rice canoe fills its niche

One of my daughters-in-law is the head booger of the Girl Scouts in the town where she teaches school. It is a little town so there aren't too many participants. Girl Scouting is a tradition in this family and my mother, who might have been one of the very first ones, ran a troop off and on for most of her life. She was a person of the woods and water and messed up the lives of many (no longer young) women. They should have wound up obedient wives who never got more than eighteen inches from civilization but because of early experience running the woods and bogging the bogs and splashing around in the water of creeks, rivers, ponds, lakes, and swamps, they didn't turn out ordinary and their husbands complained when they came home with scratches on their legs and mud between their toes and red bug (chigger) bites. Of course they *knew* what had bitten them which is a rare thing among the women of this region of the world. There is a spot on our old home place called "Girl Scout Hill" in honor of these deviants from the norm. That's where they camped out. Nowadays, Girl Scouts don't do much camping in the wild woods. I think scouting has become more of a Martha Stewart sort of thing.

Though my daughter-in-law was raised in California and South Florida she somehow managed to learn enough sense to know that scouting in a churchyard beside the highway is not quite as significant as doing it in the woods so she hauled them out here to the old home place woods and they set up a tent and went to scouting. They were supposed to go by the book and gain merits of all sorts but the woods were very fine in that spot and they ran amok. I am afraid some of them got scratches on their legs and mud between their toes and one of my granddaughters had a tick in her hair when it was all over. They climbed trees (mostly overgrown sparkleberry bushes . . . the best climbing tree in the world) and picked flowers of all kinds: plum, bay, jasmine, wild azalea, creek gentians, crab apple, blackberry brier, gooseberry (wild blueberry), violets (both white and blue), and lilies and irises of all kinds . . . even spider lilies which only grow in about three feet of water around here. On one trip my oldest granddaughter even climbed a magnolia tree and broke out one of those big flowers. In a tree she is kind of like a retrograde of the Darwin theory . . . about to turn back into a monkey. Which . . . You know most people have that wrong. There are a world of experts on Darwinian theory both pro and con who apparently never read the damn book and I advise them to do it before they open their mouths wide enough to show their asses down at the bottom of the abyss. Charles Darwin was a good writer. He explained his theory clearly enough so that anybody could understand it and what he said was not that people descended from monkeys but that people and monkeys came from the same ancestor. The theory book is sort of dry but *The Voyage of the Beagle* is just plain nautical adventure of the best kind. My favorite Darwin quote is what he said about some "savages" he saw whose "stomachs soared above all prejudices."

Anyway, after all the wildflowers had been arranged about the camp in Martha Stewart style, the girls discovered lily pad flowers way out in the pond and the flowers of pickerelweed. They also discovered the old Grumman seventeen-foot standard canoe *Wild Rice.* Though they were more than ready to embark immediately, they had to wait around while my granddaughters walked (ran) the mile back to their house to get the life preservers so I was able to hold their attention long enough to explain the origin of the name of the boat. I told them how my mother read in a magazine that Uncle Ben would give a new canoe to anybody who saved a thousand box tops of this new wild rice product they were trying to introduce. I told the girls that she conned me, in best Girl-Scout-cookie-selling tradition, into a deal. "You buy the rice and I'll eat it and give you the box tops," Mama explained. "What did the rice cost?" one future home economist asked. "About a buck a box," I replied. "You mean you paid a thousand dollars for *that!*" she exclaimed. Some future yahoo bass boat dork better watch out for that one. All my grandchildren can swim like otters (well the littlest one of them swims like a tadpole) but there were some pretty good-sized scouts in the troop who couldn't swim a stroke. I bet if they had stayed one more day they would be able to swim like otters, too, but they had to go back to civilization. They attempted to stir up all the water in the pond first, though. Not only did they partake of the lotus, they chased baby alligators to the point of exhaustion of both species. It is amusing to see a canoe full of little girls in hot pursuit of some very exciting and elusive goal when they have never had a paddle in their hands before. There was much advice given and ignored, I tell you. The little dog (actually still a puppy) couldn't decide where the best place on the bank to be was and jumped in the water five or six times only to discover that she would rather get back out and run back and forth. I'll venture an opinion about canoeing that I was able to form while I was running back and forth on the bank (no, dammit, I did not slip in). I don't believe it is possible to catch a fish out of an aluminum canoe paddled by four or five perfectly green Girl Scouts.

By the time to cook the hot dogs over the fire and settle down a little bit came they could all make the canoe go where they wanted and both the Girl Scouts and the little alligators were worn out from the lesson. The hot dogs were good, too. Do you think Girl Scouts eat Girl Scout cookies for dessert? Certainly not. That would be like feeding eggs to a dog. If you did, he would be out there goosing the chickens. Girl Scouts don't eat Trefoils and Thin Mints for dessert but they have something just about as craven. Do you know how to make the traditional Girl Scout campout dessert? What you do is take one graham cracker and put one piece of a room (tent?) temperature Hershey Bar on it and cook one marshmallow in the fire until it is good and sloppy (and possibly on fire) but a good Girl Scout's stomach can soar above a little smut. Then you place that hot marshmallow on top of the warm piece of chocolate and clamp it down with another graham cracker and pull the stick out. It is right up there with a Tagalong or a Samoa in the esteem of Girl Scouts everywhere. The name of that hot chocolate, mashed marshmallow sandwich is S'more.

It might occur to some of you to wonder if I, myself, ever became a scout. Yes I did but my association with the Boy Scouts was very brief. I am afraid I made up a poem with the title "Droopy Drawers" that might have been recited in the cadence of the Scout Oath and caused me to be passed over for promotion to tenderfoot. I started going to the movies while I was supposed to be in Boy Scouts. I got my Marilyn Monroe merit badge.

Hot Rod Trip to the Gator Hole

in which I disclose some (not all) of my secrets

Well, it was a lot of trips but I'll just hit the high spots. The Gator Hole is actually a bunch of holes way back in the swampy part of Lake Miccosukee and they are very hard to get to but it sure is worth it. The lake was the ancestral home of the Miccosukee Indians of this region before Andrew Jackson and his ilk came along and cleaned the place up so it would be safe for white people.

Lake Miccosukee is sort of peanut-shaped and arranged with the long axis sort of north and south with the two big ends connected by a narrow (maybe a mile wide) piece of water so shallow that it is completely covered by lily pads and grass. Most of the two big ends are covered by weeds, too, but there is a pretty good-sized clear hole at the north end where the boat ramp is. I don't know why but there is a tradition at boat ramps on lakes and rivers around here that usually there is a bait store/juke joint or some kind of bar in walking (and hearing) range, complete with its crew of loud drunks, litterbugs, vandals, and thieves, and Miccosukee is no exception. You see two kinds of people at the lake. One is those trashy yahoos at the bar and the other is folks who came to launch their boats and go fishing. The fishermen are just standard-issue various people . . . old men, and young, old women and young and children. Everybody belonging to various ethnic groups. Most of them fish right near the ramp in the north hole, which is very good fishing some of the time. You can just paddle out a little way from the ramp and be on one of the best bream beds in Florida. Miccosukee bream (both bluegills and fliers) are legendary for large size and dark color. There are speckled perch there, too, and some days it is possible to "limit out" in less than an hour with twenty-five big perch (the law says they have to be nine inches or better). People catch largemouth bass, catfish, pickerel (called "jacks" here), and warmouths there all the time. A lot of the people are specialists. One of the best bream fishermen is an enormously fat white woman, so big that she has a disabled sticker on her car, and thus gets the best parking place in the state lot at the boat ramp. She is always accompanied by a half-witted-looking boy about seventeen or eighteen years old who does all the work. She backs down (very skillfully using the mirrors like a truck driver) and he launches the boat and then helps her heave her vast bulk out of the car and onto a pedestal seat in the bow of the boat. Once she is situated and has her Winston lit and sucking good, he parks the car. While he is doing that he wears a diabolically devilish look like he might floor-board the old 98 Oldsmobile and burn rubber and haul ass out of the parking lot with the boat trailer bouncing along behind but he doesn't. He doesn't park straight worth a flip, either.

So this old gal fishes over the bow and the kid runs the trolling motor in the stern. Trolling motors are all very long-shaft-style and it is a good thing in this case because with that load in the bow, if it was normal length, the propeller would be about a foot from the water. They ease around out there in the bonnets very slowly and the woman catches one big bream after another with a cane pole by dipping a cricket on a short line in carefully selected holes between the lily pads. She is expert. When she catches one (two-pound Miccosukee bluegills are not uncommon) she pulls him around as she slowly swivels in her seat and presents the boy with the catch alongside the boat. He carefully nets the fish and takes him off the hook and catches another cricket out of the cage, hooks him on the hook, and the cycle repeats itself. I have never heard a mumbling word out of either one of them. After they have their twenty-five, they go home and, I imagine, fry all those bream and she eats them.

Anyway, most people don't even know what's at the other end of that old weedy lake many miles away. Only a few very knowledgeable people go there. Not only do they have to know how to do it, they have to be ready to deal with the consequences of failure to come back. I bet Andrew Jackson never made it all the way back in there. The best way to get there is in an airplane boat ("airboat") and those have been a tradition on these weedy lakes around here since the thirties. The original ones ran a real airplane engine but lately these yahoos have convinced themselves that a big, heavy, ill-suited V8 automobile engine is more macho (and cheaper) even though more than one group of yahoos has spent more time than they intended back in the wilderness because of broken crankshafts and such. I wouldn't have one of the loud sons of bitches . . . but there was a time when I would have.

I have heard about the Gator Hole all my life and always wanted to try to shove a canoe back in there just to see what Primordea looked like to the terrible Miccosukees (who, they say were very peaceable people unless somebody tried to crowd them and then they called up their homeland security).

I was gossiping around the bait store the other day when a man came in with a box full of very big speckled perch. I thought they must be from Lake Talquin (which might have the biggest black crappie in the world some say) but they were very dark. I finally wheedled around and got the man to admit that they had come from the Gator Hole. I had to threaten and abuse the man several different ways before he admitted that it was possible to take a small, narrow boat back in there if one knew what he was doing. I carefully examined his rig. It was one of those fiberglass boats built by various manufacturers trying to copy the original Gheenoe invented by Harley W. Gheen who was a rocket scientist over on the cape. I couldn't tell if this man's boat was the real thing or not because it was so beat up and raggedy but I am here to tell you a Gheenoe is a good durn boat. One of those and a beat-up nine point nine just like that man had is just the ticket for around here. If I didn't have the capability to build something at least as good, I would have one myself.

I didn't tell the man but not only do I have just exactly the boat for the duty but I know a thing or two about a thing or two, too. I trotted straight to the library and, before I got settled in the swivel chair (trying not to act fat) I had typed www.terraserver.com in the window and, before the woman at the computer next to me had finished her cell phone conversation, I had an aerial photograph of the south end of Lake Miccosukee working its way out of the ink jet printer. Old Gheen ain't the only rocket scientist in the skiffboat business.

If you zoom in on the TerraServer map you can see little trails all out through the weeds of Lake Miccosukee. There are holes of clear water all over the place that (except for rocket scientists) nobody but an expert at local knowledge would know about. The first clear day (it has been a wet, stormy spring, thank goodness) I took off down there. Sam was working on the spring boat in the shop and Jane was playing with the baby so I had to go by myself. It took me all day to get back to the Gator Hole but I did it. Then it took until way after dark to find my way back out of there. No, dammit, I did not use any GPS or cell phone. I have had a lot of experience in navigating swamps and marshes and I knew what I was doing but Lake Miccosukee has a unique characteristic that needs further investigation. I have never seen anyplace that has identical willow bushes and perfectly matching runt cypress trees before. It must be an inbreeding thing. I am going to check their DNA and calculate their coefficient of consanguinity.

It was a good thing there was a full moon or I would have been drinking lake water and licking Vienna sausage cans. When I finally got back to the boat ramp, one of the drunks over at the bar hollered loudly, "Did you catch anything?" "No." I replied politely. "Didn't catch nothing?" "*No.*" "You ain't caught no fish at all?" "*NO.*" "Well, what the hell did you go for then?" "I went to see yo momma," said I, feeling my pistol in my pocket to make sure which end was up.

I had my bearings though and, the next lull in the weather, I went back prepared to bring home the bacon. It wasn't much of a lull and I got rained on a lot but I caught four nice specks and one big bluegill. When I got back to the ramp, the half-witted boy was trying to back the trailer sort of in the direction of the water to load out. I knew that woman had her fifty and hadn't gone a hundred yards from the car. You know, there is one kind of rocket science and then there is some more rocket science.

I got it figured out the next time. The lull came in the afternoon and I didn't have but just a little while before dark and the full moon was past so it would be rising a little late. I hurried right along . . . might have pushed Jane's little Kia a little beyond what it is used to on the eighteen miles to the boat ramp because it smelled a little like a hard-ridden Ford when I got out to slide the little gray boat off the trailer. I have been running the boat enough to gain some more confidence and, though it feels a little squirrelly, the boat is actually pretty predictable running wide open with only one person in there. I had my trolling motor and a good-sized battery up in the bow and that helped a good little bit, but I am here to tell you, that's a fast dadblamed boat. The little gator trails (I have not managed to go the same way twice in five trips and still don't know where I am half the time) are crooked and very narrow, and it took quite a few miles for me to get up my attamation.

Which, that's a family word my little sister made up a long time ago. I had built a tree house way up in a big hickory tree in the backyard. I nailed about a hundred short one-by-fours to the trunk of the tree for steps with only two small nails apiece barely holding on about halfway through the bark. I had a telescope up there and all sorts of interesting things and I told them all about how wonderful it was up there with the birds sitting on my finger and all. Although she was only about four years old, little sister wanted to go up there mighty bad but about halfway up those wigglesome steps she stopped and just hung on and looked down for about three minutes. "You scared?" I needed to know. "No," she replied. "Well, what did you stop for then?" "I am just getting up my attamation." And she did and went on up there, too.

I got up my attamation and poured the coal to the little Martin and we went through the little trails like a hot rod. Bob Hicks would have et that ride up I believe. You know, old George Martin who designed the motor was a . . . well, they hadn't invented rocket science back then but that's a bad lit- tle motor. When it gets on the cam (yes, Virginia, it has valves) just right it sounds about like a bat out of hell. I think old man Martin must have del- egated some of the design of the accessories after he finished the motor part because that thing has the stupidest damn gas hole I ever saw in my life.

I got so regular with my fast trips to the Gator Hole that I felt like a race driver running the same course. I tuned the cursed Tillotson carburetor and the little thing on the magneto plate that works the throttle and the trim of the tilt (adjustable under way on a Martin) until I got all I could get out of the little rig. The boat handles so sweetly and banks in the turns so adroitly that I had all the confidence in the world with my wild rides during the brief lulls in the weather. I got to where I could get back there in less than an hour if I only got lost two or three times. Hotshot that I was, I was nowhere in the league with the 450-pound woman and her young partner. Oh, I caught a few fish and learned a little lore. One man told me something interesting. He said that fish don't bite on Lake Miccosukee when the sun is shining bright. He said that the best time was just before it starts to rain. He figured that while it is bright they fast and get hungry and then start looking for supper when the clouds of the front come. Luckily that situation is what has prevailed most of this spring. I watched the local weather (www.wunderground.com) radar to look for lulls and yesterday, I hit the jackpot. It was a bright, clear day but here came a strong, fast-moving front sweeping in from the west like a train. I dropped everything and hooked up the already loaded boat to Jane's Kia and boogied out of here. It was look- ing like some weather at the ramp and everybody else was pulling out. It was Friday afternoon and the drunks were in full cry over at the bar when I launched. "Where the hell you think you going?" one needed to know. "Going to see yo momma," I replied as soon as the damn Tillotson dribbled the dollop of gas that signified that it had finished priming. I couldn't hear what he said back over the acceleration of the little engine as it climbed up on the cam. I was gone like a Bob Hicks on a Spanish motorcycle down the little trails to the Gator Hole with my fishing pole and my minnows. It was the quickest trip yet. I didn't miss but one turn the whole way and, just as I eased into the first clearing (there are a bunch of them) it began to cloud up, the wind stopped entirely, and the air got that funny feeling. I started trolling slowly using the electric motor with a minnow on one of those curly-tailed jigs that acts like he is swimming with his sparkly chartreuse tail (the current trick at the bait store). I trolled about two miles and caught three little barely legal speckled perch. "Durn," I said. "It is fixing to get dark before I can vindicate myself for all this carrying-on." Just about that time it began to rain and blow and the speckled perch started biting. I mean I hooked one on every cast. They were slapping the aluminum lid off the live box under my seat and wetting my ass even more than what the rain was doing. Some of them were big, too. It got dark before I felt like I had enough to feed all these grandchildren (you ought to see a four-year-old Chinese girl eat a one-pound fried speckled perch). When I finally stopped fishing and started thinking, I realized that I might be in a fix. It was not just plain pitch dark and raining like hell, I had to pour six miles worth of gas into that damn stupid recessed gas hole of the Martin. I had to do it by feel but, due to the good fortune of the wind having died completely off again, I didn't get any on anything but my finger and one paper towel. I crunk up and started easing slowly in what I thought might be the right direction to the opening of the trail I had come in on. I ran into the weeds five or six times and, since I had my beautiful little bronze hot rod wheel on there instead of the weedless prop that came standard with the engine I had to shut down and tilt the engine and unwrap the grass and bonnet stems. I was looking at a real ordeal . . . maybe an all-nighter. Luckily Jane does not go to wringing her hands and dialing 911 in situations like that and I did have my water jug and a can of Vienna sausages so I figured it wouldn't be nothing but a thing as long as it didn't start hailing golf balls. As I was easing across the pitch-dark Gator Hole, the rain stopped. Then I noticed that I could see a little bit. Then the bright almost full moon rose over the trees shining through the clouds like it was looking down at Marie Lebeaux and "Yowl!" said the little Martin and I was another man done gone. We went back to the boat ramp in fine style. The drunks were tuned up, too, but the lights were so bright and the jukebox was so loud they never noticed me loading up to go. Which is a good thing. I would have hated to have to take my six-foot-long solid ash paddle over there and interact.

Gator Holes

Alligators make clearings in the weeds of shallow lakes. I have talked to certified expert herpetologists about it and they say they don't think the gators do it for the hole's sake but for the mud and weeds they dig up to enhance the place. They pile these weeds and mud in the shallows to make a good place to pull out and take it easy in the sun and bellow and breed in that season (about now, the last of March, early April . . . pollen time). Sometimes their new ground breaks loose and floats off because of the buoyancy of all the dead vegetation in the mixture. That suits the alligators fine and they continue to add material to their floating island until it gets pretty big and all sorts of vegetation grows there. Some floating islands have good-sized willow trees (all genetically identical in Miccocukee) on them. Because the water in most of the shallow lakes around here is pretty murky, the plants in the hole can't grow back anymore. Even lily pads can't store enough nutrition in their big rhizomes to force a pad all the way to the surface before it gives out so the holes stay pretty clear of weeds. When the water level falls, as it inevitably does regularly in these natural lakes, some of the floating islands ground out and the roots of the plants growing on them anchor them to the bottom and, when the water comes up, they become saturated and won't float back up. That makes a shallow place in the gator hole with weeds and grass (and big, ignorant bream and bass). The whole situation is in a continual state of change because of the whims of the gators and other vagaries of nature. Just because you think you know the geography of such a place is no reason to become confident. It all looks the same but none of it is. Those alligators and speckled perch and all don't need to know their exact longitude and latitude. They have everything they need no matter where they are. So do I . . . well almost.

Lake Iamonia Speckled Perch Bonanza

*in which a big water moccasin tries to take a bream
away from Momma and gets his comeuppance from her Game Getter*

There is a good-sized lake just over the Florida line about ten miles from the shop. Lake Iamonia (pronounced *ammonia*) is one of three natural lakes nearby that were "enhanced" by the government back in WPA days. I'll name these lakes for you because I like the sound of the words: Iamonia (nobody knows what that means anymore), Miccosukee (means "home" to the extinct Indians of this place), and Lake Jackson (named for Andrew Jackson whose human rights principles while he was working for the government are the subject of skepticism). Like Okeechobee, what they did to enhance these ancient natural lakes was to cut off the natural drainage out of the lake so the water level was supposed to stay high and stable enough to suit government purposes. Unlike Okeechobee, the grand scheme didn't work with these lakes around here. They are what we call sinkhole lakes because at the bottom end of all of them there is a big limesink where the water is very deep . . . sometimes. What happens is that every now and then, in sort of a cyclical manner, the bottom of the limesink will open up and the lake will drain absolutely dry in just a week or two. It was very perplexing to the owners of high-end real estate around Lake Jackson down within the suburbs of Tallahassee when their lake did that. All of a sudden, their view was transformed from a beautiful, idyllic Florida scene worthy of reproduction in oil paint into a mud hole with umpteen jillion beer cans and bottles littering about three thousand acres of mud so soft that nobody could walk out there to pick them up. It was a mess and it took about five years for the lake to come back. Lake Iamonia did that same thing not long ago and is just now getting straightened back up and the fishing is wonderful.

I'll get back to that in a minute but, first, I want to try to explain the sinkhole phenomenon. What the government did was to dam off the lake from the sinkhole. During the time when the lake would naturally be full, the sinkhole (called the "basin") was full, too. Big trees grew all around the basin and the water was very black and so deep that lily pads and grass couldn't grow all the way up from the bottom and the basin was (is) very beautiful. There are rumors of very big fish living in the basin but, since the dam, there is no place to launch a boat in there (except for one of my little things . . . I think the first boat in the basin at Lake Iamonia since 1935 was a tin canoe). What happened to put the government plans to naught was that, just as soon as they did all that work, another sinkhole opened up and drained the lake anyway. Nobody knows for sure the dynamics of the cyclical aspects of the draining and filling but one theory is that the porous bottom of the sinkhole gets stopped up by vegetation and root-reinforced peat while the lake is more or less empty and plants can get enough light to grow and, then, when it gets watertight enough, the lake fills up and stays full for long enough for the old vegetable material down there to gradually rot and let the water trickle through and then, all of a sudden, it all gets washed away into the cavities and underground rivers in the great Floridian aquifer from which we all get plenty of some of the best drinking water anywhere. You know, the biggest single spring in the world is down below Tallahassee in Wakulla County and was home to the people of the last ice age who killed the mighty mammoth and the colossal megatherion with the exquisite Tallahassee spear point, which (in my humble opinion) was the last exquisite thing to be named "Tallahassee."

I don't know how it is that the fish population in the lake grows so rapidly and the fish get big so quickly but in about a year and a half after the lake fills back up, it is full of big, healthy, hungry fish and it is a regular bonanza for about three or four years before it reaches the normal old equilibrium of a pretty fair fishing hole. I think all those bushes and weeds growing in the rich dirt of the bottom of the lake enhance the environment for everybody. That peat in the bottom oxidizes, too, and I know that does something. Whatever it is, it is certainly an interesting phenomenon and this year, people have been wondering what it would be like when it finally got cold enough for the speckled perch to start biting in Lake Iamonia. Speckled perch only bite down here in the late fall, winter, and early spring. Nobody knows what they do all summer long but they apparently lie around in schools in deep holes and won't bite. One of my buddies says you can look at a fish finder and see the school open up to let a baited hook pass through but they won't bite for anything. One theory is that they fill up on little shad minnows and stuff and just aren't hungry. When they start biting in the fall, they are always very fat and are developing good-sized roe so it is obvious they weren't suffering all summer long. They must grow a lot during the summer since, last spring, they were all little, hungry, and plentiful.

Well, we had some good cold weather, which was associated with the same system that brought all that snow upcountry and all the local fishermen kept trying and, finally, the specks started. Wow, it was something. They were pretty good-sized (average a little better than half a pound) and were biting like crazy. Nobody had to fish more than two hours to catch their limit, twenty-five. I hate to have to say it but a lot of these small-time speck fishermen are selling their catch. It is not illegal to sell speckled perch but it is illegal to catch twenty-five and go sell them (or hide them) and then trot right back down there but, you know, when it gets too cold for yard man work to pay off, the yard man falls on hard times and a lot of self-employed people around here have never adhered to the policies of the government when unnecessary. Independent working people have had plenty of experience with the government and only a stupid person would fail to recognize that government programs really are not set up to help small-time folks . . . black or white . . . here in the South. I'll just cite the agricultural policies for an example. None of those programs managed to elevate the small farmers of this region to any level where they could become major contributors to the campaign funds of politicians like those oil-company-style corporations that run most of the agriculture in this country. I don't know about Norwegian bachelor farmers up north but there aren't any small-time farmers down here anymore. These yard men just don't think the government is exactly on their side so they don't pay all that much attention to any rules that don't make sense to them and have been taught by experience to think for themselves. Speckled perch (crappie) are apt to overpopulate a lake in a little while and, when that happens, the fish in the lake get littler and littler and thinner and thinner until they aren't fit to eat. These in Lake Iamonia, right now, are very fat . . . and worth about one dollar each. A day's fishing is not only pleasant work but the wages beat hell out of yard man work.

So as soon as I got the word, I got the itch. Unfortunately, it is just before Christmas and we are in the throes of trying to build Christmas presents for the family children and it is a job. We always start too late and are still assembling rocking horses and little boats and all in the middle of Christmas Eve night. Old Sam is working more hours at the shop now, so he can have a little spare change for the season, too, and the baby is rampaging all over the place trying to swallow screws and things so there wasn't any time to go to Lake Iamonia and, since the freezer is filling up with venison, no real excuse. But Sam's wife took Friday afternoon off so he decided to take the baby to keep her company and that left Jane and me all alone. "Go get the minnows and I'll get the boat ready," she said as soon as Sam's car was out of sight. I hurried to the bait store/pawnshop with my little icebox but, when I got there, the roach-spraying man was there and so was a fishing tackle salesman and I had to wait. Charles (the proprietor) was teasing the roach-spraying man. "You know, I ain't gonna keep giving you twenty-four bucks a month to come spray that water around and not keep these roaches under control," he said. "You think this is water?" said the roach man. "Let me spray these crickets and we'll see," said he, sidling over to the cricket box where three thousand bream crickets were chirping their forlorn little inbred tune. "Naw, man," said Charles, "I was just playing with you but you still ain't got these roaches under control in here." "That's because they come in them TVs you are always taking in on pawn," exclaimed the spray man. "I can come in here and kill them all and then somebody will bring in a TV just full of roaches and they'll come out and eat cricket feed and multiply like vermin until I come back next month."

"Dammit, y'all," I finally had to say. "I need me some minnows."

I haven't got any use for twelve and a half pounds of speckled perch so I only got a dozen toughies. "Tuffy" is a trade name for minnows bred so as to have very tough heads so they won't sling off the hook and no brains so the hook through the head won't injure them. You know, it don't take brains to be bait. When I got back to the shop, Jane got up from where she had been sitting on a bucket the whole time I was at the bait store listening to all that nonsense and had the boat trailer by the tongue (the Grumman sport boat and its aluminum trailer . . . "Trailex" came on the UPS truck . . . don't weigh enough to notice) before I got turned around. We were gone in a flash and twenty minutes later were moseying out into the lake with the electric trolling motor. Which, one of the best things the government did was to outlaw internal combustion engines on Lake Iamonia during duck season. I used to be able to sell rowboats to duck hunters back before they invented the electric trolling motor. Jane caught the first speck before we were off the paved part of the boat ramp. Then she caught nine more. I have always wondered at that phenomenon. Here we were, both sitting in the same boat, and fishing with the exact same chartreuse crappie jig with minnows so inbred that I bet they couldn't be differentiated by a DNA test and she was catching the fish. Of course, she was fishing a Mickey Mouse Zebco and I had my Snoopy rig but the line was all the fish knew about and it was old, blue DuPont Stren four-pound test off the same spool. I was using the well-proven "Iverson slow wind" retrieve and she was using the "Jane White, lift and drop" but, in the interest of science, we switched movements and she kept catching them Mr. Iverson's way. It is mystifying. Finally I caught one or two and we went home with a nice little mess of specks. While we were getting ready to pull out, I noticed James (the yard man) come in and trot to the truck with a little six-pack-style icebox and make a deposit of what I knew was exactly twenty-five speckled perch in his big icebox back in the bushes and, before I could get backed back down to haul my boat, he was pushing off. "Going back, James?" I said. "Yep . . . got to go help my cousin." James is a Vietnam veteran and, you know, they generally have a pretty well-developed sense of skepticism.

Nearly a year later we got some cold weather which was associated with another system that brought snow up the country and all the local fishermen kept trying, then finally one day I went by the bait store on my way back from visiting the post office and there were about four or five old regulars standing around Pettis's boat looking in the icebox. I knew what was up immediately. The speckled perch had started. I drove right on by and then scratched through the floorboards of my junk Mercedes collection until I found enough change for two dozen minnows. Gas being so high, I determined not to waste any by going back for the minnows and going fishing immediately. I know when the freshwater fishing starts back, it is strictly an early-morning thing. The old saying is, "Soon as the sun hits the water, it is all over." That's right, too. So I got the boat all ready (the little gray boat . . . Grumman Sport Boat improvement project) and checked out the little old Martin to make absolutely sure all was well and alerted Jane that we needed to get to bed early so we would be ready but I had forgotten that we had made arrangements to babysit some children at a house with a TV to watch the amazing Cybill Shepherd rendition of Martha Stewart. It was way late by the time we got home and the last thing that I remember about the show was that I was able to formulate the opinion that even a brilliantly accurate portrayal of Martha Stewart was not enough to keep me awake . . . now, Julia Childs, maybe.

So we dragged out of bed after a short nap, which was spent mostly being glad that great financial responsibility hadn't landed us in Camp Cupcake and, while Jane was cooking breakfast, I drove the two miles to the bait store and got in line for my minnows. You know, when something is important the word gets around. This was no FEMA-style operation at the bait store. It was time to sell some minnows and Charles was up to the job. It sort of reminded me of when I used to work at the galley in the Navy . . . slapping that chipped beef on top of the toast for the troops. I was out of there before Jane served up my eggs and sausages.

It was a pleasant drive to Lake Iamonia. There was a light mist in the air and the moon was setting down the road (US 319 south heads due west . . . geographic confusion is a southern tradition). It isn't but about fifteen miles to the boat landing and the little Kia barely got warmed up good. It is interesting about that. The car gets exactly the same gas mileage (thirty-four miles per gallon) pulling the boat on level road as it does running naked. We have made enough trips to establish that fact and also to convince ourselves that it is a roadworthy rig . . . will drag brakes without jackknifing for one thing. We are thinking about a little trip or two. I wouldn't recommend running a small car like that with a boat and trailer if it had an automatic transmission unless you installed an auxiliary oil cooler and I don't see how you could do that on one of these little front-wheel-drive cars with that electric fan in front of the radiator. Hell they don't even have room under the hood for a real battery . . . has to have a miniature. Anyway, Jane's is a five-speed so that's a moot point. It'll pull it all right, too. You know, my mother used to pull a sixteen-foot, heavy-duty, butt-head Lone Star and an eighteen-horsepower Evinrude on an old heavy steel Gator trailer behind a thirty-six-horse VW all over the place. This rig, trailer, boat, motor, and all doesn't weigh what her old trailer did all by itself and that little Kia is a boy dog compared with a VW . . . eighty-four horsepower, y'all. That VW/Kia comparison has another evolutionary parallel. You couldn't see the engine in a VW and you can't see one in this Kia either. The difference is that the motor in the stern of a VW was covered by tin and the one in front of the Kia is covered by plastic.

The boat ramp was real crowded. It wasn't a yahoo situation with rudeness and incompetence and all, though. Yahoos don't get up before day. They sleep late and eat their Froot Loops on the run. Those people at the boat ramp knew exactly what they were doing and all was running very efficiently but there were a lot of people trying to put in at the one-lane ramp at Lake Iamonia even though it was a Monday. That was no deterrent to Jane and me, though. We unhooked the trailer and pushed it down through the weeds a good bit away from the ramp and dragged the boat to the water and loaded her up with junk and poled out to one of the boat trails, and one pull on the old Martin (me and Mr. Tillotson have come to an understanding; I got that thing Cadillacking like a Singer sewing machine set on "buttonhole") and we were idling out in the early-morning mist onto the big lake. Lake Iamonia is a great big lake (maybe fifteen thousand acres depending on what-all you measure) but it is swampy and weedy and most people don't know how to get very far from the landing but I do.

Our old home place isn't but about five or six miles to the north of the lake as the crow flies and I spent many an hour at Lake Iamonia. I remember one time my mother and my oldest sister and I were down there. My sister and I were just little children. I might have been six or seven years old. We were playing on the bank while Momma was out in a canoe fishing just outside the weed line. She was catching fly bream ("fliers," *Centrarchus macropterus*) one right behind the other on long-manure worms. Whew . . . I better get into that. Some might not know the difference between long manure and short manure . . . might think short manure comes from goats and sheep and rabbits and long manure comes from things like dogs. Long manure is fresh manure that is shoveled up from out of the milk barn or horse stall or hog pen or the dog yard or someplace and mixed with straw. It is most excellent stuff for the garden. Sometimes leaves and other sweepings get mixed in with it. These big old iridescent dark blue (almost black) earthworms just love to live in the long pile. They are very active and do not like to be stuck with a fishhook so they thrash violently all the way down and are best fished on a naked hook with no weight or cork or anything. Just flip them up alongside the weeds with a cane pole and let them sink. They won't get to sink very far, though, and fly bream will fight over them so you always get the pick of the litter and that was what Momma was doing. She was putting these big fliers on a willow switch stringer that she had wrapped into the gaps in the rail of the canoe and she already had a good many when something grabbed the bottom fish. She thought it must have been one of the yearling alligators, which were plentiful and will do that, so she decided to put the stringer in the boat since it was about time to go home anyway and the fish didn't need to be kept alive anymore. It wasn't a little alligator but a great big moccasin that had swallowed the head of the bottom bream down as far as he could before the willow switch got crossways his mouth and stopped him. You know, snakes have backward-pointing teeth and, even if they want to, it is hard for them to turn loose of something they are trying to swallow. One time I caught a big king snake that had swallowed a very big rattlesnake about halfway down. I couldn't pull the rattlesnake out and my mother and I put the whole mess into the back of the Jeep (old World War Two surplus, the low-hood kind with the flathead motor and the big gas hole) and took them home and kept them in a steel drum. It took three days for that king snake to gradually digest the big rattlesnake down until his tail disappeared. After it was over, we dumped the king snake (stuffed absolutely full . . . you could see white between all his scales) out of the drum onto the floor of the tack room in the barn thinking that he might stay and catch rats but he wasn't hungry. He spent the rest of the summer and the whole winter in there just lying on the floor in kind of a daze. When spring came he shed his skin, crapped a little bit of white stuff, and crawled off. He was as shiny as patent leather. I think he was the most beautiful snake I have ever seen.

So here was Momma with this big, dangerous snake in the bottom of the canoe. She tried to fling him back into the water with the stringer but it flung him off up into the bow of the boat instead. Any other kind of snake would have just climbed out over the side but cottonmouth moccasins are very aggressive and have the confidence that comes with being deadly poisonous. Moccasins will run right at you if you are between them and the water they are trying to get to. It is prudent to keep your eye on the uphill bank while working along the edge of the pond or river with a fishing pole. Ross Allen down at Silver Springs participated in antivenin research, which yielded a fairly good injection for the bites of crotalids (rattlesnakes) but doesn't work very well for moccasins (cottonmouths and the much smaller copperheads) so it is best not to let them bite you. Momma had that in mind when that snake started coming aft to resume his swallowing project. She tried two or three licks with the paddle but there were too many fishing poles and seats in the way to get a clear shot. She thought about trying to paddle to the bank so she could deal with the son of a bitch in a situation more to her liking but trying to hit him with the paddle had angered the snake and alerted him to the source of his displeasure so he began to advance toward her in cycles of two feet of crawling and six inches of lunging in a short strike sort of like a boxer loosening up for the knockout punch. He did not know the exact extent of who he was dealing with, though. Momma fumbled out her Game Getter (I'll come back to that) and shot his head off with the .410 barrel. Unfortunately she also shot a big hole in the bottom of the canoe but she was able to get to the bank before too much water came in and then stuff her hat in the hole and paddle us all back to the landing. She left the snake but took her fish.

That Game Getter was an interesting gun. It was a long-barreled pistol-looking thing made by Marble's Safety Axe Co., Gladstone, Michigan. It broke like a shotgun and had two barrels and a little doohickey on the hammer that selected which barrel shot when you pulled the trigger. The top barrel was .22 long rifle and the bottom was .410 shotgun (originally .44/40 shot but most had been converted to two-and-a-half-inch .410). It was the favorite gun for bird collecting and it was an ornithologist who gave that one to my mother when she was a girl. She did not like to shoot the .410 barrel because the kick hurt her hand but she used the .22 barrel all the time for shooting everything she needed to shoot. The little gun had a folding wire stock and when she was hunting squirrels she unfolded it so she could shoot straight but when it was a possum in the chicken house, she just poked the barrels through the wire and nailed him with the stock dangling. Game Getters and all folding-stock shotguns were outlawed by the BATF in the early thirties with a sweeping law intended to keep Al Capone and them from robbing banks with sawed-off shotguns and machine guns or something. Getting caught with that Game Getter would have landed my mother in Camp Cupcake for a long time but she didn't know that and they didn't know she had it. Someone busted the window out of her Volkswagen in 1956 and stole it so that was that.

My mother fixed the hole in the bottom of the canoe with a piece of tin and some roofing tar put on the outside and through-fastened to a block of wood on the inside with some little nails. Her patch outlasted the rest of the boat, which was replaced by the Lone Star about 1955. My youngest sister was out scratching around in the long-manure pile the other day and dug up that patch . . . intact. Good galvanized tin and a cypress block. I have it in my artifact cabinet right now. Some day some descendant will be poking through all that junk and wonder what the hell that thing is and what the significance of it is. Maybe I'll staple this story to it. Oh yeah, short manure is dried cow and horse manure from the pasture. The rain has worked on it and rinsed out a lot of the nutrition but it is good to enhance the tilth of sandy soil. People used to follow a wagon around in the pasture and throw the cow plops up into the back with pitchforks. Children were expected to participate in this work. That's how I discovered the most satisfactory whop upside the head one can make with an overhand throw of a green mule cupcake.

So Jane and I moseyed down one of the boat trails that generations of a few knowledgeable people have kept open on their way to and from the many little honey holes in the lake. Most people just put in and go out to the middle of the lake where it is too deep for lily pads. It is pretty good out there, particularly if you cast up alongside the weeds, but that place is only maybe seventy-five acres of the lake and the whole thing is thousands of acres and there are many little deep holes where (I guess) limesinks and stuff are under the water. The fish thrive in the weeds all over the lake and hang out in the clear holes to socialize, I reckon. Anyway, it is not only worth the trouble to learn the boat trails but interesting as well. I advise you to take a good paddle and a big jug of water before you adventure forth on your exploration because it is real hard to figure out where you are and the trails follow the same kind of logic a cow uses while she is walking across a pasture from one place to another spreading those shorts . . . you might have to wander to the west for five miles to get half a mile's worth of south and all those little islands look exactly alike. If you decide to land on one of those islands be aware that I have never seen any poison ivy anywhere as healthy as on the islands of Lake Iamonia.

Lake Iamonia has some big alligators, too. There are a bunch of them. I guess because it is so hard to get to most of the lake . . . particularly along the swampy edge of the whole thing . . . those alligators are not all that used to people and boats. You know, William Bartram in *Travels in Georgia and Florida* said that alligators who weren't used to people were not afraid of boats so he was scared of them. I don't know if Jane is scared of them or not but you know how, if a boat with a fairly long waterline is trimmed right, you can steer it by shifting your weight? Well, when we approached one of those alligators in the trail, somehow the boat urged over to the off side all by itself without me having to do anything to the tiller at all. The alligator wouldn't even move until we got real close and then he would back slowly down. Jane's neck would get about two inches shorter as we passed. You know, if someone was to decide it was time to end it all and none of the conventional means of doing so appealed and Dr. Kevorkian was still in Camp Cupcake, I can't think of a more adventurous way to do it than to mosey down one of the boat trails of Lake Iamonia until you saw an alligator with a head about five feet long and just get out of the boat and dog-paddle around for a little while. It wouldn't be like one of these young women who take the pills over and over again . . . it would be a one-shot project sort of like Momma and the Game Getter.

The place where we were heading was just a little wide place in the trail where we had had some luck the fall before. Lake Iamonia had been mostly dried up for ten years prior to summer before last and when it came back in the spring of '03 all the fish spawned in the weedless water like they had a racial memory of what joy really was. There was so much fry in the water all over the lake that it looked like the clear water was alive . . . and when the weeds came back all those baby fish hid and prospered. Then the summer of '04 came and the speckled perch appeared in the clear part by the boat ramp in pure throngs but they were real small and thin until the fall came. Then they were still small but not thin and fishermen were the ones thronging. One of the fishermen was a woman in a red Gheenoe with an old 9.9 Johnson. She was pulling those specks in like a machine. We watched her while we caught our supper (small specks fried whole are a delicacy) every day. She was throwing all the fish back. We finally saw her to talk to at the ramp and I had to, like the pedant I am, explain to her that there weren't any big specks in the lake yet and there was no point to catching the little ones in hopes of something better. She opened her live box and pointed down inside. "I ain't after specks," she said. "I am trying to catch me a jack," and sure enough there was a good-sized jack (chain pickerel, *Esox niger*) in the live box. "I always thought they were too bony to eat," said me. "They are if you don't know how to fix them," she replied opening the door of her car. "But if you do, ain't no better eating fish in the world and there are still some big ones in this lake. You know, they ain't worried by drought and shallow water. They just hide in the weeds until the lake comes back. I try to catch me one for my supper every day if these damn little specks will let me. You know, ain't nothing goes better with a glass of Chardonnay than a fillet of jack. Have a nice day." "How do you fix them?" I asked but she was had already slammed the door of her Toyota and was gone to fix her jack.

So Jane and I slid into the hole and Jane was already fishing before I cut the old Martin off and she was pulling in a speckled perch before I could get situated. By the time I got him into the live box she was pulling in another one. All I could do was stow fish and catch minnows out of the bucket. Jane caught eleven good-sized (half a pound or so) speckled perch, two big (three-quarter-pound) fly bream, and two good jacks (about a pound and a half apiece) . . . a nice mess of fish and a delight to the eyes of starving people. When we decided to go back, the old Martin hadn't even cooled off enough to have to twiddle Mr. Tillotson's tallywhacker . . . cranked on idle with half a pull of the rope.

Guess what? When we got to the ramp that jack woman was pulling out and I finally got to ask her how to fix a jack. "You fillet them like a normal fish and then cut across the fillets every half an inch almost to the skin. That way the grease can get in there and cook the bones and make them edible. You know, cooking is what makes a sardine's bones edible. Have a nice day."

Jane and I ate the jacks and fed the bream and specks to a bunch of children. You ought to see a three-year-old baby eat a bream as wide as her head. It is in the nature of children to be cautious of bones . . . of course they get mighty greasy and wind up with crumbs all over them. We didn't have any Chardonnay but we did have a big jug of "red rose" cheerleader wine left over from coast house week, which I had bought to try to keep the damn guests out of my good wine collection . . . didn't work.

How a Yard Man Launches His Commercial Fishing Boat

They have it down to an exact science. The boats are all butt-headed. In small lakes, like Iamonia, the preferred rig is a small aluminum johnboat with nothing but an electric trolling motor. But if, like James, the man fishes in bigger lakes like Talquin or Seminole, he has a bigger boat with a little shape to the bow so it won't pound and throw water quite as bad. They still prefer a butt-head configuration, though. They also like low-sided boats so they'll be easy to get into or out of. Unlike organized fishermen, who would be disenfranchised if they were seen in anything with less than two hundred hp, these independents have no use for ostentatious bass boats and the favorite gas engine is the OMC nine point nine. If they are fishing Lake Iamonia during duck season in their big-lake boat like James does, they just run the trolling motor over the bow and don't crank the nine point nine. When they arrive at the lake, they back down to the ramp immediately and get out of the truck, unhook the winch, and set out the anchor (a favorite is an automobile flywheel) on the bank beside the ramp. Then they back up fast and drag brakes with an exactitude born of much practice and the boat slides off the trailer with just the right inertia to fetch up on the anchor line just enough to stop the boat and ease it back in. The man parks the rig and trots (the invention of the riding lawn mower is taking the spring out of that trot) back to the boat. By then, it is nosing up against the bank so he climbs over the bow, gets in his swivel chair, and is fishing before the ripples from the launching are twenty feet away from the ramp.

The Big Oak

in which I get reacquainted with an old friend
and find that we have even more in common

The other day I was walking to the post office to see if anybody had sent me any money yet when I passed a big-deal backhoe operation. I had read about it in the paper. Somehow an old natural gas line had started leaking under the sidewalk right beside The Big Oak.[1] Everybody was in an uproar about what to do . . . abandon that pipe and bypass the tree by cutting through a bunch of Hysterical Society yards with a new line . . . or dig it up right there and replace it, which would take much delicate work to avoid cutting any of the roots of a tree three times as old as the city. That was what they were trying to do as I passed.

I tried to keep well out of the way, but it is human nature to look into such a project as that and I have never been one to fly in the face of natural instinct so I had to do a little observation as I passed. There were two men down in a big hole where they had torn up the sidewalk way up the street from the old tree. They were poking some roots with a shovel. Several experts in respectable clothes were leaning over looking down into the hole. I imagined that they were trying to decide if those were indeed the roots of The Big Oak. I noticed another man waiting in the seat of a big, silent backhoe with his earmuffs on. I knew him . . . had gone to school with him. We had caught crawfish together in the creek while we were supposed to be in phys ed. He had been working for the city ever since we graduated. Though he was some kind of high muckety-muck supervisor now, he was the best backhoe operator in South Georgia . . . might have invented the thing. I nodded my head. "Uh-huh," I said to myself, "I see they got The Man on The Big Oak job." I tried to wave to him, but he wasn't paying attention. Then I noticed that tears were rolling down his cheeks. "Uh-oh," I said, "must have slipped and cut a root."

Then on my way back with my bills . . . tears rolling down my cheeks . . . I noticed that he was grinning from ear to ear and nodding in gleeful agreement at something and I knew what was up. Old man was hard of hearing. That backhoe bleating in his ears for forty years had done him the same way tugboat engines and sawmills had done me. Those earmuffs were too late . . . they were just for entertainment and privacy with the radio. After I cranked up my car and my radio came on, I knew just what was making him grin too. There just ain't nothing like "Swim Through the Sea of Night Little Swimmer" to cheer you up on a bad day. I can imagine what it was that had made him cry too, probably one of those damn run-over-by-the-train songs from the fifties, you know, one with the screeching tires and the busting glass and the class ring . . . or that damn "Honey" song where she planted the tree and then died.

Because of a peculiar, familial arrangement of the ears, I can't wear ear-muffs comfortably. I have to turn the regular radio up real loud and, even then, all I get is just a hint of the song to extrapolate from (which, you know, ain't all that bad) and some funny looks from young boogie men with such a boom in the backseat of the car that you can see the vibrations in the tires. Once, a young man pulled up alongside and paid me a compliment (I can tell what people are saying): "What you doing old man? Trying to spread a little jam? Still grooving . . . that's cool."

Well, the gas line project went on all summer. My old buddy and I got reacquainted on my trips to the post office. Sometimes he would motion me over and let me climb up and listen in one earmuff at some special little tid-bit (once the "Honeychile" section of an Ink Spots song) from the only radio station in town (WPAX-AM, since 1922). I noticed that he always had that backhoe in the shade of The Big Oak while those men were grubbing around down in that hot hole trying to tunnel under yet another bunch of roots.

Then one day I came by and he was busy. I had read in the paper that they couldn't find a place where the old tree didn't have roots and had finally de-cided to elevate the whole intersection to bypass the bad section of pipe. The big backhoe was bellowing (I imagined) like a railroad locomotive and my friend was deftly twitching slabs of pavement big enough to park a car on up into a herd of dump trucks. Suspicious old women were standing in their historical yards holding their little, yapping shih tzus. He was smiling again . . . didn't even have his earmuffs on. Hot dog . . . internal combus-tion . . . big pistons working hard and speaking loud . . . music to an old twentieth-century man's ears.

---

1. The Big Oak is a very large live oak tree in downtown Thomasville, Georgia, catty-cornered from the post office. I don't know exactly but it probably has just about the widest span of limbs of any of those old trees. Back in the thirties, Dime Vaughan installed an in-tricate system of cables to help support the limbs and keep them from sagging to the ground

and onto the sidewalk and out into the street. Contrary to what some people think, live oak trees can grow pretty fast when they get what they need and the city has always seen to it that ours is in good shape so with the help of Dime Vaughan's cables (you guessed it . . . his brother was Nickel and his sister, Penny, was cruelly called two-bits), the clear land in the park all around it and all that fertilizer it steals from all the grass in all the yards of two or three city blocks, the old tree is about to take over . . . roots all over the place.

Cooking Up Opinions

in which I finally set aside my peculiar ways and
start acting like all the other old men in the world

As a boatbuilder I ought to go to boat shows more, but I can't stand it. Boat shows are hotbeds for the sprouting of opinions. The older I get, the more fond I become of my own and the less delighted I am with those of others. What happens is that when people start telling me their opinions, I find that I am backing up. I try to control it by consciously taking steps forward but the net result is that I just keep backing toward the clearing until I just ain't around anymore.

I have more opinions of my own, too, now that I am getting old (hold on just a minute while I turn Paul Harvey off). I thought it was the result of my solitary profession. Fiddling around in the seclusion of my shop, planing, scraping, sanding, and painting are the sorts of things that free up the mind and foster the growth of opinions. I was so tickled with myself that I decided to share my views. Back when I used to have employees and apprentices, I would explain while the work was actually going on. After they all left my employ in search of other ways to become upwardly mobile, I had to find another outlet for the distribution of my opinions.

I began by offering them up to prospective boat customers. At first I confined my little speeches to boat design and construction (a rich field). Someone would come to the shop to have a look at the boat in the works. "I see you have just a bit of tumblehome back by the stern," one man said. "Yes, I like tumblehome. It gives a good convexity to the topsides and curvature to the rails, which strengthens the whole boat," I said. Then I began to explain the history of tumblehome, how tumbling home the topsides made a clear run from the hounds to the chainplates for the shrouds of old ships and how tumblehome saved the poorly supported bulwarks of ships by presenting the ends of the strong deck beams to the impact of the ship with the dock. By the time I got to the part where, in small sailboats, tumblehome keeps the rails from scooping up water into the boat when it heels, I noticed that I could no longer clearly see the pupils of that man's eyes. At first I thought there was something wrong with me but then I realized that there was something wrong with him. I knew I had to try to give my opinions a wider range. I decided to write them down and send them off. Coincidentally, the boat business began to fall off and that gave me time to type.

After I had refined the crop on hand and sent them off for consideration for publication by all sorts of magazines and literary journals, I sat back down at the typewriter so as to be ready when the new opinion crop sprouted. I sat there for a long time before I realized that the ground was barren. I began to fear that I might not be able to become the Will Rogers of the new millennium. I was heartbroken. I couldn't understand it until I, fortunately, finally, received a commission for a new boat. As soon as I started, the font of opinion began to flow again. I was delighted. Then I found my aluminum hard hat.

It is funny how you can lose a thing like that and have it turn up right there in plain sight. My granddaughters had fixed it up as a dog watering dish and I guess I just got used to it sitting over in the corner by the drinking fountain. Wouldn't have noticed it at all except that while I was getting a drink, I elbowed my teeth off the edge of the cooler where I keep them handy in case a customer was to show up. They went *ploop* right in dog water in the hard hat. I used that hard hat not to protect my head from bumps but to shield it from the heat lamps that I use to facilitate the penetration of the epoxy. I heat sheathe all the planks with fiberglass and epoxy in a secret way before they go on the boat so I have to spend a lot of time with my head under the heat lamps while I spread the epoxy onto the fiberglass with a little plastic squeegee. The aluminum hard hat kept the infrared light from cooking my brains. After I lost the hat, I found that epoxy spreading was very stimulating to the opinion-forming process.

When I found it and started using it again, the opinion mill slowed down. You guessed it. Vast experience and natural brilliance were not the cause of the phenomenon at all. It was the heat of the lamps soaking through my skull and boiling up these opinions out of the depths—sort of like how the oil comes out of an old piece of cheese when you leave it out on the seat of the boat in the hot sun. It probably wasn't good for me. It never is good to push a tool beyond its normal capacity. Power tools will do a little more if you force them, but after a while they'll get hot and start stinking. Which, I believe I smell hair burning right now.

Unnatural Stenches

in which I own up to an olfactory dysfunction

I live way back in the woods far enough so that, unless I bring them home with me, I don't encounter unnatural stenches. Because my tolerance is improperly developed, I am easily irked by unnatural stenches of most any kind. To start off sort of benignly, I can't stand to walk down the soap aisle of the grocery store. I'll have the runny nose and the blind staggers before I can escape the cacophony of reeks from all the lovely scents that they put in soap to disguise the natural smell of, I guess, soap. Getting a little more personal with the grocery store experience, sometimes I have to swap aisles with my cart when a woman pushes up behind, then passes me and the wake of all that air following her voluminous skirts passes by, too, and assaults my delicate sense of propriety with the cacophony of whatever mismatch of artificial odors she has slathered all over herself in the form of colognes, perfumes, deodorants, shampoos, hair sprays, FDS aerosols, laundry soaps, other soaps and hair conditioners, and those little stinking pieces of paper she tumbled in the dryer to keep her undies from clinging . . . I can't stand it. Sometimes I believe I must be the only person alive who thinks that such a mix turns into a smell sort of like the color my grandchildren get when they mix the paint from thirty different tubes of watercolors just to see how horrible it'll look.

I don't think that my condition is something to be proud of. I won't fool myself into believing that the inability to tolerate the normal situation of our great society is anything but a dysfunction. I admire folks who live in paper mill and refinery towns . . . what fortitude. I am sort of ashamed of my weakness so I must try to prove that I am at least sort of normal by explaining that I am just as fond of certain unnatural stenches as that woman behind me in the grocery store was of her choice of olfactory decoration.

I was raised up in love with internal combustion. In my day, when the car went to hunching and blew a gout of smut out the tailpipe and a fireball out from under the hood or when the outboard motor spat like a damned cat and cut off, we didn't immediately reach for the cell phone and dial 911 so somebody less incompetent than ourselves would come with the credit card scanner and put things right again. We did the desperado work beside the road or on the water ourselves. I bet you know the old trick of how to get the gas flowing into the carburetor, when you think the battery is too weak to keep cranking until the fuel pump can do it. All you have to do is seal your lips tightly onto the gas hole and blow until the tank is pressurized. You can't do that to these modern cars with the gas hole under a little door, which I think is a corporate conspiracy by credit card companies, just like how all gas caps are not interchangeable is a conspiracy of gas cap companies. "But it streamlines the car not to have the gas cap sticking out in the wind like that," you may well say. "Hell, man," I'll rebut, "look up under the damn car at all that junk hanging down. If they wanted to streamline something, they would just slide a sheet of tin up under there and pop-rivet it to both bumpers." Whoops, sorry about that. My intention was to stick to the point. So, that old lips-to-the-gas-hole trick will work on an outboard gas tank, too, and is much more reliable for priming the fuel pump than one of those little ridiculous (stinking) squeeze bulbs. Anyway, blowing in the hole will familiarize you with the smell of gasoline and, hopefully . . . soon, with the delightful stench of exhaust. Which, in my day, the only difference in the smell of exhaust was whether it came from an automobile, diesel engine, or outboard motor. A Cadillac stank just like a Ford and an Elgin stank just like an Elto and a farm tractor stank just like a road tractor. Nowadays (have you noticed?) there are at least two different exhaust stenches generated by the internal combustion of gasoline in cars. I don't know the chemistry of the phenomenon but, when they first invented unleaded gas, sometimes a car would pass us and the exhaust would smell just like the burning fuse of a firecracker just before it exploded. We always said, "That car is burning some of that firecracker gas." Sometimes a car would pass us (because of certain preferences of ours for economy and decorum, we do not pass cars going in the same direction as we) and the exhaust smelled like burning plastic. We always said, "That car must be burning some of that plastic gas." Those two gasoline odors dominated the automotive stenches for a long time but, just the other day, we were coming out of the grocery store when a brand-new Exhibition as big as a UPS truck tooled by. The smell of the exhaust was so unquestionably identifiable that not only we, but every other person trudging to and from the cars in the parking lot, stopped and looked at the bottom of our feet. "That car must be burning some of that dog poo-poo gas," we exclaimed.

Antique Outboard Motor Enthusiasts and Talking Frogs

in which smug-looking old geezers have cornered the market

Because of certain aberrations of lifestyle dictated by my hardheaded determination to stay in the wood boatbuilding business for these forty-five years, I am pretty durn familiar with old outboard motors. An old, used boat motor is all I ever could afford but that ain't so bad. There are plenty of them around because nobody ever throws one of the damn things completely away and they have been making them ever since around the turn of the last century when Ole Evinrude rowed across the lake to get some ice cream for his sweetie and said, "There has . . . *whew* . . . got to . . . *whew* . . . be a . . . *whew* . . . better . . . *whew, whew, whew* . . . way to do this." Anyway, he built himself an outboard motor and then set to improve the model and worked on it all his life. Though I wouldn't know, I bet the very first one, "Ole Fudge Ripple," is still lying around in somebody's junkpile somewhere.

Most people don't have much use for an outboard motor but the lure is just about inescapable. They are like magic. All you have to do is shell out a few coins (a Neptune "Mitey Mite" cost $49.95 right after World War Two), clamp the motor on the stern on any old piece-of-junk skiff, and mix a Coca-Cola bottle of oil into a gallon of gas and pour it in the cute little tank and wrap a rope in the groove and fiddle with a few little doodads and make one pull and, lo and behold . . . internal combustion followed by propulsion . . . that is, if you knew what you were doing with the doodad fiddling. If you didn't, pulling the rope was followed by frustration, more fiddling, and more pulling of the rope while the ice cream melted and Sweetie sweltered under the critical view of many keen observers. When you took the motor back where you bought it, the man put it in the barrel, fiddled with the doodads, and cranked it with one patronizing pull. "Musta flooded it" was what he said as he loosened the clamps and handed it back to you.

There are some people who cannot, to save their lives (or the ice cream), start an outboard motor with any certainty . . . not one with doodads anyway. I guess, now that they have these modern ones with, like a new car, computers to fiddle with the doodads, anybody can run one but I wouldn't know . . . those kinds cost thousands of dollars. I always used to be able to find one of the old-style motors cheap. The reason is, after the initial frustration and being shamed by the man at the motor store, the original owner usually threw the thing on the junkpile in the corner of the carport with his old snow tires, camping equipment, garden tools, barbecue grill, and other useless stuff. When he died his widow dragged all that mess out by the street and had a yard sale. It used to be that you could ride down the road on any Saturday and see a bunch of old outboard motors either lying on the grass or sitting on sawhorses . . . for sale cheap . . . sawhorses and all. "It ain't been run in thirty years . . . been sitting right there on that sawhorse . . . just as good as new." I already knew that. A few powder post beetles don't hurt a sawhorse at all.

Those were the halcyon days but they are about gone. There has sprung up this new fad of collecting old outboard motors. Despite the fact that a lot of people couldn't run the durn things even though the instructions are printed right there on the front like on the heel of a boot, there have always been a good many mechanical geniuses who could. America used to be a hotbed of mechanical genius. I won't go all into it but the Wright Brothers and Edison, Harley-Davidson and Henry Ford and them, are just the tip of the iceberg. An old outboard motor is a piece of cake to one of those people. There is a smugness to being able to make one run and, since the invention of the automatic doodad, there is not much use for a mechanical genius anymore so these people all have five or six sawhorses' worth of old outboard motors. They have cornered the market . . . just so they can smugly twitch the rope and produce a little noise and some blue smoke. Nowadays, if you see an old outboard motor lying on the grass at a yard sale among the boxes of whatnots and defunct kitchen gadgets, old Coca-Cola bottles and other collectibles, when you finally get the car turned around and parked there'll be a smug-looking old geezer sniffing the gas hole to see how stale it is down in there and you'll be too late. It is pitiful. If these old boogers just wanted something to motorvate a skiff with like me, there would be a never-ending supply, but what they want to do is take the old engines out of circulation. They go to these meets where they gather around and hobnob with other like-minded old coots. Some of these codgers have to have a trailer or van or a covered pickup truck to haul their collections. Those old poots have cornered the market.

Because of my association with a peculiar little boating magazine (*Messing About in Boats,* 29 Burley Street, Wenham, MA 01984-1943. The *Boston Globe* said, "Alongside the Information Superhighway, *MAIB* is a dirt road.") I have struck up a communication with some of those guys. They even have a loose-knit club (Google "AOMCI"). I found out they are a lot alike and a lot like me. They are mostly old men with irreverent attitudes that can best be called boneheaded. In the November 15 issue of *MAIB* there is a picture of one of those people, which makes a real good example of what I am talking about.

It shows a man with messy-looking gray hair kneeling in the very stern of a boat made out of two car hoods welded together butt-to-butt. This man is just about to pull the rope on a junk outboard motor . . . you know the kind with the naked tiller sticking out the front and the naked spark plug sticking out the back. You can tell by the expression on his face and the dangle of the cigarette hanging on his lower lip that he either knows that he has his doo-dads right and the thing is going to start with the first pull, or he doesn't give a fat rat's ass if it does or doesn't. Not only that, but he is not concerned that he is barely floating in freezing-cold water in a proven deathtrap with only two inches of freeboard. It is easy to tell that his priorities are not easily influenced by government surveys or symposiums addressing safety issues.

So what does all that have to do with talking frogs, one might ask? Well, one of those antique outboard "gentlemen" sent me a joke about a man about my age and a talking frog:

Uncle Pete was out fishing when he heard a voice say, "Pick me up." He looked around and didn't see anybody so he kept on fishing. "Pick me up" he heard again and, when he looked, there was only a frog sitting on a lily pad. The frog said, "Pick me up and kiss me and I'll turn into a voluptuous woman and put something on you like you ain't never seen before."

The old man picked the frog up and, after he had examined it carefully, put it in his pocket.

"What!" croaked the frog, "You don't want to participate in none of that?" "Nah," said Uncle Pete, "I would rather have a talking frog."

The Old J 80 Johnson

in which I help a man recover his long-lost self-esteem

The main goal in my life is to get to the day when I can quit burning gasoline. When I was a young man, I loved anything that burned the stuff and chased those machines with the same fervor that some young men chase women. I guess the same physiology drives both desires because . . . well . . . anyhow, it ain't the same anymore but I still get a slight twitch when I see a little outboard motor.

An old man came to the shop with an old boogered-up outboard right about the time I shipped my last boat in August of '99. I normally stop trying to con people into letting me build them one of these boats around that time of year so I can have time to do my logging and sawmill work—and go to the coast in that wonderfully cool and biologically significant time of year—so I agreed to fix the old motor for this man just for a little spare change. He had an interesting story: It seems that when he was a young man, he had borrowed this engine from his grandfather. Because he was young and had other things on his mind, he neglected to return it until it had froze and busted. It was one of those old outboards that have a brass piston water pump driven off a cam on the propeller shaft. Since it is a positive displacement rig the water squirts out of the pee-hole in a regular, strong cyclic way at the rate of about three strokes of the piston to the squirt (is this a metaphor?) and all the water does not drain back out of the engine when you shut it off unless you take out a little tap down on the foot that says DRAIN. If you don't do that, when it freezes it makes a hell of a mess.

It was an old Johnson from back in the days when *horsepower* was just beginning to be used to misdescribe the capability of a machine. This old thing was bragged up to be about one hp in the days when people knew what a horse could do. No doubt there were some who, after trying one out, raised their eyebrows when it could hardly push the boat through a patch of weeds that a one-horsepower horse could have hauled out of the pond and spread on the field for manure. Now I have a "5 peak hp." vacuum cleaner that runs on twenty-two-gauge wire. It might blow hot air as hard as a horse but not like five—not when they are at their peak anyway. That ain't got nothing to do with this story, though.

What had happened was that my customer had ruined his granddaddy's old Johnson and all his life had felt guilty about it. Though he didn't say it, I bet his grandfather had never let him forget. Now, this man, a successful businessman, retired, and had gotten tired of looking at the old motor that he kept as some sort of override limit on his happiness. Somehow he had found out about the twitch I get at the sight of such and had brought the damn thing to me. "Can you fix it back to where it is as good as it was before it froze and busted?" he said.

"Does a sanctified Baptist love a shiny new SUV?" said me. When I got it all taken apart ("Carb Cleaner" in the aerosol can, $1.69 for two at AutoZone is just the ticket) I found out that what was busted was the pump housing in the foot, the watertight clamp thing that held the foot onto the brass pipe that went up to the head, the tubes that conveyed the water up every whichaway to the cylinder—and the damn base of the crankcase where the water went into the engine of the thing. I fixed the water pump by turning a little liner sleeve to fit the undamaged piston. I replaced the busted tubes. I welded the aluminum foot clamp after about five tries (old 1920s aluminum is strange stuff), cut new threads, and reworked the seal, but I was stymied about the busted crankcase bottom until I remembered a brilliant genius with whom I used to work back in the tugboat days. He cast a brand-new one for me. Ain't life sweet?

The old motor ran good too—first pull, hot or cold—though you had to work the choke and single-needle valve with some expertise. My grandchildren and I took it to Lake Iamonia on my old Grumman Sport Boat to see what it was like. Though it thrummed the aluminum pretty good, it didn't vibrate nearly as bad as I expected. It is one of those primitive old slow-speed, two-cycle engines that aspirates right into the cast-iron cylinder when the little two-inch piston opens the port at the bottom of the stroke. Since the fuel doesn't go through the crankcase like modern two-cycle engines, all that is lubricated by an expostulation of oil and gasoline (eight ounces, a small Coca-Cola bottle, to the gallon) from the cylinder at each compression stroke through little tubes all through the engine—kind of marvelous. There are no seals on anything (except a regular adjustable leather packing gland, "Chicago Rawhide," on the propeller shaft) and that makes it smoke out from under the flywheel a little bit while it is cold—but when it warms up, it is cleaner running than a British Seagull. It has a dry exhaust and you can see how much it is smoking and lean it on down with the big-knob-style needle valve. Got a big aluminum take-apart muffler sort of like a Model T, which it is good to avoid when you have to tilt it, that and the spark plug and the flywheel. It is a lot like handling a crab.

I had it running in my garbage can rig when the man came back. He watched it for a while, then he gave me a check and said, "You keep that thing."

Finally in Fashion

in which, fashion-wise, I end up back where I started

It seems like the men in my family have always worn the same kind of clothes every day . . . something sort of like a uniform: My father's father was an Episcopal priest and always wore a black shirt with a peculiarly rigged little white collar and sometimes a long robe . . . often with hunting boots under it. My mother's father was a woodsman and always wore very tall hunting boots laced all the way up with leather laces. His britches were specially cut so that they fit down inside the tops of his boots to keep the ticks from crawling up in there with him. All my uncles and my father were in World War Two and never wore anything but khaki pants and shirts. Somehow they all had an endless supply.

I guess it takes a powerful influence to fasten a person tightly onto something as important as a lifetime uniform . . . something like an act of God or ticks or war. For me, it was my mother. When I was a little boy, my mother (legendarily hardheaded) required me to wear denim overalls to school. I mean, brand-new, stiff, and dye-stinking overalls so wide and straight that a squirrel once ran up inside one of the britches legs and out the bib without even slowing down. All the other little boys at my school wore overalls too, but they all had a bunch of brothers and sisters and their hand-me-down overalls were about worn out and very nice. I always hoped that mine would get like that, but I was the oldest child of my generation and outgrew them before the knees even got to where they would bend. I argued and whined about it for a long time.

As soon as I got to where I could bypass my mother, I bought me some khaki pants and khaki shirts. All the other boys at my school were very uniform, too, but in a different way . . . flat-top hairdo and way-too-tight blue jeans hauled down way-too-low. I guess, as an act of hardheadedness, I had a round-top hairdo and kept my way-too-slack khakis pulled up way-too-high. It kind of had a funny effect on my social life . . . that and the model airplane glue that I dribbled or absentmindedly wiped on my britches legs sort of kept me from the mainstream of the frantic dating activity that went on around me all the way through high school. It didn't bother me any. Hell, a model airplane would run rings around any one of those uniformly frivolous frumps who were trying to pass themselves off as beauty queens at my school. I was perfectly content to wait for a real woman.

Well, I wore the khakis all my life up until about three years ago. Because of some misuse of my identity by some online entity, I somehow began to get all these surplus catalogs. In one of the catalogs were what they called "British Surplus: Her Majesty's Prison Service Bib Overalls." When I read that, I gave a strong involuntary twitch as if some old soul had given me a prod. I help-lessly ordered a pair and when they came, they were way different from the stiff denim ones of my youth. Though the 100 percent cotton cloth was thick and durable, it was soft and delightful, already broken in, cheap too . . . brown. I was so infatuated that I ordered fifty pounds of them—quite a lot—and at my age, probably a lifetime supply. They are cool in the summer and warm in the winter, just like my mother tried to tell me back in '45.

There is one thing though: My wife won't let me wear them to society de-buts. I tried to explain that people who were likely to recognize the overalls for what they were don't usually go to things like that but it didn't do any good (I wonder if there is some consanguineous cross-link that I don't know about). I argued and whined about it for a long time. I explained how I had developed a phobia that a belt cut off the circulation in my guts and that I was certain that an uninhibited vertical convection of air all the way through promoted good health and hygiene but it didn't do any good. Finally I wailed, "Well, why not then?" "Because, if you must know, they are just too damn cute, that's why." I still have to wear my khakis for all the high-society functions that we attend but I buy them big and keep my belt slack and let them sag . . . finally in fashion.

Why I Am a Hermit

*in which Unca Buddy becomes fascinated by civilization
and all its ridiculousness*

People always want to know how I turned out to be nearbout a hermit.

Well, for one thing, I had a fine example of how good it can be. My grandmother had an old boyfriend who, though he lost the race, stayed in the running after the flag. He built him a little shanty way back in our place where the big creek runs into the river. He stayed down there for seventy-some-odd years and only came out when he got so old that we thought he was liable to burn himself up down there. You know how some folks get sort of crazily obsessed with some little thing when they get old, well Unca Buddy didn't like to let his fire go down on him. When he got to be about ninety-five or so, all he wanted to do was hunt wood and burn it.

He was a mule handler in the Army of World War One. I guess he was one of the ones that kept the caissons rolling along. The only thing he ever said about it was that he didn't like it. Said that when he got back he thought about getting a job but it seemed like that was about the same kind of thing so he decided not to. He just lived down there by the river and fished and messed around all his life . . . had a little garden and one or two partially tame wild hogs. He wasn't the cleanest person I ever saw, but his lifestyle never made him sick. Hell, he is pushing a hundred right here in his chair by the stove in my shop.

Uncle Buddy is real regular around the shop now that school has started and all his other caregivers have had to go back to work. After spending all his life as an out-of-touch hermit, he is becoming fascinated by civilization and all its ridiculousness. It is just another aspect of his going too far with stuff now that he is getting close to a hundred years old . . . like how he plays the radio too loud and puts too much wood in the heater. I used to leave him by himself in the shop when I went to town but the other day, I came back and, before I could get in the door, I thought I heard somebody wailing like he was badly hurt, then I heard this soothing voice trying to calm the person. I was so worried that I dropped the groceries and hurried in to hold Uncle Buddy's hand for the last few minutes . . . but when I got in the shop, the temperature was 130 degrees, it was the Ink Spots on the radio, and old Buddy was singing right along with the soothing voice . . . "Honeychile" my ass . . . Buddy had burned up a whole set of futtocks that I had already fitted the plank lap jogs on.

So, now, I have to take him to the post office and all to keep him from burning the place up. He has begun to notice women and he is formulating theories about them. It isn't as if he had no previous experience. There have been quite a few gals who have made the long trip back through the cat briers and boggy holes to his cabin over the years. I knew one of them pretty good myself. She was a sweet old gal . . . had known Buddy for years and years. She told me that he was so ignorant that he was more like a puppy than a man.

The first thing he noticed about town gals was what a fine display they make of themselves just for other people, sort of like flowers do for bees. He thinks it is nice how all the office buildings and banks and places like that have these pretty women standing around outside for decoration. "They just go to so much trouble to be entertaining. Look-a-there, ain't that sweet how she's standing out there right by herself just so we can see her. I think her boss is nice, too, to let her off from her job to do that for us," said Buddy at the sight of this foxed-up beauty standing on the steps of the tax office. "Let's us do business with those folks, Bingey."

"We already do, Unca Buddy, don't you worry," I said but I didn't have the heart to tell him that she and all the others were out there smoking cigarettes because it was against the law to do it inside. Lately, we both noticed a big escalation of this sort of attractive display and I secretly worried that a lot more women were learning how to smoke and were fixing to kill themselves until I noticed that most of them weren't smoking at all but were talking on these tiny cellular phones. I was relieved. "You know," Buddy said. "Jack Benny used to hold his hand to his face just that way . . . looks better on a woman, don't it? Look how she is wiggling her head . . . ain't that sweet."

Next, sitting in the car outside the post office, he noticed that you could hear women coming from a lot farther away than men. "You know, you hear something sounds sort of like a pileated woodpecker beating his brains out on a hollow oak tree and you look up to see what's making all the fuss and there ain't nothing there but a little tiny woman coming down the hard path. Some of them sound like two pileated woodpeckers heel-and-toeing it down the road. Make you sit up and take notice don't it?" said he. "Yeah, shore does, Unca Buddy . . . you mean you can hear them over all this radio?

What do you think they imagine when they see an old fool like you leering out the window like that with all that loud music?" I said.

"I don't know . . . I sure do wish I could find out," said Buddy.

Well, soon he did. I had to start taking him into the post office with me after he got to hanging out the window and burned up the motor in the electric roll-up-thing with his elbow. He was so fascinated that he walked sideways like a crab into the lobby. All the women in there that get sent to pick up mail thought he was the cutest thing they ever saw in their lives. I have never understood exactly what cute was and that is probably why I was always such a wallflower. After a few of them had seen him in there a couple of times, they would hop up and down and run to fondle him as soon as he came in the door. He thinks they smell wonderful.

Even the most powerful kind of perfume is a delight to him. We can both come out of the stamp line with our eyes watering from some frumped-up fine young thing and he will talk about it all the way back to work. "Look here . . . right here," he demands, sniffing his shirt. "Smell that right there . . . that little place right there. Hell, man, not all up and down the sleeve, just this little place right here. Now, ain't that something?"

There is this one real red-lipped woman who works the drive-in window at the bank that Buddy is in love with. He is shy about her. He will hardly look at her while she is phoning to see if I have any money in the bank . . . he'll just sort of cut his eyes over that way every now and then. But as soon as the drawer opens he dives for my side. He doesn't think I know he just wants to smell that air that came out with the tiny envelope. Lately, I notice that she has been slipping a lollypop in the drawer even when we don't have any children in the car and I think I caught her flirting over my head, too. I'll know something if he starts acting like he is thinking about moving back out to his cabin in the woods. I hope she knows panty hose ain't going to hold up long in all those cat briers.

Messing About with Boats

Appeared in Classic Boat, *June 2006*

What the hell is a boatbuilder from the woods of South Georgia (that's Georgia, ex–Confederate States of America) doing on the back page of a British magazine, even if I do know a little about classic boats? Since ascending to the giddy heights of having a story or two in each issue of *Messing About in Boats* and being an irregular contributor to *WoodenBoat,* it might surely be time to rest on my laurels. After all, I am getting old . . . the oldest wood boatbuilder in Georgia . . . steady at it since 1961.

Truth is I think the editor has decided that you, dear reader, need to be agitated (like dirty clothes in a washing machine?). Some of my comments caused such a furor among the subscribers *of Messing About in Boats* that the reverberations have not stopped, even though fifteen years have passed. The title of the inflammatory article was "Plywood Phooey."

I have been obsessed with building boats ever since I was a little child. It is not just the excellence of my work that has enabled me to stay in business through the era of the flowering of the inexplicable fad of cheap-made plastic and aluminum boats, but the amazing tolerance of my wife and family for a life of poverty and squalor.

What I have been trying to do all these years is to build small boats better than those commonly available. That was easy here in South Georgia. When I was a child, the only small boats I ever saw were heavy, flat-bottomed skiffs, cross-planked on the bottom with cypress lumber . . . useless damned things.

One thing I can't understand is how anyone can think that a flat-bottomed boat is a thing of beauty? Over here in the US, there is a flat-bottomed cult. People stand around a little plywood box as enraptured as if they were in a trance. They read in expensive magazines boring articles titled "Stitch and Smear" and dream of their own finely "crafted" coffin. It is another sign of the degeneration of Western Civilization from the days when schoolboys read magazines that had the complete plans for how to build a real aeroplane or a steam engine or . . . a round-bilged boat in your own backyard. They did it, too.

Now all they do is flick through the pages looking at the Bayliner and

SUV ads. Do y'all have Jet Skis in Great Britain? Lord help us, people. So, I like a light boat. Fortunately, my prejudice against square corners has worked to advantage. Round-bilged boats can be significantly lighter than chine-style boats and they look good, too, especially if they are built in lap-strake. I live in a place where there is plenty of good wood so I was actually set up pretty well and, since I was the only boatbuilder within hundreds of miles, I was able to do just like I dadblamed pleased without fear of ridicule from my peers.

At first I attempted to learn from books written by people like Howard I. Chappelle (who I don't believe ever built a boat in his life . . . too busy pontificating), but I finally had to work it out on my own. Despite being extra-light and peculiarly built, they look like real boats and work well and hold up in rough service just fine. Ain't that the point to it?

I learned to loft from a set of another man's plans. I won't run down any more dead people but, when I got through and set up my molds, I thought I had done something wrong. Finally I got so disgusted that I just knocked the whole mess down and carved me a model, took the lines off, and built my own durn boat and I have been doing it ever since. Well, not exactly like that. I quit carving models about 1968 and just build by eye now. It is a lot easier on the knees than crawling around on the floor trying to loft up the plans . . . quicker, too.

Now, to earn my keep as an agitator, I shall state that I don't like perfectly plumb, U-shaped transoms. Put that in your pipe and smoke it.